THE RENAISSANCE IN ITALY

This book offers a rich and exciting new way of thinking about the Italian Renaissance as both a historical period and a historical movement. Guido Ruggiero's work is based on archival research and the new insights of social and cultural history and literary criticism, with a special emphasis on everyday culture, gender, violence, and sexuality. The book offers a vibrant and relevant critical study of a period too long burdened by anachronistic and outdated ways of thinking about the past. Familiar yet alien, premodern but suggestively postmodern, attractive and troubling, this book returns the Italian Renaissance to center stage in our past and in our historical analysis.

Guido Ruggiero is College of Arts and Sciences Cooper Fellow and Professor of History at the University of Miami. As an author, editor, and translator, he has published more than two dozen books on the Renaissance and related topics, including, most recently, *Machiavelli in Love: Sex, Self, and Society in Renaissance Italy* (2007) and *The Blackwell Companion to the Worlds of the Renaissance* (2002). His articles have appeared in many journals, including *The American Historical Review*, *The Journal of Social History*, *Viator*, *The Journal of the History of Medicine and Allied Science*, *Xin shehui shi* (New Social History), *Studi storici*, and *Quaderni storici*. He has also published numerous essays and articles in edited volumes. Ruggiero has won a number of fellowships, including a Guggenheim Fellowship; two National Endowment for the Humanities Fellowships; several Delmas Foundation, Orowitz, and Taft Fellowships; as well as an ACLS Fellowship. He is an elected member of the Ateneo Veneto and has been a Fellow or visiting professor at the Institute for Advanced Study at Princeton, Harvard's Villa I Tatti in Florence, and the American Academy in Rome.

THE RENAISSANCE IN ITALY

A Social and Cultural History
of the Rinascimento

GUIDO RUGGIERO

University of Miami

CAMBRIDGE
UNIVERSITY PRESS

CAMBRIDGE
UNIVERSITY PRESS

University Printing House, Cambridge CB2 8BS, United Kingdom

One Liberty Plaza, 20th Floor, New York, NY 10006, USA

477 Williamstown Road, Port Melbourne, VIC 3207, Australia

314-321, 3rd Floor, Plot 3, Splendor Forum, Jasola District Centre, New Delhi - 110025, India

79 Anson Road, #06-04/06, Singapore 079906

Cambridge University Press is part of the University of Cambridge.

It furthers the University's mission by disseminating knowledge in the pursuit of education, learning and research at the highest international levels of excellence.

www.cambridge.org
Information on this title: www.cambridge.org/9780521719384

© Guido Ruggiero 2015

First published 2015
3rd printing 2016

A catalogue record for this publication is available from the British Library

Library of Congress Cataloging in Publication data
Ruggiero, Guido, 1944–
The Renaissance in Italy : a social and cultural history of the Rinascimento /
Guido Ruggiero, University of Miami.
pages cm
Includes bibliographical references and index.
ISBN 978-0-521-89520-0 (hardback) – ISBN 978-0-521-71938-4 (pbk.)
1. Renaissance – Italy.   2. Italy – Social conditions – 1268–1559.   3. Italy –
Civilization – 1268–1559.   4. Italy – Intellectual life – 1268–1559.   I. Title.
DG533.R84   2015
945'.05–dc23   2014019659

ISBN 978-0-521-89520-0 Hardback
ISBN 978-0-521-71938-4 Paperback

For Laura

CONTENTS

ILLUSTRATIONS

ACKNOWLEDGMENTS

Ludovico Ariosto, in his classic sixteenth-century epic/romance/fantasy *Orlando furioso*, traced the origins of the Este family, who had patronized that masterpiece, back to a great female warrior of medieval romance, Bradamante, and a slightly less impressive warrior of even greater lineage descended from the heroes of ancient Troy, Ruggiero. The origins of this book, by a considerably less noble Ruggiero, cannot be traced so far back, but to do justice to the debts owed one would need acknowledgments and a tale of thanks that would approach the epic proportions of Ariosto's tale.

Undoubtedly the greatest thanks are in order to the two generations of scholars who have virtually revolutionized the field of Renaissance scholarship since the Second World War. Readers will find their work informing virtually every page that follows. Moreover, the great debates that flourished in academia over that same period, especially those over the cultural turn in the humanities and women's and gender studies more generally, along with historical controversies that swirled around the new social and cultural history and theoretical debates in anthropology and literary criticism, have left me deeply in the debt of those who carried forward those often heated discussions. Readers will find echoes of all my books and articles throughout this book. Thus I would like to thank all my publishers here, especially the most important: Rutgers, Johns Hopkins, Blackwell's, and Oxford. And I am particularly grateful to my Cambridge editors, Beatrice Rehl and Asya Graf, as well as to my copy editor, Russell Hahn, for all their help and support.

Thanking those who helped make me a scholar, often overcoming my stubborn resistance, would be a formidable task. The serious work really began at the university, however, where a number of professors stepped forward in many ways to actually launch this project, as they tried to mold an overly self-confident student into a scholar, most notably Boyd Hill at the undergraduate level and Gerhardt Ladner, Richard Rouse, and Lauro

Martines in graduate school and beyond. Once again, readers will note their influence throughout this book. Ladner's vision of reform is one of its main themes, and Martines's powerful vision of the social world of the time and his always creative approach to the subject have been a model not just for this book, but for my career.

Less formal teachers, both within academia and beyond, have also been many. But to single out perhaps the most important: Gene Brucker, Felix Gilbert, David Herlihy, Christiane Klapisch-Zuber, and John Najemy have taught me more about the history of Florence than they may be happy to admit and served as models of the committed scholarly life. The same is true of Gaetano Cozzi, Kenneth Setton, Martin Lowry, Joanne Ferraro, and Ed Muir for Venice. Moving beyond the cities most studied for the Renaissance in Italy, Nick Terpstra, John Marino, and Tom and Elizabeth Cohen have been particularly important as well. And although this is only a very limited list of all those who deserve thanks, when one moves beyond Italy the list grows exponentially. Particularly important have been Jim Farr, Donald Spivey, Mary Lindemann, Karen Kupperman, Richard Brown, Londa Schiebinger, Robert Proctor, Sophie De Schaepdrijver, Ronnie Po-chai Hsia, Matthew Restall, and Natalie Z. Davis, who in many ways unwittingly provided the most important model as well as some crucial support along the way.

Many beyond history also played a crucial role in this book. Those in literature were especially important, and to name only the most significant and appreciated among what once again would be a long list: Deanna Schemek, Valeria Finucci, Denis Looney, Margaret Rosenthal, Linda Woodbridge, Mihoko Suzuki, Frank Palmieri, and especially Albert Ascoli stand out as informal teachers, models, and much-appreciated friends. The same should be said for art historians like Deborah Howard, John Paoletti, and Karen Barzman. Although it might seem strange to include them in this list, my larger *famiglia* in Treviso also deserve a special place among my informal teachers. Over the years they have thoughtfully pushed me to remember that there is a larger world of exciting and interesting people who do not frequent the halls of academia, libraries, or archives yet are still deeply engaged with ideas and the broader issues this book attempts to address.

Obviously students and colleagues at the several universities at which I have taught over the years have also contributed in more ways than I can mention. Hopefully, as they read the book, they will recall our many conversations and see how much I have profited from their ideas. Thus, although it is much too brief to be adequate to my debt, let me at least formally thank my students and colleagues at the Universities of Miami, Cincinnati, Tennessee, Connecticut, and Syracuse in Florence, as well as the Pennsylvania State

University. Along with those great students and fine colleagues, the staffs of each institution were unusually supportive and special friends as well.

Similar thanks are in order to the granting foundations and institutes for advanced study that have supported the research and writing that have gone into this book, starting with the Center for Medieval and Renaissance Studies at UCLA and the Regents of the University of California, who awarded me a handsome University of California Regents Intern Fellowship that allowed me to complete my studies and carry out my first years of research in Venice. This was followed by a series of research grants from the Taft Foundation at the University of Cincinnati and several Delmas Foundation grants that supported more than a decade of ongoing research in Venice and Italy, until an invitation to the Institute for Advanced Study at Princeton as a National Endowment for the Humanities Fellow in the early 1980s pulled together the first part of my career and gave me the opportunity to consider the broader issues that stood behind my first two books and pointed to this work. These were followed by another NEH Fellowship for a year at Harvard's research villa in Florence, I Tatti, in the 1990s and a John Simon Guggenheim Foundation Fellowship, part of which I again spent at the Institute for Advanced Study in Princeton. There and at I Tatti in 1990–1991 I began formally writing this book. The handsome research support that I received soon after as the Weiss Chair in the Humanities at the Pennsylvania State University was continued at the University of Miami and enhanced generously by my being made a College of Arts and Sciences Cooper Fellow there. Each freed up considerable time for writing this book. Invitations to the American Academy in Rome as a Rome Senior Visiting Professor and once again to Harvard's Villa I Tatti as the Robert Lehman Senior Visiting Professor allowed me to finish it.

A special note of thanks is also due to my colleagues at each of these idyllic study centers; they have taught me much more than they realized and have enriched my life. My deep gratitude also goes to the staffs, who did so much to make my time profitable and truly special. Although once again there are many who should be named, let me note just five of the most important: Chris Celenza, director of the American Academy in Rome; Walter Kaiser, former director of Villa I Tatti, and its current head librarian, Michael Rocke, and director, Lino Pertile, along with his gracious partner and organizer of life at the villa, Anna Bensted.

Finally, thanks are due to all who have read or discussed parts of this book over the years, most importantly to the readers for Cambridge University Press, John Marino and Nick Terpstra, whose comments were both encouraging and most helpful. Colleagues who also read parts or all of the book,

Konrad Eisenbickler, Karen Barzman, Michele Laughran, Jim Farr, Mary Lindeman, and Laura Giannetti, were crucial for inspiring the many revisions that have gone into it and made it far stronger than it otherwise would have been. Laura Giannetti, who has long been much more than a colleague and mentor, not only read the whole book more than once, saved me from numerous foolish errors, and made crucial suggestions, she also lived the book with me for the last twenty years that have gone into it and made them truly special. Thus I dedicate the book to her along with all those who have contributed so much to it and made the path to its completion less epic and slightly less *furioso* than Ariosto's tale, but rich with shared pleasures and good friendship.

Map 1. Main cities of Italy c. 1300.

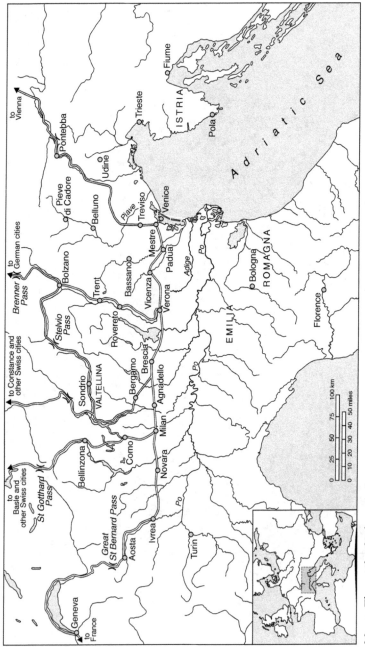

Map 2. The north of Italy c. 1426.

Map 3. The states of Italy in 1559.

xvii

INTRODUCTION: THE END OF THE WORLD AND ITS REBIRTH (*RINASCITA*) AS THE RINASCIMENTO

The End of the World

Did the world end in 1260? Was there an Apocalypse that we have forgotten seven and a half centuries later? Certainly if that were the case it would be convenient for a book that considers an Italian Renaissance or, as it is called in Italian, a Rinascimento, a rebirth (a *rinascita*) of the world in Italy that began at about that time and continued on through the last decades of the sixteenth century. Perhaps surprisingly, one thing is clear: in the middle of the thirteenth century many people were expecting the world to end. And we are not talking about those on the margins of society or the typical fringe groups that today we associate with prophecies of impending doom, but rather emperors and popes, kings, nobles, powerful clerics and merchants, as well as rural priests, peasants, and denizens of the dark alleys and warrens that often typified the Italian cityscapes of the day.

Perhaps the best place to start is with Joachim of Fiore (c. 1135–1202), an Italian preacher and prophet who, although virtually forgotten today, enjoyed great popularity in his time. In fact, he was so popular that no less than two popes encouraged him to write down his prophecies, which spread quickly not just through the learned world of theologians and church leaders, but also through the more general culture – especially that of the rapidly growing and prospering cities of Italy. At the heart of Joachim's prophecy was a discovery he had made while studying that mysterious section of the Bible known as the Book of Revelations. There, following a long tradition of allegorical reading, he found a concealed deeper truth: a hidden third gospel to go along with the Old Testament and the New – the Everlasting Gospel.

Like many others, Joachim believed that the Old Testament was the book given by God the Father to organize and guide humans in the first age of the world: from the expulsion of Adam and Eve from the Garden of Eden to the

coming of Christ. This had been an age dominated by a wrathful and vengeful God, punishing humans for the first sin of Eve and Adam. But a new age
began with the life and suffering of Christ, a new order of the world and
a new relationship with God. The New Testament was the new gospel for
that new age that was ushered in by Christ's life and death to save humanity: an age of love, a return of grace, and the birth of the Church of Rome
that Christ and his disciples established. Crucially, however, that second age
literally ended one world and began another – the whole order of reality
was changed with Christ's life and death. A world of suffering and despair
before the wrathful God of the Old Testament ended, and it was followed by
a radically new world watched over by a loving God, fully human and fully
divine, Christ.

But, significantly, the Christian view of God was Trinitarian: Father, Son,
and Holy Spirit. If there had been an age of the Father/Old Testament and
if Joachim was living in the age of the Son/Christ/New Testament, it was
logical to assume that there would be a third age of the Holy Spirit and a
new third gospel. That age, as revealed in the hidden Everlasting Gospel, like
the age of the Son, would be radically different from what had gone before.
Once again one world would end and a new one would be born, ruled over
by the Holy Spirit. In that age the Church of Rome and Christ's vicar on
earth, the pope, both of which were temporary institutions for creating a
Christian society in the second age, would be replaced by the direct rule
of the Holy Spirit. In fact, all institutions and governments would fall away,
unnecessary as humanity would live in perfect harmony with God via the
direct inspiration of the Holy Spirit. Thus the Trinitarian promise would be
fulfilled. And the last age would be one of peace and perfection awaiting the
Last Judgment and the end of time.

What changed this radical but not immediately threatening vision into
a prophecy with teeth were Joachim's calculations, based on the Bible, that
the first age, from the expulsion of Adam and Eve from the Garden of Eden
until the birth of Christ, had lasted 1,260 years. As he expected that each age
would be of the same length, that meant that things were about to get exciting because the year 1260, or 1,260 years after Christ's birth, should signal the
end of an age and a world and the beginning of something completely new.
To make this more interesting and perhaps a little less strange and unlikely,
Joachim found in the Book of Revelations a series of signs that would signal
that the last days were at hand. Among the most significant there would be:
a unification of all religions under the umbrella of Christianity, so that all
could enter the Age of the Spirit; a rapid growth of a new order of preachers with a new leader to lead the way into the new age; and in the last days

of the old age, the reign of the Antichrist that would destroy secular society and the Church. For with perfect symmetry, in the name of ultimate evil, the Antichrist would perpetrate the ultimate good, by preparing the ground for the end of the Christian era and the last age of the Holy Spirit.

All this would be only mildly amusing were it not for one troubling fact. After Joachim's death in 1202, many came to believe that his prophecies were coming true. And, significantly, they seemed to be coming true more clearly in the Italian peninsula, especially in the north, where literally dozens of little city-states in the thirteenth century prospered, struggled, and appeared to many to be on the verge of a new age and world order. In those cities a traditional medieval order, typified by what might be labeled the Great Social Divide — where society seemed to be essentially divided between a hereditary nobility and the rest — had been radically and often violently challenged by new social classes, new social and cultural values, and new wealth. In essence the power of an old nobility had been challenged and, at least in the larger cities, pretty well limited by new groupings of merchant/banker/artisan powers who usually called themselves the *Popolo* (the People).

The struggles between the *Popolo* and the older nobility were often violent and bloody and frequently meant that when one group won power, the other was exiled from the city or worse. Also, of course, some nobles deserted their peers — after all, there was a long medieval tradition of tension and fighting among noble clans — to join the *Popolo*, and in turn some members of those merchant/banker/artisan groupings were also prepared to abandon their peers in an attempt to grab power in alliance with the older nobility or merely to ape their aristocratic ways. The result was messy and violent, but usually seen at the time as pitting the *Popolo* of a city and their new wealth and power based on commercial and artisanal activities against the nobility and their more rural landed wealth. Prophecies like those of Joachim, with their prediction that these changes signaled the end of the world, thus found a wide swath of the population ready to give them credit. This was especially true because these negative novelties promised a better last age, preordained by God, where the Great Social Divide would be wiped out and replaced by a unified populace led by the Holy Spirit.

Thus when a humble preacher from the little Italian town of Assisi who would become Saint Francis of Assisi (c. 1181–1226) founded a new preaching order (quickly labeled the Franciscans) and preached what seemed to most a new and more spiritual vision of Christianity, it was soon seen as a confirmation of Joachim's prophecies of a new leader and new order leading the way to the end. But even before that was recognized, Francis's preaching caught the imagination of a wide range of the population because it had a deep resonance with the spiritual problems created by the burgeoning wealth of the cities of Italy. Preaching a spiritual life of poverty to the poor peasants of medieval Europe made little sense and had little to offer. When virtually everyone was poor, it did not seem like an impressive sign of spirituality to be poor; it seemed merely normal. But in a society where people were accumulating impressive wealth, seemingly in opposition to the poverty that Christ had preached and that the Bible endorsed, a new preacher and a new order that promoted poverty and called for a more spiritual life had real relevance, hitting at the heart of the changes that worried people, even many of the newly rich.

Francis dramatically stripped off his clothes in the main church of his hometown of Assisi to go naked as God made him – literally with no belongings – into the world and demonstrated his rejection of all property. His followers in turn wandering the cities of Italy in rags, begging their way without material possessions, were potent symbols. In a world powerfully attuned to such signs, they demonstrated the spirituality that came with a denial of worldly goods in the name of living a Christlike life of poverty. In fact, Francis's preaching was so extreme and potentially revolutionary that the leaders of the Church forced him and his followers to moderate their calls for poverty and to dress in clothing that at least covered their nakedness. They eventually settled on the brown robes similar to those still worn by Franciscans, belted with a knotted rope that suggested a commitment to the vow of poverty that remained central to the order. A number of Francis's followers, however, were not happy with such compromises, and a splinter group developed called the Spirituals – again perfectly named for Joachim's prophecy of the coming age of the Spirit. By the end of the century they were declared heretics for their commitment to complete poverty and a spiritual life. Significantly, a number of the Spirituals, when they discovered the parallel between their teachings and Joachim's prophesies, combined the two to preach the impending end of the world with success in the cities of Italy.

As if this were not enough, Francis himself seemed to have begun to fulfill yet another prophecy of Joachim. For not only did he preach Christianity to the birds and animals, he also set out to convert the pagans, actually petitioning the pope to go to the Holy Land to convert Muslims. He eventually made it to Egypt in 1219 with a crusading army and reportedly entered the Muslim camp to try to win converts. And if Francis was the prophesized new leader, right on time a candidate for the Antichrist appeared, the Emperor Frederick II (1194–1250, emperor 1220–1250). He, of course, did not see himself as such. Officially elected emperor by German electors following medieval tradition in 1220, he was much more a Mediterranean, born and raised in southern Italy. Most of his life he lived there, balancing effectively a rich rural nobility with newer urban centered merchant wealth and supporting an impressive and vibrant court.

As emperor, and thus theoretically ruler of all the West, Frederick saw himself as the ideal leader to bring peace and order (and taxation to fill his treasury) to the cities of Italy, especially the rich but tumultuous cities of the north. In fact, many cities of the north supported him in the hope that he would deliver peace and order. Others, however, were not so enthusiastic about his attempts to dominate the peninsula. Their resistance was supported by a series of popes, who saw themselves in competition with emperors for power in Italy. For the moment this long story can be made quite short: to the struggles for power in the cities of the north, Frederick brought a new series of wars in which he squared off against local powers usually aligned with the papacy – making them frequently seem to be wars against the papacy itself. In sum, much as Joachim had predicted, here was a ruler who with one victory after another seemed to be slowly but surely destroying the papacy and the Church and fulfilling the requirements of an Antichrist, ending the reign of the Church of Rome and the papacy to clear the way for the Last Age.

Was the Second Age of Christ and the New Testament coming to an end? Was the Age of the Spirit at hand? Everything seemed to point in that direction at midcentury. The Franciscans, especially their more spiritual wing, were preaching a new, more spiritual world; an Antichrist was ravaging the old Church; and the cities of northern Italy were in turmoil. Change was rife, and an old world order seemed to be dissolving in chaos and violence, just as Joachim had prophesized.

But as Frederick's victories mounted, and as the last days seemed evermore nigh, Frederick II, not the Antichrist but just a powerful emperor, died suddenly in 1250 as mere men are wont to do. Some, unwilling to give up on him as the Antichrist, claimed that he was buried along the Rhine waiting for the call to begin the true last age. Some of the Franciscan Spirituals continued Joachim's prophecies into the fourteenth century and beyond, seeing themselves as preparing the way for that last age still to come. In fact, Joachim's prophecies endured, often emerging in times of crisis or influencing religious enthusiasms that featured world-changing visions. Ultimately, true to the strangeness of his prophecy, even some of the Nazi propagandists who preached their own last age – an age of the third and last millennium, the Third Reich – still claimed in the last century that Frederick was waiting to be called to usher in their final age.

Of course, it might seem obvious that the world did not really end in 1260 as Joachim had promised. A good historian would certainly admit that it did not, yet in a way that is at the heart of this book, I would suggest that one world did end around the middle of the thirteenth century in Italy, and another was born. What has been labeled misleadingly the Middle Ages, a rural feudal world dominated by a nobility whose wealth was based on land and a medieval church whose economic roots were similarly rural, was largely superseded in Italy by a new age often labeled the Italian Renaissance. The change did not occur in a day or a year or ever completely, for the nobility continued and even the urban world of Renaissance Italy was highly reliant on the rural world that surrounded it and supplied many of its basic needs. Moreover, its culture and traditions drew heavily on medieval precedents.

And of course, this new age was not the age that Joachim had predicted: poverty did not replace wealth, and churches and governments did not wither away as humanity came to embrace the peace and harmony of the Holy Spirit. Rather, ironically in the north of the Italian peninsula and slowly elsewhere, wealth and material goods came to power as never before, and more urban-based churches and governments flourished. And obviously Joachim's promise of an age of peace and harmony remained unfulfilled. But still I would suggest that the many signs that his followers saw as indicating the imminent fulfillment of his prophecy were in a way correct, for they signaled the end of one world and the start of a new age. The culture and society of that strangely new/old/reborn age is the story of this book.

Time and Rebirth: The Rinascimento a New/Old Age

For all its strangeness to modern eyes, Joachim's prophesy was perhaps most strange to contemporaries for a claim that would go largely unnoted today – that this third age would be a *new* age and a better one because it was *new*. One of the deep differences that sets modern society and culture off from most others is that it tends to accept without question that the new is good. The premodern world, by contrast, had a deep suspicion of change and the new. In fact, in many ways it was enough to label a thing new or a change as an innovation to ensure that it would be seen as wrong and rejected. At one level there is a profound logic in this, for if one looks at the world around us, all things do seem to break down with time and change; thus, from that perspective, change over time, and the new, imply decay. In the best of worlds, then, the ideal would be to hold things as they are or, better yet, to return to their beginnings before change and decay set in, that is, return to when they were first made.

How did this vision of time come to change? This is a complex and perhaps ultimately unanswerable question, but historians usually posit two very broad cultural factors. The first was a general acceptance of a Christian vision of time, which saw it as moving forward positively from a low point with the expulsion of Adam and Eve from the Garden of Eden to the Last Judgment, when the world would end with the saved living happily ever after with God. The second key factor in this vision was the idea of progress itself, which to a large extent was merely the secularization of the Christian promise that in God's plan for the world, as time passed, things would improve. What both progress and the Christian vision of God's unfolding plan for humanity implied was that time was linear and going somewhere positive, and that meant ultimately that change and the new were good.

But many things in the premodern world and daily life contradicted this vision of linear time and the new. In fact, many still do today as we live in a culture where we tend to overlook the fundamental contradiction between a linear vision of time and a circular vision that we use interchangeably to understand change. Certainly a circular vision of time seemed natural in premodern times. Perhaps most significantly, along with the way things seem to decay with time, the cycles of the seasons and the rotations of the heavens, along with the repeating sequences of time – years, months, days, hours, and so on – all literally turn on the idea that time repeats and thus is circular, not linear. The mechanical clock, invented in the fourteenth century in Italy, is a mechanized version of such a circular vision of time. The first clocks used circular gearing to reproduce the circular motions of the heavens, which were seen as directly creating circular time. In this mimicking of the very nature of the heavens, and time, mechanical clocks seemed to have almost a magical dimension. And, in fact, they were often used in magic, before they were adopted by natural philosophers to measure time in ways that would lead to the development of what we label modern science – a particularly effective offshoot of earlier natural magic.

Although Joachim built his predictions on a linear vision of time dating from the birth of Christ in order to predict the end of the world in 1260, most of his contemporaries still had not adopted the habit of dating from the birth of Christ. In the Middle Ages dates normally were recorded using a cyclical calendar based on the ancient Roman measure of time, the fifteen-year cycle known as the indiction. These cycles were often keyed to the rule of emperors, popes, or local rulers, and just as years and weeks represented time as repeating and circular, so too indictions represented longer periods of time as circular. It was only in the fourteenth century that the more linear vision of time associated with dating from the birth of Christ began to catch on more generally, and even then documents often were dated both in indictions and from the birth of Christ.

The central point, however, is that time remained more circular than linear until the modern world, which meant that the new was seen almost unquestionably as negative and wrong. Change, in this way of seeing time, meant one of two things, either positively returning to the beginning when things were done or made correctly, or negative decay and movement away from good beginnings. The result was that those who benefited from or saw as positive the changes of the thirteenth and fourteenth centuries found it difficult to represent them as new and positive. They tended to portray and conceptualize the changes that they wished to present as good not as new, then, but rather as re-turns (going back to the first turn of the cycle of time when things were as they should be); re-forms (going back to the first, correct form of things); re-newals (going back to when things were new and first put together correctly, thus undoing the damage of time and decay); or, although the term was used less often, re-births (going back to when things first came into being). All these "re" words stressed that the changes they described were not to something new but rather a return to something old and better, because time was circular and the first times of things were the best times.

For culture, society, and even government that meant that positive change was portrayed as going back – return, renewal, reform, rebirth – to ancient, better, first times. In the first-time culture of ancient Rome, most pertinently, society and government in Italy had functioned as they should and were perceived as having been virtually perfect, a golden age of peace, prosperity, and happiness. For spiritual life and Christian salvation, change also needed to be presented as going back to the first time of Christ and the Church. Positive personal change often aimed at literally going back to imitate Christ's life itself, much as Saint Francis had preached. In fact, Francis claimed to have literally re-formed his own body and thus developed the stigmata of Christ, the wounds that Christ suffered in his passion on the Cross – an impressive personal re-forming. The Church also portrayed positive institutional change as going back to the first Church of Christ's disciples and the Church Fathers. Once again the affirmative terms were "return," "renewal," "reform," and "rebirth."

And significantly, for all these "re" words the crucial first times were often closely associated with the early days of the Roman Empire, when both that empire and the first Christian Church were born. For the flourishing cities of the Italian peninsula, especially the cities of the center and north, such a return to a glorious past was especially attractive because their citizens felt that they were occupying the same spaces, both physical and spiritual, as their forebearers of those superior first times. Frequently, in fact, they lived among the ruins and with the relics of that first Christian and imperial time – the very landscape of Italy was alive with vivid recollections of that more perfect past. Local memories, ruins of ancient Roman buildings, and relics of the martyrs and founders of Christianity (often still working miracles that attested to their potency), all supported by oral and written traditions that recalled superior first times, served as a constant reminder of those glorious first days. And thus they were everywhere available for rethinking the dangers and fears of change or the new as instead positive reforms, returns, or rebirths of a better, more perfect time, what we might call a Rinascimento.

Italy and the Rinascimento

The term more commonly used in English to label the period, the Italian Renaissance, has a number of problems that the Italian term Rinascimento avoids. First, of course, there was no Italy in a modern sense in the thirteenth century or across the period usually labeled the Italian Renaissance. The center and north of Italy in the second half of the thirteenth century were divided into dozens of little city-states, all with their own strong local traditions, loyalties, and local dialects, fiercely defended. Yet for virtually all of those little cities the business of governance was carried out in a common language, a late medieval Latin that was understood by lawyers, notaries, and bureaucrats and by the university-trained in general, as well as by a number of artisans and men of lower status. A significant portion of what was perceived as the more serious literature of the day was also written in Latin, including most prescriptive and philosophical works, religious texts, and even local chronicles. Thus, in a way, a Latin culture that was seen as rooted in a common Roman and Christian past was shared among the cities of the center and north. Of course, that Latin culture was shared more widely throughout the rest of Europe as well, but once again the cities of Italy had a special relationship with that language as they saw it as the language of their own special Roman heritage and first times.

At the level of the language that everyone spoke, however, things were more complex. Local dialects were the norm, and at times they could vary virtually from neighborhood to neighborhood. More pertinently, someone from Venice would have had some trouble understanding a person from Rome or Florence and even more trouble understanding someone from Naples or further south. But the key here is "some trouble," because it was widely agreed that in most cities the local dialects were just that, dialects of a language or at least an imagined language that was Italian. Thus Dante could write his famed poem *The Divine Comedy* in a Tuscan dialect of Italian, and although it was attacked for not being written in the learned language of Latin, it also came to be seen as a foundational work for Italian as a language that could be understood by a more general populace in an Italian cultural zone.

In fact, Dante wrote an important work on the importance of Italian (in Latin, ironically), *De vulgari eloquentia*, to convince the intellectual elites of his day that behind the many dialects of the Italian peninsula there stood a primal Italian language that informed and unified them, a topic that he had also explored in an earlier work in Italian, the *Convivio*. Although there appear to be some significant differences in their arguments, the two works agreed that this more general shared Italian language was based on shared historical and cultural experiences at least among the cities of northern and central Italy. At some moments it seemed as if Dante was referring to a language that still needed to be developed, at others it seemed as if he was referring to his own use of the language that would pull forth this underlying unifying language.

Later in the fourteenth century the famous poet Francesco Petrarch, even as he advocated writing a purer, more classical Latin, wrote his love poetry in a Tuscan dialect that he and his admirers again saw as foundational for Italian as a language. Less well known but equally indicative of this development of an Italian culture, based on the local dialects of what was not yet one language, was the decision of many poets in the north of Italy at the end of the thirteenth century to write their poetry in their own dialects rather than in Latin. In sum, for all their local loyalties, the denizens of the cities of northern Italy were beginning to see their culture and society as somehow different in terms of a still largely imagined common language, Italian.

Another measure of a developing sense of *Italianità* has been suggested by those who study the medieval Italian trading cities that sent out groups of their citizens, primarily merchants, to live in the Islamic world and in northern Europe. In both instances these merchants were treated as outsiders and identified with their homeland as Italians. In Islamic lands their separation was usually more rigorous, with their living and working conditions strictly regulated – at least in theory – often in terms that saw them as a particular people. In northern Europe regulations and limitations were usually less strict, but Italian bankers and traders were again definitely seen as outsiders and often labeled Italian. Thus although the trading and banking cities of Italy were frequently involved in intercity competition that at times spilled over into war, they ironically often found themselves abroad grouped as one people, Italians.

Moreover, of course, the Italian peninsula was regularly perceived as a geographical unit. Separated by the Alps and the sea from the rest of Europe and various peoples who spoke other languages (perceived by Italians as having less of a Roman heritage), the peninsula of Italy seemed the center of a Mediterranean world once ruled by the great Roman Empire. In a region where the technology of sailing meant that ships still hugged the coastline rather than braving long open-water voyages, that centrality was even more pronounced. And it helped make the peninsula the center of trade within the Mediterranean and a crucial entry point for northerners into that great sea, which for most Europeans was still the center of the world. Thus for all its geographical variety, Italy was seen as a particular and significant geographical entity.

Finally, as a place, the Italian peninsula was highly unusual not just for its association with the homeland of ancient Rome or its centrality in the Mediterranean, but also for its dozens of burgeoning cities and towns. It was a land heavily influenced by its rich and rapidly developing urban life, which had already dramatically changed the economy, culture, and society of the region, wiping out the Great Social Divide that was the order of the day in much of the rest of Europe. Thus the vague and largely undefined concept of "Italy" also turned on its unusual urban nature and the culture and society that went hand in hand with it. In the end, then, while there was no Italy in a modern sense, and while most people in the region thought of themselves first in terms of their local loyalties, most were aware that they were in a special land that set them apart from the rest of Europe, one with a glorious past and a rich and vibrant urban culture, unmatched by that of the "barbarians" of the North or the rich and dangerously pagan cultures of the East and the north coast of Africa. Like many Italians of the day, then, we will use the terms "Italy" and "Italian" to indicate this larger geographical, cultural, and social entity.

The other problem with the label "Italian Renaissance" is the term "renaissance" itself. One wonders what Dante or even Petrarch, who lived for a good portion of his life north of the Alps in and around Avignon, would have thought of the idea that they were living in a period that would be named using a French term, re-naissance. Both may well have been pleased to learn that a French scholar of a much later day, Jules Michelet (1798–1874), was so impressed with the culture of their day that he coined the term "renaissance" in 1855 largely to celebrate the rebirth of classical culture in an earlier age and French participation in it. But more than a century and a half later, it does seem rather strange to continue referring to that earlier time in Italy using an anachronistic term from a different, later culture and language, especially when in the twenty-first century we no longer share the same vision of the period. Perhaps, then, it is time to use a term that might have made sense to those who lived several hundred years earlier. The term that would perhaps fit most closely for someone like Petrarch or Dante would be the Latin term *Renovatio* or renewal, as both men, along with many of their contemporaries, were fascinated with the idea of renewing the Roman world and the days of the first Christians.

But its Italian equivalent, *Rinnovazione*, has the unfortunate ring today of fixing something up, an association that seems to disqualify it for the name of a period of history. *Reformatio*, another term that was often used at the time to refer to the positive change associated with re-forming past society or reform itself, has problems of another sort. We already have one Reformation, and labeling a slightly earlier and slightly overlapping period with the same name, even if one opted for the Italian equivalent, *Riformazione*, would create more confusion than clarity. Perhaps the best option, then, is to return to the term *rinascita*, rebirth, admittedly less popular at the time, but which is in many ways the "re-word" that sums up best the thrust of the way reform and renewal were used to refer positively to the changes that the urban world was undergoing. An age of *rinascita* or the Rinascimento seems a much better label for the period, even if the older term "renaissance" might be used in the sense of a more general period of European history that was heavily influenced culturally, politically, and economically by the Rinascimento. It should be noted, however, that even this term has its problems as in the recent historiography of Italy, Rinascimento has become associated with the birth of the modern era and is used to denote a period that began around the year 1500 and lasted for two or three centuries. Obviously, when the modern era began (or whether it ever actually did begin) is an issue fraught with problems beyond the scope of this book, but suffice it to say that here the term will look more at the period from c. 1250 to c. 1575 as one that with all its returns, renewals, reforms, and rebirths in Italy fits fairly comfortably under the label Rinascimento.

In Search of a New Paradigm for the Rinascimento

One problem that the period has long faced is that it lacks a generally accepted paradigm. In fact, unable to agree on an acceptable general vision for some time now, many have uneasily evaded the issue or ignored the question. At first it might seem paradoxical, but this lack of a clear paradigm is largely the result of a tremendous explosion of scholarship on the period following the Second World War. Essentially it completed the scholarly project, already well under way, of destroying the aesthetically pleasing, but anachronistic, paradigm formulated by the Swiss historian Jacob Burckhardt (1818–1897) in his classic nineteenth-century work *The Civilization of the Renaissance in Italy*, published just five years after Michelet's work in 1860. It did so by greatly expanding our knowledge of the social and cultural history of the period, in the process largely destroying the last vestiges of Burckhardt's vision of the period as foundational for the modern world – an age of epochal changes that prepared the ground for modern individualism, secularism, and states (as works of art) in the context of a flourishing of great intellectuals, artists, leaders and "Renaissance men." Actually, this new scholarship might be more accurately labeled as "overwhelming" rather than as destroying. For in many ways this outpouring of studies overwhelmed with detail not only Burckhardt's paradigm, but virtually all attempts at a broad overview.

One result of this overflowing of knowledge was the lack of new scholarly works that attempted an overview of the period – a result that evidently contributed to the problem, for without an overview it was difficult to engage with the period from a broader historical or intellectual perspective or even to teach it. A few scholars have attempted to redress this issue by providing new ways of seeing the period. Perhaps the most successful was Lauro Martines with his *Power and Imagination: City States in Renaissance Italy*: a work that, in line with the title, offered a powerful and imaginative series of essays that suggestively melded the newer scholarship on the social history of the period with a sophisticated vision of its culture. As essays, and highly learned ones at that, however, the book required considerable prior knowledge of the events and personalities of the time in order to be appreciated, and unfortunately, it ended early in the sixteenth century just as Martines was at his most imaginative and controversial best.

Another general study that revealed well the problem of producing an overview in the face of the overwhelming scholarship produced in the last half-century was John Law and Denys Hays's *Italy in the Age of the Renaissance, 1380–1530*. Topically arranged, the volume bristled with names, dates, and details that revealed both erudition and great range, but often left even readers familiar with the period wondering how things went together and who or what was being referred to – nonspecialist readers found the detail daunting and an overview difficult to see. The volume was also quite traditional in its view of politics and social history, with newer topics such as gender and popular culture essentially brief "tack-ons." Examples could be multiplied, and several recent attempts to provide an overview have much to recommend them, but none has provided a paradigm that has won wide acceptance.

Others have tried to provide an overview by collecting in one volume a series of topical essays by experts on subjects deemed central to understanding the period. Perhaps the best example of this was John Najemy's recent edited volume, *Italy in the Age of the Renaissance*. This volume worked well and was written at a level that could both stimulate specialists and be appreciated by nonspecialists in most cases; but its topical coverage made the period seem static and offered little in the way of a paradigm to pull together its various perspectives; also, newer work on gender, sexuality, and popular culture was largely overlooked or treated in rather traditional ways that left those topics on the periphery of the life of the day. Such composite volumes have flourished of late, because they allow specialists to describe the period from the perspective of their now often massive specialized literature, but once again they lack a general narrative or a paradigmatic vision to pull together the period. Thus, with a certain irony, as our knowledge of the period has grown exponentially, it has tended to dissolve and disappear.

Given the tendency in the Anglo-American academic world to focus on one or two cities in discussing the Renaissance, especially Florence or Venice, studies of these cities have often been used to provide an overview of the period. Unfortunately, however, scholars agree that neither city was typical of the period – in fact, no one city seems capable of serving as a model. Thus, although excellent overviews for Florence have been provided by a host of scholars – most notably, perhaps, by Gene Brucker and more recently by Najemy – and a similar overview for Venice has recently been published by Joanne Ferraro to replace the dated studies of Frederic Lane and D. C. Chambers, they do not meet the need for a work that radically rethinks the Rinascimento as a period.

What this book seeks to offer, then, is a general rethinking of the Renaissance in Italy as the Rinascimento: a rethinking that aims to provide not so much a new way of seeing it as a period, as a suggestion for a new paradigm built upon the impressive scholarship of the last few generations that would allow us to conceptualize it at once as a period and a movement of return and rebirth that typified the time. At the most general level it will suggest that we think in terms of two rather different urban civilizations in the period under consideration, c. 1250–c. 1575, that set the Rinascimento apart: a first civilization (c. 1250–c. 1450) centered in the cities of the center and north of the Italian peninsula – in many ways the area that comprised the theoretical kingdom of Italy (but long lacking a king) – that focused on an urban culture and the values of a new urban-centered elite often labeled the *popolo grosso* (the great people or the big people) that to a significant degree supplanted an older rural/feudal elite politically, socially, and culturally; and a second civilization (c. 1450–c. 1575) that involved the center and south of Italy as well, which turned around the morphing of that earlier urban elite and culture into a progressively more aristocratic and courtly society, but still primarily in an urban context.

The use of the term "civilization" may raise eyebrows given its association with privileging one culture over another, and Western society and culture in general over non-Western ones, but I use the term in its Latin root meanings of *civitas, civitatis* – a city-state, state or town; or the adjective *civilis* – of, connected with, arising from, affecting the citizens usually of a city or town; or, finally, a *vita civilis* – an urban civic life. In sum, I use the term "civilization" in its premodern and more classical and Rinascimento sense of that which concerns the population of a city and, more generally, the shared culture, practices, and values that bind together an urban populace and make it imaginable as a society by its members. Thus, at the broadest level, what sets the Rinascimento apart from the Middle Ages in this paradigm is the fact that it was an urban society that saw itself as a civilization/*civitas* led by a new elite made up primarily of merchants, bankers, and investors (often called at the time the *popolo grosso*) – in contrast to a medieval society that saw itself as basically rural, led by a rural nobility and, more distantly, by popes and emperors. In many ways the term *civiltà*, which gained popularity in Italy in the late thirteenth and fourteenth centuries, summed up this distinction, indicating the superior culture and society of the urban society of the day.

Cities, of course, were not new in Europe, and especially in northern Italy they had long been important, but what was new was the assertion that these cities had the right to dominate their societies and offer a crucial *vita civilis* not to be found so nakedly defended elsewhere in Europe. Significantly, however, this urban society that seems in many ways strikingly new, as discussed earlier, like most premodern societies in the West rejected its newness. Rather, this "new" *civiltà* saw itself and was careful to portray itself not as a new birth or spring, following Johan Huizinga's famous *Autumn of the Middle Ages*, but rather as a *rinascita* or rebirth of earlier first times, especially of an urban *civitas*/civilization (ancient Rome) and an earlier Christian community (the first Church) – a Rinascimento.

For by returning to first times such as ancient Rome and the beginnings of Christianity to find the sources of their modern civilization, this new society became comfortably old and gloriously traditional. It became a movement that claimed to be returning to what were generally accepted as superior cultures, societies, and civilizations that had been lost. And, nicely, the most important of those lost worlds, ancient Rome, had also been an urban society, with an urban culture and elites that were city-based; thus the new became at once safely old and clearly better. In fact, in the Middle Ages there had been numerous proclaimed rebirths of ancient Rome and ancient Roman culture, but what made this rebirth different was that it was urban and led by a new urban populace and elite, one that was, theoretically at least, largely non-noble and nonclerical, much as had last been the case in ancient Rome. Essentially it re-conceptualized the Great Social Divide of medieval society out of existence and did so without claiming to be doing anything new or radical, merely returning to a better past. Thus, crucially, this rebirth was conceived as making the cities of the center and north of Italy in many ways not just unique, but the home of a civilization superior to the rest of Europe.

That superiority was perhaps best expressed by a key term: *virtù* – a term that has a long, contested history, but that implied essentially the social practices that demonstrated that one person was superior to another. As will be discussed with minor local variations in the first civilization of the Rinascimento in Italy, *virtù* stressed reason, moderation, and self-control sliding toward cunning and *furbizia* (cleverness that is slightly immoral, self-serving, yet effective), essentially the values of an urban elite that could be shared widely in an urban environment, where older feudal noble values of direct confrontation, violence, and manly force were increasingly seen as disruptive and dangerous to a civilized existence. Once again, significantly, this new *virtù*, or at least the term and similar values, could be claimed to have been rediscovered in the classic texts of the ancient Roman world – even if its nuances were usually much more contemporary than ancient. And, crucially, it was seen and defended as a major feature in the movement to recover an earlier great civilization that had been lost.

Tellingly, however, the vision of *virtù* evolved across the period and especially in concert with the significant social and cultural changes of the second civilization of the Rinascimento. As urban society across the peninsula gradually became more aristocratic, courtly, and princely, *virtù* became progressively more aristocratic, mannered, graceful, and courtly. It placed a greater emphasis on self-display and self-fashioning and *sprezzatura* (the ability to accomplish great things effortlessly) and fostered a greater suspicion of a growing range of activities associated with work that would come to be seen as debasing. As we shall see, this was not simply a return to older noble values, as often claimed, but part of a much more complex process of adjusting to a new aristocracy and new courts that had developed in Italian urban society across the period. Although that new urban aristocracy and those courts claimed medieval and ancient roots, both were usually anything but traditional or ancient. And slowly but surely the aristocracy also began to abandon cities and move out into the countryside adopting an aristocratic life that spawned what might be called a villa culture and bringing with that expansion more modest bureaucratic attempts to discipline and "civilize" rural life, both of which paved the way for a formulation of a new aristocratic society that socially and culturally fit with greater ease with similar developments in the rest of Europe.

What often creates confusion about this second civilization of the Rinascimento is that it seems to be a rebirth of an older noble society and culture – a return to feudal and medieval forms. But in reality this second civilization was, if anything, much newer than the first. And it actually had much more difficulty denying the new in the face of new inventions (most notably the printing press, the arquebus, and the canon), new geographical discoveries (the "new world" and the coastal route around Africa to the East), new religions (the many reform sects of northern Europe, Catholic reform itself, and a lesser noted but significant influx of Jews forced out of Spain and Portugal), new economies (more efficient profit-oriented forms of agriculture, new trade routes, new "industries," new competitors), new powers (the emerging nation-states of the north, the Habsburg empire, especially Spain, and the Turks), challenging new political forms (the developing nation-state and the increasing dynastic ambitions of the leading noble families of Europe), and even new diseases (syphilis) and foods (from the "new world" and the East).

But, perhaps most significantly, the aristocracy of the northern cities of Italy was new, based as it was to a great extent on the merchant/banker urban elites of the first period of the Rinascimento and their growing aristocratic pretensions, which often contributed to the ongoing flourishing patronage of art and architecture that we associate with the period as well as the more general cultural flourishing that in many ways continued, with a more aristocratic vision, well beyond the end of the sixteenth century. And, crucially, this second civilization promulgated a new, challenging cultural mix of older urban values, ancient Roman and Greek ideals, and contemporary European noble values appropriated and adapted to fit urban Italian social and cultural realities. At the same time the social hierarchy of this new and progressively more aristocratic society became with time more strictly defined, and there reopened a virtually impassable divide between the upper aristocracy and the rest of society in the sixteenth century that might well be seen as the Great Social Divide recreated (although in its details it was quite different from the medieval one), a divide that lay at the heart of a more general European Renaissance and eventually what was once called the *ancien régime*, which would dominate Europe at least until the French Revolution.

It might be said that the Rinascimento ended simply when it became clear that the new had triumphed in Italy and the concept of a *renovatio/rinascita* could no longer be sustained. Contemporaries most often saw this in terms of new political realities, with Italy overrun by northern powers and economically weakened in comparison to expanding economies elsewhere in Europe and the world. Yet culturally and politically the Rinascimento had a long afterglow as its vision enjoyed a worldwide diaspora carried literally on the backs of Italian intellectuals, artists, bureaucrats, artisans, explorers, immigrants, and, often overlooked, aristocratic wives, who left or were sent out from Italy to make their fortunes in areas that were perceived as backward culturally, but more promising. In contrast to the Middle Ages, which has been seen as drawing to a close with a "harvest time" of medieval culture, the Rinascimento might be seen as ending with a planting season: a long period that saw the planting of the seeds of its rich culture in the rest of Europe and the broader world and deeply shaped the history of the West and the world for better *and* worse. In many ways we are the "harvest time" of that planting.

This book, then, will tell the tale of a different Italian Renaissance – a tale of a Rinascimento when, one after another, two new urban civilizations flourished in Italy in the period between c. 1250 and c. 1575: new civilizations based on new *virtù*-ous values, new economic realities, new elites, new social hierarchies, and new cultural forms. But for all their newness these civilizations and their many innovations were viewed as returns to older, tried, and proven ways – over and over again *renovatio/rinascita* and thus superior not just to the Middle Ages but to the rest of Europe and the world. Thus, although the term was not used at the time, the Rinascimento seems a particularly appropriate label for the time and the movement of return that dominated its vision of its time and of time itself.

To tell the immensely complex tale of this Rinascimento and contain it within one volume has required that many important topics be left out, and certainly many of the dozens of histories of individual cities and famous people have been skimmed over or uncomfortably ignored, but the goal has been to include the exemplary and the evocative in order to stimulate critical thought and provide a deeper and more nuanced vision of the period and its relevance. In this vein, in order to essay the Rinascimento I too have opted to attempt a rebirth of a more traditional historical format – a type of modified narrative. Thus the book is divided into two broad chronological sections representing the two civilizations of the period just discussed. And each section is divided in turn into chapters that provide a narrative that breaks down those larger periods into smaller ones and focuses on what might be seen as the most important issue in each time frame: thus Chapter 1 focuses on the question of legitimacy, both political and social, c. 1250–c. 1340; Chapter 2 on developing urban values and concepts of *civiltà*, c. 1300–c. 1375; Chapter 3 on the plague, its nature and its impact, c. 1325–c. 1425; Chapter 4 on violence and war from c. 1350 to c. 1454; and finally, Chapter 5 on imagination and the shared primary culture of the first Rinascimento, with a focus on c. 1350–c. 1475. The second half of the book continues the narrative format, with Chapter 6 tracing the development of courts and a more aristocratic society, following serially the development of courts in several cities, c. 1425–c. 1500; Chapter 7 narrates the development of a sense of self as a work of art, going back to the early fourteenth century but focusing on the period c. 1425–c. 1525; Chapter 8 traces the way the high Rinascimento dealt with the new that seemed to be breaking out all over, c. 1450–c. 1560; Chapter 9 follows the various ways in which the leading thinkers of the period dealt with the crisis that seemed to threaten the Rinascimento with the successive invasions of northern European powers in the sixteenth century, particularly during the period c. 1490–c. 1560; Chapter 10 follows the trajectory of a series of religious reforms that attempted to re-found the Rinascimento and maintain its cohesion as a Catholic society, c. 1500–c. 1575; and Chapter 11 looks at political reform and retreat as Italy became increasingly divided and disciplined and as its society and culture slowly dissolved into a broader European Renaissance, c. 1525–c. 1575 and beyond. A brief epilogue abandons the narrative format to essay the diaspora of Rinascimento culture, society, and political ideals more broadly in Europe and the world.

Although once again this return to a more traditional narrative format might slightly mask the newness and perhaps even the radical nature of the vision of the Rinascimento that underlies this book, that was not my goal. For hopefully its newness is its chief strength. As a new vision that seeks to draw out and emphasize the strongest themes of the new scholarship on the period, this volume is primarily an attempt to suggest new ways of seeing the period rather than an attempt to establish a final understanding of it. It has been written with an eye to opening debate, while repositioning the period in the central place it merits in the ongoing discussion not only of the meaning and importance of the Western tradition, but also of the fundamental questions of social organization and cultural values that all face in the increasingly global society of the twenty-first century.

In a way this book was written often thinking in terms of a Rinascimento garden – a rather crowded, messy, and at times overflowing garden in the Italian mode. As one strolls along the paths of this book's narrative one comes to realize that gardens, like societies, are constantly transforming what seems the natural into the cultural in ways worth rethinking carefully. So hopefully a wide range of readers can enjoy strolling through this garden with both its flowers and its thorns. But readers should be warned that Rinascimento gardens, as in Veronese's famous painting *Mars and Venus United by Love*, also tend to have their lurking satyrs – those classical metaphorical creatures that stress that humans are a mix of reason and passion and even at their best not always good – and of course no lack of serpents offering attractive apples. Such is the Rinascimento of this book: beautiful, attractive, and rich, yet also dangerous, cruel, alien, and certainly suggestive of a wider range of human possibilities worthy of critical consideration (see Illustration 9.1).

I

LEGITIMACY: A CRISIS AND A PROMISE
(c. 1250–c. 1340)

Pilgrimages in 1300

Imagine a German pilgrim in 1300 taking advantage of the jubilee year proclaimed by Pope Boniface VIII (c. 1230–1303; pope 1294–1303) to travel over the Alps to visit Rome. The crusty old pope had promised the remission of one's sins in return for a truly contrite confession by those who elected to make a pilgrimage to the Holy City that year, thirteen hundred years after the birth of Christ. Although his jubilee appears to have been an innovation, it was enough of a success that later popes regularly repeated it. They saw it as encouraging religious enthusiasm and stressing papal leadership in the West. It also enhanced the city of Rome's reputation as a goal of pilgrims and pilgrimages. For a German the idea of a pilgrimage would have been familiar, as it had been a popular form of piety and religious fervor across the Middle Ages. Many made short trips to nearby holy shrines. But there was also a well-established circuit of more demanding pilgrimage routes that by the thirteenth century were equipped with inns and hospitals – serving as lodgings for travelers and pilgrims – that because of their popularity offered the relative security of traveling in groups with fellow pilgrims.

Actually, a generation or so earlier a German chronicler, the Franciscan monk Albert of Stade, wrote a chronicle that spanned the history of the world from the creation to his own day, but as he neared the present his story became more complex, including a section presented as a dialogue between two imagined characters, Birri and Firri. In the midst of discussing the genealogies of ruling German families, Firri abruptly asked Tirri, "My good Tirri, I want to go to Rome, give me an itinerary." A willing and able interlocutor, Tirri proceeded to outline for Firri not one but several routes that would take him from Stade in northern Germany to Rome.

Had he not been an imaginary character Firri most likely would have been dead by the jubilee year of 1300, but we can imagine his equally imaginary son Felix making the pilgrimage for Boniface's celebration by following Tirri's suggested routes – routes that were rather different from the modern, for, of course, even roads have their history; and while all roads may lead to Rome, the paths they follow have changed over time. That definitely was the case for pilgrimage routes, as pilgrims had little reason to visit big towns and some good reasons to avoid them. Perhaps more importantly, while modern roads tend to prefer valleys and flats to hillsides and ridgelines, in 1300 the reverse was true. Valleys tended to be marshy and their rivers difficult to cross, whereas hillsides and ridgelines usually were drier and the streams that crossed them more easily forded. Many towns and hospices that put up pilgrims also tended to be located in these higher areas, in part because they were more easily defensible, in part because medieval roads passed close by. In sum, following in the imagined footsteps of Felix, son of Firri, we can begin to imagine a rather different land and world that was the home of the Rinascimento, and, taking a few liberties with the possibilities of imagined trips, we can also point out some of the important sites he would have passed along the way.

The idea of the pilgrimage, of course, was deeply ingrained in the culture of the day. Geoffrey Chaucer's *Canterbury Tales*, written at the end of the fourteenth century in England, provides perhaps the best-known imaginary account of one. Chaucer's pilgrims journeyed through England from Southwark to the shrine of Saint Thomas Becket at Canterbury and along the road told lively and human stories to pass the time. Not all pilgrimages in the fourteenth century were so down-to-earth. Perhaps encouraged by that same jubilee year of 1300 as our Felix, Dante Alighieri (1265–1321) took his readers on a personal and at the same time universal pilgrimage of self-discovery not to Rome, but rather through the spiritual realms of Hell, Purgatory, and Heaven in a work that would come to be known as the *Divine Comedy.*

At first, Dante's pilgrimage might seem a completely different kind of travel, set outside of the time and space of this world in a place to be known only after death. Yet one has only to glance at his travels through Hell with his ancient Roman guide, the long-dead Virgil, to recognize that that other time and space was deeply interwoven with the world, the people, and the quotidian conflicts of his day. Essentially this was because for Dante and his contemporaries the material world and life in it were deeply interwoven with the spiritual world; in essence they were not two separate realities, as in the modern imagination, but present together as closely related dimensions of the same Christian world in which all were merely pilgrims passing through this life. Thus our imagined Felix was traveling through a physical world that a modern traveler might still recognize even with all the material changes that more than seven hundred years have wrought; yet a modern traveler would only glimpse hints of that other, spiritual dimension that Dante and Felix lived in, largely lost today. Nonetheless, that dimension was as real and important as the physical one, and we will have to stretch our imagination to appreciate how it added a much wider range of encounters to our pilgrim's travels and the life of the day.

Of course, Felix's ultimate goal, the Holy City, was first and foremost for him a spiritual space with a very practical spiritual goal – the remission of sins promised by the pope and the jubilee. And along his pilgrimage path the spiritual world he passed through was in many ways as important as the physical cities or lands encountered. Right from the start, the Alps that Felix had to traverse to reach Italy would have taken him into the high mountains with some of the most dramatic peaks and beautiful alpine vistas of Europe. One wonders, however, if he would have seen their spectacular heights, dark pine forests, stark rock faces, and their often raging torrents in terms of the beauty of nature, or if he would have experienced them as a series of spiritual challenges testing his Christian commitment to winning salvation. Although Tirri recommended a more roundabout route, perhaps the most direct one that he discussed was the mountain road over the Alps often taken by Germans traders, the Brenner Pass. Ascending from the town of Innsbruck, it peaked out at a relatively low altitude of less than 5,000 feet and then descended the Val Pusteria past Trent and on to Verona.

One of the most often read early accounts of climbing in high mountains, in this case in the south of France, was written just a few years later by the noted poet Petrarch (Francesco Petrarca, 1304–1374). In a letter to his confessor Petrarch described his climb up the 6,000-foot Mount Ventoux, a wild terrain that above the tree line has a lunar quality, with vast fields of broken rock making climbing difficult, and that still today attracts visitors for its sweeping vistas. His account of his climb provides an interesting perspective on how one admittedly atypical person of the day saw the mountains, although Ventoux was not a pass, but rather a commanding peak. Petrarch describes the impressive views from the summit with enthusiasm, but he too thought of himself as a pilgrim; thus he soon turned to his manuscript of Saint Augustine that he had carried up the mountain. Eschewing the view and reading Augustine, he evoked the spiritual dimension of his climb, which he understood primarily as a spiritual assent in the grander pilgrimage that was a Christian's life. This world with its beauty offered seductive pleasures and dreams of glory – one might say ascents of pride – that as he read he confessed had seduced him, but the journey that mattered, the real journey, was through spiritual space to God. The beauty of the mountains, then, was merely a pilgrim's path to the beauty of God.

Perhaps Felix would not have thought so deeply about his mountain pass, and almost certainly he would not have been weighted down by a manuscript of Saint Augustine as he trudged over the Brenner. Nonetheless, as we imagine his pilgrimage it would be well to remember that he was prepared to see what he encountered in significantly different ways than a modern traveler would. His climb would have been long and slow, following the fast-flowing rivers that had carved the valleys through the mountains that created the pass. And there would have been plenty of snow on the peaks that year of 1300, because it seems that the long warm period that had typified the high Middle Ages and helped to make possible the great population growth across Europe in the twelfth and thirteenth centuries was ending. Some climatologists hold that the fourteenth century was actually the beginning of a mini–ice age that peaked in the sixteenth century, although there is considerable debate about its precise dating and nature. We do know that a few years later, from 1315 through 1318, Europe was inundated by heavy rains and cold summers that virtually wiped out summer crops and caused widespread famine. Contemporaries also reported that summer growing seasons had become less productive and more uncertain, an observation apparently confirmed by archival records.

As Felix descended from the Brenner, he would have noted that the mountains became more densely populated as he followed the Adige River down past the towns of Bolzano, Trent, and Rovereto to Verona at the foot of the mountains. Tirri had recommended cutting west over lower passes to Lake Como and down to Milan, but that was more a merchant itinerary than the most direct route to Rome. He also suggested that one could cut east in the mountains and then turn south to Padua and Venice on the Adriatic coast. But descending to Verona was the most direct route. Verona, like most of the cities of the north of Italy, he would have found larger and more alive with economic bustle and social turmoil than he was accustomed to in the north. With a population hovering in the 30,000 range spilling out beyond its medieval walls, it may well have been the largest city he had ever seen (see Table I). Its main basilica, which dominated the smaller buildings around it in the winding medieval streets, was a twelfth-century Romanesque masterpiece dedicated to the city's patron saint, San Zeno, reportedly its first bishop. Dominated by a high bell tower reaching over 200 feet into the sky, it and the cathedral were probably among the first things Felix noted as he approached and passed through the ancient Roman arch, the Arco dei Gavi,

TABLE I. *Largest Italian Cities (1300, 1500, and 1600)*

	1300	1500	1600
L'Aquila	40,000	—	—
Arezzo	20,000	—	—
Bergamo	14,000	—	24,000
Bologna	40,000	55,000	63,000
Brescia	24,000	56,000	36,000
Cremona	40,000	—	36,000
Ferrara	36,000	—	33,000
Florence	95,000	70,000	70,000
Genoa	100,000	60,000	63,000
Lecce	—	—	32,000
Lucca	16,000	—	24,000
Mantua	30,000	28,000	31,000
Milan	100,000	100,000	108,000
Modena	18,000	18,000	17,000
Naples	60,000	150,000	275,000
Orvieto	17,000	—	—
Padua	35,000	27,000	36,000
Parma	22,000	19,000	33,000
Pavia	30,000	—	25,000
Perugia	34,000	25,000	20,000
Piacenza	20,000	—	33,000
Pisa	38,000	—	11,000
Rome	30,000	55,000	100,000
Siena	120,000	—	19,000
Turin	14,000	—	24,000
Venice	110,000	100,000	151,000
Verona	30,000	45,000	—
Vicenza	22.000	37,000	—

Note: In 1300, of the twenty-two cities in Italy that had populations over 20,000, nineteen were in the northern half of the peninsula, with only three in the south: Rome, L'Aquila, and Naples.

which still stood astride the old Roman road he had followed down from the Brenner.

Confirming its ancient Roman heritage and its glory, and dwarfing all the modern buildings of the city, was the outsized Roman amphitheater. One of the largest constructed in the ancient world, it measured over 500 feet in length and 350 feet in width. Although it was in serious disrepair, it remained an impressive and haunting monument to a powerful world that had been lost. The main square, the Piazza dei Signori, rebuilt by the della Scala family, *signori* (lords) of the city in the thirteenth century and with a number of palaces that testified to their power and magnificence, would have impressed as well. One can imagine that our imagined Felix in Verona already was beginning to realize that the urban world of Italy in its magnificence, wealth, and Roman heritage was different from the largely rural world he had left behind. That would become clearer yet as he traveled on and encountered the numerous large urban centers that typified the north of Italy. Certainly there were a few cities in northern Europe of similar grandeur, but Verona was just one among dozens in Italy and far from the richest or grandest.

Leaving Verona, Felix faced several choices as the wide Lombard plain cut by the Po River and other river systems that came down from the Alps and flowed eastward to the Adriatic Sea lay open before him. Whichever way he traveled he would have found the densely populated, rich, fertile plain virtually without major forests, unlike his homeland. Almost all the arable land was farmed, with extensive systems of small canals and dikes to control and take full advantage of the abundant water that bathed the plain. Cutting almost directly south following the Mincio River he would have reached Mantua, a striking city that seems to float on a small body of water, with the Apennines Mountains (visible on a clear day) forming a backdrop to the south. Luigi Gonzaga would take control of the city in 1328 and begin a Gonzaga rule that lasted until 1707. From there he could have continued due south through lesser and more difficult Apennine passes to Pistoia or Lucca in Tuscany, or he could have continued eastward to where the Mincio entered the Po River, the main waterway of the Lombard Plain that stretched from the French Alps and passes in the west to the Adriatic Sea in the east. Following the Po east he would have reached Ferrara, which, as Tirri noted, commanded the eastern fords over that mighty river, and from there could have journeyed south to Bologna and the main passes over the Apennines – a mountain chain that divides the north of Italy from the center before swinging southward below Bologna to divide the center and south of the peninsula.

Before heading south, however, Felix might have been tempted to visit some of the other cities of the Lombard plain recommended by Tirri. He had spoken highly of the rich grouping of cities dominated by Milan and Pavia in the central plain, where in a fairly small area more than one million people lived, supported by the rich agricultural wealth of the area and a wide range of artisanal activities. The other and perhaps more convenient route from the Brenner involved cutting east in the mountains near Trent and descending to the plain at Padua, one of the most important university cities of Italy. From there it was a short day's journey to the great commercial island city, Venice, on the Adriatic Sea. Safely isolated in its lagoons off that

sea, the city commanded the main shipping routes to the rich lands of the
Middle East and the Eastern Roman Empire, which still existed, centered
in Constantinople. A short side trip to the north from Venice would have
brought our pilgrim to Treviso, famous along with Padua for its love poets
and rich culture. Again we are talking about large cities by the standards
of the day, with Padua and Treviso boasting around 35,000 inhabitants and
Venice more than 100,000, making it one of the largest cities in Europe.
Padua, as a noted university city, was also well populated with northern
students of all ages; thus our pilgrim might well have been more comfortable there as the city was used to dealing with German speakers. The same
would have been true of the larger and more cosmopolitan Venice. There,
rather than students, there was a large German-speaking population made
up of traders and middlemen engaged in both commerce between Italy and
the north and the lively Venetian trade with the Eastern Empire centered in
Constantinople and the Middle East.

Venice would certainly have seemed to Felix a very different place. First,
of course, unlike most medieval cities in both northern Europe and the rest
of Italy, it was a city without walls. Built on islands, it sat about two miles
from the mainland in the midst of lagoons, bodies of shallow water and
swamp, trapped by long, thin islands (*lidi*) from the open Adriatic Sea. The
shifting channels of those lagoons made it almost impossible for anyone but
locals to get to the city, thus obviating the need for walls and making the city
seem to float on the water. In fact, Venetians liked to speak of the lagoons
themselves as their walls. Felix would undoubtedly have been impressed by
the richness of the markets that clustered around the Rialto Bridge that
spanned the Grand Canal at its center. Then as now it might have seemed
that one could buy virtually anything there as well as along the streets that
led from the Rialto to Saint Mark's Square, the ceremonial heart of the city.
Ironically, a few of those goods may have come from as far away as China
then (and more than a few today).

Arriving in Saint Mark's Square, if Felix had not already been impressed
with the spiritual atmosphere of the merchant city – with its many churches,
shrines, and plaques that lined the streets and squares named for local favorite saints and martyrs – the glorious basilica, shimmering with its golden
decorations in the slanting rays of a late afternoon sun, would have reminded
him that this was very much a spiritual city as well as a commercial one. He
may not have been aware that this great church, dedicated to the apostle
Saint Mark, featured a series of mosaics that expressed claims of an apostolic
foundation that paralleled that of Rome, claims that proclaimed the city
as virtually as important and holy as Rome itself. But it would be hard to

imagine his not being impressed with the church's grandeur and the way those mosaics and interior spaces evoked the spiritual world of the city.

Looking to the right as he faced the cathedral, Felix almost certainly would have been struck by the magnificence of the doge's palace, the seat of the Venetian government. Although the palace had not yet gained its full Rinascimento majesty, it was still impressive. Before it lay the open harbor area, the Bacino, bustling with larger seagoing galleys unloading their cargoes or negotiating with city officials the transit taxes required by Venice. Next to the palace in the smaller open square that faced the lagoon he may also have seen a body or two of executed criminals hanging between the two columns that are still there, known as the Columns of Justice. Justice was such an important part of the Venetian vision of what government offered that its execution commanded a highly visible place at the heart of the civic and spiritual space of the city. There the offending members of society were literally cut off, both physically and spiritually, from the urban world.

As Felix walked on through the city he would have noted that although it seemed to be on the water, there were still richly dressed merchants who rode their horses through the narrow walkways and over the bridges that were ramped to make riding in the city possible. Later in the fourteenth century riding horses would be forbidden, and most bridges would quickly gain steps. He would also have noted that in many of the small squares of the city, locals still planted crops – one reason that, then as now, the squares of the city were called *campi* (fields) rather than *piazze* (squares). In addition most of these *campi* featured impressively decorated wellheads where local lower-class women and servants could be seen gathered, drawing fresh water and gossiping. These highly evolved wells collected and saved the rainwater that provided a major supply of fresh, clean water, as the lagoons were largely salt water. Salty lagoon water was actually a plus as it restricted the breeding of disease-carrying mosquitoes. Unfortunately, the freshwater streams and rivers that flowed into the lagoons tended to create marshy freshwater areas that provided dangerous mosquito breeding grounds. As a result, when the freshwater content of the lagoons became too great, malaria became a major problem for the city. Already well before Felix's visit the city had begun to oversee the ecology of the lagoon using dredging, man-made canals, and swamp clearance to maintain enough salinity to limit mosquitoes.

Moving through the city Felix may well have also realized that the islands of the city were actually largely man-made. Well into the fourteenth century Venetians were still filling in areas where there were mudflats just below the shallow surface of the lagoon in order to create new land for building. After the level of the land was raised above the level of high tide, the unstable surface of a new island was rendered steady enough for building by driving into the mud trunks of trees ferried down to Venice from the not-too-distant Alps – those trunks are still the support of most of the city. We might wonder if Felix would have noticed the smell of the city. Of course, all cities smelled rather strongly at the time, as wastes of all kind, including human, still tended to be dumped directly into the streets. The better-organized cities had gutters that ran along the edges of streets where rainwater or at times water supplied by people living there washed the wastes out of the city. Obviously, even with such systems, in most Italian cities strong odors remained a regular part of urban life. Yet as this was the norm, it may be that our pilgrim simply did not notice. Venice, however, had a more efficient waste disposal system as most wastes were dumped directly into the canals, where the incoming and outgoing tides essentially cleansed the city.

In this context it might be noted that baths and bathing were more popular in the urban centers of Italy than in much of the rest of Europe, so the real smell difference of Italian cities may have been in the relatively less odorous nature of their inhabitants in contrast to those of the north – although baths in urban Italy were still more likely to come at weekly or longer intervals. Speaking of baths, however, our pilgrim would probably have been aware that baths were not just for bathing. If Felix wandered off from the Rialto bridge into the warren of little islands and narrow streets leading to the large *campo* of San Polo, at the heart of Venice he would have come across a series of baths (*stue*) that would momentarily have given him the opportunity to forget the spiritual nature of his pilgrimage, for, like many baths at the time, they were noted for their sexual services as well. Being German and perhaps suspicious of baths, he could also have skipped the bath and simply visited the nearby communal house of prostitution sponsored by Venetian government. Such government-sponsored houses were provided in most Italian cities, offering sexual services at modest prices. He could also have sampled the independent sex artisans who often practiced their craft in the streets around the more popular churches and *campi* of the city. Perhaps, ironically, even in this we see the close intermixing of the commercial, material, and spiritual in this island city.

But leaving our imagined pilgrim's potential deviations from his spiritual path to the imagination, from Venice he would have cut across low, marshy country often covered in dense fog and swarms of mosquitoes, arriving once again at Ferrara, a city of approximately 36,000, with its fords over the Po River. This was the first city that our traveler encountered that was supposedly ruled by the pope, as the northernmost outpost of what were vaguely recognized as the Papal States. In Ferrara, however, the pope's rule was usually more theoretical than real as papal power had largely been usurped by power-ful local families. After Ferrara, heading south Felix would have soon reached the slightly larger city of Bologna, with a population of at least 40,000, once again theoretically controlled by the papacy. There he would perhaps have been impressed by the way it too was dominated by students and professors, for along with Padua's the university there was one of the most famous of Italy and Europe, particularly noted for the study of law. In a more modest way the city was also a commercial hub as it sat athwart an important north-south road that crossed the Apennines on the way to Rome and the south.

But what almost certainly would have most impressed him about the city as he crossed the last fields of the rich agricultural plains and saw it backed by the Apennines rising to the south was the way the city itself seemed to be forested by a number of high towers. The highest was the Asinelli, which in 1300 was probably only a little over 230 feet high, but which within the century would grow to more than 320 feet. Earlier in the thirteenth century the city probably had well over a hundred such towers, but the second half of the century had seen a number come down, either due to the difficulty of keeping them standing or because of civic initiatives to tear them down. Those initiatives were in response to one of their primary purposes; for they had been used as urban fortifications for fighting within the city, usu-ally between urban-living noble families and the leaders of the *popolo*. In an attempt to pacify the city many had been torn down, but certainly not all, and a few have even survived, giving the city its own modern leaning towers, although they are much higher and less ornate than the more famed Leaning Tower of Pisa. Actually, many of the cities that Felix visited had once had their own forests of towers, most of which had come down in the second half of the thirteenth century as part of a more general attempt to pacify the cities of north and central Italy.

Felix would probably have been most impressed with the university area at the center of the city, which was frequented by large numbers of foreign-ers, including many from German-speaking lands. There were virtually no university buildings per se, but professors or groups of students rented quar-ters to hold classes, and the streets were alive with students of all ages. Much of the center had porticoed walkways that allowed street life to continue when it rained or snowed or when the summer sun became too hot. A large concentration of male students, merchants in transit on the Roman roads to and from the south, and a sizeable contingent of clerics associated with the university also meant that once more the city offered a wide range of illicit pleasures, and again our pilgrim had the opportunity to forget his spiritual quest and sample more earthly ones if tempted.

Leaving Bologna, Felix again faced a choice. He could follow the line of the Apennines southwest toward the Adriatic, passing numerous small cities on the narrow coastal plain before cutting over the Apennines on one of the old Roman roads that still crossed the mountains down into central Italy. This coastal region was commercially dominated by Venice, but the whole region was at the time hotly contested by local lords fighting among themselves for local power; the papacy, trying to assert ancient claims; and Venice, attempting to secure its interests. Given these uncertainties, our pilgrim might have been better off following the road from Bologna over the Apennines directly southwest to Florence, a distance of only sixty miles as the crow flies, but more difficult to traverse than that distance might suggest.

Assuming he took that route to Florence, when Felix descended into Tuscany, he found himself in one of the most densely populated areas in Europe in 1300, both in the countryside and in the cities. Florence was rapidly rising to prominence in the region, boasting a population of approximately 95,000, which made it again one of the largest cities of Europe. The older banking center of Siena, southwest of Florence in the hills, may have been even larger, however, with a population that peaked at about 120,000 around 1300 and would fall dramatically over the next three centuries. The port city of Pisa followed, with a population of close to 40,000. The cloth-producing city of Lucca along with Arezzo, Pistoia, Prato, and Cortona all had from ten to twenty thousand souls. When one considers that at this same time there were only five cities in the north of Europe with more than 40,000 inhabitants, while Tuscany alone had two cities with populations hovering near 100,000 along with a heavily populated countryside, it is not hard to imagine that once again Felix would have been impressed by the sheer numbers of people and the size of the urban centers he encountered.

As he descended the last hills to Florence he would have found the city located toward the end of a fairly broad valley carved by the Arno River. Once again the towers that had perhaps once been the most notable aspect of the city had largely been cut down, and the great cathedral church dedicated to Santa Maria del Fiore (that today dominates the city skyline and is more commonly known as the *Duomo*) had only recently begun construction and was still a little more than a century and a great architect, Filippo Brunelleschi, from completion. Again the city was littered with churches, shrines, and Roman remains, some real, others imagined. The Baptistery of San Giovanni, which stood before the rising cathedral, for example, was widely believed to originally have been a Roman temple dedicated to Mars. Actually, however, it was built on late Roman ruins and only begun in the eleventh century. As the name implies, the Baptistery was used for baptisms, and our poet Dante began his pilgrimage through life with his baptism there, like most Florentines.

Passing through the center of the city Felix would once again have been impressed with the markets that opened up lively spaces in the narrow warren of medieval streets and perhaps have noticed the noxious smells of the chemicals used in producing luxury woolen cloth, which was becoming one of the mainstays of the city's economy. As Florence gained access to better-quality wool, that proto-industry would grow apace, and artisans producing luxury cloth would number as many as 30,000 in the first half of the century, according to the very number-conscious Florentine chronicler Giovanni Villani. Interestingly, Villani claimed that one of the things that motivated him to write his chronicle was his own pilgrimage to Rome for the jubilee of 1300; thus one might imagine that our imagined pilgrim Felix and this chronicler shared some of the same experiences. Be that as it may, most of the shops and workplaces for cloth production clustered near the Arno River, which bisected the city. For much of the year the river was too shallow to support significant shipping westward to the Tyrrhenian Sea, always a handicap for the city as a commercial power. But the river was seen as well suited for dumping the many polluting wastes of cloth production, which undoubtedly did not add to the attractiveness of the city or its general health. Felix may not have noted the countinghouses and banks that were already becoming some of the richest in Europe serving the papacy, but he would have had trouble missing the illicit world at the heart of the city, which again featured a municipal house of prostitution and very lively baths and inns.

Leaving Florence, our pilgrim would once again have faced a decision about which road to follow. One route would have taken him west down the Arno River valley to the coast of the Tyrrhenian Sea, where he could have boarded a ship for Rome. If he followed that route he would have passed through a rich agricultural plain and a number of flourishing smaller cities such as Pistoia and Lucca until he reached the important medieval trading city of Pisa, which no longer sat on the coast. It still had access to the sea because the Arno, by then navigable, traversed it just before flowing into the sea. That, however, was a mixed blessing as Florence was becoming more and more anxious to control its port and the city. Those Florentine desires, along with a series of unsuccessful and costly naval wars with its commercial rivals, Venice and Genoa, meant that the city's glory days were on the wane. Genoa, a much more powerful merchant city, perched precariously to the north along the coast of the Tyrrhenian where the Alps swept down to the sea, was yet another major city of the peninsula. With a population of about 100,000, along with Florence, Siena, Milan, and Venice it made the peninsula home to five of the largest and richest cities in Europe in 1300 (see Table I).

But Felix was headed south, and if he opted for the coastal route from Pisa to Rome, which had once been the ancient Roman Via Aurelia, he would have been hampered by marshy terrain and a number of fast-running rivers tumbling down to the sea. Aside from Roman ruins and the occasional small town or fishing village, the coast, especially in the south of Tuscany, was the least populous area in the region, with the exception of the mosquitoes that thrived there along with malaria.

Tirri recommended that from Florence south the best route involved reentering the hills below the Arno and moving on to the rich hilltop banking town of Siena, with its beautiful churches and its flourishing republican government, which was still a major stopover on the main medieval road north to the coast and north to France or south to Rome. A major banking rival of Florence, Siena would be another victim of that city's determination to dominate all of Tuscany and eliminate what were seen as local rivals. The city's hilltop location, which had offered an important defensive advantage in more turbulent medieval times, was also becoming an impediment to its continued economic success. Its heights did not offer the water resources necessary for cloth production – a key to the wealth of cities like Florence and Lucca – nor were they easily accessible for trade. In sum, the city's best days were coming to an end.

Working his way south along the ridgelines of the hills beyond Siena, Felix should have found traveling relatively easy on the primary pilgrimage route to Rome. But let's imagine that he opted to leave the hilltops to cut back to the old Roman road, the Via Cassia, to the east following the Tiber River valley to Rome. He probably would have intersected that road just south of the urban center of Orvieto, yet another hilltop town and an especially impressive one, built atop high cliffs that seem to rise directly out of the valley. Its excellent defensive position, rich hinterland, and proximity to Rome made it a city that was especially popular with thirteenth-century popes seeking a secure base in the heart of the territories that the papacy attempted to rule in the center of Italy. In fact, it had become the place where Pope Nicholas IV (1227–1292; pope 1288–1292) and Pope Boniface VIII maintained their papal bureaucracy or curia, as it was called, in an attempt to avoid the often-violent tenor of life in Rome. Once again the city was in the midst of building a majestic new cathedral dedicated to the Virgin that was begun by Pope Nicholas in 1290, which would not be completed until well into the next century.

Still a little over a hundred miles from Rome, our pilgrim was now on the last stretch to the Holy City and one-time capital of the Roman Empire. It would be difficult to be sure what he expected as he approached that city. As it was already famous for its worldly ways and corruption, he might secretly have been anticipating some more questionable illicit pleasures on the order of what Florence and Venice had offered. Or he might have been hoping that for the jubilee year the eternal city would have put on its best face, offering a powerful spiritual experience in an impressive capital that had transformed the ancient metropolis into the mother city of the great Church that oversaw Christian life in the West. Finally, after several months of travel, what lay before his eyes as he crossed the old Roman Milvian Bridge into the city was something starkly different – a town of 20–30,000 souls camped in the ruins of the ancient capital that had once hosted more than a million, with much of the land within the old Roman walls given over to farming and grazing. Pressing the capacity of the urban fabric of this city-in-the-ruins were reportedly close to 200,000 pilgrims, who swarmed the city in enthusiastic response to the pope's jubilee year. Ironically, in what was merely a large town Felix encountered once again one of the largest cities in Europe, albeit only a momentary one.

As our pilgrim arrived from the north, a number of imposing Roman ruins would have risen above the low houses and ubiquitous churches of the city. To his left would have loomed the massive structure of the Coliseum, flanked by ruins of the Roman Forum and the Quirinal Hill, once home to imperial palaces and now given over largely to pasture. Further on, the gigantic structure of the Pantheon, now a church dedicated to the Virgin, rose above the town. Across the Tiber on a slight rise stood Old St. Peter's Cathedral, where the apostle Peter was buried, and hard by it the Papal Palace, a complex that would be heavily remodeled in the Rinascimento, although major remodeling had already been begun by Popes Nicholas III (1210–1280; pope 1277–1280) and Nicholas IV with an eye to showcasing the magnificence of the papacy and the Church. The remains of the Mausoleum of Hadrian lay to the right and in front of the Papal Palace, on a bend of the Tiber, as Castel Sant'Angelo, it now served as a fortification for the papacy in times of frequent civil strife. It also loomed over the main bridge that crossed the river connecting central Rome to the area around Saint Peter's and the Papal Palace. The main cathedral church of Rome, Saint John Lateran, located on the other side of the city just up the hill from the Coliseum, however, was the official residence of the popes and the foremost church of Western Christianity. According to tradition the original Lateran Palace, an ancient Roman administrative building, had been donated to the papacy by the Emperor Constantine early in the fourth century and had become the official residence of the popes and cathedral Church of Rome.

Felix, notwithstanding his presumed disappointment at the ruined state of Rome, would certainly have visited Saint John Lateran. There he would undoubtedly have visited the pope's chapel, the Sancta Sanctorum, and perhaps finally been impressed. The chapel, which had been rebuilt after an earthquake in 1278 by Nicholas III, contained the *Acheropita*, the reputed true portrait of Christ. Nicholas had taken advantage of the rebuilding to decorate the chapel with frescoes that portrayed the stories of the various holy relics housed there and eschewing modesty for glory, had included a large fresco of himself flanked by the apostles Peter and Paul, the legendary founders of the Roman Church, presenting a model of his chapel to Christ with his own hands (Illustration 1.1). Significantly, Peter, the founder of the Roman Church, helps lift it in offering; thus the first bishop of Rome and the current bishop offered the chapel to the founder of the Christian era, Christ. Nicholas was claiming to move in very exclusive spiritual first circles. Gold mosaics, rich marble columns, and vaults all added to the impressiveness of a chapel that emphasized that Rome, for all its ruins and lack of grandeur, was still the place where ancient Christianity and the modern came together and where modern popes still drew on the power of the apostles, Peter and Paul, and Christ himself to rule the world.

If Felix visited the other great churches of the city he would have seen such messages reinforced repeatedly with recently commissioned frescoes and mosaics. If he missed the message, he may have had it confirmed verbally by Pope Boniface from his Benediction Loggia, recently added to the Lateran Palace, where he blessed those who had come to Rome in his jubilee year to celebrate the glory of the Church. The loggia, built with ancient Roman columns, again featured sculptures of the apostles Peter and Paul and rich decorations that included the pope's own family's coat of arms and baldachins (ceremonial umbrellas that harked back to imperial heraldry), thus intermixing the Christian, Roman, and recent Roman family themes that underlay his power and claims to be able to remit the sins of pilgrims with his jubilee. Perhaps we should leave our imagined pilgrim, Felix, there at the end of 1300, imagining his own spiritual renewal and his return trip north through the prosperous urban world of Italy and its flourishing society, so unlike his homeland north of the Alps.

1.1. *Nicholas III Kneeling with Saints Paul and Peter before Christ,* 1277–80, Lateran Palace,
Rome. Photo: Mondadori Portfolio/Electa/Art Resource, New York.

Dante and the Right to Rule

Felix and his pilgrimage, although hopefully providing a taste of the urban
world of Italy around 1300, can hardly hope to match the poetry of Dante's
pilgrimage of spiritual self-discovery through realms of Hell, Purgatory, and

Paradise in his *Divine Comedy*. Yet that apparently very different world turns out to be not so distant from the one Felix journeyed through; for it too was deeply intertwined with both the ancient and the modern, the spiritual and the material, and pullulating with the urban life of the early 1300s – for the dead characters that Dante encountered on his pilgrimage, especially in Hell, are alive with the urban world that Felix encountered in Italy. The people he might well have encountered on the streets or in the inns of Florence, drinking a cup of wine and arguing over politics, are there suffering for their sins and talking with the poet as he passes by, still very much involved with that world. Dante even lets his readers know that a similar fate awaited Boniface VIII, who had proclaimed Felix's jubilee, when he died.

Suggestively, our prophet of the end of the world, Joachim of Fiore, reappears in the *Comedy* as well, but in what might seem an unlikely place. For he does not appear in Hell, where one might expect to find someone who prophesized the destruction of the Church and papacy, but rather in Paradise, where Dante the pilgrim, working his way toward his ultimate beatific vision of God, encountered beatified churchmen on their way to becoming saints. Among others encountered there were two noted thirteenth-century figures who did become saints, Saint Bonaventure (1221–1274; canonized 1482) and Saint Thomas Aquinas (1225–1274; canonized 1323). Dante apparently placed Joachim in this august company because he still saw much promise in his prophecies – referring to him as "Joachim, Calabrian by birth, endowed with all the gifts of prophecy." The poet's enthusiasm may well have been influenced by a continuing Joachite tradition in Florence, where in the last decades of the thirteenth century radical leaders of the more spiritual wing of the Franciscans preached at the Franciscan Church of Santa Croce. Evidently Dante was impressed by their vision of a more spiritual age soon to arrive, where love of God would replace love of money and all would live together in much the same beatific reverence for the Divinity that he evoked in the final cantos of his depiction of Paradise.

Dante took up this issue of how people might live together in peace and harmony as good Christians in this world in a more systematic way in his less often read *De monarchia* (*On Monarchy*). Written in Latin, probably sometime around the first years of the second decade of the century, it seems today like a curious work on the cusp of the Rinascimento. Heavily based on the thinking of Aristotle and Aquinas and frequently employing a dialectical form of argumentation associated with late medieval scholasticism, it was written in a late medieval Latin that would later be criticized for its lack of classical forms. Nonetheless, its most central arguments were based on claims that called for a political rebirth of an ancient Roman imperial ideal. And throughout the work Dante's political and closely related religious vision turned not on new political or religious programs, but instead on a return or a rebirth of the political world of that crucial first time when both the Roman Empire and the Christian Church were founded.

In fact, Dante remarked early in that work that he had once been surprised at how easily the ancient Romans had conquered first their neighbors and eventually the world. But as he reflected on that success, thinking about military tactics and other, more traditional explanations, suddenly he realized that he had foolishly missed what had really happened. Roman success was actually an important part of God's larger plan for history. The success of Christ and Christianity required a world empire that made possible the spread of his message and his Church. That the two times overlapped, then, was not an accident; rather, it was by divine design, and that divinely ordained first time was for Dante a truly special time that needed to be reborn in the present. As a result, Dante based his political and religious remedies for the problems of his day on a return or rebirth of the political and religious order of that special first time when the Roman Empire and the Christian Church were founded – a Rinascimento.

In this way Dante also answered one of the most fundamental questions of political and social life: by what right does one person or one group rule over others? Today we are so inured to government and its claims of authority that we seldom ask that fundamental question. But that was not always so. And it was especially not the case in the early years of the Rinascimento, when local governments in Italy, usually centered in the flourishing urban centers like those visited by Felix, had little formal right to rule and faced many competitors for power, both within the cities and beyond their walls. As a result, the right to exercise power over others, to rule, was a matter of deep and ongoing uncertainty that significantly colored the way in which governments and other competitors for power presented themselves, claimed authority, and attempted to organize and control society. In turn, to a great extent the vision of the legitimate power of government (the competitor that eventually won) that developed in those cities lives on, the significant and largely unquestioned rationale of a modern vision of government and the state that in many ways was discovered in the Rinascimento.

Venice Claims Equality with the Pope and Emperor

Leaving Dante's vision behind for a moment and turning to the often bloody conflicts over who would rule that worried him and his contemporaries, we could discuss virtually any of the dozens of city governments that existed in the fourteenth century in the center and north of Italy. Yet Venice stands out for its powerful defense of its republican rule (with a significant future) and also because it was often in the forefront of political developments. In the middle of the fourteenth century the chief executive officer of the city's government, the Doge Andrea Dandolo (1306–1354; doge 1343–1354), wrote a chronicle that narrated the story of how Venice had developed from a humble group of scattered settlements lost in the lagoons of northeastern Italy into a major international power famed for its wealth and international trade. A central part of his account was a largely mythic tale of Venice's crucial role in an archetypal medieval power conflict in 1177 between the papacy and the empire. The pope at that time, Alexander III (c. 1105–1181; pope 1159–1181), according to Dandolo, had earned the wrath of the powerful Roman emperor, Frederick I Barbarossa (1122–1190; elected emperor 1152; crowned 1155–1190) because he had blocked Frederick's claims to imperial territory in Italy, declaring that it belonged to the papacy.

Although Barbarossa's name did not refer to his barbarous ways, according to Dandolo his response to the pope's interference was a barbarous war that forced the pope out of Rome and harried him across Italy until finally he found refuge in Venice. And while from the emperor's point of view it was a just war, from the pope's perspective the Church was completely within its rights in attempting to block his imperial designs in Italy. The issue was as simple as it was contentious: both rulers had deeply legitimate claims to rule the Italian peninsula; both intended to defend them; and at this level Dandolo's largely mythic account reflected an actual ongoing contest between popes and emperors.

The imperial claims were relatively straightforward. Frederick claimed to be the legitimate successor of the ancient Roman emperors who had conquered and ruled virtually the whole world. Actually, of course, even at ancient Rome's point of maximum expansion it was a more modest empire, but still impressive, encircling the Mediterranean Sea and stretching northward into the great Germanic forests of Europe, even reaching for a time the midlands of England and extending eastward into the Middle East. The Emperor Constantine (272–337; emperor 306–337) early in the fourth century had split the empire into an eastern half ruled from the city he had built and named for himself, Constantinople, and a western half ruled from the old capital, Rome. Progressively overrun by invading tribes from the north and overwhelmed by its own bureaucratic and economic travails, the Western Empire ceased to exist for a time as a political entity, but it endured as a political ideal. Thus toward the end of the eighth century when a line of powerful Germanic rulers, the Carolingians, conquered most of Europe, including much of the Italian peninsula, and sought somehow to legitimate their rule beyond the naked power of their armies, a renewal of the Roman Empire in the west, led by them as emperors, seemed perfect.

On Christmas Day 800, perhaps the most powerful of the Carolingians, Charlemagne (Charles the Great), was crowned Roman emperor by the pope at a mass in Rome. Charlemagne later claimed to have been surprised by the pope as the latter rather hurriedly slammed the imperial crown on his head and proclaimed him emperor while he knelt at the altar. Perhaps true, but his story also served his purpose of portraying himself as an innocent victim of papal plotting – a useful claim for the powerful eastern emperor who was not enthusiastic about competition from a new western emperor and renewed empire. In the end, however, Charlemagne and his successors fostered an imperial revival in the west that is sometimes called the Carolingian Renaissance, a rebirth of ancient Roman culture in the ninth century. This Carolingian revival was short-lived, for Europe was ravaged by new invasions from the north (Vikings), the east (Hungarians), and the south (Muslims) and the Western Empire disappeared again, only to be revived by a new group of northern German rulers, the Ottonians, in 962, when Otto I was crowned emperor in Rome. Following that revival, however, the empire in the west continued down to the time of Frederick and on through the Rinascimento. Thus Frederick could claim that he was the legitimate representative of the ongoing Roman Empire and the ultimate political authority in the west. Of course, his claims were one thing, the political realities of actual rule another. Still, claiming the legitimacy of being the true heir of the great Roman Empire was a powerful tool in asserting authority and was difficult to deny, especially when an emperor like Barbarossa showed up with a powerful army.

Theoretically, papal claims to rule Europe were, if anything, even more compelling. At the simplest level, of course, in a Christian society, the pope as God's representative on earth (his vicar) could claim authority over all Christians. Still, there were many texts in the Bible that called upon the leaders of the Christian community to defer to governments and, quite specifically, to Roman emperors. Those texts did create problems for papal claims to rule. Also, of course, popes tended to lack the armies based on feudal levies of noble warriors that were needed in order to compete when theory gave way to violence, as it did all too often. Yet the papacy did have strong claims to political power and, impressively, they were based on concessions of such power made by emperors to the papacy. The most noted of these was the famous Donation of Constantine, actually a forgery of the eighth century. The Donation related another mythic event: supposedly the

Emperor Constantine – the same emperor who divided the empire and build Constantinople – after converting to Christianity developed leprosy, one of the most feared diseases in medieval Europe. Constantine asked the pope at the time, Sylvester (pope 314–335), to pray to God to free him from this devastating malady.

And, of course, as happens in powerful myths, the pope's prayers were answered. Constantine quickly recovered. Out of gratitude, and in recognition of the fact that the pope really was the ultimate power on earth, a fact made clear by his miraculous cure, Constantine donated his rule of the empire to the papacy. Sylvester, however, more interested in his spiritual mission and guiding the Church, although he accepted the donation gave it back to the emperor to rule, but crucially contingent upon his and future emperors being good shepherds of their Christian subjects. Behind the pious resolve to protect Christian subjects, the import was clear: emperors ruled in this world only so long as they lived up to the requirements of God's vicar on earth, the pope. In the end, however, it was popes who had the ultimate right to rule; for even political power had been donated to them by Constantine. Of course, this was all too good to be true for the papacy, and (as already noted) it was not. The Donation would be demonstrated a forgery, as we shall see, by the noted scholar of the classics Lorenzo Valla in 1440. Actually, much earlier Dante had expressed his reservations about the validity of the Donation in his *De Monarchia*. Apparently never doubting the legend itself, he had taken an interesting tack that was much in line with the powerful legal arguments being marshaled in the widespread debates about who had the right to rule in the early fourteenth century, arguing that as emperor, Constantine did not own the empire, thus he did not have the legal right to give it away.

Returning to Doge Dandolo's account of the conflict between Frederick I Barbarossa and Alexander III: although largely mythic, it reflected a deeper perceived truth, that the empire and the papacy were the two recognized legitimate powers of the time and frequently in conflict about who would actually dominate the west. Frederick was so successful in the 1170s in his attack on Alexander that, according to Dandolo, he drove the pope from Rome and harried him across Italy, always about to capture him and bring the long conflict between empire and papacy to a disastrous end for the pope. Fortunately for Alexander, however, Venice came to his rescue, offering him protection and a safe haven in their island city. Actually, much of Dandolo's portrayal of the founding and rise of the city, following earlier mythic accounts, stressed how the city, safe in its lagoons, had served repeatedly as a haven for the oppressed. Thus taking in the pope was just another example of that ongoing theme.

This time, however, Venice decided to offer more than a haven. Donating money and its ships to aid the papacy, the city raised a great armada and, in a major naval battle, defeated Frederick. No matter that the great battle apparently never happened (Frederick's actual major defeat was on land, at the Battle of Legnano in 1176 at the hands of a league of Lombard cities), for the purposes of Dandolo's mythic account it was one of the greatest Venetian victories. Matched against one of the most powerful emperors of the recent past and defending one of the most important popes of the day, Venice triumphed.

Dandolo, following earlier chroniclers, reported that the pope, in thanks for this support, took a gold ring from his finger and gave it to the doge, Sebastiano Ziane, to marry the sea with his blessing on the annual feast of the Ascension. Actually, this ritual marriage to sea was a much older practice, but by tying it to Venice's great victory and the pope's gift and blessing, a major civic ceremony that celebrated Venice's special relationship to the sea, merchant power, and commercial wealth was given a deeper spiritual significance and weight. It was a significance that was aggressively emphasized in the fourteenth century as the city competed with Italian rivals to dominate the Adriatic Sea and the Mediterranean. In fact, our chronicler Dandolo as doge at midcentury every year sailed out into the Adriatic, where, after being blessed with holy water and biblical verses read by priests, he cast his gold ring into the waves to renew the city's marriage vows with the sea, proclaiming "We wed you Sea in the name of a true and everlasting dominium." Suggestively, with a ceremony rich in gender and marital symbolism, the doge as the patriarch of the city and its government wed the female sea so crucial to Venetian prosperity and survival, recreating yearly a special blessed family that in its way regularly produced many fruitful offspring for the city, in terms of both commercial wealth and important foodstuffs. Here we have a fictive corporate body, government, that, incarnate in the Doge, performed like a person, married and reproduced the wealth that sustained society and thus earned its legitimacy.

After their naval victory, according to Dandolo, a peace was negotiated between the pope and the emperor with the help of Venice. Once again in reward for the city's support the pope awarded Venice a special sword that was displayed ever after in civic processions as a sign of the doge's and the city's judicial power to literally cut out offending members of society. As providing justice was one of the most important functions of government across the period, the gift of a sword from the pope was a powerful sign of the right of the doge and Venice to exercise this central aspect of rule. Swords, however, had deeper implications when conferred by popes, because a very popular medieval sword metaphor held that there were ultimately two swords that ruled the world, the pope's and the emperor's. Thus the gift of a sword from the pope could be and was seen as a much more direct conferral of governing authority. One begins to understand why this largely mythic and largely false account of what was, from the perspective of the mid-fourteenth century, a distant medieval event had become for Dandolo such an important part of his history of the city.

After a number of other highly symbolic gifts were conferred on the Doge, continuing the celebration, the pope, the emperor, and the doge traveled down the eastern coast of the peninsula to Ancona – another important trading city at the time. There Dandolo related that the thoughtful populace of the city brought out large umbrellas (*Baldachini*) to protect the pope and the emperor from the hot Mediterranean sun. Reporting a seemingly minor detail, the Doge interrupted his narrative to note that the pope, when he saw the umbrellas, stopped everything to order, "Bring out a third umbrella for the Doge of Venice, whose merits deserve it, because he has freed us from tribulations and placed us in a cooling place which the umbrella well signifies." Once again we have slipped into the world of a mythic explanation for a civic ceremonial, and the deeper truth is in the details – for on this seemingly insignificant detail was built perhaps the most powerful and audacious claim for the legitimacy of Venetian rule. At the simplest level Dandolo was demonstrating with a seemingly innocent moment that the pope had implied that Venice was the equal of the pope and the emperor. While the others present at the ceremony humbly suffered the sun's heat, the three great powers and leaders of the world were protected from it and granted the dignity that they deserved – crucially, a dignity they *equally* deserved. The pope not only recognized this, he commanded it, and the defeated emperor acquiesced.

It might be objected that this was merely a moment of empty ceremony. But ceremony struck deep in the premodern world, illustrating for all the central connections and deeper meanings of things that were often masked by the helter-skelter of everyday life. In a world without mass media or printing, ceremony was one of the crucial areas where deeper cultural values were communicated or impressed upon a larger population – a perfect place for expressing and demonstrating the legitimacy of governments. If there is any doubt about this, the ongoing history of the Baldachin should lay it to rest. Across the Rinascimento the doge on ceremonial occasions invariably appeared in public under the Baldachin, a sign of his right to rule and of Venice's claim to equality with the papacy and the empire. Tellingly, in the Doge's palace in the hall where the Great Council of the city met, the city also decorated the walls of the chamber with the signal moments of the Venetian past. Among those pictures a prominent place was given to this mythic event, with a depiction of the three great powers of the world at Ancona under their Baldachins. And although the fourteenth-century version was destroyed by fire, in the late sixteenth century a new series of paintings was done in the chamber, with prominent place given to a painting by Girolamo Gambarato portraying the scene of the pope ordering a third umbrella for the doge. Even if it was imaginary, the moment was too important to forget.

Significantly, Venice's claims to legitimate rule were also based upon other foundational moments than the twelfth-century conflict between Church and empire. In fact, the multiple myths of founding incorporated in Dandolo's chronicle gave the city an equality with, or even priority over, both popes and emperors. First off, he claimed that the city had been founded by Trojans fleeing Troy after the Trojan War. Obviously this paralleled and undercut the myths of Rome's founding and special status, as ancient Rome had long ago claimed a similar founding. As if this were not enough, a second and third founding of Venice were claimed, respectively, by refugees from the Roman Empire when it finally fell to invading Germanic tribes and later by Roman refugees when the last vestiges of Roman rule fell to Lombard invaders. These later foundings both suggested that the city deserved to be considered the legitimate continuation of the Roman Empire as much as, or more than, the German claimants from the north.

Even that was not enough: for Dandolo used another founding myth to claim a spiritual and apostolic foundation that had the potential at least to parallel the pope's claim to rule the Church. The pope based his claim to lead the Church on the assertion that the Bishopric of Rome and thus the papacy itself had been founded by the apostle Peter, who had come to Rome to convert the pagans of the empire and had been martyred there. According to a doctrine that became known as the Petrine Doctrine, Christ, as reported in Matthew 16:18, said to his disciple Peter, "I say unto thee that thou art Peter, and upon this rock I will build my Church." As the word for rock, "*Petrus*," also meant Peter, it was claimed early on that with these words Christ had made Peter the person who would found his Church in Rome and that the bishops who followed him would continue, in a direct line from him, Christ's rule on earth. In this way the pope's claim to rule the Church descended directly from the words of Christ and the first time of the Church.

According to Venetian myths retold by Dandolo, repeated ad infinitum in the local chronicle tradition, and celebrated in a myriad of ways, Venice had

1.2. Plaque *Pax Tibi Marce*. The Lion Gate at Zadar (Croatia). © Hans Georg Roth/ CORBIS.

been founded by its own apostle, Mark, who, on his own mission converting the pagans, one day found himself lost in a storm in what would become the Venetian lagoons, when miraculously there appeared an angel of the Lord who greeted him with the famous words "Pax Tibi Marce" (Peace be with you, Mark) – suggestively, the same words, "Peace be with you," that the resurrected Christ used when he appeared to his disciples in the Bible. Mark's angel, however, went on to promise that on the very spot where he was lost a great Christian city and peaceful haven would arise to continue his work of building a Christian society. The famous Lion of Saint Mark representation of the city, with the motto Pax Tibi Marce, became, in fact, a ubiquitous marker of the city's rule and power. And it can still be encountered throughout the north of Italy and the eastern Mediterranean wherever Venetian power extended in the Middle Ages and Rinascimento (Illustration 1.2). Thus the city had its own apostolic foundation and its own spiritual mission that placed it virtually on a par with Rome and the pope.

Legitimacy and a Rebirth of First Times

While perhaps the Venetian mythic vision of the origins of its legitimate power and status were more developed than in most other cities, the crucial thing is that similar myths were constructed throughout the cities of Italy and were a significant part of the civic culture of the day. Many a sculptor, painter, or intellectual found employment illustrating in stone, fresco, or on parchment similar legitimating myths. Certain themes, however, predominated. One of the most important was the claim to be returning to an earlier and better first time, usually Roman and/or Christian, although pre-Roman and Trojan/Greek origins were also popular; thus legitimacy usually stemmed from a rebirth of those first times, a Rinascimento. Regularly fourteenth-century urban governments in Italy stressed that they had been founded by ancient Roman emperors. It was an easy claim to make in Italy, as obviously it had been the center of the Roman world, and ubiquitous Roman ruins along with local legends attested to Roman foundations. Local governments frequently claimed a founding by a superior Roman emperor who saw their city as a place well suited to continuing a true Roman society and rule. And once more lurking not-too-hidden behind such claims to imperial foundations was the implicit claim that such cities continued the empire as northern barbarian emperors never could.

Those who did not stress a Roman foundation usually opted for a founding in other superior first times. In fact, most stressed some special way in which they were connected to the first times of Christianity. Perhaps most widespread was the way they emphasized their foundation upon the relics of the great saints and fathers of the early Church. Venice, for example, claimed to have stolen Saint Mark's body, often with the corpse's aid, an event retold in virtually every chronicle of the city and an ongoing theme in civic art there. Popular oral and chronicle traditions retold the stories of how relics were brought to their cities during the Middle Ages, often miraculously, and used to consecrate the altars of local churches. In this way the sacred spaces of Italian cities were conceptualized as being literally founded on the bodies of the martyrs and saints of the Church. Much as the papacy had been founded in Rome on the body of Saint Peter, so too local governments claimed their own spiritual foundations that linked their cities directly to the first Church, often augmented by the special spiritual strength of more local and recent saints and martyrs. A great deal of late medieval and early Rinascimento religious art sought to evoke these themes that legitimated and connected the space of particular cities of northern Italy to the more spiritually central spaces of the Holy Land.

By claiming such a spiritual base as well as a founding in the great moments of secular first time, cities essentially covered the crucial bases of their legitimacy from the perspective of Church and government. In the end few could claim, as Venice did, virtually complete equality with empire and papacy, but most cities could and did claim that they shared in the legitimacy of both, sharing the tradition of the former and the spiritual continuity of the latter. And, crucially, their claims were not based upon anything that was new, but rather returned to special first and superior times, especially the glory days of the early Church and Christian martyrs or the great moments of the Roman Empire and its triumphs. Essentially, then, there was nothing new or dangerous in their claims to rule legitimately; once again everything was a return, a rebirth, a re-forming of a better, older time, a Rinascimento. And the literature, art, and culture of the day in many ways elaborated on and drove home such lessons.

Still, for all this, strong popes and emperors were difficult to deny, and most governments had to admit that they had to defer to the superior power of both. Thus most cities formally allied themselves with one or the other. In fact, local leaders were often divided over which of the two great powers they should align with, and reflecting this division, two great parties had grown up in Italy: the Guelphs and the Ghibellines. Broadly speaking, the Ghibellines supported and in turn derived their legitimacy from the emperor and the empire. The Guelphs did the same with the papacy and the Church. Unfortunately, that "broadly speaking" is crucial, for local variations were highly significant, and by the second half of the thirteenth century in northern Italy local Ghibellines and Guelphs typically were divided primarily over local issues, even if formally they were supposed to be aligned with the empire and the papacy, respectively.

The Demise of the Legitimate World Powers: The Pope

Significantly, shortly after Felix's imaginary visit to Rome in the actual early 1300s, events undermined the strength of the empire and the papacy in Italy. And with the empire and the papacy largely out of the picture, the question by what right did the cities of Italy rule themselves and who, in fact, had the right to rule became even more pressing. In fact, this remained a significant issue across the Rinascimento, resulting in the working out of many of the basic justifications of governmental authority that go largely unquestioned today – and more importantly at the time, justifications that often deeply affected the way governmental authority was deployed and defended. But theory, then as now, was usually contingent on deeds and more direct uses of power. First, then, we need to look at the events that spelled the demise of both the pope and the emperor in Italy. For that was central to the construction of the new political, cultural, and social realities of a new urban order that might be labeled the first *civiltà* of the Rinascimento in Italy, even if once again that order and its novelties were not viewed as new, but rather as old and based on the rebirth of first times.

As far as the papacy was concerned, its long medieval conflict with emperors and secular rulers over who should rule found the crusty old Pope Boniface VIII at the turn of the century locked in a fierce struggle with the king of France, Philip IV the Fair (1268–1314; ruled 1285–1314). Although the conflict could be traced further back, the easiest place to begin is with the French king's desire to secure additional revenues to help finance his ongoing conflicts with two of his most powerful vassals, the duke of Aquitaine (who was also the king of England) and the count of Flanders. Philip looked longingly at the extensive land holdings of the Church in France that in theory could not be taxed, as they had always claimed to be exempt from taxation. Philip, however, had what seemed (at least to him) a clever idea. Earlier popes had created a precedent for taxing Church lands when they allowed secular leaders to do so in order to support their crusading efforts. Actually, this precedent had been extended to wars in Europe, where popes had sometimes been willing to support one side against another and allow the side they favored to label the conflict a crusade. Thus, Philip put pressure on the leaders of the Church in France – often scions of the families of his own nobility – as well as on the pope to allow him to tax ecclesiastical holdings in order to support his wars.

Boniface VIII, however, would have none of this. For many years as a cardinal he had been the real power behind the papacy and a tough supporter of the claims of the papacy against secular rulers; thus he was not about to acquiesce to Philip's pressure, which he saw as a unilateral attempt to tax his clergy and a dangerous violation of his papal authority. After all, it was one thing when a pope declared a war a crusade and gave a secular leader the right to tax ecclesiastical holdings; it was quite another when a ruler made such a claim on his own. Boniface, reportedly outraged at the affront as well as deeply concerned about the possible precedent, issued the Papal Bull *Clericos Laicos* (*Clerics and Laymen*, 1296) – a formal pronouncement with the force of Church law – condemning Philip's actions. Boniface ruled in the bull that there would be no taxation of clerics or Church lands without papal approval, essentially destroying any hope Philip might have had to tax the Church. But Boniface, not content with making clear his refusal, went well beyond that to make a heated attack on the corruption and misrule of secular rulers in general, an attack clearly intended to intimidate Philip. In essence he had decided to draw a line in the sand in the ongoing conflict between secular rulers and the papacy about who had the ultimate right to rule. And *Clericos Laicos* made it clear that clerics and the pope came before lay rulers, especially corrupt ones. In the terms of the Donation of Constantine, rulers like Philip were not living up to their required role as shepherds of their flocks, and the pope had the right to revoke their rule.

Philip, however, was perhaps the most powerful ruler in western Europe at the time, and although he was labeled "the Fair," he was not about to be backed down by the threats of a crusty old pope, nor was he about to be restrained by fair play or more traditional ways of negotiating such conflicts. Thus he launched an aggressive counteroffensive against the pope aimed at crippling him financially and delegitimating his rule. First, he banished Italian bankers from France. This might seem an unlikely ploy, but there was a method to his apparent madness; for it was actually a not very subtle attack on the pope's treasury. Throughout Europe, Italian bankers collected the Church's revenues and sent them back to Rome; thus with one stroke, Philip seriously restricted the flow of papal revenues. Moreover, as the major banking houses of Italy held in deposits much of the pope's wealth and as being exiled from France dangerously undercut their revenues, there was a real possibility that those banks would fail. If they did, the pope would be one of the biggest losers, with much of his wealth going down with them. Needless to say, as a result the great banking houses added their fears of failure to the pope's immediate financial pinch, pressing Boniface to back down.

In addition to financial pressure Philip attempted to make use of cultural pressure, starting a pamphlet war that attacked the corruption of the Church and the questionable way in which Boniface had become pope. Particularly troubling was the fact that Boniface's predecessor, Celestine V (1215–1294; pope July–December 1294), had ended his papacy suspiciously. Celestine had been a poor, aged hermit supposedly living in a cave in southern Italy before he was apparently miraculously elected pope by the College of Cardinals. Unfortunately, the miracle largely ended with his election. As pope, he was reportedly a disaster. Not only did he lack political and administrative ability, he failed miserably as the symbolic leader of the Church, being extremely uncomfortable with the splendor and rich ceremonial that surrounded the papacy, a stance that dangerously seemed to reflect radical contemporary calls for a spiritual, propertyless Church and Joachim's prophecies. Rumor had it that he even refused to use his luxurious quarters or to sleep in his bed in the papal palace, choosing instead to live, sleep, and pray in a closet of the papal suite. More importantly, however, it was widely believed that the future pope, Boniface, had played a major role in convincing Celestine to step down from the papacy – an unheard of and questionable deed for popes. In theory the pope was elected by the College of Cardinals guided by the Holy Spirit, and he ruled until God withdrew his power on Earth with his

death. When Celestine stepped down, Boniface was with unseemly quick-
ness elected pope. Shortly thereafter Celestine died, and many wondered
whether it was God's belated Hand or poison that had intervened. Philip,
conveniently found the death too convenient, and his suspicions fastened on
Boniface.

In the end, all this allowed Philip and his pamphlet warriors to suggest
that Boniface was at best an illegal pope and at worst involved in the murder of his predecessor. Philip at the same time threatened his French clergy,
warning that he would bring them to justice and charge them with treason if they did not pay his tax. Once again he had no right to do this as
the clergy were not subject to secular law, only to the law of the Church.
Yet even if theoretically Philip should not have been able to try them, the
French clergy were acutely aware that Philip and his judges were close at
hand while the pope was in distant Rome. Moreover, Philip had the force to
carry out his threats against them while the pope had little power to protect
them, at least in the short run. In addition, many of the higher-level clergy,
coming from important noble families aligned with Philip, and often owing
their positions to him, were inclined to support him over the pope anyway;
thus, many members of the French clergy also put pressure on Boniface to
accept Philip's demands. Finally, Philip was aware that over a long career in
Rome the pope had accrued many enemies among the leading families of
the city. Boniface himself was a powerful member of the Gaetani clan, long
a force in the Church and Rome. The main opposition to the Gaetani family was led by the Colonna clan, and Philip encouraged the latter to rise up
against Boniface and his "illegal" election. Money, along with the suggestion that a Colonna might well become pope if Boniface fell from power,
sweetened the deal. Little encouragement was necessary, however, and with
the Colonna and their supporters in the streets of Rome, the pope found
himself in deep trouble.

In a first moment, then, Philip's strategies succeeded so well that
Boniface was forced to back down and grant him a crusading tax.
Obviously he was not happy with this and was anxious for any opportunity to turn the tables on Philip, the Not-So Fair from his perspective. His
chance came in 1302 when Philip attempted to try a French bishop on
apparently trumped-up charges of treason, again something that legally he
could not do. For French bishops the trial demonstrated that Philip felt
free to attack them with impunity whenever he wished, and thus many
realized that they needed a strong pope to protect their interests, a strong
pope like Boniface. Seeing his opening, Boniface called a council of all
French clergy to meet in Rome, and if there was any question about what

he had in mind, he immediately suspended Philip's permission to tax his clergy. As if that were not enough, he virtually declared war on the French king with a new, more aggressive Papal Bull: *Unam Sanctam* (*One Holy Power*, 1302). This bull was one of the strongest claims of papal power over secular rulers ever made. It insisted that the pope ultimately held both spiritual *and secular* power in this world. Taking the old medieval metaphor for power, the sword (which Venice had used in its own claims for power), and insisting that both the sword of secular rule and the sword of spiritual rule ultimately belonged to the pope, he claimed that one holy power (*Unam Sanctam*) ultimately was responsible for the rule of both the secular and the ecclesiastical realms. With his control of the secular sword the pope claimed the right to cut out the offending members of secular society, with the spiritual sword he claimed the right to cut out of the Christian community the spiritually unworthy. In sum, all power in this world belonged to the pope.

But it was one thing to claim power and another to actually exercise it. Underlining the great gap that often yawns between the two, one of Philip's henchmen reportedly commented on *Unam Sanctam*, "My master's sword is made of steel, the pope's is made of words." Unfortunately for Boniface, events were to prove the henchman right. While plans went ahead for the council of French ecclesiastics in Rome, Philip quietly sent a small contingent of his most faithful men to Italy, where they captured the unsuspecting pope at his summer estate north of Rome. Apparently the idea was to haul him back to France to try him there for usurping the papacy and probably for the murder of his predecessor as well. An audacious if totally illegal plan, it almost succeeded. But Philip's men were largely on their own a long way from France, and the pope's relatives rallied local supporters and managed to free Boniface. The pope, well into his eighties, apparently never recovered from the shock and died shortly after being freed.

Clearly what the Church needed was a strong pope to stand up to Philip. What they got instead was a weak compromise candidate, who it was hoped would not alienate Philip any further while somehow protecting the Church and the papacy's traditional prerogatives. The new pope, Benedict XI (1240–1304; pope 1303–1304), took up the crucial issue of the kidnapping of Boniface, immediately excommunicating Philip's men who had done the deed. The real question remained, however, what to do about Philip. It was clear that excommunication or even any punishment that fitted the crime would lead to retaliation by the king, who had demonstrated that there was little he would not do to protect his power and prerogatives. Thus in the end the new pope ruled that Philip was unaware of the plot and exonerated him.

Fortunately for him, he avoided the negative repercussions of that unlikely ruling by dying quickly, once again under suspicious circumstances.

When the cardinals of the Church were called together to elect a new pope, they once again faced the same difficult issue. Would they elect a strong pope to stand up to Philip, or would they elect a pope whom Philip would see as an ally, conceding to his power? This conundrum was complicated by the fact that there had been a long and close relationship between the leadership of the thirteenth-century Church and the kings of France. This meant that a sizeable number of the cardinals in the College of Cardinals electing the new pope were either French or ready to support the French king. Thus a stalemate developed, with a strong group of cardinals wishing to elect an Italian pope who would stand up to the French king, and a virtually equally strong group wanting to elect a French pope or at least a pro-French one. After a long conclave that dragged on for months without electing a pope, a compromise was finally reached with the election of the archbishop of Bordeaux as Pope Clement V (c. 1264–1314; pope 1305–1314). He had something to offer both parties, although it appeared that the anti-Philip group had gained the upper hand – for while he was French, he had been a strong opponent of Philip and a supporter of Boniface.

Appearances were deceptive, as is often their wont, for it seems that in order to win the support of the French faction the archbishop had struck a secret deal to support Philip. Quickly the new pope's betrayal of his Italian supporters became apparent, and fearing the reprisals of his former allies, he never went to Rome. After several years wandering around he finally settled his papal court and bureaucracy at Avignon, at the time just across the Rhone River from French territory ruled by Philip. The symbolism, at least, was hopeful. Across the Rhone from France, he could claim to be independent of the king, even if he was nearby. But after some weak attempts at independent action, he and his successors at Avignon settled into a fairly close working relationship dominated by the kings and leading families of France.

For Italy the results of this move would be difficult to overestimate. The popes at Avignon were too far from Italy to play successfully the aggressive role that strong popes had once played in the politics of Italian cities, even in Guelph cities that were formally allied with the papacy. This is not to say, as historians once did, that the papacy was totally removed from the power struggles of Italy, but rather that when popes did try to interfere to defend their prerogatives in Italy, they were handicapped by their distance from the action and by their increasing lack of comprehension of the complexity of local politics there. Even the city of Rome slowly slid away from real papal

control, as did most of the cities in the Papal States. The exception was the
kingdom of Naples, ruled by French Angevin kings, which was officially a
fief of the papacy and whose rulers attempted to lead Guelph forces in Italy
in part on behalf of the papacy and in part for their own advantage, but with
limited success, as we shall see.

More importantly, however, the move to Avignon helped to fan the flames
of a series of deeper problems within the Church that significantly altered
its course across the Rinascimento. First, the papacy remained at Avignon
until 1378; during that period it was much more involved in French affairs
than Italian; and French affairs in turn were much more concerned with
the Hundred Years' War (1337–1453) between France and England and the
financial hardships that went along with that conflict. In fact, all seven popes
elected while the papacy was in Avignon were French, and by 1378, 113
of the 134 cardinals of the Church were French. When finally, after much
campaigning for a papal return to Italy, Pope Urban VI was elected in 1378
promising to move back to Rome, almost immediately a second pope was
elected, Clement VI. Clearly in his name there was a promise: like his predecessor Clement V, he was pro-French, rejected the papacy of Urban, and
stayed on in Avignon. Thus began what was labeled the Great Schism (1378–
1417), a period during which there were at least two competing popes and
often more. Evidently this meant that the Church remained weak, and even
with a pope in Rome, Italian cities could play one contending pope off
against another.

At a deeper level, however, this split and its consequent weakening of
papal power meant that those within the clergy who believed that a strong
monarchical pope was a mistake could band together with like-minded
secular authorities and press for a different organization of the Church. The
Conciliar Movement, as it was called, flourished during the period of the
Great Schism, pressing the idea that the Church should be led by councils –
in some ways not unlike the councils in Italy that advised local rulers and
claimed to be the real font of governmental authority in cities like Venice
and Florence. For much of the fifteenth century popes had to face stiff competition for power within the Church from the supporters of this Conciliar
Movement. Suffice it to say for now that this also limited their ability to press
their policies on the cities of Italy, even Guelph ones.

All this division and turmoil within the leadership of the Church also
helped encourage the continued development of strong local religious traditions. Local preachers, local religious groups such as confraternities, and even
local charismatic figures all encouraged spiritual enthusiasms and holy ways
of life that were largely out of the hands of the regular organization of the

Church. Moreover, city governments in Italy, which had always stressed their own Christian roots and their role in organizing and promoting a Christian life, took advantage of the weakness of the organized Church to emphasize what might be called their own civic morality – their responsibility and ability to promote a Christian *civiltà* that in many ways sustained the religious life of their cities. In part this contributed to their claims to rule legitimately by co-opting the claims of the Church to create a Christian society; but in part it also responded to the felt needs that saw governments deeply involved in creating their own holy cities. Thus governments regularly encouraged religious enthusiasm and piety by promoting local civic ceremonials and by commissioning religious art and architecture, a patronage and a local vision that supported and deeply influenced a significant proportion of the art and spiritual life of the Rinascimento.

When finally, in 1417, Martin V (1368–1431; pope 1417–1431) was elected pope and succeeded in having his competitor popes deposed, he faced a tough problem. He found that his power base in Italy was especially weak. Thus he and his immediate successors made what appeared at the time to be a logical and particularly realistic decision: they decided to focus on rebuilding their political and economic power in Rome and the Papal States, in essence to become princelike rulers in the center of Italy. Rebuilding their power there as princes with the wealth to raise armies, they could compete with the secular powers that had for more than a century created havoc at the expense of the Church. But that was not particularly easy to accomplish, for while the papacy was at Avignon and then hamstrung by the Great Schism, local powers in Italy had effectively finished divvying up the Papal States among themselves and were not eager to return what they had gained, often at considerable sacrifice. As a result, for most of the rest of the fifteenth century the papacy, while attempting to limit the Conciliar Movement and regain control of religious reform movements and outbursts of spiritual enthusiasm, put most of its effort into rebuilding a territorial state in central Italy as its base of power, with Rome as its capital, reestablishing the papacy as a princely/monarchical power.

As the fifteenth century wound to a close and the papacy succeeded in this project, the papacy and the papal court became leaders again in a second and more courtly *civiltà* that in many ways typified the second phase of the Rinascimento. But until then, for more than a century and a half, the cities of northern Italy were largely free to develop with limited interference from the papacy and the central bureaucracy of the Church. On those occasions when the Church tried to interfere or assert its prerogatives against city governments, those governments had a wide range of options and potential allies for neutralizing such attempts. Not quite gone and not quite forgotten, the papacy was a shadow of its former self in Italy for virtually 150 years, leaving ample space for local city governments and local religious enthusiasms to color the first phase of the Rinascimento.

The Demise of the Legitimate World Powers: The Emperor

The demise of the emperor in Italy was equally dramatic and significant. Across the Middle Ages strong emperors had seen the more urban world of Italy, with its cosmopolitan society and its complex economy, as a rich and rewarding area to rule and tax. Thus there was a long tradition of imperial rule, and as late as the middle years of the thirteenth century the Emperor Frederick II had aggressively asserted it, as we have seen. Moreover, in the waning years of that century and the early years of the fourteenth, many in Italy, like Dante, tired of the squabbles within and among the cities of the center and north, actually believed that a strong emperor might bring peace, order, and stability with renewed imperial leadership. Shortly after the papacy settled in Avignon, a new emperor was elected in 1308 who seemed to have the potential ability and the will to do just that, Henry VII (c. 1275–1313; elected emperor 1308–1313; crowned emperor 1312–1313). Dante, himself a victim of local power squabbles in his native city, was typical of many when he wrote in exile about Henry and his potential as emperor, "Rejoice O' Italy … for your bridegroom comes, the hope of the world, the glory of your people, the ever clement Henry, who is Caesar and Augustus." Behind Dante's rhetoric, the strength of the Roman imperial ideal shines through with the hope that a new emperor would bring peace and a legitimate order.

Henry was actually an unusual bridegroom for Italy, with a revealing mix of strengths and weaknesses. Perhaps his greatest weakness was that he had been elected by the imperial electors in Germany because he appeared too weak and poor to be much of a factor there or to threaten the real powers in the area. This was frequently the case, as the German princes and ecclesiastical leaders who elected emperors were usually reluctant to give that power to someone who might use it to their detriment. In this case the person they especially feared was Charles of Valois, the brother of Philip the Fair, king of France. For Philip, not content with having the pope under his thumb at Avignon, also hoped to corner imperial power by pressing the electors to make his brother emperor. If he had succeeded, he would have been more than ever the most powerful ruler in Europe – exactly the reason why many electors were not eager to elect his brother. Enter Henry. From the perspective of many he was a perfect compromise candidate: he controlled little territory in his own right; thus he had limited wealth or military power. But he had grown up at the French court, spoke French, and knew Philip – weak, but perhaps with enough of a French connection to satisfy the French king, he seemed to be just what was needed.

Henry also had another advantage that with time would gain more meaning. Clement V, the new pope at Avignon, was anxious, much like the German electors, not to have Philip's brother become emperor. If that happened, he feared he would be completely at the mercy of the French king. To a great extent that was already the case, but with a weak emperor he could hope that Philip's ability to manipulate imperial authority to his own advantage and against the pope would be limited. Thus the pope aggressively backed Henry, which helped carry the day for the election of Italy's imperial bridegroom-to-be. With Henry as the pope's choice for emperor, he became a very strange bridegroom indeed. For, as we have seen, many of the local battles for political power in the cities of Italy were being fought out between local groups who proclaimed themselves Guelphs or Ghibellines. Ghibellines, of course, as the traditional supporters of the emperor, had to see Henry as their legitimate overlord and accept him as their leader. But the Guelphs, as the party of the papacy and the Church, who traditionally opposed emperors, were faced with a dilemma – he was the pope's emperor and was supported by him. In sum, Henry was that rarest of political creatures and bridegrooms from a fourteenth-century Italian perspective: a Guelph-Ghibelline. No wonder Dante was enthusiastic! In his person he seemed to promise an end to the turmoil that had torn apart the cities of Italy, for as a Guelph-Ghibelline, he was the leader of both sides in those conflicts.

There is an interesting lesson in this. To a great degree the labels "Guelph" and "Ghibelline" had been appropriated by local groups contesting local issues as rhetorical ways of adding to their legitimacy. By claiming loyalty to one of the two great powers of the world – the empire or the papacy – they had elevated their struggles by claiming that they were not really fighting for their own interests or power but merely defending traditional authority, thus gaining legitimacy that otherwise would not have been theirs. As such, the claim of legitimacy that went with these labels became a powerful ideology, very useful in building support and claiming the high ground. But at the same time these labels had the potential to become a trap. For culture and ideology can be used to gain and defend power, but from time to time both can claim their due. Simply put, from time to time someone is in the position to demand that such claims actually be met. And in this case that was Henry. When he arrived in Italy as a Guelph-Ghibelline, many local

leaders of the Guelphs and the Ghibellines were not particularly eager to
give over their hard-won local power to him, but they had little choice. As
Guelphs or Ghibellines they were trapped in their ideology and had either
to reject it – an option virtually unthinkable – or to accept Henry as their
leader and Dante's bridegroom.

Still, for all his rhetorical and ideological advantages, Henry was severely
handicapped by his lack of a real power base, especially in terms of money
and military capabilities. Henry, to his credit, realized that to escape those
problems he really needed only money. With money he could buy the mercenary soldiers necessary to have a viable army. Although many wars were
still being fought with knights who served in return for the land they held
from their overlords, following medieval tradition, in Italy battles were
increasingly being fought by professional soldiers, often drawn from a financially needy nobility. With money, if clever, Henry could pay mercenaries to
do his fighting and perhaps even finance a bureaucracy that could make his
rule more effective – and perhaps in the process become a true bridegroom
to Italy bringing peace, order, and stability as Dante dreamed. If not that, at
least his bureaucracy could effectively milk the rich cities of Italy and make
him a wealthy and powerful emperor. And if Henry was unclear about all
this, his court was soon awash with exiles, victims of the squabbles in Italy,
both Guelph and Ghibelline, eager to help him gain the resources and support needed.

As a result, Henry soon announced that Italy's bridegroom, a miraculous
Guelph-Ghibelline, was on the road to Italy. Unfortunately for Henry, he
turned out to be not quite the perfect groom he seemed to be – often the
case in weddings, then as now. His promise of peace and stability was compromised by the fact that he also needed to collect taxes and made use of
German and French supporters to do so and to help him rule. Most of these
outsiders had virtually no understanding of the decidedly different political, social, and economic situation that they had to deal with in the cities of
Italy – a clear indication of how distant they had become socially, culturally, and politically from their late medieval neighbors to the north. Henry
did have Italian advisors. But most were exiles eager to take revenge on
those who had driven them from their cities; not exactly the best sources of
information and support for bringing peace and compromise. Moreover, as
the Guelphs had been doing better than the Ghibellines in the struggles for
power in the Italian cities, most of Henry's Italian advisors were Ghibelline
exiles, which seriously undermined his claim to be a Guelph-Ghibelline.
Perhaps most significantly, however, Henry himself had little conception of
the complexity of the urban world of northern Italy that he was entering

and probably little desire to master the local politics of the myriad of cities that he was supposedly to pacify and rule. In fact, to be fair to Henry, that would have been a monumental task for any ruler, even one with much better local understanding and support.

Nonetheless, things seemed to start out well. In 1311 he went first to Milan, one of the richest cities in the north of Italy with a long tradition of alliance with the emperor. When he arrived, the Ghibellines had recently been driven out of the city, and it was ruled by a Guelph faction led by the powerful Della Torre family. The Della Torre family made a great show of welcoming their Guelph-Ghibelline bridegroom as their legitimate ruler, evidently trapped by the pope's support for Henry. But soon enough there were signs that all was not well. When the Della Torre family began searching for the Iron Crown that emperors had traditionally worn to signify their rule over the city and the Lombard plain, they claimed that it had been pawned and could not be located. After a suitable frantic search, however, the crown was located, gotten out of hock, and brought back to the city to crown the impatient emperor.

This perhaps too convenient delay allowed more significant problems to surface. Most notably, Henry's promise of bringing peace and ending the struggles between Guelphs and Ghibellines meant that shortly after he arrived in Milan, he pressed the Della Torre family to invite back to the city their archrivals, the Ghibelline Visconti clan, whom they had just driven out. The idea was that the emperor would bring peace and harmony to the two bitter rivals with a major ceremony in the main square of the city, where the Guelph leader of the Della Torre clan would exchange the kiss of peace with the Ghibelline leader of the Visconti clan. It should have been a perfect symbolic moment: two bitter rivals kissing in the main square of the city, demonstrating to all there and to all throughout Italy that the Guelph-Ghibelline emperor had brought peace and reconciliation as promised. A good ceremonial moment, then, but, of course, it was too good to be true.

Kisses were given, but peace was shattered almost immediately as fighting broke out in the streets of the city between Della Torre and Visconti supporters. Without enough troops of his own to impose order, Henry unwisely chose to enlist the aid of the Visconti to regain control of the situation. The Visconti, in turn, quickly drove the Della Torre from the city. One might say the honeymoon was already, if not over, at least seriously compromised. The lesson was not lost on other Guelph leaders. Henry came promising peace and reconciliation, but the Ghibellines had triumphed in Milan and the hard-won Guelph power there was overthrown. The Guelph cities of the Lombard plain began immediately to organize a league with the aim of driving the emperor out of Italy. They called themselves, not surprisingly, the Lombard League, a name traditionally used by Italian cities banding together against imperial claims. Henry, in turn, forced to rely increasingly on Ghibelline support, raised enough funds to field small armies to face off against league cities. But his successes were few, and his campaigns demonstrated primarily the ineptness of his German and French advisors, along with his inability to match the spending power of the cities of the league. In the end he was saved from complete humiliation by yet another traditional ally of Italians against northern invaders – the summer heat and the diseases that often decimated their armies. His adventure as Italian bridegroom ended when he died of a summer dysentery in 1313 along with many of the men in his small army besieging Florence.

Henry's tragic marriage and early death demonstrated that those seemingly small and easily taken city-states with their great wealth were not the easy prey they appeared to be to northerners used to thinking in terms of a rural society and armies manned by feudal levies. The key to their strength was their wealth and their ability to hire professional soldiers when necessary to protect their interests, and for that, large territories mattered less than large supplies of money. It also confirmed that the politics and local squabbles of those cities were a dangerous quagmire for emperors and for northern European rulers in general. And it did so in an impressive way, for many saw that Henry's greatest success there, even with the unique advantage of being a Guelph-Ghibelline, was in dying young. The emperor who had come to build his wealth and power had become instead a victim of that very wealth and power. These lessons were not lost on northern rulers.

Occasionally in the fourteenth and fifteenth centuries other emperors ventured south with plans similar to those of Henry, but with limited success. Louis IV (1282–1347; emperor 1328–1347) of the house of Wittelsbach may have had the greatest impact. After a series of wars in the north and considerable confusion there, he managed to gain enough power to venture to Italy to see what he could obtain. Entering Milan in 1327, he asserted his theoretical rights as emperor and overlord of the city and was officially crowned king of Italy – but to little effect, beyond confirming that emperors could be equal opportunity trouble for the rulers of the city. The actual ruler at the time, Galeazzo I Visconti (1277–1328; signore of Milan 1322–1327) was deposed and driven from the city with his support. Galeazzo, in exile, died within the year. But for all that, his son Azzone Visconti (1302–1339; signore of Milan 1329–1339) quickly regained his father's rule over the city and solidified it by buying from Louis the official title of imperial vicar in 1329 for a price that was reported as either 60,000 or 125,000 florins. In the end, however, he paid only 12,000 florins and settled down to continue Visconti rule. Meanwhile, Louis hurried on to Rome, where he was crowned emperor in 1328. Unfortunately, as Pope John XXII (1249–1334; pope 1316–1334) was his enemy and off in Avignon anyway, he had to make due with a crowning by a Roman noble. Still, he took advantage of his visit and crowning to try to overthrow the pope in Avignon by naming an antipope, but was soon forced to flee the city and Italy with his antipope in tow, having gained a bit of money and his semiofficial crowning as Roman emperor in Rome, and having escaped alive. He did not return.

His successor, Charles IV (1316–1378; officially emperor 1355–1378), and his Italian adventures were even less impressive. Once again his early years in the north were largely occupied with a series of wars against powerful counterclaimants to his rule. But eventually he solidified his power and, ruling from Prague, helped to foster a kind of renaissance there with impressive building projects and patronage of the arts. He first entered Italy in the 1350s, reportedly, without an army, yet still managed to be crowned emperor in Rome in 1355, this time by a cardinal and with the apparent support of the papacy. In fact, unlike Louis, he had good relations with the popes at Avignon and, after hurrying back to the north with his coronation as emperor accomplished, it was as an ally of the papacy that he returned in 1368. That second visit appeared to have the potential to be more important. Urban V (1310–1370; pope 1362–1370), a French theologian, had been unexpectedly elected pope while still just a priest noted for his scholarly interests. As pope, however, he became a vigorous reformer and, as part of his reforming program, decided that the papacy belonged in Rome and that the support of the emperor would aid greatly in that return.

That decision was encouraged by the military successes of the cardinal and general Egidio Albornoz (1310–1367), who had been pressed into service to reestablish papal control in the Papal States in the center of Italy. To consolidate those successes and to heed the numerous calls to return the papacy to Rome, Urban headed to Italy in 1367. And, in a sign of rapprochement between the papacy and the empire, he asked for and secured Charles IV's support. Charles then returned to Italy as an emperor supporting the pope, and together they entered Rome in the fall of 1368. That might have been a major historical moment, with the emperor reportedly leading the scholar/pope on a humble mule back into the holy city – the empire and the papacy uniting to return the papacy to its proper home. But once again it was too perfect; for it quickly became clear that the pope was not really able to hold Rome, especially as his real military power, in the form of his general, Albornoz, had died, and as militarily Charles was incapable of doing much more then lending moral support. Far better at leading a mule than an army in Italy that he simply did not have, Charles wisely fled back to the safety of the north. The pope followed suit soon thereafter, returning to Avignon, and dreams of a papal return to Rome were put on hold.

In sum, the emperors of the north were largely absent from the complex and contested world of fourteenth-century Italy. The most successful managed to play their cards well enough to officially be crowned emperor, perhaps gain some taxes, bribes, or momentary political advantage, and escape with their lives. But more often they found themselves used as pawns, and frequently relatively uncomprehending pawns at that, in the complex diplomatic maneuvers of local Italian powers. In fact, when Italians looked to the north, they did not tend to look with fear or even with all that much respect for the power of emperors, kings, or nobles. Rather, they were inclined to see the northerners as uncomprehending and backward players whose claims and limited powers could be used to their own advantage in the local political struggles of northern Italy.

Much the same was the case as far as the papacy was concerned. Avignon and the south of France were closer and more involved in the cultural world of northern Italy. But with French popes and French cardinals gaining the preponderance of power in the Church hierarchy, even the top levels of the Church in Italy took on a French tone, with important bishoprics and Church offices often being held by members of the French clergy. Many, facing considerable Italian hostility, did not even take up residence in their bishoprics – following in this the pope's lead as bishop of Rome living in Avignon – thus further weakening the power of the Church and papacy there. In addition, more powerful cities like Milan, Venice, and Florence took advantage of this situation by insisting on traditional claims that they had the right to nominate their own bishops and even local clergy, with considerable success, although the theory remained that these were merely nominations that had to be approved by the pope. In Rome the great baronial families that had once controlled the papacy were reduced to violently fighting among themselves and with increasingly powerful artisan and merchant groups for power within the city. At the same time the territories theoretically under papal control in the center of Italy, the Papal States, were fairly quickly lost again to locals. The popes at Avignon made the best of an impossible situation. Lacking the local power or support to hold the many small cities in the region that were eager to assert their independence from papal authority, they sold off the rule of most to powerful local families, who officially took over power as vicars of the pope. The result was that beyond moral authority – which itself was widely being questioned, given

the reported corruption of the papacy at Avignon – and the strong claims to
rule discussed earlier, the papacy had little real power to wield in Italy.

A Third Potential Competitor for Power and Legitimacy in Italy

There was, however, a third power in Italy that dwarfed the cities of the center and north of the peninsula, at least in size, and had the potential to disrupt
their claims to rule on their own, the kingdom of Naples. Our imaginary
pilgrim, Felix, if he had journeyed on from Rome to the city of Naples,
with its 60,000 inhabitants on the coastal plain and hillsides surrounding a
beautiful bay and bordered to the south by the still-active volcano Vesuvius,
might well have found that city somewhat less strange than those he had
encountered earlier. For it was the capital city of a legitimate kingdom, with
a strong noble presence and a recent tradition of German leadership. In fact,
German emperors had led a cultural and economic flourishing there that
had made the region one of the richest in Europe in the late Middle Ages,
perhaps most impressively under Frederick II, the not-quite-Antichrist, who
had ruled the south of Italy and Sicily united as the kingdom of Sicily. His
broader Italian and European ambitions, however, as we have seen, led to a
long, bitter conflict with the papacy that did not end with his death. Rather,
his illegitimate son Manfred's hopes of taking over his father's rule were
seriously hampered by a recalcitrant southern nobility and papal attacks on
his legitimacy that included the granting of his kingdom as a papal fief to
Charles of Anjou, brother of the French king, Louis IX. And in the end they
were dashed when Manfred was soundly defeated at the Battle of Benevento
in 1266, which rang down the curtain on German rule in the south.

In turn, the Angevins began almost two centuries of French rule (1268–
1442) in the south with the support of the papacy as – officially, at least –
they held the kingdom as a fief of the papacy, which was happy to see their
imperial and Ghibelline enemies finally defeated in the south. Although
Charles of Anjou preferred to rule from Naples rather than from Sicily, he
attempted to maintain the strong monarchical forms of Frederick and followed, if anything, an even more aggressive policy in the Mediterranean,
earning him the enmity of the Byzantine rulers of Constantinople. However,
the cost of his aggressive policies, along with his bringing in French nobles
to support his rule, led to ongoing conflicts. In fact, in 1282, supposedly triggered by a French soldier's insult to a Sicilian woman, a general revolt known
as the Sicilian Vespers almost toppled Charles and the Angevins from power.
Charles managed to maintain control of Naples and the south of the Italian
peninsula, but the Sicilians successfully threw off French rule with the aid

of the Byzantines and Pedro III of Aragon, who became king of Sicily. As a result, although the Angevins attempted from time to time to regain Sicily, under Aragon Sicily fell more and more into an Iberian/Mediterranean orbit. And eventually the Aragonese would use the island as a base for driving the Angevins from the kingdom of Naples in the fifteenth century, inaugurating a long process of developing Aragonese and then Spanish power in the peninsula, with dramatic results, as we shall see.

But that was still to come. Under the Angevins Naples flourished as an administrative capital of a formally French kingdom with a highly diverse nobility that included newly arrived French nobles, German nobles brought in earlier by German emperors, Normans left over from the Norman conquest of the South in the eleventh and twelfth centuries, Lombard nobles from a still earlier period, and even some Greeks and Albanians. And not unlike similar kingdoms in the north of Europe and the Iberian peninsula, those nobilities and their ruling Angevins were heavily involved in the dynastic adventures of the rest of Europe. Thus, for example, Charles I's son, Charles II, married into the royal family of Hungary, which led to more than a century of diplomatic wrangling and meddling with the affairs of that monarchy. In fact, that ongoing feuding may eventually have contributed to the fall of the Angevins in Italy in the fifteenth century. Also, while the Angevins' drive to develop a nobility that supported their attempts at centralized rule failed in the long run, it did lead to the alienation of much land that had formerly been controlled directly by the crown. This seriously compromised their revenues and weakened their rule. Thus, in a way, a government that had been relatively strong and effectively centralized under Frederick, across the fourteenth century tended to grow weaker as the nobility grew stronger and as the barons of the realm in many ways came to dominate society.

Economically the kingdom of Naples tended to be a supplier of resources, primarily agricultural, for the north of Italy. Moreover, the Angevins turned away from earlier strong trade relations with Genoa and Venice in order to work more closely with Florentine merchants and bankers, who had a strong connection to their papal overlords and an equally powerful Guelph tradition. Thus Florentine banking houses were a power in the city, and Giovanni Boccaccio, one of the most notable Florentine writers of the fourteenth century, actually worked for a time as a youth in the Bardi bank there. In fact, the Florentine connection meant that the lively court of Naples was anything but culturally isolated from the early Rinascimento. Florentine artists and intellectuals were patronized by the Angevins – the famous painter Giotto, for example, did frescoes for the royal convent associated with the Church of Santa Chiara – and exposure to the more noble and courtly south certainly had an impact on northern writers and painters who visited the city and its court to enjoy Angevin patronage.

But it would be hard to see the kingdom of Naples as deeply integrated into the first Rinascimento, at least as discussed here. Its few urban centers were dominated by a feudal nobility, not an artisan/merchant/banker *popolo*. Moreover, even the most cosmopolitan urban center, Naples, was more an administrative and transshipment center, not a city that actually produced wealth like Florence, Milan, Venice, and the dozens of other central and northern cities of the peninsula. And finally, the Angevin monarchy, although contested, like the imperial rule it replaced, could claim a legitimate right to rule and its nobility a legitimate feudal right to dominate society, unlike the problematic city-states of the north and their even more problematic *popolo*. Thus, while in Naples and the south ideals of Roman revival and various visions of returns to earlier first times could be and were evoked from time to time, royal and noble lineage and tales of medieval greatness in distant France did much of the heavy lifting to support Angevin rule and its traditional social order. That would change in the fifteenth century, when the Aragonese replaced the Angevins and began to promote more aggressively a vision of their own revival of ancient Rome that brought their court more into line with the urban courts of northern Italy. In sum, although one would not want to discount the many and often significant connections between the north and south of Italy, in the early Rinascimento the kingdom of Naples was a quite different society and economy on a significantly different trajectory. Culturally there were more similarities, but even in that area much of the culture of the Angevins was more comfortable with late medieval and French Gothic forms than with those of the Rinascimento.

It is true that especially under King Robert the Wise (1277–1343; ruled 1309–1343), the court in Naples was a flourishing center of intellectual excitement that attracted many from the north, especially Florence. Moreover, Robert attempted to play an aggressive role in northern Italian politics as a leader of the Guelph party and may have even harbored designs of uniting all of Italy under his Angevin rule, although recent scholarship has tended to downplay such claims, noting that his periodic interference in the north was determined more by his alliance with the papacy and pursuing papal/Guelph goals there than by any larger designs. Suggestively, Robert spent a good deal of his reign actually living in his territories in France and at the papal court in Avignon. And it is precisely these things that in the end made Naples so different from the urban governments and societies of the rest of Italy. The Angevin kings of the south were largely outsiders, and city-states were willing to use them as they used emperors and popes for their local advantage, but they were not interested in surrendering their local power to them. They could admire and even to a degree ape the manners and refinement of southern nobles, especially those at the impressive Neapolitan court, but they were not particularly interested in giving up to them the leadership and status that they had taken from their own local nobility. And at a deeper level they were not interested in sacrificing their vision of civic morality or an urban/*popolo*/*popolo grosso* ideal of *virtù* in order to be ruled by a French king and his foreign nobility.

Robert's relationship with Florence provides a good example of this. In 1313, with the city in turmoil and factions of the local Guelph party violently pitted against each other, Robert, as the pope's Guelph leader in Italy, was asked to become lord of the city. As the emperor Henry VII also threatened the city, he seemed to offer much-needed military support against the increasingly Ghibelline, Guelph/Ghibelline emperor. But Charles, deeply involved with problems of his own in his southern kingdom, never came to rule, and when Henry conveniently died before the walls of the city, a relieved city forgot their momentary lord. In 1325, again in the throes of internal turmoil and a deep budgetary crisis that required serious reform, the city once more appealed to Robert to bring peace to the city. This time, however, he actually sent his son, Charles, duke of Calabria (1298–1328). And unlike his father, whose name and fame more than his actual presence had served Florence a little more than a decade earlier, Charles actually came to rule, imposing tax reforms that were especially unpopular with the upper classes and a noble style of rule that quickly lost its glamour for the *popolo* of the city. His increasingly unpopular rule was cut short by his death, and Florence heaved a sigh of relief.

In sum, the Angevins of the south, used with caution, could be called upon from time to time, but in the end they were French foreigners from a very different society, even if they were Guelphs and formally the pope's primary supporters in Italy. In turn, poets, painters, sculptors, and writers could seek royal patronage by traveling to Naples, but understanding that they had left the distinctive urban world of the north behind in order to gain the advantage of royal wealth and patronage. Painters and craftsmen in the Angevin south had to adapt to a more noble and late medieval Gothic style; writers had to adapt to a more noble and royal-centered world; and for all the glory of the royal court in Naples, the underlying rules and deep perceptions of society and culture were different. The cities of the north and center of Italy in the final analysis used the Angevin kingdom much as they used the emperor and the pope, along with northern European rulers more generally, primarily as pawns in their own local power struggles, carefully avoiding deeper entanglements.

In the end, then, the cities of the center and north of Italy that our imagined traveler Felix visited on his pilgrimage to Rome found themselves shortly after his visit largely on their own for slightly more than a century and a half to develop further their own power arrangements, society, and culture. That strange world of bustling cities, violent conflicts, intense religious enthusiasms, and different social values was not about to end to make way for the last age of the Holy Spirit; it was already well along its way on a different path that set it off as the Rinascimento. The Italians Felix met were quite willing to take from their northern and southern neighbors what they saw as useful or attractive for their own society. But they did so increasingly seeing themselves as the superior society and crucially different. The uniquely urban *civiltà* that they created is what might be aptly called the First Rinascimento (c. 1250–1450).

CIVILTÀ: LIVING AND THINKING
THE CITY (c. 1300–c. 1375)

Imagining the City

Leave the city to the merchants, the lawyers, the brokers, the usurers, the bidders, the notaries, the doctors, the perfume makers, the butchers, the cooks, the pastry chefs, the sausage makers, the alchemists, the clothes washers, the builders, the weavers, the sculptors, the painters, the mimes, the dancers and acrobats, the musicians, the charlatans, the pimps, the robbers, the hosts, the frauds, the magicians, the adulterers, the parasites, and to the insatiable do-nothings always sniffing out the smell of the market.... They are different from us. Leave the rich to count their money.... There is not one reason to envy them.

Petrarch, *De vita solitaria* (written 1346–1347)

The first Rinascimento was not the Age of the Spirit, as Joachim of Fiore had prophesized, but an age of much greater urban-based wealth and a new elite and social order that such wealth had empowered: a world where new wealth, new perceived needs, and new skills had undercut and confused the Great Social Divide between a hereditary nobility and the rest of society that had typified the medieval world. But the discomfort with that new wealth, in conjunction with a strong religious tradition that many shared with Saint Francis, meant that the spiritual side of life was not forgotten. Rather, it melded with new social values and ideals of status in deeply significant ways that made that urban *civiltà* very different from its medieval and ancient antecedents, even in the cities of Italy that flourished in the twelfth century, as well as in modern urban societies. Most simply, it was an urban world where Christ, Mary, and the martyrs and saints of Christianity were very close to merchants, bankers, lawyers, and artisans. To paraphrase the historian Edward Muir, there was a Virgin on virtually every corner – the urbanscape of the fourteenth century was marked out, lived in, and even used to think, not just as a material space, but also as a spiritual one punctuated with humble religious shrines and great churches, with relics and places of holy memory, with neighborhoods named for holy figures, one where even urban time was measured by church bells and the time it took to say a common prayer. The result was a different world where the spiritual and the material were part of a continuum; one flowed easily into the other in ways that deeply colored the fabric of the city and the *civiltà* of the day.

As the quote just given suggests, the famous poet Petrarch (Francesco Petrarca, 1304–1374) could appeal to those moral and spiritual values in order to contest what he saw as wrong with the cities of his day. He was particularly concerned that the moral corruption of their citizens made them too focused on wealth and worldly power, even as he enthusiastically promoted a revival of ancient Roman culture – a culture and society that had been quintessentially urban and shared many similar values. Yet, like most who saw ancient Rome as an ideal, he wanted not the actual ancient Rome, but rather his dream of that first time – a dream that turned on his own vision of an ideal society dominated by a refined and mannered intellectual elite who, like him, preferred to live a spiritual life in solitude isolated from the bustle, hustle, and violence of the urban world. In the rebirth of the spiritual tranquility that he believed ancient Roman intellectuals enjoyed, Petrarch saw the promised leisure and peace necessary to recapture their cultural world; thus he dreamed of a learned aristocracy of poets and philosophers seeking out the lost texts of that once-upon-a-time world that would lead the return to his ideal way of life.

The merchants, lawyers, bankers, moneylenders (referred to more negatively as "the brokers, the usurers, the bidders"), "notaries," and "doctors" – or, to put it more simply, the actual emerging urban elites of contemporary cities – could serve but could not lead in this quest; for, of course, even Petrarch was not so spiritual as to believe that their wealth was unnecessary for realizing his aristocratic Roman dream. Even the "butchers," "cooks," "pastry chefs," "sausage makers," "alchemists," "clothes washers," "builders," "weavers," "sculptors," "painters," "mimes," "dancers," "acrobats," and "musicians" served their purpose and were probably acceptable at a safe distance from his country home at Vaucluse near Avignon where he wrote these lines, especially as artisans and workers who relied on their hands and bodies for their living were no challenge to his vision of elite status, which was based on the mind and spirit of true intellectuals like himself. The same could not be said for the "charlatans," "pimps," "robbers," "hosts" (of inns and drinking establishments), "frauds," "magicians," "adulterers," and "parasites." All of them constituted the dark and dangerous underbelly of the city – the satyrs

2.1. Ambrogio Lorenzetti, *Allegory of Good Government*, 1338–1340. Sala della Pace (Room of the Nine), Palazzo Pubblico, Siena. Photo: Scala/Art Resource, New York.

defiling his ideal garden – with whom he preferred not to share his ideal world.

Yet, perhaps unwittingly, in his attack on the city Petrarch provides a good picture of the main denizens of the urban world of the first Rinascimento, aside from women, who remained largely invisible in his masculine vision. Of course, not all were so negative about that picture and the urban life it reflected. Slightly earlier (1338–1340) in Siena, Ambrogio Lorenzetti (fl. c. 1317–1345) frescoed the walls of the Hall of the Nine, a committee that led local government, in the Palazzo Pubblico with a vibrant depiction of the positive side of urban life under a good government (Illustrations 2.1 and 2.2). This cycle of frescoes, often called the *Allegory of Government*, depicts the civilizing effects of an ideal good government that combined spiritual and secular discipline to produce an ordered, peaceful, and productive urban environment. All this stands in stark contrast to frescoes on the opposing wall that show the dangerous results when such governance is lacking. In the positive frescoes one again sees Petrarch's productive characters portrayed constructively at work and play in a city alive with bustling activity and

2.2. Ambrogio Lorenzetti, *Effects of Good Government in the City and the Country,* 1338–1340. Sala della Pace (Room of the Nine), Palazzo Pubblico, Siena. Photo: Scala/Art Resource, New York.

sociability – the life of a well-ruled urban *civiltà*. Harmony reigns, and people work with exactly that civic spirit and tranquility that Petrarch claimed were not to be had in the city.

That good government was posited as responsible for this is not surprising; for, of course, the fresco cycle was commissioned by the government of Siena. That government, one notes immediately, is depicted as disciplining the city by punishing with its own violence those who disrupted its *civiltà*, often the same people about whom Petrarch complained most. We see criminals being judged and the condemned having their heads cut off with a sword wielded by an angel of justice, implying that the government's use of force was legitimated by God and represented His power in the world. Recalling the claims of Boniface VIII, we see here how local governments could turn the tables on papal claims to wield both the spiritual and temporal swords of justice. Divine justice in the form of that sword-wielding angel is depicted as working directly through local government without the intervention of the papacy or the Church. We also see soldiers armed and

2.3. Ambrogio Lorenzetti, *Bad Government and the Effects of Bad Government in the City*, 1338–1340. Sala della Pace (Room of the Nine), Palazzo Pubblico, Siena. Photo: Scala/ Art Resource, New York.

ready to defend the government, and nearby bodies, presumably of criminals, hanging by the gates of the city. Angels and divine support for local government were all well and good, but the more direct power of soldiers and the grisly example of executions were also necessary and effectively displayed. Government, the divine, law, justice, and violence, then, went hand in hand in this vision of urban *civiltà* to produce peace and order.

Without good government, however, the evils that Petrarch complained about are graphically portrayed in Lorenzetti's frescos dedicated to bad government (Illustration 2.3). In those scenes the devil literally rules and justice is denied. A different violence dominates life and the images – a violence that brings disruption and disorder. Prosperity and productivity are brutally overthrown by the powerful and the dishonest, unleashed in an uncivil society that lacks good government. And true to Siena's republican tradition, bad government is depicted as tyranny, with the tyrant literally wearing the horns of the devil. Once again, as was the case with good government, the bad is deeply intertwined with a Christian vision – the ultimate evil in the world, the devil, oversees bad government. For Lorenzetti and his patrons, their Siena was a prosperous, good, and orderly civic society because of its good government, but they clearly feared much the same dangers as Petrarch.

It might seem curious that in this they agreed with someone who disagreed with them so profoundly about the positive nature of civic life and their own rule; for the rulers of Siena were exactly those merchants, bankers, and lawyers whom Petrarch felt should not be entrusted with the leadership of society. But for all the disagreement about what the best society was or should be and about who should lead it, there was a deep underlying agreement – one might say a deeply shared cultural perspective – about what dangers needed to be overcome in order to live well in the urban world of the early Rinascimento. Violence, disorder, the naked use of power for family or self-interest were the core obstacles that were seen as disrupting the urban *civiltà* of the day. And with good reason, for concentrating large numbers of people in a tightly packed urban environment, one with large disparities of wealth and power not only between rich and poor, but also between newer wealth and older, was a recipe for violence and conflict.

Social Conflict and the Ideal of Public Power over Private

In fact, conflict and violence had been ubiquitous in the cities of Italy, going virtually hand in hand with their rapid economic and demographic growth across the twelfth and thirteenth centuries. But, tellingly, things came to a head at much the same time that the removal of the empire and the papacy, discussed in the last chapter, left those cities largely on their own to deal with these problems and the underlying questions about who should dominate and rule. Looking back to medieval traditions, leadership both social and political was viewed as correctly being driven by private interests for private ends. A medieval lord protected the people that gathered around him and served him, because they served him, and to the extent that they served him, it was in his personal interest to do so. In turn, people served a lord for a host of traditional reasons, but most fundamentally because he and his private justice protected them. This reciprocity of private interests ideally provided a relatively peaceful society without the need of much in the way of government, law, or formal rule.

Of course, reality fell well short of this ideal – as is usually the case with social and political ideals. Still, in a largely rural society, with little in the way of other forms of protection, a powerful lord capable of the violence needed to protect his people was a necessity. Few were so foolish as to desire or even to conceive of living outside a relationship where everyone served someone more powerful and was in turn protected by him. Such relationships ideally structured the whole of society from the great lords – kings and emperors, for example, being served by their nobles – all the way down to peasant patriarchs, lords in their homes, protecting and being served by their wives and children. At every level this was a personal and essentially private relationship of power, even if over time an elaborate series of traditions and customary rights tailored local situations to local realities, making things more complex.

As urban life developed across Europe in the twelfth and thirteenth centuries, the problems inherent in this vision of a symbiotic relationship between private and personal power became increasingly apparent. This did not mean that such relationships disappeared; quite the opposite, for they continued and adapted to a more complex urban world in significant ways – most notably, perhaps, underlying the patronage relationships that would deeply color Rinascimento life. Yet at the same time a more public vision of power began to be articulated both by urban governments and by the denizens of the city, especially by those most active economically and culturally. Clearly this was not a modern vision of public power fully separated from the private; indeed, in many ways that latter ideal still has not been realized, despite ideological claims to the contrary. Rather, it utilized a number of corporate bodies, literally conceptual units of society that were conceived as fictitious bodies and legal persons in their own right, that sought to exercise power for the sake of some broader good: guilds, confraternities (local religious organizations), groups of families that banded together for mutual protection in clans or more formal *consorterie* (fictitious extended families), and, of course, government itself. From this perspective, a very medieval one, urban governments were just another corporate competitor in a cityscape awash with corporate bodies, all working (and often competing) to provide a peaceful and disciplined urban environment where they, rather than lords, protected and were served by individuals.

Earlier local lords and/or church leaders – especially the bishops who often ruled medieval cities – tended to see the newly rich merchants, money-handlers/bankers, and even artisans of the city as socially insignificant; thus they seemed the perfect victims of traditional private justice and other manifestations of their power. Against such private power, city dwellers banded together in self-defense in corporate organizations or "cooperations" to protect themselves from their often rapacious and violent superiors. Frequently these groupings were military and organized to contest the violence of lords or bishops with counterviolence. At times they developed in the context of artisans and merchants organized in guilds or in the context of local religious and spiritual groups organized in confraternities. Neighborhoods also frequently formed such organizations, and their militias were particularly important in many cities.

Such "cooperations" or incorporations (literally fictitious persons) with time tended to band together to overthrow the private power of local lords and church leaders and rule in common, as communes. As the name implies, the commune held power *in comune* (in common) for its members in what might be labeled a kind of corporate and more public vision of power – in essence a fictive corporate person replacing a private lord. It was a vast oversimplification, but in the thirteenth century in most Italian cities of the north, those ruling *in comune* tended to defend their rule by claiming that they were the real people of the city, *Il Popolo*. The name suggests today that the *popolo* included all the people of the city ruling together, a true democracy. At the time, however, it was a more limited ideal, claiming merely to include those people worthy of participating in ruling; significantly, in this way of seeing the *popolo*, women, day laborers, the young, the poor, the recently arrived, and the perceived enemies of the *popolo* were excluded. In fact, in most cities the *popolo* was actually limited to guild members. Guilds will be discussed in more detail later, but for now suffice it to reiterate that guilds themselves were also incorporations (fictive bodies); they were made up of artisans but also of merchants, bankers, lawyers, doctors, and other professions. Ideally they organized and disciplined their membership while protecting them from other organizations of power. But they also guaranteed the quality of their products or services, fixed prices, and kept peace among their members. Significantly, with bankers, lawyers, and merchants at one level and butchers, bakers, and used clothing dealers at a lower one, they included a large swath of urban society; thus, banding together as *Il Popolo*, they could and did claim to rule the commune in the name of all the people that counted.

Using principles drawn from ancient Roman law, which had undergone a widespread revival in Europe in the twelfth and thirteenth centuries, the *popolo* progressively discovered and deployed claims that they had the right to preserve and defend their cities for the common good. Finally, in the early fourteenth century, noted lawyers and commentators on Roman law such as Bartolus of Sassoferrato (1313–1357) and Baldo da Ubaldis (1327–1400) formalized what was already practice, arguing that a free people (*popolus liber*) in the absence of other legitimate authority had the right to rule themselves in order to assure peace and justice for their communities. That claim, of course, was made easier in the fourteenth century by the relative absence of popes and emperors who could contradict it. Significant in this defense of government, lawyers were turning once more to the Roman past to give legitimacy to the current organization of society, in this case governmental authority – making the crucial claim that such power was not new, but rather a renewal or rebirth of classical forms of rule embodied in ancient Roman law. Public power to assure peace and justice for the common good seems a remarkably modern idea for the late thirteenth and fourteenth centuries, and the reality of rule of course turned more on private competition for power within the *popolo*, as we shall see, but, nonetheless, this legitimization of power in terms of creating a civic community that served the common good helped to expand the discourse of political power in directions that would have a long (and often contested) history. The *popolo* and government, once just fictitious persons in competition with lords and bishops for private power, were slowly becoming recognized as public organizations of power serving the general good and increasingly as a significant underpinning of the *civiltà* of the first Rinascimento.

Obviously, in the thirteenth century power was not handed over to *Il Popolo* merely because they asserted it based on ancient Roman ideals or even because notaries and lawyers in their service produced legal arguments that defended such claims. The economic and demographic growth that typified the thirteenth century throughout Europe and fostered the rapid growth of dozens of flourishing cities in northern Italy created a generally confused and contested situation that involved virtually all aspects of life, from politics, social distinctions, and morality to art, architecture, and even love poetry. Traditionally, nobles whose titles were based on rural land-owning (although by the thirteenth century many lived in the city) and military service had competed with ecclesiastical officials for the control of cities, but with the rise of *Il Popolo* merchants, bankers, lawyers, and even many of Petrarch's motley crew of artisans entered the fray, contesting once again the Great Social Divide that had previously dominated society. These conflicts were often fought violently in the streets, as well as in many more subtle ways that used literature, poetry, manners, local history and traditions, and even religious enthusiasms to advance one group's claims over another.

These conflicts were once viewed as a classic contest between economic classes in a Marxist sense – an important stage on the way to modern bourgeois capitalism. As early as the end of the nineteenth century the great socialist historian Gaetano Salvemini argued that the conflicts of the thirteenth century were essentially driven by class warfare between an old feudal nobility and *Il Popolo*. In the early twentieth century the social theorist Alfred Von Martin, in a brief essaylike book, *The Sociology of the Italian Renaissance*, laid out the thesis with less detail, but clearly and powerfully. Anti-Marxist historians quickly took up the cause of disproving this thesis, and already in the 1920s a Russian historian who had fled the communist revolution in his country, Nicolai Ottokar, launched a powerful counterattack. He argued, based largely on Florentine documents, that many members of *Il Popolo* there actually came from the rural nobility and that those who opposed *Il Popolo* often included rich merchants and bankers. Moreover, many nobles whose wealth was based on rural landholding lived in the city, intermarried with powerful families of the *popolo*, and often supported their causes. In sum, he demonstrated that there was not a clear-cut economic class difference between the groups competing for power and claimed that rather than class, the real tension and conflicts were due to competition between factions or local groups that formed around local issues without a clear class or economic base.

While the debate on the nature of these conflicts has been intense ever since, the strict Marxist vision has largely lost sway, without, however, the more conservative anticlass vision totally winning out. Recently a more cultural vision of class has complicated the debate, with historians arguing that although there were not clear economic divisions between *Il Popolo* and their opponents, there was a clear division in values and in the social and cultural visions of the two groups competing for power in most cities. Even this may be too simplistic, as we shall see, but it does seem clear that, broadly speaking, there were significant issues that were more than local involved in the conflict across the thirteenth century over who would rule and who would be the leaders of society, both socially and politically. Even for Petrarch, well into the next century, these ongoing conflicts were a significant part of the reason for his negative vision of the city, and earlier they had played a significant role in Dante's hope that the Emperor Henry VII would bring peace and a just rule to end the violence.

In a way these conflicts even seemed to confirm the message of Joachim of Fiore that one world was about to end and a new one begin, a vision that in some circles continued to live on across the Rinascimento. But by the end of the thirteenth century it was becoming clear that the new world dawning would not be his Age of the Spirit, but instead the age of the *popolo* and the urban *civiltà* that they were building. Significantly, however, it would not be the age of all the *popolo*. For as the century progressed and as they won power in more and more cities, exiling or even killing their enemies, the *popolo* began to break apart. Often it is true that nothing fails like success, and that was clearly the case for *Il Popolo*. When their alliance of quite different groups of people (rich merchants, bankers, lawyers, and humble butchers, bakers, and candle makers, along with an occasional fellow-traveling noble) effectively defeated their perceived common enemies, they found that they had less and less to hold them together as a group. Simply put, merchants and bankers shared with butchers and bakers a common interest in a peaceful city and a civic society ruled in such a way that they were not victimized by governmental power used for private ends, but they were not adverse to profiting from governmental impositions at the expense of their one-time allies.

The result was that in many cities *Il Popolo*, although still ruling in the name of all, began to pull apart into competing groups. The easiest division, and the most significant, was generally seen at the time as dividing the *popolo minuto* (the little people) and the *popolo grosso* (the big people); in many cities, although not all, this pitted the lesser guilds (usually artisans who worked with their hands) against the greater (usually merchants, bankers, and cloth producers – those who essentially manipulated money or goods). The labels for these groups varied from place to place and even within cities. In Florence, for example, merchants, bankers, and cloth producers were at times referred to as the *grandi del popolo* (the great of the people) or even the *popolo grasso* (the fat people). Crucially, however, as the *popolo grosso* worked to gain power for themselves and limit the power of their former allies, the legitimacy gained by ruling in the name of all the *popolo* began to fall away, and new justifications for their power were needed. Perhaps it is not surprising that the justification that they adopted was a discourse, building on the earlier defense of the *popolo* and the Roman law ideal of a *populus liber*, that stressed that this more restricted and generally wealthier group worked not for their own private interests but for the general welfare of the commune. Around this common theme circled other, closely related contemporary ideals such as peace, stability, and an end to the violence that had disrupted urban life in the context of a Christian city guided by both secular and divine justice. In sum, they emphasized virtually what Lorenzetti had visualized in his frescos in the Palazzo Pubblico of Siena and what Dante had called for, not just in his political works but also in his love poetry and *Divine Comedy*.

The Ordinances of Justice in Florence: Virtù, Civiltà, and the Popolo Grosso

Of course, once again this legitimating discourse was often more ideology than fact. Also, it was a discourse that developed at different times in different cities and in some less prosperous ones hardly at all. But, significantly, it was a discourse that won out in the center and north of Italy over the course of the fourteenth century (even in cities where the *popolo grosso* did not clearly win power), becoming a generally shared ideal of *civiltà*. In Florence, however, there is a particular event that once appeared to historians to reflect concretely this transition: the passage of the Florentine Ordinances of Justice on January 18, 1293. The Ordinances were officially concerned with providing peace and justice in Florence: justice for those who upset the orderly life of the city – as again represented by Lorenzetti's angel of justice cutting off the heads of malefactors – and peace for those good citizens of the city who were productive and orderly members of society.

Basically the Ordinances identified a group of unruly people and labeled them magnates, promising them stern punishment if they misbehaved. These magnates – or more accurately, their families – were required to put up a sizeable pledge for the good behavior of their family members. If anyone then behaved violently, the pledge was confiscated and the family had to put down another. In theory this should have pressured magnate families to discipline their own members in order to avoid being ruined financially and thus ensured peaceful and less violent behavior. But the Ordinances and the legislation that anticipated and reinforced them in the eighties and nineties went further, for together they denied virtually all major offices in government to those labeled magnates: in essence eliminating them from direct political power. This legislation also limited the magnates' ability to hold offices in guilds, a significant restriction because most governmental offices were elected from the membership of the guilds; thus, without power in the guilds, magnates theoretically would have little power to influence those elected. In the end, although magnates could still occasionally hold minor offices and could influence politics through membership in the Guelph party (which for most of the fourteenth century also played an important role in elections in Florence), they had been essentially pushed out of government. Approximately 1,500 men and 50 large families were labeled magnates and theoretically fell under these regulations.

For Salvemini, this was a crucial moment of class conflict and signaled the triumph of the *popolo grosso* over a feudal nobility labeled and eliminated as magnates; for Ottokar, it was merely another moment in the long history of factional struggles that would continue to dominate Florence, until finally the Medici came to power in the fifteenth century. To complicate matters, recent research suggests that the Ordinances of 1293 were passed at a moment when the *popolo grosso* found their power momentarily under attack by the *popolo*, and there are indications in the Ordinances themselves of a desire to limit the power of those perceived as overly powerful across the board, including some of the major banking and merchant families. In other words, while this particular legislation seemed to have struck more directly at those labeled magnates, it may have been intended as a warning to other, more domineering families among the *popolo* as well.

In the end, however, the long debate over the class nature of the Ordinances and the broader legislation that limited magnate power may simply arise from a question badly posed. Recently it has been argued cogently that the traditional nobility of the Tuscan countryside had already lost its battle with the Florentine *popolo*, not so much in great confrontations like the Ordinances but earlier, in one small skirmish after another. And, more importantly, the old nobility had simply broken apart culturally and socially, with some of their number intermixing with those they perceived as becoming the richest and most important of the *popolo* across the thirteenth century. At the same time some of the most successful of the *popolo*, attracted by the noble status of the traditional nobility, intermarried with them, trained in arms and cavalry warfare, and bought up country estates. This created a situation similar to the one that Ottokar discovered and used to attack Salvemini, claiming that there were no essential economic or class differences between the leaders of the *popolo* and those labeled magnates. Some of those labeled magnates were newer rich men from the *popolo*, and in turn some of those who did the labeling of magnates were themselves members of relatively old families whose wealth and family tradition were largely rural.

What must be considered, however, are the social and cultural developments that stood behind this social mixing and apparent confusion. On the one hand, some of the *popolo* had become rich and powerful enough to ape the manners and style of the old nobility, seeking military titles like knighthood, displaying their wealth with urban homes that resembled fortifications, buying country estates, and adopting noble, high-handed behaviors that often mixed violence and polite manners in ways that were both disruptive and troubling. On the other hand, a number of the traditional nobility had rejected this type of behavior to adopt the more peaceful, ordered, and less violent life associated with the emerging merchant/banker elite of the *popolo*, the *popolo grosso*. Along with this came a vision of a civil urban society that put civic values above personal and family ones, at least as a legitimating ideal, and did so often with reference to the civilization of ancient Rome and the first ideals of Christianity and Christian society. One would expect, of course, some of the newly rich with social pretensions to copy the style and manners of the old established nobility with an eye to gaining similar traditional elite status. What is strange at first glance is that some of the old nobility moved in the opposite direction, not just copying the customs and style of the more *grosso* of the *popolo*, but also following their economic lead by becoming bankers, merchants, lawyers, and large-scale cloth producers.

In such moves, however, one discovers the deeper underlying class/cultural nature of the social tensions and conflicts of the day. For the emerging elite that drove the passage of laws against magnates (of which the Ordinances of Justice were merely a part) was more and more driven by the *popolo grosso*. As a result, in many ways neither the *popolo grosso* nor the *popolo* were by the end of the thirteenth century engaged in a straightforward or simple conflict with an old nobility – the Great Social Divide of the medieval world was already a dead letter in the cities of Italy, replaced by a much more complex and contested social and political world. Rather, the *popolo grosso* was emerging as a new elite, attempting to dominate both the *popolo* and the members of the old nobility that for one reason or another refused to align with them. Crucially, this emerging new elite defended its position of leadership in terms of its own vision of who the best people in society should be and how they should behave. On the one hand, true members of the elite should not work with their hands, manual labor being a traditionally negative social marker associated with peasants and artisans, in other words, the broader *popolo*. On the other, they should be urban, peaceful, careful, and rational in their approach to life. This group of behaviors that, along with their wealth, in many ways defined the *popolo grosso* was given the traditional name for those behaviors that distinguished the best men from the rest: *virtù* – a term that again evoked ancient Roman values and in this case the qualities that made ancient Rome great at the same time that it evoked traditional Christian virtues.

Significantly, in the Middle Ages, when a traditional nobility had been recognized as the unquestioned leaders of society, their vision of *virtù* dominated with a very different meaning that turned on more rural and warrior values: courage, military prowess, keeping one's word, and violently defending one's honor. Of course, there were many at the end of the thirteenth and well into the fourteenth century who still saw *virtù* in those more traditional terms, but society was changing, and along with it *virtù*. Crucially, however, those changes were conceptualized and idealized not as changes to something new, but as returns to something old, the old values that had made Rome great. In this vision Florence, as a city built by the Romans and rebuilt in the Rinascimento on those Roman foundations, was correctly to be led by a *popolo grosso* elite measured by ancient Roman *virtù*, thus becoming virtually Rome reborn. In that context it is not at all strange to see Dante in the *Divine Comedy* guided through Hell and much of Purgatory by the pagan Roman Virgil and sharing with his guide an evaluation of the lives of his deceased friends, enemies, and acquaintances in terms of their *virtù*, seen in both civic and religious terms. Ancient Roman authority and the best of pagan values exhibited by Virgil melded paradoxically with Christian values and a shared culture of urban values to allow Dante in a way his own personal Last Judgment of his predecessors and compatriots – a last judgment that confirmed a developing Rinascimento ideal of *virtù* both in the afterlife and in a Roman imperial past. In other cities and in the literature of the day, this new *virtù* once again was not presented as changing to something new; rather, it was reimagined as returning to something older and better, even if, crucially, that was usually more imagination than reality.

When read in this light, the Ordinances of Justice take on a different meaning. They were merely a moment in a longer process of defining who among those competing for elite status would be eliminated from the competition. But rather than eliminating one group of families because another had the naked power to do so, they were eliminated in the name of the values widely shared among the most powerful of the *popolo*, with the emerging elite, the *popolo grosso*, taking the lead in defining those values. Significantly, those values were contrasted with the dysfunctional values of what was by the end of the thirteenth century a largely imaginary, outdated feudal elite, imagined as the rulers of a dark age that had forgotten the true *virtù* of Italy's great Roman past. In their very name, then, the Ordinances of Justice presented a program, promising a Christian, ordered, rational, just urban environment – a *virtù*-ous and civilized urban world – in other words, an urban *civiltà* that lived up to the values of the *popolo grosso*. Thus, as Ottokar pointed out, a rather mixed group that did not really make up an economic class was labeled magnates, *and, at the same time*, as Salvemini argued, a merchant/banker elite and its values in many ways stood behind this labeling and the broader changes that were deeply transforming society. Moreover, as this was all done in the name of *Il Popolo* and for the sake of creating a Christian, safe, peaceful urban environment with justice for all, this move gained a wide consensus at the expense of those families that found themselves labeled magnates.

Yet, crucially, behind the consensus that backed the Ordinances and saw the legislation as a great defense of *Il Popolo* there lay deeply embedded, perhaps unwittingly, a defense of the ideals and ideology that were increasingly the program of the *popolo grosso*. Ideally, governmental power and power in general should be used for the common good, to create a civic culture or *civiltà* that the English term "commonwealth" expresses well. That commonwealth required peace, order, and justice for all. Of course, the *popolo grosso* did not live up to these ideals and this ideology particularly well – actually, they often fell short of upholding the common good over private interests (as in most societies) or in recreating a Roman civilization that had of course never existed as they imagined or evoked it. But with the Ordinances a program of the *popolo grosso* had begun to emerge more clearly from the general program of *Il Popolo* in Florence.

Significantly, Florence was not alone in passing Ordinances of Justice and legislation that aimed at creating a more peaceful and ordered urban Christian society. In fact, over the last years of the thirteenth and the first years of the fourteenth century, Ordinances of Justice with similar provisions were passed in most of the cities of northern Italy, with Florence actually joining the trend rather late. If anything, the city was more of a leader in violent social conflict – even as the Ordinances proclaimed a program of peace and justice for all – as over the fourteenth century Florence was dominated by tensions and at times open conflict between the *popolo grosso* and the *popolo minuto*, who did not always quietly acquiesce in their progressive disenfranchisement.

The Serrata in Venice: Civiltà *and the* Popolo Grosso *as a Nobility*

As much as Florence has been seen as being typical of the cities of northern Italy during this turbulent transition, Venice is usually seen as unusual. Yet, suggestively, it may well be that Venice was less an atypical city than one in the vanguard of developments, for its precocious economic successes brought about social and cultural change earlier in Venice than in most other cities. At much the same time that across the north of Italy the Ordinances of Justice were labeling powerful people magnates and eliminating them from government, in Venice – once more in the name of peace, justice, and a more ordered urban life – what might be deemed the local version of the *popolo grosso*, primarily merchants and investors in trade, were defining themselves legally as the dominant political and social class. Although, as elsewhere, the working out of this definition spanned several decades, Venice too had its highly symbolic defining moment, the famous Serrata (Closing) of the Maggior Consiglio (Great or Major Council) of 1297–1298.

Formally, the legislation that enacted the Serrata was merely a technical electoral reform and, in fact, one in a series of electoral reforms at the time, officially promoted as assuring access to government to all who deserved it. As originally passed it increased the number of people sitting in the Maggior Consiglio; thus, it might actually qualify to be labeled an "opening" rather than a "closing," as a noted historian of Venice, Fredric Lane, suggested in a path-breaking 1971 article that reopened debate on just what the Serrata meant. What the legislation actually did was to simplify earlier, complex electoral reforms making membership in the council automatic when males turned twenty-five, if they belonged to a group of families defined by the law as having the right to be members. Provisions were also included for adding new families that had been left out unintentionally, but, to get ahead of the story, those provisions quickly became virtually a dead letter.

Because the Great Council was officially the body that was the ultimate source of all governmental authority, it might seem that this restricting of its membership to a legally defined group served to give that group greater power. But Lane argued that the reality was that the group of people who were defined as automatically having the right to sit on the council was very large, probably including more than 1,100 men; thus the council became too large and unwieldy to function or to exercise meaningful power. Moreover, as it included virtually everyone who had participated in government before the supposed closing, it seemed to promise that no one would lose power – no magnates were pushed out of government. As a result, it appears that in the short run Venetians, when they thought about it at all, saw this change as technical and not particularly significant, as Lane argued.

What changed all that and made the Serrata a closing was the fact that over the course of the next decade the Great Council passed a series of laws that gradually commandeered for themselves the authority to elect virtually all the other important offices of government from their own membership. Thus, quietly but effectively, within a decade a process that had begun with the 1297–1298 legislation became a revolution that locked in a hereditary ruling class and locked out most of the *popolo*. And, crucially, the core of this ruling class was made up of merchants, investors in trade, and other powerful moneymen, essentially the Venetian version of the *popolo grosso*. What makes this different from the situation in other cities? First, Venice, unlike other cities, did not create an official group of magnates who were eliminated from power. As Venice was a commercial power whose merchants and investors had successfully ruled the city for centuries, its elite had long been more united in its broad economic perspectives, as well as in its rather unique blend of *popolo grosso* values and a concomitant, and seemingly contradictory, fascination with more old-fashioned noble and knightly ideals. Other Italians made fun of the tournaments and knightly displays that Venetian merchants and investors enjoyed, mocking those men as more suited for ships and countinghouses than for donning armor and jousting in the small open *campi* of their island city. In the end, however, the youth of the Venetian upper classes could play at horseback riding and jousting before and after the Serrata, but they grew up to be merchants and investors, not knights, and that had long been the case, even as one or two took the title of knight or went off to fight on horseback.

More importantly, however, a large portion of the population was legally closed out of government. And those who were, it became clear with time, were those who were losing out in most of the cities of northern Italy, the lesser members of the *popolo* or the *popolo minuto* – artisans, shopkeepers, small-scale local traders, plus a large group of Venetian sailors and boat hands. The clear elimination of this group obviously made Venice appear different from most other cities where Ordinances of Justice and similar legislation were promoted and defended as protecting the *popolo*. That apparent difference is what most historians have focused on. Yet in many ways this open political elimination of the *popolo minuto* was not so much a difference as something that put Venice ahead of similar developments in other cities – ahead as it had been, in fact, economically, politically, and socially for a long time. In other cities, as the magnates slowly ceased to fulfill the role of a dangerous other that united the *popolo*, the *popolo grosso* moved in a similar direction, also using various forms of electoral reform to limit the access of their more humble ex-allies to power. Of course, the *popolo grosso* did not always win immediately or even over time in every city, but overall they and their vision of the ideal of a peaceful and ordered civic world dominated the shared culture of the first Rinascimento.

In Venice what was unusual was the fact that its government in the end legally defined, with the Serrata and subsequent legislation, a hereditary ruling class, something that virtually no other city did. Obviously, even if the ruling group turned out to be much the same there as elsewhere, the fact that it was legally defined was a significant difference. It helps, for example, to explain the fabled peacefulness of the city, even if that peacefulness was to a degree a self-serving fiction used to defend the rule of the closed order created by the Serrata. Still, while other cities often fought out questions of power and status with bloodshed in the streets, in Venice an established ruling class settled down to defend its rule against those excluded. The Serrata also helped to color in significant ways the republican ideals of the city – republican ideals that had an important impact on the development of political ideals during the period and beyond.

This transition in Venice, however, was more than simply a political one, which makes the story of the Serrata more complex and has led to suggestions of a "Long Serrata" that took decades to complete. Evidently, political change and social change are tightly interrelated – for, as we have seen, the developing power of the *popolo grosso* as a social class was closely related to political change. And in Venice the political triumph of this group was followed by their social triumph as well. For not only did they become the hereditary ruling class, fairly rapidly they became a legally defined dominant social class as well. The events that led to this legal definition of social status were triggered by one of the few moments of revolutionary violence in

Venice during the period, the famed Querini-Tiepolo conspiracy of 1310. By that date it had become clear to many that the Serrata was not a mere technical electoral reform. The closed nature of the ruling class was underlined by the fact that virtually no new men were being taken up into the ruling group, and the laws restricting virtually all important offices to members of the Great Council were clearly eliminating others from government.

Adding to a growing disaffection with an ever-more-evident closing of government was the heavy cost of an unsuccessful war to gain control of Ferrara that had begun in 1308. Ferrara controlled the main fords over the eastern Po River, fords that had the potential to interrupt both Venice's west/ east river trade with the rich cities and agricultural regions of the Lombard plain and its north/south overland trade with Florence and the south. When factional strife in Ferrara seemed to offer an easy opportunity to take the city, Venice jumped at the opportunity. Unfortunately for dreams of an easy success, a coalition of other cities, not eager to see Venice dominate those fords, came to Ferrara's aid with money and troops; and Pope Clement V, who claimed to have the right to rule the city as the northernmost outpost of the Papal States, weighed in from Avignon with an interdict against the Venetians as well. Thus Venetian expectations of a quick victory quickly died. Not only did the war drag on with a concomitant increase in its cost, it also increased the tensions over those costs and the papal interdict. Those tensions began to have a deeper economic impact when other naval powers took advantage of the interdict to seize Venetian merchant ships, one of the punishments allowed by the interdict. In the normal order of things other cities might have ignored this possibility out of fear of Venetian retaliation, but once again, with the city involved in what looked like a long and costly war, that seemed less a danger. In sum, what had seemed an opportunity for a quick success for the ruling class became with time a serious economic and spiritual burden on the city and a black mark on its rule.

In that context those who had been excluded from government by the Serrata began to question the war, which was increasingly seen as the war of a government from which they were excluded. And for some of the *popolo* who had come to feel that their exclusion was unjust, the Serrata itself began to be more aggressively questioned. As if that were not enough, two of the most powerful families included in the hereditary ruling class by the Serrata, the Querini and Tiepolo clans, had become disenchanted with the war, government policy, and the political order. It seems that the powerful and charismatic leader of the Tiepolo family, Baiamonte Tiepolo (d. 1328), may have hoped to take advantage of the situation and the disaffection of the *popolo minuto* to take over the city and rule it as a tyrant. The result was a conspiracy to overthrow the government and the order created by the Serrata by storming the Doge's palace and deposing the doge, Pietro Gradenigo (1251–1311; doge 1289–1311). Gradenigo, as doge, was held by many to have been responsible for the Serrata and the new order it had created; thus Baiamonte hoped his unpopularity and that of the war for Ferrara would make his own conquest of power relatively easy.

Two centuries later, Niccolò Machiavelli would warn that conspiracies to overthrow governments seldom succeeded because in order to win, one needed a certain critical mass of supporters, but in order to gain that critical mass, too many people had to be trusted with the plans, which inevitably led to betrayal and failure. In this case Machiavelli's later analysis appears well founded. Several of the conspirators betrayed their fellows. Thus when Baiamonte and his supporters arrived before the Doge's palace on the morning of June 15, 1310, they found it well defended and were quickly routed with heavy losses. A brief period of reprisals followed; a powerful secret police was created – the Council of Ten, which would play an important role in Venetian politics down to the end of the republic – and peace was quickly restored with the ruling class of the Serrata more firmly in place than ever.

For that ruling group the rout of a powerful and charismatic traitor within their ranks was a great testament to the power and effectiveness of their new order. Locked in an expensive and unpopular war, faced with internal divisions and pressure from below, they had survived a conspiracy led by a popular leader and some of the strongest clans of the city. Suggestively, Baiamonte was often portrayed as a man with knightly ways and military ambitions (a virtual magnate), although this reputation may have been enhanced by the winners and their desire to portray him not just as a conspirator but as a dangerous other who had threatened the basic values of the merchant city. More significantly, as a symbol of their success the winners made June 15 a yearly festival of triumph – a Venetian Fourth of July that was celebrated annually until the fall of the city to Napoleon's troops in 1797. But they did much more. Realizing that the order created by the Serrata was becoming ever-more clear and evident, they made the decision to celebrate the closing and its creation of a hereditary ruling class.

As a result, rather than portraying the Serrata as a power grab by the *popolo grosso* at the expense of the *popolo minuto*, or even by a few more powerful families at the expense of those less powerful, they decided to glorify the Serrata, portraying it as a far-sighted decision by which the best of Venice willingly sacrificed their own self-interest and ruled for the common good of their city – once again to create a civic world of justice and peace for all, a true Venetian *civiltà*. In this they were clearly rejecting the traditional medieval vision that saw power as being exercised in the private interests of a prince or lord. Perhaps this was not quite yet a vision of public power, but it was a significant step in that direction. The ideal was that the republican government of Venice was ruled by a closed political class that ruled for the general welfare of the city itself and all its citizens, even those who were excluded from participating in government. Of course, this was primarily an ideal and even more an ideology used to defend the rule of the few against claims from those below, yet it had a major impact on the development of Western political thought because of Venice's great success and apparent stability, especially as Venetian political thinkers made it clear that this was not something dangerously new, but something safely old.

First, they claimed, building on local historical traditions, that this vision of government by a few for the common good of all went back to the first days of the Venetian republic and its founding by refugees from the falling Roman Empire. They also claimed that it fulfilled the prophecies made to the apostle Mark when he was reassured by his angel that in the lagoons where he was lost a great city would be born that would continue his mission of building a Christian society in the West. With time many other Christian, classical, and medieval examples were added to this defense of the new order, thus once again making it not something new, but something old and respected. Much later in the eighteenth century, when these mythic defenses of the order of the Serrata were fully worked out, and political thinkers were seeking models for constructing enduring republican governments or defending republican institutions, leaders like Thomas Jefferson looked to Venice and its republic as a significant source of inspiration because of its stability, longevity, and peaceful civic life. To him and many others of his day, the city seemed to represent a great historical success based on the perfect form of what a republican state should be; thus a myth originally built largely to deny the new, ironically became in many ways a reality for new republics of a later day.

There was, however, another response to the Querini-Tiepolo conspiracy, a social one. In legislation distinguishing the more dangerous conspirators from the less dangerous, the authorities made a distinction between a group of people whom they labeled "noble" and the rest of the population – in other words, a distinction between those who were perceived as being at the top of the social hierarchy and those below. Crucially, those labeled nobles were not traditional nobles from the countryside or old noble families living in the city; rather, they were members of those families who (following the Serrata) sat by hereditary right on the Great Council. In other words, the Venetian *popolo grosso* – primarily merchants and large-scale investors – had begun to legally call themselves a nobility. At first glance this might seem the height of confusion: the *popolo grosso* who in other cities had slowly but surely across the thirteenth century grabbed power from an old nobility or labeled their enemies nobles, in Venice were now claiming to be a nobility. In the face of this one might argue, as many have, that Venice was an anomaly, a city very different socially from other cities of the early Rinascimento.

Yet a closer look suggests that Venice was not so much different socially as ahead of other cities. For if one considers the use of the label "noble" for a moment, it becomes clear that the Venetian *popolo grosso* were not claiming that they were an old traditional nobility with wealth drawn from the land or even from urban rents, ruling for their private interests, but rather an elite based on wealth and productive power ruling for the common good. Lacking a better name for their newly established elite status and, in the spirit of the day, anxious to avoid any label that implied novelty, they took an old and widely recognized name for those on top of society, "noble," and applied it to themselves.

Nothing could be further from the way the old feudal nobility operated and more typical of the rising power of the *popolo grosso* across Italy; over and over again, in city after city, this group used law and government to reorder their civic world and society with themselves on top. In other cities the process would take longer and be more contested. And in cities with more fragile or more rural economies, there would be more mixing of an actual old nobility and new *popolo grosso* leadership or even moments of *popolo minuto* power. But the general trend was the development of a new social elite dominated by the *popolo grosso* and a new political, social, and cultural order that reflected the values and vision of that same group. It is important, however, not to oversimplify this transition. It was never as neat or clean as the Venetian case suggests. Yet from such fertile mixing of the new thought of as the old, and the old describing the new, and in the messy confusions between the two, there emerged slowly but surely a vibrantly rich culture and society that contemporaries saw as reborn on ancient values and traditions, Christian, biblical, and classical – the Rinascimento.

In Venice, then, the political ruling class made up of the leading *popolo grosso* families legally defined themselves as the socially dominant class, the Venetian nobility. A clear and clean overlap between political status and social status is rare, and it might be noted that the failure to match up between the two often leads to tension and conflict, especially when economic distinctions are added to the mix. Venice, however, had created a society where the match was virtually perfect and where even economic power lined up pretty well, at least for a while. It took time for these distinctions to be generally recognized, but by the early 1320s there was little question in Venice: political power and noble status were one and the same thing and limited to a legally defined hereditary class of merchants and investors, their own *popolo grosso*. Time would break down this powerful alignment, with some nobles becoming less wealthy and even poor. In turn, some non-nobles built large fortunes and developed strategies to exercise considerable political power behind the scenes. But for much of the fourteenth century there was a fairly good fit between wealth, political power, and social status in Venice. As a result, as other cities fought out who should rule and who deserved elite status, often in bloody battles in the streets, Venice settled down to defend its order. And, crucially, it did so not only with aggressive policing and control of the lower classes – although it did that – but also by aggressively defending the order created by the Serrata as uniquely just, creating a rich political ideology and civic culture that defended and celebrated that order and the rule of their noble *popolo grosso* as ideal.

Milan and the Visconti: Civiltà, *the* Popolo Grosso, *and* Signori

While Florentine and Venetian historians have debated the relative importance of such changes and how representative they were of the rest of Italy, it should be noted that as far as governmental forms are concerned neither was particularly typical. Both were republics. Yet in many ways, with the end of the thirteenth century the day of republics had passed. The future in most cities lay with one-man rule, princes or tyrants, depending upon one's perspective. Called usually *signore/signori* (lord/lords), they promised peace, order, and stability once again, in the face of the political, social, and economic conflicts that divided most cities. Certainly there was no lack of conflicts for them to settle. Once in power, however, they almost invariably worked out alliances with the most powerful local families in order to maintain their rule. This meant that where the *popolo grosso* were strong, they tended to align with them, while in less commercial cities where a more traditional nobility, or at least a powerful group whose wealth was based on land, was stronger, they leaned more heavily on them. Still, across the century the *signori* who were most successful tended to oversee a melding of the most flexible of the older nobility with the most powerful of the *popolo*, a mixing often already well under way in the thirteenth century. The result was usually a progressively more aristocratic *popolo grosso*, still urban, and still heavily influenced by widely shared ideals of an urban *civiltà*.

As *signori* typically came to power following the exigencies of local politics and conflicts, it is difficult to pick a representative example or even moment. But perhaps the way the Visconti family came to power in Milan, in its apparent serendipity and messiness, best reflects the complexity that was the norm. Milan also warrants attention because, under Visconti leadership, it was one of the most important and powerful cities of the early Rinascimento. In the thirteenth century the city was still dominated politically by an ecclesiastical leader, its archbishop. Earlier, rule by local bishops had been fairly common for cities in Italy as well as in much of Europe, as the Church had centered bishoprics in larger population centers to serve as administrative seats for its own bureaucracy. Thus, with their superior wealth and comparatively sophisticated bureaucracy, they tended to dominate the cities where they were located.

The Investiture Controversy of the eleventh and twelfth centuries had attempted to break the power of bishops, who in many places had become virtually local hereditary lords. One of the most important reforms passed at the time was a requirement that bishops be appointed by the pope; thus it was hoped that they would serve him and the Church, rather than local noble families who had gained control of the office, passing it on from generation to generation. Also, reformers attempted to eliminate clerical marriage, thus making it impossible for a bishop to marry and pass on his office to a son. Although neither reform was entirely successful, these attempts to regain control of bishops and the local church did help supply the wedge that allowed merchants and urban nobles to take power away from local bishops. Moreover, once bishops were no longer drawn from local powerful families, it was easier for locals to take over rule from foreign and often absentee bishops appointed by a pope.

The archbishop of Milan, however, was not easily displaced from power. The post continued to be a highly sought-after prize for powerful local families even after the Investiture Controversy, and it controlled enough wealth and authority that it could stand up – albeit at times with difficulty – to both popes and local attempts at secular governance. According to tradition, the great noble families of the rich agricultural Lombard plain that surrounded Milan elected the archbishop from their number with the approval of the Church, a local compromise necessitated by the nobility's power. In the thirteenth century that nobility was facing competition for control of the archbishopric from two newer corporate groups organized in the city: the Motta, made up primarily of lesser nobles who lived in the city and who were aligned with newer rich commercial and business families – an incipient *popolo grosso*; and the Credenza di Sant'Ambrogio, made up largely of artisans and shopkeepers – closer to those labeled the *popolo minuto* elsewhere. Significantly, both groups, as incorporations, were seeking power in order to protect their own private interests, much as in other Italian cities.

This conflict came to a head in the 1260s, when a powerful local noble family, the Della Torre, aligned with the Credenza. Leading the Guelph party, they rode Guelph victories in the north of Italy to gain power in Milan, led by Napoleone Della Torre, called Napo (d. 1278). Although their conquest was based upon force and Napo's widely respected military leadership in the Guelph cause, it was justified by claiming that his rule was in the name of *Il Popolo* as a whole, once again very much in the spirit of the times. But to secure his power, Napo was aware that his family had to control the archbishop. Unfortunately, he was correct; for although he was from the old nobility and a Guelph leader, his lower-class allies made him suspect. In the end neither the old nobility nor the pope supported him in his attempt to control the office; instead, an archbishop from a major rival family, Ottone Visconti (d. 1295), was elected. Napo, unhappy with this, did not allow Visconti to enter the city. From exile, however, Ottone with his supporters made things difficult, leading a harassing opposition to his rule. At first glance it might seem that we have here a classic thirteenth-century conflict, with the Visconti, representing the old nobility and their supporters, against the Della Torre, representing the *popolo*. As usual, however, things were not so simple. Both clans were far too flexible in their competition for power to follow modern models of how such conflicts should have developed.

Rather, in the last decades of the century, both families shifted their alliances among the old nobility, the Motta, and the Credenza and at times even divided among themselves, in order to gain power. To make a long, complex story shorter, the Archbishop Ottone Visconti, leading an army himself, with the aid of soldiers from neighboring cities who feared his rival's expansionist policies, finally captured Napo along with many of the Della Torre in late 1277. Napo died shortly (and conveniently) thereafter in jail. Visconti quickly moved to take control in Milan. But realizing that his original power base, the old nobility, was no longer adequate to sustain his rule in a city where merchants and bankers were amassing large fortunes and where artisans and day laborers made up a restless mass of a population, he wrapped himself in the mantle of *Il Popolo*, claiming to be their champion. As part of this he helped a charismatic young relative, Matteo Visconti (1255–1322), to become *Capitano del Popolo* in 1287 – an office that in Milan, as in other cities, was responsible for keeping the peace and protecting the *popolo* from the high-handed ways of the old nobility.

Both controlling the ecclesiastical authority of the city as archbishop and having considerable power in its secular government via his relative Matteo, Ottone was well on his way to securing Visconti rule of Milan and becoming its *signore*. Those best-laid plans, however, overlooked one of the crucial problems that all tyrants must eventually face, their own death. Ottone died in 1295, and the Della Torre family, waiting in exile for just such an opportunity, took it. They defeated the Visconti militarily, finally driving them into exile in 1302. Guido Della Torre (1259–1312) became *signore* of Milan, and the family gained control of the archbishopric as well. But almost immediately, the Della Torre family itself began to divide against Guido, a few even aligning with the exiled Visconti. All the infighting was rendered moot, however, when Italy's erstwhile bridegroom, the emperor Henry VII, arrived, bringing his promise of peace and reconciliation between warring factions as a paradoxical Guelph-Ghibelline.

Arriving at the gates of Milan in late December of 1310, the Della Torre unhappily welcomed him into the city, because as emperor he was the rightful king of northern Italy and, according to long-standing tradition, Milan was the capital of that kingdom; any power the Della Torre had, they held, at least in theory, at his pleasure as their king and emperor. Moreover, as leader of the Guelphs in Milan, Guido had to accept Henry because the pope, Clement V, the theoretical leader of his party, supported Henry and his initiatives in Italy. In turn, Henry, as the savior and peacemaker of Italy, had to make peace in the city, in this case between the Guelph Della Torre and their archrivals, the Ghibelline Visconti. Thus, much to the distress of Guido, Henry invited the Visconti back to Milan, and in late December of 1310, in a moment rich in symbolic significance, in the central square of Milan, under the benevolent eye of the emperor, the Guelph *signore* of the city, Guido Della Torre, exchanged the kiss of peace with Matteo Visconti, his recently defeated Ghibelline rival. As we have seen, fighting between their supporters broke out almost immediately.

It quickly became a full-fledged war for control of the city, and Matteo made the best of the situation. First, he sought to strengthen the legitimacy of a potential Visconti victory. For that, the emperor was useful. Henry was badly in need of money and troops to support his claims, more than ever at a moment when his rhetoric of peace and conciliation seemed to be collapsing around him. Thus when Matteo offered him 50,000 florins immediately and a yearly payment of 25,000 more in return for being named imperial vicar of Milan, Henry jumped at the offer – although taking that sum to confirm a Ghibelline in power in Milan at the expense of a Guelph rival did not help his image as a Guelph-Ghibelline peacemaker.

Matteo, however, could and did claim, as imperial vicar, to be the legitimate ruler of Milan. He merely needed to take the city, which he proceeded to do in short order. But Matteo understood that having both the force to drive out the Della Torre and the legitimate right to rule were still not enough. He also needed local support, and the group that he turned to, along with a small group of old noble followers, should not be surprising – the leaders of the Milanese *popolo grosso*. Matteo mixed members of the leading *popolo grosso* families of the city with his old noble supporters to serve as his advisors and made sure that they also held the lion's share of important posts in government. In addition, he supported the business interests of the *popolo grosso*, offering them the protection of law and the courts against private power. And all this was once more proclaimed with the rhetoric of peace, justice, and stability in a Christian city.

The older nobility who had originally supported the Visconti when they were archbishops, however, were too powerful in Milan and the surrounding countryside to be ignored. Instead, as was the case in many other cities ruled by *signori*, where the old rural nobility remained a significant factor in economic and social life, Matteo and his successors encouraged them to move to the city, take up a more profit-oriented agriculture (or often to continue in such endeavors), and to intermarry with the most powerful *popolo grosso* families. In this way he and his successors slowly but surely amalgamated the strongest and most economically aggressive of the two groups into a more aristocratic *popolo grosso* that typified the social world of Milan in the early Rinascimento as well as many other cities ruled by *signori*.

Tellingly, then, with three different stories, we still end up where we started. Tyranny or republic; closed ruling group or more open; Ordinances of Justice or Serrata; Guelph or Ghibelline; Florence, Venice, or Milan: the winners in the fourteenth century would eventually be the *popolo grosso* or some combination of older aristocratic families and this group. Local variations could be significant, but looking at the broad picture, Italy had a new political and social elite based upon wealth from trade, banking, and investment in the production of luxury products – the Great Social Divide that still dominated most of the rest of Europe was a fading and largely irrelevant memory. And, crucially, that new elite was not content merely to take power and hold it with force; it defended its power and legitimated it as old, based upon the ideal first times of ancient Rome and early Christianity. Moreover, in the name of offering peace, justice, and the rule of law in a Christian urban environment, they claimed to serve not private family interests but the interests of all in creating a civil urban society: that is, a *civiltà* much like that pictured in Lorenzetti's frescos in the governmental palace of Siena.

Rinascimento Civiltà: *Urban Government and Civic Order*

But what did the government actually look like, and how did it work behind the high ideals it espoused? With the dozens of cities in the north and center of Italy all apparently building their own governments as they went along, in response to local exigencies and problems, at first glance it appears that attempting to answer this question is a hopeless task. And, of course, that is true. In fact, the best answers have been provided by numerous studies of local political institutions. Still, the very ideology that defended and supported the rule of the *popolo grosso* and the groups that joined with them made certain institutional responses more attractive than others. Perhaps more importantly, as law and legal justice were shared themes of rule, much of the actual operation of government was carried out on a day-to-day basis by notaries and lawyers. Some were locals; many, however, were foreigners drawn from other cities who shared a relatively standard university training in law and Latin – as virtually all bureaucratic and legal business across the fourteenth century was carried on in Latin. This common training meant that even as they moved from city to city, they tended to share a legal culture and a bureaucratic vision that fit well with, and undoubtedly also influenced, the evolving vision of governance supported by the *popolo grosso*. Significantly, that shared legal culture based on Roman law and Latin training presented itself once again as modeled on and legitimated by the ancient world, yet another and particularly significant rebirth of Roman culture.

As a result, certain repeating forms and ways of operating can be seen behind local variations, providing a kind of continuity behind the daunting diversity. Most cities had a large council that officially represented the whole of the citizenry of the city, *Il Popolo*. As the *popolo* was theoretically the font of all authority, it was usually seen as the ultimate authority in passing legislation. But as such, it also regularly served as a court of last resort for the most important or potentially divisive criminal or civil cases that government adjudicated. In turn, as the font of all authority, it often created new councils and magistracies to deal with new perceived needs as they arose. In fact, across the fourteenth century, as the *popolo grosso* grew in power and governments became increasing articulated in response to calls for tighter discipline and control, a host of new magistracies and councils were created by these large councils. The Ordinances of Justice with their policing and punishing power, passed in most cities across the north of Italy at the end of the thirteenth and the first years of the fourteenth century, are merely one of the most notable examples. This mixing of legislative, judicial, and administrative responsibilities meant that Rinascimento governments were not neatly divided into legislative, judicial, and administrative divisions as they are often represented, presumably following modern models; instead, there was a much more complex and often contradictory mix of powers that created unique opportunities for corruption of government and competition for power among various councils and factions.

Elections, then, were usually overseen by the large council. In most cities they relied upon quite complex forms of drawing lots. Theoretically, this created a virtually perfect form of democracy or, more accurately, given the values of the day, rule by the *popolo* open to all, as in election by lot not even merit interfered with the opportunity of every qualified male citizen to hold office. But the qualifier "qualified" suggests immediately the way this apparent opening of government to all was significantly limited. In Florence, as elsewhere, a complex process of reviewing the names that were eligible for office to assure that only "qualified" citizens were drawn allowed the powerful to corrupt those who reviewed the names and assure that opponents were eliminated and supporters included. In fact, a particularly significant part of the political agenda of the *popolo grosso* across the fourteenth century was to assure that, at least for the most important offices of government, only their most powerful leaders would be eligible. Elections were usually held by drawing names from a bag (*borsa*) containing the names of all those eligible for a particular office; those drawn then served for what were normally brief terms, often as short as two or three months. This rapid turnover also contributed to the impression of a more open government, limiting the possibility of having only a few dominating offices. Yet in the end, in most cities, behind the democratic forms of election by lot the powerful, with few exceptions, dominated the councils of government.

Other factors also limited the apparent openness of elections. In most cities guilds had played such an important role in the rise to power of *Il Popolo* that they claimed to be and were often seen as the *popolo* itself. As a result, in those cities one had to be a member of a guild even to be eligible to have one's name put into the bag for elections. Dante, for example, although there is no indication that he ever worked as an apothecary or spice merchant, enrolled in that guild in Florence so that he would be eligible to hold office. In turn, the guild community, as it became divided between richer and more powerful guilds (dominated by the *popolo grosso*) and lesser guilds (more the domain of the *popolo minuto*), worked out agreements for divvying up how many names from each guild or group of guilds would go into the bags. Once again, because of the greater power and wealth of the powerful guilds, the tendency was for the number of names from the lesser guilds to decrease as the number from the greater increased. In moments of particular social tension or economic turmoil, however, when the lesser guilds found an opportunity to reverse this process, they did so, but almost invariably with little long-term success.

Early on, in many cases already in the thirteenth century, it became apparent that the large councils representing virtually all the *popolo* were too unwieldy to actually respond to legislative or judicial needs. Thus smaller councils, usually envisioned as representing the wisest and most important men in the city, were created to handle the most important matters in both areas. Frequently identified with the leading families of the city, with time they became associated with the ancient Roman Senate, recognized as having represented the interests of the most important Roman families. Thus, in many ways, such councils, largely dominated by the *popolo grosso*, were portrayed not as new, but as another part of a rebirth of Rome and its ideal political order. And perhaps more significantly yet, the leaders of the families that sat regularly in these more elite councils could be seen, not as a new social elite, but rather as a rebirth of that ancient Roman senatorial class based on *virtù* that had been the driving force behind the success of ancient Rome – a claim that Rinascimento scholars would rediscover as they reread classical authors like Cicero and Livy.

As governmental forms became more articulated across the fourteenth century, additional councils were set up, but in most places there were two main ones, a larger one representing the *popolo*, and a smaller, senatelike one representing the most important families. Still, even the smaller, senatelike councils with forty to eighty members were often too unwieldy and slow to respond efficiently to the rapidly evolving crises that governments faced. Thus in most cities small short-term committees were used to deal with particularly urgent problems, often with the power to sidestep or override the larger councils. These committees were usually elected by one of the larger legislative councils, and, significantly, they were usually not chosen by lot. The idea was that in crucial moments only the best men with special expertise or significant interest in the matter at hand should decide. Often these committees were called "Sapientes" (Wise Men) or some similar name that signified their recognized expertise and special status, although the term "Balìa" was also widely used. These special committees investigated the particular issue they had been chosen to consider and proposed solutions to deal with it. In turn, their proposals were voted on and approved or rejected by the larger legislative council that had appointed them. They could also be empowered, however, to deal with an issue in its entirety – investigating it, devising a response, passing whatever measures necessary, and overseeing its final resolution. Such committees were frequently appointed to take charge of a war, deal with a particularly difficult financial crisis, or handle a revolutionary moment or threat.

In a number of cities Sapientes evolved into regular councils of state or, because their concerns were ongoing, became permanent magistracies dealing with matters like taxation, administration of conquered territories, trade, or perceived threats to government, as was the case with the famed Venetian Council of Ten. Created to deal with the aftermath of the Querini-Tiepolo conspiracy, the Ten continued across our period to become a powerful and feared secret police and at times a shadow government behind the regular government of the city. Most such councils, however, served their immediate purpose and folded. But, significantly, the important men who sat on these special committees often went on to serve on one such committee after another, creating a small core of powerful leaders behind the theoretically more inclusive large councils of state. In part as a result, in cities like Florence and Venice the larger representative councils tended to become more like debating societies that took responsibility for actions that had often been decided elsewhere, reflecting a general tendency to place decision making and power in the hands of a few while spreading the responsibility for such decisions as widely as possible. Not surprisingly, in most places that "few" tended to be drawn from the most important members of the local *popolo grosso*.

Turning to justice – so important to the *popolo grosso* view of government – most cities in the thirteenth and fourteenth centuries preferred to rely on a foreign professional, usually known as a *Podestà*, who came to the city for a period (often six months) to handle the daily business of justice and policing. The idea was that a foreign professional, bringing with him the judges and patrollers necessary to guarantee order, would provide unbiased justice, being uninvolved in local politics and intrigue. Frequently these officials had trained as lawyers or notaries and provided an important source of governing knowledge that passed from city to city. In fact, it may well be that the idea for the Ordinances of Justice that proliferated in the last years of the thirteenth and first years of the fourteenth century was carried from city to city by *Podestà*. Not all *Podestà*, however, were trained as lawyers or notaries; a number were military figures. As warriors they often seemed to offer that extra potential for violence that was considered necessary to handle particularly difficult moments or unruly cities. Not surprisingly, from time to time, when the turmoil that they sought to control was great enough, or merely when the opportunity presented itself, the unscrupulous (and perhaps occasionally the scrupulous) transformed their temporary positions into permanent ones and became *signori*.

More commonly, however, the *Podestà* performed what was seen at the time as one of the most important functions of government, justice. Returning to the Lorenzetti frescoes in the council halls of Siena, justice was the key to virtually all the positive things portrayed as provided by good government. Significantly, that justice was backed up, when it was good, by angels with swords literally cutting out the offending members of society, along with an occasional bandit or malefactor hanging from a governmental gallows, overlooking a peaceful countryside now freed from their depredations. In Dante's apparently more spiritual vision, the disruptors of urban order – or at least those he saw as such – ended up, along with closely related sinners, in Hell, suffering the ultimate divine justice that stood behind the civic justice offered by government. As he encountered these men and women suffering divine punishment, many of whom he knew either by reputation or from the streets of his city, Dante commented upon their punishments with an interesting mix of pity and satisfaction that says much about the violent ideals of punishment of his day that were deemed necessary to provide urban peace and order.

On civic buildings Justice was often portrayed as a female figure holding a sword to cut off the offending members of society in one hand and a scale to weigh the severity of an offence in the other. Thus Justice was figured as a weighing of retribution rather than a simple judging matter of right or wrong. Underlining the complexity of weighing retribution, Justice was also usually portrayed as unblindfolded – in distinction to most modern representations – and looking the viewer directly in the eye. Justice, then, was neither blind nor simple. She required a clear vision of all issues involved and a correctly measured response. The fact that Justice was portrayed as a woman reflects, on one level, merely the gendered nature of the noun in both Latin and Italian, where it is a feminine noun. In fact, there was a tradition that went back to ancient Roman times that anthropomorphized the concept as a woman. Yet there may have been deeper resonances in the gendered representation of the ideal, for justice was not merely a legal concept based on divine and ancient Roman law. It was also involved in a complex competition with more informal forms of judgment, retribution, and discipline that had powerful medieval roots based on honor and vendetta.

Briefly, in that traditional system of private justice, violence or misdeeds were seen as dishonoring their victims and their families and thus required a violent response that balanced out the original misdeed, undid the dishonor, and returned things to a balance. If misdeed and violent response balanced out, honor and vendetta worked to limit the level of violence in society, maintaining a certain level of peace without more complex social organization. Before committing a misdeed, one theoretically had always to calculate what the cost would be in terms of honor and vendetta; thus many acts of violence were avoided, and those that were not were justly punished through vendetta. Significantly, it was family that largely drove this system. If someone dishonored a member of one's family, the whole family was committed to exacting a just revenge. The violent deeds of that revenge were often associated with the men of the family, which is not to say that women did not at times participate with as much violence as their men. But ideally women had another, more significant role to play in vendetta: recalling and encouraging the males of the family to avenge their dishonor and to do so adequately. In essence they were the *ultimate judges* of family dishonor and the just retribution. Thus unblind justice, in this traditional system, was ultimately in the balance of women, just as it was in Rinascimento civic representations of governmental justice.

The primary problem with the honor/vendetta system of justice turned on the correct evaluation of the amount of violence necessary to overcome a dishonor. If the response was too severe, it would require more violence in turn, and violence could spiral out of control in blood feuds that went on for generations. In this context it was hoped that the *Podestà*, as an outsider, could judge these conflicts, weighing the honor issues and violence involved with his eyes wide open, and impartially settle them by balancing the claims for retribution and reestablishing honor. Thus his judgments, or those of the judges he brought with him, usually spoke in equal measure about what both honor and law required for a just outcome. Historically speaking, in fact, honor often came first, and as judicial forms developed, honor remained an important part of legal rhetoric and procedure.

In many cities, then, the legal description of a criminal case began with the evaluation of the dishonor that it had caused for God, followed by a similar evaluation of the dishonor to the *popolo* of the city or its government; it then considered the dishonor to the victims; and only in the end did it turn to the crime itself. What such rhetoric suggests is the deep and enduring way in which the justice of government was seen as building out from and taking over the earlier honor/violence dynamic of social discipline. In sum, it was not just divine law, ancient Roman law, or local legal traditions; it was all of those to be sure, but it was also a continuation of a traditional honor/vendetta system in a theoretically more controlled and balanced form via a foreign *Podestà*. This complex mix in the cities of the early Rinascimento seemed to promise a more secure and less violent form of social discipline, one that was necessary to provide a more stable urban environment in which commerce, banking, and artisanal production could be carried out in peace.

From this perspective local Ordinances of Justice might be seen as creating a major breach in this system of governmental justice based on the *Podestà*. Not only did they create new laws designed to limit the violence and high-handed ways of the powerful, they also created, or gave new power to, a local official who usually combined policing and judicial powers in order to enforce these new rules. This official was called the *Capitano del Popolo* or a similar title that suggested that he was the defender of the *popolo* against those who would disrupt the peace of their cities. At times these officials could be very powerful, and, much as was the case with *Podestà*, from time to time a powerful *Capitano del Popolo* could transform his office into a permanent one-man rule and become a *signore*. More commonly, however, the *Capitano* was an early step toward a more permanent, locally controlled judiciary and patrolling apparatus that by the fifteenth century in most of the major cities of the north would replace the earlier *Podestà* system of justice. The title *Podestà*, however, continued to be used for officials sent out to provincial cities from a dominant central city as many of smaller cities fell to their larger neighbors across the fifteenth century.

The progressive elimination of the *Podestà* system once again was in many ways anticipated by the Venetian system of justice, which already at the end of the thirteenth century seems to have developed a different approach to crime and justice. Less enthusiastic about Roman law than most cities, Venice was more committed to its own local legal traditions and the wisdom of its own unblindfolded judges, who were instructed by law to weigh each case carefully, taking into account the social and political issues involved. In part the rationale for this judicial freedom was that it allowed a more careful balancing of the honor involved. But it also appealed to a strong local pride in the peacefulness of the great commercial city and its own honor, which had to be maintained. After all, right from its legendary founding the angel of the Lord had promised the apostle Mark, "Pax tibi Marci" ("Peace be with you Mark"), and with that peace a great and prosperous city would grow up and flourish, thanks to local law and judges.

A multiplying series of magistracies dealt with less serious civil litigation and organized a number of policing bodies that patrolled the streets, levying fines for petty infractions. When a more serious crime was encountered, they arrested the culprits and threw them in jail until their crimes could be formally tried. Most important among these magistracies were the *Signori di Notte* (Lords of the Night), who, as their name implies, were primarily responsible for patrolling and keeping the city safe after dark. By the fourteenth century, however, their patrollers in ever-increasing numbers were patrolling night and day, handing out summary justice for petty violence and

carrying arms illegally. But they also had taken on more significant responsibilities, investigating murders that involved immediate explosions of violence rather than more considered homicides. The latter were investigated
by the *Avogadori di Comun* (state attorneys) and tried before the Council of
Forty, a body that dealt with more serious internal matters, both legislatively
and judicially.

The *Signori* also investigated cases of a crime labeled "sodomy," a newer
concern of governments, which apparently had become worried about the
danger of suffering the fate of Sodom and Gomorrah that such crimes created for their cities. Officially, in Venice as elsewhere, sodomy was a catchall
crime that included any nonreproductive sexual practice, but prosecutions
tended to focus on male/male sex. Their investigations generated some
very interesting documentation of such relationships, for the *Signori* were
interested in weighing the intent involved – as intent was the key to the
seriousness of a sin or a crime. A momentary desire or mere compliance
as a passive partner in sodomy made the deed unwilled and thus less sinful
from a religious perspective and less culpable from a judicial one. In this
context, then, the *Signori* carefully chronicled the sexual history of those
accused of sodomy to see whether their deeds were a willed sexual practice
or merely a passing moment of passion, creating mini–sexual biographies
of those accused. They were also quite intent to discover whether those
involved accepted a passive role or took an active one, a telling distinction
in all sexual relations. Again, intent seems to have been a key here, as the
passive partners, usually younger, were punished much less severely, whereas
the active were almost invariably executed, apparently because they acted
with intent and willed the deed.

A number of other patrolling bodies also policed and provided immediate justice in the form of fines in the streets of the city, creating a city with,
at least on paper, a particularly high density of patrollers. What pulled this
complex system together into a model for other governments was the creation of the Council of Ten in 1310. As noted, they were originally just a
temporary ad hoc committee of *Sapientes* created to deal with the aftermath
of the Querini-Tiepolo conspiracy. Quickly, however, they used their virtually unlimited authority to develop into a powerful, permanent, and largely
unlimited secret court with an extensive policing apparatus of their own.
With time they brought the other policing bodies of the city under their
direct control and asserted the right to take over virtually any legal proceeding that they saw as involving the security of the state, a right they slowly
expanded to include almost all important matters. Already by the last years
of the fourteenth century they had created a powerful centralized system of

policing and justice in Venice that was run by the most important men of the city – a system that when necessary could override older, more messy and overlapping forms of justice that in the normal order of things allowed for a more personal and perhaps popular justice.

Across the fourteenth century, as noted earlier, other cities began progressively to substitute local judicial and policing bodies for those provided by a *Podestà*. It may be that this occurred earlier in civil courts dealing with minor litigation, where a large number of cases involving smaller sums were heard – the volume of cases heard presumably overwhelming the capabilities of a *Podestà* system. But certainly the process was accelerated by the creation of offices like the *Capitano del Popolo* and eventually of smaller councils or committees responsible for public security like the Venetian Council of Ten. Local patrollers also joined and eventually replaced the *Podestà*'s foreign patrollers. Almost certainly, as a result, the streets of most late fourteenth-century cities were more secure than the streets of the thirteenth century in the cities of Italy. But this came at a price. Beyond the rhetoric, the sterner discipline of more heavily policed cities, often involving arbitrary justice imposed in the streets, and a socially biased justice system that hit property crime and the lower classes more heavily, meant that justice could often be heavy-handed and repressive. Thus patrolling bodies quickly developed the negative stereotypes in the popular imagination often associated with those who operate at the level where governmental power has a direct impact on the denizens of a city. Moreover, it seems clear that this negative vision was reinforced by the petty graft and intimidation often used by policing bodies, which also victimized the lower classes. Not surprisingly, a significant proportion of the cases of prosecuted urban violence of the fourteenth and fifteenth century involved attacks against those very patrollers responsible for keeping the peace.

Such daily encounters with the often violent power of government were reinforced in most cities by the often violent nature of punishment for crime. Crimes involving property – as might be expected in cities dominated in many ways by merchants, bankers, and rich artisans and their guilds – were harshly punished. Robbers could count themselves lucky if they lost just the hand or hands they used for their crime; in most places repeat offenders lost their head as well or found themselves hanging outside the city gates, as depicted in Lorenzetti's fresco in Siena. Capital offenses were many; murder, robbery, counterfeiting, and treason usually headed the list. Particularly serious cases frequently were punished with elaborate symbolic mutilations followed by execution involving rituals that stressed the justice of the state, its defense of its honor, and the literal undoing of the crime.

Less serious crimes were punished by fines, which provided additional income for a *Podestà* and his staff, as usually they were given a percentage of the take, with an eye to encouraging them to work diligently to control such crime. In cities like Venice that used local patrollers, they too often received a portion of the fines collected. One significant problem with fines, however, was that many minor criminals could not pay their fines immediately, especially if they were poor or the fine large. Traditionally the response was to put them in jail until they paid. Certainly, given the conditions of most jails, that provided a strong incentive to pay as quickly as possible. Yet many were unable to raise the money to pay. Thus, to help deal with the problem of jails overflowing with petty criminals unable to pay their fines, governments in cities like Florence and Venice began to count time in jail as a way of paying off all or a part of a fine.

It was only a matter of time before such cities took the logical step of imposing jail terms instead of fines. And already in the fourteenth century in those cities courts were directly imposing jail sentences for crimes. Traditionally scholars have held that the use of jail sentences to punish crimes was a much later development of the Enlightenment and the penitentiary system, which was theoretically designed to make criminals penitent and reformed before they reentered society. Although he was not the first to make such claims, Michel Foucault, in his important study *Discipline and Punish*, portrayed this way of treating crime as a powerful measure of modernity. Evidently the fourteenth century was not modern as it lacked the ideal of creating a penitent and reformed criminal, yet with its emphasis on creating a peaceful and moral urban environment, it shared very broadly some ideals with (what has perhaps been overly optimistically labeled) the modern. And for all its lack of modernity, in some cities of the day jail was at least seen as a useful alternative to fines and corporal punishment for less serious crimes, and thousands of fixed-term jail sentences were handed down well before the modern scholarly tradition believes that could have happened.

Much as was the case with the system of justice in most cities, what might be labeled the executive part of government became more highly articulated over the early Rinascimento, with an eye to providing a peaceful urban environment conducive to economic prosperity. Usually a small executive committee, serving for short terms of two to six months, led the government. It had the responsibility for implementing governmental policy and frequently for deciding it, albeit normally with the approval of the larger, more representative councils. This chief executive committee usually had a membership that ranged from six to a dozen men and, because of its importance, often also included ex-officio members drawn from other important organs of government; the entire group was then called the Signoria (the City Lords, one might say). In Florence and many other cities the smaller elected executive committee was known as the Priors, or the First Men of the city. With a rich symbolism in Florence they actually left their homes to live in the *Palazzo dei Priori* (the Palace of the Priors) for their short terms, theoretically thus leaving their family and personal interests behind to live in the palace/home of the city and its government.

In many other cities the members of this small central committee were called councilors, especially where they served a *signore* as his councilors or, as was the case in Venice, the doge, the formal head of state. But even in the case of *signori*, their councilors played an important role, not only carrying out much of the daily work of organizing government and implementing policy, but also filling the important role of advising the ruler and spreading the responsibilities for governmental decisions more widely. Naked power in fourteenth-century cities might rule for a time, but, as Machiavelli noted later in *The Prince*, a *signore* or prince could not rule for long without winning and holding broader support. Fear and a willingness to use violence, when required, helped, but true stability required a rule that was widely seen as representing the interests of the city or at least of those who mattered in the city, whether it was formally ruled by one man or a republican government. Thus, in either case, a small council representing the most important families of the city was essential at the heart of government.

As noted, this small council, when it met with the *signore* or a limited number of other functionaries, was usually called the Signoria, a rather confusing term because of its similarity to *signore*. In most cities the Signoria was the real focus of executive power – running a growing regular bureaucracy, overseeing relations with other governments, developing and implementing taxing policies, and leading an often rich ceremonial life. Not surprisingly, this group was usually heavily dominated by the *popolo grosso*. From time to time, especially in moments of civic turmoil, a member of the *popolo minuto* might serve a term among such heady company, especially in cities like Florence whose governments maintained close ties to the guild community. In other cities, like Milan, where older noble families had moved to the city they also made it into the Signoria. Still, a telling measure of the progressive dominance by the *popolo grosso* of the political life of the city (and more generally) can be seen in the way they dominated such executive councils at the heart of one city government after another in the fourteenth century. As the century progressed and as the bureaucracy of government grew, these central committees tended to hand off many of their responsibilities to lesser committees acting in their name. At times it almost seems that the response to every problem was to create a new magistracy or committee, and many seemed designed more to express an ideal than to actually do much of anything.

One area in which actually accomplishing things remained extremely important, however, was in the collection of revenues to finance government. With minor variations collection followed the same general pattern from city to city, perhaps once again reflecting the shared legal culture of the itinerant bureaucrats who frequently staffed governmental magistracies. In theory, the most important sources of revenue came from direct taxes and state monopolies on certain basic staples. Taxes on goods entering, leaving, or just passing through a city or its territory were important everywhere and obviously a significant source of revenue for large commercial hubs such as Venice, Genoa, and Florence. But governments also attempted to control staples such as salt and grain, usually in the name of assuring a constant supply even in times of shortage. In fact, grain offices selling grain at or below market value in times of dearth were early on seen as a highly important fire wall against social unrest, as bread and porridge-like gruels were the staples of lower-class diets. Still, such monopolies also offered governments an easy and secure way to make money on the sale of staples; thus, in many cities the salt office and/or the grain office quickly became, if not the governmental treasury, an important adjunct to it.

Direct taxes, however, were seldom enough to cover the costs of government, especially in times of crisis or war, and virtually all cities turned to loans to cover shortfalls at such moments. Deficit spending thus became central to governmental functioning and to the general economy of the day. Ideally, loans were given voluntarily by the wealthy in return for payment of a regular rate of interest. In theory this was usury, a serious sin, and in many cities also a crime. But with the excuse that these loans were insecure and a service to government in time of need, the question of usury was quietly overlooked. The most evident problem with this system was the fact that voluntary loans often were not forthcoming, especially in difficult times. Thus across the fourteenth century we find voluntary loans progressively replaced by forced loans that were based on the estimated wealth of families.

This system had several advantages. First, it allowed the bureaucrats running the system to calculate how much money would be raised by a loan, thus matching demands to needs. Perhaps equally attractive, but less straightforward, was the fact that the estimates of wealth upon which forced loans were based could easily be manipulated in the favor of those who dominated government. This was yet another reason for the rich and powerful to make sure that they were well represented in government, but it also meant that much of the burden of paying for government fell on the shoulders of the less powerful. Of course, even they were not simply handing over their money to government, as everyone received, in return for their forced loans, both a promise of repayment and a relatively secure yearly rate of interest, which was usually fixed at about 5 percent. It quickly became apparent, however, that the promise of repayment was at best a distant one as the public debt grew to what seemed like astronomical levels. In fact, then as now, the burgeoning public debt of most governments was viewed as one of the primary problems of the day.

In many cities the government's debt was called simply the *Monte* (the Mountain), and most governments in larger centers spent most of the fourteenth century and the early years of the fifteenth perched insecurely on the edge of default. Complicating matters, the less wealthy who had shares of the debt were often unable to hold on to them and profit from the interest paid; thus, there rapidly developed a market where shares were sold, obviously at a fraction of their face value, by those who needed to recover at least a portion of their forced loan. In turn, when the sale price of shares fell low enough, they became a very attractive investment for the wealthy, as they continued to pay interest on their full face value. Thus, for example, if the market value dropped to half the face value of a loan, as it might in hard times, one could buy shares, say, for 100 ducats of debt at 50 percent of their original cost. This meant not only that for 50 ducats one held 100 ducats of debt, but also, more significantly, as that debt earned a relatively secure interest of 5 percent on its original value, that one would receive 5 ducats of interest per year on an investment of 50 ducats, or a handsome 10% return on one's investment.

Not surprisingly, payment of the interest due on the *Monte* was one of the highest priorities of government; for, of course, government was controlled by many of the same *popolo grosso* who were rich enough to buy up loans. Moreover, as these forced loans were collected as often as the government needed money, and that could mean several times in a few months when there was a crisis or a war, the rich, who were already paying less because they could manipulate the estimates of their wealth upon which their loans were calculated, were able to buy up shares cheaply and thus to secure obligations often paying impressive returns. In essence the public debt based on forced loans turned the government into another and significant producer of revenues for the *popolo grosso*. On the one hand this helped to ensure strong and enthusiastic support for government on their part, as long as it was capable of paying interest on the *Monte*; on the other, it often distorted the priorities of government and certainly made the ideal that government worked for the greater good of the whole community an ever-more-distant dream. Finally, in times of great crisis, especially ongoing wars, when forced loans quickly followed one another, the system accentuated social tensions, and it is not surprising that most revolutionary changes of regime were associated with such moments.

It should be noted, however, that government was not the only power interested in collecting revenues, overseeing trade and artisanal production, and assuring justice and a peaceful urban environment. Especially important in each area in most cities were the guilds, which in many ways organized urban economic life more directly and often attempted to control government as well. The complex organization of guilds will be examined in more detail in Chapter 3, but suffice it to say that most had their own courts and councils that not only attempted to manage production and laborers, but also settled disputes, punished violence between guild members, and usually provided charity as well. Guilds more concerned with trade, finance, or highly profitable products like wool cloth and led by large investors were often as important in setting economic policy as government itself. Competition between the two was largely an illusion, however, for the same families tended to dominate both the powerful guilds and the government. Times of crisis, however, tested the relationship between guilds and government. When rifts developed among powerful families and factions formed, the potential for competition frequently came into play. In Florence, noted for its civic turmoil in the fourteenth and early fifteenth centuries, such competition often occurred and was further complicated by the organization of the Guelph Party, which also had its own governing council and committees concerned with protecting the "Guelphness" of the city. As we shall see, they used that power to influence and at times to compete with government, creating a complex triangular competition among government, guilds, and Guelph Party.

If all this seems like a very complex and unwieldy system for controlling a multifaceted, dynamic, and often violent urban life, the simple response is: exactly. Behind the complexity, however, there stood a common evolving vision of the *civiltà* of the Rinascimento that helped to foreground a number of shared goals. That vision increasingly stressed that city life needed to be ordered and peaceful; governed for the general well-being, via both the laws and the bureaucratic forms that guaranteed it; and should offer a Christian civic morality for a Christian city. All these novelties, however, were not seen as new, but rather viewed as being based on the model of the great civilization that had once dominated the area and the world, ancient Rome, now fortified by those very Christian values that the pagan empire had lacked. Significantly, however, these shared values provided a dramatically different set of parameters for governance than the medieval ideal of private power for private ends, parameters that live on at the center of modern political thought.

Behind those ideals with a future, of course, there lay a more messy mix of government, guilds, parties, families, and bureaucratic forms, all fought over by a fractious *popolo* and an increasingly dominant *popolo grosso* with an eye to controlling the economy and mobilizing the potential for their wealth in a rich urban world. And as far as government was concerned, the *popolo grosso* progressively controlled the real centers of power and provided a certain continuity with their broadly shared values. At a day-to-day level, their governments employed a largely university-trained cast of notaries and lawyers who staffed the ongoing and rapidly growing bureaucracy that actually ran things. Their Latin culture and training in the classics and Roman law neatly melded with both the ideals of the *popolo grosso* and their more practical goals for government; thus, as the Rinascimento and its culture developed, they became increasingly important players not just in government but also in the cultural explosion associated with the period. They also gave stability to government and were crucial for cutting through its intricacies when necessary in order to make it work with an efficiency that was certainly not modern, but decidedly different from its medieval precedents.

Yet in many ways, it was not government that was really crucial in the early Rinascimento as much as it was the social and economic groups and organizations that empowered it. Petrarch was correct to point out what a confusing, apparently conflicted, and messy world the cities of his day were, but what he missed from his safe retreats and intellectual isolation (occasionally interrupted by passing political enthusiasms of his own) was the way the leaders of the world he looked down upon were building a new urban society and culture, a *civiltà* in the name of a rebirth of ancient worlds both Christian and pagan, a Rinascimento. Ironically, although the first times and ancient worlds that they sought to recreate were often deeply contradictory and decidedly different from the *civiltà* they were actually creating, it was in that fertile mix, created in the name of return and rebirth, that many of the most exciting and significant aspects of the day were being born, if not actually being reborn as claimed.

Rinascimento Civiltà: *Consensus Realities, Self, and Discipline*

After this discussion of government, it might seem paradoxical to argue that government has frequently been overemphasized as a player in the organizing and disciplining of life in the early Rinascimento. Certainly there is no question that government was a hotly contested prize across the period. Moreover, wealth and power were often deeply contingent upon who controlled it, and normally it literally had the power of life and death over its subjects. But, as we have seen, governments were just one corporate group among many that were competing to control and discipline society. Yet behind that competition there lay highly significant disciplining forces that are less visible from a modern perspective, distracted by a vision of government as the primary focus of power and discipline in society. There is room for doubt about such claims today, but there is no question that during the Rinascimento government it was much less significant than it is often presented as being, especially in terms of its control over and disciplining of everyday life.

In fact, looking behind the forms of government and claims of contemporary ideals to examine the informal play of power and discipline across society – a play often to be found represented in the most unlikely places – offers a rich perspective on the complexity of Rinascimento life. From this perspective the widely shared vision of the urban *civiltà* of the Rinascimento was central, because it helped empower a series of richly evocative discourses that people believed in, tried to live by, and attempted to hold others to – in sum, discourses that served to discipline without much help from or need for government. Actually, we might claim that government and the other corporate groups that competed for power at the time often attempted to piggyback on those more significant disciplining discourses in order to legitimate their own claims to rule and to reinforce their own ability to do so. Not surprisingly, the literature of the day returned over and over again to these discourses – not just prescriptive literature, but also the poetry and short stories so popular at the time. Simply put, these discourses were engaging and worth returning to because they focused on and frequently queried the deeper roots of power within society, where government was at best peripheral. In this, then as now, literature tended to examine the very DNA of society and culture, returning continuously to the deepest and most powerful ways in which life was organized and disciplined.

From this perspective, then, it might not seem quite so unlikely to consider the deeper disciplining realities of urban society, using a group of much-too-aristocratic-to-be-real storytellers: a youthful *brigata* (group of friends) who withdrew from Florence to tell apparently fanciful tales of love and pleasure. Yet the fourteenth-century storyteller par excellence, Giovanni Boccaccio (1313–1375), a one-time *popolo grosso* banker turned writer, has ten such aristocratic and mannerly youths run off to escape the Black Death in 1348 in his *Decameron*. To pass the time and forget the horrors of the plague, they tell one hundred tales that, even as they replay a medieval past or an often fanciful present, pullulate with the central disciplining discourses of his day. His strange novella of Lisabetta da Messina – the fifth of the fourth day of tales – illustrates well the most important of those discourses that disciplined daily life at the time. In most ways Lisabetta was depicted as a typical fourteenth-century young woman and a happy one at that. Living with her three brothers, she had fallen in love with a certain Lorenzo, a young man who worked with her family of Tuscan merchants in Messina. Yet as their relationship had developed into one where sex was involved, they had begun to cross behavioral boundaries that were troublesome. For although it could be portrayed as a small *natural sin* for young lovers, as Boccaccio frequently did in the *Decameron*, Lisabetta's affair presented bigger problems for her brothers. First, it threatened their family's honor, as her behavior was seen as reflecting on the honor of her family as a whole. It also, of course, threatened the honor of Lisabetta and, if it became known, might ruin her chances to marry and become a wife, the honorable status required of adult women.

Already three disciplining forces loom large in the story: marriage, family, and honor. To protect her family, its honor and her own, Lisabetta should have avoided her affair with her more humble lover and awaited an arranged marriage with a partner selected by her family who would have allowed her to have a correct sexual relationship and produce the correct heirs for all involved. And virtually immediately, although sympathetically presenting her natural sin, Boccaccio's story follows those disciplining imperatives to a first logical, if tragic, conclusion. For her brothers, fearing that her affair would become known, did the honorable thing and secretly killed her lover. To cover their crime they let it be known among their business associates and neighbors that they had sent the young man on a business trip, and life quietly returned to normal. The story might well have ended there, with Lisabetta, sad because Lorenzo never returned, marrying correctly and the honor of all preserved. In that case, honor and family would have disciplined invisibly – a safe happy ending – without government or other corporate bodies interfering or even being aware of the quiet, if murderous, upholding of social order. The murder, the affair, and the potential dishonor, unknown, would simply not have existed, and thus life would have returned to its regular disciplined order.

But that overlooks Lisabetta's youthful love, which in life as in literature often ripped apart the ordered flow of life with its uncontrolled passions. As the days slipped away and Lorenzo did not return, Lisabetta began to suspect that something was wrong. Those suspicions were confirmed one night in a dream, when Lorenzo's ghost appeared to her and sadly revealed that he had been murdered by her brothers and told her where they had buried him. Moved by now much more dangerous passions, she breached once again the boundaries of behavior required by honor and social norms and journeyed with a servant to the place where he was buried and dug up his body. But even in her grief she realized that she could not bring the body back for proper burial, because that would reveal to the community all their sins and crimes; thus, she instead cut off his head and secretly brought it home. Back safely in the privacy of her room, she covered it with kisses and tears, finally placing it in a large vase and planting over it a basil plant to cover the odor of its decay.

Day after day she lovingly tended her potted head and its basil, watering it with the finest distilled waters or, more regularly, her own free-flowing tears. So lovingly cared for, the plant flourished. Yet as it grew ever-more lush and green, her sadness grew apace, and she became ever-more pale, thin, and hollow-eyed. Her neighbors and her brothers, noting her decline and her strange attachment to the plant, began to worry that there was something amiss and that in some way the flourishing herb was involved. Hoping to reverse her rapid decline, her brothers finally stole her basil plant. When they discovered the decaying head that fertilized the herb, the disciplining power of government threatened to intervene in the tale, as Lisabetta's brothers realized that she had discovered their murder, and her unstable behavior meant that at any moment she might make public their crime. As a crime of honor it might have elicited sympathy from the community and most probably leniency from the courts, but there was real danger in moving from the realm of private discipline where they were in control to a more formal governmental one where they lacked it. Realizing that, they secretly buried the head, discarded the basil, and in an unbrotherly fashion abandoned their sister, fleeing for less dangerous climes. Alone, Lisabetta had only her tears and her laments about her lost basil plant and its secret treasure, Lorenzo's head. Having lost both, she continued to decline and shortly thereafter died. No one knew the reason for her death, and as she died without family or friends, no one mourned her passing.

As a merry tale to lift the spirits of its listeners – one of the purported purposes of the tales told by Boccaccio's *brigata* – the story seems to fall rather short of the mark. In fact, much like jokes from the past that no longer seem funny, it seems to require something more to comprehend what made it meaningful and moved Boccaccio to tell it. One simple answer is that, as a tale told on the fourth day of storytelling, it gorily fit the day's theme – tales of lovers whose love had an unhappy ending. Certainly the deaths of Lisabetta and Lorenzo at first appear a perfect fit. Yet in many ways their tale seems out of place in the context of the other tragic love stories of the day. Most notably, most of the other lovers in the tales of that day are ennobled by their tragic loves, and when they die their deaths are heroic – judged and celebrated as such publicly, both in the tales and among the *brigata*. Publicly not so much in the modern sense of a public sphere, but rather in the sense of the groups – family, neighbors, friends, peers, fellow workers, fellow confraternity members, and broader communities and solidarities – who evaluated each person and negotiated with them a Rinascimento sense of worth and identity.

These groups formulated and nourished what I have called in an earlier book, *Machiavelli in Love*, "consensus realities" about their fellows – imagined realities, but no less real for that, and shared within the groups that to a large extent constituted an external negotiated sense of self and personal identity during the period. More than Stephen Greenblatt's famous formula of self-fashioning, "consensus realities" evokes a complex and ongoing process of self-negotiation and self-measuring against a series of personal publics that surrounded an individual in the small, intimate, urban world of the Rinascimento. In this context the secrecy of all involved in Lisabetta's affair and Lorenzo's death takes on a deeper meaning. If their behavior at each stage of the evolving tale had become known, the groups that surrounded them in society would have intervened to question and discipline their behavior. In fact, that is exactly what happened when what was perhaps the most important group that evaluated a person's behavior and identity and disciplined both at the time, Lisabetta's family, in the form of her brothers, learned of her dishonoring affair. They secretly ended the affair and protected their honor by murdering her lover. Thus their crime did not become one; it did not become available for the other groups that surrounded them or government to judge. Their private justice was done, and with one private violent act order was quickly and efficiently restored.

In the modern world, where evaluations of self have become more internal, Lisabetta's brothers would have had to deal with their guilt and their own deep awareness of their crime – and perhaps fears that more effective governments might discover and prosecute their deed. The tragedy of the story would have had that additional dimension. But as presented by Boccaccio, evil deeds that were unknown, unjudged by the groups that surrounded one in society, and thus not entered into the calculus of one's consensus reality, simply did not exist. As we shall see, it was primarily in the public venue of evaluation of ideals like honor and *virtù* (and related terms of evaluation) that people perceived themselves and their worth. In turn, they disciplined their behavior in order to avoid the negative judgments of those groups with whom they interacted; and if they did not, they were shamed, ridiculed, or more quietly pressed to correct their ways. This was the discipline of everyday life in the close and intimate spaces of cities where consensus realities were constantly being formed, re-formed, and evaluated, and to a great extent those evaluations determined how one lived a disciplined life within those groups.

But what was this thing called *virtù* that was constantly being safeguarded and negotiated in Boccaccio's tales? As we have seen, at one level the answer is simple: in the Rinascimento, as in the Middle Ages and in ancient Rome, *virtù* was a term that identified the range of behaviors that made one person superior to another and thus marked out the best. But the simplicity of that definition dissolves before the fact that because it was such a telling term, its meaning was highly contested and, in fact, changed considerably over time, place, and social divides. As discussed earlier, in a warrior society like that of the Middle Ages many saw *virtù* in aggression, direct action (often violent), physical strength, blood line, and blood itself, even as at the same time moralists and philosophers tended to see it in terms of Christian behavior that eschewed violence and aggression. In the Rinascimento the discourse of *virtù* was first expanded, then increasingly dominated, by a vision more suited to the new merchant/banker elites and urban life of the day. For many, *virtù* tended to be seen as requiring the control of passions – in contrast to the medieval vision, which often celebrated strong passions directly expressed. That control of self in front of the consensus realities that surrounded one required peaceful, mannered conduct that turned on reasonable, calculating (at times sliding into cunning) behavior that controlled the present and the future as well.

Significantly, from this perspective Lisabetta's tragedy seems to stand even more alone in the tales of the fourth day, for *virtù* appears largely absent, and it seems that evil fortune wins over a sad and mourning love that has nothing ennobling or *virtù*-ous about it. Even her potentially ennobling tears over her basil plant are narrated without positive comment and apparently without positive results of any sort beyond the flourishing of the basil. Indeed, sad, uncontrolled tears are virtually always a sign of lack of *virtù* in the *Decameron*, a sign that one has given in to emotions and lost control of self and situation. And curiously, in the end even her love itself is hardly mentioned, forgotten or at least overwhelmed by her suffering and tears. Looking more closely at the tale from the perspective of consensus realities, Lisabetta early on did exhibit what might be considered a certain *virtù*, but only in private, where it really did not exist for her consensus realities. When she found her lover's body, rather than collapsing in tears – giving in to strong emotions – she managed to marshal the self-control to cut off his head and get it home, all done secretly so that neither her brothers nor any larger public were aware. Then she hid it in a vase and planted basil over it so that the smell of the plant covered the odor of decomposition. Whatever deeper implications these deeds might have had, a Rinascimento reader would have seen in them a way of acting that was associated with *virtù*; but, crucially, unseen and unjudged, it hardly existed at all. From that point on, however, a different dynamic took hold in her developing relationship with her potted head. Most notably, perhaps, her ongoing tears publicly proclaimed that she had lost control of her life and lacked the *virtù* necessary to make her love and her story heroic if they ever came to light.

Some have argued that Lisabetta's mourning over her potted head was what kept her alive and that from this perspective, when her brothers took it away they inadvertently caused her death. The argument runs that Lisabetta's lover's head in death gave birth to a basil plant, which in turn gave life to Lisabetta, as long as she worshipped it. Unfortunately for this romantic hypothesis, Lisabetta's basil plant did not give her life. In fact, the tale makes it clear that, rather like a vampire, it sucked the life out of her. As she worshipped over it, she actually became weaker and sicker. It was her decline as she worshipped it that attracted the attention of her neighbors and her brothers – those closest to her who judged her – and they took it away from her in the hope that doing so would stop her decline.

The contrast with another lover's body part is instructive. In another tale of the fourth day, the wife of Guiglielmo Rossiglione was served the heart of her lover for dinner disguised as a gourmet dish. Her husband, after secretly murdering her lover, to avenge his honor lost to adultery, cut out his heart and gave it to his cook, asking him to make it into the best-tasting dish possible. A perfect fictional cook, he created a wonderful dish, much to the satisfaction of Guiglielmo's wife, who unbeknownst ate it with relish. But when her husband, savoring his revenge, announced that the dish that she had just enjoyed so much was the heart of her lover, she did not waste time on tears or mourning, declaring nobly: "As God would not wish that anything be added to so noble a dish like this heart of so valiant and noble a knight … no other dish will ever [pass these lips]." And she promptly jumped out the window to her death. Strong *virtù*-ous words followed by strong *virtù*-ous deeds demonstrated her deep love and made her death truly noble and heroic. Tellingly, the tale ends noting that with "the greatest sadness and tears the two bodies [of the lovers] were brought together [by the public] and … buried in the same tomb inscribed with verses that explained who were buried there." In burial the consensus reality of their community was expressed. The lover's adulterous love in its *virtù* was judged positively and won them – in the fictional world of Boccaccio's tales, at least – nobility and public approbation.

Lisabetta, however, followed a different path. Rather than performing a heroic deed like the wife of Guiglielmo Rossiglione, Lisabetta demonstrated in the end neither *virtù* nor heroism, giving in to tears and mourning over the death and her secret tragedy. The key to reading the tale with a Rinascimento vision was that her potted head and its basil were literally a dead end. As empty tokens of her private loss, they worked all too well. Lisabetta was trapped by them in her uncontrolled mourning. Her strong emotions and tears turned inward, and in continuously recreating the emotions associated with her loss, she was overwhelmed by them and lost to *virtù*. In the end alone, deserted by her brothers, isolated from her neighbors in her tears and without her lover, Lisabetta had no public or urban world with which to interact, no consensus realities to negotiate with to reformulate a sense of self and a life after the death of her lover. Ultimately her tears and uncontrolled mourning had only one exit: a slow decline and a sure death.

In sum, her potted lover's head and her mourning were ultimately meaningless in an urban world where both *virtù* and honor were measured publicly and disciplined by consensus realities. They offered only an anonymous, meaningless, and tragic final oblivion – a salutary warning for Boccaccio's youthful group of storytellers fleeing the mourning and suffering of the plague to create with their friends a safe haven of new consensus realities with their tales of pleasure, love, and *virtù*. In her grief and mourning over her lover's head Lisabetta had essentially thought herself out of the city, its *civiltà*, and life itself. Her actual death was a mere formality. And, crucially, the power of government paled before such informal discipline. At best governments attempted to ride on the broad shoulders of such social realities with a rhetoric that imagined its own honor, its own ability to form consensus realities, and perhaps most curiously a fictitious personality of its own. Living and thinking the city and its *civiltà*, with its intimate spaces and judging and disciplining groups that surrounded a person turned honor, *virtù*, and consensus realities into the true quotidian disciplining and ordering powers of Rinascimento social life.

3

PLAGUE: DEATH, DISASTER, AND THE *RINASCITA* OF *CIVILTÀ* (c. 1325–c. 1425)

Apocalypse Now: Portraying the Plague and the Breakdown of Civiltà

I say, then, that there had passed 1348 years after the incarnation of the Son of God, when in the famous city of Florence ... there struck the deadly plague (*mortifera pestilenza*). Whether caused by the stars or the wrath of God to correct the sins of humanity, it had appeared a few years earlier in the East, killing an infinite number. Moving terribly to the West .... [when it arrived in Florence] it appeared in a different form. In the East if any-one had blood coming from their nose, it was a sure sign of death; but [in Florence] instead in both men and women it began either in the groin or under the armpits with certain swellings, some of which grew to approxi-mately the size of an apple, others to that of an egg. They were called by common people *gavòccioli* (plague sores). From those two parts of the body quickly they grew and spread over the whole body.

After a while, however, the nature of this disease changed with black spots or livid patches which appeared in great number on the arms, the thighs and all over the body, some were large and distant from each other, others small and close together. As the plague sores were a certain sign of death, so were these later symptoms.... Actually virtually everyone within about three days of the appearance of these signs died and most without a fever or other symptoms.... Oh how many great palaces, beautiful houses, noble residences once full of families, of lords and ladies became vacant.... Oh how many important families, very rich inheritances, famous fortunes, were left without their just heirs! [Boccaccio, *Decameron*, Day I Introduction]

If some people had thought the world was coming to an end in 1250, many more thought that the end had arrived in 1347–1348, when the first wave of the plague, often referred to today as the Black Death, carried off from one-half to two-thirds of the population of Europe. Giovanni Boccaccio (1313–1375), in *The Decameron*, began his storytelling with this account of the earthshaking event. It hardly seems a fitting way to begin a collection of at times rather racy and playful tales, and Boccaccio actually apologized for doing so. Yet it was such a powerful moment of social dislocation and disorientation that for him it provided the virtually required temporal setting for his tales, which were offered to women and lovers, as noted in Chapter 2, to raise their spirits and alleviate the somber sense of mourning and loss in the wake of that tragic event.

His account is one of the more detailed and oft-cited eyewitness reports of the plague's devastating impact on one of the leading cities of fourteenth-century Italy. Large urban centers like Florence, Venice, Genoa, and Milan, whose populations before the plague had hovered around 100,000, were reduced to 30–40,000 souls or fewer, leaving the survivors in once-flourishing cities camped among Boccaccio's hauntingly empty palaces, mass graves, and corpses. It must have seemed to many that the apocalypse had arrived. In reality, however, the first half of the fourteenth century had been punctuated by a series of famines and natural disasters that, following the economic expansion and prosperity of the twelfth and thirteenth centuries, had prepared the ground for such dark thoughts and fears. The Florentine chronicler Giovanni Villani (c. 1276–1348), who died in the plague, reflecting on those earlier disasters, warned: "Note, reader, that the aforementioned calamities and earthshaking disasters are great signs and judgments of God and have not happened without divine judgment and permission. These were the signs and miracles that Jesus Christ prophesized to his disciplines that would appear at the end of time." To many, the arrival of the plague and its terrible slaughter following those earlier dark signs signaled that fears of the end of time had finally been realized.

Certainly the economic and social order of an earlier prosperous age appeared to have broken down completely in its aftermath. In addition, the very rules of social life and traditional values seemed to have been overthrown by the cruel die-off, almost as if the new *civiltà* of the Rinascimento had already come to an end at the hands of a vengeful God. Boccaccio was particularly struck by this. His long introductory description of the plague and its impact repeatedly returns, with a haunting obsession, to this breakdown: "With the city so beset and miserable, the sacred authority of the laws was virtually totally lost and destroyed. [This was] because the magistrates and enforcers of them, like other men, were either all dead, ill or left without agents, so that they were not able to carry out their responsibilities. This meant that everyone was free to do as they pleased." But perhaps more important than the breakdown of law and government, in Boccaccio's vision, was the breakdown of what most at the time considered the central institution that bound society together and ordered its functioning – the family, the primary measurer of consensus realities. He lamented: "such great fear had captured the hearts of men and women, that brothers abandoned each other, uncles their nephews, sisters their brothers, and often wives their husbands. And what is even worse and hardly believable, fathers and mothers [abandoned] their children almost as if they were not theirs." Governments could break down, but families ceasing to function signaled the ultimate collapse of society and was a sure sign of the end.

Yet, in apparent contradiction to this devastating psychological, demographic, and economic disaster and in the face of this tremendous human tragedy, the Rinascimento did not just continue, it rose like a phoenix from the ashes, and in many ways its urban life and *civiltà* flourished. And, significantly, the social and political order of the *popolo grosso* came through the crisis if anything more firmly in place, triumphant, and confident. Even Boccaccio's stories, which begin with the grim devastation of the plague, quickly turn to laughter, the pleasures of life, and sex. More telling yet, they present a largely confident picture of a society that was dominated by the *popolo grosso* and their vision of an urban *civiltà* where their *virtù* remained the measure and in many ways ruled via consensus realities. For, as we shall see, in Italy, unlike the situation in much of the rest of Europe, after a relatively short period of fear and gloom following the plague, an optimism and a self-confidence returned that continued to set off the early Rinascimento from the rest of Europe. The urban leaders of Italy seemed, if anything, evermore confident that they had that special *virtù* that made them better than others and capable of leading and dominating not just their land but the larger world as well. How and why that happened is probably ultimately an unanswerable question, but one worth considering, as it is crucial for understanding the Rinascimento, its culture, and its economic and social order. But to set the stage, first a word is necessary about the plague, its victims, and its purported culprits.

Bubonic Plague? A Defense of Rats and Fleas

Once historians were quite certain what the plague of 1347–1348 was. In 1894 the Swiss scientist Alexandre Yersin, a student of Louis Pasteur, studying a bubonic plague outbreak in China, identified the plague bacillus that had caused it and that would eventually be named *Yersinus pestis* in his honor. While he did not understand how the bacillus was transmitted and misunderstood many things about the disease itself, he was convinced that he had discovered the bacteria that had caused the great plague of 1348 – a suggestive reminder of how deeply the memory and fear of that great plague had lodged in the Western imagination. His conviction quickly won wide support among doctors and historians, becoming the accepted vision of the Black Death. The Black Death at the turn of the twentieth century had for all extents and purposes become the bubonic plague.

As research on the modern bubonic plague progressed, this vision influenced in many ways what historians saw and did not see in Rinascimento descriptions of the plague, as the historian Samuel Cohn has shown in a series of revisionist studies. And as he has argued, in a curious reversal, what historians thought they knew about the plague in that distant time had a significant impact on modern research on the bubonic plague. For instance, although the modern bubonic plague moves quite slowly across space, it is not highly contagious and does not involve large population losses; many modern researchers studying it well into the twentieth century tended to assume that the reverse was true notwithstanding the contrary evidence, in part because that was how the plague was reported to have spread in accounts from the fourteenth century. In fact, one reason why so much time and money was spent on studying the bubonic plague at the turn of the twentieth century was because scientists and, perhaps more importantly, governments feared it would take off, spreading rapidly around the world, creating massive mortality as it had in the Rinascimento.

At the same time, following the progressive discoveries of the etiology of the modern bubonic plague, historians reread the accounts of the fourteenth century and saw working there the signs and symptoms discovered by modern medicine. Thus the standard account became that the plague was actually three closely interrelated diseases. The most famous was the bubonic, which is spread by fleas from infected rodents, usually rats, to people. As the bacteria proliferates in the human host, buboes or swellings appear, usually in the groin area or the armpits, a high fever develops, and the victim either dies within a few days or recovers. Clearly there are strong similarities between these symptoms and those reported by Boccaccio and others in his day. Moreover, as scientists gained an understanding of the rat-flea-human vector of the disease, the devastating spread of the disease from the east to the west seemed to confirm that it was the bubonic plague. Rats and fleas following the lines of trade, so the account ran, carried the disease from the east to the west in a type of deadly biological exchange similar to that which the Americas would suffer in the sixteenth century with the arrival of European explorers and their diseases.

Historians tied the plague to the growing current of international trade – the very growth that made the *popolo grosso* truly *grosso*. Briefly stated, the argument was that as the European population peaked in the fourteenth century, the ever-present partner of human civilization, the rat population, also peaked. The trigger, however, was international trade with Asia, which created a new biological zone that slowly but surely integrated Asia and Europe. As medical and social historians pointed out cogently, even bacteria and diseases have a history and historical movements of their own, and this seemed a perfect case in point. With the right level of trade and with rats traveling on ships from areas of Asia where the bubonic plague was endemic, such as the Caucuses (where it is still endemic), they, along with their fleas, brought the disease to the port cities of Europe. There the disease-carrying fleas found a rat population dense enough that they could pass on the bacillus, and it rapidly flourished in rat populations across Europe. In turn, fleas infected humans, and the plague spread like wildfire – a deadly biological exchange that turned into a demographic nightmare.

There were, however, problems with this scenario. One that historians noticed early on was that in the accounts of the fourteenth-century plague many, including Boccaccio, reported that it seemed to spread directly from one human to another, something that was simply not possible for bubonic plague, where a rat flea had to infect a human. Moreover, many accounts stressed that when one human passed the disease to another, death came quickly, often almost immediately, without the formation of buboes, the patient losing blood from the nose or coughing up blood. That too could not happen with bubonic plague. But researchers on the modern plague came to the rescue and seemed to resolve this apparent anomaly. They discovered that there were two secondary infections associated with the modern plague that were much more deadly than the plague itself: septicaemic and pneumonic infections. The former is rarely seen today and did not seem to fit the bill. But the latter, the pneumonic, although fairly rare, has an etiology that appeared to fit perfectly fourteenth-century descriptions like that of Boccaccio. Pneumonic plague infections piggyback on bubonic plague infections in a population, and when they get going, the disease is passed directly from person to person, with pneumonia-like symptoms that include coughing blood and high fever, followed by rapid death. All this seemed to match so well the accounts of the plague that both historians and doctors were satisfied that they had discovered yet another proof that the great plague was triggered by new biological contacts, intercontinental trade, and perhaps even a darker side of a proto-worldwide capitalist economy – with rats, fleas, and *Yersinus pestis* being the distasteful culprits. Most historians and doctors still agree that the case is settled and that the plague of 1348 was the bubonic plague and its related pneumonic plague.

Yet for once rats and their fleas may have been unjustly maligned. And world economies have probably more than enough to answer for without being responsible for the Black Death. Recently scholars have begun to undercut this virtual certainty about the plague, pointing out several additional problems. A number of them, for example, have noted that in modern bubonic plague epidemics, rats die in great numbers before the plague gets started in any significant way in humans. The reason for this is that the flea that passes on the bacteria much prefers rats to humans – *de gustibus non disputandum est.* It will leave a rat host only when it is dead and no longer capable of supporting it to move on to a human body, and then only until it can find another rat host. Thus rats must die in large numbers in order for humans to die in any number. But troublingly, when historians looked for accounts of rats dying before this great epidemic, they found silence. In fact, the animals that were reported as dying in conjunction with the plague were usually large farm animals such as sheep and pigs, frequently reported to have caught the disease from humans, not the other way around. Many dismissed this troubling lacuna in the sources, suggesting that the death of so many people caused observers to miss what was happening to rats, or that rats were so unimportant in the worldview of the time that their deaths went unnoticed. Still, modern populations in India and China have regularly noted the dying off of rats and associated it with the bubonic plague, actually well before medical researchers identified the rat-flea-human vector of the disease. It is perhaps more troubling that while Rinascimento observers correlated an impressively wide range of phenomena with the appearance of the plague, no one thought to mention hundreds of thousands of dying rats.

Equally troubling was the reportedly rapid spread of the plague. That could not be so easily blamed on the panic of the victims. Either people were dying or they were not. The problem is that the bubonic plague moves very slowly geographically in modern outbreaks. It can take years for it to travel fairly short distances, and it has never raced around the world, as it was feared it would in the late nineteenth century based on fourteenth-century accounts. Also, modern bubonic plague is not very infectious. It actually moves quite slowly. Pneumonic plague is more infectious, but, as noted earlier, it is relatively rare. Moreover, this latter form usually occurs in cold, damp seasons, whereas the great waves of plague, at least in Italy, focused on the summer months and usually ceased in the fall. But, as we have seen, pneumonic plague was necessary to explain human-to-human infection and the massive mortality.

At least two other problems are even harder to ignore. Recently, as part of his ongoing study of the plague, examining a large number of accounts of the disease from the fourteenth and fifteenth centuries, Cohn has noted that many do not mention buboes at all. Moreover, even many of those that do, tend to stress another set of symptoms, reporting that the victim's body was covered with spots, often black or red, of various sizes. These were more often seen as the sign of impending death. Boccaccio, it will be remembered, noted: "After a while, however, the nature of this disease changed with black spots or livid patches which appeared in great number on the arms, the thighs and all over the body, some were large and distant from each other, others small and close together." Such symptoms, however, are not associated with either bubonic or pneumonic infections.

Finally, and most significantly, modern human populations seem to have no natural resistance to bubonic plague, which means that each time the plague hits a population, deaths are relatively evenly spread across that population, and the plague can continue for years in one region. In the Rinascimento, however, the plague came back only at intervals of ten to fifteen years. Moreover, after the first outbreak, which killed people of all ages, genders, and social ranks, when it returned it hit hardest the young. This appears to indicate that there was a natural resistance in the population to whatever caused the plague, impeding its return until a new generation of nonresistant victims had been born. Such a pattern is observable with many infectious diseases, but tellingly, it is not true of the modern bubonic plague.

One thing militates against this apparently overwhelming evidence: recent DNA studies of apparent plague victims from the Rinascimento seem to show that they have traces of the same DNA as the modern plague virus. If such findings turn out to be accurate, we are faced with an even greater apparent anomaly, a virus with the same DNA as the modern bubonic plague with a different set of symptoms and manner of spreading. In the end, then, perhaps the only thing that is clear is that there are too many things that do not fit to make any confident claim about what disease the great plagues of the Rinascimento were; and, as some have cogently suggested, maybe they were not one disease at all but several different ones. Perhaps in this there is another and more secure lesson about the history of disease, rats, fleas, and even microbes – they too have their history, and a very important one at that, even if it is hard to know. We see today that microbes and diseases can mutate quite rapidly. In light of this it is becoming harder to imagine that any disease of several centuries ago is the same disease we know today, even when the symptoms do seem to match. In fact, the same lesson is crucial for the history of biology and of nature itself. We tend to assume that both are unchanging, the same in the past as they are today, but virtually every time we look more closely at either we find that things are not so simple or fixed. Not just microbes but plants, animals, even rats and fleas have changed in a myriad of ways over the last six hundred years, in part through mutation and apparently "natural" processes and also, crucially, in interaction with humans and their economic, social, and cultural attempts to control and transform the world to meet human needs. Simply put, the biological and natural world we live in today is not the same as the one that people of the Rinascimento lived in, and we are just beginning to explore the ramifications of that history.

Economy versus Culture: The Plague as a Malthusian Check

It may be that we will never know what exactly the plague was, but one thing is clear: it killed off massive numbers of people, and that has led to the claim that it had a devastating effect on the economic, social, and even psychological world of its day. In fact, some have labeled it the crucial turning point on the road to the modern world, ending the Middle Ages and inaugurating the modern era. Such large claims, however, seldom work when looked at more closely, and the plague provides a good example of the danger of proclaiming firsts and beginnings of the modern world. First, of course, such a dramatic die-off of friends, relatives, and neighbors must have been immediately devastating, as virtually all contemporary accounts agreed. In a world where life expectancy was relatively short, infant mortality high, and medical care not particularly effective, death was a common and virtually everyday experience. But the plague brought death on an unprecedented scale, so much so that contemporaries broke down and actually called it something "new," a term that the age was loathe to adopt for any change, aside from the most negative. The survivors, however, found that there were positive signs even in such a great mortality. First off, of course, they were the survivors, and that was no small thing in the face of such terrible devastation. Moreover, as Boccaccio and others noted, once the momentary breakdown in society was righted, the survivors stood to inherit the wealth that was untouched by the plague. Although it would be difficult to calculate exactly how much wealth remained, it was a considerable pie to be divided among a much smaller population.

We can be more certain about the fact that the population loss in the cities of northern Italy may not have had as devastating a short-term effect as once thought. Although, as noted, the first wave of the plague struck the population without preference for age, class, or gender, it returned periodically, and in those regular reappearances it struck mainly the young. This was a tragic reality that may have made society cherish children even more

and see them as an even more valuable asset to the family than previously.
At the same time, however, it was a reality that in economic terms was less
devastating, because children were more quickly and easily replaced than
adult workers. In fact, after each wave of the plague demographers note that
birth rates jumped dramatically, suggesting that families that had lost children quickly moved to replace them, in both the city and the countryside.
Moreover, after the first wave of the plague and subsequent returns, city
governments repeatedly passed legislation designed to attract laborers to the
city, making it easier to join guilds and even to become citizens. As many
in the countryside suddenly found themselves without family or family ties
and thus free to move to the city, many, it seems, did just that, especially the
young.

     In turn, although the urban population was smaller, the productive work-
ing population quickly recouped a significant part of its losses thanks to
immigration from the countryside. This also helps to explain why land rents
in the countryside and food prices in the city did not decrease as significantly as might be expected. What appears to have happened instead is that
marginally productive land in the countryside was abandoned, because there
was no longer a glut of agricultural laborers available as there had been in the
more densely populated days of the twelfth and thirteenth centuries. Thus
only richer terrain continued to be farmed, and poorer land was allowed
to go fallow. Those peasants who had not died or been lured off to the city
continued, then, to pay higher rents for the more limited amount of highly
productive land that remained in cultivation. And significantly, this seems
to have meant that although rents were high, and less was produced overall,
what was produced was produced more efficiently and easily, perhaps with
those who remained to farm the land garnering more for their labor and
living better than before. The same appears to have been true in the cities,
where the need for labor tended to make laborers more valuable and their
working conditions better. Local variations could alter this general picture
significantly, however; for example, recent contested studies of Tuscany suggest that an especially aggressive Florentine policy of exploiting the countryside seriously reduced agricultural production and the quality of life of
peasants there, even after the plague.

     Still, from a macroeconomic perspective this population loss created a
significant decrease in markets. There was no way around the fact that fewer
people meant fewer consumers. This in turn meant greater competition for
those markets that remained and smaller profits. In fact, the level of international trade probably did not return to the levels of the late thirteenth and
early fourteenth centuries until the very nature of the European economy

changed with the "discovery" of the "New World" and the development
of a much broader economic base that built on a budding Atlantic and
world economy. In northern Italy, in many ways, the increased competi-
tions and smaller levels of profit at the macro level also help to explain
the startling failure of cities to survive independently across the second
half of the fourteenth and the first half of the fifteenth century. By the
mid-fifteenth century there were essentially only three major urban powers
dominating the northern half of the peninsula: Venice, Milan, and Florence,
along with the administrative center of the Church, Rome. Smaller courtly
centers survived, but the real urban economic motors of the period had
been largely reduced to the big three. Economically the little fish had been
cannibalized by the big, which had been able to recover more competitively
and to dominate international and regional markets. Thus, while from a
macroeconomic perspective the decline caused by the plague is evident in
area after area, both in the big cities and at the local rural level its impact
was less negative than the macro picture might seem to suggest. In fact,
those members of the *popolo grosso* who survived and their workers in the
great cities may have found their situation better and generally improving.
This may help to explain the optimism and self-confidence of the cultural
flourishing that typified Italy in the late fourteenth and fifteenth centuries,
even in the face of returning waves of plague and less-than-impressive macroeconomic figures.

But, of course, this is the typical history of the winners and survivors. There
were no lack of losers as well, and a look at their situation is also instructive.
Fortunately, one of the most important economic historians of the last century, David Herlihy, studied in detail the impact of the plague on the little
city of Pistoia. Near Florence, at the foot of one of the secondary passes that
connect Tuscany and the center of Italy with the Lombard plain, Modena,
and Milan, it was a small but vital urban center in the thirteenth century.
One of the things that led Herlihy to study the city was its excellent archival
records, which allowed him to construct long-term profiles of population
change and the impact of recurring waves of the plague. Somewhat surprisingly, he found that the population of Pistoia and the rural areas immediately
around the city peaked well before the first wave of the plague. In 1244 the
population there was approximately 31,000 souls, making it a modest-sized
city, not all that much smaller than Florence had been just a few generations
earlier. By 1344 the population had declined by about a third, to 24,000; tellingly, this was before the first wave of the plague struck in 1348. In 1383 the
population had dropped further, to 14,000, reflecting the mortality of the
plague along with, presumably, some recovery of population afterward. Yet

in 1404 the population had declined still further, to 9,000. Only in 1427 was there a slight increase in the population, to 12,000 inhabitants.

Evidently these figures demonstrate a tremendous population loss in Pistoia. It had declined by two-thirds from the mid-thirteenth century to the early fifteenth century, from 31,000 to 9,000 at its lowest point. But clearly this was not entirely due to the plague, as the data reveals that the population decline was well under way before it hit and continued afterward, although progressive returns of the plague undoubtedly played a role in the continued decline. Herlihy asked, then, what these figures meant. First, he noted that this massive die-off occurred in an unusually densely populated area. Looking at the broader territory around Pistoia, he calculated that there were approximately 44,000 people living in a 600-square-mile area that included the city, which meant that there were about 66 people per square mile. Although the area around Pistoia was probably somewhat less densely populated than most of Tuscany, Herlihy used these figures to calculate a minimal population density for all of Tuscany, concluding that it was well over a million people. That level of population, he noted, was not reached again in the area until the nineteenth century, when health care, food production, and life expectancy were all more favorable to sustaining such numbers. Struck by these figures, he argued that in the fourteenth century in Pistoia and Tuscany there was a catastrophic population collapse that ended an era of population growth and very high population densities.

Did this reflect a basic Malthusian check on population, he wondered. The eighteenth-century economic theorist Thomas Malthus had argued, in what was labeled at the time the "dismal science," that it was unfortunate but necessary to keep the working classes at a subsistence level, for if they were paid too much and lived too comfortably, they would overreproduce and create a population density that was unsustainable. Higher wages meant more reproduction, and that meant eventually disaster: famines, plagues, and diseases – what became known as Malthusian checks on the population that would return it to sustainable levels. To avoid such "natural" disasters for humanity, Malthus recommended that employers restrain their altruism and keep pay low: subsistence wages actually protected and were best for the laboring classes in the long run. This vision was clearly popular with many employers and had a significant influence on the budding new social science disciplines, especially economics.

Actually, at the time when Herlihy developed this data, the idea of a Malthusian check was already popular among economic historians and often used to explain the demographic losses of the fourteenth century. And it still has proponents today. Herlihy, however, was unconvinced. On the one hand, his figures clearly showed a catastrophic population loss following an era of very high population density. Moreover, there was plenty of information to suggest that this dense population had been living on the margins of subsistence, both in the cities of Tuscany and in the countryside. Our very numerically oriented fourteenth-century Florentine chronicler, Giovanni Villani, for example, was deeply troubled to report that in 1330 the poor living at or below the level of subsistence in Florence made up about a quarter of the population. It may be that Villani exaggerated for effect, but it is clear that across northern Italy population densities and poverty levels were unusually high before the plague struck. From a Malthusian perspective it seemed self-evident that the main victims of the plague were those people literally on the margins of society and of life itself.

Herlihy, however, felt that his data did not fit a Malthusian model. Tellingly, he asked: if Pistoia was overpopulated in 1344 at 24,000 souls before the plague struck, was it still overpopulated in 1392 when the population had fallen to 11,000? That would be hard to imagine, especially in light of the fact that it had a population of 31,000, almost three times greater, in 1244. Yet its population continued to decline, reaching a mere 9,000 in 1404. And if 9,000 was the "natural" base level of the population, Herlihy wondered how it had ever reached 31,000 a little more than a century and a half earlier. Moreover, he pointed out that the plague did not hit a rapidly expanding population, as a Malthusian model required; rather, the population of Pistoia had been declining, and rather dramatically, for some time before the plague hit. In addition, although the data was not as good for other areas, it seemed that similar declines had been under way across Tuscany, northern Italy, and much of Europe well before the plague. Herlihy thus felt forced to conclude that the plague was not a Malthusian check.

The question then became: if it was not a Malthusian check, and the plague was not enough to explain the ongoing population decline, what had happened? Herlihy found his answer in a most unlikely place – the customs and everyday culture of society, especially the strategies regarding the basic economy of the family and its reproductive practices. It is often assumed that the reproductive rate of premodern societies was uniformly high, approaching the biological maximum, especially in Catholic countries. Without birth control, and under the dictates of a Church that saw sexual intercourse as licit only when it was aimed at reproduction, such birth rates seemed almost inevitable. But when Herlihy began to examine the *Catasto* records of Florence and Florentine Tuscany, he found again some suggestive surprises. The *Catasto* was essentially an inventory made in 1427 of all the people and wealth of the territory in Tuscany, including

Pistoia, under Florentine control at the time. This massive survey was created in order to apply more effectively the forced loans based on wealth that were needed to finance the city's ongoing wars. These records provided Herlihy with a statistical snapshot of Florence and its territories in the early fifteenth century.

Significantly, the *Catasto* listed not just family assets, but also the children of each family and their ages. This allowed Herlihy to compare the number of children per family to that family's estimated wealth. Clearly such figures need to be treated with caution, as families were not anxious to reveal their wealth when those figures were to be used to assess forced loans to the government. Still, even assuming that wealth was underreported, the figures seriously challenged the assumption that people were reproducing at or near a biologically maximum rate. Herlihy found that at the lowest assessments – those families that had less than fifty florins of assets, by far the greatest number of households in Pistoia and its surrounding countryside – the number of children in the household averaged only 1.43. Families that had no reported wealth in the *Catasto* actually did a little better, with 1.47 children per household. But significantly, even families with up to 100 florins of wealth averaged only 1.85 children. Evidently those at the bottom of society were not reproducing at anywhere near their biological potential, and, tellingly, they were not even reproducing at the level needed to replace their parents. Moreover, Herlihy noted that as the wealth of a family increased, the number of children increased in a direct correlation to wealth: families with wealth that totaled 101–150 florins had 2.14 children; 151–200 florins, 2.44 children; 201–250 florins, 2.46 children; and over 250 florins, 3.21 children.

Things clearly were not working as common assumptions about premodern populations required, and it seemed evident to Herlihy that these figures, especially the strong correlation between wealth and birth rates, required an admission that members of this population were limiting their birth rates in a way that reflected their perceived ability to sustain children. The question was how. Herlihy turned to culture and custom over nature and biological necessity for his answers and in the process rejected Malthus's "dismal science." First, he noted that marriage was highly contingent on being able to offer a dowry, and, of course, being able to offer a dowry was in turn contingent on the wealth of a family. Even at lower social levels it was difficult to marry a daughter without a dowry, and thus – at a statistical level, at least – the cost of dowries created a form of birth control for poorer families. Even the Church recognized this. In 1425, for example, the famous preacher and eventual saint Bernardino of Siena (1380–1444) attributed the still-dwindling populations of Siena and Milan to the failure of thousands of young people to marry for lack of a dowry.

This alone, however, would not have been enough to create the dramatically low and economically sensitive birth rates the *Catasto* reveals. It seems clear that a lack of economic resources was also leading families to limit the number of children they had. One gets an inkling of this in the observation of the Pistoian chronicler Luca Dominici, who noted after yet another wave of the plague in 1399–1400: "In this time many women became pregnant, which was good because there were many that had been barren for a long time and some had never made children." What he seems to be describing is a situation in which families that had been limiting births "for a long time" suddenly found themselves able to choose to have children again – a conscious limiting of births, then, followed by an equally conscious decision to have them in order to replace those who had died in the plague. Such family planning would have helped make possible the close correlation between wealth and family size that Herlihy discovered.

Some have claimed, in the face of Herlihy's statistics and analysis, that these figures were caused by sexual abstinence, arguing that there were no other means available to lower-class people to limit births. But this seems to seriously underestimate the everyday culture of the day and the intelligence of peasants and lower-class urban populations. If we speak of controlling births rather than birth control, there was a wide range of options open to families for limiting the number of children they had. First, as already discussed, dowries often delayed or blocked marriage. Beyond that, however, criminal records that deal with sex crimes and ecclesiastical records that deal with family problems reveal that various forms of birth control were well known. The most obvious form was *coitus interruptus*, a technique apparently widely known and practiced. Of course, this practice was not totally secure, but if extensively used it would have had a statistically significant impact on births. Contemporary reports suggest that many believed it was highly effective and used it as part of their strategy to limit births. Also, although the Church frowned upon this and other nonreproductive sexual practices, such as anal intercourse and masturbation (and although preachers railed against both with increasing vociferousness), literature, criminal documents, and the continuing refrain of condemnation from ecclesiastical sources suggest that such practices were understood and used.

It seems likely that many families also used abortion to limit their children, especially when it was clear another child could not be supported. It may be, however, that the practice was often not viewed as abortion. Midwives and women healers, it appears, often induced menstruation in women who were suffering from late periods – a fairly common problem in societies where malnutrition is high and physical labor for women heavy and demanding. The remedies used by women to induce late periods – often poisons or rudimentary forms of herbal abortifacients – indicate that the treatment in reality frequently terminated a pregnancy, whether or not the patient or the healer realized it. Male doctors and surgeons also understood and administered abortifacients to terminate pregnancies. Usually these abortions, recognized as such, were done at the behest of husbands or the males responsible for single women. I have argued elsewhere that this created a significant divide in medical culture between women's healing networks that cured late periods and men's medical networks that procured abortions. In both cases, however, fewer pregnancies came to term, and fewer children were born.

Many poor families were also forced by their economic position to abandon children whom they felt they could not support. There was, in fact, a long tradition in medieval Europe of abandoning children in the hope that a more prosperous family would discover the abandoned child, take it in, and raise it. Although many historians are loathe to consider it, the abandonment of female babies may account, in fact, for the unbalanced sex ratios found in records of the time, where males frequently significantly outnumber females. Usually this imbalance is explained in terms of the underreportage of females because of their perceived lack of importance or by the higher death rates of women in pregnancy. It may well be, however, that these figures also reflect a society that still abandoned unwanted or unsupportable female children. In addition, the noted Rinascimento charitable institution, the foundling home, seems almost certainly to have been a response to the ongoing abandonment of unsupportable children. Most cities had one or more foundling homes where children could be left to be raised by the institution rather than simply abandoned.

Unfortunately, however, the survival chances of children left in foundling homes were often low. Where human milk was unavailable, many babies died because there was no adequate substitute for it at the time. Moreover, in the close and often unhealthy quarters of the foundling homes, contagious diseases regularly swept through the children, to deadly effect. In the best of foundling homes, like the famous Innocenti in Florence, reported survival rates could be relatively high, but in poorer houses abandonment tended to be a delayed death sentence. It should be noted, however, that families that left children at foundling homes often hoped to be able to reclaim them at a later date when their financial situation permitted it – frequently they identified the baby left in such a way that it could later be reclaimed, even recommending special treatment or promising to return for the child when things got better. Significantly, a large proportion of the babies left were female, indicating again the negative vision of females and their cost to the families that had to rear them and eventually provide them with dowries.

A more subtle form of postpartum birth control that also seems to have affected girls more than boys grew out of the institution of the *balia*. The term is frequently translated as "wet nurse" – in other words, a woman who was paid to nurse a child – but it usually involved more. At the upper levels of society hiring a *balia* to nurse a family's children was a common practice, in part because if a mother was incapable of nursing, a substitute was necessary to provide milk for her baby. More often, however, a *balia* was used because it had become customary to pass on this time-consuming task to menials if a family could afford to do so. The Church, preachers, and even some civic leaders preached against this, but *balie* were widely employed nonetheless. In fact, if one looks at the literature of the period, *balie* are often important maternal figures, especially in sixteenth-century comedies, where, suggestively, they regularly played a much more visible and maternal role than mothers.

What, one might well ask, did *balie* have to do with birth control? At times too much. First, while breast feeding, a woman usually cannot become pregnant. That meant that lower-class women who breast-fed the children of others in order to earn money tended to have fewer children. In turn, upper-class and more well-to-do women, who did not breast-feed, could return to reproducing more rapidly. It might be tempting to jump to the conclusion that this had a significant impact on the perceived correlation between wealth and the number of children per family, but upper-class women did not produce anywhere near enough children to confirm such a hypothesis, and, of course, not enough lower-class women worked as *balie* either. More significantly, hiring a *balia* could be costly. To save money, many families, rather than bringing a *balia* into their household, sent their newborn child out into the countryside to the home of a peasant woman who fed and raised the child until it was weaned, usually quite late, at about three.

The problem with this was that infant mortality rates were normally high, and *balie*, far away from the control of their employers, could cut corners; so a distant child's death could be written off as normal. Studies of the contracts made to hire *balie* reveal that families tried to make sure that their child would be well cared for and that only the child paid for would be fed, but the very repetition of such clauses in contracts suggests that this was not always the case. We also see a troubling gender bias in such contracts. Female children, especially second and later-born females, tended to be sent farther away into the countryside, or at least to have contracts in which the *balia* was paid less. Males, and especially first-born males, tended to have *balie* who were much better paid and lived either in the home of the child's family or nearby, where their feeding could be controlled and the baby's health monitored. All this suggests that hiring cheaper *balie* farther from the city meant that a number of children would not return, swelling the statistics of infant mortality, a fate that almost certainly befell more girls than boys. Thus, as was the case with the foundling home, the institution of the *balia* had a negative impact on survival rates for children less desired.

Although we have almost no evidence on this, it is also probably necessary to ask how those peasant women who were being paid to nurse the children of the urban well-to-do were able to have the milk available to do so. A traditional explanation is that when they had weaned their own children, they simply continued to feed others as *balie*, never interrupting the flow of their milk. Usually the hiring of a *balia* was carried out by men: the husband or father of a woman who still had milk would contract with the father of the child to be fed, and the negotiations often included an examination of the women and the milk involved. Needless to say, fathers could be quite aggressive, especially when important male children were involved, making sure that the *balia* was capable of feeding and caring for their child. Thus younger, healthier women with a good supply of milk were preferred and commanded higher prices. In fact, such women were a considerable asset for a peasant household and in the best of cases could become not only an important source of income, but also an important connection to the rich and powerful.

A peasant baby that died unexpectedly (or conveniently) or was sent to the foundling home must have seemed a great boon to some families. How often such events occurred, particularly when there was an opportunity to earn a handsome stipend and to build ties with a powerful urban family, or when a family's need was great, we cannot know; but there were strong economic incentives involved, and many upper-class children were well fed by healthy young *balie* without children of their own to feed. At the lower level of the trade, poor mothers may have been tempted to feed their own child along with the child they were being paid to care for – at times openly, at times surreptitiously. This may have led to trying to feed a peasant child with substitutes – often a bread and cow or goat milk mixture, referred to as *pappa*, was used – but if overdone this could be deadly, and it tended to produce malnourished and weaker children, less likely to survive. Of course, the child paid for could also fall victim to such treatment, but as those children produced an income, they had an economic advantage in the competition for survival. When all is said and done, as noted earlier, a significant number of children nursed in the countryside did not return to their urban families.

In sum, there was a wide range of practices that help to explain why poorer families had fewer children, which makes Herlihy's data showing a virtually perfect correlation between wealth and family size an eloquent, and often sad, testimony to the way families controlled their own destiny. Simply put, in the face of the high rents and overpopulation in the countryside and the problems making ends meet in the city, well before the plague struck, peasants and the urban poor were making hard decisions about how to limit their family size and survive. This meant that a general population decline was under way in Italy from the last decades of the thirteenth century, well before the plague struck – as the data confirms. And in turn, it meant that although there may have been momentary reversals of this downward trend – immediately after the plague, for example, when poor families felt they could replace lost children – over the longer run the downward trend continued, because it had become customary to limit births, and the survival of children, in response to economic needs. Thus, even when the Malthusian reasons for population decline had long since disappeared, the population of Italy continued to decline.

Herlihy, in the face of this decidedly wider and more complex reality, returned to the Florentine chronicler Giovanni Villani, that noted counter of people and things who tried to make sense of this in his own way. Villani asked whether the suffering of Florence and Tuscany in the 1330s, well before the plague, was the result of natural causes or the sins of Florentines, especially their avarice, greed, and economic oppression of the poor in the countryside and the city. And, for all his modern-seeming counting and social analysis, he opted for sin. At first, this might seem like a typical medieval point of view and a rather moralistic one at that. But, as Herlihy pointed out, if we rephrase Villani's choice as one between natural and economic forces (Malthus) on the one hand, and people, culture, and custom on the other, we have a cultural claim that is less easily dismissed. Although it is largely irrelevant to Herlihy's path-breaking cultural analysis, it would be unfair to him not to point out that later in his career, he became quite unhappy with what he and others perceived as the "fuzziness" of such cultural explanations; yet his own early forays into the area revealed that cultural analysis opened important new vistas and moved historical analysis well beyond the sometimes too narrow vision of the supposedly "hard" social sciences.

Simply put, the economic and natural imperatives of the fourteenth century did not overwhelm the culture of survival, which was already well established in the face of earlier overpopulation and the general impoverishment of the lower classes. People, rather than submitting to nature, in Villani's terms, made their decisions – Villani's sins – and in the end continued to live in a complex dialogue with natural and economic forces – a central part of the developing and dynamic *civiltà* of the first Rinascimento. This helps to explain why, on the one hand, the population declined much further than would have been required by Malthusian models in order to rebalance natural resources and the number of people living in Tuscany and in northern Italy more generally, and why, on the other, the few who remained found that in the short run their survival strategies often allowed them to live, after the disasters of the fourteenth century, with a certain optimism and even at times better than before. In the end the traditional dichotomies of nature versus nurture, economy versus culture, and even material reality versus the human spirit, from a historical perspective are all too simplistic; rather, what we see at work in the travails of fourteenth-century Italy is the complex interaction between culture, biology, and nature that makes human society and makes it at once so fascinating and rich with potential, and also so sad and troubling.

The Wealth of the Rinascimento: The Example of Florence

To understand how this worked, however, we need to look more closely at the economic world of the day, a world in many ways shaped by the *popolo grosso*'s vision of how the economy might best function. This was no small matter, obviously, for the *popolo grosso* saw the production of wealth as crucial for their power and status. Speaking very generally, there were four great motors of economic growth that created wealth in the cities of the day: banking, both international and local; trade, again both international and local; the production of luxury goods, especially woolen cloth; and, often overlooked but crucial, a more aggressive, capital-intensive agriculture. To a great extent these were the sources of wealth that made the *popolo grosso/grasso*, big and fat, providing the wealth that underpinned the vital urban society of the period and its flourishing culture and distinguishing the cities of the north and center of Italy from most of the rest of Europe and from the south of Italy as well.

Right from the start, however, two popular myths should be laid to rest. First, for all the triumph of the *popolo grosso* and all the wealth that they controlled and displayed, the fourteenth century was not a particularly prosperous time. In fact, many have argued that it was a time of economic decline or at best stasis. Second, the *popolo grosso* were not in favor of "hands-off" unlimited economic development. Rather than "free markets" and "free trade," which are often assumed to be crucial for the first stages of a market economy and premodern proto-capitalist development, the Rinascimento was a period when one of the primary purposes of the corporate organizations of society, in the form of both guilds and governments, was to control and regulate the economy, at best in the name of creating a prosperous *civiltà* and, more realistically, with an eye to creating a more controlled and predictable economic environment tilted in favor of the *popolo grosso*. After all, they had fought too hard, and often bloodily, to gain political power not to use it to further their interests – even if, not surprisingly, they frequently saw and virtually always expressed their interests in terms of what was good for their city as a whole, and in terms of a return to better first times modeled on the successes of imperial Rome and the values of the Church Fathers and Christ himself.

Florence is often seen as one of the leading cities of the time in terms of its economy. In reality, however, its economic growth came relatively late. In the thirteenth century it found itself in competition with neighboring cities that seemed to have a more prosperous future than the largely landlocked city in the center of Tuscany. The Arno River, which bisected it, was for much of the year too shallow to support shipping of any significant proportions, and the city lay in a valley surrounded by mountains on two sides, north and east, and by rolling hills not easily traversed with heavy goods to the south. The hinterland to the west and south did offer some potentially rich but often contested farm land. Little of this seemed to augur well for the city's economic success. Perhaps its biggest economic advantage was that it stood on one of the main north-south roads and near the southern base of a mountain pass over the Apennines. The northern side of the pass was controlled by a much more important city, Bologna, famous for its university and especially its faculty of law (so central in the *popolo grosso* vision of creating a just and ordered civic world). Nearer at hand, and apparently more competitive economically, were Pisa and Siena. Pisa was a port city that controlled access to Tuscany for international trade and had been one of the leading international trading cities in the West for much of the Middle Ages; Siena, if anything even more landlocked than Florence, sitting on top of hills, was an important banking city in the twelfth and thirteenth centuries and for much of that period one of the richest and largest cities in Italy. With such competition and its evident geographic liabilities, Florence's economic future was not bright.

Like many smaller cities in the eleventh and twelfth centuries, Florence focused on building wealth by investing in the countryside around the city – the *contado*, as it was called. Central to this was the gradual replacement of long-term leases for peasant farmers with shorter ones. In the early Middle Ages, as a result of the devastations of barbarian invasions, incessant local war-fare, and perhaps even a mini–ice age, the countryside had become severely underpopulated. This meant that local lords who controlled the land found that their primary problem was securing labor to farm it; thus, they offered long-term rents in order to bind peasants to the land. These leases were called *libelli* (*libellus* singular), following ancient Roman usage, and were normally for a lifetime, usually defined as thirty-three years, the theoretical life expec-tancy of a peasant. (Actually, it appears that the average medieval peasant lived slightly less than thirty years.) In the twelfth and thirteenth centuries, however, Europe saw an impressive demographic growth, with many areas of Italy, including Tuscany, becoming densely populated. The reasons for this growth are debated, but undoubtedly better nutrition based on cultivation of a wider range of foods that enriched the bread and gruel of the traditional peasant diet, a warmer climate, and a *relatively* more peaceful and settled society all played significant roles. This more densely populated countryside allowed landlords to slowly change the nature of leases, moving to shorter ones that required peasants to pay higher rents for land to farm and playing a significant role in the peasant impoverishment discussed earlier. Eventually, short-term leases were replaced in many areas by a system of leasing called *mezzadria*. *Mezzadria* contracts required the peasant to give a portion of the agricultural production to the landlord – often half, thus the *mezza* or half of *mezzadria*. All this meant that landlords progressively realized greater profits from the farming of their land; they thus had more wealth and could live a life of greater luxury, creating growing markets for luxury goods.

This growing wealth and interest in a more luxurious lifestyle for the upper classes, however, helped foment a second motor of economic expan-sion, lending money. As local lords began to live a more expensive life, they often found that their immediate income did not match the costs of the products and services that they desired. In turn, the building capital base extracted from peasant labor meant that some could use that capital to lend money at interest to those temporarily short of funds. This helped build a limited proto-banking business based on loans made primarily to locals. Needless to say, in the long run it also impoverished and destroyed many noble families, who fell into debt and often lost their lands, and at times even their noble status. This contributed in turn to a noble reputation for vio-lence; for not only did their traditional military roles and social values tend to make them violent, the progressive deterioration of their economic sta-tus at the hands of non-noble city dwellers encouraged violent displays and violent retribution against those same people. This frequently involved what might be politely termed direct forms of wealth redistribution – more aptly labeled, from the perspective of the *popolo*, noble robbery and banditry.

Finally, interconnected with all of this, there grew up a more significant local trade to supply the luxury goods that this growing wealth made possible. Luxury cloth was an important driving factor in this trade. Light, relatively easy to transport, and particularly useful for demonstrating one's wealth via expensive clothing, luxury cloth was virtually an essential luxury. Spices and perfumes were also seen as increasingly necessary. And they were very expensive, as the most sought-after came from the Middle East or more distant lands. Local trade, however, primarily involved basic staples, such as the salt and grain that Florence, like other cities, tried to monopolize. All three of these economic developments – more intensive, profit-oriented agriculture; the growth of local banking; and the rise of a local luxury and staples trade – made Florence in the early thirteenth century just another growing town like dozens of others.

What changed all that was a series of political and economic conflicts that jumped Florence ahead of its rivals in the middle years of the thirteenth century. And in the thick of it all was our old friend the Emperor Frederick II (1194–1250), who, while he did not live up to his destiny of becoming the Antichrist, did play a significant role in the rise to economic prominence of Florence. Briefly put, Frederick, in his wars with the papacy and the Guelph cities of Italy, was so successful that in city after city the Guelph party was driven out and replaced by his Ghibelline supporters. Even Guelph cities that survived were afraid to cross him too openly for fear that they would suffer his wrath. This had serious repercussions for papal finances. In the past, cities like Siena had been leaders in handling the pope's banking needs, which were many, as the wealth of the papacy was drawn from across Europe and required international banking experts both to collect revenues and to transfer them to Rome. Also, of course, such banks were quite willing to lend the pope money when he needed it for the daily operation of his court and expensive lifestyle, another source of impressive profits. Frederick's success meant, however, that cities like Siena became reluctant to offer these services to the pope, forcing him to seek new bankers.

Florence was one of the primary Guelph cities that stepped into the breach, risking imperial wrath for papal wealth. When Frederick died suddenly in 1250, his Ghibelline plans to dominate Italy died with him, and the papacy and Guelphs in many cities quickly reclaimed much of their lost power. But the resurgent papacy did not forget Florence's loyalty, nor did the Florentines allow it to do so, and by the 1270s papal banking was largely in Florentine hands. Using the city's central role in papal finances while also piggybacking on the papacy's international administrative network of bishops located in the major cities of Europe, Florentine bankers became international financial leaders, lending large sums to kings and nobles across Europe. The resultant rapid financial growth of the city in the second half of the thirteenth century transformed Florence. No longer was its wealth based on exploiting the surplus production of peasants in its hinterland. Suddenly it was drawing wealth from the whole of Europe.

Crucially, its ability to draw wealth from a European-wide base was one of the key underpinnings of Florence's economic power and its amazing intellectual and cultural flourishing during the Rinascimento. Like ancient Athens, which drew the wealth of the eastern Mediterranean into one city; ancient Rome, which drew the wealth of that whole sea into one city; late sixteenth and seventeenth-century Madrid, which drew the wealth of a large part of the Atlantic world into one city; eighteenth-century Paris, which drew the wealth of a major nation-state into one city; nineteenth-century London, which drew the wealth of a world-spanning empire into one city; and twentieth-century New York, which drew the wealth of a rich nation-state and an incipient world economy into one city, Florence drew a significant portion of the wealth of Europe into an unlikely landlocked city in the back corner of the Tuscan plain to create its flourishing Rinascimento *civiltà*. This great pooling of wealth allowed a large number of people there to commit their efforts and lives to the artistic, cultural, and intellectual endeavors that are often seen today as the essence of the Rinascimento.

Papal banking offered many opportunities for profit beyond simply skimming papal revenues or lending money to the pope at interest. There were handsome profits to be made in both, of course, but being papal bankers meant that Florentine banks established branches throughout Europe to collect papal revenues. Where their people were not actually in place, they frequently worked through the administrative structure of the Church itself. Though obviously not a modern bureaucracy or particularly effective by modern measure, it was by the standards of the day, nonetheless, quite impressive, with administrative officials in major towns and cities across Europe gathered around the bishops established there. These officials were able to read and write, keep records, and thus organize and keep track of the Church's complex operations locally while at the same time responding to directives from Rome. The Church also had highly organized monastic establishments sprinkled through the countryside, where it played an important role in the more rural life of the north. Thus in both cities and countryside the Church was often the point of reference for and well connected to the most powerful people in Europe. In sum, it provided an ideal entry into the local society and economy for bankers eager to extend their reach beyond Italy.

Being able to piggyback on this extensive network of connections that blanketed Europe made Florentine banking houses like the Bardi and Peruzzi much more than banking houses. It made them international financial companies in what was for them, in a way, a first European common market. Through their contacts they learned the needs and possibilities of local markets as far away as the north of England and the principalities of eastern Europe – a tremendous advantage not just for banking but also for international trade. For Florentine development, one of the most important advantages gained was the ability to purchase the raw materials necessary for improving Florentine luxury cloth production. In the thirteenth century Florence had developed a small luxury-cloth-producing industry. This production, guided by the Calimala guild (the "evil-smelling street" guild, probably referring to the odor of the chemicals used in its shops on that street), was based on refinishing cheap cloth bought at the Champagne fairs in France into a higher-quality cloth, primarily for local consumption. There was little chance of penetrating larger markets, because the cloth produced was not of a high enough quality to compete with luxury cloth produced elsewhere.

What changed this was the access to superior raw materials that became available via the international networks built up by Florentine bankers. In that context, the banking houses, when collecting papal revenues in the wool-producing regions of northern England, the Low Countries, and Spain (where the finest wools were to be found), instead of collecting money, which was often still scarce in those regions, offered to accept wool instead, which was relatively cheap there. This fine wool was then shipped back to Florence, where it was much more valuable as the raw material for developing a true luxury-cloth-producing industry dominated by the Lana (wool) guild. Florentine merchants then shipped this superior product throughout Europe, following the market advice and networks of their banks, perhaps even selling it to the same raw-wool-producing lords of Spain and England who wanted a more refined cloth than that produced locally. To make the whole process more profitable yet, if those locals did not have the cash on hand to pay for the luxury goods, local Florentine bankers were willing to give them credit and make still greater profits. This was virtually a vertical monopoly Rinascimento-style, where Florentine bankers in conjunction with Florentine guilds controlled the production of wool all the way from the fields to the fashionable dress of a northern noble.

Things could be considerably less neat and favorable to Florentine bankers, merchants, and cloth producers, however, for they dealt regularly with rich and powerful nobles and monarchs in the north, who often felt less bound by the laws and contracts of the Italian *popolo grosso*. Still, once they became papal bankers, the way was clear for Florentine investors to become major entrepreneurs in three of the major profit-producing areas of the day: luxury cloth production, international trade, and banking itself. Significantly, this meant that although we use terms like "bankers," "merchants," and "cloth producers," they are somewhat misleading: the reality at the highest level of finance was that men of wealth tended to invest in all three areas. In Florence the three were so closely intertwined that it would sometimes be hard to distinguish which area was responsible for a person's wealth. All three endeavors, however, enriched an increasingly powerful and wealthy group of men who on the whole were the leaders of the *popolo grosso* economically, socially, and politically.

Turning to the Florentine cloth industry, our Florentine chronicler, Giovanni Villani, again counting in a way typical of his *popolo grosso* peers, estimated that by the 1330s more than 30,000 of Florence's approximately 90,000 inhabitants were employed in the cloth "industry." Calling this large-scale production an industry, however, is somewhat misleading, for while large number of workers, often low-paid and living at the margins of survival, were employed, making up what some have even labeled the first proletariat, most of the production was done at home. Both the spinning of the thread from wool (often done by women) and the weaving of cloth (usually done by highly skilled artisans, both men and women) took place at home in a system similar to what would later be dubbed in England a cottage industry. In Florence there were few cottages, but the practice was similar, with the raw material put out by factors to local homes, where the thread and cloth were produced.

But there was much more to the production of luxury cloth in Florence and other cities. To produce yarn and woven fabric required sophisticated treatment involving expensive chemicals and dies, usually done in large factorylike buildings by day laborers, who were not considered artisans. Early on in Florence these large buildings were clustered along the Calimala and near the Arno, as many of the chemical processes involved required a large amount of water. Thus, while this system of production cannot be equated to modern industrial production, it had some significant parallels: a large, relatively unskilled, and low-paid workforce; often dangerous and polluting manufacturing processes; and a portion of the labor carried out in large buildings dedicated to the industry. At the same time, however, it maintained more traditional modes of production: farming out work to homes, where it was done at times by women and families; employing highly skilled artisans for the crucial procedures; and placing an emphasis on a luxury product rather than mass production.

The emphasis on luxury production was an especially important difference between what we might call Rinascimento neo-industrial production and modern industrial capitalism. In England in the eighteenth and nineteenth centuries, what drove the cloth industry and the industrial revolution there, beyond the opening of new worldwide markets and the invention of new technologies of production, was the development of new technologies of transport that made both possible. Larger, more oceanworthy ships; a system of canals in Europe, and to a lesser degree elsewhere, that allowed heavy barge traffic; and eventually the railroad, all allowed the relatively inexpensive transport of large quantities of cheaper cloth and other materials, which when sold in quantity produced small returns per unit but high overall profits.

In the Rinascimento, lacking those technologies of transport, trade had to be carried out on a smaller scale, and that meant that luxury, high-quality products were the key to profitability. Spices, a mainstay of medieval long-distance trade for cities like Venice and Genoa, are a perfect example. Light and relatively inexpensive at their source, their price could be greatly marked up after their long journey to Europe, where they were otherwise unavailable and seen as a luxury. This produced large profits on relatively small quantities of goods. The same was true for luxury cloth, where quality, not quantity, ruled. This may help to explain why, although the period arguably had the mechanical and technical skills to construct complex geared machines such as clocks and mills, it did not see an industrial revolution. Its luxury-based economy and more limited transportation potential meant that large-scale production of products at low cost was generally not profitable or perhaps even conceivable. And actually, in those few areas where machinery was suited to luxury production, it was widely adopted and perfected.

It is easy to underestimate the importance of luxury cloth today, when a wide range of clothing is available at relatively modest cost. In the Rinascimento, however, luxury cloth was much less simple than modern cloth, involving elaborate weaves and dying procedures, creating a product much richer and finer. In fact, high-quality cloth and clothing for most upper-class people across Europe were the main discretionary expenses, often requiring as much as a quarter of a family's disposable income. In many ways the luxury cloth industry functioned like the modern luxury car industry. And like luxury cars today, fine clothing was an important social and economic marker – clothing literally did make the man and the woman. Indicative of this is the fact that throughout this period Italian cities passed over and over again sumptuary legislation limiting the cost of clothing that might be worn legally. Such legislation, officially touted as a means of conserving wealth because of the high cost of clothing, was often more concerned with enforcing the social distinctions that dress marked for society. Upper-class people like the *popolo grosso* could display their wealth within limits via their clothing, but lower-class people were not to attempt to confuse the issue by aping their superiors in their dress.

One thing that made this a potential danger was the fact that cloth and clothing were so well made that there was a lively trade in used clothing. In Florence, as in many other cities, there was even a guild of used clothing merchants, the Rigattieri. Thus lower-class people, especially those on the rise who were trying to claim a place among the *popolo grosso* by demonstrating via their clothing their growing wealth and status, could do so by buying cheaper used clothes. Interestingly, as mature males tended to dress soberly in order to stress their modesty and *virtù* – even if with expensive fabrics – the most visible display of upper-class wealth and status in clothing focused on the dress of women and to a lesser degree on that of youths, both male and female. In a way, *popolo grosso* women via their dress, became advertisements for the wealth and power of their families when they appeared in public, often in costumes featuring the newest styles or made with fabrics that showcased the most expensive dies or interwoven threads of gold and silver. In this context women's bodies were used to establish family standing: they were literally clothes horses, wearing clothing often invested in and owned by their husbands to show family power and status. All of which meant that the luxury cloth that Florence produced found a highly profitable market across the cities of northern Italy, as well as throughout much of Europe, where dressing expensively was also required of the nobility. It also meant that in Florence and other luxury-cloth-producing cities a number of skilled artisans earned substantial wages – almost certainly not enough to enter the ranks of the *popolo grosso*, but enough to give perhaps a greater weight to the *popolo minuto* there.

Historians usually see the guilds of Florence and other cities of the day as structuring economic life. In many ways that is true, especially if we mean by this that they disciplined the quotidian activities of work. At the highest levels of commerce, banking, and even cloth production, however, in most cities the guilds followed the lead of the most powerful *popolo grosso* families in a symbiotic relationship in which guilds were empowered by those families and in turn normally served their interests. At the lower levels of economic activity the interference of the *popolo grosso* in guilds was often more indirect and less clear. A closer look at the hierarchy of guilds in Florence provides a better sense of this dichotomy. The number of guilds in the city fluctuated throughout the period, but a representative sample is provided by the list of twenty-one guilds officially recognized by the Florentine Ordinances of Justice in 1293. Three levels of guilds were listed: the *arti maggiori* (major guilds), including Lawyers and Notaries, Calimala (merchants, dyers, and finishers of foreign cloth), Cambio (bankers and moneylenders), Lana (wool producers and merchants), Por Santa Maria (silk weavers and merchants), Medici e Speziali (doctors and apothecaries), and Furriers; the *arti medie* (middling guilds), including Butchers, Shoemakers, Blacksmiths, Builders, and Rigattieri (used clothing dealers); and the *arti minori* (minor guilds): Retail Wine Dealers, Inn Keepers, Sellers of Salt, Oil and Cheese, Tanners, Armorers, Ironworkers, Girdle Makers, Woodcutters, and Bakers.

Several things stand out in this ranking of guilds. First, the major guilds clearly were the domain of the *popolo grosso*. The large-scale wealth they produced is what fueled their economic, social, and political prominence. Lawyers and notaries might not seem to fit the mold, but a university degree and the ability to serve a crucial role in the legal and record-keeping regime of the *popolo grosso* meant that the leaders in this guild were often leaders in the city – their skills provided in a way both the technology of rule and commerce as well as the social and political ideology that went hand and hand with it. On the other end of the scale, furriers might seem to be relatively low-level craftsmen working with animal skins, but that actually was more the activity of the tanners (in the minor guilds), whereas the furriers focused on the international trade in luxury furs, a business that required a large capital investment and dealt with many of the same issues as the luxury cloth guilds.

At the middle level it might seem surprising to see butchers, as their craft involved rather bloody manual labor, but meat too was a luxury item, and thus butchers, with a more expensive product – and with a reputation for the violent defense of their place in society – found themselves ranked higher than bakers, whose craft supplied a basic everyday staple of life, the price of which was intentionally kept low. Shoes were also a relative luxury, as the poor usually wore wooden clogs; thus the shoemaker's higher status. At the lower levels clustered guilds that supplied everyday necessities, including wine, salt, oil, and cheese, along with the humble innkeepers who dotted Florence serving wine by the glass (or usually the cup), cheap food, cheap lodgings, and frequently cheap prostitution. Again it might seem strange to see armor makers and ironworkers in this group, but in Florence, both were minor industries making rather modest products for a largely local market. In other cities, where such production was more central to the economy, such as Milan, armor makers were a much more important craft and guild. Still, in this guild hierarchy one can see a general reflection of the economic, social, and political order of the city, and the *popolo* already dividing into *grosso* and *minuto*.

In its apparent clarity, however, this image of the guild world is deceptive. In Florence, for example, as was the case in most cities, the number of guilds misrepresents the number and range of craft activities in the city as well as the social divisions within the guilds themselves. Many no longer really involved craftsmanship in the traditional sense of the term, most notably the guilds of notaries and lawyers, bankers, and used clothing merchants. Moreover, many included multiple crafts. A good example of this is the guild to which Dante belonged, the guild of the Medici e Speziali (doctors and apothecaries), which included at the time of the Ordinances not only doctors and apothecaries, but also small-scale retail merchants, saddle makers, purse makers, and painters. Perhaps the most misleading thing about this guild hierarchy is the way in which, at the higher levels of wealth in the city, investors moved beyond guild structures by financing cloth production, investing in trade, or becoming partners in banking and credit operations. Thus, someone who was officially a member of the Cambio guild might actually be heavily involved in trade or cloth production, while an apparently humble butcher or even baker might have invested some surplus wealth in international trade or in land in the countryside. But such messiness at the individual level always undermines historical generalizations. On the whole, the key to understanding the upper levels of the system is to recognize that large investors or investing families from the *popolo grosso* worked through guilds at the same time that they also used government and informal networks of powerful families to control and drive the economy in their interests.

It is also important not to confuse these guilds with modern craft unions. Most of Villani's 30,000 workers in the cloth industry were disciplined by the Lana and Calimala guilds, but had no say in their operation. Many of them actually saw these guilds as their oppressor. To the extent that the guild set their low wages, ordered and defined their often difficult or even dangerous working conditions, and sternly disciplined resistance to those conditions, they were probably correct. Most guilds were actually dominated by the masters of the craft, and from their perspective the goal of the guild was to discipline those below, secure a monopoly of production for themselves, and assure a product that would be competitive in terms of price and quality. Guilds, like government, therefore saw nothing positive in higher wages or free markets; rather, they sought to corner markets, control workers, direct production, and organize trade to protect profits and assure the ultimate authority of masters.

Actually things were more complex yet. In many ways the operation of guilds during the period is still unclear, waiting for the patient study of scholars willing to work through the voluminous records that the guilds maintained, even if the impressive studies of scholars like John Najemy working on Florence have taken our understanding to new levels. More humble craft guilds appear to have been organized in a way that fits fairly well the ideal vision of a medieval guild. If we look at the baker's guild, for example, we find master craftsmen on top and apprentices learning the trade below them. The masters – those who had mastered the trade – had full voting rights in the guild and set the standards for the product, the levels of production, and the rules and disciplinary procedures for the guild and its members. The apprentices, usually younger men, who were learning the profession from the masters, had no voting rights in the guild, but were under its jurisdiction and largely at its mercy.

Yet even in such guilds, by the fourteenth century, things were no longer so simple, if they ever had been. Many apprentices, although they had mastered the craft, never became masters to open shops of their own. Because part of the goal of the guild was to control levels of production in order to maintain prices, keeping a constant level of masters and shops was important. Too many apprentices becoming masters and opening shops of their own was not seen as positive and was not encouraged. Moreover, low-paid apprentices had trouble saving the money to open a shop on their own and become a master. The result was that many apprentices remained apprentices long after they were qualified to become masters. A significant side effect of this was that the daughters and widows of masters (who inherited shops) often became highly sought-after marital partners for apprentices, as such marriages offered the possibility of gaining master status. In this way lower crafts leaned toward becoming virtually hereditary castes, at times through matriarchal lines. Also complicating the picture was the fact that much of an artisan's work – for example, a baker's craft – could be done by family members, especially wives and children. Thus, although women were officially excluded from most guilds, it appears that they could at times play a significant role in various crafts, both as workers and as the conduit through which some apprentices gained shops and master status.

When we look at the major guilds, things are even more complex and unclear. The Lana guild, for example, was run by "masters" who, rather than being master craftsmen, were usually the large-scale investors who dominated wool production. At the same time their guild included master craftsmen and apprentices who had mastered or were mastering the several craft skills involved in producing luxury cloth. The interrelationships among these groups within the guild is unclear, aside from the fact that the investors at the top controlled the guild, and the apprentices at the bottom had no say in running it. Moreover, even at the craft level of the guild, its activities were divided among various specialized skills organized around spinning, weaving, dyeing, and finishing the cloth. Finally, much of the actual labor was performed by unskilled laborers called *sottoposti* (literally, "those at the bottom"). Moreover, much of the work carried out for the guilds in homes, especially spinning, but also some weaving, was done by women and even children, who were often prized for their smaller, quicker hands. All of these people were in one way or another under the control of the guild, but had no say in its operation. Even if it is unclear how all this went together, we are evidently light years away from a craft guild of masters and apprentices working together in one trade.

Examining how the guilds were run reveals that these corporations were quite similar to the many other corporate bodies that typified the period and competed with each other for power. Normally guilds were run by an elected executive committee of the most powerful members, much like most governments. In addition, they usually had a large council made up of all masters or an elected body representing them that discussed and approved the suggestions of the executive committee or passed legislation on its own. This legislation not only regulated the practice of the craft, it also often regulated the life of those under the guild's control, imposing fines for misbehavior or requiring brotherly behavior. There were also guild courts that dealt with everything from economic disputes between guild members and infractions of guild regulations concerning production to the odd brawl, punch, or stabbing. They even had small magistracies concerned with internal finances, dues, fines, guild charities (including poor relief for workers), and, with growing significance, artistic commissions.

If this seems all rather like a government, it is because in many ways, as corporations, guilds were just another corporation competing for power, like government itself. As time passed governments would attempt to assert their superiority over other corporations and in the process transform themselves into the state – the corporation that dominated all the others in the name of the well-being of society. But that discovery of the state still lay largely in the future – an ideal of how government should be understood that developed during the Rinascimento and slowly became more powerful and dominant, as we shall see. In the early fourteenth century, in Florence and elsewhere, it seemed to many – and it was regularly claimed – that the guilds actually ruled the city, both in terms of controlling their own membership and in terms of their power over government. Officially, in fact, Florence was a guild republic, as the great guilds dominated elections and the formal structure of government, even if they themselves were largely dominated by the powerful rich of the city, the *popolo grosso*.

There was yet another competitor for power in Florence and in the Rinascimento more generally, and that was the often unrecognized elephant in the room, money. Needless to say, money was one of the central concerns of the *popolo grosso*, the guilds, and the government. But for all its importance, money in Florence, in other Italian cities, and across Europe was in its own right an extremely complex, often contested, and difficult-to-understand cultural creation. Virtually every city, principality, and kingdom in Europe had its own culture of money, its own monetary system and often coins in multiple forms composed of silver, copper, and (as time went on) gold, along with multiple levels of fictive (and thus culturally created and sustained) wealth as well. These various monetary systems made international trade especially difficult, and once again this was a situation that placed Florentine bankers working for the papacy at a considerable advantage over their rivals. With their networks of agents and allies spread across Europe dealing with local currencies and monetary cultures, Florentine bankers could make informed decisions at a level that most of their competitors simply could not match.

In the Middle Ages coinage was limited, with the larger coins used for trade being made with silver, primarily because silver was fairly widely available in Europe. The monetary system according to which these trading coins were conceptualized was based on the ancient Roman system of money, where twelve *denari* (*denarius* singular) equaled one *solidus*, and in turn twenty *solidi* equaled one *liber* or pound. This meant that one pound equaled 240 *denari*. These divisions, however, were essentially theoretical as most trade was carried out with silver coins usually described as multiples of a *denarius*; and local exchange, when it was not done in kind, often used copper coins or even more base metals that were conceived of as fractions of a *denarius*. In 1235 Florence began making a silver *solidus*, giving rebirth to a long dead form of Roman coinage. This was a move well suited to the expanding volume of trade in that century, as attested to by the fact that the move was quickly copied by other cities involved in trade and banking.

Shortly after the death of Frederick II, and as its banking firms were becoming established as papal bankers, the city began issuing a radically new coin in gold, the Florin, which was originally valued at one *liber*. By making the value of their Florin equivalent to the ancient Roman *liber*, they cleverly made their new coin once again safely old – a rebirth, a *rinascita*, not a dangerous novelty, even if (of course), it was new. The gold Florin rapidly became one of the most important trading coins in circulation, because it was ideally suited to the larger sums needed for international banking and trade. And the city jealously protected the reputation and honor of its new/ old coin, almost as is if it were a fictitious person, and a special citizen of Florence at that. Protecting its physical identity was extremely important because cutting off pieces of a coin, "clipping" or "shaving" (sanding off the edges) was widely practiced. Florence, like other cities, however, imposed stern penalties on clippers and shavers, including cutting off their hands, branding, and even death for repeat offenders, very similar penalties to those for assault and murder of actual citizens.

Protecting the honor of the Florin paid handsome dividends for trade and banking, but it also added complexity to the monetary system, which created the possibility for additional profits. For with the gold Florin, Italy and Europe went on a bimetallic system, especially as other major trading and banking cities began minting gold super-coins of their own. At the simplest level, with smaller coins in silver and larger coins in gold, the relationship between the value of silver coins and gold coins did not remain stable. As silver was regularly being mined in Europe, the supply of the metal was increasing steadily, which meant that its intrinsic worth was declining. At the same time the supply of gold in Europe was quite limited – hence its relatively stable, higher value – with only small amounts of new gold coming in, primarily from Africa and the Middle East. This meant that gold coins tended to hold stable or increase in value as silver coins slowly decreased in worth. In turn, the relationship between silver and gold coins and the old *denarius/solidus/liber* system broke down as silver coins decreased in worth and gold coins gained. For example, after 100 years in circulation a gold Florin that had originally been worth one *liber* or 240 silver *denari* was actually worth approximately 720 silver *denari* or three *libri*. Florentine bankers and moneymen recognized the advantage of this system, paying their workers and their daily expenses in depreciating silver coins while carrying on their own business in gold Florins. Thus they kept their profits steady, stable, and, perhaps most importantly, calculable in a fairly constant currency, while at the same time they allowed the real wages of their workers and their daily living expenses to slowly decline.

Not content with this advantage, and in an attempt to rationalize the complexity of the wide range of coinage that they encountered throughout Italy and Europe, Italian merchants and bankers saved the ancient Roman *denarius/solidus/liber* monetary system as an ideal money or, as it became known, a "money of account." Money of account was essentially a fictitious currency whose value was held constant against real coins of all types and metals. Bankers with international connections, like the Florentines, pegged individual coins and currencies to this theoretical money, regularly adjusting the exchange rate to reflect changing values in local currencies. This was even better than using gold coins, because if bankers were well informed, contracts could be written and trading carried out using this fictitious money, guaranteeing that a constant value would be maintained. Thus, for example, if a merchant signed a contract to deliver a shipment of wool cloth in London for 1,000 *libri* in money of account, he would know that whatever real local coin he would be paid in, it would be worth 1,000 *libri* in the end. As a result, if he bought that cloth in Florence with gold Florins worth 500 *libri* in money of account, and his shipping costs were paid, say, in Venetian ducats (another important gold coin) worth 200 *libri* in money of account, he could calculate that his real profit would be 300 *libri* in money of account, no matter what currency he was paid in. Not only did this system guarantee an ability to clearly calculate profits and avoid inflating or deflating real currency, it greatly increased the significance of bankers like the Florentines, who, with their network of agents and contacts spread across Europe, could best calculate the exchange rates that were key to the functioning of this system.

But money of account had another and even more significant impact. For as long as everyone involved had faith that real value stood behind it, it actually did not have to be retranslated into coin. Instead, this fictitious cultural construct was traded on its own as if it were real hard coin. Florentine merchant X who was owed 1,000 *libri* in money of account in London was credited with that 1,000 *libri* in his bank in Florence. He could in turn use that credited sum to buy 1,000 *libri* worth of cloth to ship to London to sell there at a price of 1,500 *libri*, and continue to repeat the cycle, slowly building up a larger and larger supply of wealth in his Florentine account without converting it back into gold Florins. After all, although one gold Florin was easier to cart around than 240 silver *denari*, converting them into actual coins was a problem when large sums were involved. Clearly it was much easier to move paper between banks than to move large hordes of metal coins. But, significantly, trading with money of account, as if it were real metal coins meant that Italy and Europe were no longer operating with the metallic and material wealth they actually had. Money of account essentially increased the wealth of Europe, making it extend as far as people's faith in money of account extended – culture in this case dramatically extending and transforming the material world.

There was one serious problem with this system of expanding European wealth, however – it required that those who believed in the fictitious value of money of account continue to believe. If they stopped believing and demanded their money in gold or silver coins, there simply was not enough gold or silver in Europe to cover the fictitious wealth. Unfortunately for Florentine bankers, that is exactly what happened in the early 1340s. Big banking firms had lent large amounts of money to the rulers of Europe, especially the king of England, and apparently at the same time had over-extended their investments in land in Tuscany. Although there is debate about whether the problem ultimately hinged on loans to European rulers or a dangerous overinvestment in land, when in 1342 the king of England reneged on his debts, major players in Florence began to demand that the money of account that the banks held for them be transformed into hard coin. But it simply did not exist. In fact, it could not have existed, since money of account had expanded the culturally created wealth of Europe well beyond its metallic or tangible wealth – nature, it might be said, finally had its revenge on culture. Without the resources to meet the demand, the banks collapsed; many fortunes were lost, and Florence entered a period of crisis that seemed to threaten *popolo grosso* power in the city. But in the end Florence revived, in part perhaps thanks to the great die-off and economic dislocation created by the plague in 1348. Florentine banking did so as well, with new banks replacing the old and once again drawing on the wealth and connections of the papacy.

But such reneging on debts, which brought many low, raises the issue of credit and the profits that Florentine banks made from loaning money. Credit had a special problem of its own in the Middle Ages and Rinascimento, for loaning money at interest was seen as the sin of usury, which, in theory, was highly frowned upon by the Catholic Church. Of course, the pope was quite willing to leave his money in Florentine banks, allowing it to accrue interest, and also quite capable of asking for loans that required interest payments. But this was actually not quite as hypocritical as it might sound, as bankers had worked out a number of ways to get around the sin of usury, lending money in ways that theoretically returned a profit without charging interest. The most widespread and successful strategy turned on exchanging currencies; thus the name used for banks and banking during the period (and still today in Italian) was *cambio* or exchange. Such exchange turned on the changing of one currency into another at a distance and over time in such a way that a profit could be made on the money originally paid out.

The most common form of fictitious exchange that covered a hidden
loan was the letter of credit. Essentially, a branch of a bank issued a letter of credit worth x amount in a local currency in another city. Ideally,
the person then went to that city and collected the money stipulated
in the letter and used it for his business there. He then returned to the
place where he had originally received the letter of credit and repaid the
value of the original letter in the currency of the city where it had been
issued. In theory, then, this was a simple exchange of money over time
and distance that put the banker's own money at risk. But the key to the
real nature of the arrangement was the time and distance involved and
the rate of exchange, all of which could be manipulated to make a hidden loan. As it took time to go from the original city of the loan to the
city where the money was to be delivered, carry out the transactions and
return, the letters could set a future date for repayment that in reality was
the period of the loan. The exchange rate could be set in such a way that
when the loan was repaid in another coinage, there was a hidden interest included, and this could be defended by the risk factor involved in
exchange rates potentially changing over the time involved in the travel
and trading. Thus a letter of exchange drawn up in Florence might call
for x number of Florins to be paid out in London as y number of English
pounds, which would then be repaid as x Florins plus the hidden rate of
interest in Florence six months later. In the end no one actually had to go
anywhere, as it was possible to merely return after the contracted period
to the Florentine bank where the letter had been drawn up and pay the
contracted amount, the distant city and the foreign currency becoming
just convenient fictions.

This was a truly ingenious way of lending money at interest. But because
there was actually some risk involved, as exchange rates could and did fluc-
tuate, bankers built a higher rate of interest into the exchange to try to assure
that they would make a profit whatever happened. As a result, the system
tended to mean that money that might have been lent at a straight return of,
say, 7 percent was lent at a higher rate of, say, 10 percent in order to assure a
profit. Also, because it was a very theoretical exchange, a convenient fiction,
it created considerable worry about its sinful nature, even among bankers.
Many, in fact, attempted to pay off their ultimate debt to God by admitting
their usurious practices in their wills and donating a portion of their sinful
gains to the Church or charitable causes, a practice that helped to enrich
churches and support their building and art patronage – sin nicely fueling art
and culture, as is surprisingly often the case. But it was a doubly costly system in terms of higher rates of interest and higher rates of sin – a curiously

unmodern combination that reminds us how different the period was, for all its seeming familiarity at times.

While the letter of credit was the most common form of loan at interest, many other ways of escaping the sin of usury were devised. In Venice and other maritime cities, the sea loan or variations on the theme were also popular. Basically, this employed a fiction whereby one partner was credited with a greater portion of the investment in a trading venture than had actually been contributed, because that partner was, in fact, covering via hidden loans one or some of the other investors' contributions. The larger return on that partner's investment actually repaid the hidden loan at a rate of interest that could be roughly calculated and would assure a profit on the money loaned. Again, however, because of the risk involved, that rate of interest was higher than it would probably have been with a straight loan.

Virtually from the first these papers of hidden credit also began to be traded as if they were money. For example, a bank did not need to hold a letter of credit for the full term of the loan, but could immediately turn around and sell it to someone else for a portion of the profit, or the person who owed money via a letter of credit could exchange it for another letter that matured later and at a higher rate of interest in order to extend the period of the loan. In this way what we might call an early form of commercial paper circulated and, much like money of account, expanded the pool of wealth available in Italy well beyond the amount available in the form of coins or material goods. Once again, however, this required that everyone accept the fiction that the wealth was really there, that the paper was actually redeemable at some time in the future. Not surprisingly – even if this is not a prevalent part of the myth of entrepreneurial economies – right from the start failures of nerve and faith in the culturally agreed-upon fictions of the economy meant that there would be repeated cracks and crises punctuated by bank failures and financial collapses.

From money to banking, merchant endeavors to luxury cloth manufacture, artisan production to grand entrepreneurs, Florence was a major player in the economic world of the early Rinascimetno, and the wealth the city gained in many ways pooled a significant portion of the wealth of the rest of Europe and the Mediterranean into the city, transforming it from a not-very-promising competitor in Tuscany at the beginning of the thirteenth century into one of the leading cities of Italy by the end of the fourteenth. This in turn helped to make it one of the leading cultural and artistic centers of Italy in the fifteenth century. Wealth perhaps did not directly produce its culture and art. But it certainly helped to make it possible in a number of ways that extended from simply freeing up human labor to pursue both, to creating the means to pay for it, and on to fomenting the social competition that used culture, art, and display to confirm social and economic status. But, perhaps most importantly, it helped draw the best and brightest to Florence and other rich Italian cities to pursue their dreams of fame and fortune. And in many ways it served, even with its all-too-fictitious nature at times, as the real catalyst that allowed greatness to blossom in the aftermath of one of the worst demographic disasters Europe ever faced. In the end the world did not end with the Black Death, whatever it really was – instead, the Rinascimento and its unique *civiltà* flourished.

4

VIOLENCE: SOCIAL CONFLICT AND THE ITALIAN HUNDRED YEARS' WAR (c. 1350–1454)

The New, New Men, and Violence

It might seem strange that in the century after the first wave of the plague and the demographic, economic, and social disruptions that followed, the Rinascimento enjoyed a cultural flowering that was flush with the sense of the superiority of its urban *civiltà*. Central to this was the fact that the *popolo grosso* had finally come to dominate most of the major cities of Italy as a political and social elite. And their victory was idealized and defended as an ongoing rebirth of first times and cultures that had been the best of times – thus the best of times were returning, literally being reborn. Such claims, and the political and social reality that stood behind them, never totally triumphed, however; in fact, if anything, the uncertainty about the extent and permanence of their victory played an important role in fueling the cultural flourishing of the time and the optimistic claims of the superiority of Italy's urban *civiltà*. And, significantly, such uncertainty was accompanied both by a wide range of open conflict and violence that, in an apparent paradox, also typified the cultural flourishing and by a sense of superiority that rose from the ashes of demographic disaster, social conflict, violence, and apparently unending war.

One challenge the *popolo grosso* perceived as particularly dangerous after the plague was the "new men" who seemed to threaten to destroy the order of urban life in city after city. These "new men" were often associated with large numbers of rural youths attracted to cities by opportunities to replace the ranks of artisans and workers lost to the plague. Their ranks were also swollen, however, by dislocated urban males who were suddenly without significant family ties or who had moved from one city to another seeking better working conditions. To a degree, as we shall see, imagination also increased their ranks, for their newness made them a convenient scapegoat for apparently growing levels of urban disorder and violence that turned on broader social and economic tensions. The violence of these young males was attributed in part to their youth, in part to their lack of acculturation to the more orderly civil life required in densely packed urban spaces – now legally required by the restrictions that urban governments had promulgated and attempted to enforce with their policing patrols. The few recorded criminal statistics that we have for the period reveal that crime rates after the plague remained virtually the same as before and continued at similar levels into the fifteenth century – data that seem to suggest that "new men" and their youthful, rural ways actually were an important factor in the violence, managing to make up (at least in terms of violence) for smaller urban populations.

This was almost certainly the case. But to a degree this startling continuity in crime in the face of large population losses may also be attributed to the fact that governments, for all their growth in the first half of the century, never had the capability to prosecute all the violent crimes committed. In reality few societies do, even modern, much more efficiently policed ones. Thus, pre-plague prosecutions represented merely the tip of a larger iceberg of violence. From that perspective, when a large part of the population died off, the bureaucracy merely dug deeper into that iceberg, and prosecutions continued at much the same level – essentially the level bureaucracies were able to sustain both before and after the plague. Yet after the plague many young males did take advantage of the increased demand for urban workers and moved to the city, creating an unusual concentration of young men lacking urban living skills. This almost certainly created a more violent urban environment and, in turn, more concern about youthful violence, followed by more aggressive attempts to maintain and strengthen bureaucracies in order to repress such violence. It comes as no surprise, then, that the number of policing magistracies and patrols in most cities continued to increase in the second half of the fourteenth century, even in the face of dramatic population declines. Moreover, it was during this very period that in many cities the older *Podestà* system of justice, discussed in Chapter 2, was augmented by local policing and judicial bureaucracies.

Much of this violence, when lumped together and considered from a statistical perspective, seems the senseless violence of youth in response to perceived minor slights or moments of petty conflict. And that is an accurate picture of the situation in many ways. But behind such generalizations lie the deeper tensions of an urban world that was especially difficult to cope with for young men, especially when they were fresh from the countryside, without family support or the discipline created by consensus realities for those better integrated into the urban social fabric. Moreover, masculine ideals, in both rural and urban society, expected young men to be active, masculine, and powerfully male. But the reality of their economic and social existence meant that they were often poor, dependent on others for their work, and in precarious positions that they and others perceived as not particularly masculine at all. In that context every slight, real or imagined, every minor offense, every petty conflict offered the tempting opportunity to demonstrate aggression, power, and masculinity, and the records of violent crime suggest that many young men did just that – probably many more than the records indicate.

Of course, this was not just a question of gender or masculine identity. Much violence was predicated upon real or perceived economic and social issues; for while most youths came to the city to secure economic and social advancement, and some actually succeeded, most were doomed to live on the economic and social margins, where violence was often a response to that fate. Finally, obviously, violence could also be a useful skill: often the strongest and most aggressive males, with their ability to dominate and intimidate others, were seen as valuable by those who could use their violence for more profitable ends. A physically powerful and violent young man could be a valued client or *bravo* for the powerful who felt the need to protect their families or their enterprises from the violent tenor of city life, or who wished to use violence for other purposes of their own.

Rising expectations are often cited as yet another reason for a higher level of violence. The need for workers following the demographic losses of the plague created a deeply conflicted situation. Governments and guilds were forced to raise wages, lower requirements for guild membership and citizenship, and offer a range of other incentives in order to attract labor from other cities and the countryside. This certainly raised the expectations of those attracted by such incentives. But at the same time governmental leaders and guild masters were not eager to give up too much to the new men they attracted with the promise of a more secure economic life and the possibility of advancement. Thus they quickly invented ways to keep new men in place and to limit their access to wealth and power. It was a dangerous balancing act between reward and regulation – often in the name of peace, order, and stability – and when it broke down, as it often did, the result was again violence on both the individual and the collective level. Actually, it might be suggested that this difficult balancing act contributed to the fear of new men as much as their actual violence. For the leaders of society were almost certainly aware that, although they wanted to attract new men with promises of labor and wealth, they were not really all that eager to share their wealth with them in any significant way.

The New, the Old, and the Ciompi Rising in Florence

Florence provides a good example of this situation. New men – real and imagined – became a negative theme of the political, social, and economic struggles of the city after the plague. As elsewhere, they were blamed for virtually all the problems confronting the city, as they in turn pressed to secure their place in their new urban world. The result was growing tension marked by an ongoing series of conflicts, which came to a head in the summer of 1378 with what appeared to many at the time to be an attempted revolution led by new men and the *popolo minuto*. As usual, things were not so simple. For in many ways old men – from the powerful old families of the city – were equally if not more responsible, even if the first wave of open violence seemed to feature those at the bottom of society. On June 22, large numbers of guildsmen and workers who were not voting members of the guilds for which they labored but under their control nonetheless – the *sottoposti* discussed earlier – went into the streets and, with considerable violence, burned the houses of a number of the older families of the city. Their violence was not random, for the houses they burned belonged to families whom they feared were using the Guelph party apparatus to control the government and implement policies that they believed were victimizing them. As will be discussed more fully later, those fears were not without some basis and suggest a political awareness among the lower classes that is often discounted.

Yet another form of violence typical of the day, war, made this explosive moment yet more explosive. As discussed briefly in Chapter 1, in the 1360s the warrior Cardinal Egidio Albornoz had had considerable success temporarily regaining for the papacy much of the Papal States in central Italy. His successes created tensions with Florence's own program of territorial expansion to the east and south, as the two powers' borders came uncomfortably close, with concomitant conflicting territorial claims and ambitions. Although things were more complex, as we will see, in the face of this situation Florence decided to fight a war against the papacy, which would become known as the War of the Eight Saints (1375–1378), named after the special committee or *Balìa* of eight that led the war effort. As the name Eight Saints suggests, a war between a traditional Guelph city like Florence and the pope, the official leader of the Guelph party, created problems politically, rhetorically, and in terms of the legitimacy of government. Labeling the leaders of the war efforts "saints" was a way of claiming that Florence was following the truly Christian path in this war while the pope and his generals were not: Florentine saints were squared off against a corrupt pope and Church.

Needless to say, at such moments the tradition of associating government with civic morality and creating a truly Christian urban *civiltà* proved useful, greatly aiding such claims. The pope was distant and corrupt; Florentine government was close at hand, moral and committed to defending a truly Christian city. In the early stages of the war this vision found wide support in Florence, but as the war dragged on, the leadership of the local Guelph party began to mobilize discontent and question the saintliness of the conflict in an effort to gain control of government. Their goal appears to have been to secure power for a limited number of older families and to eliminate new families and lesser guildsmen who had become more competitive after the plague. The key to their strategy played upon the party's traditional power to disqualify from holding governmental office those perceived to be Ghibelline traitors. In addition to blocking access to offices in this way, they also made use of *ammonizioni* (official warnings issued by the party) that alerted individuals to the fact that the party suspected them of being Ghibellines. If one ignored the party's *ammonizione* and was demonstrated to be a Ghibelline, the penalties could be severe, including banishment and confiscation of a family's property. What gave teeth to this threat was the fact that, because they had supported the war against the papacy, most people in Florence could be charged with secret Ghibelline leanings as that party traditionally opposed the papacy.

Things came to a head as 1377 ended and 1378 began with literally thousands of denunciations being processed by the Guelph party and almost one hundred citizens, mostly from the newly rich, being warned via formal *ammonizioni* not to attempt to hold office. Still, at least in theory, the guilds of Florence dominated government and should have been capable of standing up to the Guelph party. Guild membership remained necessary for holding virtually all offices in the city, and guild leadership, especially of the more powerful guilds, tended as a result to overlap closely with city leadership. Following the plague, however, the lesser guilds and those workers controlled by the larger and more powerful cloth guilds – the majority of the *sottoposti* – had begun to press for more power in government and for new guilds to represent even the *sottoposti*. That, crucially, would have changed them from *sottoposti* to guild members with voting and political rights like the other members of the guild community.

Thus, to make a complex and rather fluid situation more straightforward than it ever was, when the Guelph party used its power to label people Ghibelline with moderation, as it did before the War of the Eight Saints, the power of the richer and more traditionally powerful guilds was unthreatened, and they tended to work with the Guelph party to maintain *popolo grosso* control of government, even if occasionally a lesser guildsman or a newer man held an important office. When, however, the Guelph party over-reached and began to label leaders of the major guilds and a few members of the *popolo grosso* itself as Ghibellines in the late 1370s, that alliance broke down and the more powerful guilds turned to the lesser guilds, evoking traditional guild solidarity against Guelph party pretensions. In this delicate balancing act, real new men, perceived new men, and the lower levels of the *popolo minuto*, with their demands for greater power, were the catalysts.

The breaking point came in the hot summer days of June 1378 when Salvestro de' Medici (c. 1331–1388) – a family name with a future – as Standard Bearer of Justice called for a renewal of the old Ordinances of Justice. Originally passed at the end of the thirteenth century to eliminate from government those families labeled magnates, as we saw in Chapter 1, the Ordinances were still officially the law of the land, even if they had largely fallen into disuse. It appears that behind this particular rebirth lay a plan to use the Ordinances and their provisions against magnates and to turn the labeling game against the leaders of the Guelph party. If those leaders were labeled magnates by the terms of the Ordinances, they faced stern punishments, both politically and economically. This threat, wrapped in an appeal to return to the great guild and *popolo* traditions of the city that the Ordinances exemplified, was not lost on the leaders of the Guelph party, who quickly mobilized their supporters in government against Salvestro's proposal. It was at this moment that the workers went into the streets, attack-ing and burning not just any houses of the rich, but those of the most impor-tant leaders of the Guelph party. Virtually as those palaces were burning, the government approved a Balìa – a special committee with the full power of government – headed by Salvestro and the leaders of the city's guilds to deal with the deeper issues involved.

Using the Ordinances of Justice, as he had threatened, Salvestro and the Balìa labeled several leaders of the Guelph party magnates. In turn, they declared that a number of those recently labeled Ghibelline were actually good Guelphs and thus eligible to hold office. This relatively contained strike against the Guelph party quickly got out of hand, in large part because the driving force behind the violence that had been used to initiate it was based on an appeal to a renewal of guild power and traditional *popolo* ideals. But, while those ideals served well the *popolo grosso* in power in their struggle with the Guelph party, they also could serve the lesser guilds in their demands for more power. And the appeal of such ideals did not stop there, for new men and *sottoposti* under the control of the larger guilds saw in the reasser-tion of guild power a rationale for creating guilds of their own in order to participate in the political and economic life of the city. Thus, the agitation in the streets did not stop with the elimination of the powerful leaders of the Guelph party, but continued to simmer as a hot June slid uneasily into July.

Things came to a boil in mid-July, when a number of leaders of the *popolo minuto* were arrested and tortured in response to reports that they were holding secret meetings to demand that new guilds be created for the *sottoposti* and that the forced loan policies that favored the upper classes be eliminated. This brought large masses of people back into the streets on July 20. Again, select palaces of the rich were burned. Negotiations were attempted, fitfully interspersed with violence in the streets, until on July 22 Michele di Lando (1343–1401), one of the more charismatic leaders of the *popolo minuto*, leading a large crowd, took over the halls of government and declared himself Standard Bearer of Justice. As bells rang throughout the city signaling their victory, Lando and his supporters declared the old Priors deposed and radically reordered the government, placing new men and leaders of the *popolo minuto* in many of the key positions of power.

But what most impressed contemporaries and gave this revolt its name and the flavor of a truly radical revolution was the creation of three new guilds for the *sottoposti*: one for dyers, washers, and other skilled workers in the cloth industry; one for shirt makers, tailors, and others lesser artisans in clothing production; and one for unskilled textile workers (the mass of the *sottoposti*), who were called the Ciompi – perhaps in reference to the noise their wooden clogs made as they marched through the streets. This was the moment of maximum success for what would become known as the Ciompi rising or revolution. One contemporary estimated that the Ciompi guild alone included 9,000 workers and that altogether the three new guilds comprised 13,000 men. When added to the approximately 9,000 in the older guilds, all of a sudden the guild community grew to approximately 22,000 men in a population of 55,000 men and women. If these numbers are correct, they imply that the vast majority of men in the city had become actual voting members in guilds and had the right to be elected to communal government. One hesitates to speak of democracy, but this was probably as close to that ideal as any government ever came in the Rinascimento. New men were in; *sottoposti* were no longer *sottoposti*; the guilds and government were in the hands of virtually the whole *popolo*. Political reality appeared for once to have caught up with rhetoric and ideology.

Yet this was far too radical a revolution to survive in a world where, economically and socially, things were stacked heavily in favor of the *popolo grosso*; and to make its survival even less likely, the revolution did not stop. In August, leaders of the new guilds, especially the Ciompi, attempted to interfere more aggressively in elections, apparently in an endeavor to assure that their new power would not be challenged. For many of the older, richer, and more traditionally powerful guilds, this seemed to confirm that they were in danger of losing power to the lesser guilds. Fighting soon broke out in the streets, with the older guilds, led now by Michele di Lando, squaring off against the Ciompi. Unfortunately for the Ciompi, even the other two new guilds broke ranks to align with the older ones, and they found themselves outnumbered and overwhelmed by the better-organized guild militias rallied against them. At the end of the day a number of Ciompi leaders were killed in the street battles, and most of the rest quietly disappeared.

On September 1, 1378, the Ciompi guild was formally abolished and the twenty-three guilds that remained divvied up control of government among themselves. For the moment it seemed that a still fairly representative guild government ruled the city, one with room for members of the *popolo minuto* and new men. But the reality was that the leaders of the major guilds and the *popolo grosso* had learned their lesson. Slowly but surely they rolled back the gains of the revolution and put in place reforms that secured their control of the city. By 1382 most of the reforms of the revolution had been undone; the *popolo grosso* were back in the driver's seat, having incorporated into their number a few of the richest and most powerful of the newer families and newer men; and behind the scenes, one powerful family from the topmost ranks of the *popolo grosso*, the Albizzi, was soon playing on anxious memories of the Ciompi and rising to corrupt the electoral process and control government using techniques that would be adopted and perfected by the Medici in the next century.

Although few other cities had revolutionary moments that were so visible – or successful, for that matter – the violence encountered in many cities in the second half of the fourteenth century and the early years of the fifteenth often had strong overtones of social and economic conflict, with new men, imagined new men, and the lower classes arrayed in various alliances against the ever-more in control and progressively more aristocratic *popolo grosso*. At the same time it also served the purpose of the *popolo grosso* to label those who opposed their power "new men," as the label suggested their dangerous and negative novelty. From this perspective, much as suggested earlier, a significant portion of the apparently senseless petty violence in the streets of cities, much decried at the time, was not without a social dimension. At the same time, however, violence in the form of warfare often played a role in such social conflict, for its cost and its impact on the urban lower classes and the rural peasantry often brought to the fore and strengthened deeper social tensions.

The Italian Hundred Years' War (c. 1350–1454)

Although the name has not been used before, much like the famous Hundred Years' War in northern Europe between France and England (1337–1453), a period of approximately one hundred years of almost continual strife among the city-states of northern Italy from 1350 to 1454, which might be labeled the Italian Hundred Years' War, had a profound impact on the society and economy of Italy as well as on the cultural flowering of the day. Actually, to a certain extent, the northern European Hundred Years' War helped to make Italy's own Hundred Years' War possible. First, as that northern war occupied the military and aggressive energies of two of the most powerful realms in Europe north of the Alps – France and England – and captured much of the attention of the rest of the region, it left the city-states of Italy relatively free to pursue their own local aggressive expansion without outside interference. Perhaps the most significant exception to this overly broad generalization was the papacy, which first from Avignon and then from Rome attempted to reestablish its territorial power base in Italy, contributing to the ongoing warfare.

Moreover, although many of the battles of the northern Hundred Years' War were fought by feudal levies of noble warriors and their retainers, with increasing frequency and success professional soldiers were used. Early on, during lulls in that ongoing series of conflicts, many of those professional soldiers found their way to northern Italy, where they fought in the Italian Hundred Years' War, and many stayed on to make their fortune in Italy. Known as *condottieri* – the name given to mercenary soldiers in Italy – they were joined by locals from old branches of Italian noble families like the Visconti of Milan or by the *signori* of smaller cities. Many, however, were northerners like Sir John Hawkwood (c. 1320–1394), an English mercenary who had fought in the north of Europe, but after moving to Italy enjoyed a long, successful career leading a mix of Italian and northern soldiers known as the White Company (Illustration 4.1). The most important *condottieri* armies were called the Great Companies and were often led by elected leaders (once again corporations or corporate groups much in the spirit of the day) who sold their services to the highest bidder and wielded great power.

In many ways these mercenary armies, with their elected leaders, were like great mobile guilds or even cities made up primarily of young men and their supporting camp followers, who were often as numerous. Normally they lived off the land, utilizing a mix of violent appropriation of local wealth and pay from contracts that were awarded them to fight for (or not against) the territories they traversed. In this way they could be as much of

4.1. Paolo Uccello, *Sir John Hawkwood*, 1436, Florence Cathedral (Duomo). Photo: Scala/ Art Resource, New York.

a burden on the cities and countryside of Italy in peacetime as when they fought, for, much like feudal armies, they were often a moving plague on the countryside. This extra cost of premodern warfare is often forgotten, but the passing of armies regularly meant a generation of dearth as peasants labored to rebuild lost herds and flocks, recover seed stocks taken, and even to replant trees and vines that had been destroyed. Actually, *condottieri* armies were frequently more devastating in this respect, because, unlike feudal levies, they were less likely to disband and return home after a campaigning season, instead living off the countryside they traversed for long periods.

While Hawkwood was one of the best-known *condottieri*, fairly early on Italians came to dominate the trade. The victory of Alberico da Barbiano (c. 1344–1409) and his Company of San Giorgio in 1379, against a powerful French army that was threatening Rome, is often cited as a moment that confirmed the superiority of Italian *condottieri* and their tactics. Those tactics favored a mix of highly skilled warriors who fought on horseback, using complex cavalry formations and maneuvers that less well-trained feudal levies had trouble matching, and well-armed and equipped foot soldiers whose training and experience made them superior to local militias, especially in facing cavalry charges. Alberico's camp became in a way the training ground for those who would master this Italian *arte* of *condottieri* warfare. Perhaps the most noted *condottieri* trained there were Braccio da Montone (1368–1424) and Muzio Attendolo (1369–1424), who became better known under his nickname, Sforza. They, in turn, founded the two most famous schools of Italian *condottieri*, the Bracceschi and the Sforzeschi, each of which developed its own traditions, loyalties, and techniques of warfare. Although drawn from all classes and all parts of Italy, especially important were the petty nobility from the more rural regions of the center and north, especially the Romagna and the Marches. They found in *condottieri* warfare a way to continue the military traditions that had once made their families a powerful nobility.

The system also offered some opportunity for upward mobility, with even peasants occasionally rising to lead great companies. Francesco Carmagnola (1380–1432) is one of the better-known examples. He played an important role, serving at different times both Milan and Venice in the early fifteenth century before coming to an unhappy end at Venetian hands, as we shall see. The lords of smaller cities also were often involved in *condottieri* warfare, at times to consolidate their local political power with their military prowess, and regularly to supplement their revenues with military earnings. Most notable in this were the Gonzaga lords of Mantua, the Malatesta of Rimini, and the Este of Ferrara and Modena, all willing to hire themselves out to lead armies from time to time and thereby earning both money and fame to aid their rule. Even an occasional church leader became an outstanding *condottiere*, perhaps most notably Cardinal Giovanni Vitelleschi (c. 1390–1440), who fought for the papacy and became virtual *signore* of Rome for a time in the late 1430s.

In Italy, then, *condottieri* warfare became the norm. The marginalization of the old warrior nobilities, and the slow but sure incorporation of their richer and more flexible peers into the *popolo grosso*, meant that there no longer existed a sufficiently large or well-trained noble military class in or around the major cities to fight their wars. More importantly, those who wished to continue that life had to adapt to a new, more commercial approach to warfare that was more suited to cities ruled by the *popolo grosso*, who much preferred to pay for warriors rather than submit to their power. Most cities also had civil militias, usually based on neighborhood and/or guild militias, and had on the books formal provisions for training and arming them. In fact, these militias were used regularly, especially to aid in the defense of their cities or to swell the numbers of foot soldiers put into the field for decisive battles.

But by the second half of the fourteenth century (and usually well before) city governments had come to realize that professional soldiers, with their superior tactics, training, and skills, were the key to victorious campaigns. In turn, that meant that money to pay *condottieri* was the sine qua non of successful warfare. Thus, significantly for a merchant-banker *popolo grosso* vision of the world, warfare became largely a matter of successful management of funds and investment for return – investment in *condottieri* to increase a city-state's territory and markets, and often to eliminate competitors. In this way warfare was transformed from a form of violence that was an integral part of the way of life of a medieval nobility to an investment in violence with an eye toward economic gain; and thus it was neatly reintegrated into the way of life of the new *popolo grosso* elite of the Rinascimento.

At a very general level, the primary cause of these one hundred years of Italian warfare – always with local variations and conditions – was the competition for markets and territory among the many little cities that dotted the north of Italy. In this respect the Italian Hundred Years' War tended to be quite different from the dynastic wars of northern Europe or the south of Italy, driven by family and claims of inheritance. For as cities expanded their control over the territory farther and farther from their city walls in order to gain secure food supplies, exercise control over land and over lines of communication and trade, and dominate markets, they invariably encountered neighboring cities following the same trajectory of expansion. From time to time momentary accommodations were worked out, but without higher authorities such as the papacy or the empire to negotiate disputes over boundaries and territorial aspirations, warfare was a common solution. Reduced populations following the plague, increased competition for markets, along with the significant number of mercenary soldiers available – often aggressively pressing for contracts to fight – all accelerated the aggressive expansion of larger and more powerful cities at the expensive of their weaker neighbors.

The Florentine War of the Eight Saints and the Italian Hundred Years' War

In many ways Florence's strange War of the Eight Saints with the papacy suggests the complexity of these wars. Although Florence prided itself on being a Guelph city, in the mid-fourteenth century the papacy had begun a campaign to regain the papal territories in central Italy as well as Rome, which had fallen out of papal control while the papacy was in Avignon. Pope Innocent VI (c. 1282–1362; pope 1352–1362) in 1353 appointed a legate and tough warrior, Egidio Albornoz (1310–1367), to regain control of Rome and the Papal States, where many cities had been taken over by powerful local families ruling as *signori*. Albornoz, with a mix of military force and diplomacy, slowly reestablished papal authority in both. Florence, however, was not happy to see the return of papal power in the Papal States, in part because much of the area bordered their own territories and in part because a renewed powerful papal neighbor interfered with their own dreams of expansion. Weaker local *signori* seemed far less dangerous as neighbors and far easier to manipulate than a renewed Papal State slowly expanding on their borders.

Things came to a head in 1375 when Pope Gregory XI (c. 1329–1378; pope 1370–1378) was freed from a military conflict with Milan that had taken much of his attention and resources. Florence feared that this meant he was also freed to turn his aggressive interests to their common borders. Making matters worse, Gregory's main *condottiere*, John Hawkwood, was lurking near those borders with a large army that they feared might be used to "liberate" towns subject to Florence and perhaps to attack the city itself. Thus, in the spring of 1375, just before the campaigning year was to begin, the Florentines made what they saw as a wise investment. They hired Hawkwood for themselves for the princely sum of 130,000 Florins. Actually they hired him not to fight for them, but rather not to fight against them. How the pope felt about this is unclear, but his feelings toward the Florentines were definitely undermined when they appointed a special Balìa of eight important civic leaders to find the money; for, far too cleverly, the Balìa decided that the cost would be covered by a forced loan on the local clergy in Florentine territories. Clearly this did not sit well with the local clergy or the papacy. But before either had time to react, in July the Balìa definitively broke its traditional Guelph alliances to align with the leading Ghibelline city of the north, Milan. No one missed the significance of this, and war broke out immediately.

But with Hawkwood safely bought, little was accomplished, and the war settled down to a few bloody sacks of hapless small towns; meanwhile, Florence worked diplomatically to undermine the pope by fomenting revolts throughout the Papal States. The pope, in turn, trotted out his spiritual heavy guns and proclaimed an interdict against Florence. Florence responded with its own ideological weapons, claiming to be defending republican liberty and the guild regime of the *popolo* against the return of papal tyranny and corruption in Italy. Such claims had a particularly strong resonance for many of the little cities of the Papal States, which had, over the years, with the papacy at Avignon, established independent governments of their own. In fact, such claims even garnered sympathy in cities where local *signori* ruled, often with the support and cooperation of the *popolo* and guilds. Better a local lord who had some understanding of, and need to appease, local interests than a distant powerful one whose agendas were driven by the dangerously distant concerns of Avignon and French cardinals.

Thus when the soon-to-be-famous Florentine chancellor, Coluccio Salutati (1331–1406), wrote letters to cities that were formally part of the Papal States like Bologna and Perugia, he deployed his developing rhetorical powers, claiming that papal claims to rule them were illegitimate because, as cities with a strong guild and *popolo* tradition, they deserved their liberty from the tyranny of a corrupt papacy. He argued that, like Florence, they had been and should continue to be ruled by "merchants and guildsmen, who naturally love liberty" and should not be subjected to a distant and corrupt lord like the pope. Later in the century Salutati would return with greater insistence to these same claims when Florence faced off against Milan and its lord, Gian Galeazzo Visconti, as we will see. But for the moment he supported Florentine war efforts with a series of impressive paper battles that helped to consolidate widely shared ideals of Rinascimento *civiltà* in a powerful synthesis that stressed that only as an active citizen in a republic could one live a full and meaningful Christian life. Such expressions of civic morality – the morality fostered by living a civic life in a Christian city – were not new and not solely Florentine, but rather the much more general

phenomenon of a legitimating ideology associated with republican governments and guild regimes.

But, returning to the War of the Eight Saints, neither propaganda nor
minor massacres moved the war ahead. The pope's interdict, however, with
time became a festering wound that made a difference. It forbade all priestly
functions in the city, including masses, communion, last rites, burial in
consecrated ground, and a whole host of public religious events that punctuated daily urban life. For a while it was successfully ignored. As the name
given to the leaders of the war effort, the Eight Saints, suggests, Florentines
claimed aggressively that they were the true Christians and their leaders the
true saints, not the corrupt and worldly pope, living in distant Avignon in
lordly exile from his bishopric in Rome. Thus the interdict at first touched
off in the self-styled Christian republic a great outpouring of spiritual fervor,
with religious festivals, pageants, processions, and fasting, along with public
prayer and displays of holiness, becoming the order of the day. But for all
that, masses, communion, and the other services normally provided by the
Church were effectively stopped, which in the long run gradually allowed
the interdict to weigh on the population and create unrest.

Over the long run the interdict also had a significant economic impact as
it forbade rulers throughout Europe to do business with Florentine bankers. While this was a serious threat, Florentine banking was an important
base for much of the commercial economy of Europe, so it was not readily
accepted. Moreover, the ability of Florentine bankers to sustain rulers with
regularly needed loans when revenues fell short of expenditures often made
them more necessary allies than a relatively weak and distant pope. As a
result, using a series of clever ploys, rulers and bankers survived the interdict, although not without some real losses and difficulties. The real problem
developed when Florentine authorities counterattacked on the economic
front, confiscating and selling Church property to finance the war. This was
not just a clever and profitable strategy; it was a dangerous precedent and
serious threat, as the Church was one of the largest owners of property not
just in Florentine territory, but across Europe. And while the property confiscated was a costly loss, it was even more damaging as a precedent that
might tempt other rulers.

Compounding the problem was a continuing current of religious thought
that claimed that the Church should not own property and that its wealth
and property were a major reason for its corruption. This position had been
pressed by more radical Franciscans and their recently declared heretical
offshoot, the Franciscan Spirituals, who saw themselves as continuing Saint
Francis's call for a life of Christlike poverty, not just for individuals but also

for the Church. Similar ideals of a propertyless church had also long perco-
lated in Florence itself, where this ideal was now to a degree encouraged. In
this context, war with the papacy also helped to revive the Joachite prophecy
of the proximate arrival of the third and last age of the Holy Spirit. As will
be remembered, that last age, according to Joachim's prophecies, would be
preceded by the destruction of the corrupt Church and papacy, an event that
Florence certainly seemed to be doing its best to bring about. Not surprisingly, then, a number of proponents of such prophecies, led by well-known
supporters of the Franciscan Spirituals, began to appear in Florence and take
an increasingly prominent role in the religious life of the city.

We see here once again that the violence of war was rich with dangers for
the status quo, well beyond the more easily appreciated economic dangers
caused by the cost of *condottieri* armies. Florence, in appealing to guild republicanism and *popolo* values, opened the door for both to be turned against
the status quo, as we have seen in the Ciompi revolt. Similarly, attacks on
the corruption and worldly wealth of the Church provided an opportunity
for much more radical attacks, not only on the Church and the papacy, but
also on property and the social order of the day – ironically, in the name of
a rebirth of first Christian times. Behind such deep disjunctures in a shared
cultural vision lay the seeds of revolution and violence and, at the same time,
of cultural creativity and flowering. Both were the order of the day.

Meanwhile, the pope had attempted to return the papacy to Rome with
limited success. Arriving in Rome in January of 1377, he was forced to flee
the city from May to November while pursuing the war with some notable
success. In the spring his armies actually retook Bologna, a key city in the
old Papal States that crucially controlled the primary pass road that connected Florence to the north of Italy. And in the early fall, with mounting
concerns in Florence about the lack of regular religious services, the government there took the radical step of ordering the Florentine clergy to defy
the interdict and begin saying masses. Rather than solving the problem, this
merely exacerbated it and further strengthened the pope's position.

Few were really satisfied with the order. Most priests and clergy submitted,
but many, both clergy and laity, harbored doubts about whether the renewed
religious services were valid, given the papal interdict. To make matters
worse, a few church leaders refused to obey and fled the city. Confiscation
of Church property accelerated, seeming also to confirm the government's
support of the Spirituals' call for a Church shorn of its property. Making
matters worse, it was precisely at this moment that the Florentine Guelph
party began more aggressively to label their enemies Ghibellines and use the
ammonizione to force many out of government. As virtually everyone who

had supported or continued to support the war with the papacy was suscep-
tible to such charges, the old guard leadership of the Guelph party may have
seen government as theirs for the taking – a serious miscalculation that the
Ciompi rising, which followed in short order, made violently clear.

As 1377 slid uneasily into 1378, the divisions within Florence and the weight
of the continuing cost of the war seemed to make the dark clouds of the
first spring rains loom darker yet. But March showers brought the death of
the pope, and although April did not bring the flowers of peace, a settlement
was finally agreed to in July. It cost Florence dearly, requiring an indemnity
of 250,000 florins. In addition, on the difficult issue of confiscated Church
property, the Florentines agreed to return all the land and wealth taken *eventually*. The problem was that the government also agreed to first repay those
who had bought Church property for their loss. With the communal treasury
empty, that meant that the restitution would be *very* eventual. Meanwhile,
Florence promised to pay the Church 5 percent interest on the estimated value
of the property and wealth taken, until it was returned. Thus, significantly and
unexpectedly, the Church found itself defending Florentine interests in the
end, as Florentine success guaranteed its regular 5 percent return on what had
become essentially its large investment in the Florentine public debt.

Perhaps if the papacy had been stronger, the long-term commitment to
restore the confiscated wealth of the Church would have been a serious
brake on the Florentine economy and a long-lasting legacy of a small war
that turned into a costly disaster. Fortunately for Florence, however, the new
pope, Urban VI (c. 1318–1389; a pope 1378–1389), had a plethora of more
immediate problems to deal with. Most notably, his election and his commitment to also return to Rome caused a split in the College of Cardinals,
with a splinter group electing a second pope, Clement VII, whose election
began the almost half-century of multiple popes known as the Great Schism.
Florence took advantage of this division in the Church, playing one pope
off against another; thus thirty years after the peace that officially ended the
war, it has been estimated that almost 90 percent of the land and wealth
confiscated by Florence still had not been returned. In the long run, then, it
is not clear who won the War of the Eight Saints. In the short term, however,
peace did not stop the accelerating divisions in Florentine society that war
had accentuated, and, as we have seen, the war and its peace were deeply
intertwined with the violence in the streets and the attempted revolution of
the Ciompi rising and its aftermath.

The violence of that attempted revolution was, however, just a short
and frightening interlude for Florence in the broader context of the Italian
Hundred Years' War. In fact, at much the same moment that Florence's war

with the papacy was entering its darkest days in 1377, a new *signore*, Gian Galeazzo Visconti, was raising much more dangerous storm clouds in the north; as the ruler of Milan, he would come very close to taking advantage of those wars to unite the north and center of Italy under his rule. His storm clouds would not be so easily overcome, in many ways providing the central tempests of the Italian Hundred Years' War.

The Count of Virtù and the Central Phase of the Italian Hundred Years' War

In Milan, the Visconti family, who had regained power in the first years of the fourteenth century, when the emperor Henry VII invited them back to the city as part of his program of a Guelph-Ghibelline peace, had long since consolidated their power as *signori*. While they had failed Henry's kiss of peace with their rivals the Della Torre, they had stood the test of time well, flourished, and built for themselves a mini-state in the heart of the Lombard plain. As the century progressed, however, their territorial expansion brought them into conflict with their neighbors to both the east and the west. Thus, in Milan, when Galeazzo Visconti died prematurely in 1377, his relatively young and inexperienced son, Gian Galeazzo (1351–1402), was unexpectedly catapulted into a difficult leadership role, surrounded by enemies both beyond his borders and closer at hand.

Closer at hand, those enemies were in fact his own family, for his father up until his death had divided the territorial state they had built up around their capital cities of Milan and Pavia with his rapacious brother, Bernabò. Ruling from Pavia, Galeazzo had focused his aggression toward the west, while Bernabò, from Milan, pressed to the east. Gian Galeazzo succeeded his father in Pavia, but most did not expect him to last long given his aggressive uncle, who clearly had designs on ruling the whole of Milanese territory in his own name, seeing little need to divide it with his inexperienced and reputedly incompetent nephew. Actually, in a rather curious foreshadowing, the scholarly young Gian Galeazzo was known as the Count of *Virtù*, not because of his intellectual abilities, cunning reputation, or sympathy for the *popolo grosso*, but rather because he had obtained, as part of a dowry in his first marriage, a county in Champagne known as *Vertus*, rendered in Italian as *Virtù*. Yet *virtù* was exactly what Gian Galeazzo needed in order to survive against his more powerful and more experienced uncle: he had to become the Count of *Virtù* in deed as well as in name.

If Bernabò had plans to take over all of the Visconti mini-state, they were quickly tested when Gian Galeazzo, in 1377, after the death of his first wife, unexpectedly announced that he had arranged to marry Maria of Sicily (1363–1401). As the fourteen-year-old daughter and sole heir of King Frederick IV of Sicily, who had died in July, she was the heir to the kingdom of Naples and Sicily; thus, the marriage would have catapulted Gian Galeazzo from being the weak heir of half of the Visconti lands into a major figure in Italian and European affairs. As king of most of the south of Italy and Sicily and as *signore* of a small but significant part of the north, he would have dwarfed his uncle and been in a position to dominate not just him, but perhaps the whole Italian peninsula. Unfortunately for Gian Galeazzo and his not-quite-best-laid plans, although he had secured a contract to marry Maria, marriages were not valid until actually consummated. That required that the bride and the groom meet, something that virtually every powerful ruler in Italy and Europe, including his uncle, was anxious to prevent. As others maneuvered to keep them apart, the king of Aragon solved the problem by kidnapping Maria, eventually marrying her to his grandson, in a move that served to gain the south of Italy for his family and to keep it in a more European dynastic orbit.

From Gian Galeazzo's perspective, this failure may well have taught him an important lesson; it at least confirmed a strategy that he would follow for the rest of his life – never reveal plans until everything is nailed down and enemies have no opportunity to block them. Actually, this was a lesson that most city-states were learning and that was typical of the developing ideal of *popolo grosso virtù* in governance and war. Careful and secret diplomacy could reduce the danger and cost of conflicts between states, especially when such conflicts required costly *condottieri*. Gian Galeazzo had not done his diplomatic homework; thus, with most of Europe ranged against him, the straightforward aggression of the king of Aragon made sure that his marriage remained unconsummated, and his grand plan failed. Many thought that this would end Gian Galeazzo's precocious career. But instead, Gian Galeazzo decided to take the somewhat simpler path of dealing with his powerful enemies nearer to home, who had also worked to block his marriage, before tackling his more major projects.

The problem closer to home was clearly his uncle, Bernabò. Gian Galeazzo's approach to dealing with him was typical of what would become his strategy of rule and the newer style of governance favored by the *popolo grosso*. Rather than confronting his uncle openly on the battlefield with honor and military valor – a traditional approach that honor seemed to require – he understood that with wars fought by *condottieri*, things turned less on valor and honor than on resources and money. Money, however, required putting one's economy in order, so as to maximize income and minimize unnecessary expense. Thus, he resided quietly in Pavia, making no waves that would give his uncle an excuse to act, and put his economy in order, relying heavily on more efficient bureaucratic professionals – those same notaries and lawyers so popular with the governments dominated by the *popolo grosso* elsewhere. Together they began to centralize and rationalize taxes and to eliminate as much corruption as possible in the name of creating a government that served its subjects. Much of this, of course, was rhetoric and show designed to win support, but he still managed to cut taxes and increase revenues and began to paint himself as a true Count of *Virtù*.

To cut the cost of the war that he realized might be necessary to overcome his uncle, Gian Galeazzo committed to making diplomacy a central tool of his plans. If one could isolate one's enemy and make victory as secure and quick as possible before showing one's hand, costs could be contained and reliance on often-unreliable *condottieri* limited. Gian Galeazzo thus turned first to the current Roman emperor, Wenceslaus, who was induced for a relatively modest sum to give him the title of imperial vicar. Although it was largely an empty title, as neither he nor Wenceslaus had the power to back up its claims against Bernabò's powerful hold on Milan, it did make his rule more legitimate; for in theory, of course, all power to rule devolved from the Roman emperor. Gian Galeazzo then turned to the Swiss lords who controlled the Alpine passes to the north of Milan and made a secret agreement with them not to allow any enemies to pass if war should break out. This was followed by a similar agreement with the French nobility, who controlled the Alpine passes to the west. Turning southward, he secured ties with the Florentines, who feared Bernabò's designs on Bologna and also his meddling in Tuscany. To the east, Bernabò's aggressive policies had already alienated the city-states of the plain and Venice; thus, Gian Galeazzo's work had already been done for him, and he could count on their support against his uncle. As a result he had quietly isolated his uncle, and Bernabò was virtually unaware of his imminent demise.

All this had taken eight years of planning and diplomacy, but in 1385 Gian Galeazzo was ready to take care of his family problems. He announced that he was going on a pilgrimage and would pass by the city of Milan, where Bernabò ruled, but that he would not enter the city. His uncle apparently read this as well-deserved respect for his strength. Shortly thereafter, Gian Galeazzo arrived outside the city and set up camp with an unusually large bodyguard. Bernabò may well have seen this as another sign of respect, which in part it was. Gian Galeazzo humbly invited his uncle and his cousins to his camp for a parley, and Bernabò unwisely accepted. When Bernabò arrived, he was quickly arrested, and Gian Galeazzo rode back into Milan with his troops, where – given those troops, his uncle's arrest, and the lat-ter's unpopularity – he was welcomed as a liberator. The Milanese had little choice in the matter, but Bernabò, with his costly wars of expansion and his high-handed ways, had not been a popular ruler. Gian Galeazzo certainly increased his own popularity by almost immediately distributing a portion of his uncle's treasure to the population. In turn, rather too quickly for appearances, Bernabò died in jail, of unknown causes, and Gian Galeazzo's careful diplomacy stood up well in the face of his fait accompli; thus, with a minimum of expense and violence, he had become the leader of the whole Visconti state and the Count of *Virtù* indeed; that is, in deed as well as in name.

Gian Galeazzo was now a north Italian power. Imperial vicar of Milan, he held a strong mini-state at the heart of one of the richest regions in Italy and Europe. His next goal appears to have been to become a truly European power, which meant gaining control of the rest of the Lombard plain by tak-ing over the rich city-states to the east, which had formerly been the chosen prey of his uncle. His most powerful enemies in the area were two impor-tant *signori*, the young Antonio della Scala, lord of Verona (1362–1388), and Francesco da Carrara, lord of Padua (1325–1393). Neither was a particularly easy opponent to overcome, but they shared one fatal weakness that Gian Galeazzo exploited to the full – they feared and hated each other more than they feared him. Shared borders and long-standing hostility between their two families prepared the ground for the Count of *Virtù*'s clever – nay, *virtù*-ous – maneuvers. Turning first to Francesco da Carrara, he secretly proposed that they divide up the territories of della Scala, a logical proposition as Carrara's Padua-centered lands bordered della Scala's Verona-centered lands to the east, while his own Milanese territories bordered them to the west. Carrara agreed, and, striking quickly before della Scala had time to protect himself from this powerful alliance, he was defeated and his lands divided between Milan and Padua.

Unfortunately for Francesco da Carrara, he had made one major miscal-culation in eliminating della Scala, for he had substituted for the youthful and aggressive Antonio the much more powerful and aggressive Gian Galeazzo. Visconti wasted no time teaching him that lesson. Virtually as soon as Verona had been divided, Gian Galeazzo turned to Venice, Padua's most power-ful neighbor to the east, and suggested that they work together to elimi-nate their common enemy, none other than his erstwhile ally, Francesco. As the Venetians had been suffering from Carrara's expansionist policies at the expense of the limited territories they controlled on the mainland, and as they were also frustrated with Carrara's interference with their trade up the river systems that opened both the rich Lombard plain and some of the most important passes to northern Europe, they were tempted. Moreover, Visconti suggested that for Venice it would be much better to deal with one lord of the Lombard plain, and an ally on matters of trade, than with a host of little warring city-states, a position that had its supporters in Venice, apparently even a few quietly paid off by Gian Galeazzo. Suddenly Francesco found himself isolated in Padua, and as he wisely fled the city, realizing he was no match for Milan and Venice, Gian Galeazzo's soldiers rode through its open gates in the fall of 1388, taking it without striking a blow.

Reviewing Visconti's rapid rise: his father had died in 1377; he had eliminated his uncle in 1385; and three years later he was in control of virtually the whole of the Lombard plain. In eleven short years, with only minimal expense for *condottieri*, he had conquered his powerful rivals and become the most important ruler in the north of Italy.

There was only one major obstacle to his control of the Lombard plain – the city of Bologna. Theoretically one of the northernmost cities of the Papal States, with the papacy hamstrung by the Great Schism it was caught up in virtually interminable local factional squabbles. This allowed Gian Galeazzo to weaken the city internally by playing on local conflicts while working once again to isolate it. But Bologna was not easily isolated, in large measure because the other city-states of the north, led by Florence and Venice, were not eager to see Visconti's power expand yet further. Florence was especially concerned because, as noted earlier, the crucial north-south trade route that crossed the Apennines began its way over the mountains immediately to the north of Florence and descended through Bologna onto the great northern plain cut by the Po River. Venice shared Florence's concerns and suddenly was also worried about its rapacious new neighbor.

The standard historical view of what happened next was that the two remaining great republican cities of the Rinascimento, Florence and Venice, banded together to protect republican liberty from the threat of evil tyranny in the form of Gian Galeazzo Visconti, poised to gobble up not just Bologna but also Florence and perhaps all of Italy, cutting out the very heart of the Rinascimento. The reality of the situation was somewhat less black-and-white or mythic. To simplify greatly, the Venetians soon realized that in destroying Francesco da Carrara, they had created a more powerful and dangerous neighbor by far, one who would require careful, and often costly, watching and diplomacy, at best, and perhaps expensive military intervention, in order to protect their mainland territories and their trading interests. Both Florence and Venice were also deeply concerned about the power that controlling the north-south trade routes would give Gian Galeazzo. And finally, both were worried about his potential interest in dominating not just the Lombard plain, but the whole of the northern half of Italy, especially Tuscany.

Significantly, this concerned Florence because it had also embarked on its own program of taking over the other city-states of Tuscany, including many republics – significantly undermining its high-minded claims to defend republican liberty. What made the city's concern more pressing was the fact that in preparing to isolate Bologna, Gian Galeazzo realized that he had to neutralize Florence. As Florence's neighbors in Tuscany correctly feared that city's expansionist policies, he saw them as easily won allies who could be used to isolate that city, at least for the time it took him to take Bologna. Thus, in return for his promise to protect them against Florentine expansion, most of Florence's neighbors allied formally or informally with him. What we have, then, is not so much a battle between republican liberty and tyranny as a messy battle between powerful expanding states, as they slowly but surely eliminated their smaller weaker neighbors, leaving the victors to turn their aggression on each other.

With Florence apparently isolated, and with supporters in the city of Bologna ready to undermine the government there, Gian Galeazzo showed up with his *condottieri* outside the walls of Bologna, apparently calculating that Venice, being a maritime power without a ready army, would not be able to come to the city's aid before he took it. But Venice thwarted his plans for yet another quick and inexpensive success; for Francesco da Carrara had earlier fled with his sons to Venice as Gian Galeazzo took Padua. Now Venice gave Carrara's son, Francesco Novello (the New) Carrara (1359–1405), a few troops and set him loose to retake Padua. As Visconti had drawn off his troops from that city to help take Bologna, and as the locals had already become restive under his new rule and new taxes, Padua welcomed back the new Francesco with open arms. That quick success led much of the rest of the eastern Lombard plain to rise up in revolt as well. Even without a major army, Venice had outflanked Gian Galeazzo and threatened virtually all that he had accomplished. Evidently, Venice could also play the game of *virtù*, and the Count of *Virtù* was forced to withdraw his troops from Bologna in order to put down the revolts fomented by the maritime city.

At considerable expense in terms of money and bloodshed, Gian Galeazzo squashed local resistance and reestablished his control, more straightforward violence for once replacing *virtù* as well as diplomacy to secure his ends. He then returned to his plans to take Bologna. This time, however, he proceeded with greater caution, attempting once more to isolate Florence and to neutralize Venice. Florence, however, realizing the danger of its situation, decided to strike first. With the arrival of the campaigning season of 1391, the Florentines launched a major offensive against Gian Galeazzo. With substantial promises and bribes, they induced the French to invade Milanese territory from the west. In turn, mobilizing as much wealth as possible, they hired a large army led by their old client, John Hawkwood, who, passing over the mountains and through Bologna, marched up the Po River valley from the east. Thus Gian Galeazzo found himself caught in the middle in a slowly closing trap between the French and Hawkwood and badly outnumbered as well.

Things looked bad, but Gian Galeazzo's response once again showed his *virtù*-ous ability to understand and manipulate wartime situations. Mobilizing his resources, he put the largest army he could into the field. But rather than waiting for his enemies to close their trap, he committed his whole force against Hawkwood. As the armies neared each other, instead of engaging immediately, he sent small contingents behind the advancing enemy to open the dikes along the Po and its smaller tributaries, flooding the plain behind Hawkwood's army. Much as he expected, this caused Hawkwood to pull his troops back toward Bologna; for, as Gian Galeazzo understood well, the *condottiere* was not prepared to fight a battle where, if he lost, his retreat was cut off.

As Machiavelli would later note, professional soldiers were not in the business of fighting wars in order to die needlessly; in fact, they seldom earned their wages at the cost of shedding their own blood, preferring battles that were easily won or, if necessary, quickly lost with minimal losses. For Machiavelli, as well as for those who hired *condottieri*, this was regrettable, but logical, as the main resource of a *condottiere* leader was his men, and if he lost too many, he was out of business. With the plains flooding behind him, Hawkwood wisely chose retreat in order to fight another day under less threatening conditions. This meant, in turn, that the number of enemy troops that Gian Galeazzo had to face was temporarily cut in half. Taking full advantage of this, he rapidly marched westward to face the French in one of the most famous battles of the Italian Hundred Years' War, the Battle of Alexandria in July of 1391.

The French troops he faced were a mix of French nobles and professional soldiers. Visconti's *condottieri* were primarily veterans of fighting in the north of Italy and well-trained in *condottieri* techniques of war. Perhaps because of their superior experience and tactics involving fighting on horseback in close formation (rather than in individual combat between nobles as was the medieval ideal); perhaps because of superior technology, including a sterner bit that allowed a rider to control a horse more effectively and thus to fight in formation; perhaps simply because many were fighting closer to home and with greater incentive, Visconti's troops won a decisive victory. As a result, the Battle of Alexandria was widely seen as yet another proof of the deadly danger for foreigners of becoming involved in Italian affairs and the superiority of Italian *condottiere* warfare. In war, as in wealth and cultural display, Italy was claiming, and seemed to be demonstrating, its leadership role in Europe and its superiority to those from beyond the Alps, who lacked its command of true *virtù* and its urban *civiltà*. And who better to teach that lesson than the Italian Count of *Virtù*.

Perhaps more significantly, however, the Florentines without their French allies found their tactical and numerical superiority gone and sued for peace. Both sides saw the treaty signed in 1392 between Florence and Milan as temporary and planned to use it to rebuild their resources and return to battle as soon as possible. But, of course, Gian Galeazzo was not content merely to sit quietly, waiting for his treasury to recoup his losses in order to finance another war. Once again he turned to diplomacy in order to isolate his enemy and to gain a superiority that would guarantee a swift and relatively inexpensive victory when open warfare resumed. A crucial success came when he signed a secret agreement with Venice that promised that that city would not interfere with his plans for Bologna and Florence, provided that he committed to leave the Carrara in Padua as a buffer state between Milan and Venice. Apparently the Venetians believed that Florence and Milan were fairly equally matched; thus, sitting on the fence, they could avoid the costs of war, and even profit by supplying both contenders, while protecting themselves with a new tough Carrara lord in Padua. Events would soon show that their calculations were clever but ultimately incorrect. Meanwhile, Gian Galeazzo turned to Tuscany to isolate Florence. Once again taking advantage of Florence's neighbors' fear of her aggressive policy of expansion in the area, slowly but surely he gained their support against his enemy and even formally became the *signore* of Pisa, Siena, and Perugia. As the new century dawned, Florence was effectively isolated in Tuscany.

Bologna, however, came first. And Visconti had been working behind the scenes there to foment factional strife that he could exploit in order to gain the city at minimal expense. Thus, in the early summer of 1402, when the city suddenly dissolved in civil war, it was probably not by chance that a sizeable contingent of his soldiers was lurking in the vicinity. When the gates of the city were opened, they quickly entered in the name of restoring peace. And, not surprisingly, peace came with a new *signore*, Gian Galeazzo Visconti, the Count of *Virtù*. Thus, once again with hardly a battle and with a treasury still largely intact, he finally took Bologna. But more importantly,

with Bologna in hand it was now Florence's turn. With a large army Gian
Galeazzo moved rapidly south over the Apennines to finish off his rival once
and for all and consolidate his control of Tuscany and most of the rest of
northern Italy. Florence's situation looked hopeless. It had almost no army
and no opportunity to hire one. It had no allies who were in a position to
come to its aid. And it had virtually no time to prepare to face the large army
that Visconti had gathered to assure its demise. It appeared that *virtù* would
finally make the Count of *Virtù* master of the northern half of the peninsula
at fifty-one, changing the course of Italian history and the Rinascimento
irrevocably.

But that was not to be. For, as Machiavelli would later point out cogently –
and as was already a commonplace – *virtù* had one implacable enemy, *fortuna*.
The best-laid plans, the most cunning schemes, the most carefully worked
out strategies – all of which Gian Galeazzo seemed to have – were trumped
by evil fortune. For as bad luck would have it, as his armies were approaching the walls of a desperate Florence, Gian Galeazzo himself fell ill and died.
Cruel fortune had triumphed over the Count of *Virtù* and *virtù* itself.

Visconti's troops retreated to Milan to squabble over who would dominate the heartland of Milanese power, and slowly the balance of power in
Italy shifted. Florence eventually gobbled up Tuscany. Venice, tired of squab-
bling with petty tyrants in the eastern Lombard plain, took advantage of the
situation to take much of that territory and create a mainland empire that
balanced her maritime empire in the east. Milan was confined to the central Lombard plain and eventually found a Visconti, Filippo Maria Visconti
(1392–1447), capable of defending it and holding Venice and Florence at
bay. This rebalancing of the political equilibrium, however, required a series
of additional conflicts that continued the Italian Hundred Years' War until
midcentury. Once again it was fought almost exclusively by *condottieri*, who
pressed the finances of Venice, Florence, and Milan (the main combatants)
to the limit, repeatedly devastated the countryside, and slowed the demographic recovery from recurring bouts of the plague. They also drove these
city-states to experiment with organizing more effective bureaucracies of
rule and warfare, and colored significantly the cultural flowering of the first
Rinascimento.

At the time, however, the most significant impact of the wars following
the death of Gian Galeazzo would have seemed to most to have been the
carving out of territorial states and broader spheres of influence around what
had become the three great powers in the north, Florence, Milan, and Venice.
Venice appeared to have undergone the greatest change: a profound reori-
entation of its relationships with its Italian neighbors and its commercial

empire in the Adriatic and eastern Mediterranean. For most of the four-teenth century it had largely avoided involvement in mainland politics in favor of protecting its maritime empire, which had entailed an increasingly costly conflict with an expanding Ottoman Empire. From that perspective the island city's move onto the mainland following 1402, creating a mini–Venetian empire that included most of northeastern Italy, seemed to indicate a radical shift in Venetian economic and diplomatic policy.

Recent scholarship, however, has suggested that this move onto the main-land, or *terraferma*, as the Venetians called it, was neither as radical nor as new as once thought. First, as noted earlier, Venice, much like other cities heavily involved in long-distance commerce, always balanced it with local trade. Thus they were especially interested in protecting access to the Po River, which with its tributaries gave access to the Lombard plain, and to the more local Adige River that flowed through Verona and on toward the passes to Austria and Germany; to the Brenta River, which led to Padua and eventually Belluno in the low Alps; to the Sile River, which bisected Treviso and the rich Trevigiano plain; and to the Tagliamento River, which opened the poorer plains of the Friuli region and the eastern passes to Austria, to name only the most important. In sum, Venice had long had an interest in the mainland cities that dominated those rivers that were so important both for its local trade and for its overland luxury trade with northern Europe. When these interests were threatened, as we have seen in the wars with Gian Galeazzo, Venice was ready to spend the money necessary to protect its inter-ests and even to wage war on the mainland. Less often recognized, however, is the fact that the Venetian nobility had already begun investing in country estates and more profit-oriented agriculture, especially around Treviso, in the fourteenth century, a quiet economic expansion onto the mainland that was made easier when Venice took over the rich little city itself in 1339.

Still, the traditional view that holds that in the turmoil following Gian Galeazzo's death, Venice decided that a more aggressive approach to the mainland of northeastern Italy was necessary clearly has much to sup-port it. Debates in the Venetian Senate reveal that a powerful group sup-ported taking a more direct hand in controlling that hinterland, in order to protect both traditional trade interests and Venetian investments there. In addition, Gian Galeazzo picked an unusually good time to die, not just for the Florentines but also for Venice. For in 1402 the Ottoman Emperor Beyazid I (1347–1403) was captured by Tamberlane (c. 1336–1405), a new Middle Eastern conqueror from the plains of Asia. Fortunately for Venice, this new threat from the east and the ensuing confusion created a momen-tary reprieve from Ottoman pressure on the Venetian maritime empire in the eastern Mediterranean, which allowed the city to redirect its military resources and wealth to dealing with perceived problems closer to home: what would become their *terraferma*.

The War of Chioggia and the Venetian Attempt to Dominate Italian Mediterranean Trade

That distant victory by Tamberlane over the Ottoman emperor, however, opens a more Mediterranean perspective on the Italian Hundred Years' War and the transformation of Venice from a primarily commercial metropolis into a city-state also committed to profiting from its *terraferma* empire. While most histories of the period focus on the wars fought in the center and north of Italy, much of the wealth that paid for those wars came from international trade and banking, both of which relied heavily on the great maritime cities of Italy. By the second half of the fourteenth century fierce competition had reduced the rivalry to dominate long-distance trade to essentially two northern Italian cities: Genoa and Venice. Actually, although Tamberlane's victory would temporarily slow the growth of Ottoman power in the east, the Ottomans had been the other major player in that competition.

Early on, even without a navy, the Ottomans had repeatedly demonstrated their military superiority in land battles, defeating crusading armies, crushing the Eastern Empire's attempts to thwart their advance on Constantinople, and pushing aggressively into eastern Europe. In a way, the result was an ongoing unofficial conflict between the Italian naval powers and the Ottomans, though there was often considerable difficulty actually engaging in military confrontation, as the Italian navies and the Ottoman armies literally lacked a common battleground. Eventually the Ottomans would become a sea power as well, which would give them the upper hand in the conflict as the fifteenth century progressed. But that lay in the future. To a great extent the conflict during the fourteenth century was fought out in terms of Italian naval raids and Ottoman attacks on Italian trading outposts and naval bases.

In what was then essentially a three-way conflict, at least Venice and Genoa could fight at sea. And fight they did, on and off for at least two centuries. What are normally considered the conclusive last two wars, however, were fought in 1350–1355 and 1378–1381. The ability to fight those two wars was severely limited once again by the demographic devastation of the plague; for both cities lacked the manpower to man their war fleets, which were made up of galleys that were still rowed and thus required large crews. Most war galleys were also equipped with sails, but rowing was preferred for battle as it gave ships more maneuverability, especially important for ramming, the preferred method of disabling enemy ships. Cannons had been introduced in midcentury, but they were still highly inaccurate, and their weight and unreliability limited their number on the relatively small, swift galleys. Much more effective and significant in battle were crossbows firing steel bolts as oarsmen maneuvered ships in and out of firing range. Hand-to-hand fighting when ships were grappled together was often the last stage of battle, in a way transforming sea battles into land battles. It appears there were also attempts to burn enemy ships using various burning compounds based probably on naphtha, quicklime, sulfur, niter, or perhaps even adaptations of the closely guarded secret Greek Fire. The danger of using such incendiaries was that they could set both fleets on fire, as well as destroy enemy ships that, if captured, were highly valuable prizes. Most battles, then, involved maneuvering aimed at coming within crossbow range with the enemy downwind, ramming, or grappling, with experienced rowers, crossbow men, and soldiers for boarding being crucial.

Before the plague, Venetian crews were drafted from the sailors of the commercial fleets and boatmen of the city. But the population losses of the plague forced the city to recruit sailors from its trading outposts in the east and other maritime cities in order to man even the smaller war fleets it put to sea. In fact, in the war of 1350–1355 the city was so short-handed that they actually rented twelve fully equipped and manned galleys from the Aragonese for 12,000 ducats a month. The Aragonese, given their traditional enmity with the Genoese in the eastern Mediterranean, promised to supply an additional eighteen galleys at their own expense. A similar deal was worked out with the Byzantine emperor to rent another eight galleys. Significantly, Venice was able to make such investments in men and ships because it was rich enough and well-organized enough in terms of its taxing abilities to raise the funds necessary to finance its war, thus in a way, transforming naval warfare into just another investment, much as was the case with *condottieri* warfare on land.

It was not just plague losses, however, that made recruiting foreign sailors and renting ships necessary. Many non-noble Venetians who had once served willingly in the Venetian fleet were no longer willing to do so. Thus it had become the practice to allow those with the means to do so to avoid service by paying to hire a replacement, and many of the better-off below the nobility took advantage of that possibility. Clearly, many who could pay preferred this to the risky business of fighting at sea. But it appears that there were also deeper social tensions involved, not unlike those Florence experienced with its Ciompi rising or those in other mainland cities where tensions continued between artisans and the more wealthy *popolo grosso*. Local chroniclers reported that by the 1350s lower-class antagonism had begun to be manifested in Venice against the closed nature of the ruling class and its *popolo grosso* nobility. Their high-handed ways, their absolute control of government, and their handling of what were seen by many as their wars heightened the dissatisfaction. War only heightened such tensions, and in 1355 it appears things came to a head with a mysterious conspiracy to overthrow the closed ruling order and nobility of Venice.

Most of the records dealing with the event were destroyed by the Council of Ten, Venice's secret police council that dealt with conspiracy. But it seems that in 1355 the new doge of Venice, Marin Faliero, himself a successful naval commander who was highly popular with the lower classes, decided to take advantage of that popularity and lead the lower classes and new men of the city in eliminating the most high-handed nobles and establishing himself as *signore* of Venice. Unfortunately for him, a number of those he attempted to recruit for his conspiracy informed the Ten. Paradoxically, as doge, Faliero sat on that body as an ex-officio member. Thus he actually participated in the first stages of the investigation that eventually led to the Ten ordering his secret execution. In the face of what should have been, given Venetian ideology, this unthinkable crime, a concerted effort was made to eliminate the doge from the civic memory of the city; even his portrait was removed from the chambers of the Great Council, where the portraits of all Venetian doges were displayed as a reflection of civic pride.

Real tensions were not eliminated, however, by eliminating Faliero or the memory of his failed conspiracy. If anything, they emerged even stronger in the last Genoese war of 1378–1381, known as the War of Chioggia. Behind the battles that involved galleys and ports from the Bosphorus and the Black Sea to Sardinia and the Tyrrhenian coast, in the city and its fleets there festered a deep antipathy to Venetian government, the nobility, and the war itself. When added to Genoese military successes and naval forces that seemed virtually unstoppable, those internal divisions seemed to spell the end of the proud republic and its pseudo-nobility. In this context it is suggestive that the two Venetian naval leaders who emerged as the popular heroes of the war, Carlo Zeno and Vettor Pisani, both had troubled histories with Venetian government and the noble families that dominated it. From important noble families themselves, both had followed career trajectories that definitely established them as black sheep and made them at least appear to contemporaries as lightening rods of anti-noble sentiment.

Zeno was destined by his family for a career in the Church, but while studying at Padua, according to the rather romantic accounts of his early life, he reportedly enjoyed his student days too fully, wasting the funds that had been earmarked for his studies on the pleasures the city offered. Eventually he was forced to flee his family's wrath, running off to join a *condottiere* company. After several years soldiering, he returned to Venice and his family. And, then, as should befall the prodigal son in such romantic stories, he was forgiven and shipped off to serve in an ecclesiastical position that his family had secured for him in Greece. There his military experience came in handy in fighting the Turks. His soldiering and his involvement in duels, however, soon led him to desert the Church, marry, and move to Constantinople as a merchant. The successes that followed meant that this rather atypical noble, who had begun as a professional soldier and cleric, was eventually appointed one of the admirals of the Venetian fleet that faced off against Genoa.

Vettor Pisani was an even less likely admiral. He was a nephew of Nicolò Pisani, who, after winning a brilliant victory against the Genoese in the war of the 1350s, had lost perhaps the crucial battle of that war at Porto Longo in 1354. As was typical of the Venetian government in such cases, Nicolò was prosecuted for his defeat, sentenced to pay a large fine, and permanently banned from military command. His young nephew, Vettor, also took part in that battle and, like his uncle, was tried, but acquitted. After that war, Vettor continued to sail with Venetian commercial fleets. Apparently his skillful seamanship and popularity with his crews led to his being named a commander of the commercial fleets, a major post that put him in line for military command in time of war. But his reported run-ins with his noble peers in defense of his non-noble crewmen have a romantic air that makes them seem almost mythic. In one telling incident, widely remarked upon at the time, he assaulted one of the most powerful nobles of the city, Pietro Corner. Corner had questioned his defense of one of his non-noble galley masters, and Pisani was so outraged at the affront to his honor and his galley master that he attacked Corner with a dagger. Fortunately for both men, Corner escaped, and Pisani was fined 200 ducats and deprived of an important state office to which he had just been elected. Whether or not defending a non-noble galley master against the insults of a high-handed noble was his actual motive, Pisani clearly had his issues with the leaders of the Venetian nobility who had condemned him and his uncle. In turn, many non-nobles, who saw him in this light, had good reasons for seeing him as a sympathetic leader.

In the first phase of the 1378 war, Pisani had actually risen to be the Captain General of the fleet and had considerable success in the western Mediterranean attacking Genoese shipping. But things turned against him when the Venetian government refused his request to return to Venice for the winter to refit his fleet. In the spring his small fleet of approximately twenty-four ships encountered a Genoese fleet of about the same size in the

southern Adriatic. Although Pisani was reluctant to fight, feeling that too
many of his ships were unfit for battle, he engaged the enemy and actually
managed to capture the Genoese admiral's galley and kill him. But reportedly the inferior repair of his galleys caused the tide of battle to turn, and the
Venetians were soundly defeated, with Pisani managing to escape with only
a half-dozen ships. As might be expected, given his uncle's fate and his own
defeat, Pisani's return to Venice was not pleasant. He was put on trial for his
role in the defeat, and although his powerful noble enemies pressed for his
execution – a penalty legally required for a commander who fled from battle
before it was over – the Doge Andrea Contarini, apparently aware of Pisani's
popularity with the sailors of the fleet, recommended merely a fine and a
ban from offices and commands. In the end he was sentenced to six months
in jail and permanently banned from offices and military commands.

Meanwhile, back at sea, the Venetian government had committed to an
aggressive policy and had sent off their other black sheep, Carlo Zeno, with
a small fleet to harass the Genoese in their home waters. After Pisani's defeat
they actually sent Zeno reinforcements, hoping to force the Genoese fleet
to leave the Adriatic and return home to defend their city. Unfortunately,
that strategy failed. With Pisani's fleet destroyed and Zeno's off threatening
Genoa, the Genoese fleet stayed on and took control of the Adriatic. To
make matters worse, Francesco Carrara, the lord of Padua, came to the aid
of Genoa, moved by his own expansionist policies, blockading Venice on
the mainland. The king of Hungary, who was interested in controlling the
northeastern coast of the Adriatic and who was thus in perennial conflict
with Venice in that area, joined the fray, blocking the supply lines of Venice
to the north. Thus the Venetians in 1379 found themselves in much the same
situation the Florentines would find themselves in later, in 1402. They were
totally cut off from supplies and any possible support.

Their one hope was the lagoons themselves – a wide expanse of shallow waters dotted by mudflats and traversed by shifting channels that made
access to the city difficult for war galleys, unless guided by local pilots. The
lagoons had long protected the city from conquest, and the Venetian government hoped that they would continue to do so. The Genoese and their
allies, however, planned to make the matter of the lagoons moot by simply waiting and starving out the city. To increase the pressure and secure a
base that would allow their fleet to come into harbor, the Genoese, with
the aid of Carrara, attacked the Venetian port city at the southern edge of
the lagoons, Chioggia, and took it in August of 1379. The fall of Chioggia
stunned Venice. Totally isolated, the once great maritime power seemed on
the verge of defeat.

It is at such moments that governments are tested, and Venice was no exception, for at precisely that moment the deep rifts within the body politic became clearest. The Venetian government ordered a general conscription of the populace to serve in the fleet that was being rebuilt and in the civil militia. But when those called to serve on the sixteen galleys that remained reported for duty, they were only enough to man six. Essentially, a large portion of those called refused to serve under the new Captain General of the fleet, who was seen as representing the worst of the nobility. Instead, according to the chronicler Daniele di Chinazzo, they insisted that they would serve only under Vettor Pisani, "head and father of all the seamen of Venice."

The problem was that the "head and father," Pisani, was in prison, condemned by that same nobility and government that were now trying to press their lower classes to fight to support their regime. It appears that the lower classes, especially the sailors, saw Pisani as their defender and as the nobility's scapegoat for the earlier defeat. From their perspective he had been forced to fight, and many of their comrades to die, handicapped by the lack of support from Venetian government; thus, he and they were victims of that government, as were the lower classes in general. Certainly there were significant differences between this lower-class resistance to Venetian government and the Ciompi revolt that occurred at much the same time. But in a real way the sailors of Venice were its *sottoposti*, and Ciompi and their refusing to fight, as well as their rallying behind popular leaders, suggests again the way in which war tested the fabric of society and the challenges that the Italian Hundred Years' War posed for ruling classes made up largely of the *popolo grosso*.

Supported by the Doge Andrea Contarini, who apparently saw that compromise was necessary to pacify the city, Pisani was released from jail, and a series of reforms and rewards were promised the lower classes once the war was won. Cheered by mobs who called out "Long live Vettor," Pisani avoided a potentially revolutionary moment, going immediately to the doge to assure him of his loyalty and his readiness to serve and defend the honor of the city. Tensions remained, however. When a large contingent of men came to the ducal palace to enroll to fight under Pisani and were told that they would have to serve under the unpopular Captain General who remained in command, they reportedly replied with shouts so seditious that the chronicler refused to report them. When eventually Pisani was given command of six galleys, it was reported that he was overwhelmed with men volunteering to crew for him. Finally, the aged Doge Contarini personally took over the command of the navy, naming Pisani his chief of staff, and regained the necessary support of the city's lower classes.

In essence, the war was back in Pisani's hands. And his strategy demonstrated once again a masterful use of *virtù*. Rather than directly facing the enemy, he simply reversed the siege, besieging the Genoese fleet in Chioggia by blocking the channels to that city with sunken ships, thereby cutting it off without supplies. Begun in December, the counter-siege succeeded so well that soon the Genoese fleet found itself a nonfleet unable to get to sea and trapped and starving in Chioggia. Carlo Zeno returned to the Adriatic in the new year with a series of important successes. After harassing Genoese shipping in the western Mediterranean, he had sailed on to Constantinople and back to the Adriatic and Venice, winning a number of naval battles, greatly aided by the fact that the heart of the Genoese battle fleet was blockaded in Chioggia. Upon his return, although some called for an immediate confrontation with the Genoese fleet, Zeno settled down to defend the blockade strategy of Pisani and the doge. Much of the conflict focused as a result on skirmishes involving smaller boats adapted to the shallow waters of the lagoons and mercenary soldiers hired by the Venetians to intercept attempts to supply Chioggia over land. With his youthful experience as a mercenary, Zeno was reportedly particularly effective in working with and holding the loyalty of those hired troops. In the end, in June of 1380 the Genoese fleet in Chioggia was forced by the siege to surrender, and Venice, without winning a truly major battle in the war, snatched victory from the jaws of defeat.

The war was formally ended by a peace signed in Turin in 1381, which on paper did not appear to be particularly favorable to Venice. But Genoa's power as a maritime city was severely handicapped, especially in the eastern Mediterranean, with their trade there never again reaching even a quarter of Venetian totals. At home the city was also torn apart by factional strife led by the great families of the city, suffering some thirteen uprisings between 1413 and 1453. Population also declined slowly but surely across the fifteenth century, driven in part by recurring waves of the plague, in part by the less attractive economic climate of the city. To make matters worse, the city's geographic position, huddled at the base of the mountains on the Tyrrhenian Sea, which made it such a fine port, meant that there was a limited hinterland to support the city and even more limited space to develop the kind of proto-industrial production that gave cities like Florence and Venice more balanced economies. Without entirely giving up on their naval power in the western Mediterranean, in the end the Genoese played perhaps the one card they had to play, focusing on banking and finance and developing a close working relationship with the ruling powers in the Iberian peninsula and the nearby south of France. In the sixteenth century they would flourish again as they became the bankers of Spain and the riches that flooded Europe from the "new world," becoming major financial players, as we shall see.

But for the moment, with Genoa in decline in the eastern Mediterranean, peace allowed Venice to recoup economically via its powerful merchant fleets and to restabilize its government and social order. Perhaps more significantly than most have recognized, the very popular Vettor Pisani died at sea in 1381 fighting to reestablish Venetian control of the Adriatic after being named Captain of the Sea. With his death, a military leader who had won the popular imagination as no other, and who might well have inspired a viable revolution against the nobility of the city, passed from the scene. Carlo Zeno followed him as Captain and was kept busy, and well rewarded, reestablishing Venetian trading lanes in the Mediterranean.

In turn, shaken by the war, the Venetian nobility at least appeared to deliver on its larger promises. Most notably, the *Serrata* or closure of government was momentarily undone, with thirty new families added to the Great Council and the nobility. Most were rich *popolo grosso*–type families who had had enough money to make major economic contributions to the war effort, but a few were men who had served the city well during the war. And in both groups were men who could be seen as "new men." To many this seemed to indicate that the closed nature of government was not quite as closed as it had seemed. The reality, however, was that this was the last major addition of new families to the closed nobility during the Rinascimento. Perhaps more importantly, many of the old nobility had been seriously weakened economically by the war, and while the richest tended to survive and recoup their losses, a number fell into decline, which made the nobility seem a little less privileged. With less to lose, the lower classes also had less to recover, and with the renewed commercial and artisanal activity of the city after the war, they may have recovered more quickly and successfully. For once poverty had its advantages, although clearly it remained poverty. In sum, the period following the war was one of slow recovery, where the gap between rich and poor might have seemed to narrow, even if the richest were probably richer and more solidly in control.

Venice and Milan Divide the Lombard Plain

When Gian Galeazzo died in 1402, his Lombard state, following Visconti tradition, was divided among his three young sons. The oldest, Giovanni Maria, at only thirteen, was made duke of Milan and Lombard territories to the east. In turn, Gian Galeazzo's favorite son, Filippo Maria, at ten, was given much the same territories his father had started out with, Pavia and

territories to the west. A third, illegitimate son, Gabriele Maria, was made
signore of a small central region that featured the smaller but important cities
of Crema and Piacenza. As all three were too young to rule, formal power
fell to a council of sixteen tutors. Behind the scenes, however, the real struggle for power appears to have been between Gian Galeazzo's wife, Caterina,
and his powerful chancellor, Francesco Barbavara.

These divisions at the heart of Gian Galeazzo's Lombard state made it particularly ripe for dismemberment. Immediately Francesco Novello Carrara,
the city of Florence, and Pope Boniface IX (1359–1404; a pope 1389–1404)
stepped up to take advantage of the situation. Carrara made the first move,
attacking Verona, his traditional enemy and neighbor to the west. The new
Francesco, however, reversed his family's traditional policy of animosity to
the della Scala family. Rather, he took under his wing two of the illegitimate
males of the line, Brunoro and Antonio, offering to reestablish them as the
rulers of Verona in return for their submission to him as overlord. It was a
deal too good for them to pass up; thus as Carrara's troops moved towards
Verona with Brunoro and Antonio in tow, promising to "liberate" the city
from the Visconti, a badly divided Milan found itself unprepared to respond.
Without troops and with little to offer Francesco to buy him off, they turned
to the Venetians and offered them a number of small but significant towns
along the passes over the Alps controlled by Milan in return for aid against
Carrara. The offer was too little and too late. Venice declined, and in short
order Carrara took Verona, installing the della Scala as his vassals.

Carrara then turned his eyes to Vicenza, another rich city that lay midway
between Padua and Verona. It was clear to all, and especially to the leaders of
Vicenza, that Carrara would not leave them free right in the middle of his
new mini-state for long. Thus, as Carrara laid his plans for taking over their
city, they too turned to the Venetians and asked them to become their overlords, clearly preferring the distant rule of a hopefully lighter-handed Venice
to submission to their rapacious neighbor. The offer of a significant city like
Vicenza was considerably more attractive, but it also appears that Venice,
with the fall of Verona, had come to fear that the new Carrara was as bad
as the old, who had been a long-term thorn in Venice's side. Vicenza's offer,
then, was seen as offering an opportunity to eliminate the Carrara once and
for all and gain a *terraferma* state that would stretch from the lagoons and
Treviso to Vicenza and potentially beyond to Verona. Some desultory negotiations ensued, in which Carrara tried to convince Venice that interfering
was not in their interest, sweetening the deal with offers of a few small cities
of his own on the passes to northern Europe that he hoped might win over
Venetian commercial interests.

But Venice opted for war and took up arms. Much like Gian Galeazzo, they understood the virtue of using *virtù* in waging war. Reason, careful planning, limiting costs, and cunning, once again, came before valor, honor, and blood. Moreover, they demonstrated a particular taste for making use of military engineering – yet another form of *virtù* – to reshape the field of battle and gain unexpected advantages over their opponents. First, they mobilized their resources to isolate Carrara by fortifying the mouths of all rivers entering the Adriatic from Paduan territory. With Milanese territory to the west and an effective Venetian blockade to the east, Padua was perhaps not completely isolated, but its options were severely limited. Venice then bought one of the best *condottieri* money could buy, Pandolfo Malatesta (1370–1427), along with a number of lesser-known *condottieri*. But in typical merchant fashion they assigned two Venetian nobles to advise Malatesta and also to keep track of him in order to make sure they were getting their money's worth. As they worked to further isolate Carrara by diplomatically closing the passes to the north of Padua, they used their investment in *condottieri* to harass his forces in the countryside around both Padua and Verona, but avoided major confrontations.

As these troops pillaged their way over the countryside, their costs to Venice were limited, thanks to the spoils taken – a cost that Carrara, committed to defending the same territories, obviously could not escape. By forcing the less wealthy Carrara to face Venetian forces on two fronts and to defend a long border, the Venetians essentially used their superior wealth to strain his resources to the limit. Thus the war had a David and Goliath tenor from the start, with the distinction that in this case Goliath would win. Things came to a head in the campaigning season of 1404, when Venice made good use of its engineering *virtù* to soundly trounce Francesco in the field. Francesco was camped on the plain not far from Padua behind fieldworks that he deemed impregnable, only to find himself suddenly attacked by a large Venetian force, thanks to engineers who had secretly constructed a bridge across a swamp that guarded one of his flanks. As Francesco was unprepared and without defenses on that flank, the battle was lost almost as soon as begun. Seriously wounded, Francesco retreated with the remnants of his army to Padua, where Venice clamped on a tight siege. With his other army similarly besieged in Verona, things quickly unraveled. Verona fell first, on June 22, 1405. Taking the city, the Venetian army was on its best behavior; atypically for *condottieri* armies, there was virtually no sacking – a lesson not lost on those suffering the siege of Padua. Rather, the Venetians promised that Verona's laws and liberties would be protected and upheld by a Venice committed to protecting them.

With the fall of Verona, Venice turned all its military might on Padua. But it was hardly necessary: plague had broken out in the city, and, according to chronicle accounts, hundreds were dying daily as July turned into August. Francesco, finding himself fearing for his life at the hands of his own citizens, made a last desperate attempt to save himself by offering to sell Padua to the Venetians in return for a safe conduct to Florence for himself and his sons. Apparently Venice was disposed to accept, as the price asked appeared to be less than the cost of keeping their armies in the field. At this point, however, Florence, fearing Venice's growing power and anxious to preserve Carrara as a counterbalance to the Visconti in the Lombard plain, apparently stepped in, offering to help Francesco. Thus suddenly, in the midst of negotiations, with the promise of Florentine support, Francesco launched an attack on the besieging Venetian troops. But it failed, and no Florentine help showed up to save the day. The siege dragged on. Once again, however, the Venetians used their engineering skills to advantage. The engineer Domenico da Firenze managed to divert the course of a fork of the Brenta River that ran through the city, thus seriously depleting the city's water supply. Finally, on November 23, the gates of Padua were simply opened, and Francesco Novello Carrara was handed over to Venice. Once again the Venetian troops entered with minimal looting and violence, promising to protect the laws and liberties of Padua and to keep the peace.

Venice now became a mainland power with a *terraferma* mini-empire of its own that would quickly grow to encompass virtually all of northeastern Italy, with a few notable exceptions. As they developed their ruling techniques for that Italian mini-empire, the Venetians followed in many ways the techniques they had developed in the Middle Ages for ruling their maritime empire in the Adriatic and eastern Mediterranean. That empire had been aimed less at direct exploitation of conquered territory than at creating a peaceful and ordered environment favorable to trade and development, with perhaps just that pinch of graft needed to ensure profits and make things run smoothly. There was little interest in exerting more heavy-handed control as a way to extract revenues, as the Venetian vision always leaned toward making money by controlling trade and related commercial activities rather than via direct rule.

Thus, as they took over Verona, Padua, and Vicenza, with minor variations in each city, the Venetians left in place local laws and governments, merely adding at the top of the administration a rector or *Podestà* to oversee the highest levels of civil justice and act as the chief executive officer of the city. As the final arbiters of civil justice, these officials played a significant role in assuring that commercial activities were conducted in an orderly and legal fashion, or at least in a fashion that served Venetian interests. In addition, they appointed officials responsible for the policing and defense of the city, both always seen as a measure of good government. Many of the smaller towns in the area that had been under the control of Verona, Padua, or Vicenza continued to be ruled by those cities, but once again Venetian oversight of their rule tended to make it less heavy-handed and corrupt. In sum, although it would be unwise to be too idealistic about Venetian rule, it seems that, broadly speaking, while leaving each city at least looking as if little had changed and functioning much as it had previously, they made sure that what might be labeled a *popolo grosso* program of rule would obtain. Peace, order, and law were all to be guaranteed with an eye to protecting and encouraging the economic prosperity of the new cities of their new *terraferma* mini-empire. Over the long run Venetian rule tended to become more centralized and more exploitative, but with a few significant exceptions, it remained remarkably intact until 1797, when the city and its *terraferma* were finally conquered by Napoleon.

A Condottiere *Wins: Milan, Francesco Sforza, and the Art of the Double-Cross*

Venice's relatively rapid successes were not so easily matched by either Milan or Florence. Both had been financially exhausted by the wars with Gian Galeazzo Visconti, and both had felt forced by events to demonstrate to their neighbors, and to their intended victims, a more aggressive and unattractive vision of what awaited them if they should fall under their power. For Milan and its Lombard mini-state, Gian Galeazzo's death was the signal to rise up in revolt, as we have seen. When we left Visconti territories to pursue the *terraferma* successes of Venice, a group of tutors was theoretically ruling there in the name of Giovanni Maria Visconti, the teenage son of Gian Galeazzo, while in fact his mother, Catarina, and one of his father's chief administrators, Francesco Barbavara, wrangled for power behind the scenes. Given the situation, it is not particularly surprising that things went badly for Giovanni. In fact, by the time Giovanni's unhappy rule was cut short by his assassination in 1412, most of the chief cities of his father's old mini-state either had set up their own local *signori* drawn from powerful local families or had been taken over by *condottieri* who had once served Milan. This process of disaggregation was aided by enemies who sought to assure that the Visconti would not rebuild a dangerous Milanese state, often with military intervention.

In a way, then, Giovanni picked the right time to be assassinated. Even for Gian Galeazzo's preferred son, Filippo Maria, the future did not appear especially bright. When his brother was killed, he was besieged in his own castle in Pavia, while the city itself was controlled by a powerful local family, the Beccaria, supported militarily by one of his father's old *condottieri*, Facino Cane. Actually, Filippo had not lost power to them, for to a great extent he never had been able to claim it. Moreover, not yet twenty, and reportedly sickly, socially withdrawn, and timid, he did not seem to have the ability to extricate himself from his dire situation. But whatever his personal flaws or strengths, he, like his father, quickly became a master of that *virtù* that brought success. Soon after his brother's death, *fortuna* also came to his aid, as Facino Cane died unexpectedly – luck that in this case may have been aided by *virtù* in the form of an effective dose of poison.

Filippo quickly took advantage of the situation, marrying Cane's widow, who needed a husband to help her maintain control of the territory Cane had taken. He also rapidly won over to his side one of Cane's main captains, Francesco da Carmagnola, who provided the force behind Filippo Maria's slow but sure reenactment of his father's strategy of isolating and then gobbling up former allies. By 1426, together they had retaken the core of his father's old Lombard mini-state. Moving out from Pavia and Milan, he had reestablished his power from the Mincio River in the east to the old western borders; while to the south, retaking Parma and Piacenza, he moved into the lower Lombard plain, and in the north he drove the Swiss back north of the Alpine passes. In the process, in 1422, he also captured the traditional maritime power, Genoa, still weakened by internal divisions and its wars with Venice. The emperor Sigismund, who had been dabbling in Visconti affairs, signaled perhaps most clearly the status of Filippo Maria when he invested him with the duchy of Milan in 1426, recognizing him as the dominant power in the area.

Not all were so willing to accept Filippo's success. Florence was especially concerned about the Visconti resurgence, and with some reason. First, although Filippo was not responsible for it, they felt exposed by the loss of their Carrara allies, whom they had counted on to contain Visconti aggression and to keep open the main north-south trade routes across the eastern Lombard plain and over the Alps. Under Venetian control things were much less certain. They also worried that that city, seen as a wily and potentially dangerous commercial competitor, could not always be counted on to ally with them against Filippo, as the Carrara had been virtually forced to do, given their hostile relations with Milan. More immediately, the Visconti conquest of Genoa had moved Milan directly into the shipping lanes in the Tyrrhenian Sea that were crucial for Florentine sea trade with northern Europe – the main route that their luxury cloth trade followed tracked the coastline of that sea and passed Genoa. It also gave him control of a maritime trading and banking city with the ability to compete with Florence in both areas.

But that was not the only area in which Filippo seemed to threaten Florence, for he also reinstituted his father's policy of dabbling in the politics of Tuscany, thwarting once again Florence's own plans for expansion. Actually, he went one step further, dabbling more aggressively in the troubled and violent lands to Florence's east, the Romagna. The Romagna was a less developed area with many little city-states, most of which were theoretically part of the Papal States. Perhaps best known as a breeding ground for *condottieri* and for its almost constant state of local conflict, it was also much too close to Florence and Florentine expansionist ambitions to allow it to fall into the hands of old enemies like the Visconti. As a result, with an eye to stopping Filippo's growing power before it was too late, Florence declared war on Milan in 1423.

The first two years of fighting produced little in the way of military successes, but did quickly deplete Florence's typically strained treasury. This in turn put considerable pressure on the conservative inner group of Florentine families led by the young and inexperienced Rinaldo d'Albizzi (1370–1442), whose family (led by his deceased father, Maso [1343–1417]) had fairly effectively cornered power in Florence for a generation after the Ciompi revolt. In the face of this situation, Rinaldo felt forced to put aside what had become a virtually traditional distrust of Venice and attempted to win their support for the war with Milan. His ambassadors, however, found themselves dealing with a divided Venice. On the one hand, a significant number of noble families felt that Venice had expanded far enough on the *terraferma* to secure their interests and that the Mincio River, which marked the western edge of their territories, provided a natural and defensible border with Milan. Moreover, with Florence and Milan involved in a war that was exhausting the resources of both, Venice could sit safely on the sidelines and not have to worry about the territorial ambitions of either; even commercial competition would be tilted in Venice's favor by the ongoing war. On the other hand, a group of nobles saw the expanding territorial pretensions of the Visconti, especially in the Romagna, which bordered Venetian territories to the south, as dangerous, reawakening fears of a Milanese state that might dominate the north of Italy. Visconti control of Genoa, a traditional mercantile enemy of Venice, was also a novelty that worried many, especially as Genoa was still feared as a rival.

Finally, in 1425, the unusually aggressive and young doge, by Venetian standards, Francesco Foscari (1373–1457; doge 1423–1457), came out in support

of war, and Venice aligned with Florence against Milan. The early campaigns
of the new alliance went well. Troops led by Francesco da Carmagnola, once
Filippo's main *condottiere* (who had jumped sides, apparently fed up with
broken Visconti promises), won first the city of Brescia in 1426, then the
city of Bergamo in 1427, pushing the Venetian border with the Milanese
state west all the way to the Adda River. At this point, with Milan's army
decisively defeated, the end seemed to be nigh for Filippo. Carmagnola had
merely to sweep up the Adda into the inner core of Milanese territory to
secure a final defeat of the Visconti, making Venice the ruler of the whole
Lombard plain. But, inexplicably, Carmagnola at this point stopped. He
appeared to be stalling on purpose. And as time dragged on without further
advances, rumors began to spread back in Venice that he had secretly been
bought by Milan or was trying to hold up Venice for more money, just as he
had apparently tried to hold up Filippo earlier.

Venice tried to press Carmagnola to resume his advance, but to no avail.
Thus, they found themselves in a delicate situation, one often noted as a significant problem with wars fought by *condottieri*. As Machiavelli would later
point out, *condottieri* were frequently more loyal to money and their own
interests than to their employers. But, as warriors, they controlled the direct
force that was necessary to win wars in the absence of citizen armies. Thus,
when they decided that it was not in their interest to follow the orders of
their employers, their employers had little recourse but to renegotiate, accept
the situation, or lose their army. Many a city would have liked to fire a recalcitrant *condottiere*, but the trouble then became how to secure new ones in
the midst of war. In Venice there was considerable debate about what to do
with Carmagnola. Was there a way to encourage him to return to his aggressive winning ways? Was there perhaps a way to force him to fight? Or was
punishment perhaps necessary, even in the face of the danger that he would
then jump back to serving his ex-master, Milan?

As these discussions raged in Venice, the Council of Ten took the initia-
tive, quietly pressing the Senate to invite Carmagnola back to Venice for a
discussion of strategy. It might have appeared that this invitation was aimed
at discovering what Carmagnola really wanted and what it would take to
get him back into the field. If this is what Carmagnola expected when he
accepted the invitation, he was badly mistaken. For, as soon as he entered the
city, he was arrested by the Ten and quickly executed. From the Ten's perspective the problem was eliminated with his death. The lesson was clear: Venice
expected results for its investments, even in *condottieri*, and investments that
did not pay off could be terminated, in this case literally. Moreover, Venice
flexed its financial muscles and quickly found new *condottieri* willing to take

the risk of replacing Carmagnola. They were not as effective as hoped, however, and the war dragged on with neither side regaining the upper hand.

With the demise of Carmagnola, Filippo Maria Visconti was in a stronger position, at least in theory, as he had managed to hire the leading *condottieri* of both of the two main schools of *condottiere* warfare: Niccolò Piccinino (1386–1444), leader of the Bracceschi, and Francesco Sforza (1401–1466), leader of the Sforzeschi. It might be more accurate to claim that they were in and out of his camp, as he too was having trouble holding on to his *condottieri* and getting them to fight. Most significant for the future of Milan were his problems with Sforza. Earlier, unhappy with his performance against Carmagnola, Filippo had fired him. But he soon decided that he needed him; thus, in order to secure his loyalty, he decided to betroth the thirty-one-year-old *condottiere* to his own eight-year-old daughter and only heir, Bianca Maria, in 1432. Betrothal, however, was not marriage. And as time went by, it became clear that Filippo was reluctant to deliver on the promise of marriage. In turn, Sforza was busily following his own military interests, carving out a small territorial state for himself at the expense of the papacy in central Italy. Growing tensions between Sforza and Visconti were finally rendered moot, however, when Sforza accepted a Venetian offer of better pay and jumped to the Venetian camp.

Paradoxically, although the ensuing war was officially waged to control the Lombard plain, perhaps the most important battles were naval battles. This might have given the Venetians an advantage, were it not for one significant qualification: the battles were fought not on the Mediterranean, but rather on an inland lake, Garda. This actually gave Filippo an advantage as he had only to sail his ships from Mantua up the Mincio River to Garda or to build them there, as the lake was in territory he controlled. The Venetians faced a more difficult problem. If they wanted to take advantage of their skill at naval warfare, they had to figure out a way to transport a war fleet over the mountains to the lake. Needless to say, Filippo must have felt confident that that flank was one of his most secure. But after considerable debate the Venetians devised a highly unlikely plan to carry a fleet over the low mountains that divided the Adige River, which they controlled, to Lake Garda on rollers, in the winter. Improbable as it seems, they succeeded. It required over 2,000 oxen, but in the end a small fleet of 6 galleys and 25 smaller long ships was hauled over the mountains in 15 days in the winter of 1439.

This unlikely task was carried out by the Venetian naval officer Niccolò Sorbolò, and once again demonstrated the Venetian willingness to experiment with major feats of engineering and technical virtuosity in order to garner strategic advantage. For all that, however, their fleet was defeated in the first major battle on the lake, and only Sforza's land army, now serving Venice, prevented a total rout. Still, the Venetian fleet was established on Garda, and in the following year they won a series of major victories that established their control of the lake. With the support of the now victorious Venetian fleet, Francesco Sforza took the main town on the lake, Peschiera, and moved south to push back Milanese armies that had been pressing nearby Brescia and Bergamo. Piccinino, now the main *condottiere* general of Milan, tried to create a diversion by attacking Florentine territory in Tuscany in the hopes of drawing off Sforza to defend Venice's ally. But his attempt failed rather dramatically when Florence, led by their new leader, Cosimo de' Medici, and his wealth, fielded a strong army of their own and defeated Piccinino at the Battle of Anghiari in June of 1440, a victory that would live on in Florentine memory as a great Medici moment.

Pressing Milanese finances to the limit, Piccinino raised a new army and returned to the north to face off with Sforza on the Adda River, the last barrier on the road to Milan. The impending battle appeared to have the potential to become the classic confrontation of the Italian Hundred Years' War. At question was the heartland of the north of Italy, fought over by the two greatest cities of the north, Venice versus Milan, and with their armies led by the recognized leaders of the two greatest schools of Italian *condottieri* – the Sforzeschi, led by Francesco Sforza, and the Bracceschi, led by Niccolò Piccinino. But once again the complex realities of *condottiere* warfare denied this perfect confrontation. Piccinino apparently saw the moment as a good one to hold up Filippo Maria Visconti for a city of his own to rule. He demanded Piacenza as a prize for his loyal service, a jewel that Visconti was reluctant to cede to a general who had not been doing particularly well in the field. Thus, it appears that Visconti decided he would rather keep the city and instead finally give up his daughter, Bianca Maria, to Francesco Sforza in order to induce him to desert Venice. Francesco did just that, abandoning Venice to marry Bianca Maria, whose dowry was sweetened with the promise of two cities, Cremona and Pontremoli. Soon after the marriage took place, peace was declared in December of 1441, with Venice lacking a major general to pursue the war and both sides financially exhausted. Yet, in its own strange way, the classic battle that was never fought between Venice and Milan was actually the truly representative moment of these wars, with all its typically complex intrigue and double-dealing.

Once peace was signed, again much in that spirit the war was almost immediately renewed. Filippo soon revealed himself to be his own worst enemy, for although he could not take his daughter back from Sforza, he attempted to keep him from taking over the cities promised. Fed up with his new father-in-law, and never the most loyal of generals, Sforza jumped back to the Venetian side, and by 1446 he and his Venetian armies had crossed the Adda and were on the road to Milan. Once again, it seemed that finally things had become clear. Sforza and Venice would take Milan, and the Visconti would be eliminated from the Italian political scene once and for all. But that was much too simple for the realities of *condottiere* warfare and the messy political scene of the day. To make a much more complex story of intrigue and double-dealing as brief as possible, suffice it to say that Filippo lured Sforza back to his side one last time and shortly thereafter died in 1447, perhaps exhausted by all his double crosses.

As Sforza was his primary heir, thanks to his marriage to Bianca, it looked like things had finally come together for this powerful *condottiere* with his inheriting the biggest prize of all, Milan and the heartland of northern Italy. Obviously, that would have been too logical and straightforward. Instead, the Milanese took advantage of the situation and declared themselves the Ambrosian Republic. Quickly they worked out a deal with the jilted Sforza. He would fight for Milan once more against Venice, lured by vague promises of future rewards and good pay. Perhaps Sforza did not have the courage to claim his due as heir, but it appears more likely that he felt that this arrangement would place him in the ideal place to double-cross his new employers and press his claims to rule Milan once Venice and Florence were actually defeated. And, in the long run, he would gain the strong support of the people of Milan, something that he could not have counted on had he tried to overthrow the Ambrosian Republic and assert his claims immediately.

He served for fourteen months, then, as the new republic of Milan sought to defend itself against Venice. His "loyal" service was rewarded in the end by the republic attempting to strike a secret deal with Venice for a peace that would have cut him out of the picture. Before things could come to a head, however, Sforza jumped to Venice again, and peace talks stalled. More double crosses quickly followed, until finally Venice and Milan agreed that their best course of action would be to eliminate their dangerous *condottiere* Francesco Sforza. Thus, in September of 1449, the folly of the war and its multiple betrayals was brought to its illogical logical conclusion with Venice and Milan joining together to declare war on their most famous general, none other than Francesco Sforza. The growing unreality of it all, however, was finally brought up short before the toughest reality of war, money. The cost of the war had exhausted the treasury of the Ambrosian Republic, and it collapsed bankrupt. The city was forced to turn to its Visconti heir, *condottiere*, and frequent opponent, Francesco Sforza, and accept him as their new *signore* in February of 1450. A much reduced Milanese state remained the dominant power in the western Lombard plain now led by its new lord, Francesco Sforza, not quite a new Count of *Virtù*, but at least the master of the Rinascimento double cross.

The Costs of War: Debt, Fear, and the Rise of the Medici in Florence

Before the Italian Hundred Years' War could end, however, Florence had to come to grips with its internal problems, exacerbated by years of warfare and a concomitant burgeoning public debt. Significantly, the one thing that was perhaps most critical in bringing at least momentary peace and prosperity was the rise to power of the one family that would dominate Florentine political and social life up to the eighteenth century, the Medici. The best way to begin the tale is to return briefly to Florence's Ciompi revolt of 1378. At its most revolutionary, it seemed as if the dominance of the *popolo grosso* might actually be broken by a guild regime that included in government a much broader proportion of the *popolo*, including the large Ciompi guild made up of the thousands of unskilled workers in the cloth-producing industry. But that regime was too democratic to last, and by 1382 a conservative reaction was well under way, with the leading families of the city, having survived a scare that would not be forgotten, putting aside their differences to band together to rule. At the head of this group emerged a successful leader, Maso d'Albizzi, who led quietly behind the scenes with a careful mix of compromise and corruption, building a solid base of support in a progressively more aristocratic and narrow group called the Ottimati (the Best). The Ottimati were drawn from the richest and most powerful of the *popolo grosso*, who, rather like the Venetian nobility, claimed to represent the oldest families of the city; once again the ideology was that they were not new, merely the best and oldest.

Whether or not they were actually either, Maso led with their support by essentially corrupting the electoral system of the city. As was the case in many cities, Florentine elections were conducted by lot, with the names of candidates elected to each office being drawn from bags. The key to corrupting the system was getting to the names in the bags before they were drawn, and, although the process was complex, essentially Maso did this by having his people cull the bags periodically to make sure that the names of his followers dominated. Thus, although from time to time a humble artisan might be drawn to serve, even in a major office, with impressive continuity the names drawn were those of his supporters. Luckily escaping certain defeat thanks to Gian Galeazzo's death in 1402, Maso's hold on the city became ever stronger, until his own death in 1417 brought on a transition crisis. A number of his long-time supporters, who had taken more of a leadership role in his last years, were ready to step in to replace him, but his son Rinaldo, not without resistance, asserted his leadership of the Ottimati. Rinaldo, however, was less content to rule quietly behind the scenes, adopting a much more princely style, which did not sit well with some of the older members of the Ottimati, who felt that they were more deserving to rule.

Nonetheless, Rinaldo managed to rule, not so quietly, nor so successfully, for almost two decades, until that great destroyer of governments, war and its expenses, stepped in to bring him down. A major factor in this was Filippo Maria Visconti, who, it will be remembered, had rebuilt his father's power in the north successfully enough that he was again perceived as threatening Florence. Not a patient behind-the-scenes manipulator content to carry out the long, involved intrigues necessary to isolate or outmaneuver enemies, like his father or Gian Galeazzo, Rinaldo instead successfully pressed for a declaration of war against Milan in 1423, as fears about Milan's expansionist policies grew. But the war that was supposed to nip Filippo's power in the bud dragged on, and the costs of maintaining *condottiere* armies in the field placed increasing burdens on Florentine revenues and the public debt. And tensions within the city built. The princely Rinaldo, with his more open style of rule and lack of military successes to bolster his fading support, found himself in a difficult position. To make matters worse, when expenses outran revenues, as they regularly did in times of war, he was forced to rely on forced loans to cover expenses.

Based on estimates of a family's wealth, these forced loans, if the estimates had been fairly done, would have fallen evenly on everyone. But, of course, one of the reasons for supporting Rinaldo, and his father before him, in power (or most other governments, for that matter) was that they rewarded their supporters with lower estimates. In the regular order of things, such privileges could pass largely unnoticed, but when wars dragged on and loans were required monthly and at times weekly, the unequal distribution of the burden became much more obvious. Moreover, those who benefited from this favoritism were in a position to buy up loan shares at a fraction of their original cost, yet still earn interest on their full face value, thus turning them into lucrative investments. In sum, as others struggled to survive, the protected few flourished. Needless to say, as such favoritism became more evident during the ongoing war with Milan, the economic and class divisions within society weighed more and more heavily on those who saw themselves as the victims. And this in turn put Rinaldo and the Ottimati in a decidedly precarious position.

Finally, in 1427, a group of the Ottimati, fearing the revolutionary potential of this situation, lent their weight to widespread calls for reforming the
forced loan system. Reluctantly, Rinaldo's government took on the task
of making a serious and honest census of all the property and wealth in
Florence as well as in the areas of Tuscany that Florence controlled. This
Catasto of 1427, as it was called, attempted with considerable success to enu-
merate all the people and measure all the wealth and property of the region,
with the goal of using this new, more accurate measure of wealth as the base
for imposing forced loans. (This virtual snapshot of Florentine Tuscany, its
population, wealth, and property, for all its problems and biases, has become
a valuable source for historians, as noted in Chapter 3.) And it actually did
provide a basis for extracting increased revenues from forced loans in a manner that was at least less unfair. But many of the Ottimati were unhappy
about losing their tax advantages, blaming Rinaldo, while many in the larger
population realized with the compiling of the *Catasto* just how unfairly they
had been treated in the past and blamed him as well.

As a result, no one was particularly happy with Rinaldo. If anything,
tensions in Florence increased following the reform. In turn, Rinaldo and
his inner circle seemed to be caught in what might be labeled an escalat-
ing paranoia, an increasing fear that resentment about taxation, war, and
his own high-handed rule might lead to the growth of an opposition that
would attempt to overthrow them. Fear grew so rampant that those viewed
as potential opponents were actually required to swear on the Bible that
they would not be divisive and instead think only of the honor of the city.
Religious confraternities were shut down, as it was feared that their popularity with a wide spectrum of the population and their enthusiasm for civic
morality might make them foci of resistance or revolutionary agitation.

Things were quickly falling apart. To Rinaldo's credit, he appears to have
been aware that a dramatic success was necessary to reunite the city behind
him. Given the mixed results of the city's expensive and ongoing war with
Milan, a quick and inexpensive military victory might have seemed just
what the situation required. Thus, in 1429, when the nearby rival cloth-
producing city of Lucca seemed to be dissolving in internal turmoil of its
own, it must have appeared to Rinaldo and his remaining Ottimati supporters an opportunity too good to pass up. War was declared, with an eye to
taking over their cloth-producing rival. And Rinaldo, anxious to be seen as
leading a triumphant war effort for a change, took a prominent role in the
campaign. Unfortunately for plans of a quick, easy, and, most importantly,
inexpensive victory, the Florentine attack reunited the Lucchese. Moreover,

it rallied support from other independent cities in Tuscany that continued to fear Florence's aggressive tendencies.

As a result, a theoretically short, successful war morphed relentlessly into a long, costly one. Rumors swirled through the city, as 1432 slid painfully into 1433 without any victory in sight, that an opposing faction was forming with the goal of finally throwing out Rinaldo and the Ottimati. The most likely leader of any such faction was seen as the rich and powerful Cosimo de' Medici (1389–1464), son of Giovanni da Bicci de' Medici (1360–1429). Cosimo, like his father, had largely avoided political activity in the city and for the most part had been a tacit supporter of the Ottimati. But, unlike Rinaldo and the Ottimati, he was not perceived as an enemy of the lower classes. This was in part because he was a relative of Salvestro de' Medici, who was remembered as a supporter of the Ciompi in 1378, and in part because his banking and cloth-manufacturing activities provided jobs for a significant number of the city's artisans and *popolo minuto*. From this perspective he seemed a natural rallying point for those opposed to what were perceived as Rinaldo's wars and their costs.

Rinaldo attempted to blame the war with Lucca on Cosimo and his financial interest in cornering Tuscan cloth production, and there may have been a kernel of truth in his claims. But even peace conspired against him; for Cosimo was a leader in negotiating the peace with Lucca that ended the war in April of 1433, thus at one and the same time increasing both his popularity with the war-weary city and Rinaldo's fear of him. A few months later, in September, when a group of Priors was drawn that was strongly pro-Rinaldo – something that was relatively easy to do as the bags were still filled with Albizzi supporters – Rinaldo decided to take decisive action and had Cosimo arrested for treason. Apparently the plan was to have the Priors appoint a special Balìa made up of the strongest supporters of Rinaldo to try Cosimo and execute him.

Rinaldo got his Balìa, and Cosimo was duly arrested. But then things went wrong, as even Rinaldo's Balìa was uncomfortable about taking responsibility for an unpopular execution of Cosimo. Moreover, a number of Florence's most powerful allies stepped in to warn against such an extreme action. Venice, with its close ties to the Medici bank and Medici international trade interests, made it clear that they were not enthusiastic about the potential risk to its economy were the Medici bank to fold – something that it saw as a distinct possibility if Cosimo were executed. The pope, Eugenius IV, whose finances had been controlled by Cosimo's bank and who was heavily indebted to him, expressed similar concerns. As a result, although Rinaldo continued to insist on execution, his Balìa let him down, voting merely to exile Cosimo to Venice.

Cosimo survived. And unsurprisingly, with his survival, any hopes that there was not an anti-Rinaldo, Medici-led faction died. In Venice, Cosimo continued to lead his economic empire succored by that city, while back in Florence many of Rinaldo's supporters, seeing the writing on the wall, slowly deserted to the swelling Medici camp. Finally, in the summer of 1434, even with the bags still corrupted and supposedly filled with Albizzi supporters, a new group of Priors was drawn who were ready to openly switch sides. They appointed a new Balìa to deal with the political turmoil of Florence, which asked Cosimo to return. Rinaldo understood all too well what that meant – his own men, drawn from his own corrupted bags, had deserted him and invited back to the city the man he had failed to execute. Intelligently, he fled the city into an exile of his own.

In turn, on October 5, 1434, Cosimo returned to Florence, ostensibly merely as a once-exiled citizen now restored to the city he loved and wished to aid. But few were fooled. With his supporters Cosimo had driven out a leader who had attempted to kill him and divided a ruling group that for almost five decades had dominated the political scene. Still, Cosimo was careful not to repeat Rinaldo's mistakes. Rather, like Rinaldo's father, he worked quietly behind the scenes, making good use of his own group of supporters (who would become known as the Palleschi – after the six balls [palle] on the Medici coat of arms) and his own corruption of elections, which adopted and expanded many of the strategies used by the Albizzi, as we will see.

Meanwhile, the war dragged. Milan and Venice divvied up the Lombard plain, and Francesco Sforza out-double-crossed his employers until he became signore of Milan. Finally, in 1454, with perhaps the most famous peace of the Rinascimento, the Peace of Lodi, the new political realities were confirmed, with Venice and Milan dividing the north between them and Cosimo's Florence controlling much of Tuscany directly and exerting considerable influence over the center, even if the Papal States were formally confirmed there as well. Although in many ways this peace and the division of Italy among five great powers – Venice, Milan, Florence, the Papal States, and a Neapolitan kingdom in the south – was not as neat or complete as it is often depicted, the political picture of Italy was clarified and to a great degree stabilized after more than a hundred years of almost continuous war.

New men, social turmoil, violence in the streets, and the violence of warfare had transformed the northern half of Italy, bringing the once dozens of proudly independent cities under the rule of a handful of powers. In turn, the social and political significance of an increasingly self-assured and aristocratic popolo grosso had survived and flourished in the face of numerous travails and, as we shall see, in the process constructed a cultural vision and program that consolidated their claims to lead society. The peace that had arrived would last, with a few significant exceptions, for forty years, from 1454 to 1494 – forty years often depicted as the high point of the Rinascimento. Thus for a little more than a generation Italy was relatively at peace: Italy's own Hundred Years' War was formally over.

5

IMAGINATION: THE SHARED PRIMARY
CULTURE OF THE EARLY
RINASCIMENTO (c. 1350–c. 1475)

One thing is clear when we look at the cultural world of the early Rinascimento. There were no humanists. And the supposedly central cultural accomplishment of the period, humanism, was unknown. It simply did not exist. The term was coined only in the nineteenth century by a German teacher in the *Gymnasium*, as the great twentieth-century scholar of the subject Paul Oscar Kristeller pointed out long ago. The label "humanist," however, did begin to be used in the late fifteenth century, apparently first by university students to refer to professors who focused on the *studia humanitatis* – that is, grammar, rhetoric, history, poetry, and moral philosophy – rather than on theology and law.

Less obvious, but in many ways more significant, is the way the search for humanism and humanists in the early Rinascimento, before they existed, has skewed the way scholars have looked at the cultural world of the fourteenth and fifteenth centuries. Perhaps most importantly, it has created a canon of works and writers who are deemed to be pre-humanistic or even simply humanist that seriously distorts the range and complexity of the cultural world of the day. Moreover, many writers and thinkers have largely been overlooked (or consigned to the Middle Ages, a kind of humanist hell) by scholars because they do not fit into the anachronistic and rather procrustean mold of an imagined humanism. In turn, many luminaries who have made it into the canon have become curiously disjointed by a scholarly desire to highlight their supposed humanistic writings at the expense of their broader oeuvre.

Petrarch (Francesco Petrarca, 1304–1374) provides a good case in point. Those who would see him as the first humanist tend to focus on his search for ancient Roman texts, his call for a Roman revival, and his enthusiasm for the recovery of an ideal ancient Latin based on Cicero to replace what he saw as corrupt medieval Latin. But as Ron Witt showed in his pioneering work *In the Footsteps of the Ancients*, all of this had crucial antecedents in a group of notaries and lawyers from the northeastern cities of Italy, perhaps most notably in love poets, chroniclers, and scholars such as Lovato Lovati (c. 1240–1309) and Albertino Mussato (1261–1329). Witt terms these scholars and statesmen as the first humanists, but his own work shows that their actual interests were much more broad-ranging and rich than the label normally would imply. Returning to the better-known Petrarch, his important religious speculations, heavily reliant on Saint Augustine, with a dose of the Franciscan spiritualism popular in his day, along with his rejection of the commercial culture of the cities of Italy have been relatively neglected or simply dismissed. Even what were probably Petrarch's most famous works, his love poems, eventually collected in his *Canzoniere*, created problems for some who label him the first humanist, because they were written in Tuscan vernacular, rather than in classical Latin. In many ways they seemed little interested in a classical revival, fitting far more comfortably – and dangerously, from the humanism-search perspective – into a late medieval tradition of love poetry and its vision of an ideal, refined, mannered way of life.

In the end, as a pre-humanist Petrarch becomes considerably narrower than the famous and influential figure of his day; and his fascinating complexity either drops away or creates problems for accounts of him as the first humanist. When we turn to Dante or Boccaccio, things get, if anything, worse, with the former disappearing back into the Middle Ages and the latter apparently unable to resist the lure of the vernacular, writing a number of his most important works in Tuscan rather than in Latin. In sum, we might do better to focus on the much more complex and fascinating cultural world of the early Rinascimento and leave humanists to a later day.

Rethinking the Culture of the Early Rinascimento without Humanism

Turning to that culture, if we think of it as a series of loosely interconnected, loosely shared imagined discourses – imagined, at times, in a consciously reflected way or merely accepted as the given and obvious modes of understanding life and the world – the project of doing cultural history becomes suggestively different. From such a perspective much of the discussion in earlier chapters becomes cultural history; for we have looked at a series of evolving ways of living in and imagining the urban *civiltà* of the early Rinascimento that did not turn on a shared single vision, but rather involved loosely shared discourses on the nature of a number of themes central to the times: the significance of the society's place in time and the primacy of first times; the social importance and disciplining power of *virtù*; the meaning and acceptance of social hierarchy and a hierarchical society; the implications of melding into a form of civic morality Christian ideals, civic traditions, and what might be labeled Rinascimento family values.

These central discourses were *to a degree* shared across society and provided the cultural lens that reduced the complexity of everyday life to discernible patterns that allowed action, reflection, and communication. But "to a degree" is a crucial caveat and one that complicates the picture significantly, because it is difficult to know in a precise way how deeply or consistently these discourses were shared across the highly differentiated society of the day. Did rural illiterate peasants imagine the world as did Dante or Petrarch? The latter obviously were educated men who were arguably comfortable reading Latin and conversing with the ancients, at times literally, while most peasants were illiterate and knew little of the urban world that was in many ways the motor of Dante and Petrarch's cultural and social world. Yet the distance may not have been as great as it appears at first, and if one considers the urban lower classes, sharing the closer confines of the narrow streets and lively market squares of their cities, a great deal more may have been shared than is often assumed.

But, of course, as we can encounter those ways of imagining the world only indirectly half a millennium later, via written and material records such as artifacts (including what we label anachronistically "art"), distinguishing the degree to which a particular way of imagining life or the world was shared becomes a difficult *and* intriguing question. In the discussion that follows we will attempt to consider such issues precisely because they are as interesting as they are difficult. And one thing is fairly clear from the start: the new cultural history has provided a range of suggestive new perspectives and methodologies that help to reveal that complexity. Newer visions of the way culture functions in complex societies, for example, have tended to reject the traditional vision of culture as moving from high to low in society and the very labels "high culture" and "low culture." In part this is because of the value judgments implied in "high" and "low" and related terms like "common," "popular" and "vernacular" that are used to label culture. But more pertinently, it is because a circulatory model of culture seems more appropriate, especially in premodern societies, where the desire and the ability to impose one culture upon another were less developed and more limited by technologies of communication that were less easily monitored and controlled. This is not to argue that in the Rinascimento motives were lacking for pressing one way of imagining reality over another or that this was not attempted. In fact, most of the ways of imagining that we have presented as central to the period served the *popolo grosso* in one way or another and were pressed as ideal by writers and scholars drawn from their ranks or in their service. But that does not mean that they originated with the *popolo grosso* or were always consciously seen as serving their interests at the expense of others. In some instances that was the case, but many elements of these central discourses were much more generally accepted, and often taken up from other social milieus or even from other cultures such as that of the Middle Ages or the classical world.

For the Rinascimento a circulatory model of cultural diffusion creates some different questions about how such dissemination worked. Scholars were once confident that most cultural activity, and thus the dissemination of ideas, was oral, as levels of literacy were assumed to have been very low. Recent studies, however, suggest that the commercial nature of urban life in Italy had led to an impressive growth of literacy, at least in the cities of the north and center of the peninsula, even before the fourteenth century. The Florentine chronicler and inveterate counter Giovanni Villani, whom we have already encountered counting the number of laborers in the cloth industry, reported that in the 1330s there were more than 70 teachers in Florence alone, teaching elementary reading and writing to approximately 10,000 children. Paul Grendler, in his important study of schooling in the Renaissance, estimated that that meant that between 67 and 83 percent of Florentine males went to school and had some rudimentary knowledge of reading and writing.

Although these figures seem particularly high given earlier assumptions, they are supported to a degree by the famous Florentine *Catasto* drawn up almost a century later, in 1427, to help finance the war with Milan. The *Catasto* required the heads of households throughout the territories controlled by Florence to submit a written declaration of their family's possessions. A full 80 percent signed their returns in their own hands. Also noteworthy was the growth of the number of teachers on public payrolls during the period; a partial list with the dates on which public stipends began includes Ivrea (1308), San Gimignano (1314), Treviso (1316), Turin (1327), Pistoia (1332), Savona (1339), Lucca (1348), Bassano (1349), Feltre (1364), Vigevano (1377), Sarzana (1396), Modena (1397), and Udine (1400). A number of cities even offered free education to all children of citizens. Missing from this list, however, are the more major cities such as Venice and Florence, where it appears teaching remained in the hands of private teachers and where education remained a matter of family investment and privilege rather than public policy. By contrast, in lesser cities the legislation that created public stipends often referred to the opportunity that education provided for promoting economic development and a city's competitiveness.

The education provided by these teachers was usually elementary and functional, focusing on learning to read and write the basic business Latin necessary for writing contracts and carrying on business. In most cities, then, literacy meant a rudimentary knowledge of a practical late medieval Latin used by notaries and lawyers for commercial activity and by governmental bureaucrats for governing. This suggests why many writers in the fourteenth century, eager to establish their superior intellectual and social status, attempted to distinguish themselves from ordinary notaries and lawyers and the practical Latin that was used for their work. Petrarch was merely a leader of a more general movement that sought to create a separation of a literary elite from that business world. A purer ancient Latin based on the best Latin of the ancient world was the vehicle that marked out a supposedly superior intellectual attainment, and it did indeed create a significant scholarly/social divide. Just as working with one's hands distinguished artisans from the *popolo grosso*, so too did working with one's mind and writing true classical Latin (even by a select few lawyers and notaries) begin to distinguish true poets and intellectuals from more common notaries and lawyers and the larger mass of the population who read and wrote what was increasingly labeled an inferior medieval Latin.

Although obvious, it is worth pointing out that this new, supposedly superior cultural tool of ancient Roman Latin and the new literary elite it identified were thus presented not as new, but rather as old – a rebirth of the first perfect Latin along with a rebirth of cultural leaders based on that ancient culture. Significantly, Petrarch and many of his fellows made a point of noting that while they had been pressed by their families to study law, they had found it distasteful and escaped its common drudgery and corrupt Latin to focus on rediscovering the classics and, through them, a lost classical language. As a result, Latin actually became two languages: one a widely shared, practical language of law, commerce, and governance, and one a superior ancient language limited to an elite few. Across the fifteenth century, however, the two languages would eventually meld to a degree, as more and more lawyers and bureaucrats mastered a more refined classical Latin and integrated it into the more important documents of government and society. In turn, at much the same time many of the more common documents of commerce and everyday governance began to be written in the vernacular, in part because classical Latin lacked the rich vocabulary of late medieval Latin and was less capable of describing the full complexity of the modern world.

At first this might seem to imply that there was a deep rift between an elite world dominated by classical Latin, which had the potential of opening the culture of the ancients to a select few, and the wider literate urban populace without the ability to participate in that discovery of the past. But once again the gap may not be as great as often assumed. Obviously, for all their claims to the contrary, the masters of classical Latin still lived in the urban world of their day. Few had the luxury of attempting to live in rural isolation from its quotidian cultural demands, like Petrarch. And even the fortunate few were able to read only a limited number of classical texts in manuscript before printing made a wider range of literature available. Many would-be elite scholars were limited to working with a few classical texts, like Ovid's *Metamorphoses*, that offered brief sketches of particular aspects of ancient culture or compendia of ancient thought, compiled in the Middle Ages. These compilations – often called *florilegia* or little books of flowers of ancient wisdom, both classical and Christian – were a source of knowledge easily transferred to the oral culture of the day, and along with tales of the lives of Church Fathers (obviously set in the ancient Roman world), Christian martyrs, saints, and local legends of Roman foundations and important historical events, they created a largely oral-based rich imaginary of the ancient world that was widely shared across society. Perhaps more significantly, the material remains of that ancient world were all around and, at times, imagined to be even more around than they actually were (when medieval ruins were assumed to be ancient). Eventually scholars would sort all of this out and make the divide between an elite Latin culture and a less learned one come closer to what Petrarch thought it should be, but that was still in the future.

In fact, before printing, culture was primarily oral. Even written texts retained essential features of oral communication in a way that is hard to fully appreciate today. The letter, the short story or novella, and, of course, even poetry, which intentionally mimed the rhythms and feel of speech, all retained a familiar orality. From that perspective a letter was merely a moment of oral communication frozen and transmitted over space and time, and given its shorter length, it could be and was regularly melted back down into oral communication. Letters often were meant to be copied and spread widely in that way. And, of course, they were frequently read out loud and thus returned to that oral culture. Much the same was true of the novella. Boccaccio's *Decameron* is just the most famous example. Most of its stories were taken from an oral tradition that stretched back to the Middle Ages and earlier. But the popularity of the tales Boccaccio took from that tradition meant that they returned to the oral culture of his day, where they had a history of their own, popping up repeatedly and being recrystallized in many literary genres and cultural traditions. At first glance Petrarch's love poetry seems distant from the rougher world of the streets of the cities of his day, as he no doubt intended it to be, but it should not be forgotten that his love poetry, like that of others was often converted into popular songs sung in those same streets, and almost certainly echoed the imagery of both at times.

Moving beyond written texts, one of the most important areas of cultural transmission was storytelling – a favored way of imagining the world and conveying knowledge. Neighborhood, street, shop, market, home, even church were all places where stories were exchanged, not just to pass the time, but also to imagine it, explain it, and even discipline it. And especially in the home, but also in church, markets, and streets, women's voices played a significant role in passing on family traditions, lore, and that special disciplining form of rhetoric misleadingly labeled gossip. For gossip, as a form of social evaluation orally conveyed, was a powerful tool for imposing traditional values and discipline; in a way, it was the Greek chorus of everyday life and culture itself. When used wisely, it offered great power to those who deployed it, men as well as women. The market was also a special place for stories. The famed mountebanks (literally, those who mounted stages/banks to sell their goods) often attracted clients for their wares and nostrums with elaborate tales of their miraculous powers or exotic origins, putting a premium on their ability to capture the imagination of marketgoers and their ability to orally manipulate a shared culture based on their command of popular or intriguing stories.

Oral abilities, then, were widely respected, carefully cultivated, and provided a significant vehicle for conveying a shared culture. Streets and shops were also significant venues for stories, especially as work time was not yet clearly separated from play time, and thus both streets and shops pullulated with people ready to talk and relate the stories of the day. Finally, of course, churches were exceptional places of imagination and stories. The artwork that decorated them, the relics and ex votos that enriched their spiritual promise, and the sermons – one of the most popular forms of storytelling of the day – all had a particularly fecund ability to stimulate the imagination, creating stories often quite different from those intended – not to mention the gossip and stories told by the parishioners in this crucial place of social contact. But in all these venues it was the story that formed the human imagination of the world, creating modules of shared knowledge that could be endlessly recombined, making sense of life and its meaning, and helping to convey a shared culture.

Ennobling Love Poetry and Imagining Refined Desire and Elite Status

Perhaps the most important imaginative literature of the early Rinascimento was the poetry of love, because there were so many contradictory emotions associated with it. Actually, love poetry had been an important fascination of medieval literature, and if we include mystical poetry, with its love of the Divine, in many ways it was the first and most important poetry of that era. But the more mundane poetry of love between young people really gained momentum in Italy in the thirteenth century, stimulated by Provençal poetry carried to Italy by Troubadour poets. Fleeing the devastations of the Albigensian Crusades (that in many ways literally destroyed a flourishing Provençal culture), first at the medieval courts of the kings of southern Italy and Sicily, then more slowly in the north, attracted by the small but flourishing courts there, they introduced their love poetry in Provençal, the language of their homeland. It was a vital, rich, and at times quite earthy poetry that expressed the strong emotions of young love, both positively and negatively, and it found a responsive ear in Italy. In the flourishing urban centers of the north such as Treviso, Vicenza, Verona, and Padua, locals wrote love poems of their own in Provençal in imitation of the Troubadours, as well as in their own local dialects and even in Latin, to give it a higher tone. In Italy, given the oft-times violent social and political conflicts of the day, this poetry was not without a political and social agenda as well, which emphasized a refined love that demonstrated a nobility of manners and more traditional measures of status.

Beyond poetry, refined manners and love were often associated with a defense of the (largely imagined) more refined aristocratic ways of old elites, distinguishing them positively from the more direct and rough-hewn manners of the *popolo* (again largely imagined). In fact, for a time in the second half of the thirteenth century Provençal was for some with aristocratic pretensions the refined language par excellence, challenging the commonness of the vernacular and the working-world Latin of lawyers and notaries. It appears, however, that not all were content with this displacement of Latin and local vernaculars or with the implied dominance of Provençal and aristocratic cultural models that seemed to go with it. This was undoubtedly accentuated for some by a desire to escape what they saw as the intellectual influence of the clerical culture of French universities, which had been so important for medieval high culture, and perhaps Angevin influence from the south.

In the end, then, there was a reaction against French and Provençal culture and the love poetry associated with it, a reaction that stressed local traditions,

both in Latin and the vernacular, while co-opting the uplifting and aristocratic nature of love to agendas that did not serve an old nobility so easily.
Two of the most recognized love poets of the day, Dante (1265–1321) and
Petrarch, might be seen in this light. Both were influenced by the Provençal
tradition, but like many of the Italian love poets who preceded them, both
tended to move their love poetry away from the more earthy and sensual
forms of that tradition toward a more spiritual and ennobling vision of love.
In fact, it is often noted, with considerable justice, that the ennobling aspect
of their poetry was at times more significant than their claims of love. Dante's
love for the virtually nonexistent Beatrice – whom he claimed to have seen
only a few times in his life and to have met just once – and Petrarch's love for
his equally distant Laura stress the ennobling spiritual aspect of their passion.
Beatrice and Laura remain primarily imagined, and imagined in ways that
demonstrate repeatedly the spirituality of Dante, and Petrarch's aristocratic,
refined nature. In essence they served as literary signs for forming consensus
realities that confirmed the poets' superiority. In turn, their way of imagining
love served as a lesson on how passions might be disciplined so as to lead a
refined person – a true noble – to a Christian and peaceful life, something distant, one might note, from the violence traditionally associated with nobles.

Dante in his *Vita nuova* (*New Life*) wrote a work that was innovative in
that he included his own commentaries as a prose frame around his love
poems, explaining their deeper and ultimately ennobling spiritual meaning. As such, it was a clever innovation that attempted to assure that no one
would miss the consensus reality he sought to create of his love-induced
spiritual superiority. Comprising thirty poems, most in sonnet form, plus an
unfinished one on the death of his love, the "new" life that Dante refers to
in his title was the spiritual discovery of self that his love for Beatrice awoke
in him, giving him a new life. The poems are surrounded and explained by
what might be labeled an emotional and spiritual self-fashioning that details
the story of his first meeting with Beatrice, when he was nine and she eight,
and then follows his love for her up to her death. At a deeper level, however,
they present the story of a pilgrimage of self-discovery driven by love in
which Dante's love of beauty leads from the love of the beauty of Beatrice
in the material world to the love of true beauty in the spiritual world and
eventually to the love of God – the ultimate beauty and the one true life,
loving God. This involves a deep rebirth of self, and for Dante that personal
rebirth is possible only because of Christ's life and loving death and rebirth
to save humanity, the ultimate *rinascita*.

In his more famous *Divine Comedy*, virtually the whole early fourteenth-
century civic world of Florence and the medieval intellectual tradition are

melded in another personal pilgrimage. The work is a tour de force pilgrimage that traverses the spiritual universe of the early Rinascimento from
Hell, through Purgatory, and on to Paradise, where the love of Beatrice
leads Dante once more to the one true love – the love of God – with much
the same conclusion, his personal rebirth. This journey seems in many ways
a Christian rewriting of the classic pagan myth of Orpheus that had been
quite popular in the Middle Ages, with a positive twist. Orpheus, the god
of song and music, in the ancient story lost his newlywed Eurydice to death
and decided to journey to the underworld to try to win his love's resurrection with his singing ability. Dante, also a singer with his poetry, pursued
his love Beatrice, also lost to death, beyond this life to the next in order
to recover her love as well. Orpheus's songs in Hades were so moving that
Eurydice was restored to him on the condition that he lead her out of Hell
and back to life without either one looking back. But as they left Hell,
she could not resist looking back, and thus, tragically, he lost her to death
once more.

Like Orpheus's songs, Dante's singing poetry was so moving that with
the aid first of Virgil, a messenger sent by Beatrice to guide him through
Hell and Purgatory, and then of Beatrice herself, who was waiting for him
in Paradise, he also recovered his lost love. But from that moment the stories
diverge dramatically. Beatrice, in Paradise, rapt with the love of God, showed
Dante that his love of her was not the end of true love, but rather merely the
path to the one true love of God. Rather than returning to this world with
Beatrice in tow and losing her at the last moment, then, he returned to this
life with the true Christian love for God to guide him. And rather than the
tragedy of lost love – the fate of Orpheus – Dante's song had a happy ending,
making it a comedy rather than a tragedy, a *Divine Comedy*.

While in this rapid summation it might seem that Dante was operating
light years from the urban *civiltà* of his day, Dante's poetry comes alive with
that world in the people he encounters on his pilgrimage through Hell,
Purgatory, and Paradise, especially those in the violent and disturbing circles
of Hell. In fact, although there are rural moments in each of those three
realms, they all have an urban and even a Florentine feel, densely populated
with the denizens of his city who have passed away, yet are still alive with
its passions and conflicts. It is almost as if Dante could not imagine life even
after death without the teaming life of the urban world he knew and that
formed his cultural context at its most basic level. Thus his comedy is both
high culture at its highest and most transcendent – a spiritual pilgrimage to
paradise and God – and at the same time deeply embedded in the real nitty-
gritty political and social world of the cities of his day.

And while the love of Beatrice ennobles and ultimately promises salvation for the poet, his more mundane love of friends, city, and homeland, and the strong negative emotions that his enemies evoke, suggest how powerfully this highest form of literature was filtered through the everyday shared culture of his time. Dante's spiritual pilgrimage and Christian song frequently disappear, overwhelmed by the factional strife, loves, and hates of his city that he could not imagine escaping even in the afterlife. Yet love also ennobled, in the best sense of the term, a non-noble *popolo grosso* like Dante. At an historical moment when elite status remained a matter of hot debate and often violent deeds, here in the imaginary world of his *Divine Comedy* we see how love could become truly transcendent and how it marked him out as truly noble, safely numbered among the saved. And at the same time love (and hate) deeply colored his relations with his contemporaries and provided a crucial passion that bound him to his city and his fellow citizens, for better or worse.

For Petrarch, the discourse of love was apparently both less embedded in the civic world of his day and more physical and sensual in its description of his beloved Laura. And to that extent, at least, it was more erotic. Yet even with his often evocative descriptions of Laura, and his repeated admission of desires that he found troublingly nontranscendent, he too evoked divine love and transcendent passion. Given the ideals of spiritual love that the Italian love poetry of the day tended to exalt and that were deeply engrained in the discourses that circled around the powerful emotions of desire and love, it would have been difficult for a deeply Christian writer like Petrarch to avoid such connections. Perhaps what distinguished his poetry from that of Dante, which built upon similar Christian ideals, was the fact that Petrarch seemed incapable of completely making the jump to the spiritual love of God and finally accepting Laura as merely the path to a truer love of God. Or at least this is the way Petrarch chose to present his love in his poetry, in his self-examination in his many literary letters, and in his autobiographical and self-fashioning spiritual self-portrayal in Latin, the *Secretum*.

In each genre he returned over and over again to the fear that he ought to move on from his love of Laura to the ultimate love of the Divine, while confessing his inability to do so. In this he portrayed himself, for all his attempts to distance himself aristocratically from the everyday world of his day, as much like the adulterous lovers encountered in the criminal records of the fourteenth century – people who found love of another man's wife such a powerful passion that they could not resist its pull, even when they were well aware that it was a dangerous and disruptive emotion. For Petrarch, however, it is precisely this heroic and deeply self-reflective battle to overcome this dangerous emotion for his Laura, who was married to another, that makes him in his self-presentation a spiritual and ennobled lover. Skating on the edge of dangerous self-destruction and fully aware that the stakes might be his own salvation, he created a refined poetry that sensually evoked all the contradictions and dangerous beauty of his emotions. This rich mix of a widely shared everyday vision of love as a powerful and dangerous emotion and its potential to be spiritually ennobling, self-destructive, or, paradoxically, both at the same time, in many ways set the stage for the development of an aristocratic form of love poetry that would come to dominate the genre and the clichés of romantic love right up to the present. In fact, it is difficult to read his poetry today with a fresh eye, as over and over again one encounters his best lines with a sense of tired déjà vu – they surround us, and often drown us, in the saccharine world of romantic sentiments hawked in greeting cards and the romantic fantasies of popular romance, not to mention great literature.

Boccaccio (1313–1375), for all his more earthy sensuality in the *Decameron*, was definitely influenced by both Dante and Petrarch, and his love poetry owes much to both. Along with poetry he wrote a number of romances and love stories early on that tended to play on his portrayal of his own love in the 1330s for Fiammetta (a code name or *senhal*, meaning "the flame," for his love, who was apparently actually named Maria). She is often identified as a Neapolitan lady of substance, whom he came to know while working in the Florentine Bardi bank in Naples as a young man; and, as was the case in most of the love stories of the day, his love would have been adulterous if consummated, as she was married. That love seems to have influenced much of his early writings: several lyrics, two longish poems – the *Filostrato* (*Destroyed by Love*, based on the medieval tale of the Trojan lovers Troilus and Cressida) and the *Teseida delle nozze d'Emilia* (*The Theseid of the Marriage of Emilia*, an attempt to realize Dante's call for a classical epic in the vernacular) – the *Filocolo* (*Love's Labors*, a long, episodic narrative of love), the *Elegy of Madonna Fiammetta*, the *Ameto*, and the *Amorosa Visione*. While all of these works evoke Boccaccio's passion for Fiammetta, sometimes rather tenuously, they swing through a wide range of emotions associated with love in the shared culture of the day, evoking everything from uplifting desire and pure passion to more earthly desires and lust, along with a deep appreciation of the negative emotions that love was seen as inciting: jealousy, melancholy, envy, and even hate. Boccaccio even explores a woman's feelings in the *Elegy of Madonna Fiammetta*, making Fiammetta the narrator.

The last work of Boccaccio's early period, which ended more or less with the first wave of the plague, was the pastoral romance *Ninfale fiesolano* (*The

Nymphs of Fiesole). Finally leaving Fiammetta behind, it is set in the hills above Florence in much the same area where the *Decameron* would be set. It retells the tragic love of a shepherd named Africo for a nymph named Mensola. Africo eventually seduces and impregnates Mensola, but then, consumed by shame for taking the virginity of a nymph dedicated to virginity, he commits suicide by a brook that is then named after him, the Africo. Poor Mensola is punished by the goddess she serves, Diana, who, finding her weeping for her sins, transforms her into another brook that flowed into the Africo, the Mensola; thus presumably she and her tears of repentance, in the form of the Mensola, would join the Africo eternally. Yet even this mythic tale of the dangers of love, with its romantic conceits apparently so distant from the urban world of Boccaccio's day, circles back to Florence and its origins: for the son born to Mensola eventually founded the city of Fiesole on the hills above the two streams. Fiesole, in turn, founded Florence. Thus, even in this pastoral tale, the urban world of Florence underpins the tragic romance with a brilliant future and a founding myth. Rather ironically for romance and Boccaccio's founding myth, today both streams have been redirected to make way for cars and urban development and have largely ceased to flow – tragic tears replaced by modernity.

The hills above Florence where the Mensola and Africo flowed provided the setting for Boccaccio's most famous work, the *Decameron*. As noted earlier, he collected and retold 100 tales largely from the oral tradition of his day, many from the common lore of the streets of Florence. The collection is set in a frame story that features ten upper-class youths who, to overcome the sadness and horror of the Black Death raging in the city, have decided to pass their time telling tales, each relating one novella a day for ten days. This was not as callous as it might seem at first, as common wisdom supported by medical authorities recommended distancing oneself from the plague, both physically and spiritually, to avoid the dangers of melancholy and contamination; thus their flight, mannerly courting, pleasant surroundings, and light storytelling actually offered not just physical safety but also a form of emotional recovery, where youthful love played an important role.

Boccaccio's stories, although they often seem to the modern eye more lusty than loving, also provide a window on how love could be imagined as ennobling the *virtù*-ous. An excellent example of love's positive power to ennoble is provided by the first tale told on the fifth day, where the hero, a young Cypriot, started out so boorish and ignorant that he went by the name Cimone, because, as the tale explained, "he was never able to learn either letters or good manners and ... [thus he went about] with raucous, deformed speech and with manners more befitting a beast than a man; as a result virtually in mockery everyone called him Cimone, which in their language had the ring of our dumb animal." One day, wandering like a beast through the forest, he came upon a lightly clad young woman, Efigenìa, sleeping with two servants beside a pool, and he was literally un-dumbfounded by the sight of her beauty and the sudden love that overcame him. "In his brutish heart, which a thousand lessons had been unable to penetrate with civil pleasures (*cittadinesco piacere*), he felt suffused with a thought which his coarse and rough mind suddenly realized, she was the most beautiful thing ever seen." In a manner that echoed Dante's vision of the ascent from beautiful things and the love of individuals like Beatrice to the beauty of true knowledge and on to the love of the Divine and truth itself, Cimone's suddenly kindled thoughts ranged over her physical beauty with loving desire, "and in the end he … he came to realize that divine things were more worthy of reverence than the earthly." From a dumb animal he had been transformed by beauty and love into a philosopher.

In short order he became "the most elegant and mannered youth in Cyprus with a wider range of *virtù* than any other." In the face of this miraculous transition Boccaccio's narrator stopped the tale to query, "What, lovely ladies, are we to make of Cimone?" and proceeded to answer with a short but telling disquisition on the oft-noted tension between *Fortuna*, *Amore*, and *Virtù*: "It is clear that … invidious Fortuna had bound in a tiny corner of his heart with the strongest of ties that great *virtù* placed in his soul by heaven. These bounds were … overthrown by Love, for He [*Amore*] was so much more powerful than Her [*Fortuna*]." An audacious claim indeed, that Love's power is so great that He easily defeats *Fortuna*, but one that the tale forcefully underlined, for with his newly released *virtù* Cimone overcame one by one the obstacles that *Fortuna* placed in the path of his love and eventually married Efigenìa to live happily ever after, inspired by a passionate love that had transformed him from a dumb animal into a civilized citizen of his urban society – a master of the *virtù* of the *popolo grosso* and a full participant in their *civiltà*. In retelling the tale of Cimone, its classical themes are refashioned to speak directly to contemporary conceptions at the very center of the shared culture of the day – fortune, *virtù*, love, and the *civiltà* of urban world of the Rinascimento.

Yet Boccaccio was also clearly impressed by the more traditional courtly graces and refined manners of the aristocratic nobility of Naples, where he had lived and worked as a young man. As a result, in the *Decameron* there is a suggestive mix of love, manners, and aristocratic refinement that Boccaccio found attractive, both in the stories told and in the frame narrative, and at the same time, paradoxically, a clear commitment to the superiority of *virtù* and the values of the *popolo grosso*. These essentially conflicting visions make it difficult to read the *Decameron* in any simplistic manner. Nonetheless, the way he consistently reworked the tales he told suggests that Boccaccio was seeking to ennoble a widely shared discourse on love in order to make it attractive to a *popolo grosso* elite increasingly anxious to distinguish themselves from their *popolo* roots. Tellingly, more questionable desires and more lusty passions, although also labeled love, were reserved for artisans and questionable characters like corrupt clerics, while refined love was the preserve of more elite characters who usually displayed *popolo grosso* behavior that, as in the case of Cimone, brought them success. That curious mix may have made the fortune of the tales, for it appealed to a future that would see the post-plague *popolo grosso* become progressively more aristocratic across the fifteenth century. But clearly, for all the difficulty of interpretation, his portrayal of love reflects, even in the rather stylized settings of many of the stories, a deeper connection to the urban values and world of the day than any imagined by Petrarch.

It should be noted, however, that virtually as soon as he finished the first draft of the *Decameron*, Boccaccio wrote a virulently anti-woman, anti-love work, the *Corbaccio* (*The Ugly/Evil Crow*, 1354–1355), that seems to brutally contradict that ennobling and positive vision of love. Its portrayal of women and love is so negative that it has led some scholars to attempt to rethink his earlier vision of love and the *Decameron* itself, trying to find a sterner moral meaning underlying the amorous and often laughing stories told there. In turn, it would be tempting to argue that the *Corbaccio* was not actually written by Boccaccio, especially as it frequently seems to copy word for word earlier texts of his, twisting their meaning into a negative vision of love and women. But rather than tackling that unlikely argument here, it might be claimed that it simply reflects darkly the other side of the coin of the strong emotions that Boccaccio, and the shared primary culture of his day, associated with love and women, and the dangers of both. From that perspective, women (and the love they were seen to evoke) could be at one moment ennobling and transcendent, yet quickly become dangerous, destructive, and demeaning – *Ugly/Evil Crows*.

Violence, in fact, was often seen as going hand in hand with love, especially as it was imagined in literature, where it was frequently depicted as a violent and uncontrollable passion. Dante, Petrarch, and Boccaccio all ruefully admitted this from time to time, even as they celebrated love – for they recognized that it presented a real danger to the ideal of a peaceful urban *civiltà* that they dreamed of. Yet at a deeper Christian level, all three evoked strains of a discourse that saw a more Christian love promoting peace, friendship, and ultimately an ennobling and mannered life. Of course, Dante's violently suffering sinners from the urban world suggest that even God's love was ultimately intertwined with forms of discipline that could be brutal and violent. But, more pertinently, the optimistic, almost certainly overoptimistic, association of love and *virtù* that all three writers shared with their cultural world promised a more peaceful and positive self-discipline that ennobled young lovers, bound society together, and ultimately promised salvation.

First Times and Places: Finding the Old in the New

Significantly, as we have seen, the violence and disorder of the urban world of the Rinascimento was more surely associated with the new – new men, new ways of behaving, new institutions, and new values. With the plague wiping out large masses of the population and seemingly threatening to overthrow the old moral and social order; with new men and women migrating to the cities to replace population losses among the laboring and artisanal classes; with new men rising from those classes with new wealth struggling to join the ranks of the *popolo grosso* and even the political elites; with new economic realities emerging across society; with some cities expanding and gaining new territory and prominence and others falling behind, creating new alignments of power; and with new leaders emerging virtually everywhere, the new seemed to be breaking out all over. Yet even earlier – with the conflicts among the nobility, *popolo*, and *popolo grosso* in the second half of the thirteenth century – many had seen the problems of the day turning on dangerous innovations that had upset the established order and violently disrupted urban life. Simply put, over and over again the shared culture of the day imagined the new as decidedly bad.

Essentially the new was denied by framing change and innovation as old, the return and rebirth at the heart of the Rinascimento as a movement. And although such denial had existed much earlier, it accelerated across the period, becoming ever more firmly one of the major themes of intellectual life and political and social ideals. At all levels of society it played a central role in every area, from philosophy, theology, classical studies, and literature to the more humble world of sermons, chroniclers, and people telling stories and discussing life in the shops, squares, and markets. Ultimately the rejection of the new in favor of the old turned on a very traditional way of seeing the world that stressed that in the beginning, when first created, things were well made and good, but that with time they began to deteriorate and break down – a general vision shared in many societies and seemingly confirmed by everyday life, where material things invariably seem to deteriorate with time unless they are renewed, re-formed, or even reborn.

This vision was confirmed at more theoretical levels as well. Significantly, from a widely shared religious perspective God created things correctly in the beginning when they were perfect. And, as Genesis revealed, Adam then named those things with their true names – names that were not mere metaphors for what things were, but what they actually were. With the Fall humanity lost that original perfection, was exiled from the earthly paradise, and entered a material world of change and decay, where even language itself lost its direct connection to things, becoming merely metaphorical. The ultimate goal of history and Christian society was to return, renew, and reform history itself, regaining paradise and ultimately perfect communion with God.

Christianity, however, could be viewed in a totally different way that actually empowered the new, for the coming of Christ had opened a *new* age, as Joachim of Flora and others had claimed. From that perspective it could be argued that mankind was on a path of improving relations with God and of positive change headed toward the end of time, a Last Judgment that would reward the saved with eternal life at God's side in paradise. Although the two views of time coexisted in the Rinascimento, it would not be until much later that time would be consistently imagined as linear, moving ahead toward a positive end and salvation – in sum, as progressing. Only then would the new gain a positive valence and "progress" really compete with tradition, reform, and rebirth.

Suggestive of the traditional shared vision of return and rebirth was the fact that in the fourteenth century circular ways of measuring time still predominated. Dates, in fact, were often given in indictions: a circular, repeating standard cycle of years of ancient origin associated with the reigns of emperors or rulers, rather than (or as well as) in years from the birth of Christ. Suggestively, the first large mechanical clocks, perfected at midcentury in cities like Padua and Venice, were actually conceived of as mechanical recreations – astronomical machines – of the circular movements of the heavens that were the base of cyclical time. They measured with circular gearing the repeating cycles of time that we still imagine today: hours, days, weeks, months, seasons, and years. And, as such, they were viewed not so much as new but as merely recreating the movements that had always been there from the first of the cosmos.

Looking at the urban world of the day with an eye to discovering first times, it is evident that cities were awash with remembrances of and connections to a range of first times that really mattered. Even at the level of the parish churches that marked out neighborhoods, each was founded on a central altar where the fundamental ritual of Christianity was repeated regularly and involved the literal rebirth of Christ in the miraculous transformation of bread and wine into His body and blood. In turn ingested by the faithful in the sacrament of communion, it literally re-formed them spiritually and physically, reforming them freed from their sins. All this was imagined in terms of returns to crucial first times: the first time of Christ and his promise at the Last Supper; the first time of the individual sinner, when after baptism he entered the Christian community reborn as a member of the flock of the faithful. And, of course, the need to repeat the sacrament was required by the repeated cycle of falling away from renewed first times on the part of sinful individuals, which necessitated another sacramental return.

That, of course, was only the most central cycle associated with the churches that dotted the urban landscape. For under the altar upon which the mass was celebrated were the relics of saints, which had been collected for centuries and which were believed to make the altar an even more significant spiritual space, ensuring its connection at a deep and direct level to crucial first times and spaces of Christianity. Relics of the first great Christians, whether they were apostles, Church Fathers, saints, martyrs, or even merely the especially holy, were required for the very foundation of an altar and a church – connecting both to key first times. Such connections were hard to miss, as the lore of the day was rich with stories of saints' lives and the miracles that they and their relics had performed. The ties they offered to better first times were ubiquitous and overdetermined, not just for theologians and clerics, but for all.

If we think of relics in a broader context, the most important dead of a community were also entombed in churches, often with inscriptions that recorded the impressive deeds of their first times, and the more humble were buried in the churchyard, also reinforcing a church's connection to the past. Tombs and commemorative chapels were often supported by frescoes, statues, stained-glass windows, and other forms of decoration that also evoked the deep connections between the spiritual space of a church and the first times of religion. All this was enhanced in virtually every church with a collection of ex votos that thanked God and the saints for the little miracles of everyday life, often attributed to the power of relics or to the connection of a church to the various first times of Christianity. Hymns and the music of the mass also powerfully evoked the first times of Christianity. In a way, then, the churches of a Rinascimento city offered a form of spiritual time travel in their ceremonial, their relics, their decorations, and their very structure – a time travel that took the faithful back to the various first times of Christianity when God interfered with or even directly entered the world.

But that was just the beginning, albeit a ubiquitous one. In addition, the geography of the city was mapped onto the stories of religious first times, with districts, neighborhoods, streets, and squares named after saints, apostles, martyrs, and local holy people and evoking the stories of the oral tradition that went with their names. Neighborhood shrines commemorating all of the above also dotted the byways of cities, along with the ubiquitous crucifixes that decorated both the facades and the insides of houses, where religious images often adorned the basic accoutrements of everyday life as well. In turn, urban time was marked by church bells, and people even thought of the duration of time not in seconds or minutes, but in terms of the amounts of time it took to say basic prayers such as the Lord's Prayer or a Hail Mary. The beginnings of many of the regular cycles of daily life were also marked by prayers – meals and going to bed being only the most obvious. Healing, food preparation, and even passing through thresholds or boundaries in the home involved prayer or ritualized signing, such as making the sign of the Cross. In sum, Christianity as a lived religion was largely dominated by a discourse of first times: the first time of Christianity itself; the first times of the Bible, both the New and Old Testaments; the first times of saints, martyrs, and the local holy; the repeated first times of the mass and sacraments; and the repeated first times of everyday life. All these first times were disseminated and disciplined by oral traditions and the urban space of the day itself, which was rife with religious recollection and stories crystallized in architecture, images, shrines, sounds, and place names.

Along with this Christian vision of first times, the early Rinascimento shared a general vision that the ancient world was an earlier and virtually perfect first time or series of first times that had been lost and, crucially, might also be recovered or reborn. This vision was aided by the fact that in much of Italy the impressive remains of at least the Roman part of the ancient world were ubiquitous, reminding people of earlier and more perfect civilizations. In addition, there was already in place a strong and highly articulated medieval conviction that the ancient world had been dominated by a superior civilization that needed to be recovered in order to bring society back to its ancient perfection. Significantly, that vision had been deeply incorporated into the rationale for and justification of the urban *civiltà* of the early Rinascimento, as discussed earlier. Virtually every city boasted and celebrated its own founding by ancients from better first times. The law codes of most were based on Roman law, in large part because of its oft-touted perfection. Often the political structures of government were, if not modeled on, at least justified in terms of copying superior Roman models. And when that was not the case, origins were found in other significant first times, often biblical. Local powerful families tried, often with impressive imagination, to trace their origins back to famous Roman figures or important families. Even local conflicts were explained in terms of ancient animosities.

From this perspective Dante's guide, companion, and at times judge through Hell and Purgatory, Virgil, serves as a kind of living (if dead) model of an ancient Roman point of view, providing an ancient consensus reality that gives added weight to Dante's experiences and judgments. The modern would-be great Christian and Italian, Dante, is first saved from the despair of being lost ("in a dark wood") by that great ancient, whom many, at the time, believed had prophesized the crucial first time of the coming of Christ in his writings. Then together they begin the journey that will eventually return Dante to his first love, Beatrice, and Paradise.

On their spiritual pilgrimage the pagan Virgil and the Christian Dante share a quite mundane vision of what is wrong with the modern world, meeting and evaluating those sinners who had disrupted it as they pass through Hell. Not surprisingly, then, although Virgil is a pagan and Dante a Christian, in most cases they agree, because their shared goal is a return to that *virtù* that Dante *imagined* a great ancient like Virgil shared with him – precisely because he imagined *virtù* as that ancient measure reborn, even if in fact his vision of it was more contemporary *popolo grosso* than ancient Roman. Virgil, then, needed to be there not just to showcase Dante's classical knowledge and disarm critics who might complain that he wrote in Tuscan dialect rather than in Latin. More significantly, he joined Dante's pilgrimage to demonstrate that Dante's path led not toward a dangerously new world but to a safely old one, a return to proven first times that included not just Christian first times, but also the first time and *virtù* of the great civilization of ancient Rome.

Petrarch's famed search for the lost manuscripts of ancient Roman authors to serve as his own guide to a rebirth of ancient *virtù* as he imagined it was merely the most noted aspect of his ongoing self-presentation as a cultural leader committed to recovering the lost culture and the language of that first time. For Petrarch, however, this recovery was not envisioned as a goal for all or even a large part of humanity. Only an elite few were capable of recovering his imagined Roman past. And in a way this elitist vision was to become the dark companion of the recovery of classical culture for many intellectuals across the Rinascimento and beyond. As noted earlier, by insisting on a return to a first perfect Latin like that of Cicero, Petrarch managed to cut out most of those educated in a more practical legal and commercial Latin, rejecting them as unequipped to gain a true knowledge of the ancient world and its superior learning. In this way his return to first time was tightly tied to a vision that rejected much of the world of his day and eliminated most people from his dream of returning to the glories of ancient Rome.

Only a select group of intellectual aristocrats patronized by a few powerful notables could live in that imagined world. Of course, there had long been a strong tradition that knowledge was only for a chosen few who were capable of understanding deeper truths; this esoteric vision underlay much medieval thinking about religion and nature and had deep roots in the ancient world. In fact, it was still a significant element of Dante's writing, although his use of the vernacular, which made his work more readily accessible, may reflect a greater willingness to share at least aspects of his learning and vision more widely. For Petrarch, however, his esoteric and elitist vision of ancient language and knowledge led him at times even to disavow his love poetry in the vernacular as not serious enough or up to the standards required for a return to the great days of ancient Rome. Be that as it may, he was anxious to be crowned in Rome as Roman poet laureate for his Latin epic poem, *Africa*, and the crowning was carried out there on Easter Sunday – yet another returning crucial Christian first time – April 8, 1341, in the palace of the ancient Roman Senate on the Capitoline hill. Petrarch reportedly followed his crowning with a laurel wreath that evoked the ancient symbol of victory and fame, in this case his own, with a speech that called for a rebirth of ancient Roman culture and poetry, interlaced with Christian motifs, including a literal recital of the *Ave Maria*.

Roman revival was always more than just a cultural ideal, even for Petrarch. Perhaps most notably, his desire to avoid the squabbles of urban life and politics was momentarily put aside when he publicly championed Cola di Rienzo (c. 1313–1354), a controversial leader who proclaimed himself tribune of the Roman people in 1347, promising to make Rome once again the capital of Italy and the world in the name of recreating the ancient Roman Empire. With the papacy at Avignon, the Roman nobility had essentially been ruling the city, when not tearing it apart with internecine strife. In 1347, however, Cola, with the support of the *popolo* and especially of the land-holding merchants (a form of Roman *popolo grosso*), had himself proclaimed tribune on the Capitoline hill – the ancient governmental center of the city, where just a few years earlier Petrarch had been crowned poet laureate. In ancient Rome the tribunes had been responsible for protecting the plebeians against the senatorial class. By claiming that title for himself,

Cola was consciously harking back to that first time and promising to do the same in modern Rome.

Petrarch's vision of Roman rebirth seemed to fit well with Cola's claims, and his support for him suggests why seeing him primarily as a precursor or the father of a later movement that modern scholars have labeled humanism limits our understanding of him. For in Petrarch's letters Cola became a liberator and a defender of contemporary republican values, planning to bring peace and prosperity to Italy not as something new, but as something safely old. In fact, the masking of the new in several quite different earlier first times is well illustrated by Petrarch's instructions to Cola in a letter of 1347. Along with calling on him to rule for the good of the people and to overthrow the tyrants of Italy and the nobles of Rome, he reiterated some more practical advice for living a life of *virtù*, asking him to be a good Christian:

I hear … that every day since you became ruler of the Republic … it is customary for you to receive the Sacrament of our Lord's Body, with sincerest devotion and after a most searching examination of conscience. This is doubtless as it should be.... That most illustrious of Rome's generals [Scipio Africanus] would have followed the same course, I believe, had he lived today. For he was as correctly committed to his sacred duties as his day permitted, *an age shrouded in darkness* and lacking the knowledge of heaven. [italics mine]

It is noteworthy that here we see that Petrarch's call for a rebirth of Rome was not acritical and could feature the same "age of darkness" topos more usually associated with his condemnation of the Middle Ages as a time of ignorance and darkness. In the end, both kinds of darkness needed to be eliminated, and that required Christ and Christianity and their first times as well as Rome. In addition, Petrarch recommended that Cola pursue reading – not just any reading, but reading the history of the deeds of "*virtù*" of his ancient Roman predecessors. In this he counseled imitating Augustus (whose status as the first Roman emperor who destroyed the republic was quietly overlooked), who, according to Petrarch, even while eating and drinking had history books read to him. In sum, a significant daily dose of Christianity and its recurring first times along with a similar adherence to Roman models were necessary in order for Cola to succeed in his project of giving birth again to republican Rome.

But few were as enthusiastic as Petrarch about Cola's plans for a rebirth of Rome or about his leading Italy. While there was a general agreement that a return to Roman greatness and first time was a worthwhile goal, there were understandably quite different opinions about what that might entail. Local *signori* were quite willing to discover that their cities had been founded by Roman generals and to have their own rule defended as a renewal of such imperial founding. Republican governments were equally willing to stress their city's founding by the late Roman republic and modern renewal. Even local powerful families were eager to stress their ancient Roman roots. But evidently few were interested in stepping aside or even sharing their hard-won power with Cola. When he tried to revive a pro-papal, pro-Roman Guelph alliance in the center of Italy, calling the leaders of the cities there to a general "parliament" in Rome, the responses were few and unenthusiastic.

Much like Petrarch, Cola freely mixed his ancient Roman and Christian ideals in order to advance his claims. Thus he styled himself not just tribune, but also "Candidate of the Holy Spirit." And in the name of allowing all the people of Italy to be protected by the Holy Spirit and Rome, he made them all Roman citizens – a move unlikely to win the support of local rulers who were not eager to share their subjects even with the "Candidate of the Holy Spirit." These spiritual claims were equally unappreciated by the papacy. In fact, Pope Clement VI (1291–1352; pope 1342–1352), although he had originally supported Cola from Avignon as a counterweight to the Roman nobility, moved by Cola's growing messianic pretensions deserted his cause and ordered his removal from power. It did not help that Cola had also begun to make claims that seemed to echo Franciscan Spiritual calls for a propertyless Church. More immediately, however, the Roman nobility, led by the Orsini family, were unenthusiastic about Cola's rule as well as his dreams. In turn, the harsh measures that he had imposed as Tribune to pacify the deeply divided and violent city cost him the support even of many of the *popolo*.

All this came to a head in the last days of 1347, when Cola was driven out of Rome, fleeing into exile. To many, rather than an ancient Roman tribune reborn, he had become just another tyrant using the rhetoric of Roman renewal and rebirth to mask his grab for power. Paradoxically, however, Cola was reborn with papal support in the 1350s, when he became a part of the new Pope Innocent VI's (c. 1282–1362; pope 1352–1362) plan to reestablish his own authority in Rome. Forgiven for the presumed heresy that lay behind his earlier claims of special affinity with the Holy Spirit, he was sent to Rome by the pope as papal senator in 1354. New title, much the same game – but things went no better for Cola reborn as a senator. This time the Roman nobility eliminated him once and for all – he was assassinated by supporters of the Colonna family in early October 1354. Even with the support of Petrarch, his return to first times and the rebirth of ancient Rome was one that would not prevail.

Boccaccio might appear to be the least likely advocate of a return to first times, especially as his *Decameron* seems to draw heavily on tales from a more recent past. But, like his friend Petrarch, he is not so easily pigeonholed. He apparently first met Petrarch in 1350, when he was in his late thirties and Petrarch in his late forties. Although he had already read and been influenced by the latter's love poetry, it appears that Petrarch encouraged Boccaccio's ongoing interest in his own two most favored first times, ancient Rome and the early Church. Thus Boccaccio began to overlay his discussions of *virtù* with a classical veneer, although, like Petrarch and Dante, his vision of it drew heavily on the values and imagined verities of his day. His *De casibus virorum illustrium* (*On the Fortunes of Famous Men*), *De claris mulieribus* (*On Famous Women*), and a virtual encyclopedia on the ancient gods, *Genealogiae deorum gentilium* (*The Genealogy of the Pagan Gods*), were all reworked completely. Each work in its way returned to crucial first times and in classical Latin explained what made men and women gain fame or, more often, lose it in those first times.

In his *On Famous Women* and *The Fortunes of Famous Men* the tension between *virtù* and *fortuna* is the key to a gendered reading of ideal and ennobling behavior and the loss of same, with the ancients serving as examples. With a strong Christian tone, Boccaccio's famous pagan women tended to be chaste, obedient, and self-sacrificing, although he did include an occasional heroic or magnificent figure. The fortunes of his famous men were largely negative, primarily because, rather than following the dictates of fourteenth-century *virtù* and living lives of moderation, reason, and self-control, they succumbed to evil fortune, overcome by the violent emotions that his contemporaries saw as disrupting their society – love, jealousy, hate or a desire for vengeance – and destroying *virtù*. In his compendium on the origins of the gods, he presented the first times of the pagan gods but drew Christian lessons from that pagan first time. Like Petrarch, he held that behind such myths and stories, even if the pagans were unaware of it, there lay a Christian truth – for all truth was ultimately God's (the first and ultimate truth from his perspective) and thus Christian. That way of seeing truth in first times made all of these works that focused on pagan lives and values suitable as models for and defenses of contemporary Christian values – and, as such, they were among Boccaccio's most popular works in his day.

In this context a quick mention should be made of another first time to which Boccaccio returned repeatedly in later life, one that to some extent he constructed: the first time of Dante as the first great poet of the Tuscan vernacular. Not only did Boccaccio pen one of the first biographies of Dante in the 1350s, he wrote some of the most important early commentaries on the

Divine Comedy. He even copied the poem by hand – a long labor of love – and gave the copy to Petrarch. Finally, late in life, in the 1370s, he took up a post where he lectured on Dante in Florence. In all this he played an important role in transforming Dante from a noted poet who wrote in a language unsuited to great literature, into a first in his own right: the first to elevate his Tuscan dialect into a language worthy of great literature on a par with classical Latin. Ironically, and partially as a result of this, Boccaccio, along with his friend Petrarch and the Dante he idolized, would become in the fifteenth and sixteenth centuries the writers of a first time of Italian as a literary language capable of expressing great ideas, albeit not without considerable opposition. One could go on, but the point is clear: for the Rinascimento the understanding that the old was good, and the new dangerous and bad, was a deep structural element of a primary shared culture, widely accepted and rarely questioned. It was enough to argue that something was new to demonstrate that it was bad. Positive change, then, was invariably framed in terms of renewal, revival, or rebirth.

Virtù, *the Measure of Status and Behavior*

As much as the old was an uncontested marker of the good, the concept of *virtù* was a generally accepted marker of status and the correct way of doing things. Yet at the same time, exactly what that meant was often highly contested and at the heart of many a contemporary debate. For craftsmen it was the skills that made the work of one person better than that of another and that ideally marked out the creations of all guild masters. For theologians and many writers writing in a more traditional moral vein, it was the opposite of vice and described by the traditional Christian virtues, even if the number and nature of those virtues could be contested. In the material world it was that inner quality that made things behave as they should and be what they were. Acorns become oak trees over time thanks to their inner *virtù* that makes them potentially oak trees.

But perhaps most significantly, as we have seen, the term was used widely as a measure of social status and behavior, and this had long been the case. In chivalric literature and in the context of more traditional medieval warrior values – which had not entirely disappeared, especially among older noble families and rural elites – it denoted a range of direct, forceful behaviors associated with masculinity. The warrior heroes of medieval epics and the popular genre of chivalric romance come immediately to mind, with their direct rough-hewn manners, straightforward and open speech, and ready use of violence; although in the chivalric romances of the Rinascimento the more extreme forms of this vision of *virtù* were often treated with irony. As we have seen, the *popolo grosso*, and many of the *popolo* as well, had their own quite different vision of *virtù* that tended to stress rational and moderate behavior over the more direct ways they associated with the old nobility and the urban lower classes and peasants. An ability to control the future and one's emotions, guided by reason rather than emotion, was key and seen as more suited to urban life and the economic complexities of the day. At times this ideal behavior could fall well short of Christian virtue, as in this *popolo grosso* vision *virtù* tended to slide off into the clever, cunning, and often formally sinful behavior that one sees laughingly presented in many *novelle* of the time.

The various ancient and medieval philosophical visions of the term also played a role in the debates about the nature of *virtù*. The Greeks and the Romans had agreed that the behaviors associated with *virtù* were ideally what should mark out one person as better than another, but had then disagreed about what those behaviors should be. Medieval writers, like Saint Thomas Aquinas, had continued the discussion, basing their arguments on classical authors such as Aristotle (Greek and pagan) and Saint Augustine (Roman and Christian), while also referring to contemporary ideals. In sum, *virtù* had long been a contested term, and in the first centuries of the Rinascimento it was anything but an easily defined element of its shared primary culture, even if it was widely agreed that it was a crucial measure of what made one person better than another.

The contested meaning of *virtù*, and at the same time the power of love and the denial of the new in the fourteenth century is nicely illustrated by a well-known novella of Boccaccio: the tragic love story of Ghismonda and Guiscardo that opens the tales of the fourth day of the *Decameron*. With its stories of tragic loves and death, that day at first seems hardly appropriate for storytellers one of whose stated goals was to take heart from their tales in the face of the plague. Significantly, however, many of the day's tales of the heroic deaths of tragic lovers transform mourning into a celebration of the ennobling *virtù* of lovers (and of love itself) and, in doing so, seem to suggest that love and *virtù* were as central to transcending the horror of the plague as they were to the shared culture of the day.

The tragic love of Ghismonda for Guiscardo is set in a time and place different from the urban world of Boccaccio's Florence – an apparently earlier time in the southern city of Salerno at a court ruled by a medieval prince, Tancredi, Ghismonda's father. Tancredi had married his daughter at an early age to an older noble, who had quickly died, leaving her a youthful widow. As was often the case, she returned to live with her father and to wait patiently for another marriage alliance to be arranged by him in the interests of his family and his rule. To this point the story, if a bit sad, could not have been more normal and banal from a medieval noble or an urban *popolo grosso* point of view. But after several years of waiting patiently for a new marriage, things began to go awry. Ghismonda, noting that her father was not anxious to remarry her, apparently because he enjoyed her company too much and seemed unable or unwilling to find a suitable match for her, decided to take a lover rather than let her youth slip away.

This was the first of what would have been seen as unacceptable decisions for a young woman. Both medieval and Rinascimento literature were fascinated by such tales of formally illicit love outside of marriage. In many ways love outside of marriage was seen as the only true love – as was the case for Dante, Petrarch, and young Boccaccio – because it was based on the emotions of the couple involved, not on the calculations and reasoning of parents or relatives. Yet when women initiated such relationships in medieval literature, they were usually presented as at best flighty girls or lustful adults overwhelmed by strong passions or, at worst, as evil, licentious creatures leading men to their downfall. Ghismonda in Boccaccio's telling, however, fits neither stereotype. Instead, he portrays her as intelligent, thoughtful, brave, and capable of devising clever strategies in order to have the lover she desired safely and secretly. The word he uses to describe this group of attributes is telling: *virtù*.

Ghismonda moved on almost immediately to a second, even more questionable deed, picking as her lover a young man who had attracted her attention at the court of her father, Guiscardo. Handsome, brave, mannerly, and also intelligent, Guiscardo had one overwhelming fault: he was not a noble. In fact, he was a *new* man and a mere page of base background at that – in sum, for all his attractive qualities he was at once new, base, and unworthy of the daughter of a prince and just the type of man Boccaccio's Florentine contemporaries feared most. Nonetheless, in the short run he was a fine lover from Ghismonda's perspective, and they spend many happy days and nights together making use of a hidden entrance to her chambers and their careful planning to keep their affair secret. Unfortunately, according to Boccaccio, *Fortuna* – widely recognized as the nemesis of *virtù* – envious of their love, led her father to observe the lovers enjoying themselves in bed unbeknownst to them. Soon thereafter he threw Guiscardo in jail and, with tears in his eyes, reproved his daughter for her misconduct, focusing on what he saw as her major fault – not her affair, but rather her choice of a new man of base social condition as her lover.

Although the tale was set in the past, it turned then on a new man rising above his station to take the most precious possession of an aristocrat, his daughter. That crime was too great for even youthful love to negate, and in the end both lovers were doomed to tragic deaths, Guiscardo secretly murdered and Ghismonda heroically committing suicide after being presented with her lover's heart in a golden chalice. From a medieval perspective it could be argued that this was a perfect, if tragic, ending to the tale; for justice had been done, and Tancredi, dishonored by his daughter's affair and her base lover, had heroically exacted a cruel, but necessary, vengeance on the servant and the daughter who had dishonored him and his family. In the process he had literally eliminated the dangerously new and defended the social order he was required to protect as a prince. In sum, he would have been the hero of the tale and an exemplar of an earlier vision of *virtù* that still had its proponents in the fourteenth century.

Yet in Boccaccio's telling of the tale Guiscardo and Ghismonda are the heroes, and her father is both the villain and the tragic victim of his own tears, wrath, and sense of honor. The point is made over and over again, but perhaps most clearly when Ghismonda defends her love to her father. "It's true that I loved and love Guiscardo and as long as I live – which will not be for long – I will love him," she forthrightly explains; then continues, "This, however, is not a result of my feminine weakness but rather your lack of desire to marry me and Guiscardo's *virtù*." Shortly thereafter she offers a long description of what that *virtù* entails:

> But let's move on to consider the *origins* of this situation. You will note that we are all made from the same flesh and created by the same Creator with souls of equal strength and potential and equal *virtù*. *Virtù* was what *first* created distinctions among us, who all were born and are born equal; and those who had the most *virtù* and demonstrated it the most were named nobles and the rest non-nobles. And even if later contrary practices have hidden this law, it has not been eliminated, or overturned by nature or good manners; for this reason the person who demonstrates *virtù* reveals to all his nobility and those who call him otherwise are in the wrong.... Look carefully at all your nobles and examine their lives, their manners, and their ways, then consider Guiscardo.... If you judge honestly you will admit that *he is most noble and that all your nobles are peasants.* [italics mine]

At the simplest level Ghismonda was claiming that her evaluation of Guiscardo as noble and worthy of her love was not based upon some dangerously *new* appreciation of the merits of a new man but rather on his *virtù* – and that judgment, she made clear, was tellingly *old*, going all the way back to the original social order created by God himself. Crucially, then, rethinking social distinctions on the basis of *virtù* was not new, but rather old, God-given, and thus not dangerous at all. Ghismonda's argument also evoked the old at a deeper and not so immediately apparent level, for it was very similar to the arguments that Aristotle and medieval thinkers like Saint Thomas Aquinas had advanced for the way social distinctions should be drawn, even as both admitted it was often overlooked in favor of wealth, family status, and tradition. Thus the *virtù* card had the advantage of an ancient heritage as well as a medieval defense, and both again made the new safely old.

From this perspective, the true victim of the tale is Tancredi, whose way of understanding *virtù* Boccaccio presents as outdated and ultimately self-destructive. In his rage and unreasonable desire for vengeance, "crying like a baby," he caused the death of his daughter, the person he loved more than any other, and the story stresses that he never quite realized that it was all unnecessary had he only reasonably (*virtù*-ously) considered his daughter's logic and married her to the truly noble and not new at all Guiscardo. In this way the novella subtly allows the reader to conclude that this vision of *virtù*, with its emphasis on reason, self-control, mannered/measured behavior, and an ability to plan in order to deal effectively with the future, would have saved Tancredi from his tragic fate – if only he had been a Florentine *popolo grosso* rather than a medieval prince of Salerno. A story that in the Middle Ages could have been the sad but honorable triumph of a noble prince, thus became in Boccaccio's fourteenth-century retelling a parable on the value of a particular contemporary vision of *virtù* that typified the values of the *popolo grosso* and a defense of that vision of things as not new and not dangerous, but rather as old and safe.

In fact, the theme of *virtù* runs deep in Boccaccio's *Decameron* and helps to explain much of the often cruel humor of the tales. Those who do not practice *virtù*, because they are victims of their passions, are portrayed as the deserving victims of harsh jokes that reveal their lack of true *virtù* and subject them to demeaning laughter or worse. Many of the more tragic tales also turn on demonstrations of the sad things that happen when *virtù* is replaced by the direct violent emotions associated with medieval warrior elites of an earlier day (or with contemporaries who still aped those more direct ways); when lovers' passion are not moderated by *virtù*; or when the foolish and gullible, lacking *virtù*, do not understand the true nature of religious faith.

Of course, older visions and understandings of *virtù* did not simply disappear. Rather, the shared primary culture of the day tested the concept and wrestled with it frequently, seeking its true nature in earlier, more perfect times or literature, especially in the writings of the ancients and the Church Fathers. But with the progressive dominance of the *popolo grosso* across the century and the integration of many of the old noble families into the urban, merchant culture of the day, the discourse on *virtù* came to be increasingly dominated by one fairly unified vision. Old, both God-given and defended by an appeal to classical culture (not always warranted), and ultimately reasonable in itself, it turned on reason sliding into cleverness, exercising self-control over violent or strong emotions, and progressively more mannered and graceful behavior. And although in many ways this went well beyond the requirements for living successfully in an urban, merchant world, it fit well with that life.

The triumph of this way of imagining *virtù* and the active life in civil society associated with it was neither easy nor smooth in the fourteenth century. A contrasting vision, with strong Christian and classical roots, one that still had many supporters, insisted that a life of *virtù* required a withdrawal from the everyday turmoil of urban life to pursue a spiritual life in isolation – the ideal contemplative life. Such a life was ideal for both clerics and scholars, for it provided the peace and freedom, *otium* (positive leisure), to pursue study and give full attention to the development of one's mind and spiritual well-being. Boccaccio's friend and regular correspondent Petrarch was a stout supporter of this position. And his dream of a return to the glorious days of ancient Rome envisioned a rebirth of an ancient *virtù* significantly different from that envisioned by Boccaccio in the *Decameron* and a society dominated by cultural heroes who lived a perfect existence focused on great ideas, safely withdrawn from the hustle and bustle of *popolo grosso virtù*.

Petrarch saw this as true of ancient Rome, because its great leaders and wealth had made it possible for a select few to live such lives and to create a literature that recorded that way of living for the future, where it could be rediscovered and revived. Petrarch's mission was to do just that. A central component of his program of recovery of the ancient was a rediscovery of the works of Cicero, whom he saw not only as a great thinker and moral philosopher, but also as a great Latin stylist. Style and content went hand in hand, because he, like many in his day, believed that truth and beauty were deeply intertwined, if not merely the same thing seen from two different perspectives. What was true was beautiful, and what was beautiful was true. This was because it was the truth in a thing that created a harmony and a simple being-what-it-was that superior people perceived as beauty. Ideas expressed beautifully, then, were more likely to be true. Significantly, this implied that ideas expressed in corrupt and inelegant medieval Latin were not only ugly, but also, lacking the beauty of ancient Latin, almost certainly incorrect. In Cicero's Latin, Petrarch discovered what he considered the most beautiful form of the ancient language, and he campaigned for replacing the

Latin of his day with it. Actually, he was not the first to do so, but he used his position as a cultural leader to campaign for this and was supported by a number of like-minded scholars who shared his vision.

Petrarch spent much of his life tracking down Ciceronian texts and was especially interested early on in his letters. Letters were ideal in part because they were relatively short and thus easily copied and circulated. They were also attractive as they required the maximum of elegance in the minimum of space, something for which Ciceronian Latin was well suited. In many ways they were the poetry of prose. Shorter and more evocative than a closely argued medieval tome, they offered greater rhetorical brilliance and beauty. Cicero's letters also attracted Petrarch because they were known primarily through a collection, the *Tusculan Disputations*, that portrayed Cicero as virtually a withdrawn Stoic sage, one who had left the confusion and turmoil of his Rome to retire to his country estates and live a contemplative life of *virtù* focused on his own moral and spiritual development. This Cicero fit perfectly with Petrarch's ideal for his own life and the ideal he advanced for contemporary scholars. And although Cicero was clearly a pagan, Petrarch could imagine his *virtù* as being consonant with a Christian vision – once again just an earlier moment of the one truth that ultimately originated in God, reinforced by the beauty of Cicero's ideas expressed in an elegant Latin and by the fact that Cicero's ideas were old, not new.

Thus, as Petrarch sought ancient texts across Italy to help revive ancient culture and his vision of ancient *virtù*, discovering additional letters of Cicero was a major goal. Unfortunately for Petrarch's imaginary Cicero, the real ancient writer and many of his other letters did not match up well with those of the *Tusculan Disputations*. One can imagine his dismay when in 1345 he discovered in the Cathedral Library of Verona a series of letters to a certain Atticus that presented a very different picture of his hero. In those *Letters to Atticus* Cicero wrote as an active citizen of republican Rome, forced out of public office, much to his regret, when Julius Caesar came to power. Moreover, they presented a Cicero who had plotted against Caesar, and who after his death was an active participant in the civil wars that ended with the triumph of Augustus and the fall of the republic that he had supported in words and deeds.

Poor Petrarch, his very being shaken, the actual ancient world having betrayed his dreams, did something that reveals how close he felt to his fallen ancient hero: he wrote Cicero, dead for more than a thousand years, a letter. Or, more accurately, he wrote his ghost, now safely consigned to Hell, a bitter letter. "Why did you involve yourself in so many contentions and useless quarrels and forsake the calm so becoming to your age, your position

and ... your life?" he asked reprovingly. And continued, "what vain splendor
of fame drove you ... to a death unworthy of a sage[?] ... Oh how much
more fitting would it have been had you ... grown old in rural surroundings ... meditating upon eternal life ... and not aspiring to consular offices
and military triumphs!" In the end, however, Petrarch was too clever to be
cornered by history or ancient texts. He explained away his hero's misdeeds,
claiming that Cicero was "an historic example of a citizen who against his
own will bore testimony to the superiority of the contemplative life," arguing that his greatest works had been written in the "*solitudo gloriosa*" of his
exile from power and the civic world of his day. Thus the activist Cicero was
safely returned to a role model for Petrarch's brand of *virtù* and his vision of
the superiority of the contemplative life over the active.

Later in his career, however, Petrarch came to modify his stance somewhat. In his spiritual and psychological autobiography written in Latin, the
Secretum (begun in 1342), he suggested that worldly *virtù* – the key to success in the active life – is found by turning inward. At first, this might seem
simply a non sequitur: the contemplative life leads to success in the active
life. But restated in a way that comes closer to Petrarch's vision – as a claim
that a strong inner, spiritual life brings strength even in the active world of
everyday life – it sounds less contradictory; closer to the vision of another of
his heroes from the ancient world, Saint Augustine, and similar to the compromise between Christianity and merchant capitalism worked out more
fully by later Protestant theologians: inner purity and spirituality lead to
earthly success, and that success is a sign and confirmation of inner purity.

Petrarch's defense of a withdrawn, contemplative life also led him to conclude that in the ancient world the Roman Empire had been superior to the
Roman republic. As long as there had been a republic, he argued, the civil
strife of the republic had prevented the best and the brightest from dedicat-
ing themselves to a tranquil, scholarly life. The violent turmoil of the republics of his day once again seemed to confirm his contention. Needless to
say, this antirepublican stance was an opinion that won wide approval from
the many *signori* who were gaining power in the city-states of central and
northern Italy and once again it did not hurt in the least that it presented
their newly and often violently won rule not as new, but as based upon
the ancient Roman Empire and its superior civilization. Not surprisingly,
Petrarch was supported over the course of his later career by a series of *signori*
and ended his career advising the rather bloody Paduan tyrant Francesco
Carrara, albeit from the safety and isolation of his hillside retreat in Arquà in
the hills just south of that city. Obviously, the leaders of republican cities that
had held out against the rise of tyrants in the fourteenth century were less

enthusiastic about this aspect of Petrarch's thought, even as most claimed to follow their own programs of classical revival and visions of *virtù*.

As we have seen, however, republics like Florence and Venice had their own traditions that stressed the importance of an active civic life and republican forms over despotic ones. These traditions, however, were tested and crystallized as a powerful republican ideology as the fourteenth century drew to a close and in the first half of the fifteenth in the context of the long series of wars between those republics and the *signori* of Milan, discussed earlier as part of the Italian Hundred Years' War. Florence, Venice, and Milan did not fight those wars just with money, professional soldiers, and diplomatic maneuvering; they also mobilized the intellectuals who staffed their bureaucracies and the cultural leaders of their cities to defend and legitimate their cause. Writers in both Florence and Venice stressed the importance of life in a republic and republican values for sustaining true *virtù*, using classical literature to defend their position. In this they squared off against writers in Milan, who, following in the footsteps of Petrarch, stressed the freedom and support that *signori* could give to those who withdrew from the troubles of the world to live a life of more contemplative *virtù*.

Clearly these verbal battles of the Italian Hundred Years' War, often based on a close reading and interpretation of texts from the ancient world, were not merely intellectual exercises or even simply sophisticated scholarship. They were at times both, of course, but, crucially, they also grew out of more bloody battles and were deeply intertwined with the everyday life of their times. In fact, in these debates one sees an excellent example of the complexity involved in doing intellectual or cultural history well: it is possible to tell the tale of this defense of republican values simply as a series of responses to and debates on texts from the ancient world. But that misses a much more complex, messy, and rich picture that sees these writers as intimately involved in the life and primary shared culture of their times, using their readings of past texts to defend and reimagine the novelty of their cities as old, good, and necessary to live a meaningful life of *virtù* – and as a verbal battlefront in a series of long and disruptive wars.

Perhaps the best-known defense of republican values and a civic life of *virtù* is found in the advocacy by the Florentine Chancellor Coluccio Salutati (1331–1406) of the superiority of an active life of civic *virtù* at the end of the fourteenth century in the midst of the wars with Gian Galeazzo Visconti. Salutati was one of the most noted examples of a growing desire in Florence, Venice, Milan, and elsewhere to have not just competent scribes and bureaucrats staffing the highest secretarial offices of government, but also scholars trained in the classical tradition, capable of writing letters and documents that came ever-closer to Petrarch's ideal of capturing the elegance of classical Latin – letters and documents that demonstrated in their elegant prose both a deeper truth and a rebirth of the Roman past in city-states with a superior *civiltà*. Salutati, in fact, was widely recognized in his day as a powerful Latin stylist and thus a powerful representative of the superiority of his city. Even Gian Galeazzo Visconti recognized his importance, noting that a letter from Salutati could be as effective as a troop of 1,000 horsemen. Hyperbole or merely respect, Salutati's impressive rhetoric set the tone for defending republics as the only places where one could live a fully civilized life – an active life of service to one's city and one's society, a life of true *virtù*.

Salutati turned to the Roman past to defend this vision, which in many ways had earlier typified the *popolo grosso* vision of a moral social order and *civiltà* built upon the civic morality of *popolo* power. He was aided in this by a new set of letters by Cicero discovered in 1392 that became known as the *Familiar Letters*. Once again they revealed Cicero to have been an active political participant in the civic life of ancient Rome. Moreover, they stressed the importance of such a life and participation in the civic world in fully realizing one's moral and cultural potential – in becoming a truly *virtù*-ous citizen in a truly *virtù*-ous city state. Salutati's Cicero became virtually the opposite of Petrarch's, a citizen of a republic who held that an active life in the service of one's city was the duty of every citizen and good person. From this Salutati went on to insist that in order to live a true life of *virtù*, a full and meaningful life, one had to participate in a republic as a good moral citizen, a good officeholder, and an active supporter of one's government. In turn, he argued that it was impossible to lead such a life in a city ruled by a *signore*, because under a tyrant the active life was either a sham or no longer existed; thus only in a republican city such as Florence could one live a full and active civic life. In sum, looking to the past and Cicero's letters demonstrated that contemporaries should defend republics not for any newfangled reason or simply to protect the interests of the *popolo grosso*, but rather because the great Roman society of the ancient world had at its best and most powerful been based on the active civic involvement of its citizenry. That had made Rome superior and allowed individual Romans to lead a meaningful and moral life. True life and *virtù*, then, were available only in a civic context, a republican one like that of contemporary Florence – not quite a thousand horsemen perhaps, but an effective rallying cry for Florence's wars with Milan.

"Civic Humanism" or Republican Ideology and Civic Morality?

This vision, as articulated by Salutati, his pupils, and followers has been labeled "civic humanism." Yet as neither humanists nor humanism had been yet conceptualized, it might be less anachronistic to see this stress on civic life, using classical and early Christian texts for its defense – while moving well beyond them – as just another facet of the much broader rebirth of classical culture and first times in general, already well established and expressed in terms of *civiltà* and civic morality. In fact, even in its particulars this vision was not particularly new, but as it became increasingly codified in Florence, Venice, and more generally, it became an important defense of republican values that would long outlive the Rinascimento and play a significant role in the formulation of modern republican theory. As it crystallized at the end of the fourteenth and beginning of the fifteenth century, however, it also helped to stimulate a significant rethinking of the traditional vision of the superiority of the Roman Empire – a vision obviously central to the many earlier medieval revivals of the Roman Empire and still of great weight.

Defenders of civic morality and republican values, following Salutati's line of reasoning, began to argue more aggressively that the Roman republic was actually superior to the Roman Empire, because under the republic people had the opportunity to live full civic lives and thus were superior to those who had lived under Roman emperors. This encouraged many to reconsider the Roman origins of their own cities. As noted earlier, in a search for legitimacy and a way of claiming parity with contemporary Roman emperors from the north, many cities had discovered their own Roman foundations, usually by noteworthy emperors and often with an implicit or explicit claim that such foundations made them continuations of the empire on a par with contemporary German emperors. Now, however, Florentines suddenly discovered that their city had been founded not by an emperor at all, but rather during the last days of the republic; thus, in a way their republic was a continuation of that superior political, social, and moral way of life in a world increasingly dominated by tyrants and would-be rulers of mini-empires like Gian Galeazzo Visconti.

The neatness of the fit with contemporary events might suggest that this was merely propaganda, but it struck deeper chords. First, and crucially, the vision of *virtù* embedded in civic life, with its stress on a public and active life in an urban environment, almost perfectly overlapped with the values of the *popolo grosso*. Second, the emphasis on public service for the public good helped to reinforce the growing vision of the idea that public power for the public good was, in fact, the true goal of government – an ideal already well developed in Venetian republican ideology and elsewhere. Third, this vision was enfolded in and reinforced by a Christian and moral context that saw both public service for the public good and an active civic life as crucial elements of a civic morality that made life in the city superior to other ways of living. And last but not least, civic cultural leaders, using the Roman classics to defend this republican vision of civic morality, had proved their metal and merit to those in power, as even Gian Galeazzo had to admit.

This triumph of civic ideals couched in classical thought and the *popolo grosso*'s vision of the active life and civic morality, given its many resonances with modern civic and political values, has engendered much study. One of the most ambitious and influential has been Hans Baron's *The Crisis of the Early Italian Renaissance*, written in the mid-1950s in the heat of the cold war, a moment when republics faced authoritarian regimes in an apparent battle to determine the course of Western civilization, a moment when the military and cultural battles between the tyrants and republics of the Rinascimento seemed particularly relevant to an age that also saw its great conflicts involving republics defending their traditional values against authoritarian states. Yet, while those issues may have added weight to Baron's interests, he was too good a scholar to let them dominate, and, in fact, another significant historical issue drove his interest in the topic: the question of the relationship between the history of ideas and political and social history. In *Crisis* he attempted to show the direct relationship between political change and intellectual change, believing firmly that the two were intimately and deeply intertwined.

For Baron, Leonardo Bruni (1370–1444) was the central figure for explaining the timing and triumph of what he labeled "civic humanism." And it is interesting to follow his argument, as it still provides a suggestive reading of Florentine intellectual developments of the early fifteenth century. Like many of those involved in the move to find classical precedents for contemporary political agendas in Florence, Bruni did not come from an elite Florentine family, but rather from a provincial family from Arezzo involved in the grain trade. Salutati noted the young man's talent in Latin and classical studies and made him a part of his chancellery staff. This allowed Bruni to move into the elite circles of Florentine cultural life and bureaucratic power.

When in 1396 the Greek scholar Emmanuel Chrysoloras arrived in Florence and began to teach Greek, Bruni rewarded Salutati's faith in him by being one of the brightest and most successful of his students. Mastering Greek was the logical extension of the return to the classical past in order to find and defend the present, as most contemporaries believed that ancient Greek culture had been the base of Roman culture. Moreover, it was widely accepted that the Greek philosophers had discovered many fundamental truths independently, without the benefit of Biblical inspiration or Christ's teachings. From this perspective a lack of knowledge of ancient Greek texts in the original Greek was a handicap in investigating the origins of Roman culture and the true first times more generally. Bruni's successes in Greek, then, brought him into closer contact with Florentine intellectuals from elite families who were also interested in garnering a deeper knowledge of the classical world by learning Greek – men like Roberto de'Rossi, Palla di Nofri Strozzi, and Niccolò Niccoli.This ongoing wedding of men of power and wealth with public servants and leaders like Salutati and Bruni meant that such interests encouraged a shared vision of an active life in service to the state as the best life imaginable – a highly significant, if imagined, reality.

Was this the first glimpse of a future humanism? Perhaps. But evidently the term's nineteenth-century coinage makes humanism an unlikely measure of an intellectual moment that occurred four or five centuries earlier. Actually, for Baron's central thesis such labels were less necessary than demonstrating that the history of ideas did not develop in a political or social vacuum, simply as ideas passed down from one great thinker to another. The real issue was showing the way in which political events and ideas interrelated at a concrete historical moment. And for those deep connections two of Bruni's works were especially important: his *Laudatio Florentinae Urbis* (1403–1404) and his *Dialogi ad Petrum Paulum Histrum* (written, Baron argued, in two parts, the first in 1401, the second between 1403 and 1406).

The *Laudatio* was labeled by Baron "[t]he pioneer to which must be traced the development that leads through Bruni's *History of the Florentine People* to Machiavelli and the other great Florentine historians." There are aspects of the *Laudatio*, however, that appear to fall rather short of "pioneerhood." First, as the title suggests, it was part of a quite traditional late medieval and early Renaissance genre of works lauding a city – a tradition that often referred to a city's classical foundations and the way its current organization and practices recreated those of the ancient world while also, of course, fulfilling Christian ideals. Bruni, however, was original in that he was one of the first to use a Greek source as a model for constructing his panegyric: the *Panathenaicus* of the Greek orator Aristides, a work that lauded ancient Athens. Although modeling a laud of Florence on an ancient text praising Athens might at first seem unlikely, Baron noted that Bruni stressed the parallel between the two as republics. Republican Athens in the Persian Wars defeated Persian despotism and saved Greek liberty from tyranny, much as republican Florence had just done by defeating the tyrant Gian Galeazzo Visconti. No matter that it was more fortune and disease that had defeated Gian Galeazzo, once again the classics had been imaginatively brought to bear on the present. Moreover, Bruni made the crucial point for Florence's sense of destiny that just as Athens had become the political and cultural leader of the Greek world after its victory, so too Florence was destined to lead Italy. It would do so, however, not as a new power but as the rebirth of the glory days of another first time, that of ancient Athens – yet another *rinascita*.

Following Aristides again, Bruni noted that Athenian successes, both against the Persians and as leaders of the ancient world, were predicated upon the fact that they had always been a free people. This gave him the opportunity to point out that the same was true for Florence, provided, however, that he reject earlier traditions that had claimed that the city had been founded by Caesar – now demoted to the status of a tyrant. Thus, he marshaled historical evidence for reimagining the founding of the city by the republican general Sulla. This allowed him to claim that Florence deserved to lead Italy because the Florentines had also always been a free people from their very founding – a dubious claim, but a powerful rhetorical one that again fit well with the project of making the new old.

Turning to political institutions, Aristides, following Aristotle, had argued that Athens was a perfect example of the ideal of a mixed government, an ideal widely shared in Bruni's day as well. According to this vision there were three basic forms of government, each of which had a fatal flaw: republics, which tended to devolve into mob rule; aristocracies, which tended to become oligarchies; and polities ruled by princes, who tended to turn into despots. The best governments were ones that included a balance or mix of all three forms, so that the weakness of each would be limited by the strengths of the others. It took some fairly clever reasoning to demonstrate that Florentine government was a republic with a perfect mix of the three, but Bruni made the attempt. More realistically, it might be argued that forcing Florentine government into an Aristotelian model of mixed government (already a traditional vision for Venice) was yet another clever rhetorical ploy that, much like the claim of republican foundations, had little to do with what actually was the case. Yet as a way of reimagining power, it was again a particularly potent use of the past to legitimate the present: Florentine government was not some new combination of magistracies and councils, judges and policing bodies developed over time, it was a rebirth of an ancient and proven ideal – creating a perfect urban environment in which to live an active life of *virtù*.

Bruni's *Dialogi* (*Dialogues*) according to Baron's much-questioned dating, were written at two different and significant moments: the first in 1401, during the darkest days of the war with Gian Galeazzo, and the second sometime between 1403 and 1406, after Florence had survived his threat to its independence. In the first the young turks, Bruni, Niccolò Niccoli, and Roberto de' Rossi, led by Niccoli, argued that the great authors of Florence's recent past – Dante, Petrarch, and Boccaccio – should be discarded because they were inadequate as Latinists and classical scholars. In the second, however, they retracted that radical conclusion, albeit in Niccoli's case reluctantly. Their original arguments turned on their insistence that earlier scholars had relied too heavily on medieval authority and Aristotle, and more damning yet, that they had worked with ancient texts that were corrupt, badly transcribed and translated. Behind all this lay an essential failure – they had not mastered classical Latin well enough to realize their errors. Ironically, Petrarch's insistence on perfect classical Latin had come back to bite him.

Implicit in this argument was the insistence that establishing perfect classical texts was a crucial end in itself. It came before dealing with contemporary issues or even the analysis of current problems – a premise that had a logic, if one accepted the vision that ancient culture had been virtually perfect and offered the answers to all questions. In a way, this mode of seeing the ancient world has strong parallels with certain religious fundamentalists, who see returning to the sacred texts of the Bible or the Koran as all that is necessary to live correctly. Yet from a scholarly perspective, this call for developing the most accurate classical texts ultimately made it possible to develop a deeper understanding of those texts and the classical world itself – an understanding that, with a certain poetic injustice, would eventually undermine the myth of a perfect classical past. But significantly, the call to establish perfect texts before using classical knowledge for a broader range of intellectual and practical purposes reflected a growing desire on the part of some to separate classical scholarship and an elite culture from the shared primary culture of the day.

This rejection of everything not ancient, including earlier Florentine greats such as Dante, Petrarch, and Boccaccio, suggests a dangerous closed-mindedness. No matter that in Bruni's second dialogue the young rebels backed down, for in their appeal to a higher order of learning that disqualified most of their predecessors and contemporaries, they were making a disciplinary move that would be at the heart of what many of the later humanists saw as their intellectual mission. Earlier classical enthusiasts such as Petrarch had made similar claims, perhaps even with similar dreams of restricting scholarship and culture to an elite led by themselves. But in many ways Baron was correct in seeing Bruni's *Dialogi* as representing a sea change, for many who studied the ancient classics – especially certain lawyers, scribes, and notaries, along with a group of teachers and tutors and a number of the increasingly aristocratic elite – began to develop a more disciplinary approach to their studies that would earn them the label "humanists" as the fifteenth century came to an end. A deeper and more technical knowledge of ancient texts, rhetorical skill, and a highly demanding standard of writing in Latin, along with some Greek or even Hebrew, would become recognized as the essentials for a true sixteenth-century humanist. For these scholars, their learning and its discipline would increasingly become a mark of elite status, both intellectually and socially, with an aristocratic program of classical studies eventually becoming a movement that dominated Western high culture and learning, even if the term for their discipline, "humanism," was coined only in the nineteenth century. Suggestively, this elevation of their studies into a marker of status was paralleled by similar developments in a number of arenas – certain artisans, for example, were becoming artists, and even elite prostitutes were becoming courtesans, as we will see.

Not all were content with this self-proclaimed status of sixteenth-century humanists as the intellectual elite of their day, especially the increasingly narrow and stringent standards for membership in their new intellectual aristocracy that they defended. In fact, already in the sixteenth century humorous and often quite biting attacks on humanists demonstrate that there was a perception that in their striving for elite status they had all too often defined themselves out of the world of practical concerns and meaningful cultural debates. Often these attacks are dismissed as early forms of anti-intellectualism. At one level they were just that, but they were often expressions of real concern about the narrowness of humanist scholarship as well, especially in the context of claims to set the standards for and dominate intellectual life. Pietro Aretino (1492–1556), one of the most virulent critics of the first half of the sixteenth century, who at times tried to display his own humanist credentials in order to garner posts and patrons, provides a typical send-up of the stereotypic self-satisfied humanist scholar who is laughed at as a pompous learned fool in his bitterly witty comedy, *Il marescalco*.

The comedy concludes with a humorous marriage scene involving the lead character, the Marescalco, who hates women, much preferring young boys. Throughout the play he has been resisting a match arranged for him by his local *signore*, the duke of Mantua, which allows Aretino to laughingly reprise traditional debates about whether it is better to marry or to avoid the entanglements that marriage entails. Unbeknownst to those summoned to the wedding celebration, the duke has provided the perfect bride for the Marescalco, a young male page dressed and passing as a woman. To add to the humor of the moment and the suffering of the Marescalco, the duke has also asked the Pedant – a character in this comedy already on the way to becoming a stock character of laughter at the expense of humanists – to deliver the marriage ceremony, which he proceeds to do with equal amounts of misplaced enthusiasm, and misplaced classical knowledge, and a large amount of learned foolishness, all buoyed by a misplaced sense of his own elite status.

Tellingly, the Pedant immediately begins on the wrong foot: "[L]et us begin *latine* (in Latin), because Cicero in his *Paradoxes* says that we should not speak of holy matrimony in the vulgar tongue." The use of Cicero as an authority on marriage ceremonies, even if Cicero never wrote a work called *Paradoxes*, as well as the insistence that his speech must be given in Latin, immediately identifies him as a humanist, and a particularly pompous one at that. At the same time, the mistaken reference serves to undercut any claims to true intellectual accomplishments. The duke's man interrupts, undoubtedly underlining what a reader or an audience must have been thinking at the prospect of hearing the Pedant deliver the marriage ceremony in Latin, ordering him to instead "[s]peak to us as much as you can in everyday language, because all this '*ibus, ibas*' [Latin case endings] business is too constipated to be understood."

But, of course, that would undermine the Pedant's claims to superiority, and he objects: "Do you want me to lose the gravity of my oration? One must first pace a bit, glancing now up, now down, in the manner of the followers of Demosthenes." The perfect imperfect humanist rhetorician, he then begins his peroration, returning to Latin and literally starting at the beginning with Creation and the Garden of Eden. This drags out the ceremony with a ridiculous play of preening and misplaced, misused Latin, until the audience is saved from his foolishness by the revelation that the Marescalco's bride is actually a boy, whereupon the laughter at the Pedant is lost in a tide of broader laughter, and the comedy ends with a transgressive humor true to Aretino at his best. Yet clearly behind the clever send-up of the Pedant's pretensions lies a deeper dissatisfaction with, and mocking of, the claims of intellectual superiority of humanists and their overreliance upon classical texts as the measure of all things.

And although it would be difficult to take much seriously in this send-up of the Pedant, his attempt at high Latin rhetoric calls attention to one aspect of classical scholarship of an earlier period that is often seen as setting apart "proto-humanists" as a group well before the label existed – a fascination with rhetoric and writing and speaking with classical style. Aretino's pedant's failures in this area draw laughter, but from early on some intellectuals, in the broader return to the classics and first times, sought to separate themselves from their peers by stressing their mastery of Latin rhetoric. Hand and hand with this went an attack on more traditional forms of medieval argumentation and rhetoric that lacked the style and grace that ancient masters such as Cicero were held to have epitomized. Particularly disliked was the scholastic method of argument associated with medieval universities and medieval interpretations of Aristotle. Although it is a great oversimplification, at its height in the Middle Ages – perhaps best exemplified by Saint Thomas Aquinas's *Summa theologica* – this style of analysis, based on a rigorous use of dialectic and close reasoning, took theology and metaphysics to new levels and to many at the time seemed capable of answering all questions, or at least all questions that could be answered rationally. But it also produced heavy and turgid prose that could become quite mechanical and make for arguments that were anything but elegant or beautiful in terms of language.

Rinascimento writers, who prided themselves on their mastery of rhetoric, much preferred other forms of argumentation, such as the letter and the dialogue. The letter, with its short form, required masterful style to convey its message; the dialogue offered an opportunity to create beautiful speeches that evoked actual debates and often real intellectual figures. But these and other forms of writing that demonstrated rhetorical ability and the truth of ideas via their beautiful expression were often less capable of developing complex ideas; thus, it is frequently assumed that more technical or complex subjects such as theology and philosophy suffered because of this rhetorical turn. Not all were won over to the rhetorical turn proclaimed by Petrarch, however, and many of those who claimed they were did not consistently eschew close analysis for rhetorical elegance. Still, rhetorical skill and the beauty of a text became an increasingly significant criterion that defined certain writings as intellectually superior. And there was a deeper logic to this position, for, as we have seen, beauty and truth were often seen as interchangeable. What was true was beautiful, and what was beautiful was true, and that meant that ideas expressed in beautiful Latin could be presumed to be true. In the face of such claims, however, Aretino's Pedant and the many other pedants of sixteenth-century comedy should not be forgotten; their laughable attempts at rhetoric revealed more vanity and folly than truth and beauty.

The establishment in the early fifteenth century of a new program of education outside the universities – the *studia humanitatis* – is often portrayed as playing a major role in establishing a higher standard of classical Latin and rhetoric. Among the leaders in this movement were two noted scholars and their schools: Vittorino da Feltre (1378–1446) at Mantua, supported by the Gonzaga lords, and Guarino da Verona (c. 1374–1460) at Ferrara, with the support of the Este rulers there. Guarino was well known for his study of Greek and for the years he spent in the east searching for lost ancient Greek manuscripts and perfecting his command of that language. Upon his return to Italy, he settled for a while in Bologna, where he met another student of Greek, Leonardo Bruni, who helped him secure a post teaching in Florence. After teaching there for five years, he moved on to Venice, where he founded a school for the sons of rich Venetian nobles and worked with Vittorino da Feltre, whom he also tutored in Greek. Presumably the two men shared ideas about the ideal form of education for scholars and civic leaders, one that stressed ancient languages and reading the classics in both Latin and Greek. In 1429, after a failed attempt to move his school to his home town of Verona, Guarino was invited by the duke of Ferrara to tutor his son Leonello, and at the age of fifty-five opened a school there. With the duke's patronage, it flourished, and Guarino's educational program quickly became a model for what would become known as the *studia humanitatis*.

Once again his innovations were presented as traditional: in place of the typical medieval university education based on the *trivium* (grammar, rhetoric, and logic) and the *quadrivium* (arithmetic, music, geometry, and astronomy), he took his students back to the classical world via an incremental program of study divided into three levels. The first level, as might be expected, focused on classical Latin. The second went on to study advanced Latin grammar and style, in both prose and poetry, along with basic Greek. These skills were then used to read history and ancient literature. The final level considered rhetoric and philosophy, seen as the highest accomplishments of a truly educated person. For rhetoric, Cicero was the measure, but a wider range of noted Roman orators was studied as well. For philosophy, Greek philosophers, especially Plato and Aristotle, were central. Accompanying this course of study Guarino commissioned a series of teaching manuals and wrote a widely used treatise of Latin grammar.

Pupils came from all over Italy and Europe to study at his school. And as many of them were the sons of notable and powerful families, they spread the fame of his school and of the *studia humanitatis* as a superior form of education, distinct from traditional university education. Guarino, to his credit, insisted that his training should be open to the less well-off, and the dukes of Ferrara supported his vision with the patronage necessary to bring in a few promising students from more humble backgrounds. But in the end it was a training that really made sense only for the sons of the upper classes and bureaucratic elites seeking to move up in the intellectual/scholarly world. Few sons of the lower classes could hope to find the powerful connections or support to move ahead as scholars or high-level bureaucrats in the Church or government – those few who did were the exceptions that proved the rule.

Vittorino da Feltre, although he had studied Greek with Guarino in Venice and was slightly younger, actually opened his school in Mantua in 1423, six years before Guarino. After studying literature and the natural sciences at the University of Padua, followed by Greek with Guarino, he won a chair in rhetoric at Padua. He too opened a school for the sons of nobles in Venice, but when Gian Francesco Gonzaga, lord of Mantua, invited him to educate his sons *and* his daughters – the latter an idea that was gaining ground, even if many opposed it on moral grounds – Vittorino jumped at the opportunity. In many ways his school was even more traditional as it stressed the *trivium* and *quadrivium* associated with university instruction, also emphasizing a more stoic ethos of self-mastery in a Christian context. Thus students spent considerable time in physical exercise and reading religious texts that stressed self-control, obedience to the dictates of religion, and moral values. The ideal was that teachers and pupils would live and work together and once again that the school would be open to all ranks of society. It too quickly attracted students from all over Italy and Europe as well as patronage from a wider circle of aristocratic supporters. Success followed rapidly, as an impressive number of scholars and civic leaders studied there and the school continued at least another twenty years after Vittorino's death.

If those who had studied in the schools that stressed the *studia humanitatis* had set themselves clearly apart from the vast majority of fifteenth-century people who appealed to the classical world as the basis for their arguments and ideas, perhaps we might identify among their number a group that might be labeled proto-humanists. But although many who embraced this educational ideal were successful, they usually followed the *studia humanitatis* not as a separate and superior path to knowledge, but as, at best, a superior manifestation of the general fascination with and respect for the ancient world. Actually, scholars and intellectuals of the fifteenth century who are labeled humanists by modern scholars tend to be individuals who seem particularly important or successful, rather than the group who studied with Guarino or Vittorino. Not surprisingly, then, mediocre figures are seldom identified or studied as important precursors – ironically, even in humanism's imagined lineage only the elite find a place. To avoid the pitfalls of this anachronistic popularity contest, perhaps a better way to look at these figures is to focus on the fact that most of those now labeled humanists saw themselves until late in the fifteenth century as merely part of a much broader movement that sought to place ancient language, literature, and rhetoric at the service of a society and a shared culture that valued above all returning to better first times – in sum, in the service of a Rinascimento.

As humanists at the end of the fifteenth and across the sixteenth century developed their scholarly interests into a discipline that created and identified a superior intellectual elite, the *virtù* associated with intellectual leadership narrowed in a way that transformed the use of ancient texts and ancient languages from a significant aspect of virtually every field of knowledge to the scholarly discipline of an elite few – a discipline that sought to dominate all other knowledge. Those who had not mastered that knowledge, who could not demonstrate that they possessed that *virtù*, were progressively defined out of the world of knowledge that really mattered, at least from the perspective of humanists. Thus when it became absolutely necessary to know exactly what Aristotle had said in the original Greek about the nature of government, or what Galen had held on the humors, without turning to other disciplinary traditions such as medieval political theories or the observations of surgeons, a widely shared faith in the superiority of the ancient world had splintered off to become a discipline that would accomplish many positive things, gain wide respect, but at the same time become the butt of jokes and be seen by its naysayers as both narrow and an impediment to knowledge.

Fifteenth-Century Classical Scholarship

If we look at those often labeled humanists or proto-humanists from the fifteenth century, most again had a wider vision of their classical scholarship, even those who prepared the ground for a more disciplinary approach to such scholarship. One scholar often singled out is Lorenzo Valla (1407–1457). His proof that the Donation of Constantine was a forgery is often seen as an early triumph of humanistic discipline. It will be remembered that the donation of the Roman Empire to Pope Silvester, supposedly made in 324 by the Emperor Constantine in return for the former's curing him of leprosy, had been one of the primary documents defending the papacy's claims to temporal authority. By the 1440s, however, when Valla proved that it was a forgery, it was in many ways a dead letter, as no secular rulers were ready to deliver up their lands and power to popes on its authority. Still, Valla's proof that it was a forgery was a disciplinary tour de force. He demonstrated that the Latin of the text contained a number of words that were not in use in the fourth century, when it was supposedly written, and showed that several of the key phrases were particular to the much later Carolingian period. But his analysis went beyond the text's Latin, also exhibiting a perceptive historical awareness, as he pointed out that leprosy was relatively unknown in Constantine's time. Only in the early Middle Ages had it become the scourge that the Donation invoked as the reason for Constantine's gift. In sum, the search for an understanding of the way Latin developed, along with a more scholarly understanding of the past, had allowed Valla to prove that what had once been a key text of the Christian tradition was not at all what it seemed. It should be noted, however, that this proof, often pointed to as one of the triumphs of early humanists, was largely ignored – for when Church figures listed claims for papal authority, the Donation still regularly appeared, Valla's proof notwithstanding.

A closer look at this widely recognized "humanist" hero of the fifteenth century once again suggests some of the problems involved in creating humanists for this period. Certainly much of Valla's scholarly production qualifies him as one of the most important classical scholars of his day, yet he was much more, and strongly influenced by medieval mysticism and his own brand of Christian Epicureanism. At the same time that he wrote on the development of ancient Latin and taught rhetoric at Pavia in the 1430s, he argued for a form of Epicurean Christianity that stressed the mystical pleasure of the search for union with God as the highest Christian good, something that had a long medieval tradition, albeit with a classical pedigree recognized already in the Middle Ages. In his *De voluptate* (1431) Valla attacked the contemporary vision (that could be traced back to ancient Stoics) that had dominated Christian thinking at least from the time of Petrarch's enthusiasm for Cicero, claiming that rather than control of one's emotions, the cultivation of pleasure was the true goal of a Christian life. Pleasure was not something to be avoided as a sin, but rather a God-given emotion that taught the true path to a good life. Like everything else created by God, it was good and natural to humans and served a holy end. When correctly understood and pursued, it actually led to a moral life and ultimately to God.

Moving from court to court seeking patronage, Valla eventually settled at the court of Naples, becoming secretary to Alfonso I, king of Naples. While there, his defense of Epicureanism caught up with him, and the Inquisition attempted to try him for heresy. Thanks to powerful protectors, he escaped that danger and actually soon found himself at the papal court, where from 1448 he served as secretary to a series of popes. In that capacity he augmented his fame as a student of the classics, translating a number of Greek texts into Latin, most notably works by the historians Thucydides and Herodotus. Yet he also continued to work on theological issues and expanded his theories about the essentially Epicurean nature of Christianity, attempting to sidestep the materialistic and atheistic underpinnings of that classical philosophy. Recovering perfect texts in that context did not mean accepting or attempting to recreate in the modern world everything they taught; in fact, it required a careful rejection of much of their teaching and a deep rethinking of the rest in terms of contemporary Christian thought and values. What stands out in his long and successful career serving some of the most powerful masters and patrons of his day, then, was that while he made important contributions to what was developing toward a humanist discipline, he worked well beyond those interests, using his classical knowledge eclectically to serve his wide-ranging interests in Christian mysticism, legal theory, and history.

Still, perhaps his most important work from the perspective of that future tradition was his *Elegantiarum Latinae Linguae* (1435–1444), which attempted in a systematic way to look at how Latin grammar and language had developed over time and to eliminate from contemporary Latin what he saw as the medieval corruptions that had disfigured the language. In that work he drew a clear distinction between his own day and an earlier, less learned time. And that distinction turned on what he labeled a "rebirth" of ancient culture in his modern urban world – a *rinascita*, however, that he argued was much more wide-ranging than a mere revival of classical languages or its disciplinary imperatives. Noting that painting, sculpture, architecture, and the other liberal arts, along with literature, had long been "virtually dead," he claimed that "now they are reawakened to a new life and flourish among an *impressive group of excellent artisans* and learned men of letters." [italics mine] And he continued to enthuse, "[H]ow much happier we ought to be about our epoch when if we work just a little harder, I am confident that soon we will restore even more than the city, the language of Rome and with that all the disciplines (*discipline*)." Significantly, although the recovery of Latin was central to this vision, it was a much broader recovery that he dreamed of – and in many ways less elite, including artisans and manual arts as well as philology and scholarship.

In this light Leon Battista Alberti (1402–1472), another noted figure frequently labeled as a proto-humanist, also had a close relationship to the artisan culture and to the more practical disciplines of his day. Rather like Boccaccio, who in his *Decameron* uplifted the popular *novelle* from the shared primary culture of the day, giving it that touch of refinement that made it more palatable for elites, Alberti frequently took the practices of artisans or the commonplaces of a shared primary culture and gave them the theoretical basis and the classical finish needed to transform them into something more suitable to a more aristocratic society. Yet it might be suggested that frequently his classical veneer was just that. Most notably, for example, in his famous work written in Italian, not Latin, that explained the mathematical

underpinnings of perspective, *Della pittura* (*On Painting*, 1436), his theories
relied extensively on medieval theories and practical knowledge, rather than
on classical authors. In fact, his explanations of optics were heavily based on
the eleventh-century Muslim thinker Alhazen (Ibn al-Haythan), made more
widely available in the West by thirteenth-century Franciscan thinkers such as
Roger Bacon and John Peckham. Tellingly, they also drew extensively on the
practical skills of the artisan-painters of his day, who were actually working
out the techniques necessary to create the impression of a three-dimensional
space on a two-dimensional surface. In this case as in many others, one is
forced to wonder whether we are seeing Alberti as a neo-humanist, then, or
as a much wider-ranging intellectual using the past to inform and uplift the
present in the spirit of a more general and ongoing Rinascimento.

Yet perhaps what made Alberti's work most original at the time was his
own deeper understanding of mathematics and his ability to use it in many
of his technical treatises to help explain artisanal techniques or classical theories. This was especially true in his works on architecture and painting,
particularly his *Della pittura* and *De re aedificatoria* (*On Building*, 1452), which
harkened back to the classical work of the Roman Vitruvius. These skills
were also displayed in his books on mathematical games – *Ludi mathematici*
(*Mathematical Games*, 1450–1452) – and on cryptology – *De componendis cifris*
(*On Writing Codes*) – as well as in his reported collaboration with the noted
Florentine scholar Paolo Toscanelli. Toscanelli is perhaps best known today
for his map claiming that the Far East could be reached by sailing west, a
copy of which Columbus carried with him on his first voyage, but he was
most noted in his day as a mathematician, astrologer, and astronomer.

Alberti was also not averse to the ultimate sin of humanists from the later
disciplinary perspective writing in Italian, even when he gave some of his
works Latin titles. Worse yet, he produced a Tuscan grammar, *Grammatica della
lingua toscana*, as if that dialect were capable of gaining the stature of a truly
learned language comparable to Latin. Still, from an early age he also made a
name for himself as a master of Latin style, even passing off a Latin comedy
he wrote at the age of twenty, *Philodoxeos* (*Lover of Glory*), as the work of
an ancient Roman comic poet. A partial list of his other writings, however,
suggests his range of interests and the way treating him as a humanist limits
his much broader cultural explorations: *De commodis litterarum atque incom-
modes* (*On the Advantages and Disadvantages of Literary Studies*) (1428 or 1432);
Intercoenales (*Table Talk*, c. 1429); *Vita S. Potito* (*Life of Saint Potitus*, 1433);
De iure (*On Law*, 1437); *Vita* (*Autobiography*, 1437); *Apologi* (*One Hundred
Aesopic Tales*, 1437); *Pontifex* (*The Bishop*, c. 1437); *De amore* (*On Love*, c.
1437); *Theogenius* (*The Origin of the Gods*, c. 1440); *Profugiorum ab erumna libri*

III (*Remedies for Misfortune*, c. 1441); *Canis* (*My Dog*, c. 1440); *Musca* (*The Fly*, c. 1440); *De equo animante* (*On the Life of the Horse*, c. 1440); *Descriptio Urbis Romae* (*Rome Described*, 1440s); *Momus o del principe* (*Momus, or On the Ruler*, 1450); and *De iciarchia* (*On the Ideal Ruler*, 1468).

Not content merely to write on a wide range of topics, he also attempted to practice many of them, although with what success remains a matter of debate. He advised several popes on their plans for rebuilding Rome and collaborated on a number of major architectural projects in Florence and elsewhere. He also worked as a painter, although critics have not been enthusiastic about the limited number of works attributed to him. All this was augmented by an aggressive program of self-fashioning and by laudatory reports about his good looks, witty conversation, athletic abilities, and wide-ranging learning. In what is believed to be his own brief autobiography (c. 1438), he boasted that he was capable of jumping with his feet together over a standing man; throwing a coin so high in the *Duomo* that it touched the ceiling; taming wild horses; climbing mountains; composing music; and playing the organ, among other feats. Clearly he was a man who attempted to capture the imagination of his contemporaries, and in many ways succeeded.

Alberti's illegitimate birth is often pointed to as his one handicap, and frequently analyzed for its impact on a psyche that clearly was driven to succeed and to set its master apart and above the rest of society. Such theories are interesting, but it should be noted that illegitimacy was not all that rare during the period and that the drive to sustain a more aristocratic status and glory was ubiquitous. Perhaps more significant for Alberti was the fact that his branch of the Alberti family had been exiled from Florence, which meant that, much like Dante and Petrarch, for much of his life, and especially during his formative years, he was an outsider. In addition, and perhaps more important for those who would consider his psyche, his father never legitimated him, as he might have done before his death. Thus when his father died, the young student Alberti suddenly found himself, according to his account, cut off from his rightful inheritance and the support of his family, forced to struggle on his own for what he saw as his deserved place in society. Something that he clearly did with an impressive drive and success.

Alberti's troubled relationship with his family has recently led to reevaluations of his treatise on the central role of the family in the Rinascimento, *I Libri della famiglia* (*The Books of the Family*). Once seen as a paean to patriarchal values and the patrilineal ideal – the centrality of the male line of descent within a family – it seemed to argue that this form of the family was the very building block of the *civiltà* of the period. As such, it was viewed as a fundamental text on what we might call Rinascimento family values and the way in which the family was seen as underpinning and upholding civic morality. The fact that most of the defenders of this vision portrayed in the book are members of the very Alberti clan that Leon Battista felt had betrayed him and with whom he had troubled relationships has led to questions about just how seriously he used such figures to defend that vision. Moreover, the work is presented as a dialogue, which makes reading it as a defense of any specific point of view still more problematic.

Yet reflecting on the popularity and nature of the dialogue as a literary form may actually offer a way of reading Alberti's work that allows one to think more clearly about the issues presented and perhaps also to read the many other works written as dialogues during the period. For in many ways the dialogue is the most oral of the written forms of the period and tends to reflect the range of the shared discourses on a topic. From this perspective the different Albertis portrayed present a series of positions from the discourse of the shared primary culture on family and family values, allowing readers to evaluate them based on the characters who argued them. Then as now, the point was not necessarily to correctly identify the real people behind the characters, but rather to judge their arguments based on their individual characteristics. Thus some of the old scions of the Alberti line come across as crusty and decidedly anticivic in their hard-line defense of the great family line over all else, and both they and their logical arguments are decidedly unattractive. Others are presented as more moderate, attractive, and more attuned to the civic values of their day and win sympathy.

Leon Battista portrays himself as an unmarried young man who speaks more from his reading than from experience. Yet rather than being disqualified by that fact, he seems a compelling young scholar whose learning and knowledge of the ancient world make him attractive and make his comments particularly relevant. Moreover, as the shared primary discourse of the day privileged classical culture and ideals over contemporary practical experience, his lack of experience in family matters was not particularly significant. In fact, one might argue that the practical experience of the more senior members of the family, who may well have mistreated him in real life, from this perspective is trumped by his superior knowledge of the ancient world, which underpins his defense of the family as the basic building block of society.

All this is perhaps best seen when Leon Battista puts speeches in the mouth of his similarly young, impressive, and scholarly relative Lionardo Alberti, perhaps better known at the time for his knowledge of classical literature. Lionardo draws on that knowledge to provide a virtually "pre-Rousseauian" explanation of the genesis of the tight relationship between the family and the society and the *civiltà* of his day:

Families increase in population no differently than do countries, regions and the whole world.... And for the procreation of children, no one can deny that man requires women. Since a child comes into the world as a tender and delicate creature, he needs someone to whose care and devotion he comes as a cherished trust.... Woman, therefore, did *first* find a roof under which to nourish and protect herself and her offspring. There she remained, busy in the shadow.... And since woman was busy guarding and taking care of the heir, she was not in a position to go out and find what she and her children required for maintenance of their life. Man, however, was by *nature* more energetic and industrious, and he went out to find [these] things.... In this way it seems clear to me that *nature* and human *reason* taught mankind the necessity of having a spouse. [italics mine]

Here a highly gendered and traditional view of marriage in the name of first time, reason, and nature – all key measures of the shared primary culture of the day – posits the patriarchal family as the crucial foundation of a well-ordered society. Women should remain at home, weak but nurturing, while men, "more energetic and industrious," leave the task of continuing the family line and ultimately the social order itself to those very same weak women. The misogynistic illogic of this vision notwithstanding, Lionardo builds the case for this marriage-based family unit as the basic building block of social discipline and order, which in turn serves as the base for all other corporate organizations, including government. The discussion, in fact, begins by noting that familial reproduction was not just a matter of concern to the family, but had crucial significance for "countries, regions and the whole world." Earlier this had been stressed when he pointed out that not only did families produce the future citizens of society in terms of procreation, they also produced them by training them to live together peacefully and successfully: "Children whose character is excellent are a proof of the diligence of the father, and an honor to him. It is generally thought better for a country, if I am not mistaken, to have upright citizens of *virtù* rather than many rich and powerful ones."

What might at first sound familiar and relatively ahistorical here begins to take on more specifically Rinascimento resonances, with marriage, procreation, family, child rearing, morality, and citizenship coming together in a vision of a society based on *virtù*. Clearly this was more ideal than real, as a number of the older and more experienced members of the Alberti clan lament. Yet as an ideal based on both classical ideals and contemporary values, it was rich in explanatory power, for if fathers did not train their heirs in the *virtù* that Lionardo envisioned; if honor as practiced was often less concerned with a good civic order and more with private family goals; and if citizens were not particularly moral, then what we have called civic morality, theoretically inculcated by the family, would not be capable of effectively disciplining the vibrant and chaotic cities of the Rinascimento. This seemed patently true to most observers; thus, Lionardo provided both the theoretical explanation for the travails of his day and a solution that his contemporaries could hear and accept. Like Leon Battista himself, his young relative showed how ancient learning and common wisdom overlapped to provide a powerful vision for explaining and perhaps even mastering their everyday world.

The Venetian noble and scholar of ancient languages Francesco Barbaro (1390–1454), after an earlier visit to Florence in 1415, wrote a similar treatise, *De re uxoria* (*Concerning Wives*), on the centrality of marriage and the family, with, if anything, an even more patriarchal and aristocratic vision of civic morality. Once again, however, even as he proudly displayed his classical learning in this and other works, Barbaro was much more than a proto-humanist. Destined for a significant political career, he early on made a reputation for himself studying with some of the leading scholars of his day, including Vittorino da Feltre. His rich and powerful family and their inter-regional connections also gave him the opportunity to travel, and in 1415 he visited the Florentine banking family the Medici, where he befriended both the young Cosimo de' Medici, future ruler of the city, and his brother Lorenzo. It was in this context that he penned *De re uxoria* as a gift for the marriage of Lorenzo and Ginevra Cavalcanti, the social event of the year in Florence.

As the title suggests, the work focused on the choosing and training of a wife, but the central concern with picking and training wisely turned once again on the premise that the family was the base of the political, social, and moral order. In fact, not far behind the sternly patriarchal vision of women as silent and obedient, virtually childbearing vessels of aristocratic status, the real concern of Barbaro's treatise was the husband – for he had to pick, train, and discipline his wife in order to ensure her *virtù* and that of *his* family and household and eventually of *his* civic world itself. If the husband accomplished this, his sons would be *viriliter* (manly), successful, and capable of serving their family and their city, thus playing their part in ensuring an orderly and prosperous society. As might be expected given Venice's closed ruling class, Barbaro placed more emphasis on noble lineage and the way nobility flowed "naturally" from noble parents to noble offspring. Noble lineage was not absolutely necessary, he conceded, but it offered much greater security as new men were far less stable, lacking that very family tradition that allowed *virtù* to be imbibed virtually at the breast of a noble mother and the disciplining hands of a noble father.

A child's early years were crucial. In a well-ordered household a noble wife's dignity, prudence, and thrift taught children the basics of *virtù*: "The child's moral education ..." he argued, "in infancy continues under the mother's guidance, until a pious, dutiful, and self-restrained young person is prepared for intellectual training under his father's direction." At that point a father has to lead his sons beyond the feminine world of the household to the civic world that will be their arena as adults, impressing on them the discipline and reasoned approach that will allow them to serve and prosper in the broader society, in many ways imagined as merely the noble family writ large. Treatises on the family replaying these themes could be easily multiplied, for even if the veneer was rediscovered ancient truths, the driving force was an emphasis on civic values and a contemporary vision of *virtù*. In the end, in the early Rinascimento *virtù*, honor, love, and the central values of the shared primary culture of the day all circled back to the family and the civic morality that it underpinned.

Returning to Florence and the ability of writers like Alberti to give the shared primary culture and artisanal skills a classical veneer, a more openly positive view of the world of artisans was presented by a slightly younger Florentine contemporary of Alberti, Antonio di Tuccio Manetti (1423–1496), not to be confused with the better-known Giannozzo Manetti (1396–1459). Tellingly, the more famous Giannozzo is often portrayed as an important humanist and the less well-known Antonio as merely an architect, a biographer of famous men, or the mathematician who mapped out mathematically Dante's *Divine Comedy* and its deeper numerological symbolism. Both Manettis, however, again led the highly variegated life of fifteenth-century scholars who used the classics in the service of a much broader range of interests. In fact, Antonio is best known today for his biography of the noted Florentine architect and sculptor Filippo Brunelleschi and for his funny but troubling novella about how that same Brunelleschi, with the help of some of the most important artisans of his day, tricked a gullible young wood carver into believing that he had been turned into someone else, the *Novella del grasso legnaiuolo* (the *Novella of the Fat Woodcarver*).

In each work he celebrates Brunelleschi's *virtù*. Suggestively, however, that *virtù* turns not just on his technical skills and mastery of his crafts, but also on his clever understanding of the world and his ability to overcome all obstacles to reach his goals, even in the case of the hoax that convinces the poor fat woodcarver that he has lost his identity. That tale is a masterful celebration of the Florentine's beloved *beffa*, the clever, often cruel, trick that rewards those who have *virtù* and thus are truly superior at the expense of those who lack same. Although the biography of Brunelleschi and the novella are often treated as separate works, the novella actually seems to have served as an introduction to the biography, and the former ends by offering the biography to those who want to learn more about the clever author of the *beffa*. Significantly, both works celebrate the superior intellects and skills (*virtù*) of a group of artisans in Florence in the early to mid-fifteenth century, men whom Manetti portrays as deserving that superior status – in his telling they are heroes of Florentine arts and production and are well on their way to becoming artists rather than artisans.

The story of the downfall of the fat woodcarver at Brunelleschi's hands is a novella that seems totally contemporary, especially as it turns on a deep and thoughtful understanding of and familiarity with the everyday world of an artisan in Florence. In fact, the tale can be read as a virtual guided tour of the masculine spaces of work there, as I have argued elsewhere, offering virtually the touch, the feel, the sounds of the city. It appears that nothing could be further from classical culture, until one realizes that it is also a clever spin-off from the tales of a highly popular classical text, Ovid's *Metamorphosis*. With a good dose of sex, quick action, and plenty of references to other ancient literature, that work is a collection of stories about people who have lost or changed their identities in "marvelous" ways – exactly the fate of the fat woodcarver as engineered by Brunelleschi and his friends. Much like Boccaccio, then, Manetti once again took the traditional Florentine *beffa* and uplifted it into a novella with a classical veneer. One could enjoy it without realizing its classical precedent; but superior people, those in the know, were also aware of how it replayed Ovid's transformations in the familiar world of Florence, with its artisan heroes playing the main roles and demonstrating their thoroughly modern *virtù*.

More often cited today as an early humanist, Antonio's older namesake, Giannozzo Manetti was if anything more eclectic in his use of the classics and an even less likely candidate for that title. His knowledge of ancient languages, not just Latin and Greek but also Hebrew, certainly marked him out as a classical scholar of note. But he was a man of many masters and many interests that required a much broader range of skills. He first worked as a banker in his youth, then moved on to serve several princely rulers, including Alfonso I of Naples, Pope Nicholas V, and Cosimo de' Medici. For the pope he began collecting Hebrew manuscripts for the Vatican library; for Alfonso he translated the Psalms of the Bible from Hebrew; and he is often seen as one of the pioneers of a more rigorous biblical scholarship with his new translations of the New Testament from Greek. He too was a biographer whose interests went well beyond the ancients: along with his moralizing biographies of Socrates and Seneca, he wrote on a number of the most important "moderns," including Dante, Petrarch, Boccaccio, and his patron Pope Nicholas V. The moralizing nature of his biographical writings reflects his apparently deep Christian faith and the way he believed a careful reading of ancient culture, including the first texts of Christianity, revealed the deeper moral truths shared by pagan and Christian culture.

What is often seen as his most important and pioneering humanist work, *De dignitate et excellentia hominis* (*On the Dignity and Excellence of Man*), fits well in this broader context. While it can be read as a paean to the possibilities of humanity and human creative powers, those powers ultimately, *and always*, were the gift of God, a vision having strong affinities with medieval theology. Still, the work was criticized in its day as giving humans Godlike powers and skirting the edge of heresy, if not crossing the line. For historians who saw humanists as emphasizing the importance of the humans in this world and their ability to act and create with almost Godlike powers, such accusations helped Manetti's work gain its pioneering humanist label. But that vision has been successfully attacked for ignoring the strong Christian dimension of the culture of the day (and of later humanist thought as well), and Giannozzo's work, when looked at more closely, illustrates why. Humans may be more creative and powerful, even Godlike, for Manetti, but this was because God made humans in his "image and likeness" and gave them the power to create. This is certainly a positive vision, but, crucially, the power of humans that Manetti evokes was neither secular nor based on man; it was divine, and it came from God and only from God.

Once again what is most striking about Giannozzo is how much broader his interests were than a later humanist discipline would have permitted. In fact, many of the writers that we have been considering have been labeled "civic humanists" for their supposedly new emphasis on the vision that the best life was one of service to government and society, a service that was enhanced by the rhetorical and literary skills that the study of ancient culture and thought offered. But, as we have seen, in many ways this label misses the fact that this vision of an active life actually dips well back into the early Rinascimento, with everyone from chroniclers, notaries, civic leaders, preachers, and prominent literary figures weighing in on whether the ideal life should be an active one in service to one's family, community, or city or a withdrawn life of Christian contemplation. That this vision was often defended using classical thinkers and classical texts, both Christian and pagan, did not make it proto-humanist – it was much too complex and richly intertwined with contemporary life, Christian values, civic morality, and a *popolo grosso* vision of *virtù* and the urban *civiltà* of the day to be reduced to such a simple formulation.

A Powerful Dream of First Times: Marsilio Ficino and Knowledge

Marsilio Ficino (1433–1499) and his followers have often created problems for those who would label the most important thinkers of his day humanists. For his fascination with the relationship between Platonic and Neo-Platonic philosophy and Christianity seemed distant from the rhetorical and philological interests of later true humanists and from those of the supposed civic humanists. Even the attempt to label him and his followers "Christian humanists" seems to fall short, as in reality they created a series of religious and philosophical discourses about the ultimate significance of first times and what those first times revealed about the meaning of life and truth, discourses much more typical of the broadly shared interests of the primary culture of the day. Of course, Ficino's studies were aided by a close analysis of classical texts. Yet crucial for the reading of those texts was a generally accepted and traditional religious belief that God had given humans such as Adam, Moses, and Solomon, along with other early thinkers, the true knowledge of things in various first times. This way of seeing the world made the knowledge of first things – whether it be first philosophy, religion, or language – extremely valuable, because each had been given by God and thus offered the ultimate truth. The study of first things was not merely a religious or historical concern, then; it was self-evidently the best approach to knowledge available.

Although Ficino had been trained in the medieval Aristotelian tradition, like many philosophers and theologians of his day, in his early twenties he learned Greek and became fascinated with Plato, whom he began to translate into Latin. The quality of his translations and his impressive insights into the deeper meanings of ancient Greek texts earned him wide recognition in learned circles in Florence and the attention and support of Cosimo de' Medici, perhaps helped by the fact that Cosimo's personal physician was Ficino's father. With time and Medici patronage, his translations of and commentaries on Plato's dialogues, along with treatises inspired by Neo-Platonic ideas on the immortality of the soul and love, made him the darling of the circle of intellectuals that surrounded three generations of the Medici family. But as the intellectual historian Francis Yates pointed out more than a generation ago, Ficino offered much more, and the Medici and their circle were if anything more fascinated by his broader, more esoteric writings. In fact, at the same time that Ficino was being encouraged by his Medici patrons to translate Plato, he was being pressed more aggressively to translate a series of texts that were believed to be more ancient – first texts that were ultimately the source of Plato's philosophy.

No matter that most of those texts actually came from the Hellenistic period in the first centuries after the birth of Christ and represented later Neo-Platonic traditions in a syncretistic mix with various forms of religious and magical thought popular at the time. What impressed Ficino, his patrons, and his peers was that these texts came with the claim that they had been written down at a time very close to the beginning of the world itself and thus seemed to come as close as possible to the first knowledge from God Himself. This knowledge, the *Prisca Theologia* (the First Knowledge from God), offered the ultimate answers to all questions. And significantly, these texts made it absolutely clear that knowledge was power, much as has been suggested by modern thinkers. And indeed, how could it be otherwise, for these texts were essentially God's instructions for understanding and using the world.

Some sense of the excitement and importance of Ficino's understanding of these texts can be garnered by a quick overview of how they intersected with and enriched the widely shared primary cultural concepts of time and metaphor. First time, of course, had always been one of the greatest and most important times for understanding the true nature of the world, for in the beginning God made the world, and He made it good, as the Bible and many other texts insisted. This meant that in the first time things were made perfectly as God intended. In the Garden of Eden, Adam was instructed to name the things that God had made, which was, of course, the beginning of language. But it was much more, because it was the beginning of meta-phor, as names were not the things named themselves but a representation of those things. Yet because God had given Adam the power to give things their true names, they were not mere arbitrary signs or empty metaphors; rather, they were deeply true to the very nature of the things named and thus in many ways participated in the power of the named thing itself. Over time humanity had lost track of the true significance of things, their names, and the metaphorical relationship between them; thus words and language had lost their power and became merely descriptive. Modern metaphors, even in Latin, therefore, were at best pleasing but merely hollow echoes of the first true language and true metaphors.

Especially important for recapturing first names and knowledge were the writings of Hermes Trismegistus, supposedly an ancient Egyptian from around the time of Moses – a critical first time when God was busy passing His knowledge to humanity in various forms, including the Ten

Commandments. This writer stressed the close and metaphorical relationship between God and humanity, for humans were literally a metaphor in this world for God, who existed beyond it. God had created humans in his image and likeness once more – literally as a metaphor for Himself. Moreover, the essence of humans was that they were Godlike and creative – for as God created the world in the beginning, humans recreated it daily, both physically and imaginatively. No small claim, but, suggestively, not only did it have a certain logic given the metaphoric way of seeing the world and first time, it was an idea that in the fifteenth century had wider resonances with a similar metaphoric vision of nature and widespread magical practices. Unfortunately for all this, Hermes Trismegistus was not a contemporary of Moses as claimed; he was actually a composite pseudonym given to a series of Hellenistic texts from the second century after Christ, texts that were heavily influenced by the Neo-Platonic thought of that period and by many of the same religious currents that had had an important impact on early Christianity.

Ficino, however, did not base his ideas on Hermes alone. He was also deeply impressed with ancient Greek religion and the philosophers who preceded Plato, especially the number philosopher Pythagoras. Once again, however, he knew most of them, and particularly Pythagoras, largely via Hellenistic texts which pictured him as a thinker fascinated by the metaphoric quality of number, who purportedly argued that the underlying reality of number demonstrated that there is just one God – the One above and beyond all numbers guaranteeing their order and the unchanging rules of mathematics. In turn, as the most perfect and ordered system of knowledge known, number seemed to be one of the most basic underlying metaphorical systems of this world, very similar to the original true language of Adam – a vision that appears to have strong echoes in modern physics. Be that as it may, for both Pythagoras and Ficino the power of number was reflected in and revealed by the close relationship between numbers and music. The pleasure one felt in hearing music and its beauty were not an accident, but rather tied to the way in which good music reflected aurally the basic rhythms and numerical order of Creation itself. And once again, in creating such harmonies based on number humans were acting as a true metaphor for God, creating in the here and now the deep harmonies of truth, just as God had created them.

The metaphorical vision of Ficino, in turn, made time relatively easy to explain. Time became just a metaphor for change. All things seem to break down and pass away. That process is seen as time, which is thus merely a metaphor for the constant change of things. For Ficino, then, without change there is no time. And at a deeper level both change and time were ultimately the result of motion – all change requires movement that transforms one thing into something else. Crucially, however, all motion and thus all change descended from God. To be more specific, God initiated movement without moving Himself, as medieval theologians had long argued; His first movements descended through the stars (dominated by decans, demigods associated with the 360 degrees of the basic circle of the outer shell of the cosmos), then through the circles of the planets (Saturn, Jupiter, Mars, the Sun, Venus, Mercury, and the Moon) to arrive at the center of the cosmos, Earth. Significantly, if all motion descends and that is the root of all change and time, then the wise man or magus who understands how this works can predict, and perhaps even influence, change in this world.

Each of the planets and decans had their own metaphoric qualities and their own metaphors in the world that influenced or actually drove change below. For example, Saturn was associated metaphorically with intellectual contemplation, Jupiter with discursive reasoning, Mars with emotions and imagination, and the Sun with words, songs, and sounds. Moreover, the decans not only pass down motion and change to the world, they literally do so with a crucial responsibility to "form" the world. To understand how this works we have to return to Ficino's conception of Platonic forms. For Ficino, as for Plato, the problem with this world was that it was constantly changing and thus ultimately impossible to know – change and time again. Simply put, the thing we knew a minute ago or an hour ago changes, and thus the moment we think we know it, it becomes something else, and our knowledge becomes false. This is the ultimate predicament of knowing anything in a material world of time and change.

The solution for Plato, his followers, and Ficino, along with many others in the Christian tradition across the Middle Ages, was the realization that the material world is simply not the real world – it cannot be real, because it has no permanence or knowability. What we encounter in this world, and mistakenly take for real, is constantly changing. In the true immaterial world beyond time, space, and – crucially – change, there exist eternally unchanging things – forms. As these forms are not made of matter, they do not break down with time, which means in turn that nothing changes in that *real world*. These forms, then, are the real, unchanging reality – the real things – upon which the unstable things we encounter in this world are modeled as metaphors; thus a chair, in the classic example, is a passing materialization of the eternal form of chair, a cat a similarly temporary materialization of the form of cat, and so on.

As material things in this world, cats and chairs come and go, change over time, and pass away; yet for all their change, we still can know cats and chairs if we discover the real eternal forms behind their changing manifestations. If, for example, we mistakenly identify a chair as a cat, Plato and Ficino can explain our error – we have mistaken the form that stands behind a chair for the form that stand behind a cat. Useful, perhaps, for those who tend to confuse cats and chairs; but all this becomes much more significant when one realizes that Plato and Ficino believed that behind more abstract ideas, such as beauty and good, stood eternal forms as well; thus, those much more value-laden labels, which might seem dangerously relative and subjective otherwise, were anything but. Philosophers and those with a knowledge of the forms could identify true beauty or true good as they were reflected metaphorically in this world just as surely as they could identify cats and chairs – no small accomplishment.

Ficino, however, took things a significant step further by putting these ideas firmly into what he saw as a Christian context. For him, reality itself involved a tripartite scheme based on the Trinity. Before time, everything existed in the oneness of God. With the Creation that unity was separated out as unchanging forms in the Holy Spirit, which Ficino saw as equivalent to Hermes' Nous or Spirit. Finally, in the last created material world, matter was formed into impermanent metaphors for the forms, what we think of as things, like cats and chairs. And it was that world of change that Christ entered with a human material body as fully God and fully man – one of the most fundamental tenants of Christianity. Thus God, the Holy Spirit, and Christ played out in Creation as the One (God), the underlying spiritual reality of forms (the Holy Spirit), and the savior of the material world of time and change (Christ). In its symmetry and its apparent perfect fit with what Ficino and his followers saw as the deeper meaning of Christianity, this interpretation of the ultimate order of things was a beautiful and appealing vision of breathtaking symmetry and order that made sense of everything.

But, if true, it offered much, much more in Ficino's eyes: the ultimate power over this world. For if a magus or philosopher could learn to influence or control change – holding things to their forms or even manipulating their constant forming – he could influence or even control it. Chairs could become cats. More significantly and practically, the high-minded magus could help to form justice in a ruler or beauty in the dreary routine of daily life. Clearly this was a very positive vision of human power over the universe, in many ways not unlike a modern scientific vision: know the reality behind change, its origin, control it, and one controls the material world. Of course, it was also a dangerous knowledge, as power could fall into the wrong hands, but once again one that has its parallels with modern scientific knowledge. Perhaps the most telling difference was that in the Rinascimento most agreed that this knowledge should remain esoteric – in other words, a secret knowledge limited to an aristocratic, intellectual elite – whereas in the modern world there is the faith that the open dissemination of scientific knowledge is positive – a faith that has increasingly been challenged, however, as the dangerous implications of much of what science has accomplished has reawakened promethean fears.

This potential power that the magus had was evoked with poetic optimism in a work known as the *Egyptian Genesis*, attributed to Hermes, which Ficino translated; it described God's creation of the cosmos with a powerful promise of human power: "Now the Nous, father of all beings being life and light, brought forth a Man similar to himself whom he loved as his own child. For Man was beautiful, reproducing the image of his Father [note the God/man metaphor], as indeed it was with his own form [in Man] that God fell in love and gave over to him his works." Man at this point was still outside of time, space, and the material world, but

> Then Man, who had full power over the World … leant across the [heavenly] spheres … and showed himself to Nature below in the beautiful form of God…. Nature smiled with love….And he, having seen this form like himself in Nature [again a metaphor], reflected in the water, he loved her and wished to dwell with her.The moment he wished this he accomplished it and came to inhabit the irrational form [i.e., matter].Then nature having received her loved one embraced him, and they were united, for they burned with love.

Here the Fall – a literal fall into matter and the material world – is not a result of Original Sin or a turning away from God in the Garden of Eden, but rather a result of human love positively depicted. Man fell in love with the form of God in himself and, seeing it reflected in nature, out of love willingly united with nature and entered this world of matter, time, and change. As such, it was a fall of sorts.Yet rather than being a punishment, as it was in Genesis, it was a voluntary act of love for nature and God. Humanity is portrayed even more positively as a metaphor for God and literally his reflection in the material world of nature. We are here a long way from original sin, serpents, and apples, or the vision of humans as alienated pilgrims passing through a strange and sinful world hoping to win salvation.

Those who understood this deeper secret knowledge or gnosis (the ultimate secret knowledge at the heart of religion) knew how to draw on the connections reflected in the metaphors found in the material world to control what happens and even its very nature.This is the power that the magus commands in a number of ways. First, and in a way most simply, because the magus knows how all motion and thus all change descends from the outer spheres, through the stars and their constellations, down to the planets and eventually reaches Earth, he can use the observable motions of the heavens to predict what changes will happen on Earth. Observable repetitions of the motions of the great stellar constellations and the planets will produce similar repetitions of events on Earth. This science – one of the most potent based on observation in the premodern world and perhaps more responsible for the faith given to an empirical methodology than normally realized – was the basis of a long tradition of astrology. But once again Ficino's studies of Hermes seemed to confirm this science, demonstrating that it came from the very first writers, who had learned it virtually directly from God. Like many before him who had made similar claims, Ficino used this knowledge to cast horoscopes and was so noted for his skill that he was commissioned to write them even for popes.

More active power turned on the fact that our own spirits are part of the Nous, the Spirit of the Universe – in Ficino's Christian terms, the Holy Spirit. As the Nous is everywhere in everything as the ordering principle giving things their form and meaning, our spirits have potentially great power. Actually, they are nothing but pooling places for this ordering force of the universe; this explained for Ficino how we think and act. Using this spiritual force within us, we are capable of employing our understanding of the reality that stands behind this world (the forms) to perform correct and powerful deeds. When we understand correctly the essentially metaphorical nature of material things, we interact with them as they should be interacted with – we do not try to sit on a cat or pet a chair. More significantly, we do not expect justice from an unjust person or beauty when we encounter something ugly. But the magus goes beyond this by trying to use his understanding of the true reality of things outside of time and space to draw as much as possible of that true reality into this world. In this the magus is literally drawing the out-of-time into time and maximizing the reality of the things in this world of change – in a way making the metaphorical quality of things as real as possible.

Crucially, Ficino's way of seeing reality could be traced back to his discovery of what he believed were first texts and the *Prisca Theologia*; yet his belief in their significance was firmly rooted in a Rinascimento conviction that first times were best and in traditional ways of seeing the world. And virtually all agreed that the best of all first times for ideas and a spiritual life was the first time when God freely gave men the knowledge necessary to live successfully in His creation, whether it was God allowing Adam to use His knowledge to give things true names and thus with language to create the true metaphors between things and forms; or God giving Moses the Ten Commandments to order the social life of humans according to His plan for human society; or God giving to Hermes Trismegistus and the earliest philosophers the secret metaphorical order of nature and the real world beyond it.

All these firsts warranted – no, they required – a return to their first truths and a rebirth of a first time that had been lost, a *rinascita*. Once again, in what might seem rather esoteric and thoroughly unmodern ideas we find the underlying shared primary culture of the Rinascimento. And, crucially, to reduce Ficino's complex use of ancient texts, his complex ideas, his deep involvement in his society and culture, and his powerful influence on the intellectuals of his day to a mere strain of later humanist thought (or to dismiss him as a deviation from mainstream humanists) is to put him into a box that dangerously ignores much of what he was about and much of his attraction for his contemporaries. His most important contributions to the modern world are often seen as his translations and commentaries on Plato, but his contemporary impact was much greater, even if it was all a magnificent misunderstanding based on texts that were not first at all.

Ficino and other thinkers who followed in his footsteps or who moved in a more otherworldly direction – seeing this world as a mere reflection of and metaphor for the real world outside of time and space – returned to what we might still label the classics of the ancient world, but they were a different set of texts than those sought out by the more civic-oriented classical scholars of an earlier generation and the early Rinascimento. Yet the more withdrawn, contemplative, and elite intellectual life they envisioned was frequently better suited to a more aristocratic and courtly society and to the educated courtly elite that was developing in his day. Such ideas were more satisfying to those who had less opportunity to contest political power openly, offering instead the more nebulous promise of influence and power via the hidden metaphors of Creation for those in the know. Often labeled magic, such hidden powers are frequently seen as power for the powerless and the lower classes; yet it may say something about courtly society and the princely regimes of the high and later Rinascimento, which we are about to look at more closely, that this new/old approach to power attracted even the best intellectuals and the most powerful. And once again this attraction was the new viewed as the old – rebirth, not change. Still, in its search for the underlying reality that stood behind change and time and the power and *virtù* that such knowledge offered, it queerly anticipated a very different future and faith, modern science and the modern itself.

6

COURTS: PRINCES, ARISTOCRATS, AND QUIET GLORY (c. 1425–c. 1500)

A Great Turning Point Forgotten?

On July 6, 1439, the famed architect Filippo Brunelleschi's (1377–1446) recently domed Cathedral of Santa Maria del Fiore, which dominated the cityscape of Florence and the imagination of many as the engineering and spiritual marvel of the day (Illustration 6.1), was the setting for an earthshaking proclamation. Under the remarkable free-standing dome referred to as *Il Duomo* (the Dome), along with the relatively new leader of Florence, Cosimo de' Medici (1389–1464; "in power" 1434–1464), in attendance for the historic moment were the Greek emperor John VIII Palaeologus (1390–1448; emperor 1425–1448); the Patriarch of Constantinople, Joseph II, arguably the most important leader of the Eastern or Orthodox Church; a host of eminent Greek churchmen; Pope Eugenius IV (1383–1447; a pope 1431–1447); numerous cardinals; a large group of leaders of the Western Church; and a sizeable contingent of local notables. With impressive festivities and pageantry they were regaled with the formal announcement that the Church Council originally convened in Ferrara in 1438 and now meeting in Florence had concluded an agreement to reunite the Eastern Orthodox with the Western Catholic Church, ending almost a millennium of discord that had divided Christianity.

It seemed to be a great turning point in history. Making the reunion of the two churches even more significant, and in many ways making it possible, was the hope that a unified Christianity would be able to face the menace of an expanding Turkish Empire in the east, which threatened the Eastern Roman Empire centered in Constantinople. A crusade, it was hoped, would stop Turkish expansion in the east and strengthen the Eastern Roman Emperors in the bosom of a now unified Christianity. And it was not by chance that this agreement was reached in Florence, for the newly completed architectural masterpiece of Florence's great *Duomo* was not only

6.1. The *Duomo* in Florence (Santa Maria del Fiore). Photo: Scala/Art Resource, New York.

a testament to Rinascimento spiritual enthusiasm, artistic leadership, and technological *virtù*, it was a very visible measure of that city's wealth, power, and leadership in Italy and Europe, all of which were deeply intertwined with the great wealth and European reach of its new leader, Cosimo de' Medici, who had come to power in Florence just five years earlier.

In a way, then, Brunelleschi's masterpiece, the *Duomo*, stood not just at the heart of Florence but at what was one of the main economic foci of the West. In fact, that was one reason why Pope Eugenius had moved his Church Council to Florence. Florentine wealth, and specifically a series of Florentine loans, had made the council possible, supporting the Greek leaders' visit and aiding the pope with the considerable expense of hosting such a large gathering. Actually, Eugenius had been living in Florence for some time. Medici support, both financial and military, offered him a safe haven from a competing antipope, Felix V (1439–1449), and an aggressive Church Council that had dragged on for years in Basel (1431–1449) challenging Eugenius's power. From that perspective, an additional motive for calling the council had been the hope that an embattled Eastern Empire and Eastern Orthodox Church would agree to a reunification of Christendom that would significantly reinforce papal authority in the West and the pope himself.

Of course, Medici support had its price. Papal banking, already heavily reliant on Florentines, now fell even more completely into the hands of the leading banker of his time, Cosimo de' Medici. That, in turn, reinforced his informal but very real power in Florence. In essence, Florence under Cosimo could be touted as the city that brought together the greatest leaders of Europe and forged a peace that promised their eventual victory over the Turks. It was a mythic moment much like that much earlier mythic moment in 1177 when Venice had supposedly provided refuge for Pope Alexander III against the emperor Frederick Barbarossa, demonstrating its equality to those two great world powers. But this moment actually happened.

One might well ask why this potentially great event has not become a symbolic turning point in history. The answer is simple and at first seems straightforward. The union of Christendom dissolved almost as soon as it was announced. Within a short time the only remnants of that theoretically glorious reunion were a few major figures in the Eastern Church who joined the Western Church; a few leaders who continued to call for a crusade against the Turks; and a perhaps heightened interest in learning Greek among Western intellectuals. To make matters worse, the religious divisions and the lack of unity among European rulers was soon confirmed by Turkish successes in the east that culminated with the fall of Constantinople in 1453 and the collapse of the Eastern Empire, which had endured more than a thousand years. The Eastern Orthodox Church survived, albeit much weakened, living under Ottoman rule. Many of its leaders fled to the West. And a number moved north to Moscow, which soon was styling itself the Third Rome. In sum, what had seemed a momentous triumph, rich with symbolism for the future, turned into merely another moment of false hope or, worse yet, a telling harbinger of the inability of a deeply divided Christendom to work together to overcome even the most pressing threats.

Yet that moment in Florence's impressive new *Duomo*, engineered in many ways by a cooperation between an aggressive pope trying to reestablish papal power and an aggressive new ruler in Florence, also reflected deeper changes that did have a future. First, it showcased Cosimo de' Medici as a major player, not just in banking or in Italian affairs, but on a European scale. It also showcased what was becoming increasingly his Florence – a rich, lively city and cultural center, made richer yet by his patronage, banking, and investment in cloth production. Equally importantly, it highlighted the fact that the papacy was truly back in Italy. Eugenius IV was far from being a strong pope. And although he spent most of his papacy as a client of the Medici, living in exile from Rome in Florence (1434–1443) with his court, he aggressively fought to make the papacy a significant player in Italian and European affairs once again, with some success.

The Papal Court in Rome: Quiet Glory and a New/Old Courtly Aristocracy

The popes were back. Theoretically, of course, they had been back since the reign of Martin V (1368–1431; pope 1417–1431), who took office alone as pope in 1417, officially ending the Great Schism (1378–1417), and shortly thereafter, in 1420, returned to Rome. But when he returned he found a city badly damaged by the ongoing battles between local nobles, and a generally violent tenor of life. Establishing peace and his rule in the city and in the former Papal States became a top priority. This he saw as necessary in order to effectively establish Rome as a secure and safe base from which to rule the Church. In turn, in the Papal States this meant reestablishing papal power at the expense of locals who had usurped control while the papacy was away in Avignon or occupied by the Great Schism; and at the same time it required building broader diplomatic alliances that protected his power and rule. In this way Martin was refashioning himself as a prince, admittedly of the Church, but nonetheless acting much like any other princely ruler anxious to establish a firm power base and defend it. Regaining the Papal States, however, was not easy. Early on the death of the powerful *condottiere* and lord of Perugia, Braccio da Montone (1368–1424) – one of his main rivals in the area – led a number of prominent cities, including Perugia, Assisi, and Todi, to resubmit to papal rule. In short order they were joined by other cities further from Rome, beginning the long and conflicted process of reestablishing the traditional boundaries of the Papal States.

Martin also arranged a series of profitable marriages for members of his own important Roman family, the Colonna. One of his brothers became duke of Amalfi and prince of Salerno, creating an important foothold and a loyal defender in the south. Yet another brother became count of Alba. This form of nepotism, as it was negatively labeled by opponents, would also become a regular strategy of the popes seeking to secure their power and rule in Rome. And although it was without doubt nepotism, especially as Church revenues played a major role in furnishing the large dowries and special favors that smoothed the way for these advantageous marriage matches, it was also a tried and true princely form of diplomacy. What better way to extend one's influence and protect one's power than to extend one's family networks via marriage into the powerful families of Italy and Europe.

Family, land, and political power, however, were not all a prince required in the Rinascimento. To be a true prince, one had to be princely. Yet if one had not been born a prince, and in many ways was really supposed to be a pious leader of a spiritual church, not a prince, one had to find ways to demonstrate merit in as unobjectionable a manner as possible. In Martin's case, if he needed any examples, he found himself surrounded by *signori*, lords, and princes of questionable pedigree who demonstrated through their courts and patronage of the arts and learning their own *virtù*. Such patronage demonstrated what might be labeled the quiet glory of *virtù* – not greedy display or sinful consumption, but visible and laudable support of the most impressive cultural achievements of the day. In Martin's case, he proclaimed that he was leading a rebirth of Rome and papal power as a prince of the Church, his own papal *rinascimento*. More generally, similar forms of patronage, displays of learning, and demonstrations of princely demeanor were becoming the order of the day at the courts that would-be notable princes gathered around themselves throughout Italy.

At first glance fifteenth-century Italian courts might seem merely a continuation or renewal of earlier medieval courts. But although to a degree they looked back to those earlier courts, in crucial ways they were different. First, as was the case with the culture of the Rinascimento, they were invariably urban, and they did not move about the territories that a prince controlled, following his peregrinations. Medieval courts, by contrast, tended to be rural and moved through the lands ruled by a noble or a prince, living off the wealth of the various underlords visited. Significantly, the denizens of medieval courts were usually a warrior nobility legally tied to their overlord in ways that ultimately turned on the military commitments that stood behind and legitimated a medieval nobility. Rinascimento courts, by contrast, encompassed a greater social mix, especially in the fifteenth century, with at times artist/artisans mixing with self-made bureaucrats, old noble families, and *popolo grosso* families who had risen to power and wealth in the more recent past, to form a decidedly new courtly aristocracy.

In fact, many members of these new courts comprised an increasingly aristocratic segment of the *popolo grosso* who had gained wealth and power across the fourteenth century. From this perspective, as discussed in Chapter 2, members of the Venetian merchant banker class who labeled themselves nobles in the early fourteenth century were not so much anomalous as ahead of the social developments elsewhere in their aristocratic pretensions. As the economic, social, and political leadership of the *popolo grosso* became progressively more secure at the close of the fourteenth century and in the early fifteenth, they became progressively more aristocratic as well. This transition was at times helped along by intermarriage with older noble families, especially in the smaller towns and economically less advanced areas. But, on the whole, the trajectory that had seen the *popolo minuto* lose ground to the *popolo grosso* gradually saw the *popolo grosso* divide between a more prosperous and increasingly aristocratic core, on the one hand, and a lesser group of wealthy families who did not measure up to the newer standards that stressed grace and refined manners as central components of *virtù* and requirements for elite status, on the other. These were not new attributes of status added to the vision of *virtù* so much as they were traditional attributes that were being more strongly emphasized at the expense of what might be seen as the more utilitarian values of fourteenth-century elites, such as calculation, reason, and cunning.

The papal court, as it was reconstituted in Rome after the papacy's return, provides a particularly good example of this, with certain significant caveats. Most notably, the papal court was both clerical and masculine, in contrast to courts elsewhere where women, at least in theory, played a central role and clerics were less dominant. In addition, the papal court tended to be an unstable entity, changing, often dramatically, from one relatively short-lived pope to the next, whereas the secular courts of Italy usually enjoyed a certain dynastic continuity, both in the ruling family and in the local families that participated. Martin V found it difficult even to get his court to join him in Rome after his return. Many were not particularly enthusiastic about moving to the relatively small town with less than 30,000 inhabitants that Rome had become, camping in the ruins of an ancient city that had once boasted a population of well over a million.

Poggio Bracciolini (1380–1459), the roughly contemporary book collector and classical scholar (recently made famous by Steven Greenblatt in his *The Swerve: How the World Became Modern*), described the city: "The hill of the Capitol ... formerly the head of the Roman Empire ... has fallen.... The path of victory is overgrown with vines, and the benches of the senators are concealed by a dunghill.... The forum of the Roman people ... is now enclosed for the cultivation of herbs or thrown open for the pasturing of pigs." Rome also was not particularly attractive because its environment was decidedly unhealthy, in terms of both disease and urban violence. The nearby swampy lands of the Campania, once drained by Roman emperors, had long since returned to being breeding grounds for swarms of mosquitoes that made malaria virtually endemic in the city. In turn, internecine warfare between noble families had become the order of the day in the absence of the papacy, with armed bands of supporters of various clans battling in the streets or from their own fortified compounds, often nestled in the ancient ruins. To make matters worse, the most powerful of those noble families had once dominated the College of Cardinals and the papacy itself; and many feared that in returning to Rome they would regain control of both. Martin, as noted, was a scion of one of the most powerful of those old Roman families, the Colonna, which only intensified such fears.

In the end, with all these things stacked against him, it is not surprising that Martin's attempt to reestablish his court in Rome did not go particularly well. His successor, Eugenius IV, seemed only to confirm these negatives. Immediately problems with Martin's powerful family forced him to flee to Florence, where he lived with his court, supported in part by Medici wealth for most of his papacy. Those years in exile, however, exposed Eugenius and his court to the vibrant cultural and artistic world that Cosimo, his supporters, and the city itself were cultivating as a demonstration of their own wealth and importance. The impressive hosting of Eugenius's Church Council and the leaders of Christendom was just one example of the power of such display and of Cosimo's own growing quiet glory.

Life at Eugenius's court was described by a young scholar, Lapo da Castiglionchio, in his *De Curiae Commodis* (*On the Benefits of the Curia*), shortly before his untimely death at the age of thirty-three in 1438. In a recent study of Lapo, Christopher Celenza sensitively portrays this relatively unknown scholar's description of the papal court, with its suggestive mix of a vibrant intellectual life and wealth, which so attracted him, and its highly visible vices, which troubled him. Perhaps trying to improve his chances for advancement, and certainly demonstrating his rhetorical cleverness, he often attempted to explain how even those vices might be seen as virtues. For example, speaking of gossip at court, he opined, "But whenever a conversation about lighter matters comes up, if it turns towards jest and gossip (for a great liberty and license is allowed in the Roman curia for reproaching and abusing) no one is spared, whether he is absent or present, and everyone is equally attacked.... Dinner parties, tavern life, pandering, bribes, thefts, adultery, rape and shameful deeds are publicly revealed." Without missing a beat, Lapo smoothly turned this critique into yet another positive aspect of the court: "From this one acquires not only pleasure but also the greatest utility, since the life and character of all is thus placed before your eyes." The result, he claimed, was that members of the court knew each other intimately and thus knew exactly how to deal with each other and "live[d] more wisely and more securely."

He also praised the riches to be won at the court – although not always honestly, he admitted. Such wealth, for all its admitted negative attributes, he also defended as useful at least as far as it enhanced the glory and power of the Church. His highest praises, however – as might be expected, given his own scholarly pretensions – he reserved for the intellectual life of the court, which in his eyes included the greatest thinkers of the day, singling out as the most important Poggio; Giovanni Aurispa (1376–1459), another book collector and translator of Greek texts; Flavio Biondo (1392–1463), the noted historian of Italy, both ancient and medieval; and Leon Battista Alberti (1402–1472). Significantly, Lapo never speaks of any of them as a humanist or even as a follower of the *studia humanitatis*. Biondo is portrayed as an erudite writer of history, Poggio as an urbane and witty writer, and Aurispa as so learned in the *bonis artibus* (perhaps a reference to the liberal arts) that little escaped his notice. Alberti is lauded as one whose mental power and wide range of abilities were unmatched. For Lapo, then, these luminaries of the papal court were men of great learning, eloquence, and doctrine whose enviable intellectual range was much broader than simply the *studia humanitatis* or what would have fit under a label like "humanist," had it existed. Simply put, their cultural interests were much broader, as were those of the court of Eugenius and the day.

Eugenius's successor, Nicholas V (1397–1455; pope 1447–1455), might be seen as the real architect of the rapid rise of both papal power in Rome and the papal court. A Tuscan by birth, trained at Bologna first in law and later in theology, he surrounded himself with a number of the leading intellectuals and artisans of his day. Many were drawn from Florence, where he had met and known them while he served there in pope Eugenius's entourage. Reportedly he met daily in his Florentine days for scholarly discussions with the likes of Poggio and Giannozzo Manetti, among others. Back in Rome, his goal was to establish a glorious court that would attract the most creative artisans and intellectuals of the day. To make the city more attractive to such men, he began to build what would be the nucleus of a papal library based on his own collection of ancient authors and Christian authorities, including both the Church Fathers and Scholastic theologians of the Middle Ages, which reportedly came to include more than 5,000 volumes. In this endeavor he took advantage of his leadership of the Church to press clerics across Europe to search for little-known works in monastic and cathedral libraries and secure copies for his library. He was particularly interested in the Greek writers of the early Church and their predecessors in the ancient world. In turn, his library and court were enriched by scholars he recruited who were capable of translating those works into Latin in order to make them available to the majority of Western scholars still unable to read them in their original Greek.

This program was aided by a steadily growing flow of Greek scholars and churchmen fleeing the East, as the Turks advanced inexorably on
Constantinople. When the city fell in 1453, that flow became a flood, with
many of the refugees finding a place at Nicholas's court. They brought with
them important manuscripts, some of which also found their way into
Nicholas's library and many of which added to the excitement of a Greek
revival in Rome. Thus, along with Nicholas's drive to make Rome the new
capital of the world, he and his supporters also began to portray his court
and Rome as Athens reborn. As the glory of the classical world was seen as
having shifted from Athens to Rome with the rise of the latter, that trajectory could now be seen as having completed a cycle, with his Rome giving
rebirth to both ancient Athens and Rome.

Such a grandiose vision, and an only slightly more modest rhetoric of
renewal, was matched by a revival of art and architecture in Rome that was
orchestrated by Nicholas and that demonstrated his increasingly princely
stature and at times not-so-quiet glory. On a practical plane he rebuilt the
walls of the city and repaired many of its bridges and aqueducts. On a more
spiritual but still utilitarian plane, he also repaired and redecorated many of
the churches of the city that had fallen into disrepair; cleared and straight-
ened the streets leading to the Vatican; rebuilt the papal palace itself; and
began work on repairing Saint Peter's Cathedral. To carry out these projects
he brought to Rome a number of the best builders and architects of the
day and apparently made use of Alberti and his architectural vision to plan a
rebuilding of the city that, if realized, would have made it truly a capital of
the world. And significantly, of course, all this novelty and aggressive aggrandizement of papal rule in Rome was once again packaged as anything but
new or innovative. It was dominated over and over again by the now familiar
"re" words: renewal, reform, rebirth. Rome was undergoing a rebirth of her
ancient glories – no matter that it was led by a new pope, his new court, and
a host of new painters, architects, and scholars.

One of the keys, however, to this papal *rinascimento* in Rome was yet
another recall of the past – the fact that the city, like the papacy itself, could
be seen as built on the body of Saint Peter, who had been martyred there and
whose body was entombed in Saint Peter's Cathedral. In this light, Flavio
Biondo in his *Roma instaurata* (*Rome Renewed*), written in the mid-forties,
had earlier, asserted that it was a mistake to see ancient Rome's greatness as
stemming from the bloody victories of her armies, as many contemporaries
believed. Instead, he insisted that it was the blood of Christian martyrs that
had made Rome a true capital of Christianity and the world. The true first
"emperor" was Jesus Christ. He had passed his reign down to his apostle

Peter, promising that upon that "rock" (a play in Latin on the double meaning of *petrus* as both rock and Peter) would be built his church. Biondo used
this long-stressed doctrine of the Petrine or Apostolic Succession to promote
Rome as a unique spiritual place with the mission of leading Christianity.
Moreover, he noted that the city was exceptional because its monuments
and churches were over and over again founded literally on the bodies of the
martyrs of Christianity. What other city could boast that it housed the bodies
of the apostles Peter and Paul, found in the Vatican, or the many other relics
to be found under the altars of its churches.

Actually, many others made similar claims based on their own relics,
bought or stolen over the centuries. But none, not even Venice, with its own
apostolic claim to house the body of Saint Mark in Saint Mark's Cathedral,
could come close to Rome's rich heritage, with trophies like the chains
that held Peter in Herod's prison in Jerusalem, now found in San Pietro
in Vincoli; the ring sent directly from heaven to Saint Agnes; the grill on
which Saint Lawrence was roasted; or, for that matter, the "fountains of sweet
water" that rose from the spot where Saint Paul's head fell when he was martyred in Rome. Most of these claims were not new, but now that the papacy
had returned to Rome, they were marshaled aggressively by papal courtier/
scholars, who emphasized them as part of a program that aggrandized the
pope and his princely rule while associating the special destiny of the city
with his role as the direct successor of Christ and the apostle Peter – virtually a papally inspired civic morality for urban Rome, stressing its renewal
or rebirth as the capital of Christendom. With a paradoxical irony, then, the
very civic morality that city-states had earlier developed in order to create
parallel and essentially independent spiritual claims to legitimate their rule
against the spiritual claims of the Church, was now being reinvented to
empower papal claims to a special spiritual primacy.

Adding to such claims and to papal revenues as well, Pope Nicholas V
declared 1450 a jubilee year for the Church. This was not an innovation on
his part, as popes had been declaring jubilees every fifty years since the 1300
jubilee that brought our imaginary German pilgrim, Felix, to the city. But
Nicholas used it to showcase the glory of his renewed Rome and his leadership of the Church. It was claimed that more than 40,000 pilgrims came to
the city to take advantage of indulgences earned by visiting, and while the
reality may have been more modest, the pope made the most of the event
with a series of major processions and celebrations that proclaimed that
Rome and the papacy were back and leaders of Europe. At the same time,
the jubilee helped to refocus attention on the monuments and Christian
heritage of the city and in turn helped to stimulate the revenue-producing

potential of the city itself. For with better administration; rebuilt walls, churches, and streets; and a less violent tenor of life, Rome was ready to become one of the first tourist cities of the world. Of course, it had always been an attraction for those hardy pilgrims who braved the dangers of medieval travel to visit the holy city. What they had found, however, was another matter, for to many the holy city appeared to be only a holy village camped in the ruins of ancient Rome. Those who came for the jubilee of 1450 discovered a flourishing court and growing city that was on the way to becoming an impressive capital of Christian Europe.

Nicholas also increased the papacy's role as a leader of Christianity following the fall of Constantinople in 1453 by calling a meeting of the main leaders of Italy to promote peace between them and once more to plan a crusade against the Turks. These were the last days of the Italian One Hundred Years' War. The main belligerents were financially exhausted and ready for a peace that would stabilize their gains or limit their losses. Thus, although the pope's meeting failed to gain more than rhetorical support for a counteroffensive against the Turks or a general peace, shortly thereafter, in 1454, the Peace of Lodi was signed, and the major parties to the conflict joined an Italian League that was pledged to maintain the peace in Italy for twenty-five years, officially ending the Italian Hundred Years' War. Although the pledge was not always honored – mini-wars for territory in the Papal States, led by popes, were among the most significant breaches of the pact – a relative peace reigned in Italy until the mid-nineties, and the papacy attempted to demonstrate its leadership of the Christian West by championing a crusade against the Turks.

In fact, the popes that followed, Calixtus III (1378–1458; pope 1455–1458) and Pius II (1405–1464; pope 1458–1464), were less concerned with building the papal court or the city, preferring to focus on developing crusading plans. Calixtus of the Catalan family of Borja (Borgia in Italian), old and sickly when he gained the papacy, had played a long and significant role in establishing Aragonese power in the south of Italy and as pope continued calls for a crusade against the Turks. Much in what would become a Borgia tradition, he was also eager to aggrandize his family, appointing his nephew Roderigo cardinal (eventually he would become the notorious Borgia pope, Alexander VI [1492–1503]). In that context Calixtus also turned on the Aragonese, claiming that the kingdom of Naples was a papal fief, apparently in the hope of granting lands there to members of his family. Pius, a noted intellectual and classical scholar, spent more time building up Corsignano, his birthplace in Tuscany, into a beautiful little Rinascimento gem that he renamed Pienza, than he did on Rome or the papal court. Also, for a man who had been elected pope in the hope that he would maintain the peace finally gained with the Peace of Lodi, he spent much of his papacy deeply involved in war and diplomatic wrangling.

More curious at first glance, but more significant for his crusading initiatives, was the account that Pius provided in his autobiographical *Commentaries* of his welcoming of the apostolic head of Saint Andrew to Rome. It had been safely deposited in the Greek city of Patras, but had been forced to flee the Turkish invasion of the area in 1460, aided in this by Thomas Palaeologus, lord of the Morea. Pius offered Palaeologus sanctuary at the papal court and a pension to live comfortably as a lord in exile, in return for the head. But it had to wait to enter Rome until large new statues of the apostles Peter and Paul were placed in the square before Saint Peter's Cathedral and until the square itself had been redone to provide a suitable setting for the reunion between the apostolic brothers Andrew and Peter. Once all had been prepared, the head was brought to a place just outside the gates of the city on the day after Palm Sunday, April 12, 1462, where it was met by the pope and a large entourage of cardinals, churchmen, important dignitaries, and an enthusiastic populace.

Pius notes in his autobiography that, overcome by tears, he welcomed the head, crying out, "You arrive at last, most sacred and adored head of the holy Apostle.... This city that you see before you is mother Rome, blessed by your brother's precious blood. To this people gathered here [to greet you] your most loving brother the Apostle, Saint Peter and with him the chosen vessel, Saint Paul, gave rebirth [*regeneravit*] to Christ's Rule." The message was clear: this Rome, Pius's Rome, was the destined final resting place of the apostles of Christ and quite literally the rock on which the Church and its mission were built. But he ended his welcome with a solemn prayer that made his vision of the Church's mission clear: "Omnipotent and Everlasting God, Who rules Heaven and Earth, Who has today deigned to grace us with the arrival of the precious head of Saint Andrew, Your Apostle, grant, we pray, that through his merits and intercession the insolence of the faithless Turk may be crushed, all infidels may cease troubling us, and Christians serve You in freedom and safety. This we ask in the name of Christ our Lord." The assembled host, he reported, replied, "Amen."

Adding weight to the pope's plea to defend Christians and "Christ's honor" with a crusade against the Turks was the fact that Saint Andrew was often seen as the apostle to Greece, and thus in a way his head joining his brother's in Rome seemed to reinforce the idea that the Eastern and Western Churches were reuniting and ready to defend Christendom as a whole. In his autobiography he put the call for a crusade in the mouth of the famed

theologian and intellectual Cardinal Bessarion (1402–1472), himself a refu-
gee from the East and a convert to the Western Church. Bessarion made an
impassioned speech to the head of Andrew when the Apostles were finally
united in the cathedral, once again before a large crowd of the faithful.
"What will you do now?" he queried the head face to face.

> Will you be unmoved or slow against the impious Turks.... Will you accept
> such deeds? You have today a successor [Pius II] who besides his other
> virtues cherishes in his heart this supreme purpose, this desire to avenge by
> righteous punishment the innocent blood of Christians that has been so
> cruelly shed. Now plowshares must be beaten into swords.... Now must
> your zeal blaze forth ... and the Church founded on the rock that is Christ
> may prevail against the gates of hell.

And if anyone had missed the point, he ended his speech by exhorting
Pius to call the princes of Europe to a crusade that the pope himself should
lead. In this he was evidently well coached, as that was exactly what Pius
had been planning and almost certainly was why Pius had brought the apostle Andrew's head to Rome. With great difficulty Pius actually managed to
bring together a crusading army and fleet at the Adriatic port city of Ancona.
But, old and sickly, he died shortly after joining the troops who had reluctantly gathered there and who were melting away even before he arrived;
thus, he never led his crusade and never got a chance to test the mettle of
Andrew's head or the bones of Paul and Peter in battle. Instead, his crusade
dissolved in bickering between its secular leaders and never left Italy.

Paul II (1417–1471; pope 1464–1471), who succeeded Pius, has not fared well
at the hands of historians or many of his contemporaries, for that matter. He
was a patron of the arts and had his own rebuilding program in Rome, but he
was troubled by the growth of the papal bureaucracy and the way in which
offices were increasingly sold and traded. Thus he fired many of the scholars and
intellectuals in the papal bureaucracy, a move that was not popular with them
or their fellows and that seriously weakened his court. Adding to his negative
reputation in the eyes of scholarly contemporaries, he was reportedly not a
good Latinist. Some even claimed that he conducted too much of the business
of the Church in Italian, a signal sin in the eyes of fifteenth-century intellectuals
proud of their mastery of a revived classical Latin. Adding to his negative repute,
it appears that he was not particularly enthusiastic about the classics or pagan
culture more generally, which he saw as undermining Christian piety.

In this context Paul was especially worried about a group of intellectuals
who met regularly in what some called the Roman Academy. Apparently he
feared that in their enthusiasm for classical antiquity they were more pagan

than Christian. No doubt the pope's concern was accentuated by a number of scurrilous poems and invectives attacking him that had reportedly been written by members of the academy. Given that many of them had been dismissed from their posts as part of his reforms, such rumors had their logic. Tensions came to a head in 1468 when he dissolved the academy, accusing its members of a conspiracy against him as well as paganism, heresy, and sodomy, throwing a number in jail and even torturing a few. This clearly did not improve his image with the academy or its supporters and earned him a number of posthumous biographical sketches that portrayed him as ignorant, moody, grasping, and corrupt.

His successor, Sixtus IV (1414–1484; pope 1471–1484), for all his famed nepotism, his battles with Florence, and his role in the founding of the Spanish Inquisition (1478), was nonetheless portrayed by the scholars at his court in a much more positive light. An avid patron of the arts and scholarship, perhaps more than any previous pope he has been given the credit for establishing Rome and the papal court as a leading force in the Rinascimento. This may well have been because he undid the short-lived reforms of his predecessor, rebuilding the papal bureaucracy and staffing it with many of the scholars and intellectuals that Paul had fired and reinstituting the system of buying and trading offices. Labeled "veniality," this system may be traced back at least to Bonaface IX (1359–1404; a pope 1389–1404). At first it was a fairly informal practice, but it soon developed into a system whereby the person originally appointed to a post in the papal curia withdrew, giving it to another for a fee. As the fee was regularly paid over time, it became a form of revenue for the original holder of the post.

Things quickly became more complex and corrupt. People began to pay the pope directly for an office. Thus the pope immediately gained needed revenues. Over time, however, the officeholder earned enough in office to turn a profit on his original investment, thus making the payments something very close to a hidden interest payment on a hidden loan to the papacy. These offices, however, were not limited to the first buyer, and that created a lively business in resales. To make matters worse, as the offices sold were to be held only for the life of the buyer, a range of scams developed designed to hold onto the office after the death of the original buyer. All required a dose of corruption to work and created a series of mini-intrigues that made the system even more profitable for those who knew how to play it. When Paul briefly abolished the whole mess, the system had already become so regularized that the papal bureaucracy itself was actually charging a tax on many of these highly questionable transactions, and such fees had become a significant source of revenue.

Most offices of the papal bureaucracy that were more administrative than spiritual came to be capitalized in this way, with the family of an office-holder having the right to sell the office at his death as long as the correct fee was paid. Under Sixtus, the approximately 300 offices involved before Paul's reforms grew rapidly to over 600. By the papacy of Pope Leo X in the early sixteenth century, they had ballooned to over 2,000. The system was so lucrative for all involved that it actually endured down to the early twentieth century and was copied by many other bureaucracies during the early modern period. The negative impact of this practice has been well rehearsed by both modern scholars and contemporaries. Not only did it encourage what was essentially the buying and selling of Church offices – the much decried sin of simony – it also meant that many rich and powerful families treated some of the most important offices of the Church as private investments.

But for all the negatives of the system, it frequently benefited scholars and courtiers. Some offices could be bought directly by patrons for their protégées or awarded by the pope directly to noted intellectuals. The most successful could amass large fortunes; the more humble could at least find a relatively secure income and the freedom to pursue their scholarly interests. Thus the system not only increased papal revenues, it also significantly increased papal glory and magnificence, expanding the number of intellectuals and writers who graced a pope's court. From this perspective, Sixtus, like Nicholas V, was especially interested in building the glory of his papacy, his court, and Rome itself by emphasizing once again that all three were undergoing a renewal of their ancient glories. Like many of his predecessors, then, he spent freely on the city's walls, roads, aqueducts, and bridges – most notably the elegant *Ponte Sisto* constructed over the Tiber, named after him – with an eye to improving the living conditions in the city and its appeal to visitors. Perhaps most significantly, he had built the Sistine Chapel, which was to become the ceremonial center of the Church. Reportedly he played a significant role in choosing its decorative themes – parallel events in the life of Moses and Christ – and brought in from Florence a group of some of the best artists of the day to paint the frescoes he envisioned.

Glory was the story: artisan/artists competing for glory; the Sistine chapel representing the glory of Sixtus himself; and the whole package representing to a broader world the reborn glory of Rome and the papacy. Sixtus also continued in the footsteps of Nicholas V, expanding the papal library as a resource for scholars and a repository for the most important manuscripts of classical and modern authors. He added as well a number of less prized, but still significant, newly printed books. The library was moved into new quarters and was graced with the leadership of a major scholar, Bartolomeo

Platina (1421–1481), who previously had been imprisoned and tortured by
Paul II for his alleged role in the antipapal plot by the Roman Academy.
Nothing could be more indicative of Sixtus's rejection of Paul's suspicion
of scholars of the classics and what he saw as their dangerous fascination
with paganism. Not only had Sixtus reestablished the Roman Academy and
encouraged its celebration of the city's ancient past as part of his own program of Roman aggrandizement, he had placed the supposed ringleader of
that dangerous pagan revival in charge of the Vatican library itself. He then
forcefully demonstrated his commitment to the library and its collection of
the classics by having his favorite artist, Melozzo da Forlì (1438–1494), do
a fresco for the library representing the pope giving the office of Vatican
librarian to Platina, with several of his prominent nephews in attendance
(Illustration 6.2). Platina, like the good courtier that he was or at least had
become in the pope's service, reciprocated with a literary campaign that
once again stressed Sixtus's glory and his renewed Rome.

But what exactly was Sixtus's court? At a technical level the answer is
relatively simple: the papal court was formally made up of his *famiglia*, just
another fictive corporation or family that included dependents, both lay
and clerical, who assisted the pope in his religious, administrative, cultural,
and personal life. But having said this, things rapidly become less clear. On
the one hand, many members of the papal *famiglia* were menials, hardly the
courtiers that discussions of the papal court normally focus on, even if they
may have frequented it as servants and lesser functionaries. On the other,
the extensive staff of the papal bureaucracy or curia, as it was known, was
also closely involved with the *famiglia* and the court, some even officially
becoming members of the *famiglia*. Usually, however, when outsiders, or
even Romans themselves, referred to the papal court they were alluding
more to an imagined community than to the actual papal *famiglia* or the
curia. In some ways this imagined nature of the papal court actually worked
to the pope's advantage, because the glory of his court and his own glory
could be increased by notables, leading cultural figures, and even artisan/
artists working in the city who often had a rather distant relationship to
the pope, or no relationship at all. Artists whom Sixtus IV called to Rome,
such as Botticelli, Ghirlandaio, Perugino, Pinturicchio, and even Melozzo da
Forlì, or papal secretaries with scholarly reputations who served him were
imagined as significant players at his court. But the reality of their role and
the very nature of courtly life at the papal court remain elusive.

Moreover, it was not the only court in town. Following the return of the
papacy to Rome, cardinals also established elaborate courts of their own
there. Actually, notable cardinals had had courts at Avignon as well, but now

6.2. Melozzo da Forlì, *Sixtus IV Confirming Platina as Papal Librarian*, 1477, Pinoteca Vaticana, Rome (originally in the Vatican Library). Photo: Scala/Art Resource, New York.

they established them in the eternal city, often in competition with each other and at times with the princely glory of the papacy. Perhaps the most magnificent cardinal's court in Sixtus's day was that of his favorite nephew, Pietro Riario (c. 1445–1474). Riario was made a cardinal (as well as archbishop of Florence and Patriarch of Constantinople) by his uncle at the age of twenty-six, shortly after the latter's elevation to the papacy. Pietro's court in its heyday employed 500 people and had an annual budget of about

150,000 *scudi*. According to the rather fawning account provided by one of his courtiers, Ottavio Cleofilo, the young cardinal held lively discussions there in which he personally participated along with an impressive circle of poets, architects, painters, singers, physicians, astrologers, philosophers, and classical scholars. Hyperbole or mere description, these gatherings added to the prestige of Riario, who seemed well on his way to succeeding his uncle and becoming pope himself until his "untimely" death in 1474, perhaps helped by Venetian poison, cut short the intrigues that swirled around him. Riario's princely glory died with him, but not before it added significantly to the notoriety of the courtly life of Rome, as did the courts of a number of other cardinals.

That notoriety was, as Riario's demise suggests, not always positive. The search for visibility and glory, for example, was also part of a larger competition for power between cardinals, who used their courts as one more tool in the ongoing jockeying to win the papacy. But the obverse was true as well: belittling, mocking, or even the more direct defeat of another cardinal's courtiers in street battles were also seen as advancing one cardinal and his court over another. Thus poets, writers, and scholars could be used to attack opponents, both verbally and at times physically, as well as to sing the praises of patrons. In fact, the high level of violence that remained in Rome after the pacification programs of the fifteenth century were often attributed by contemporaries to such violent confrontations between the members of various cardinal's courts. Moreover, with cardinals often dividing along dynastic or "national" lines – Italian, French, Spanish, and German being the most common – the potential for competition and open conflict was greater yet.

Even the old noble families of the city entered the courtly competition. The most important usually had a cardinal or two among their number, and family courts could then be integrated into their households. But when that was not the case, the more powerful of the old Roman families tried to emulate the courts of cardinals. In addition, a few of the most successful bankers in the city followed along in building courts to proclaim their glory, perhaps most notably the powerful Chigi family. Fifteenth-century Rome, then, with its cacophony of courts, rich patrons, seekers of power and glory, and a renewed papal prince was being transformed from a sleepy ghost town into an impressive reborn ancient Athens, classical Rome and a new/old Holy City that would play an increasingly central role in a more courtly and aristocratic second phase of the Rinascimento. The papacy was definitely back, and its increasing glory and impressive courts were quietly and not so quietly proclaiming its pope/prince as at once a spiritual leader and a powerful ruler.

Naples and Its Courtly World

Papal claims to rule the center of Italy, however, often brought it into tense contact with its neighbors: Florence to the north, Venice to the northeast, and Naples to the south. In the early Rinascimento the kingdom of Naples had been in many ways an anomaly from the perspective of the cities of northern Italy, for in the fourteenth century it was under the control, and in many ways the cultural leadership, of the French in the form of Angevin rulers and a more traditional social order that featured a complex combination of feudal forms and Mediterranean commercial contacts. Naples itself had a rich court life mixing French, Italian, Norman, and Mediterranean influences that had attracted the likes of northern artists such as Giotto and greatly influenced the young Boccaccio, who saw in its courtly graces an attractive, uplifting ideal for his own *popolo grosso* world. But although it was one of the larger cities in Europe, it was essentially an administrative capital, more like London or Paris than the productive urban centers of the north and center of Italy. Thus it remained largely a city that consumed rather than produced and featured an elite dominated by a more traditional nobility, with artisans and *popolo* remaining relatively weak, both socially and politically. To a degree its language and its proximity to and commercial ties with the rest of the peninsula made the break less stark than it has at times been portrayed – and there was plenty of interchange between the north and the south – but in the first Rinascimento, Naples and its kingdom remained a curious hybrid, too Mediterranean, rich, and Italian to fit easily into the world of northern Europe and at the same time too agricultural, noble-dominated, and rural to fit into the urban, *popolo grosso* world of the Rinascimento.

The kingdom of Naples had already built important bridges to the culture of the Rinascimento in the fourteenth century. But the process accelerated as the north of Italy became more courtly and aristocratic in the fifteenth century and as Naples became more deeply involved in the affairs of the north. Perhaps the moment that best symbolizes this is the triumphal entry in February 1443 of Alfonso I (1396–1458), son of Ferdinand I of Aragon, into Naples in a golden chariot through a hastily constructed Roman triumphal arch. Alfonso was already king of Aragon, Sicily, and Sardinia, making him, along with the Turks and the Venetians, one of the primary powers in the Mediterranean. Yet what is striking about the moment is that we find the son of a king from Aragon, with little or no Italian/Roman heritage, claiming the throne of the kingdom of Naples in a ceremony that harkened back to ancient Roman triumphs and echoed the imperial claims of many of the *signori* of the northern city-states.

Therein lies another complex tale of what is frequently called "bedroom diplomacy" – marriages between ruling families arranged to secure dynastic territorial goals – stretching back at least to the thirteenth century. To make that long story as short as possible, the key moment arrived in 1282, when the bastard son of the Emperor Frederick II married into the royal family of Aragon in order to gain their support for his attempt to secure control of Sicily. The house of Aragon, one of the most powerful on the Iberian peninsula, had long been interested in playing a major role in the Mediterranean, and they viewed a Sicilian connection as a strategic asset in that context. Following that marriage and descending through a long complex chain of at times rather questionable inheritances, an Aragonese claim to Sicily, and more vaguely to the south of Italy, was kept alive until finally, in 1443, Alfonso (already king of Aragon) conquered the kingdom of Naples, settling the matter by force.

His legal claim to rule, however, was rather tenuous. It seems that in 1420 the ruling queen of Naples, Joanna II, had been convinced by the latest in a series of her colorful lovers to adopt Alfonso as her son and heir in return for his military support in quelling the unrest among her nobility. But that dynastic alliance was short-lived, as Joanna found her new "loving" son pressing a bit too hard to rule before she had actually passed away; thus she disinherited him and in 1423 found a more patient son and protector in Louis of Anjou. When Louis died shortly thereafter fighting to defend her kingdom, she took his brother René as her heir, and things finally seemed settled. Eventually she did die in 1435. And at that point Alfonso reappeared to press his doubtful claim to the throne as her first adopted son, even if he had been disinherited. After a series of unlikely turns of fate, he finally defeated René in 1442 and took Naples in 1443. Pope Eugenius IV then became involved and – perhaps unwisely, given the future tensions between Naples and the papacy – recognized Alfonso as ruler of Naples and his illegitimate son Ferrante as his heir in return for Alfonso's recognition of the pope as his feudal overlord. Needless to say, he did not do this out of the kindness of his heart or because of the quality of Alfonso's claim to Naples, but rather in return for Alfonso's support against the Conciliar Movement that was contesting his own power as pope. Tangled webs indeed.

Machiavelli would later discuss Alfonso's strategy for ruling Naples as an ideal example of the way a new prince should govern. And one might claim, ahistorically, that Alfonso reciprocated, as he was in many ways a perfect Machiavellian prince *avante le lettre*, preferring to be feared rather than loved, but seeking to be both as much as possible. He was ruthless in putting down noble unrest, but at the same time patronized an impressive court and pressed to make Naples a lively cultural capital in competition with Rome, Florence, and Venice. Much in the spirit of the Rinascimento, he stressed his connections to and close affiliation with the ancient world, as even his entry into the city through a faux-Roman victory arch in 1443 proclaimed. If anyone had missed the point, when he rebuilt the great fortress that dominated the city, he incorporated into its Gothic structure a larger-yet Roman triumphal arch as its entry gate. Wedged rather inelegantly between dark battlements, the arch's contrasting white marble sculptures depicted his earlier triumphal entry into the city. Their classicism echoed the depiction of ancient Roman triumphs to be seen on numerous classical columns and buildings in Rome, Italy, and throughout what had once been the Roman Empire. Rich in symbolic details that attached Alfonso to various crucial first times often evoked during the Rinascimento, he even depicted himself protected from the sun by an umbrella that recalls those of the pope, the emperor, and the Venetian doge – a traditional symbol of rulership.

An inveterate warrior who was frequently at war with his neighbors, Alfonso also used his court and patronage to depict himself as a deserving prince rather than a mere conqueror and tyrant. His search for a glorious reputation was carefully enhanced by the classical scholars and noted artists whom he attracted to his court with the goal of giving it a decidedly Rinascimento reputation. Naples, as a large European capital with a lively court, had always attracted northerners searching for patronage, but now, with an increasingly courtly world in the cities of the north, a circulation between courts became easier and parallels between the various courtly cultures of the peninsula more meaningful. One of Alfonso's most prominent and enthusiastic courtiers was the classical scholar Antonio Beccadelli, called Panormita (1394–1471), who wrote a laudatory biography of him. Panormita had lived a well-travelled and rather colorful life before joining Alfonso. Born in Palermo, he studied in Siena along with another famous classical scholar, Eneas Silvio Piccolomini, later Pope Pius II. Their reportedly wild student days are often seen as a partial source for the erotic and racy material to be found in his perhaps most famous, or infamous, work the *Hermafroditus* (1425), a series of epigrams in Latin verse that drew heavily upon the ancient Roman poet Martial. After serving as court poet and historian at the court of Filippo Maria Visconti in Milan, he joined Alfonso in 1434 and followed him on his successful quest to take Naples. During that period he served as Alfonso's secretary, tutor to his son, and occasionally as a diplomat as well.

Yet, perhaps more significantly for his patron's classical cultural pretensions, Panormita reported that every day he read to his prince Livy and other ancient authors, because Alfonso loved the classics so much that he could not go a day without his revitalizing dose of ancient culture. Moreover, he claimed that even when Alfonso was in the field, he required his daily measure of classical readings and declared that he had learned more about warfare from Caesar and other ancient authors than from practical experience in battle. Such claims certainly won the hearts of many scholars, then as well as now, but, more importantly, they helped place him squarely in the midst of the cultural world of the cities and princes of the north of Italy.

Adding to his Rinascimento reputation, Alfonso also patronized and protected the often-controversial Lorenzo Valla (1407–1457). From 1437 to 1448, when he left to go to Rome to serve as papal secretary, Valla thrived in Alfonso's entourage, producing some of his most important works, as discussed earlier. His famous proof that the supposed Donation of Constantine was a forgery and his *Elegantiarum Latinae Linguae* (*On the Elegance of the Latin Language*), which traces the development of ancient Latin, were both written during this period. He also wrote works attacking clerical corruption and defending the idea that salvation was gained by God's grace and faith rather than by works; all of which seems to make him more of a precursor of Luther than a proto-humanist. Less controversially, he also wrote a laudatory life of Ferdinand I of Aragon, Alfonso's father, that once again glorified the family. One modern critic decried it as a work "lacking in the critical spirit with which he approached classical texts," but then that was required of him as the client of a prince with an unlikely Roman heritage who sought glory and legitimacy, and the controversial Valla needed that support.

Alfonso also patronized noted scholars like Poggio Bracciolini, whom he rewarded handsomely for translating Xenophon's *Cyropaedia*, a treatise on the education of King Cyrus of Persia and princes in general. And he even invited the noted Florentine classical scholar and statesman Giannozzo Manetti (1396–1459) to his court in 1455. Reportedly Manetti had once induced the *condottiere* Sigismondo Malatesta to desert Alfonso to fight for Florence against him, but, more eager for glory than holding a grudge, he welcomed Manetti to his court as yet another master of ancient languages, as well as a noted biblical scholar. This open-handed support of scholars certainly contributed to his reputation as "Alfonso the Magnanimous." It was even reported in glowing prose that the aristocrats of his court attended the daily classical readings he sponsored and that his commanders enjoyed similar pleasures with his army in the field. Be that as it may, it does seem that the more powerful of his barons living in Naples aped his princely ways and classical interests, also patronizing scholars and artists, who contributed in turn to making the city a vital cultural center. It should be remembered, however, that this glory was costly, and the title "magnanimous" applies less well to his need to extract revenues from the peasants and barons of his kingdom. Peasant unrest and baronial resistance, in fact, often kept him and his armies in the field, as did his ongoing wars with his neighbors.

At his death his less-than-magnanimous reality contributed to the problems his illegitimate son, Ferrante (c. 1431–1494), faced. A wide range of opponents materialized who were anxious to deny his claims to the throne, including the house of Anjou, now led by Jean of Anjou, along with much of the local Neapolitan nobility eager to escape what they saw as the heavy hand of the Aragonese. In a first moment the pope, Calixtus III, who had been a longtime supporter of Aragon in Italy, claimed that the kingdom should revert to the Church in the absence of a legitimate heir, as noted earlier, apparently with an eye to divvying it up among the members of his family. But after his death, Pius II, hoping to find a crusading ally, one perhaps more substantial than the apostle Andrew's head, supported Ferrante's claim, both verbally and militarily. Also important were marriage alliances made between the Neapolitan Aragonese and the Sforza rulers of Milan, who came to his support. Thus, with some of the most powerful papal *condottieri* at his side, he eventually defeated Jean of Anjou and put down his rebellious nobles after six years of fighting. His reign followed much in the pattern of his father's, with perhaps a heavier dose of repression and taxation, and with a more prominent northern Italian role in both his bureaucracy and court. All of which underlined the fact that Naples, and with it Aragon, were moving from being a powerful neighbor of the urban world in the north to becoming central players in the developments of Italian society and culture in the second Rinascimento.

At his court, Ferrante spent heavily to attract some of the leading lights of his day, including Panormita, Pontano, and a younger Sannazaro (1456–1530), all of whom, like most hired-gun intellectuals of the day, celebrated their patron's rule, giving local traditions and his power a glorifying coat of classical brilliance and Roman ancestry. Panormita, as already noted, had served his father and, along with his other duties, had been Ferrante's tutor. In later years he served as a learned diplomat for him. Pontano, who had studied at Perugia, joined Panormita in the service of Ferrante's father early on, and the two collaborated closely, starting an informal classical academy that, under Pontano's leadership, would eventually become known as the Neapolitan Academy, although like most such "academies" at the time it was apparently quite loosely organized. Learned in Greek and Latin and noted for a wide range of works – from poetry to philosophy and prescriptive literature on love, the family, and social issues, to satire, astrology, rhetoric, and botany – Pontano became a close advisor to Ferrante and eventually his learned chancellor in the mold of the learned chancellors of the north, famed for their rhetorical skill and Latin learning.

Jacopo Sannazaro succeeded Pontano as leader of the academy and, like him, was a noted Latin stylist who with classical inspiration wrote on a wide range of topics. His most famous work was *L'arcadia*, a classical pastoral tale of love written in Tuscan in both verse and prose. In selecting Tuscan rather than Neapolitan dialect for his classicizing tale of the love of the young shepherd Sincero, who goes to Greece to live an idyllic life among the shepherds there, Sannazaro once again placed Neapolitan literature at the center rather than on the periphery of Italian intellectual life and glory. For the Neapolitan court and its prince, however, such glory could not overcome the one thing that brought down even the most successful of princes – death.

And Ferrante chose exactly the right moment to die, for Aragonese glory and the classical *rinascimento* in Naples have brought us to 1494, a tragic year in the history not just of Naples but of the Rinascimento as a whole. In that year Italy's long relative freedom from invasion from the north came to a brutal and unexpected end with the invasion of Italy by the young king of France, Charles VIII. Although that invasion will be discussed later, suffice it to say here that Charles had begun his invasion in order to reclaim Naples from Ferrante, whom he once again depicted as an illegitimate bastard who held the kingdom illegally. Within the year Charles's claims were vindicated as he rode triumphantly into the city with his troops, much as Alfonso I had done fifty-one years earlier, but as a French king, not as a pseudo-Roman Aragonese Rinascimento prince – and with rather different results, as we shall see.

The Gonzaga Court in Mantua

Meanwhile, in the northern half of Italy, as papal expansion and the wars of the first half of the fifteenth century eliminated many of the independent cities that had been such a distinctive feature of the early Rinascimento, a few survived and flourished. In fact, the wars actually contributed to their survival, because they were ruled by *signori* who served the larger powers as *condottieri*, augmenting their revenues with their warrior's wages and winning them the protection of the larger neighbors they served. At times clever and quite flexible diplomacy and rapid shifts in employers were also necessary for survival. In turn, in cities ruled by *condottieri* lords such as Ferrara, Urbino, Rimini, Pesaro, and Mantua, their *signori* built up courts that once again demonstrated their glory and presented them as more than warrior/

tyrants. And in this regard they and their courts played a crucial role in fashioning the second, more aristocratic and courtly era of the Rinascimento.

Although smaller and often poorer than their Roman or Neapolitan counterparts, their courts were also vibrant centers of a new and more aristocratic cultural flourishing that once again was viewed, albeit with some difficulty, as not new but old. Classical Roman precedents, of course, had to be found and stressed, but often these smaller courts played on local medieval traditions with a militaristic emphasis that drew on the first times of the Middle Ages as well. Those largely mythic first times had been kept alive in the more general imagination by the highly popular tales of Charlemagne, his various knights, and their romantic adventures, along with the equally popular cycle of stories of the adventures of King Arthur, the knights of his Round Table, their loves, and their search for the Holy Grail. Although Mantua was probably not the most important of these cities, and while the Gonzaga who ruled there were not the richest, they were the most long-lived and most successful in the long run, ruling the city first as Captains of the *Popolo* from 1328, when they wrested power from earlier *signori*; then as marquises of the emperor from 1433; and finally as dukes of the emperor from 1530 until 1707.

Mantua is a smallish city on the Mincio River in the center of the Lombard plain on one of the routes that Felix might have followed on his pilgrimage to Rome in 1300. As the Mincio runs in a southeasterly direction from Lake Garda in the north to eventually join the Po on its way to the Adriatic, it was blessed with a central location for transport in some of the richest agricultural territory of a fertile agricultural plain. Well before the rise of the Gonzaga family, the marshy territory around the city and frequent floods caused by the Mincio had been tamed to a degree by hydraulic works that surrounded the city with a series of lakes, which also helped to protect it from invasion (giving it a distinctive and beautiful setting). Unfortunately, those same lakes and the lowlands that surrounded them were also ideal for the breeding of mosquitoes and contributed to problems with malaria that dogged the city. Geography, however, did place it in a fortunate position during the wars of the fifteenth century, as it sat conveniently at the outer limits of both Milanese and Venetian territorial claims; thus its rulers were able to play one city off against another and use their skills as *condottieri* in the service of first one and then the other in order to sustain their independence.

As Machiavelli later opined, a ruler was most likely to survive if he was loved as well as feared. As *condottieri* the Gonzaga had the military power to be feared and were willing to use it as necessary. To be loved, however, required more. A brilliant court once again, along with a beautiful city and the quiet

glory of impressive scholars, artists, and architects, all went together to make
a ruler seem a true prince or at least to broadcast the claim. Already in the
fourteenth century, after taking over the city with considerable violence, the
Gonzaga garnered their first moments of glory. Guido Gonzaga, for example,
who ruled in the 1360s, brought the poet Petrarch to the city several times.
His grandson, Francesco I (1366–1407), began a series of major rebuilding
projects that associated the religious and cultural life of the city more closely
with the Gonzaga family and in the process patronized noted architects
from both Milan and Venice. Much in the spirit of the Rinascimento, he also
took over one of the city's most important relics from Christian first time,
the *sacra pisside*, a pix that held a small amount of Christ's blood, reportedly
brought to the city by the Roman centurion Longinus in 37 A.D. This had
long been safely locked up in a local monastery, but Francesco brought it
out and displayed it for the Feast of the Ascension in 1401, an event regularly
repeated thereafter. Sponsored by the Gonzaga, it attracted large numbers of
pilgrims and once again associated their rule with one of the key first times
of their city.

The pix of Christ's blood became a continuing refrain in the celebration of the glory of the Gonzaga. When the emperor Sigismund visited Gianfrancesco Gonzaga (1395–1444; ruled 1407–1444) to invest him
as marquise in 1433, he confirmed the imperial connection by marrying
Gianfrancesco's son and heir, Ludovico, to his niece Barbara of Brandeburg.
To celebrate the occasion Gianfrancesco issued a silver coin that on one
side featured a mix of Gonzaga and imperial heraldry and on the reverse
a stylized rendition of the city itself, surrounded by lakes and punctuated
at its heart by an out-of-scale and dominating depiction of the pix. As the
business of the city was transacted with its coins, its special first time, imperial connections, and Gonzaga glory were all reiterated over and over again.
The message was so powerful and so perfectly Rinascimento – with money,
religion, and ideology all forged into the everyday – that it was repeated by
virtually every generation of the Gonzagas, with each ruler minting his own
version of the coin that offered an image of the sacred blood of Christ at the
center of their city.

Gianfrancesco utilized an eclectic mix of the ancient and the medieval,
almost always, however, stressing first times and the rebirth of their original glory. Perhaps motivated by his new status as marquise, he initiated a
series of building and redecorating programs to upgrade the many family
villas that dotted the countryside around the city as well as the Palazzo
Ducale. Freely mixing classical motifs, scenes from chivalric romances, and
hunting and agricultural vistas, the result was a testament to the warrior's

self-presentation as a cultured warrior-prince. Perhaps the most discussed of these renovations is the Sala del Pisanello in the Palazzo Ducale, named after the painter Antonio Pisanello (c. 1390–1455), who had worked at many of the most important courts of the day. Although badly damaged by later redecoration, and much contested by art historians after being uncovered in the late 1960s, the main subject of the unfinished work appears to have been drawn from popular French medieval romances based on the legends of the first time of King Arthur and the knights of the Round Table. Jousting knights and fair princesses share the scene with Gonzaga warhorses (a favorite subject of Gianfrancesco), shining armor, Gonzaga banners, and heraldic colors. At first apparently distant from the Rinascimento, it fits comfortably with the topos of returning to superior first times. And for a noted *condottiere* like Gianfrancesco, clearly his military first times filled with stories of the great deeds of mythic first rulers like Arthur and Charlemagne do not seem so strange from the perspective of our broader Rinascimento.

For Gianfrancesco, this first chivalric world and its glory evidently lived on with relative ease along with his other Rinascimento interests. For at the same time he was actively supporting the revival of ancient Rome in Modena as well – and so visibly that Alberti actually dedicated his volume *On Painting* to him in an effort to gain his patronage, a ploy that eventually bore fruit with a number of architectural commissions. In this context Gianfrancesco was also an important patron and supporter of Vittorino da Feltre's new school in Mantua, with its emphasis on the *studia humanitatis* discussed earlier. In fact, his son Ludovico studied for a time at the school, as did Ludovico's wife, and their studies played a significant role in the cultural life they encouraged in the city and at their ever more glorious court.

Once again nicely suggesting this mix, Ludovico (1412–1478; ruled 1444–1478), soon after he succeeded his father in 1444, had Alberti strike a series of commemorative medals in the style of ancient Roman coins that featured members of his family along with the city's famous educator Vittorino da Feltre. He had himself presented on one side of his medal with a classical Roman haircut in a half-bust pose that recalled ancient Roman generals and emperors, and on the other side in tournament armor that evoked once again the chivalric world of the Middle Ages. Of course, both poses also reflected his growing reputation as a *condottiere*; thus the mix was perfect for the glory that he sought to represent to the many contemporaries to whom he sent copies. In fact, the genre became quite popular in the later fifteenth and sixteenth centuries, especially among rulers eager to stress their own ennobling connections with the ancient world.

As a warrior Ludovico backed up his militaristic claims with deeds, fighting for the major cities of the day, including Florence in 1447, Venice in 1448, Naples in 1449, and Milan on and off from 1450 until the Peace of Lodi in 1454 ended the Italian Hundred Years' War. While he was off fighting, his able wife, Barbara of Brandenburg, oversaw court life and the administration of the city and its territories. Perhaps it was his military reputation, perhaps the growing fame of his court, but certainly it was his wife's family connections with the emperor that helped Ludovico convince Pope Pius II to convene a congress in Mantua in 1459 to plan his crusade against the Turks to free Constantinople. Pius knew he needed the emperor's support and hoped Barbara could help win it. As noted earlier, Pius unfortunately died, and the crusade agreed upon in Mantua dissolved before it ever left.

Although the pope's crusading plans came to naught, Ludovico was anxious to make the city as impressive and attractive as possible, engaging Alberti to redesign and upgrade the most important buildings of the city in a classical mode. The actual work, however, was carried out by less well-known Florentine architects and builders who realized Alberti's ambitious plans with local artisans and relatively inexpensive local materials. Ludovico also sought to bring in one of the most promising young artists of the day, Andrea Mantegna (c. 1430–1506), whom he first contacted in 1457 to work on decorating his residences for Pius's crusading congress. The painter did not make it to Mantua until 1460, well after the congress was over. But once he arrived, he became a fixture of the court and served three generations of Gonzaga lords, producing some of the most important paintings of the period.

Mantegna's paintings featured a kind of sculptural classicism, with figures that seemed more like modeled stone barely contained within the frames of his works, and thus moved painting in Mantua away from the more chivalric and idealistic painting of earlier times and other courts to the very cutting edge of his day. Finding Ludovico a parsimonious patron, Mantegna's early rewards were modest at best. An early agreement stipulated that he would receive a monthly salary of fifteen ducats, along with lodging, firewood, and grain to feed his family. But as his fame grew, Mantegna found his patron more generous with property and privileges, which were more available to Gonzaga than cash. Thus he eventually found himself with a rich house in the center of town, a number of properties in the countryside, and various titles that allowed him to present himself as more a gentleman or noble than a craftsman. His social and financial success became a model and a goal for other painters who were increasingly anxious to transcend their humble

6.3. Mantegna, *Camera Picta* (court scene), 1465–74, Castello San Giorgio, Mantua. Photo: Scala/Art Resource, New York.

status as artisans to become members of the elite, "artists" rather than artisans. Still, as court painter Mantegna was an artisan, and he not only painted the great works for which he is famous, he also designed festive decorations for the court, floats for pageants, wall hangings, and even silverware and table adornments.

Perhaps his most famous and influential painting was the series of frescoes in the *Camera Picta* (Painted Room), more commonly known today as the *Camera degli Sposi* (Bridal Chamber), begun in 1465 and finished in 1474. Located in the *Palazzo Ducale*, the room actually served both as Ludovico's bedroom and as a reception chamber for foreign dignitaries, a dual function that was not unusual at the time. The room is painted with a series of illusionistic scenes that seem to make the court life that went on in the halls of the palace come alive on its walls. We see Ludovico dressed informally, seated with his wife, their children, his courtiers, his servants, and the various accoutrements of court life, apparently discussing some important matter or awaiting the arrival of a notable visitor (Illustration 6.3). From across the room in another fresco his servants and dogs look on, and next to them is another depicting his brother Francesco being made a cardinal in a rural setting surrounded by family members and supporters (Illustration 6.4).

6.4. Mantegna, *Camera Picta*, 1465–74, Castello San Giorgio, Mantua. Source: see Fig. 6.3.

It almost seems as if the figures could step off the wall into the room at any moment, an effect heightened by Mantegna's sculptural styling of the figures as well as by the *trompe l'oeil* effect of drawn-back painted curtains and architectural details such as columns that seem to be real parts of the room. The vaulted ceiling, with its stucco work and classical motifs painted in monochrome shades on a gold-colored background, depicts the first eight Caesars and once again connects the courtly space below with a militaristic Roman past. But court and palace were places of play as well as display, and the crowning aspect, quite literally, of the illusionistic space is a faux oculus in the ceiling that seems to open the room to the sky above. A few puffy clouds float by as the viewer enjoys a playful vision of putti dangling dangerously above, a pot perched precariously ready to fall, and smiling peasant girls (one might almost imagine) laughing at the elegant pretensions of the room below and Rinascimento courts in general.

Mantegna continued to work for the Gonzaga court after the death of Ludovico, serving his son Federigo I (1442–1484; ruled 1478–1484) and his grandson Francesco II (1466–1519; ruled 1484–1519) as well as his wife, Isabella d'Este (1474–1539), one of the most famous and interesting women of her day, who will be discussed more fully later. By the time of Francesco and Isabella, the Gonzaga were well-established masters of a leading courtly city, one of the most important in Italy. Francesco's letters show him as a military man with pretensions of learning and the unquestioned assurance of his own status, along with an earthy bluntness whose sexuality mixed easily with his piety. Isabella's more extensive correspondence (a significant portion of which will soon be published by Deanna Shemek) reveals her as similarly self-assured in her aristocratic status, learned, and masterful in her connoisseurship and patronage. It also demonstrates that while her husband was off fighting – which was usually – she was the real ruler of her city, with her glorious court setting a high standard for the courts of Italy and those of Europe as well.

A Medici Court in Republican Florence? Cosimo's Quiet Glory and Sprezzatura

Bankers holding court? The very idea of rethinking courts in terms of bankers is useful for gaining a deeper appreciation of what was new about the courtly "revival" of the Rinascimento. Usually, taking at face value Florentine self-presentation in its myriad conflicts with more recognized courtly powers, such as the papacy and the Visconti and Sforza in Milan, the city is seen along with Venice as an anticourtly bastion of republican values. And, of course, there is more than a little truth to this, if one is speaking of ideals, but the reality was rather different in both cities; for, in a curious way, behind the imagined courtly world of Rome and the largely unimaginable courtly world of Florence and Venice, many of the forms of social and cultural life looked remarkably similar. In each case, however, the court and the courtly life of the city were driven by rich aristocratic patrons – the pope, cardinals, and powerful families in Rome; the Medici in Florence; and the most powerful of the nobility in Venice – who surrounded themselves with those they supported and who in return bathed them in a shared cultural glory that was becoming a necessary accoutrement of truly elite status.

Turning to early fifteenth-century Florence, as we have seen, the city had become one of the strongest and richest in Europe. When Cosimo de' Medici returned from exile in 1434, he took over the system of electoral corruption perfected by Maso d' Albizzi as well as his quiet, behind-the-scenes style of rule. Quiet, behind-the-scenes rule did not mean, however, that Cosimo was not ready to act decisively to solidify his position. Most importantly, he was well aware that he had to deal with those who had remained loyal to the Albizzi and, while he was at it, any families that appeared to pose a threat. In this he was aided by the Balìa that had invited him to return, for they took the bull by the horns and exiled most of his potential opponents for five years. Cosimo cleverly took the high ground and merely suggested that everyone be treated with moderation. But lest one be taken in by this and assume that Cosimo did not mean to rule behind the scenes, it should be noted that after those exiles expired in 1439, most found their banishments extended to 1499. A few families who were merely of questionable loyalty were declared magnates and thus placed under the regulations of the old Ordinances of Justice. This had the obvious advantage of eliminating them from political life, at least in terms of holding office, but, more subtly, it reminded everyone of the Medici tradition of supporting the *popolo* against aristocrats, as the Ordinances were seen as the great legislation that had proclaimed and protected the victory of the *popolo* over aristocratic pretensions.

Much like the *signori* ruling elsewhere, Cosimo realized that he could not rule Florence, even behind the scenes, without the support of the most powerful families of the city. As a result he worked to build a ruling group of his own made up of the Ottimati who had deserted the Albizzi, along with a few powerful families who had always kept their distance from the Ottimati and several newer rich families. While Cosimo, like Maso, avoided holding office as much as possible, he led this group of his supporters by making use of the system of electoral corruption already in place and expanding it thereby making it more effective yet. In this way he controlled the men who held the most important offices of government. With that came the ability to use government to reward loyal followers, encourage potential supporters, and punish, when necessary, opponents. With time the result was a solid core of supporters, known as the Palleschi (after the six balls [*palle*] on the Medici coat of arms), who replaced the old Ottimati as the inner group that ruled the city, overseen by Cosimo.

Beyond creating a political elite of his own, Cosimo sought to build a more nebulous broad support for himself among the general populace. In this he attempted to create the impression at each social level that he was work-ing in its interest. For the lower classes, the story of how an earlier Medici, Salvestro de' Medici, had been a leader in the Ciompi rising and attempted to protect the lower classes, was picked up, polished (with less appetizing details conveniently forgotten), and invoked to show the traditional ties of the Medici to the *popolo minuto*. Such selective historical memories were reinforced by a Medici policy that attempted to keep grain prices low and grain available in times of shortage and famine. While this was a sage policy widely followed at the time, what mattered for the lower classes of Florence was that Cosimo seemed to be on their side, especially when hard times arrived, as they regularly did. Cosimo also gained popular support as he was seen as having driven out the Albizzi, who were held responsible for having undone the gains that the *popolo minuto* had won with the Ciompi rising and for imposing a progressively more aristocratic and closed government that had brought on costly wars and ruinous taxes.

Cosimo also won support from the other end of the social spectrum. Although he had a few aristocratic Ottimati families declared magnates, he also had a number of the old magnate families declared *popolani*. This freed them of the stigma associated with magnate status, allowed them to participate in government, and, of course, tended to make them his supporters. But perhaps the area where Cosimo most aggressively sought support was among the new men and especially the new rich. The economic turmoil of Italy caused by recurring waves of plague and the ongoing costs and devastation of the Italian Hundred Years' War had ruined many old families, but it had also created an economic climate in which a group of new families had gained wealth. This newly wealthy and potentially powerful group had for the most part been prevented from holding governmental offices and, more subtly, been kept out of the Ottimati, as the Albizzi rule had quite consciously aimed at protecting and succoring the "old" families against the pressure from those perceived as their social inferiors. Cosimo moved the more prosperous and powerful of these new men from the outside looking in to the inside of his ruling group. As a result, to the degree that these men and their families saw themselves as Medici-made, they tended to become strong supporters. In sum, support was everywhere, although some of it was dangerously new.

Yet – as many at the time, including Cosimo, were anxious to point out – nothing had changed, even if that was patently not the case. For him and his new supporters, the city remained what it had always been, a republic, and continued to portray itself as the last bastion of republican liberty against the tyrannical rule of *signori* and their aristocratic courts. And an important corollary of that self-portrayal continued to be a traditional civic ideal, based on a fourteenth-century vision of *civiltà* and reinforced by ancient texts that proclaimed that Florence allowed citizens the freedom to participate in government and civic life, thus creating better human beings, a better Christian community, and a better, richer, flourishing culture. This meant, however, that the merchant-banker Cosimo had another important reason, beyond his own interest in art and culture, to make Florence a thriving cultural capital. He had a tradition and an ideology to embrace that demonstrated the benefits of republican rule and Florentine civic morality, even as he worked behind the scenes to corrupt both.

Thus, although Florence as a republic officially lacked a court, Cosimo and his followers, along with the bureaucracy of the government that he controlled, were the leaders of a Florentine cultural world that in many ways was truly courtly. This was especially true when considered in comparison to Rome, where, as we have seen, the papal court as a cultural entity was less a formal reality than an imagined ensemble of various familiars of the pope, whether they were scholars and intellectuals employed in his bureaucracy; artists and architects brought to Rome to carry out architectural and decorative projects for him; or musicians and others he gathered around him to add to his glory. One key difference, at least, on the surface, was that the papal court tended to be dominated at the highest levels by clerics, most of whom were heavily invested in advancement within the Church. In Florence that was not the case, although many of the men who added luster to Cosimo's Florence had entered minor orders of the Church to study and were deeply interested in many of the same ethical and moral issues as the intellectuals gathered in Rome by the popes. In fact, right through the fifteenth century and well into the sixteenth, intellectuals, artists, architects, and musicians moved with relative ease and frequency between Florence and Rome, taking up minor clerical orders and even at times becoming a bishop or a cardinal in order to forward their careers.

The key and strongest similarity between the Florence of Cosimo, the developing papal court at Rome, and the courts of the *signori*, however, was the use all made of patronage to win glory – glory for one's city, of course, but more importantly, glory that demonstrated the aristocratic merit and princely refinement of a ruler. *Virtù* was once again a key in this, even as the term was slowly but surely shifting in meaning. Along with glory and more courtly values, it too was taking on a more aristocratic coloring. Manners and grace, which had played a role in the evaluation of *virtù* in the fourteenth century, were now slowly gaining place at the expense of reason and self-control, without totally displacing them. But, more importantly, magnificence and glory, paradoxically expressed as modestly as possible, were gaining place as measures of true merit. The impressively flexible renaissance term *sprezzatura* nicely captures this developing ideal of quiet glory. Essentially the term described the way a true aristocrat did great things, seemingly effortlessly and naturally – perhaps the ultimate measure of aristocratic *virtù*. In many ways Cosimo's patronage and quiet rule behind the scenes might be seen as an attempt to realize a ruling *sprezzatura* – dominating Florence without breaking a sweat.

Cosimo, however, was also an astute businessman, an effective politician, and a wily player on the European stage, displaying many of the attributes of an older *popolo grosso* vision of *virtù*. He was well educated as well, with a wide range of cultural interests. Pius II remarked about him that "he was more cultivated than merchants usually are and had some knowledge of Greek," perhaps intending to damn him with faint praise. Be that as it may, Cosimo was an avid collector of manuscripts, even planning as a youth to go to the Holy Land along with Niccolò Niccoli and the Venetian noble Francesco Barbaro to look for classical manuscripts. Although his youthful plans were cut short by the more immediate requirements of the Medici bank, he built up an impressive private library over the years. And when in 1437 his friend and erstwhile youthful companion to the Holy Land, Niccoli, died leaving a collection of about 800 manuscripts, Cosimo bought it and used it to found a library in the monastery of San Marco, which he had recently paid the architect Michelozzo Michelozzi (1396–1472) to rebuild. Open to scholars, some consider it to have been the first public library in the West since ancient times – whether first or not, it might well be seen as yet another *rinascita*. He did, however, keep a number of the more important manuscripts for his private library, which eventually became the Laurentian Library, housed in the family church of the Medici, San Lorenzo.

When in 1439 Cosimo met the Greek philosopher George Gemistus Plethon, he became attracted to the spiritual vision of the ancient philosopher Plato, whom Plethon, along with a number of other Greek intellectuals, was championing over the more traditionally popular Aristotle. Plato's thought had a real advantage in a period like the Rinascimento when returning to ancient traditions seemed to promise so much. For while most of the original Platonic texts were not available to medieval theologians, who relied more directly on Aristotle (Plato's student), Plato's ideas were literally inscribed in the very DNA of Christian theology. Saint Augustine, the fourth-century Roman thinker and Church Father, was merely the most distinguished and perhaps most important early churchman who used the philosophy of Plato and his followers to provide the base for his theological explanations of the core meanings of Christianity. Thus when medieval theologians and scholars in the Rinascimento returned to the classic texts of the early Church, they were often working with texts heavily influenced by Platonic thought, whether they realized it or not. Thus, crucially, when Platonic texts were studied anew in the fifteenth century, first by Greek scholars in the East and then translated and studied in the West, something very powerful happened. For from the perspective of the Rinascimento, what scholars thought they discovered was that this ancient Greek philosopher had thought much like the Fathers of the Church, but well before Christ and his teachings. This seemed to demonstrate the validity of going back to discover the original truths to be found in first texts, even pagan first texts, and, equally importantly, revealed that there was one truth to be discovered in all.

It is hard to imagine the power of such a discovery today, but imagine a fifteenth-century reader encountering the pagan Greek texts of Plato written almost two millennia earlier and finding in them many of the deepest truths of what appeared to be the totally independent Christian tradition based on the teachings of Christ and the Bible. For Cosimo, then, Plethon and his fellow Greek Platonists may have seemed to be offering the next, and perhaps final, step in what had already been a very fruitful *rinascimento*, a complete rebirth of first times and first knowledge. There is some indication that Cosimo's enthusiasm for the project of recovering Plato led him to consider founding a Platonic Academy in Florence, but, more importantly, it led him to patronize the young scholar of Greek philosophy Marsilio Ficino. Ficino, as discussed earlier, over the course of his life translated and commented upon the most important surviving works of Plato, his *Dialogues*, and in many ways his commentaries still form the basis of modern interpretations of them. In 1462 Cosimo encouraged him to pursue this work by giving him a significant collection of Greek manuscripts, including many of the more strange and syncretistic works of the Platonic tradition that were crucial for his later thought. In addition, he gave him the use of a villa at Careggi, in the Tuscan hills, where he could work in peace. With time it became an important retreat for those who shared an interest in Plato and the Platonic tradition of the ancient world. And after Cosimo's death it continued to garner the support of Cosimo's son Piero and his grandson Lorenzo, becoming the jewel of Platonic scholarship in the Rinascimento and the center of a rather informal Platonic Academy. That academy promoted Platonic studies, sponsored public lectures, threw parties, and even celebrated Plato's birthday, gathering together leading thinkers of the day, including Ficino, Pico della Mirandola, Cristoforo Landino, Poliziano, and Lorenzo de' Medici himself.

That was still in the future. For the moment, building seemed to have been more important for Cosimo than his patronage of intellectuals or his collecting of manuscripts. In fact, this was the case more generally for most Rinascimento rulers seeking to add to their reputations for magnificence – as buildings had the ability to showcase glory. And although as buildings they were silent, ironically they often shouted power and dominance. Even before he came to power, Cosimo's father, Giovanni di Bicci de' Medici (1360–1429), had played a leading role in the reconstruction of the family's parish church, San Lorenzo. In the 1420s the old church was torn down and a new one was built on the site, designed by perhaps the most famous architect of the day, Brunelleschi. While Giovanni was just one of the group that chose Brunelleschi for this commission, his selection emphasized just how important the rebuilding of the Medici parish church was. Brunelleschi at much the same time was completing the work of placing the gigantic dome on the main cathedral of the city (1419–1421) and had taken on the commission to design the Innocenti, the famous foundling hospital of the city.

Work on San Lorenzo, however, stalled during the turmoil of the later twenties and thirties, the cost of war and internal factional strife that swirled around Rinaldo d'Albizzi taking precedence. Finally, as the thirties came to a close and Cosimo's position of power in Florence became more secure, he personally took up the project of rebuilding the church with his own money. One person taking on the expense of finishing such a large and significant church was unheard of in Florence, and such economic display might at first glance seem to contradict the ideal of ruling behind the scenes and quiet glory. But displays of piety, especially in the context of endowing chapels in one's parish church, were a traditional way in which the rich and powerful demonstrated their patronage and merit. Cosimo, however, went well beyond such traditions by taking on a church and not just a chapel. And much of the decoration of the church can be read as a conscious expression of the way the Medici fortunes, those of Florence, and those of the Christian Church itself were portrayed by Cosimo as deeply intertwined.

Throughout San Lorenzo, from the tomb of Cosimo's father and mother, which lies at the heart of the old sacristy, to the bronze doors and illustrative stucco reliefs and roundels designed by the noted sculptor and artist Donatello (1386–1466), Medici iconography is connected directly to the family's patron saints of Lorenzo, Cosmas, and Damian and for the first time explicitly to two of the patron saints of the city itself, Saint Joseph and John the Baptist. Donatello's bronze doors, commissioned by Cosimo and his brother Lorenzo (not to be confused with Cosimo's more famous grandson of the same name), may have suggested still more impressive claims, as the figures representing the patron saints of the Medici are pictured there as the equals of saints Peter and Paul in the great mission of the Christian Church. How strong a message all this was meant to convey is unclear, but it is clear that the Medici money spent to rebuild their parish church was invested with virtually as much meaning as one was willing to or capable of reading into it. And in an age carefully attuned to the visual presentation of deeper meanings, viewers were undoubtedly aware of Medici claims to piety, wealth, power, and glory – all conveyed as princely and deeply involved with the destiny and sanctity of their city. In this case, money talked, hand in hand with power, piety, and buildings.

6.5. Fra Angelico, *San Marco Altarpiece*, c. 1440, for the high altar of San Marco, Florence, Museo di San Marco, Florence. Photo: Erich Lessing/Art Resource, New York.

Shortly after his return to Florence in 1434, Cosimo also hired the noted sculptor and architect Michelozzo Michelozzi to rebuild the Dominican monastery of San Marco. Once again the church and the cloisters were heavily imbued with Medicean messages of spirituality, with much of the artistic decoration done by the ethereal hand of the Dominican painter Fra Angelico, whom Cosimo also patronized. Perhaps the most discussed work there is the San Marco altarpiece, which at first glance seems to present a traditional *sacra conversatione*, with the Virgin Mary and Christ Child enthroned surrounded by Saints and Church Fathers (Illustration 6.5). A vaguely realistic Cosimo, in the guise of his namesake, Saint Cosmas, kneels in the front right of the painting, looking out at the viewer as other members of the family, represented as holy figures, gather around the Virgin and Child.

6.6. Fra Angelico, *Annunciation*, 1438–45, dormitory corridor, San Marco, Florence.
Photo: Gianni Dagli Orti/The Art Archive at Art Resource, New York.

Suggestively, the tilt of Cosimo's head seems to echo in reverse the tilt of
the Virgin's head, as she looks down protectively at the Christ Child. But,
significantly, Cosimo's echoing gaze is down toward the viewer and perhaps
the city of Florence itself, which he protects in its own sacred mission just as
Mary protects Christ. From this perspective his hands, which at first might
merely seem strangely crossed, appear to assert a crucial connection, with his
left hand, like Mary's, calling the viewer's attention to Christ, while his right
hand, with virtually the same gesture as Mary's, reaches with Madonna-like
succor toward the viewer. This may be claiming more than was intended,
but suffice it to say, once again the Medici, with Cosimo's artistic patronage,
placed themselves in the very first time of Christianity, and they did so in a
way that allowed them to showcase their glory, their wealth, and their role
as protectors of Florence.

The dormitory of the monastery, which Fra Angelico also decorated with
frescoes commissioned by Cosimo and his family, contains one of his most
beautiful and evocative works, *The Annunciation* (c. 1440), a work that finally
seems to be free of Medici symbolism (Illustration 6.6). It speaks with a delicate grace of one of the greatest mysteries of the Christian Church, with the

angel Gabriel kneeling with rainbow-colored wings before a humble Virgin to inform her of her destiny to become the mother of God. Yet, suggestively, the placement of this fresco creates the illusion that the portico in which the scene is set is a continuation of the newly built porticos of the dormitory itself. Thus this central event of the deepest mystery of the Church visually appears to have been replaced by Cosimo and his patronage in a contemporary space that the monks and visitors to the monastery experienced every day as a part of their regular Florentine life. Quiet glory and *sprezzatura* at their most impressive.

While Cosimo supported a number of other building projects that helped to mark the city with Medici glory, perhaps the most impressive was the family palace that he commissioned, again from Michelozzo. A story circulated that Cosimo had originally approached Brunelleschi to design a new family palace, but when Brunelleschi's design was too grand, and moreover placed the palace right next to the Medici parish church, San Lorenzo, to create a kind of Medici center at the heart of the city, he opted for a more humble structure less centrally located. Whether true or not, the tale once again stresses the mythic lack of princely ambition and modesty of Cosimo. For all that, however, the palace that Michelozzo built for Cosimo was the largest and most princely in Florence. And others who would later compete with the Medici would see it as a benchmark of the grandeur necessary to outdo them.

On the outside the palace seemed quite traditional, with a heavy rusticated first floor, often described as fortresslike, and progressively lighter upper stories – stern and traditional, virtually an ideal self-representation of Cosimo – but on the inside it was rich and princely, sparing no expense. Actually, although Cosimo was the patron, the person who oversaw its building and decoration was his son Piero (1416–1469). Frescoes, paintings, sculptures, and bronzes by the greatest artists of the day, not to mention classical antiques and gems, made the palace a princely treasure trove, the match of any courtly palace in Italy or in Europe, for that matter. In the chapel of the palace both Fra Filippo Lippi's *Adoration of the Christ Child* (late 1450s) and Benozzo Gozzoli's fresco of the Magi coming to visit the newborn Christ (c. 1459) stressed once more the family's piety and the providential role of Medici leadership for Florence. Among other treasures, in the living areas of the palace, a cycle of battle scenes associated the military greatness of Florence with the Medici, including the famous oil painting by Paolo Uccello (1397–1475) of the Battle of San Romano (c. 1430s); and, to top it all off, Piero commissioned the sculptor Mino da Fiesole (1429–1484) to do marble portrait busts of himself and his brother that in their severity and lifelike intensity seem to echo ancient Roman portrait busts of emperors.

But perhaps the most famous and debated work in the palace was placed in the courtyard, where it could be glimpsed from the street: Donatello's bronze statue of David in triumph over the fallen giant Goliath (Illustration 6.7). Virtually nothing is certain about this quite sensual youthful figure. It has been dated from as early as the 1420s and as late as the 1460s; it has been seen as an ode to the beauty of youth; as a relatively open celebration of male/male sexual attraction; and as an evocation of the strength and prowess of Piero's young son Lorenzo, who would soon take up the Medici rule of the city. And, in fact, there is good reason to consider it all of the above, but one thing it most certainly was: yet another appropriation of Florentine civic imagery for the Medici family and their rule. Actually, Donatello had earlier done a much more modest David, which in 1416 had been placed in the Palazzo della Signoria as a civic image of the city's defense of republican liberty against evil tyranny. This new Medici David thoroughly upstaged that work, and if, as appears likely, it evoked a youthful Lorenzo and the future of the Medici clan, its expense, its exquisite workmanship, and its mixture of grace, beauty, and confident strength offered a potent image of Medici rule.

The sensual and seemingly effeminate nature of the statue has troubled commentators over the years and to some has seemed to disqualify it as a symbol of Medici power. Recent scholarship, however, suggests that such reservations say more about modern stereotypical ways of seeing masculinity and male/male sexual attraction than about perceptions of same at the time. In Rinascimento Florence, as elsewhere, young males in their early teens, the age of the biblical David, were seen as relatively interchangeable with young women and capable of being every bit as beautiful, with light bodies, delicate lines, and an innocent sensuality that the period found particularly attractive. When these youths matured later in their teens, with heavier, more muscular bodies, lower voices, and growing beards and body hair, they became less beautiful and took up the active, aggressive ways required of adult masculinity. But all males went through that earlier stage, when they were as beautiful as women, and in that beauty there was great power and truth, which was regularly celebrated and admired. In fact, a figure like David triumphing over Goliath perfectly associated that exterior beauty with precocious strength and courage, and perhaps suggested an inner beauty and grace that would remain beneath the more masculine body of an adult. In this context, a David that in the early 1460s suggested the youthful beauty of a Lorenzo – the future Magnificent, then in his teens – was a virtually perfect symbol

6.7. Donatello, *David*, 1460s, Museo Nazionale del Bargello, Florence. Photo: Scala/ Ministero per i Beni e le Attività culturali/Art Resource, New York.

of all the promise of his and the Medicis' future. And even if the statue was not meant to represent the young Lorenzo, it served as a splendid and very different Medici appropriation of a traditional self-conception of Florentine republicanism placed at the heart of their new palace.

Returning to Cosimo's quiet, behind-the-scenes rule: in his later years, as he grew older and apparently more tired of the corruption necessary to control elections, he seems to have become more withdrawn and less attentive to potential enemies. It may be that he felt that his patronage, both artistic and economic, had really made him the *pater patria*, the father of his fatherland, as he and his supporters claimed, and thus untouchable. But there were those who were unhappy with his not-so-hidden rule; his co-option, both culturally and politically, of the civic world of Florence; and his increasingly less quiet glory. They may have hoped to use unease about what they styled these princely innovations to push out the aging Cosimo. It may be also that some feared that his sickly son Piero was unfit to succeed him and thus were waiting for the right moment to ease out both the aged father and the ailing son. The moment seemed right in 1454, shortly after the Peace of Lodi. Peace seemed to require less in the way of a strong leader, making a return to more republican forms of government, still a powerful ideal in Florence, appear a possibility.

Two novelties, closely related to the peace, also contributed to the moment. First, toward the end of the wars, Cosimo had made a dramatic switch in Florence's time-honored alliances, aligning the city with its traditional enemy, Francesco Sforza and Milan, and turning away from Venice. Many, including some of Cosimo's staunchest supporters, were troubled by this switch. Those less supportive styled it an open sign of the abandonment of Florentine civic and republican values, as traditionally the alliance with Venice had been idealized as one between the last great republican states against tyrants — tyrants exactly like Francesco Sforza. The David of Florence's mythology was losing his status as a symbol of the small but courageous republic taking on the evil giant of tyranny and becoming the princely youth glimpsed from afar in his tantalizing beauty in the sumptuous private gardens of the Medici palace.

Equally important, with the coming of peace more and more Florentines began to complain about the unfairness of the system of forced loans that had financed long years of warfare. Similar complaints had destabilized the rule of Rinaldo d'Albizzi in the twenties, leading to the famous *Catasto* of 1427. Forced loans were still based on that *Catasto*, but, tellingly, over the generation of Cosimo's rule the wealth of the Palleschi and his other supporters had tended to increase significantly, while others, especially perceived potential Medici enemies, had seen their wealth decline. The result was that the new riches of the Palleschi did not exist, as far as the *Catasto* was concerned, and remained untaxed, while many others were carrying the burden of taxation or being taxed on wealth they no longer had. In the short run this had been a useful strategy to build and hold the support of the Palleschi, but over the long run it created growing resistance from the general populace and increasing calls for a new *Catasto*.

The quiet rule of Cosimo quietly ignored such calls. But there was another unlikely yet real potential danger for the Medici rule; for although the electoral system had been corrupted, elections continued, and the formal structure of a republican government remained. As discussed earlier, elections were held by lot: names of future officeholders were drawn from bags filled with the names of the eligible, and as long as the bags were primarily filled with the names of Medici supporters, Medici supporters were drawn and dominated government. But with Cosimo interfering less in the process, in 1458 something went wrong, and out of the bags that were used to elect the Signoria – the executive council that oversaw Florentine government – there were drawn a group of names that lacked a clear majority of Medici supporters and evidently included the names of a number of men who were ready to end their rule. Almost immediately this group demanded that a new *Catasto* be drawn up. Obviously, this was perceived as a threat, but neither Cosimo nor his supporters were in a position to tackle it head on. In fact, Cosimo, worried about losing support by opposing a measure that had such widespread support, kept a low profile, prompting the Milanese ambassador to write to his master, Francesco Sforza, pessimistically, "At the moment Cosimo may not go into the Palazzo and cannot in any way use as much pressure as he did formerly." It seemed as if the not-so-hidden rule of the Medici was about to disappear before a reassertion of republican rule.

But, with a certain irony, those same republican institutions came to Cosimo's rescue, for in July of 1458 out of the bags still stuffed with the names of Medici supporters came the name of Luca Pitti, one of Cosimo's strongest supporters, for the crucial post of *Gonfalonier* of Justice. This lucky event for Cosimo seems, with the advantage of hindsight, almost too lucky to have been entirely by chance. Be that as it may, the *Gonfalonier* was the official entrusted with protecting the rights of the *popolo* against magnates and other powerful men who might attempt to overthrow their rule. Pitti took advantage of that responsibility immediately, accusing the leaders of the opposition of treason against the *popolo*. Under torture they confessed, although it is hard to imagine how they could have been involved in treason against the *popolo* when it was Cosimo who had already quietly made sure that they did not rule. Pitti then called a general Balìa to investigate further, deal with the conspirators, and to rule Florence for six months until things returned to normal. There were protests, but with the support of troops supplied by Francesco Sforza, Cosimo's new ally, peace was maintained in the city, and the attempt to return to republican rule was over.

The city remained a republic in its own fantasies and illusions; elections, although once again carefully corrupted, continued, seemingly confirming republican traditions. And, with a certain irony, as a largely illusory republic, it actually came close to living up to the ideology that proclaimed republics superior for encouraging intellectual and cultural achievement. But, of course, that was just another illusion, for to a great extent it was Medici wealth and patronage, plus a newer, more aristocratic elite eager to display their merit and wealth, along with the general prosperity of their city, that attracted the best intellectuals, artists, and architects to Florence and made it one of the jewels of the Rinascimento, much as was the case in other courtly cities. In fact, in most of those courtly cities, their formally quite different governments and their increasingly aristocratic upper classes with their patronage of culture produced a quiet but glorious magnificence at every level – from filling their private homes and villas with luxurious material goods and works of art to patronizing the cultural accomplishments of the famed (and less famed) in real and imagined courts. This *virtù*-ous glory came at a price, however, as republican ideals became ever-more theoretical and the *popolo*, especially the *popolo minuto*, shared little more than the reflection of that glory, as the gap yawned wider and wider between aristocratic elites and those at the base of society.

When Cosimo died after thirty years of rule in 1464, power passed, not without some opposition, to his son, Piero the Gouty. Often portrayed as a weak ruler, he was seriously handicapped by a crippling disease thought at the time to be a form of gout. Recent analysis of Medici bones, however, appears to confirm that rather than gout, it was a hereditary form of arthritis. Whatever it was, it is becoming clearer that Piero was actually more important than once thought. Perhaps most significantly, he played a major role in Medici patronage and co-opting of civic symbols in the building of the Medici palace and other buildings around the city during his father's rule. He was also heavily involved in running the Medici bank in the last years of Cosimo's life. Nonetheless, some of the most important Palleschi attempted to take his place as hidden leader of the city after the death of his father. Bedridden and sickly, his decisive action in the face of that challenge, along with the support of both Milan and Venice, however, won the day, allowing him to exile his most powerful opponents. On the quiet glory front, he was an avid book collector and supporter of scholarship, perhaps most notably continuing and expanding his father's support of Marsilio Ficino and the circle of scholars who surrounded him. In the end, though, he was too sickly and died too quickly to accomplish much in the few years he ruled on his own.

While Piero's reputation has tended to grow, that of his son, perhaps the most famous ruler of the Renaissance (who once again never actually officially ruled), Lorenzo (1449–1492; ruled behind the scenes 1469–1492), often styled "the Magnificent," has tended to lose some of its luster. Obviously, it is rather difficult to maintain the heroic fame once ascribed to him before the probing and unforgiving eyes of generations of historians anxious to diminish a reputation that is almost impossible to defend. But there are some more substantial reasons for downsizing Lorenzo. Perhaps most telling were his failings as a banker, a story often overlooked in the celebration of his more princely and courtly rule of Florence. The Medici bank, which he inherited, was already showing signs of weakness, troubled by powerful international competitors; bad loans (especially to rulers and elites of the emerging nation-states of the north); a papacy more aggressively in competition with Florence; and a number of senior employees who mismanaged its funds. Branches in Bruges, London, and Lyon failed or had to be recapitalized, and, more importantly, the revenues of the main branch in Rome, which had traditionally returned the greatest profits, declined precipitously under his leadership. To make matters worse, Lorenzo was not averse to using the bank to help with Florentine foreign policy, something that his grandfather Cosimo had religiously attempted to avoid. Thus he made unwise loans to rulers and nobles whose support he needed as leader of Florence, often at the cost of considerable losses to the bank. As a result, while Cosimo had used the bank's profits to add to the glory of Florence (and himself) and even occasionally to support the city in moments of crisis, Lorenzo at times "confused" the revenues of the city with the capital of the bank in order to keep the latter afloat.

Shortly before his father's death in 1469, however, Lorenzo married Clarice Orsini, a marriage that certainly added to his magnificence. Traditionally the Medici, like many of the leading families of Florence, anxious to avoid any identification with foreign nobility that might have implied magnate leanings or antirepublican pretensions, had married their children to other members of the Florentine upper classes. But Clarice broke that tradition. She was the daughter of an old Roman noble family, the Orsini, famous for producing cardinals and *condottieri* and deeply involved in papal and Church politics. While the marriage was officially celebrated with great festivities and widely lauded, there were those who complained that this was yet another princely turn away from the solid *popolo grosso* world of Florentine merchants and republican values to embrace an alien world of old nobles, warriors, and

Church politics. No matter that Cosimo had already dabbled in building ties to each and had effectively made republican institutions a sham, Lorenzo's marriage seemed to proclaim that the Medici were openly taking up a more courtly and princely rule and style.

But it should be remembered that although the Orsini could be labeled alien and a medieval warrior nobility, there was little that was actually traditional or medieval about them, aside perhaps from that label "noble." Warfare had changed, as had the nobles who led *condottieri* armies; in turn, nobles who prospered, in order to compete with the new wealth of urban elites, had imposed more profitable regimes of agricultural production on their lands; and finally, the Church had grown into a very efficient producer of wealth for its popes and high officials like the Orsini. From this newer perspective, war, land, and the Church were profitable investments. And, in fact, Lorenzo's marriage was very profitable indeed – for this move outside of Florence into the wider aristocratic world of princely popes and nobles with trans-city-state and transnational power bases paid off quickly. As early as the first years of the sixteenth century, two Medicis won the papacy: Popes Leo X (1513–1521) and Clement VII (1523–1534). And to a great degree they were responsible for rebuilding the family fortune and reestablishing Medici rule in Florence after their fall from power there in 1494.

Another often-cited sign of Lorenzo's shift away from traditional values associated with Florence was his subtle transfer of Medici patronage from scholarship that celebrated republican values and civic participation to areas that reflected more courtly and princely values. Again, this was not all that new. Both Cosimo and his son Piero had worked to co-opt the republican ideology of the city and associate it with the Medici family and Medici power. Lorenzo, trained in the classics and having mastered both ancient Latin and some Greek, was well schooled in the ideology that saw those Latin and Greek roots as underpinning the republican glory of Florence and its culture. But for him, and for many of the intellectuals he patronized, the imagined Roman *virtù* and highly prized *vita civile* of the recent past morphed into a vision of a life of refined, aristocratic, and courtly manners quite distant from the messy world of politics and business – *virtù* itself was becoming more aristocratic and courtly. Some have argued that Lorenzo encouraged this shift because the active life advocated earlier in republican cities like Florence and Venice was dangerous to the hidden Medici rule. Things were undoubtedly more complex and the shift more general, as we shall see, but certainly it came easily to Lorenzo, a more openly princely and aristocratic leader.

On a more practical level, however, the political realities of his day often left Lorenzo looking more like a rather mundane tyrant than a prince. And Lorenzo's rule illustrates well how a ruler, even an unofficial one, could easily slide back and forth between the two. A couple of years into his rule, in 1472, the Tuscan city of Volterra, which was under a form of Florentine protectorate, revolted. The dispute turned on the question of who would profit from the rich alum deposits recently discovered in Volterran territory. As alum was essential to the Florentine cloth industry, it appears that Lorenzo was anxious to make sure that control of the mining operations remained a Florentine monopoly. Volterra had other ideas and attempted to throw out the city's Florentine "protectors." In response, Lorenzo dispatched one of his best *condottieri*, Federico da Montefeltro, to quash the revolt. Faced with a besieging army that they had no hope of overcoming, the Volterrans sued for peace and, in return for an agreement that there would be no sack, opened the gates of the city. When Federico's troops entered, however, they ran amuck, murdering an unspecified number of civilians and sacking the town.

The role Lorenzo played in this episode has remained a subject of debate ever since. Some claim that he supported the sacking as a lesson to anyone who might contemplate revolting against Florentine authority, others that Federico, often noted for his violent ways, acted on his own. Certainly such "lessons" from tyrants were not rare. And it is true that in the debates before the attack, Lorenzo had publicly called for doing "whatever it takes" to "make them understand their error." Federico claimed in turn that there had been no plan and that he had simply been unable to control his troops; but Volterrans pointed out that the sacking, for all its destruction and violence, had been strangely limited, lasting just twelve hours, with the troops then making an orderly withdrawal from the city. Perhaps the last word in this brief account should not be left to Lorenzo, who later commented, "[W]e won't say anything more about the sack, in order to forget it as quickly as possible. Perhaps they merited this because of some sin of theirs. We must be content with our own conscience and the actions that we and [Federico] … took to prevent this evil from happening." Evidently he was well aware that brutal massacres were not what he wanted to base his magnificence upon, even if he may have seen them as necessary for maintaining the wealth and power of his Florence, like many a tyrant.

Tyrant or prince? Who was this complex person who claimed to be merely the first person of his beloved city? Certainly he is a figure who fascinated many of his contemporaries and many since, so much so that his day was once referred to as the Laurentian age – a usage that has to some degree fallen out of use, along with the traditional fascination with the history of

Great Men. Yet there was much to this paradoxical republican-tyrant-prince that appealed to contemporaries and moderns as well. In fact, Lorenzo appears to have been enthusiastically interested in virtually all the scholarly, intellectual, and artistic excitement of his Florence that made the city in many ways one of the cultural and artistic capitals of his day. He encouraged the growth of the Studio of Florence, a not-quite-university that specialized in training the Florentine upper classes, and patronized an impressive group of scholars, even if he had less money to do so.

Their number included Christoforo Landino (1424–1492), who taught poetry and oratory and was perhaps best known for his philosophical work *Disputationes Camaldulenses* (c. 1475). This dialogue portrayed a discussion between Alberti, Ficino, and Lorenzo himself on the relative merits of the active versus the contemplative life that concluded that both were equally important, but that the contemplative came first – a significant break from older Florentine civic values. He also wrote an important commentary on Dante's *Divine Comedy* that continued to add to that poet's foundational reputation for Italian literature. In addition, Lorenzo patronized Demetrius Chalcondylas (1424–1511), who taught Greek at the Studio and edited Homer and a number of ancient Greek authors. Angelo Poliziano (1454–1494) was also a client who taught Latin and Greek eloquence; noted as a brilliant translator and critic as well as a poet in his own right, he served as an on-again-off-again tutor of Lorenzo's children. His *Miscellanea*, as the title suggests, is a group of studies on literature and philology that claimed to record conversations with Lorenzo and the circle of intellectuals that surrounded him. Perhaps most famed and impressive among them, however, was Ficino, who taught philosophy and, as noted earlier, was a major interpreter and translator of Plato and other writers believed to have been from crucial first times.

Along with Landino, Ficino, and Poliziano, he encouraged the young philosopher Pico della Mirandola (1463–1494), whose youth, intelligence, and desire to bring all knowledge into a synthesis that might unite Muslims, pagans, and Christians around the one truth of God was cut short by his early death. The poet Luigi Pulci (1432–1484), an older contemporary noted for his witty and irreverent verse, at times even at Lorenzo's expense, was also an on-again-off-again favorite. His send-up of the highly popular tales of Charlemagne in his mock epic *Morgante maggiore*, which featured the often ridiculous and regularly gluttonous deeds of the giant Morgante, along with the deeds of one of the traditional heroes of the Charlemagne tales, Orlando, was perhaps his best-known work. Noted painters such as Sandro Botticelli (1445–1510), Domenico Ghirlandaio (1449–1494), Antonio Pollaiuolo

(c. 1430–1498), and Andrea Verrocchio (1435–1488) were also seen as important ornaments of his circle. And for a time the young Michelangelo (1475–1564) was also cultivated by Lorenzo, along with Leonardo da Vinci (1452–1519), before both men left the city seeking more supportive patrons. In addition, highly reputed architects such as Giuliano da Sangallo (c. 1455–1516) and Benedetto da Maiano (1442–1497), also known for his sculpture, along with Andrea della Robbia (1435–1525), best known for continuing his family's innovative work with terra cotta, were patronized by Lorenzo. While with some of these figures Lorenzo's association was more formal and limited and his patronage less princely than once assumed, still his enthusiasm for the arts and learning was clear. And that meant that at the time and thereafter the names of the great cultural figures who made the second half of the fifteenth century in Florence such a period of cultural flourishing were associated with Lorenzo and his magnificence and seen as part of a courtlike entourage, whether rightly or wrongly.

Actually, Lorenzo made an effort to contribute personally to many areas of that cultural flourishing with some success, even if, like many rich men, it may be that not all that was attributed to him was actually his. A poet of some note, his poetry spanned the gamut from refined love lyrics in the Petrarchan tradition to more earthy popular songs, often associated with carnival. Many of the latter survive and display a lively and playful mind that moved easily from classical conceits to obscene metaphors. And they were performed both at his princely table for elite guests and on the streets of Florence for the apparently admiring ears of the citizens of his city. A good example is provided by a song that featured a group of young peasant women who had come to the city for carnival, supposedly looking for their husbands and offering their "wares" in exchange for help in finding, if not their husbands, at least what Lorenzo suggests they were really seeking. They sing: "Cucumbers, large ones, we have brought, / All rough outside and strange to view. / ... / First take the fruit in hand. / ... / Open your mouth and suck. For those / Who know the way, it does not hurt at all." Things proceed downhill from there, with melons and vegetables offering pleasures both culinary and erotic, and end with the women protesting that if they are not helped by their listeners, "We'll find some other means so that / Our land does not remain unplowed. / We long to join Carnival!"

Poetry and song in Florence were a popular public activity often performed in the squares of the city. And Lorenzo was reportedly ready to join in reading and singing his lusty carnival songs even in the Piazza of San Martino, noted for its lower-class poets and humble, popular atmosphere. One wonders if Lorenzo rubbed shoulders with the lower-class workers there as a form of noblesse oblige or out of a genuine youthful pleasure in joining the playful life of the streets. In fact, it may be that the erotic and illicit were areas where upper-class men still moved regularly and with relative ease across class and cultural boundaries that were becoming stronger divides in the aristocratic world of his day. Still, not all of his more popular work was racy; in fact, many of his poems and songs, following in the tradition of street performances in Florence, focused on religious and moral themes. In this context he wrote a number of popular *sacre rappresentazioni*, popular religious plays usually performed during religious festivals, as well as poems and songs with religious themes.

Although this might seem a curious mix of the moral and the immoral, the Rinascimento, as we have seen, was a time when sexual pleasures, spiritual enthusiasms, and love in its many forms were often intertwined without a second thought and could transcend social boundaries – the garden of the Rinascimento tended to contain both satyrs and beautiful flowers. Of course, there were preachers and moralists who railed against this relatively easy coexistence, but sex, even what was seen formally as illicit sex, was still generally perceived as involving relatively minor, very human and unavoidable sins; thus an audience could shift fairly easily from laughter at obscene metaphors and lewd mimicry to tears and contrition before the deeds of martyrs and saints.

Lorenzo's poetry and play, however, were often overwhelmed by the harsher realities that faced the Medicis' not-so-hidden rule – most significantly, looming on the borders of the territory that he ruled were lands claimed by an ever-more-aggressive papacy that was not particularly impressed with his reputed magnificence. As noted earlier, one of the key goals of the renewed fifteenth-century papacy was reestablishing its authority over the Papal States in central Italy, and that brought it inexorably into troubled contact with Florence's own territorial claims and expansionist policy. Things came to a head under the papacy of Sixtus IV, who, coming from a relatively humble Genoese family, was eager to build its fortunes by distributing Church offices and territory among his relatives. Lorenzo worked behind the scenes to block those plans when they seemed to threaten Florentine interests, especially in the nearby Romagna. As part of that strategy, he switched allies, replacing Naples with Venice in the alliance system that Florence had maintained with Naples and Milan to keep the peace in Italy after the Peace of Lodi. That switch seemed to threaten the pope, because Venice was the other main opponent of his expansionist policies in the Romagna, which also menaced Venetian territories and territorial ambitions.

In response, the pope aligned with Naples and as a sign of his displeasure named a scion of an exiled Florentine family in bitter conflict with the Medici, Francesco Salviati, as archbishop of Pisa. As Pisa was one of the more important cities of Tuscany under Florentine control, Lorenzo correctly perceived this as a challenge and responded by not allowing Salviati to take up residence there. The battle was under way. Petty challenges, slights, and border skirmishes proceeded quietly until tensions boiled over in 1478 with an assassination plot against Lorenzo. Although historians debate whether or not Sixtus IV was actually in on the plot, his nephew Girolamo Riario and Francesco Pazzi, leader of the rival Florentine Pazzi bank, which had replaced the Medici bank as the primary repository of papal wealth, were ringleaders along with Archbishop Salviati and his family.

The problem that the plotters saw as paramount was that if Lorenzo were killed, his popular younger brother Giuliano would take up the Medici rule and undoubtedly do so with increased support from his Florentine subjects. That meant that both brothers had to be assassinated, preferably at the same time. Thus, with a certain irony, they decided the one time this would be possible was when both brothers attended mass, one of the few moments when they regularly appeared in public together. The perfect moment arrived on Sunday, April 26, 1478, when a nephew of the pope, the eighteen-year-old newly minted cardinal, Raffaele Riario, visited Florence. Diplomatically he had been asked to say a mass in the *Duomo*, an event that, for all the tension between the Medici and the papacy, Lorenzo and his brother simply could not miss; thus, it provided a perfect moment for a double assassination.

The plotters, however, encountered one last-minute hitch: the professional soldiers they had hired to do the deed, when they learned that it was to be carried out in church during mass, refused to commit such a sacrilege. Thus, with the young cardinal celebrating the mass, at the moment when the host was elevated and the bell was sounded announcing the presence of Christ in the transubstantiated wine and bread, two priests, presumably more comfortable working during the mass, jumped upon Lorenzo with drawn knives. But as murder during the mass was presumably not one of their specialties, they managed only to wound him. At the same time Francesco Pazzi along with an accomplice struck down Giuliano, stabbing him, according to reports of the event, nineteen times in such a fury that Pazzi wounded himself seriously.

When the uproar in the church settled down, Giuliano lay dead in front of the altar in a pool of blood; Lorenzo, wounded, had fled to safety. Supporters of the conspiracy rode through the streets crying "Popolo!" and "Libertà!"

But the crowds that had gathered as word of the attempt spread, learning that Lorenzo lived, responded with loud cries of "Palle! Palle!" – the rallying cry of the Medici and Palleschi. What followed was a bloodbath. Francesco Pazzi was quickly captured and taken to the Palazzo della Signoria along with Archbishop Salviati, who had been at the mass, and a number of other suspected plotters. Crowds gathered outside the palace, angered by the death of Giuliano, demanding that the conspirators be turned over to them for instant vengeance. The authorities one by one hanged Pazzi, Salviati, and the others from the windows of the palace, apparently trying to quench their fury.

But this deadly defenestration, with conspirators hanging from the Palazzo, did not satisfy the crowds, and the bodies were cut down, dragged through the streets, mutilated, dismembered, and desecrated with a violence that is a testament to what vengeance could still imply during the Rinascimento. Even burial did not bring peace to the bodies of the conspirators. They were dug up, further mutilated, and fed to the pigs and dogs that had the run of the streets or thrown into the Arno. Only the young Cardinal Riario was spared. Some claim that he seemed too young to be in on the plot, and as unlikely as that may seem, given his eighteen years and the violence of much younger upper-class youths of the day, he was also a cardinal and a nephew of the pope. With an archbishop, a papal banker, and a host of others executed with what could barely be termed summary justice, it may have seemed best to save someone in order to have a minimal claim to legitimacy for the violent response to what would become known as the Pazzi Conspiracy.

If that was the goal, it did not work, for the pope, learning of the failed plot and massacre, excommunicated Lorenzo, placed Florence under an interdict, and declared war on the city. This has led to ironic comments that the pope excommunicated Lorenzo for failing to allow himself to be assassinated. A Florentine notary close to the Medici described the pope not too delicately as that "wicked man ... who does not want to grant us absolution ... ass's prick that he is." But, of course, the pope had no shortage of excuses for his response, perhaps most notably the execution, if it could be called that, of Archbishop Salviati. Long tradition required that clerical misdeeds be tried by the Church, and the archbishop certainly had not been granted that privilege. The desecration of the bodies of the conspirators also provided ample excuse for punishing Florence and Lorenzo, even if Lorenzo claimed that he had tried to restrain the populace.

Sixtus's war against Lorenzo and Florence went well from the start. Naples, his new ally, sent troops to his aid, while both of Florence's allies, Milan and Venice, were unable to do so. Venice was occupied with the Turks. Milan was deeply involved in civil strife caused by the assassination of its ruler, Galeazzo Maria Sforza, in 1476 and the minority of his eight-year-old heir. As a result, the pope's troops encountered little resistance as they cut easily through Tuscany heading toward Florence in the late fall of 1479. But just a few miles south of the city, with winter coming on, they decided to retire for the winter, perhaps just a bit too conveniently. It may have been the cold, rainy days of late November that led the allies to halt their advance, or the resistance they feared the Florentines might put up, but it seems also that not all were really anxious to see Florence and Lorenzo totally defeated by the pope.

Ferrante, the king of Naples, while happy to have the pope as an ally after Lorenzo had deserted their traditional alliance, was not particularly eager to see the pope become the undisputed ruler of central Italy. That would have freed the land-hungry Sixtus to look to the south for additional territories that he might claim for his family, a much less appealing situation for someone who officially held his kingdom as a fief from the pope. Moreover, the idea of a balance of power that was the underpinning of the Peace of Lodi still made sense, and that required a relatively strong, if chastised, Florence to keep the pope's aggressive tendencies in check. Whether that was his reasoning or not, the troops of the pope's allies, who just happened to be led by Ferrante's son, Alfonso Duke of Calabria, decided that the end of the campaigning season had arrived and stopped their advance. Once again Florence had escaped, theoretically saved by nature: winter in this case, disease in the case of Gian Galeazzo Visconti.

Lorenzo clearly saw this as an opportunity to escape an untenable situation. Thus in December he secretly left Florence to sail to Naples and plead for peace for himself and his city. Before he sailed, however, he left a letter for the government and his fellow citizens that showed him at both his humblest and his princely best. After apologizing for leaving without consultation, he wrote:

> As I am the person against whom the attack of our enemies is primarily aimed, by delivering myself into their power I may be able to restore peace to my fellow citizens.... Perhaps God wills that this war that began with the bloodshed of my brother and myself, should be ended by my hands. My desire is that by my life or my death, my misfortunes or my success, I may contribute to the wellbeing of our city.... I go full of hope, praying to God to give me the grace to perform what every citizen should at all times be ready to perform for his homeland.

Apparently a heroic gesture of a perfect prince, taken at great personal risk to save Florence, Lorenzo's letter underlined the injustice of the attack on the city and himself and set the stage for either a heroic failure or an even more heroic triumph. Adding to the letter's impact, Ferrante was well known for his often whimsical and heavy-handed cruelty. He had recently murdered, for example, the *condottiere* Jacopo Piccinino, who had come to Naples under a safe conduct to parley with him. Thus, Lorenzo going alone to face the lion in his den seemed impressively heroic.

Lorenzo's dramatic action ended in triumph. In Naples he negotiated a difficult but real peace with Ferrante and lived to return to a joyous Florence. Unfortunately, it appears that this moment of princely heroism was more staged than real. Diplomatic correspondence in the Medici archives indicates that Lorenzo's dangerous solo flight to Naples was actually carefully negotiated with Ferrante beforehand and much of the peace already worked out. Essentially Lorenzo had convinced Ferrante that a total victory for the papacy and Naples would upset the balance of power in Italy and free the pope to pursue his interests in Neapolitan territories. Also, as the secret negotiations were going on, the strongest of the contenders for ruling Milan, Ludovico Sforza, known as Il Moro (1452–1508), had finally won the regency and begun ruling in the name of his nephew. That implied that aid from Ludovico might also change the nature of the confrontation. Finally, Lorenzo offered Ferrante a very profitable peace. The cities and strongholds taken in the south of Tuscany would be controlled by Siena, a traditional enemy of Florence and a close ally of Naples; Alfonso, Ferrante's son and leader of his troops, was to be hired for a number of years by Florence as their *condottiere*, in effect paying him off for winning the war; and finally, the members of the Pazzi family held in prison were to be released. But peace with Naples seemed definitely worth the price.

Triumphant, popular, heroic, and more magnificent than ever, Lorenzo, within a few weeks of his return, took advantage of the situation to solidify his rule yet further. On April 8, 1480, he turned to that well-established tool for taking power, the Balìa, and set up a special one to reform Florentine government. In short order it created a new Council of Seventy, superior to all previous governmental councils and essentially the final arbiter on all matters of state. Membership on the council was for life, and to no one's surprise, most members were drawn from the leading supporters of the Medici. In sum, while old councils and old forms remained, real power was yet more solidly and openly in Lorenzo's hands. This more complete control of the city may have seemed necessary to him, for although he had gained a peace with Ferrante and his popularity in Florence had been bolstered, his enemy, the pope, was not ready to concede peace and still had the resources to put considerable pressure on a vulnerable Florence.

Perhaps, then, it was lady *Fortuna* aided by a little secret and questionable international and interfaith diplomacy, but whatever it was, in August of that same year a Turkish fleet unexpectedly landed Muslim troops on the southern tip of Italy and they quickly took the town of Otranto. Panic spread rapidly throughout the peninsula. The Turks had arrived. Ferrante withdrew his troops from Tuscany to meet the threat, and Florence quickly reestablished control over the territories that were to have been under Sienese control according to the peace. Sixtus, anxious to face the threat with a unified Christendom, suddenly saw the wisdom of peace with Florence, and by December it had been worked out. Within a year the Turks were driven out of the small toehold they had won in the south, peace reigned, and Florence remained a republic more and more openly ruled by a prince and his unofficial court and courtiers.

Lorenzo's later years, despite his careful corruption of Florentine republican institutions and diplomatic successes, were once again not quite as magnificent as once claimed. Troubles with his bank hampered both his role as a patron and his ability to support his more open princely glory. In fact, it seems that he actually dipped into governmental funds to keep his bank and other investments afloat. He also inherited his family's arthritic disease and was forced to be much less visible in the city, a retreat that may have been related as well to the death of his brother and to his more suspicious rule thereafter. But the city and Italy were changing. For even as Florence gloried in its cultural leadership, lively social life, and rather wide open illicit culture, which featured an earthy male- and youth-centered sexuality, it was being more aggressively criticized by those troubled by its distance from the still widely held ideals of Christian and civic morality. Stoked by moral doubts and fire-breathing preachers like Girolamo Savonarola (1452–1498), a deep cultural conflict was brewing. In his last days, as Lorenzo lay dying, Savonarola actually visited him, apparently to warn him to repent of his sinful ways. One wonders if Lorenzo resisted – recalling his youthful, playfully erotic songs – or if on his deathbed he gave up his magnificence to finally become a repentant pilgrim as had Dante almost two centuries earlier.

Be that as it may, in the face of the one-time magnificence of Lorenzo, the renewed Rome of the popes, and the flourishing of Italian courts, one is tempted to ask why such impressive cultural accomplishments suddenly exploded in Italy in the fifteenth century. Where did all those impressive figures come from, and who or what was responsible for their unusual creativity and vitality? Someone like Ficino may have explained the flourishing as a fortunate conjunction of the stars combined with the rediscovery of the ultimate truths of *Prisca Theologia*. The nineteenth-century Swiss historian Jacob Burckhardt, much like Petrarch, would have seen it as the result of an aristocratic world that created and sustained genius. More recent historians would tend to stress the more impersonal forces of economics and patronage, with Italy draining the wealth of Europe into a few cities where a goodly portion could be invested in patronizing and cultivating artistic and scholarly activity. More culturally oriented historians might argue that a paradigm shift, based on a more aristocratic view of life, opened new cultural vistas and encouraged an outburst of creative exploration of relatively new questions, questions that seemed particularly attractive to the aristocratic world that followed. All these explanations have considerable weight and have been suggested here, hopefully without the value judgments, aside perhaps from the fortuitous conjunction of the stars. And even that, if one sees behind it the seldom-used, but often fairly accurate "things just seemed to fall together well" explanation, has some merit.

But it might be suggested that this flourishing was not quite as top-down and aristocratic as such explanations seem to imply and as the emphasis on more visible leaders in this chapter might seem to confirm. For many of the most creative leaders of this explosion of culture were new men whose skills had elevated them from the ranks of artisans or the ranks of more modest bureaucrats and notaries. Even many of the popes of the fifteenth century were relatively new men who had risen up through the ranks of the Church, and a significant number of the courtiers whom they supported had followed a similar trajectory. In Florence much the same was the case; even the Medici, in a way, were relatively new to their riches, power, and increasingly aristocratic ways. Of course, there were also scions of older families who contributed, especially in the area of scholarship. Yet the arts, with the exception of a few figures like Leon Battista Alberti, were more patronized by upper-class families than practiced by them.

What I am suggesting, then, is that there was a tremendous wellspring of creativity that swelled up from below and allowed the rich patrons of the fifteenth century in Rome, Florence, Venice, and elsewhere to cultivate and nourish a rich lower-class pool of talent. This pool of talent, if my hypothesis is correct, was extensive and ready to explore new horizons – and this opens a whole series of questions about the cultural flourishing associated with the Rinascimento. For example, one wonders what there was in the everyday culture of the lower classes, and especially the artisanal *popolo*, that made them so ready to experiment and so creative when they did. Could it have been simply the lure of aristocratic patronage? At a deeper level, given the apparently high per capita level of creativity of fifteenth century society, especially at lower-class and artisanal levels, what was the real potential of the nonelites who made up the largely unknown masses of the Rinascimento?

It almost seems as if the pool of talent to be drawn from the lower classes in the fifteenth century grew in direct proportion to the wealth that was committed to developing that talent. If that is true, the implications are immense and directly undercut the rationale of aristocratic societies across time that insists that only a select few are capable of leading society culturally and intellectually. Be that as it may, one thing is clear – in fifteenth-century Italy the creative power released in the cultural flourishing of the day uncovered a much deeper base of creativity in society than might be expected even today. Although that talent was to a large extent supported by aristocratic wealth and tastes, its roots went deep in a society and a shared primary culture that we are still just discovering, as we delve into the complex society that lay below the more visible and apparently more glorious world of Rinascimento aristocrats and courts.

7

SELF: THE INDIVIDUAL AS A WORK
OF ART (c. 1425–c. 1525)

Reversing Burckhardt

Two of the most important elements of the paradigm that Jacob Burckhardt envisioned as distinguishing the Italian Renaissance were its discovery of the individual and its creation of the state as a work of art. More than a century of scholarship has largely demolished both evocative claims. Yet they were and are so pregnant with implications that they are often evoked today, perhaps because they seem to make the period so central to what many see as the very foundations of modern society and the modern sense of self and state. In many ways, however, one might argue that these claims actually work quite well in light of recent scholarship, if we merely reverse them: for it might well be argued that the Rinascimento discovered what we think of as the state and created the individual as a work of art.

Even if claims of discovery always seem to prove dangerous, still, as we have seen repeatedly from diverse perspectives, political power was reconceptualized during the period, becoming, if not quite public, at least envisioned in terms of an ideology that saw it as based on a shared *civiltà*: a type of urban civic morality melding communal and Christian values and serving a more general shared common good. Even *signori* felt it necessary at least to nod at such shared values, and many, including Machiavelli, wrestled with the problems created by such an ideology. In turn, especially in the aristocratic world of the fifteenth and sixteenth centuries, as far down the social scale as such pretensions existed (and perhaps farther), the individual became a more and more carefully considered and significant cultural construct, in many ways a work of art, painted socially in a series of complex negotiations that turned around consensus realities and the various groups with which an individual lived and interacted. The key here is "negotiations," for in the negotiations that people wittingly or unwittingly carried out with the groups that surrounded them in society, self-fashioning became a more nuanced and complex ongoing *social process*. And it thus fit more comfortably at the very heart of premodern social life and individuality, making both less modern and more Rinascimento. Family relationships and social solidarities – from neighbors to fellow confraternity members to friends, lovers, and imagined fellows – all played a role in the building of the individual, and increasingly, especially for the upper classes, that construction could take on the appearance of a work of art.

Suggestively, this could be true quite literally. It is an old saw, but across the period artisans, who created what we label art, and their patrons became fascinated with representing the individual in virtually all mediums – frescoes, paintings, sculpture, as well as on coins and medals. In fact, when one thinks about how the individual was represented, many portrayals tended increasingly to reflect, draw upon, and reinforce the artfulness of being an individual. From this perspective, looking at the way individuals were represented as contemporaries would have looked at them, although a highly hypothetical project, becomes one well worth the effort. For if we are correct in positing that consensus realities were crucial for constructing and maintaining a sense of personal identity during the period, it is suggestive to consider how various forms of representation play upon such ways of understanding individuals.

Of course, representations of individuals were not new, just as notions of the individual were not invented during the Rinascimento. The simple physical separateness of the body, never mind the Augustinian notion of the individual will as defining an individual vis-à-vis sin and God, are merely the most obvious examples of a tradition of recognizing the individual that endured across the medieval period. For, of course, the final goal of Christian salvation was the individual triumph of a lone pilgrim on the way to finding God, as experienced by Dante in his *Divine Comedy*. And, significantly, in that journey Dante's truth was continuously evoked in his interactions with interlocutors along his pilgrimage route who reflected the opinions of many of the groups that evaluated and reinforced his sense of self; from this perspective, the work becomes virtually a literary representation of the way consensus realities worked, and Dante becomes a uniquely self-fashioned work of art.

Still, in the close and highly personal urban world of the Rinascimento the groups that measured and negotiated consensus realities multiplied as compared to what had been the case in an earlier, more rural society. In addition, the nature of that measurement changed, with community, family, honor, and *virtù* all sliding toward new meanings, first more in tune with *popolo* and *popolo grosso* values and later with new/old aristocratic ones. If one looks at medieval depictions of people, it seems evident that they were more often metaphors for a deeper underlying reality that stood behind the messy and particular disorder of everyday life in this world. This is especially true of the representation of holy figures: apostles, saints, martyrs, angels, and even Christ, Mary, and the Holy Family. All tended to be iconlike – that is, evocative of deeper universal spiritual realities rather than individuals, even if, in the West, the icon per se had been replaced by representations that were usually more complex and articulated. Individual physical characteristics, from this perspective, were largely irrelevant and actually threatened to distract viewers from what the image really represented. Thus images tended to be highly stylized and included signs to identify who was being portrayed, signs that at the same time stressed metaphorically the deeper spiritual truths of those depicted. A medieval viewer, as part of a Christian community – the ideal consensus reality–forming group for such images – was supposed to know the holy figures depicted in terms of their places in Christian history. To that group, the figures presented ideally represented God's power or grace much more than individuals; for in a way every image portrayed not an individual holy figure but rather a particular moment of God himself in the world.

Yet one might wonder how well informed viewers actually were and how many actually judged such images "correctly." Many viewers, for example, often treated iconic representations as having more immediate and particular personalities of their own, capable of exceptional deeds, both positive and at times negative, apparently quite independently of God's greater plans or eternal truths. For some, iconic representations, much like medieval relics and saints, could have living personalities of their own and be quite willful and individualistic. Certainly there were other responses, perhaps closer to our own, but one of the advantages of thinking in terms of consensus realities is that it begins to explain the range of meanings that could be negotiated with an image and the way even images were not fixed but rather had a life of their own, over time interacting with the various groups that viewed them and judged them. The point remains, however, that aside from an occasional ruler or religious figure – themselves typically quite stylized and supplied with iconic references – most medieval representations were relatively uninterested in the physical particularities of the person portrayed.

The Individual as a Work of Art: Replacing Icons with Portraits

That emphasis on the transcendent over a particular individual began to change in Italy in the thirteenth century, although clearly it was merely a change in emphasis, for the transcendent long retained a central role in most images. The early explorations of rethinking the representation of space with various forms of perspective were also important in this respect, as they made pictures begin to seem more in and of this world. This, in turn, changed and expanded what a viewer could imagine, for as icons were replaced by individuals placed in more everyday space, a wider range of understandings became possible – familiar space left room for familiar understandings and misunderstandings. In fact, this growing negotiability of religious images may have contributed to the waves of heresy and lower-class religious enthusiasms typical of the period.

Art historians often point to painters in Rome, such as Pietro Cavallini (c. 1245–1330), and others in Assisi with close connections to Rome who used early forms of architectural perspective and modeling techniques, created with light and shadow, in order to give more attention to the physical details of the figures and spaces they portrayed. Although still far from what might be labeled portraits, one does see more individualized faces, with popes in Rome and Saint Francis in his hometown of Assisi becoming somewhat less iconic and more physically human. Significantly, the figure often associated with the introduction of perspective, Giotto (Giotto di Bondone, c. 1267–1337), was also famed for his lifelike portrayal of individuals. Born and raised in Florence, he visited Rome early on and worked in Assisi; in both of the latter cities he was exposed to the techniques of architectural perspective and more individualistic representation. Contemporaries often commented on how he made his paintings and the figures in them come alive for his viewers. It was not just the illusion of depth that he created or the modeled bodies and revealing individualistic portrayals of biblical figures that caught the imagination of his viewers; his keen attention to expressions allowed him to make the faces he depicted evocatively human, expressing emotions that reportedly did elicit spiritual responses in those who viewed, judged, and negotiated the consensus realities of the figures portrayed. In a very real way his frescoes, rather than being solely medieval windows onto another transcendent time and space, were contemporary windows that looked out at the urban world of his day.

The Scrovegni Chapel in Padua, painted in the first years of the fourteenth century (c. 1305), is often cited as an example of this (Illustration 7.1). Giotto's frescoes there are usually seen by critics as a crucial moment in the development of both linear perspective and the representation of a more material and individualistic humanity in what was still a strongly spiritual context. The chapel was built by the moneylender Enrico Scrovegni as a form of penance for his family's wealth, gained through what he apparently hoped was not usury. As discussed earlier, bankers and moneylenders had

7.1. Giotto, Scrovegni Chapel, Padua, c. 1305. Photo: Gianni Degli Orti/The Art Archive at Art Resource, New York.

developed various ploys to lend money at interest without exactly doing so, but doubts always remained about how sin-free such strategies actually were. And Enrico was not the first, nor the last, to attempt to hedge his bets by performing pious deeds – usually involving the restoration of a portion of the questionable wealth gained via bequests, patronage, or holy building. A significant portion of the religious art and architecture of the period was financed by such bequests and seemed to aid in demonstrating repentance not only to a judging God, but also to the judging groups that evaluated a person via consensus realities. As far as Enrico is concerned, the local legend goes that he had the chapel built next to his family's palace in order to avoid prosecution for usury by Church authorities.

Whether or not that was the case, the chapel features an imposing Last Judgment scene over the main entrance that portrays Enrico himself kneeling before three haloed figures and the Cross, offering up the chapel in the form of a small model that he is holding, as the Last Judgment unfolds around him (Illustration 7.2). Although donor portraits were one area in which more individual physical traits had been expressed in the Middle Ages – as if, ironically, even then money spoke of the individual – in this case

7.2. Giotto, *Last Judgment* (detail of Enrico Scrovegni), Scrovegni Chapel, Padua, c. 1305.
Photo: Alfredo Dagli Orti/The Art Archive at Art Resource, New York.

Enrico does not display much in the way of individual features. Moreover,
the Last Judgment, although impressive and powerful (especially the depiction of Hell, which calls to mind Dante's description from much the same
period), seems almost traditional, with its limited use of perspective, its choirs
of angels, seated apostles, saints, and the beatified all arranged on a vertical

plane with the judging Deity at the center. There are individual faces in the crowds, but the transcendent and the Last Judgment definitely dominate.

At the same time, however, the Last Judgment might be seen as representing the ultimate consensus-reality measuring of an individual, with God being the final arbiter of who an individual is, saved or damned. And, suggestively, in this vision not even God stands alone, for He is surrounded by the most crucial holy groups that judged an individual, ranged in the hierarchy of their importance, consensus realities in this case literally to the last. The people in the crowds of saved and damned, however, are the people of Padua. Their faces may not be clearly individualized, but they are implicitly there, and the picture speaks to them as well, informing them and their consensus-reality judgments that Enrico and the Scrovegni will be judged in the end and judged as saved. If God and the most important groups of Heaven have decided, how could the groups that made up Paduan society form or maintain other opinions? Here the individual Enrico Scrovegni with his donation re-forms himself and his family and reassures both of their correct status in their city.

Actually, when one looks carefully at the way the complex representational program of the chapel unfolds on its other walls, it returns again and again to judgments of *virtù* and salvation in ways that emphasize the positive nature of Enrico and the Scrovegni for his contemporaries, preempting other possible evaluations. The frescoes on the side walls are also much less traditional in their depiction of people, with many individualized faces that express a fascinating range of personal emotions and reactions to the scenes that narrate Mary's life, the birth of Christ, and his passion and resurrection. Thus, while the scenes return to first times and depict the safely old, for a fourteenth-century viewer they must also have seemed safely innovative, making the crucial first times of Christianity come alive – as later Rinascimento commentators noted. But they did so not merely in a symbolic way, for the figures appeared to be real individuals, as did the emotions expressed and the familiar spaces in which they were expressed. Here the transcendent was coming to be located more aggressively in the individual; and, equally significantly for the religious feelings of the day, it was located not in some distant and unreachable space and time, but in the familiar everyday space in which people lived, imagined, and evaluated biblical figures, much as they did their neighbors, friends, and fellow citizens.

This is not the place to trace the development of the progressively more individualistic and detailed representation of people in the art of the Rinascimento, already well discussed by art historians. As their studies have shown, that development was also conditioned by the development of more

sophisticated techniques for creating frescoes and of painting more generally, which allowed for more detail and greater modeling of forms. Earlier
techniques required that color be applied in the wet plaster used to make
a fresco, which meant that it was difficult to create fine details or to overpaint. In the fourteenth century, using egg yoke as a binding material for
colors allowed the colored plaster to dry more quickly and thus allowed
overpainting and the use of layering techniques. Unfortunately, while this
made more detail possible, it was also less permanent than traditional fresco,
as the binding tended to break down over time, with the plaster of the fresco
peeling off in patches. In the fifteenth century the introduction of oil-based
painting on canvas or wood panels – techniques copied from Flemish art at
midcentury, it appears – allowed more layering of paint to create modeling
effects, with light and dark and overpainting used to generate greater detail
and thus more individualistic and "realistic" portraits. In addition, oil-based
paints adhered better, if correctly made, and dried relatively quickly, making
more detailed layering and overpainting techniques feasible.

Yet "realistic" portraits are less significant for our analysis than the way
depictions appealed to consensus realities and interacted with them to help
visualize the individual as a work of art. And, of course, "realistic" is an anachronistic value judgment, for a sophisticated medieval observer would have
argued that an iconic figure evoking the transcendent and eternal was much
more real than an image that merely represented a material body. In fact,
as time passed some rich patrons and rulers even became less interested in
realistic depictions of their own or their family's physical particularities, preferring more idealized images that presented an artistic fashioning of themselves that spoke to viewers – those whose consensus realities they wished to
mould – of their *virtù*, nobility, and right to be at the top of society.

Broadly speaking, however, for most of the fourteenth century the increasingly individualistic portrayal of people in frescoes was largely confined to
group scenes, often holy, where donors, important locals, and even a scholar
or a painter might appear. What might be called group portraiture had the
advantage of using the groups portrayed and their responses to the main figures in the work as a way of suggesting the correct response to those groups
viewing an image. Tommaso di ser Giovanni di Simone (1401–1428), known
as Masaccio (the Big Ugly Maso), perhaps for his slovenly or aggressive ways,
is often seen as having taken the individualistic representation of figures
in his paintings to a new level during his short career in Florence. Many
of his works have been lost, but perhaps his most impressive frescoes were
also done for a chapel, the Brancacci Chapel in Florence's Santa Maria del
Carmine. In 1367, Pietro Brancacci left a bequest to create a series of frescoes

in the church with a theme that would emphasize the life of Saint Peter, his namesake – once again money, the individual, and the divine intermixing. But for complex reasons, the work was not actually begun until early in the following century.

The commission was apparently first given to an older artist, Tommaso di Cristoforo Fini (c. 1383–1447), known as Masolino (the Little Maso), noted for his more traditional frescoes in what is often referred to as the Gothic style, featuring rich gold work, iconic images, and a more vertical, hierarchal representation of figures. He and Masaccio had worked together on a number of commissions, and the younger man joined him on the project in the mid-1420s. Much discussion has been given to the way the newer, more modeled, and emotionally sensitive style of Masaccio contrasted with Masolino's more traditional style in the frescoes they did together in the chapel. Recent scholarship, however, has tended to emphasize their cooperation. Without entering into that debate, it seems clear that the frescoes, perhaps more influenced by Masaccio, show individualistic personal features often dramatically modeled by light and shade, giving them an almost sculptural feeling. In fact, it has been suggested that Masaccio was much influenced by contemporary sculptors like Donatello who were working in Florence at the time. This crossover between genres seems all the more likely given that artists and their workshops often produced work involving a range of crafts – painting, sculpture, architecture, metal casting, and the more ephemeral decorations of pageants and even housewares.

The fresco of *Saint Peter Healing with His Shadow* in the Brancacci Chapel is particularly interesting for our discussion (Illustration 7.3). In it we see Saint Peter striding confidently through a narrow Rinascimento urban street that recedes convincingly into the background, providing the architectural perspective that was becoming virtually required for the more cutting-edge painters of the day. Sunlight from his left not only models the saint's body and face, it also casts a shadow, which, according to the tale depicted in the fresco, healed the cripple kneeling at his left. All the faces are individual, demonstrating different personal emotions at the passing of the apostle, including a burly and slightly disheveled figure with his hands raised in prayerful worship who has been identified by many as Masaccio himself. If his name refers to an unkempt appearance and his stature as a large man, the identification certainly may have merit. Once critics were quite sure who the figures represented were, but debate has left their actual identities uncertain. Recognizable contemporaries or just lifelike faces, as the current scholarly debate about their identities suggests, viewers apparently tended to see and evaluate them as individuals in a "realistic" urban setting. It might

7.3. Masaccio and Masolino, *St. Peter Healing with His Shadow*, 1424–1427, Brancacci Chapel, Santa Maria del Carmine, Florence. Photo: Alfredo Dagli Orti/The Art Archive at Art Resource, New York.

be suggested as well that the familiar urban setting of this fresco and many others of the period – often dismissed as reflecting a lack of understanding of the historical distance of the ancient world – actually evokes a familiarity with the ancient heritage on the part of a contemporary *civiltà*, a familiarity that says much about the way the urban groups who patronized and viewed such works felt at home thinking of and judging the first times of biblical events and figures as essentially a part of their own world.

Sculpture from Remembrance to Celebration of Power

As noted earlier, Masaccio's modeled, almost sculptured figures suggest a close relationship between sculpture and the representation of individuals. Perhaps originating in the sculptures and reliefs on tombs or family funerary monuments and death masks that commemorated important medieval figures and that recorded the personal features of the deceased, sculpture, for all its stylized nature in the late Middle Ages, had already begun to wrestle with representing the individual. This may have been because death was one of those physical realities that most called attention to the individual, especially as it evoked the crucial issue of individual salvation. Family, neighbors, community, church, and other groups and their consensus realities all played significant roles in evaluating a death, but in the end, of course, it was the individual who died and was judged by God.

In the Rinascimento, however, yet more individualized and physically detailed representations became the order of the day in statues of the living and the dead, both in marble and in bronze, with more personal features gradually overshadowing the more symbolic and iconic. Perhaps the most noted and influential figure in this transition was Donato di Niccolò di Betto Bardi (1386–1466), known as Donatello. Over a long career he produced noted marble statues, incised reliefs, bronzes, medals, and even significant wood carvings. Reportedly in his midteens he went to Rome with Filippo Brunelleschi, his good friend and nine years his senior, to study the architecture and art of the city. If this is true, their suggestive age difference may imply that they were more than friends, something not all that unusual at the time. Whether that was the case or not, we know that in the early fifteenth century Donatello was in Florence working with his slightly older contemporary Nanni di Banco on sculptures of the twelve Old Testament prophets for the north-facing buttress of the Duomo, which would soon be domed by his friend Brunelleschi.

At about the same time the Church of Orsanmichele was also being decorated with statues on its exterior commissioned by the most important guilds in the city in competition with each other. Donatello, Nanni, and their better-established and slightly older contemporary Lorenzo Ghiberti (c. 1378–1455), noted for the bronze doors of the Florentine Baptistery, were hired to produce statues reflecting each craft. The idea of using the church to demonstrate the grandeur of Florentine guilds had originated back in the 1330s, but economic crisis, plague, and war had all led to postponing the work for more than eighty years – a good indication of the problems that went along with guild and corporate patronage of art; for when groups were flush with wealth, they were excellent pooling places for the resources necessary to tackle major projects, but when times were hard, they were much less forthcoming.

Ghiberti's statue of Saint John the Baptist, done for the Calimala Guild (wool merchants guild), and his Saint Matthew, done for the Cambio Guild (bankers), although they display some individual features, show more attention to the details of draperies and appear fairly traditional. In this case, of course, the primary groups whose consensus reality not only judged these images, but paid for them, were the guilds; and thus, it may be that Ghiberti's more traditional carving was exactly what they demanded. Donatello's Saint George, done for the armorer's guild, by contrast, looks more like an individual warrior, with an aggressive youthful face and a masculine body beneath the saint's armor and cloak, all suggesting courage and strength. In the end, however, Nanni's *Four Crowned Saints* for the stone carvers' and woodcarver's guild appears to outdo both his competitors, as seems only just, as that guild may well have expected the most cutting-edge work from one of their peers. The four quite individual figures seem to face each other in conversation. Classical Roman hair styles and formal stances recall ancient statues, while the individual features of each make them seem to come alive, even if the fascination with rendering the undulations of the cloth of their clothing largely eliminates their bodies. Controlled, stern, thoughtful countenances make them men of *virtù*, be it ancient Roman or Florentine *popolo grosso* – virtually the Rinascimento vision of itself, and one that would have made them come alive for those who saw them.

Donatello, however, was just finding his style. It is only with his statue of the young David, discussed earlier, that his mastery of the free-standing human body and the individual as a work of art seemed to set him apart and above his contemporaries (see Illustration 6.7). His David is no everyman, no transcendent moment of God's power (although he could perhaps be read in that way); instead, he is a slim, beautiful, and quite sensual youth typical of the Florentine ideal of the young male figure of the day. In this case the statue was cast in bronze, a medium that allowed for a much more detailed and articulated figure than marble. Traditionally it has been dated to the 1430s, but some have placed it as early as the 1420s and others as late as the mid-1460s. An inscription that accompanied it, now lost, but reported in a manuscript from the day, proclaimed its civic message: "The victor is whoever defends the fatherland. God crushes the wrath of an enormous foe. Behold! A boy overcame a great tyrant. Conquer, O citizens!" The reference to the ongoing wars with the tyrants of Milan seems clear, although which and when are less so. Still, the youthful sexuality of the figure merely empha-sizes David's great triumph and invokes a youthful and beautiful Florence, whether it was a fatherland, motherland, or perhaps boyland. And David's carefully rendered and impressively realized physicality seems light years from medieval representations of iconic biblical figures.

The dating of a rather different male figure, Donatello's equestrian statue of the noted *condottiere* Gattamelata, is more secure, as he completed it while he was in Padua from 1444 to 1454 working on a complex sculptural pro-gram for the altar of the Basilica of Saint Anthony. Once again this bronze statue is suggestive when considered from the perspective of consensus realities (Illustration 7.4). The first surviving equestrian statue since ancient Rome, it seems likely that Donatello based his work on ancient models he saw in Rome, perhaps that of Marcus Aurelius, still standing. Donatello's tough, grizzled warrior is no slim feminine youth, and, astride his massive horse, he exudes the adult masculine power of an aggressive warrior com-manding all he surveys. Placed before the church that contained the remains of the patron saint of Padua, his dominating gaze may not have been entirely unintended. For the warrior had served Venice in the Italian Hundred Years' War, and, of course, Venice had conquered Padua in those same wars; thus the Venetians ruled the formerly independent city thanks to warriors like Gattamelata. Here the consensus reality that the rulers of Venice would have judged positively may well have been at odds with what many Paduans felt, even if in theory the monument merely represented a noted *condottiere* and Venice's commitment to defend their city.

Not all *condottieri* were so fortunate in commanding bronze equestrian statues that virtually recreated them as classical works of art. In fact, one of the most famous, Sir John Hawkwood, was promised such a statue by the Florentines in 1393, just before his death. It too was to have been placed before the main cathedral of the city as a reward for his service defending the city and its republican liberties. The cost of bronze, plus the perennial Florentine shortage of funds, however, led them to reconsider their promise. In the end they substituted a much less expensive fresco of Hawkwood on horseback painted by Agnolo Gaddi and Giuliano d'Arrigo, less ostenta-tiously placed inside the church. Reportedly it was judged of such poor quality that in the 1430s Paolo Uccello (1397–1475) was commissioned to do a new fresco to replace it (see Illustration 4.1). Uccello was a painter much in the tradition of Masaccio, greatly interested in perspective and sculptural

7.4. Donatello, *Equestrian Statue of Gattamelata*, 1447–1453, Santo Padua. Photo: Scala/
Art Resource, New York.

modeling. Thus, although long dead, in 1436 Hawkwood finally had what
most judged to be a quite exceptional equestrian statue, albeit painted by
Uccello. Working in monochrome of shades of green, the fresco appears
to be virtually a real equestrian statue of the *condottiere* in the Roman tradition, very similar to Donatello's Gattamelata. And, nicely for the financially
strapped merchant city and its ongoing costly wars, Hawkwood's pseudo-
statue was much cheaper than Donatello's bronze.

Portraits of Status and Power

It is in images of power, celebrating the noteworthy, rulers, great families,
and symbolic moments of state and Church, that we see the most imaginative use of the new techniques of portraiture and perspective in the fifteenth
century. The Medici, as discussed earlier, made particular use of such images
to broadcast to the various groups that supported them in Florence, and
to foreign visitors and dignitaries as well, their quiet (and at times not-so-
quiet) glory, religious commitment, and power. In the 1450s Piero de' Medici
commissioned one of his favorite painters, Benozzo Gozzoli (1420–1497),
to fresco the small chapel in the Medici Palace, where his father, Cosimo,

7.5. Benozzo Gozzoli, detail of the right wall of the Medici Chapel, showing one of the Magi in arrival, Medici Chapel, Florence. Photo: Erich Lessing/Art Resource, New York.

frequently received visitors to the city, with a crucial first-time moment of deep political significance, the arrival of the three wise kings, the Magi, to worship the newborn Christ Child (Illustration 7.5). Winding through a stylized and rather stark landscape is a procession crowded with recognizable Medici portrayed as the Magi, along with Medici supporters and even the painter himself, peering out from the crowd at those viewing and judging his work, perhaps with just a hint of concern on his serious visage.

The Medici connection to the biblical Magi evoked in this series of frescoes was based in part on the fact that the young Lorenzo de' Medici, son of Piero and future leader of the city, had been born on the feast day of the Magi, January 6. Moreover, the Medici had long been prominent members of the local confraternity dedicated to the Magi. And, perhaps most importantly, the Church of San Marco, with which they were closely associated as patrons, contained supposed Magi relics. In sum, the Magi connection was an easily recognized and powerful one; and Gozzoli represents it in a way that stresses both the family and the individuals who made it great. Even the stark landscape is somewhat domesticated by the presence of Rinascimento hunters and their dog, depicted chasing a deer, as a rabbit hides in the lunarlike folds of a hill. Once again this is a biblical first time made familiar that speaks in a way that could be understood by the contemporary groups who formed consensus realities about the Medici.

Adding a deeper meaning to the fresco is the way it echoes an earlier depiction of the Magi done by Gentile da Fabriano in 1423 for an altarpiece commissioned by Palla Strozzi, a leader of that powerful family exiled by Cosimo in 1434 when he returned to rule. Done in a more traditional Gothic style, with ornate gold work and a more hierarchal arrangement of figures, the painting also features the Strozzi family as the Magi, evoking for viewers their wealth and power. Clearly a part of the attraction of the Medici fresco was to trump the Strozzi's Magi connection. And it did not hurt that their fresco series was larger, more innovative, and more ambitious. Now they, not the exiled Strozzi, as the real Magi, were there at the very beginning of Christianity – and not just as any family, for the individual Medici that really mattered were strikingly presented as the dramatic leaders of those who worshipped the Christ Child and Virgin.

In Venice, by contrast, both the traditions of the city and the climate conspired against the production of such paintings. The leading families there, as we have seen, stressed an ideal of selfless service to the city that made expressions of familial or individual glory suspect. Also, the stronger influence of Byzantine art encouraged a more traditional approach to painting. Finally, the damp climate of the city, built literally on the water, meant that frescoes did not dry properly or quickly enough, and many of those produced did not survive long. But in the middle years of the fifteenth century, with the introduction of oil painting on wood panels or canvas, works that aimed at representing individual figures and personalities that could be understood and judged as such took off in the city. In many ways oil as a medium was superior to fresco, for, as noted earlier, oil allowed a craftsman to build up layers of paint to create more detailed and evocative plays of shadow and light. The layering effect also allowed the painter to create a heightened sense of texture in a painting. In addition, it permitted a larger palette of colors, and Venetian paintings would become noted for their innovative and evocative use of color. Finally, oil allowed painters to overpaint, adjusting the details of their paintings to create exactly the effect sought.

Antonello da Messina (c. 1430–1479) is often credited with introducing the techniques of oil painting to Venice in the 1470s, although it seems clear that oil paintings were being produced there earlier. There is some debate about where Antonello learned his techniques, but it appears that working at the court in Naples he had encountered Flemish painters and quickly assimilated their techniques. Although he was in Venice only for a short time, his highly evocative paintings had a strong influence on better-known Venetian painters such as the Bellini family and their workshop. Recent scholarship has questioned it, but the conventional account is that the brothers Bellini, Gentile (c. 1429–1507) and Giovanni (c. 1430–1516), grew up working in their father Jacopo's shop, creating a family tradition that deeply influenced Venetian art. Jacopo (c. 1396–1470) studied with the Florentine Gentile da Fabriano and painted at many courts of northern Italy, demonstrating an eclectic ability to work in both traditional and more innovative styles. While working at the court of Ferrara he not only befriended a painter from Venetian territories, Andrea Mantegna, briefly discussed earlier, but eventually married his daughter Niccolosa to him, thus creating a close tie with one of the most innovative painters of the day. In Venice the Bellini workshop produced a plethora of works that helped change the direction of Venetian painting, moving it toward becoming what is often seen as a distinctive Venetian tradition that used the medium of oil to foster a more adventurous use of colors, a softer modeling of shade and warm light, and a less strict, more impressionistic use of perspective.

An attention to the physical details of the human anatomy in their work enriched even their more traditional paintings of religious themes. For example, in Giovanni's depiction of the Christ Child in one of his many renditions of the Madonna and Child, known as *The Madonna Lochis* (1470s), while echoing traditional iconic symbolism, the painting comes alive with a very human baby Christ Child struggling in the arms of his pensive mother, who clasps him in such a way that her robes cover, but still suggest, his genitals (Illustration 7.6). This detail, to which the movement of the figures and the folds of the Virgin's robes direct the eye, calls attention to the humanity of Christ. For those genitals, even if almost completely hidden, insist that Christ was fully God and fully man, as the Nicene Creed taught – one of the central tenets of Christianity. It may be that they also reassured a masculine society that the Godhead was always masculine, even when he was in the hands of a powerful mother figure, one who for many had become so important in everyday perceptions as to have become almost a divinity in her own right. Her pensive passivity and his lively willfulness, while evoking real restless children, also contrasted Mary's motherly compassion with his willfully accepted future passion and death on the Cross. And in the end Bellini's portrait speaks in the language of everyday people and emotions, making Christ close, familiar, and fully human, as well as divine.

But the Bellini family's brushes, like those of all painters of the day, were for hire, and the powerful patrons they depicted in their paintings also spoke

7.6. Giovanni Bellini, *Madonna Lochis*, 1470s, Accademia Carrara, Bergamo. Photo: Erich Lessing/Art Resource, New York.

7.7. Giovanni Bellini, *Votive Picture of Doge Agostino Barbarigo*, 1488, San Pietro Martire, Murano. Photo: Scala/Art Resource, New York.

to the consensus realities of their contemporaries. One of the less well-known and more interesting paintings of Giovanni Bellini using oils was a portrait of the Venetian doge, Agostino Barbarigo (1419–1501; doge 1486–1501), originally commissioned by the doge himself for the Ducal Palace, but now in the convent Church of San Pietro Martire on Murano. Known as the *Votive Picture of Doge Agostino Barbarigo* (1488), at first glance it seems a fairly typical votive painting in a genre often used by doges to represent themselves as committed to the Divine, whose power they merely reproduced on earth as rulers (Illustration 7.7). Even the music-playing angels that produce the celestial harmony of just rule in the background seem to echo this traditional theme. And, of course, the Christ Child blessing the kneeling figure of the doge confirms it all.

But for those who saw the picture and judged it via Venetian consensus realities, Bellini, undoubtedly at the doge's bequest, had included some unsettling details – details that recalled the fact that Agostino and his brother Marco, who had been doge before him, had taken on a more princely style of rule that troubled many. That troubled sense was reinforced by a number of sculptures, paintings, and building projects they had patronized that suggested not only a more princely status for themselves, but also that their family might deserve to rule the city permanently. Ideally, of course, doges were supposed to avoid princely claims and individual or family glory, but the Barbarigo brothers and Bellini's painting seemed to push the limit. The key to that reading was that traditionally in such paintings the doge was sponsored, as he kneeled before the Virgin and Christ Child to receive their blessings, by his name saint, who stood behind him offering him to Christ. Of course, Agostino's name saint, Saint Augustine, was an unusually prestigious saint, and it would have seemed to contemporaries that Agostino should have been content to be sponsored by that important Father of the Church. Saint Augustine, however, is consigned to the left side of the painting, looking on from the wings.

Instead, behind the kneeling Agostino there stands a youthful, bearded Saint Mark. With his right hand positioned just behind the doge's right shoulder, the apostle and patron saint of Venice seems to be offering the doge to Christ and the Virgin. To be sponsored by one's name saint was one thing, to be sponsored by the apostle and patron saint of the city was quite another. To make matters worse, Saint Mark was the name saint of Agostino's brother, Marco, the doge who had preceded him. Worse yet, Agostino does not even look at Christ and the Madonna, who are giving him his rule; rather, he looks down and off the canvas, apparently at the Venetian nobles as they entered the council chambers where the portrait was to be hung. Agostino's carefully orchestrated presentation of himself could be judged, then, as an artfully presented claim of his princely status and his claim that Barbarigo power had been handed on from one doge to the next with the approval of the apostle Mark. A painting that traditionally presented a doge had become one that seemed, dangerously, to present a Venetian prince.

That contemporaries read the painting in this way is suggested by the fact that there was considerable resistance to placing it in the hall of the Great Council. Although this was not to occur until after his death, it may have been that Agostino, seeing the writing on the wall, avoided open conflict by willing the painting to the Convent of Santa Maria degli Angeli on the nearby island of Murano to be displayed there on the high altar. This avoided a confrontation and meant that the painting would have less visibility, even as it waited on Murano for a political climate perhaps more favorable to the Barbarigo family. Although their pretensions were never realized and Bellini's portrait is rather lost on Murano, it does serve as a reminder that virtually every portrait of the powerful conveyed an image not just of an individual claiming to be worthy of a form of individual pictorial representation, but also of a person seeking to have himself or herself artfully represented to the consensus realities of the groups of viewers that judged and negotiated their identity.

Suggestively, even painters used their works to present themselves as important individuals and works of art in their own right. An intriguing

7.8. Sandro Botticelli, *Adoration of the Magi*, 1470s, Uffizi Gallery, Florence. Photo: Erich Lessing/Art Resource, New York.

Medici crowd scene painted by Sandro Botticelli (1445–1510) in the 1470s, *The Adoration of the Magi*, illustrates well the way an image of the painter in a Medici crowd scene seemed to demand recognition, almost stepping off the panel surface to claim its merit (Illustration 7.8). An aged Cosimo, as the leading Magi, kneels before the Virgin and Child in humble supplication. But at the center of the picture, directly beneath the Virgin, there kneel, as the other two Magi, Cosimo's sons, Piero and Giuliano, in rapt conversation, perhaps about the miraculous birth, but with expressions that would have been no different had they been discussing Florentine politics or bank business. Piero's orangish-red cloak echoes the color of the Virgin's blouse and draws attention not only to his regal figure, but also to his wealth and status, layering status sign upon status sign and glory upon glory. All three scions of the Medici clan were actually dead when Botticelli portrayed them as Magi, but they were regally resurrected in order to celebrate Medici piety and rule.

Dominating the left front of the scene, in a pose that literally oozes pride and princely self-appreciation, stands the preening figure of the young

Lorenzo de' Medici, presented as more youthful than he was when the picture was painted. In virtually every way he seems visibly destined here to become the Magnificent. His sometime tutor Poliziano, in a blue cap with a hand placed on his shoulder, appears to be explaining to him the significance of the moment, as does the figure with the reddish hat identified as Pico della Mirandola, who seems to be gesturing toward the Virgin and Christ Child. Or is he perhaps gesturing toward the Medici Magi kneeling just below and to the Medici tradition that Lorenzo has taken in hand? Lorenzo's self-assured, almost cocky stance, hands clasped over his sword, which stretches between his stocking-clad legs – the only legs so portrayed in the picture – seem to promise much more. One could go on, as it is a painting that clearly was meant to be read, negotiating consensus realities about Medici rule with its viewers, but certainly all the Medici in this group portrait seem to be carefully constructed individual works of art.

Significantly, if Lorenzo's haughty glance is directed at anyone, it is directed at the slightly larger and slightly less haughty figure directly across the frontal plain of the picture. In fact, the two figures virtually frame the panel. That figure, dressed in rich saffron-colored robes, perfectly at home with the greats of the Medici world (never mind this crucial first moment of Christianity), looks out of the picture at the viewer, as if encouraging our judgment of him – and of his painting, for the figure is a self-portrait of the artist. Botticelli seems almost to be insisting that he is the equal, in his own creative sphere as a painter, of the rulers of Florence – no craftsman peering humbly from the background. No, he stands impressively up front with Lorenzo, detailed and large as an important individual.

There are only two other figures who look out at the viewer, both farther back in the crowd, witnessing the scene – once again as a part of a group judging and forming a consensus reality of this holy Medici moment. They too stand directly across from each other, and while the figure on the left has not been identified (as far as I know), the figure on the right is the donor, Gaspare di Zanobi del Lama, a banker and Medici supporter who had commissioned the painting for a family chapel in Santa Maria Novella. The contrast is telling: the person who paid for the painting remains in a back row even as he points to himself, as if calling attention to his role in depicting this great moment, but the Medici and Botticelli dominate the scene. It seems almost as if Botticelli is preparing to step off the painting to claim his status as a work of art in his own right.

If anything, Andrea Mantegna (c. 1430–1506), one of the most notable artists of the second half of the century, took such claims even further in his artistic self-portrayal both in his art and in life. Working for most of his career for the always cash-strapped Gonzaga lords of Mantua, he was willing to take payment in land rather than money, attempting to build up estates that would give him a claim to higher status, albeit with only limited success. He did, however, hold on to some prime land in the center of Mantua, where late in life he built a stately residence and styled himself an aristocrat. In this context he also designed his own tomb and funerary chapel in the Mantuan church of San Andrea, which made clear the self-image that he wished to display to those who judged his identity after his death. As one enters the chapel one's eye is caught by the bronze bust of Mantegna, whose stern gaze commands the viewer's attention in a classic pose that recalls that of ancient Roman emperors, an association emphasized by the purple porphyry and white Istrian stone in which the bronze is set. Crowned by a laurel wreath, the image has an inscription that makes absolutely clear the painter's intentions and claims to a unique glory. In Latin it proclaims: "You who view the bronze image of Mantegna, know that he is the equal if not superior to Apelles." Thus the painter figured himself not merely as an aristocrat of Mantua or as one of the greatest painters of his day, but as the equal of the ancient Apelles, widely accepted as the greatest painter of antiquity. In such works and with such self-styling, artisans were becoming artists, a long-drawn-out transition that would gain ground as the fifteenth century closed and across the sixteenth century with figures like Leonardo da Vinci, Raphael, and Michelangelo.

Leonardo da Vinci (1452–1519) was in many ways ideally suited to being made into not just an artist, but an eccentric genius. For it might be suggested, with a touch of irony, that among his many exceptional skills he had one often-unrecognized attribute that particularly suited him to being lionized – he completed so little of what he set out to do that he was virtually a blank slate upon which others could inscribe their vision of his greatness. Yet aside from a time in Rome, where he was outshone by a group of painters and sculptors led by Raphael and Michelangelo, he always managed to shine, perhaps because he was also a consummate courtier, full of ideas and ready to offer his patrons whatever they desired, whether it be decorations for festive events, feats of engineering, military secrets, or major works of art.

Born near Vinci, he was the illegitimate son of a notary and (reportedly) a peasant woman – clearly well below the level of an increasingly aristocratic social elite. Like more fortunate illegitimate children, however, his father raised him as a regular member of the family and apparently attempted to prepare him to be a notary. His eventual rejection of that career may explain his late apprenticeship at the age of fifteen to the Florentine artist Andrea del Verrocchio. One of the few certain things about this period of his life is that he was still a member of Verrocchio's household nine years later, when he appears in archival records at the age of twenty-four accused and acquitted of a charge of sodomy. Verrocchio and his shop were well known for stressing design and draftsmanship, and both played a major role in Leonardo's career. His sketches of virtually everything that caught his interest and his intensive use of drawing and draftsmanship to represent his ideas in his much-studied notebooks suggest that he mastered these techniques early on and to impressive effect. Interestingly, however, the early paintings or parts of paintings attributed to him done with Verrocchio seem to take design in a different direction, eschewing the sharply modeled forms of his drawing for softer forms that play with light and shade and often seem to dissolve into background shadows – a technique associated with his mature style, labeled chiaroscuro (literally, light to dark or shaded).

Giorgio Vasari (1511–1574) in his *Vite de' più eccellenti architetti, pittori e scultori italiani* (*Lives of the Most Famous Italian Architects, Painters and Sculptors*), first published in 1550, which in many ways established the canon of the great painters of the Rinascimento, ever ready to make Leonardo legendary, reported that sometime in the 1470s Verrocchio asked his pupil to help him with a commission for a painting of John the Baptist baptizing Christ (Illustration 7.9). In the lower left-hand corner of the painting there are two angels painted in decidedly different styles. The angel on the right, nearest Christ, has sharply defined features and clothing; the one on the left is much more ethereal, with soft shading defining his features and clothing, demonstrating a chiaroscuro technique. They seem to cry out for the explanation that Vasari provided, or at least part of it: for he reported that Verrocchio painted the angel on the right, while his pupil did the angel on the left, an attribution that many have accepted. But he then went on to claim that Verrocchio was so depressed by the superiority of Leonardo's angel that he never painted again. Whether true or not, this again was clearly the stuff of legend – making the artisan Leonardo both an artist and a work of Vasari's literary art as well.

As much of Leonardo's work from this early period was done in the context of Verrocchio's workshop, it was unclear which works or which parts of works were actually by him or were merely recognized as such at the time. In fact, much of the painting that is attributed to him today was not attributed to him then; in turn, as his reputation grew, a considerable amount of work attributed to him apparently was not his. It seems, however, that from the first, Leonardo enjoyed the designing of paintings more than the actual painting; thus he produced dozens of drawings before embarking on a work and frequently lost interest thereafter, leaving the work unfinished

7.9. Verrocchio (and Leonardo), *John the Baptist Baptizing Christ*, 1470s, for the Monastery of San Salvi, now in Uffizi Gallery, Florence. Photo: Erich Lessing/Art Resource, New York.

or to be completed by others. The most noted example of this is yet another Magi painting, his uncompleted *Adoration of the Magi* (Illustration 7.10). It was to be a major painting on that theme so popular with the Medici in the Monastery of San Donato not far from Florence and suggests that by that date (1480) he already had enough of a reputation to garner such a commission. What remains of the project are a number of preliminary drawings and what appears to be his preparatory underpainting in monochrome variations

7.10. Leonardo da Vinci, *Adoration of the Magi*, 1481–82 unfinished, for San Donato a Scopeto, now in the Uffizi Gallery, Florence. Photo: Alinari/Art Resource, New York.

of brown. That underpainting, now hanging in the Uffizi, seems rich with unusually intense expressions and violent movement, which, had the work been completed, would have provided a highly original and expressive treatment of the subject.

But Leonardo left it unfinished when in 1482 he moved on to one of the most promising courts of the day, the Milanese court of Ludovico il Moro Sforza. Apparently growing restless in Florence and perhaps anxious to escape the task of finishing his painting, he wrote Sforza a letter offering him those skills he hoped as an artisan/courtier would win him Il Moro's patronage. He began by promising military "secrets," which he knew would appeal to a ruler whose power still turned on his military abilities and whose position in Milan was rather shaky. The extensive list of military machines and techniques that he offered as secrets that he alone knew, however, eventually gave way to broader claims: "In time of peace I believe I can give full satisfaction equal to anyone in architecture and planning buildings.... I can do sculpture in marble, bronze, and clay and also painting." He continued with a point that he knew was close to the heart of Sforza, offering to work on the large bronze equestrian statue that Il Moro was planning in honor of his father, Francesco Sforza.

Once again it seems clear that at thirty years old Leonardo already had enough of a reputation to garner Ludovico's attention and patronage. When he arrived in Milan, Sforza entrusted him with a number of major projects, including the major equestrian statue. The project was particularly important in Ludovico's eyes because it stressed his direct descent from the first Sforza ruler of the city, at a moment when he was not eager to give up his rule to his young nephew Gian Galeazzo Maria Sforza, the legitimate ruler of Milan, who was coming of age and ready to claim his rule. The planned statue was to have been truly monumental, over 20 feet high and requiring more than 200 tons of bronze. Drawings by Leonardo indicate that he originally wanted to innovate on traditional equestrian statues, which were modeled on Roman exemplars that featured a ruler mounted in a regal pose on a magnificent but static charger, opting instead for a much more dynamic rearing horse and warrior twisting in the fury of battle. The problem was how to arrange the weight of such a large mass of bronze with the horse standing only on its hind legs. Had he worked out the technical problems, the statue would have been a massive monument not only to Francesco Sforza, but also to the creativity and technical ability of Leonardo. In the end, however, he opted for a more traditional horse, standing safely on all four legs, and fashioned a large mock-up of the statue in clay showing what glory he had the potential to add to his patron and his court – and, in turn, showing him as an exceptional artisan/courtier. Unfortunately, it was never cast as Il Moro found he had other, more pressing needs for the bronze in the form of cannons.

During this period Leonardo also painted a number of portraits, although again more were apparently attributed to him than he actually completed. The most famous, and almost certainly his, is *The Woman in Ermine*, often identified as a portrait of Cecilia Gallerani, Ludovico's mistress. He also did the central panel of an altarpiece in the Church of San Francesco Grande, known as the *Virgin of the Rocks*. Apparently the picture was repainted in several different versions, but the one now in the Louvre displays Leonardo's use of shadow and light to define his figures in the brooding and evocative setting of a glade bounded by strange and haunting rock formations – a picture that has evoked wonder and a wide range of interpretations (Illustration 7.11). But his most famous painting during his stay in Milan

7.11. Leonardo da Vinci, *Virgin of the Rocks*, 1483–1508, Louvre, Paris. © RMN-Grand Palais/Art Resource, New York.

7.12. Leonardo da Vinci, *Last Supper*, 1494–98, refectory, Santa Maria delle Grazie, Milan.
Photo: Scala/Ministero per i Beni e le Attività culturali/Art Resource, New York.

was his *Last Supper* (1494–1498), painted in the Church of Santa Maria delle
Grazie (Illustration 7.12). Unfortunately, although for once he actually finished it, it began to deteriorate almost immediately. Leonardo had always
been interested in experimenting with new mediums, and in this case he
attempted to use a mixture of oil and tempera painted on dry plaster, which
would allow finer detail than traditional frescoing techniques. The problem
was that while it allowed him to repaint and develop finer detail, the paint did
not adhere well to the plaster. Even in his lifetime, then, the work began to
break down, with paint peeling off in spots. Still, for the short time it lasted,
the picture was a marvel, especially with its masterful use of perspective,
portrayal of powerful emotions, and figures in motion, all with Leonardo's
famous use of the evocative play of shadow and light in chiaroscuro to give
the figures a soft human glow. Vasari, a half-century later, while declaring it
one of Leonardo's greatest works, lamented that it had become little more
than a spot on the wall.

In Milan Leonardo also worked assiduously on depicting and playing with
his ideas in his notebooks, where one can see him working on plans for
building churches, monuments, fortifications, and even cities; constructing
various kinds of weapons and engines; and studying the human body based
upon dissection. But he was careful to keep his notebooks secret – in the
tradition of artisans keeping their technical skills secret – and thus they were
virtually unknown until rediscovered in the modern era. Safely secret, however, they did indirectly add to his fame in his day as they remained secrets

he could offer to his potential patrons to glorify them and their courts. In that context, the marriage of the young Beatrice d'Este to Ludovico il Moro in 1491 made his court an even more important stage for Leonardo's growing fame as more than an artisan. Although she was only fifteen when she came to Milan, this younger sister of Isabella d'Este quickly enlivened the court life of the Sforzas. And she conscripted Leonardo as the perfect artisan/courtier to use his artistic and engineering skills to glorify the court. Pageants, great dinners, and the games and play of the court all displayed and made use of his fertile creativity. Unfortunately, much of what he created for the court was ephemeral and has left little but enthusiastic reports. Still, at the time such works also added to his reputation, especially at the courts of the Este in Ferrara and the Gonzaga in Mantua. At the latter, Isabella d'Este, sister of Beatrice, would pester him for years to do her portrait, and her pleading letters speak eloquently of his by-then impressive reputation.

Leonardo's Milanese days and his Sforza patronage were cut short when the French invaded Milan in 1499. For a time Leonardo journeyed around Italy seeking a new court and patron. A short stay in Mantua probably provided the opportunity for him to do his sketch of Isabella now in the Louvre; he then moved on to Venice, where he seems to have served as a military engineer working on defensive works; but after a short visit to Rome he was back in Florence in 1501, about to turn fifty and securely established as one of the leading figures of his day. By the summer of 1502 he had returned to his military and engineering interests, joining Cesare Borgia as he attempted to carve out a state for himself in the Romagna. With the death of Cesare's father, Pope Alexander VI, in 1503 and the collapse of his rule, Leonardo returned to Florence, where he worked on a number of large projects for the city, including developing plans to make the Arno navigable from Florence to the sea; designing fortifications; and perhaps even working on a scheme of Machiavelli's to isolate Pisa by diverting the Arno from flowing through that city.

During this same period he embarked on one of his most potentially impressive commissions. After the fall of the Medici, the republican government experimented with reforms with an eye to creating a lasting republic. One of their schemes was to create a Great Council on the model of Venice; thus, in the Palazzo della Signoria they built a large chamber where the council could meet, and by the early 1500s they had decided to decorate it with large murals depicting Florence's great victories, presumably influenced in this by a similar series of paintings in the Great Council chambers in Venice. Thus the city fathers decided to hire two of the most famous painters of the day to do major paintings depicting important moments of Florentine glory on facing walls of the chamber – Leonardo and his younger contemporary Michelangelo. Each painting was to be about twenty-three feet high and fifty-six feet wide, with Leonardo doing the 1440 victory of Florence over Milan at the Battle of Anghiari and Michelangelo doing the 1364 victory over Pisa at Cascina.

This direct confrontation caught the attention of contemporaries and suggests how their artistic reputations had lifted both, as individuals of genius, high above the common herd of artisan painters. Unfortunately, what had shaped up to be a classic artistic confrontation managed to fail on almost every front. Michelangelo did some preparatory drawings, but then the new Pope Julius II insisted that he return to Rome to work on a previously commissioned monumental tomb project. Leonardo got further, apparently even beginning to paint, but he too soon left for other commissions. The final failure was that the Grand Council, and the Florentine republican government itself fell to the Medici in 1512, as we shall see. Ironically, whatever Leonardo actually painted on the wall of the Grand Council chamber was eventually covered over by frescoes of other battle scenes, painted in the 1560s by none other than the painter/critic Vasari, who so touted Leonardo's glory. This failed confrontation of greats did generate, however, numerous copies of the two artists' preliminary drawings that were put on public display. Peter Paul Rubens, for example, did a powerful sketch apparently based on Leonardo's work, which is fascinating for its depiction of the emotions of battle, for both men and horses, and the violent motion and contortions of the figures. Had the final pictures painted had this intensity, the confrontation would have been truly impressive.

Over the next few years, as a noted artist and engineer, Leonardo moved restlessly between patrons and cities, mainly Florence, Rome, and Milan, taking on major engineering projects, most of which were not completed, and painting, apparently with less enthusiasm. To this period, however, probably belong his most famous paintings: his *Saint John the Baptist* and *Mona Lisa*. Both, however, were little viewed in his own day and were known largely by reputation. In fact, scholars have pointed out that Vasari's laudatory account of the *Mona Lisa* is so inaccurate that it almost seems to be describing a different picture – not surprisingly, as the painting had left Italy with Leonardo for France when Vasari was still a child. That trip to France to serve the new French king, Francis I, was the final confirmation of Leonardo's greatness for contemporaries. Benvenuto Cellini, the noted sculptor, who had trouble accepting the greatness of anyone but himself, could not help but admit that the French king, "being extremely taken with his great *virtù*, took so much pleasure in hearing him reason, that he was apart from him but a few days a year." Still, Cellini could not resist suggesting that Leonardo did not impress the king so much because of his accomplishments in "sculpture, painting, and architecture" as because he was an impressive courtier.

Those accomplishments were enshrined, however, in Vasari's account of Leonardo, which proclaimed him as the artist who finally accomplished the rebirth (*rinascita*) of ancient art after two centuries of preparation. Much in the spirit of the day, Vasari claimed not only that Leonardo's work was a gift from God and divinely inspired, but that his very person was imbued with God-given beauty, grace, and talent. Once again in such compliments physical beauty was not just an attribute, it was an outer sign of inner perfection and in this case the power to create true art – in turn making the artist a genius, unique, and almost literally a work of art. His extensive descriptions of Leonardo's art, however, asserted Vasari's deeper vision of what separated the artist from the artisan and the work of art from a mere painting – *disegno*.

The term might be translated as "drawing," but that falls rather short of what Vasari was trying to evoke. For while he was enthusiastic about the way Leonardo's drawing allowed him to reproduce the natural world so precisely and seemed to make his painting and the figures depicted come alive, true art and true *disegno* involved more. It required seeing the deeper true reality – the *disegno* – in Platonic terms, the true eternal Form behind the material form of an object, and literally drawing it forth in a painting; thus, it required that a painter go beyond technique to discover the deeper truth in things and in the composition of a painting. Crucially, for Vasari and his peers a mere artisan was incapable of such a deep understanding and was thus limited to technical ability at best. *Disegno*, however – requiring, as it did, a rare and deep understanding of the very nature of things – was the skill of the great ancient artists reborn in modern artists and their art – an artistic *rinascimento* in Italy that made it unique and glorious, along with an elite group of artisans who had become artists and works of art themselves.

Aristocrats as Works of Art: Dress and the Display of Power and Status

Yet for all the claims of Vasari and of figures like Mantegna, Botticelli, Leonardo, and other would-be aristocratic artists, they were merely a sidelight of a much broader tendency to fashion individuals as works of art, closely tied to the increasingly aristocratic world of the second phase of the Rinascimento. In a more easily visible way, clothing, jewelry, material accessories, along with perfumes and cosmetics – for men as well as women – all helped to materialize and create the individual as a work of art. Returning to Botticelli's *Adoration of the Magi*, one thing that breaks down the anonymity of his small crowd of participants (along with faces, expressions, and gestures) is their clothing and the accoutrements that go with it. Hats are quite variegated, with skull caps interspersed with narrow-brimmed, multicolored hats flaunting an occasional jaunty feather, a couple of turbanlike headdresses, and a broader-brimmed hat in the background whose gold underside catches the light. The Medici, however, are hatless, as perhaps the situation warrants; and as the three Magi they sport hairstyles that are shorter and closer to the head than those of the other figures in the painting, especially Cosimo and Piero. Virtually all the others, including the young Lorenzo, wear their hair longer, covering their ears and reaching down to their collar or below, with fuller volume. Perhaps this was an allusion to a newer masculine hairstyle, underlining the fact that the elder Medici were from an earlier generation and already dead, or perhaps that they were older and more mature leaders.

The clothing of the Medici also set them apart from the crowd of their supporters. Cosimo's dark, dignified robe is ennobled by gold work on the shoulders, while Piero wears a virtually royal reddish robe, lined, it appears, with ermine or some other expensive material that makes him seem virtually imperial. But once again the picture is framed by two figures whose clothing along with their expressions and poses make them stand apart, the young Lorenzo de' Medici and Botticelli. As noted earlier, Lorenzo expresses a youthful magnificence that his stylish clothing highlights. Just as his father and his grandfather stand out from the crowd not just because of their positions, expressions, and poses, but also because of their clothing, so too does Lorenzo, whose short purple doublet, stylishly slitted to reveal a glimpse of his bottom; form-fitting hose, which leave no doubt about his shapely legs; and suede boots all virtually shout that he is quite a work of art. Moreover, in virtually all these things he is notably different from his father and grandfather. He is a Medici, but he is much more – virtually a Lorenzo the Magnificent – as his clothing proclaims.

Yet perhaps the most intriguingly dressed figure in the painting is Botticelli himself. Certainly, for all his foregrounding, his baggy ochre/yellow robes, which today look more like a bathrobe than the elegant costumes that surround him, appear to suggest a kind of humility that everything else about his self-portrait seems to belie. In fact, their cut suggests monkish robes and perhaps a humble religious place in a scene that is as much about political power and family importance as about religion. But his proud look and the rich border at the bottom of the robe create doubts about such a reading. A tempting but admittedly more problematic reading has been suggested, however, for yellow was the color that prostitutes were required to wear to distinguish themselves from honest women on the streets of many cities.

Was Botticelli boldly distinguishing himself from the Medici by suggesting the parallel between the craftsman, who sold his labor and himself to the powerful for money, and the prostitute, who did much the same? Of course, his yellow robes might have been seen as gold or interpreted in any number of other ways by contemporaries, but in the end that is the point. Clothing also served to individuate people, and, in modes of dress, the upper classes especially found an important venue for creating themselves as individual works of art.

Of course, as Botticelli's picture underlines, clothing and the accoutrements of dress were also crucial for family identity. In fact, most accounts of dress during the period tend to focus on the ways families used clothing to demonstrate their social place and power. Recently this way of seeing dress has been suggestively expanded by arguing that the emphasis on style and on dressing elegantly was itself the beginning of modern consumer society in the Rinascimento, with clothing becoming the first form of conspicuous consumption. Some have gone a step further and argued that things like elegant dress, along with a growing use of cosmetics and perfumes, were an important means for women to express themselves as individuals during a period that stressed female silence and passivity. Certainly these broader ways of seeing dress, consumption, and women's relationship to both add suggestive new topics for research, even if one must always be wary of firsts of anything, especially something like modern consumer culture. It may be more useful to think simply about the role of consumption in the culture of the time and not worry about firsts. For it is clear that the way in which dressing well and using cosmetics related to upper-class women and their expression of self and power was particularly important in the increasingly aristocratic world of the day.

Any broad claims, however, are complicated by the fact that even the trajectory of the development of style and ways of dressing across the period is still difficult to trace, especially given local, class, and gender variations and the sources, which are so variegated and dispersed that it is hard to generalize. On a very general level, however, it seems that across the fourteenth and into the fifteenth century, with significant variations from city to city, men's clothing became shorter, tighter, and exposed more and more of the body, while women's clothing moved in the opposite direction, becoming longer and covering more of the body. Older men tended to stick with long, free-flowing robes, at times consciously compared to the ancient Roman toga, even if in fact quite different. But the younger and the more stylish tended to opt for shorter and shorter doublets over stockings that fitted the legs tightly and often incorporated leather patches under the foot that served as a shoelike protection.

Moralists worried about the exposure that such short doublets and tight stockings created; even Boccaccio noted rather delicately that when women looked "at their lower parts … it is easily understandable that they are male." One prominent Franciscan preacher of the fifteenth century, referring to the same exposure caused by tights, was less reserved, fuming, "[B]oth in front and in back [they serve] to display the parts most obscene and dishonest, almost as disgracefully as if they were nude." In the second half of the fifteenth century the effect was literally augmented with the addition of the newly fashionable codpiece (*braghetta*), which in theory covered, but often displayed, the male genitals and was often imaginatively designed to enhance them.

Women's clothing seemed to go in the other direction, with upper-class women wearing longer and longer dresses, often with a high waist that pushed up the breasts. A great deal of legislation attempted to restrict the resultant exposure of cleavage, apparently with some success if the high necklines of women in many paintings are any measure. Preachers, however, continued to rail against the ongoing exposure and, in what might seem a countertendency, some art also suggests that breasts were seeing the light of day above fashionable dresses as never before. Long trains that necessitated hitching up the dress when climbing stairs and allowed the possibility of a brief glimpse of a shoe or even an ankle were also popular among the upper classes. They also required trailing servants to keep their expensive fabric out of the mud and dirt of the streets. "Expensive" was key, as the fine fabrics used for upper-class clothing was very costly, and the more of it a woman displayed, the richer she, her husband, and his family appeared. A layered look with expensive blouses of fine fabrics under looser-fitting overjackets, often with detachable sleeves that allowed several different-colored sleeves to be attached, created different color combinations and looks and offered the opportunity to exhibit additional wealth. Later in the period puffy outer sleeves that often grew to impressive size were added, and it became stylish to slit them to allow the high-quality fabric beneath to show through. In sum, it was display, display, display, even as, paradoxically, men became less covered and women more.

In one area, however – footwear – the trajectory was shared between the sexes, as the fascinating studies of Michelle Laughran and Andrea Vianello have shown. There had been a time, as many preachers and moral commentators were apt to recall, when more humble ancestors were content to go about barefoot or with simple wooden clogs. In the fourteenth century, if not a bit earlier, that began to change, with upper-class males adopting shoes with a long pointed toe made of leather, cloth, or a combination of both.

The more delicate of these were often worn on top of wooden clogs to protect them from the dirt and grime of the streets. As the style caught on, the
length of the point tended to grow to what some lamented were virtually
phallic proportions. Again moralists decried these phallic shoes and lamented
their impact on morality. The felt danger of such shoes, in fact, seems to suggest deeper concerns, perhaps related to uncertainties about male development and sexual performance.

Curiously, in this one area, women's fashions followed men's; for as the
fourteenth century progressed, women in city after city began to take up this
phallic shoe style as well, with the long pointed toes of their shoes sticking
out from under their long, flowing robes. Perhaps to protect these expensive fashion statements or perhaps to show them off more effectively, taller
and more elegant clogs were developed that, when the shoe was inserted in
them, lifted the shoe and wearer above the less elegant and the grime of the
streets. With time these *chopines* (called in various cities *pianelle, zoccoli, sibre,
calcagnetti, chiapinetti*) grew from an original few inches to a foot or more in
height, raising the women who wore them above most men and requiring
yet longer dresses and trains of servants to help them move about the city
(Illustration 7.13). Eventually they became fashionable throughout Europe,
but they were particularly popular, famous, and infamous in Venice. Already
in the fifteenth century male visitors to that city were intrigued and troubled
by upper-class women who paraded regally through the streets, towering
over everyone. Size clearly did matter, and not just in codpieces and pointed
shoes, but also in the commanding presence of a richly dressed woman – a
work of art once again – literally sailing placidly above the lesser folk who
crowded the streets. Such stature involved multiple dangers in the eyes of
commentators, threatening social order, gender distinctions, and merely stay-
ing erect, not just in Venice, but across the cities of the peninsula and later
across Europe.

The fourteenth and fifteenth centuries, however, found governments giving more and more time and attention to trying to control the way people
dressed and presented themselves in public. Once again consensus realities
came into play, because the laws that were passed to control dress and other
forms of consumption, usually labeled sumptuary laws, were almost exclusively aimed at social moments of display – banquets, weddings, parties, and
even funerals – that is, the venues where groups formed consensus realities
about a family or an individual. These laws were often passed in the name of
civic morality, stressing that excessive display undermined the moral fabric
of the city because it was immodest, sinful, and also because it wasted wealth
that could be used for the betterment of society. Yet there was a deep tension

7.13. *Chopines*. Life-shoes. © Mark Blinch/Reuters/Corbis.

in this vision. For while too much display was a waste of wealth and potentially sinful in its appeal to vanity, at the same time clothing and festivities were seen as legitimate and virtually required markers of status in the socially more complex world of the time.

Clothing and display not only made (and identified) the man (and the woman) and the family, they were also essential in doing so in a society where status was judged and negotiated via consensus realities. Alberti expressed this tension well in his *Intercenales* (*Dinner Pieces*), a series of short essays and dialogues presented as if they were for reading during dinner. In one of these dialogues, which discusses poverty, one of the speakers offers, "Consider what the public must think when they behold a prominent man's family clothed with insufficient decorum, his horses neglected, and the master himself attired with not enough dignity – in short, the entire house less sumptuous and elegant … than public customs and standards require." With the reference to "public customs and standards" we are clearly in the realm of consensus realities, judging a family and its individuals via their dress and display. Failing to display same implied that one was poor, and the speakers in the dialogue agree that appearing to be poor is a disgrace not to be countenanced: "… we must completely shun the very name of poverty. For hand in hand with an indigent condition, there goes the reputation for instability, impudence, audacity, crimes and vices…. He [the man who appears to be poor] is excluded from friendships, and driven from the intimate and habitual familiarity of other citizens…. He walks about in gloom, unwelcome, suspect, abject, and derided." Again consensus realities determine the social reality of an individual, and not dressing and displaying oneself correctly leads to social disaster.

Of course, clothing had long served the purpose of identifying who mattered. Yet, as Alberti's speakers reveal, what had changed was that in the more economically mobile, more socially complex, and more judgmental urban world of fourteenth and fifteenth century Italy, such evaluations had become the very measure of a man and his family; making clothing and display evermore significant markers. Moreover, as portions of the *popolo grosso* became more aristocratic and intermixed with those among the older nobility who had maintained some status and wealth, and as new men and their families rose up to positions of power and prestige, the calculations of who truly belonged on top of society required a veritable social calculus to work out who really mattered. In such complex calculations, dress and display played a crucial role, and governments, while they were interested in limiting the wasteful and immoral aspects of both, recognized at the same time that both were necessary to identify true aristocrats. Thus sumptuary legislation was a tricky business, seemingly always balanced on the knife edge of a difficult-to-determine golden mean between too much display and not enough.

This may explain why it appears that while much legislation was passed and repassed, it was rarely enforced. Approximately 300 programs of sumptuary legislation survive from the forty largest cities of Italy between 1200 and 1500. More than sixty sets of regulations on women's clothing alone exist from the fifteenth century, mainly concerned with assuring that women dressed correctly for their social position. Aristocrats needed to be aristocratic, without being unnecessarily so, although what that meant was a matter for debate, especially in the fifteenth century as competition for status became more and more intense. Display at lower social levels, however, tended to be increasingly restricted, especially when there appeared to be some danger of the lower classes dressing and passing as their "betters." Actually, the high quality of upper-class clothes helped make this possible, as they tended not to wear out, fostering a significant market in used sumptuous clothing, which allowed some people lower down the social scale to buy the kind of finery that indicated higher status. The newer rich also could use clothing and jewelry to insist upon their new, higher status. But perhaps the most feared crimes of display, as we might call them, were associated with upper-level prostitutes, who often bought or were given by their patrons clothing that allowed them to pass as, or even seem to surpass, upper-class women. Such social confusion was anathema, not just because of its challenge to the hierarchical vision of society, but also because it threatened to undermine the moral basis of society and, once again, its civic morality.

But, crucially for our analysis, what stands out in all this is the way an individual by dressing fashioned himself or herself in a public display of personal and family identity, becoming in the end a complex work of social art presented for all to judge. It is significant in this context that sumptuary laws, often in conjunction with fire-breathing preachers, singled out women for condemnation: daughters of Eve (who, with a certain irony, supposedly committed her original sin unclothed) who in their vanity wasted the wealth of their husbands and their families in order to make themselves seductive and superior. This was the height of the negative vision of the individual as a work of art, for from this perspective an individual woman by her mode of dress was capable of threatening a host of the central tenants of civic morality and social order. She might squander the resources of her husband and his family; could seduce other males from their duties, wives, and families; might set a dangerous example for others; could disrupt the community with her vanity; and would certainly undermine its prosperity; and all that with the added danger of losing her soul for the numerous sins involved. Daughters of Eve indeed.

Obviously not all agreed with these sentiments, especially women. In 1453 the Bolognese noblewoman Nicolosa Sanuti, mistress of Sante Bentivoglio, *signore* of the city, and wife of Nicolò Sanuti, the count of Porretta, took umbrage at the sumptuary law promulgated by Cardinal Bessarion, papal legate to the city at the time. Bessarion, probably pressed by popular enthusiasm whipped up in the city by the Lenten sermons preached against the vanity and sinful dress of women, issued his laws in May of that year. As a result, he soon found himself the addressee of a short treatise in Latin by Nicolosa, not just defending a woman's right to wear what she wanted, but also defending women from the unjust order of the day, as she saw it. Or at least upper-class women – for her text makes clear that the women she was referring to most directly were upper-class women like herself, not all women. Sanuti began her defense proclaiming, "[W]ho would be so weak or passive, what woman so lacking in learning, what woman so lacking in spirit, that she would not speak in favor of the restoration, defense, and preservation of her adornments." Custom, honor, and *virtù*, she insisted, all required that upper-class women dress richly, and not simply for their own honor, but for the city itself: "[Given that] virtually all *popolo* ranking below us in fame and dignity employ these signs of *virtù*, would it not be dishonorable and evil for the women of Bologna who are most deserving of such adornments to be denied them [?] ... If we exceed others in *virtù*, should we not be able to match them or even surpass them in that display which is the proof of *virtù*?" Cleverly, Sanuti had turned the defense of civic morality to her support and implicitly suggested not only that the requirement of having well-dressed women was necessary for the reputation of the city, but that women and their *virtù* were an important part of the civic community in their own right.

And not content with that implied claim, returning to first times and firsts, she outlined a number of things that women had contributed to society, including reading and writing, agriculture, and the working of cloth. But she concluded more modestly: "The *virtù* [of women] should have its due. Allow her the use of her just signs. Even conceding lesser importance [for women] their dignities should not be unjustly taken away. Offices are not given to women, nor do they compete for priesthoods, military triumphs or the spoils of war, for these are the traditional rewards of men. Still adornments and decorations we will not allow to be taken from us, for they are the signs of our *virtù*." Sanuti stresses throughout her treatise that clothing serves as a sign of the most important things a woman possesses, ultimately even her *virtù* – no small claim. Bessarion, from the height of his masculine power, did not respond to Sanuti, but with time laxity won out over enforcement, and the most aristocratic women of Bologna continued to display the signs of their *virtù*, at least in dress.

To a great extent, however, attacks on women and their expenditures on clothing and vanity were a red herring. For although some aristocratic women did buy clothing, and some may have made it for their trousseaus, in most cases clothing, jewelry, and other adornments for women were bought by men. It was in their interest and the interest of their families to present their wives in public in a way that demonstrated their wealth and power. As was the case in portraits, but on a more daily level, the dress of a wife helped to create her as a work of art that spoke directly to the groups that judged individuals and families via consensus realities. Thus, although moralists and preachers tended not to focus on it, usually the men who bought women's clothing and adornments did so carefully calculating the way such clothing served as an investment: first, obviously, in terms of the simple value of the goods involved – both jewelry and expensive clothing held their value and could be converted back into money when necessary – and, more importantly, in terms of status and display; and finally, not to be overlooked, as a sign of respect and perhaps even affection for a wife who was socialized to appreciate such gestures.

Crucial for all of this was the cost of clothing, especially the sumptuous clothing required to demonstrate upper-class status. In many ways clothing was the Rinascimento equivalent of the modern car – the area where the greatest amount of a family's disposable income was displayed. Estimates vary, but it appears that more than a third of the expenses of an upper-class family went for the purchase of clothing, and it was not rare for a fine dress to cost more than the yearly salary of an artisan. And when decorated with pearls or interwoven with threads of gold or other precious metals, it could equal the cost of a small house. In this light it is not surprising to note that most of a wife's clothing belonged to her husband, and unless specified otherwise in his will, when her husband died the clothing returned to his family, leaving a widow with only what she had brought to the marriage in her dowry or with what her husband decided to will to her.

For the lower classes there was obviously less opportunity to use dress to create oneself as a work of art, although sumptuary laws reveal a fear of the possibility. But there were other ways to create a distinctive self in the urban world of the Rinascimento that we are just beginning to appreciate. Most colorful, perhaps, were the many mountebanks, charlatans, and hucksters who moved on the margins of more normal society and who carefully crafted themselves as interesting works of art in order to sell their products in the squares and markets of the day. More integrated into society were the many lower-class women healers and cunning women who are virtually invisible in the historical records. All these, and undoubtedly others whose lives are largely lost to us today, survived by creating identities that set them apart in some significant way and made them valuable, respected, or dangerous members of their communities – and this often required a careful self-fashioning and negotiation with the groups that surrounded them to become individual works of art.

Constructing Scholars and Intellectuals as Works of Art

Yet it is scholars and intellectuals who seem to cry out to be labeled the most complex and significant individuals created as works of art in the Rinascimento. In some ways the rethinking of a number of outstanding artisans as artists that began in the fifteenth century, and that reached a sort of climax with the famed artists of the sixteenth century, merely followed a trajectory similar to the earlier development of the scholar and the intellectual as special categories of individuals with an exceptional *virtù* that warranted a certain elite status. Of course, outstanding scholars, writers, and thinkers were not a novelty during the period. In the Middle Ages there had been a flourishing group of great thinkers, writers, poets, and scholars, but they were invariably associated with the few great courts, as scribes or bards, or with the Church and its universities. In fact, most were seen as part of a clerical community that dominated the intellectual life of the day or as humble servants of princes or high nobility. Only the most prominent gained greater status, but virtually never were they confused with the social elite or the ruling classes.

With the Rinascimento that began to change. Even in the thirteenth century in the cities of northern Italy, following in the tradition of troubadour poets and southern Italian court poets, writers, often from a scribal or legally trained university background, began to make a name for themselves writing poetry in Latin and the vernacular, as we have seen. A few notaries, scribes, and others among the *popolo* who could write were also penning works that celebrated their cities' past, present, and future and again making a name for themselves doing so. But it was perhaps the association of their ideas and writings with the ancient world, both Roman and biblical, that accelerated their recognition as a new form of elite, because, of course, that association made their status claims not new, but safely old, not a novelty but just another *rinascimento* – a rebirth of the elite scholars and intellectuals who had made the ancient world great, a claim that would be pressed still harder as humanists emerged at the end of the fifteenth century and attempted to assert their intellectual discipline and leadership.

But once again the process was much more broadly based, for across the Rinascimento universities founded in the Middle Ages in Italy and throughout Europe continued to be important centers for intellectual life. In addition, the Church not only continued to support intellectuals, but consciously expanded its support of some of the most important of the day by giving them positions in its increasingly scholarly bureaucracy. But for all this tradition that could be traced back to earlier times, a sea change was occurring, for many of the intellectuals who served in the Church bureaucracy moved in and out of that service in pursuit of scholarly careers and recognition as intellectuals that warranted an elite status in its own right, not merely as "humble" servants of the Church, as we have seen. The same was true of university professors, who moved in and out of universities as finding rich and powerful patrons permitted or as places at courts opened up. Perhaps the most significant sign of the change, however, was the way in which a number of members of the upper classes and social elites also took up intellectual pursuits – fashioning themselves as complex works of art that were to be viewed as significant for much more than their family wealth, their birth, or their power in the world. In sum, they began fashioning themselves as part of an intellectual elite and shared that status with poets, writers, and thinkers, whose intellectual accomplishments were allowing them to transcend their more humble origins. The unlikelihood of that strange alliance between intellectuals drawn from aristocratic families and intellectuals of more humble origins is often taken for granted in the Rinascimento, perhaps masking the fact that such an unlikely alliance was remarkably new and strange.

From that perspective, Petrarch's careful and almost obsessively pursued self-fashioning takes on a richer meaning. He not only carefully revised his letters and poetry, or created his spiritual biography, to present himself to his various judging publics as a unique work of art, he literally reconstructed his entire life to this end, transforming himself from the son of a scribe into an intellectual leader of his society and his day. And, not surprisingly, his program turned on stressing his own intellect and superior sensibility via his love poetry – which often seems to pay more attention to his love of self than his love of Laura – and his search for classical texts and call for the revival of a lost ancient, noble Roman world. Notably, he imagined that world as one in which his intellectual heroes were cultural leaders and members of a singular elite, like himself. And, of course, the contemporary consensus realities that judged him as an individual largely agreed. Dante had earlier followed a similar ennobling strategy, with perhaps a bit more humility – although it must be admitted that the hubris of a member of the *popolo grosso* of Florence (and an exiled member accused of embezzling funds at that) imagining himself as singled out to be led by Virgil through Hell and Purgatory on the way to his own private beatific vision of God and Paradise, aided by his childhood love, Beatrice, is amazing at the least, and decidedly artful as well.

These famed writers should not blind us, however, to the fact that in the fourteenth century there was a much broader scribal world supported by other literate members of the *popolo grosso* who were also taken by the idea of recovering, reusing, and celebrating first times and garnering status by doing so. Local chroniclers returned over and over again to first times and celebrated the origins of their cities, earning them local recognition, fame, and sometimes even status. The Venetian Grand Chancellor Raffaino Caresini, for example, was legally granted noble status in part for his exceptional service to the city during wartime and in part for the fame he had earned as chancellor and as author of a laudatory chronicle of the city. It seems, however, that this was taken to new levels by the circle that surrounded the Florentine head of the chancellery, Coluccio Salutati (1331–1406), as we have seen. Not only was Salutati a scribe whose classical knowledge and skill in writing Latin marked him out as a cultural leader, he was recognized by his contemporaries as a powerful intellectual who created around himself an elite group of fellow scholars whose intellectual activities focused on the recovery of first times, Roman, Greek, and biblical. And significantly, that group included not only upwardly mobile scribes seeking to transform their learning into wealth and status, but also individuals who were already scions of rich and powerful families, like Niccolò Niccoli, who shared a deep interest in the same cultural revival.

Niccoli, from the perspective of the social order of his day, had no need to be considered a part of an intellectual elite, but nonetheless that goal was a driving force in his life, as was the case for a growing number of a progressively more aristocratic *popolo grosso* who saw in a life of classical scholarship and intellectual activity an additional elite status worth pursuing. For some already on top of society, a growing sense that status required more than wealth and family clearly contributed to this, as did, of course, the excitement of discovering a rich ancient culture that seemed capable of refashioning the very way of life of the day. For the more humble, who were, one might say, the shock troops of this new cultural elite – safely perceived, of course, as old – learning and intellectual attainment offered the possibility of status as well as the possibility of the patronage of the rich and powerful, who saw their services as increasingly necessary for their own prestige. Here in this complex mixing of status with cultural achievements and the more traditional claims of wealth, family, and power, Rinascimento intellectuals were forged as works of art on the road to that modern anomalous creature who asserts a certain elite status on the basis of intellectual merit, the scholar/intellectual.

Constructing a Few Upper-Class Women as Works of Art

It might seem an unlikely claim that women, both as rulers and as intellectuals, should be numbered among the most artfully created individuals of the day. Yet, as argued earlier, women, especially at higher social levels, were regularly dressed and adorned with care in order to demonstrate a family's wealth and social position and in the process became works of art themselves. This use of women, as virtual billboards of status, made individual women stand out from and, with *chopines*, even above the crowd. But what was true for upper-class women in general was even more important at the highest levels of society, especially as demonstrating glory increasingly became a measure of elite status. Especially in two areas, this use of women to project glory or status was shifting the generally negative discourse on women in interesting directions, without, however, eliminating traditional negative stereotypes that made them the second sex. First, some families were beginning to celebrate their women writers and intellectuals as a way to increase their own status, supported in this by a few male intellectuals eager to piggyback on newfound female fame. Second, at more and more courts where male rulers earned their keep as warrior princes, women often ruled while they were at war. In doing so, a number not only gained, but also fashioned, glorious personalities of their own. As writers and rulers, then, a small but significant group of women emerged at what might be seen as the highest level of the individual as a work of art.

Virginia Cox, in her path-breaking study of women authors in the Rinascimento, *Women's Writing in Italy 1400–1600*, impressively demonstrated the unrecognized depth and breadth of women's writing during the period. But she also argued that in many ways the most noted secular women writers were often "constructions" of the male intellectuals who trumpeted their glory. Tracking this constructed vision of the female intellectual "hero" back to Petrarch's letters and Boccaccio's *De claris mulieribus* (*On Famous Women*), she traced a tradition of male writers celebrating women, both as exceptional rulers and as writers, in large part in order to advertise their own learning and to bond with like-minded male scholars celebrating women. Although these idealizations of women also tended to emphasize traditional values and negative stereotypes, they nonetheless stressed that some women of the past, and a few in the present, were capable of exceptional deeds.

Particularly important in this promoting of women as heroic – and as practically equal to men – was the genre of the letter, a literary genre, as noted earlier, ideal for gaining wide circulation and visibility. At one level letters by men praising exceptional women tend to read as quite conventional contributions to a traditional debate on the worth of women, often labeled the *querelle des femmes*, which was especially popular at the time. Often they reduced the women discussed to iconic stereotypes who displayed little beyond a limited range of *virtù*, at times even labeled "masculine." But therein lays the ambiguity of such writing, and its potential for creating a woman as a work of art: for even if such encomiums tended to reduce impressive women to stereotypic *topoi*, eliminating their actual individuality, in celebrating their exceptionality they also refashioned them imaginatively as heroic individuals, effectively as works of art, and significant ones at that. Thus, even if written down as *topoi*, they could walk off the page to be imagined as exceptional individuals in a society where few such women were presumed to exist.

Moreover, unlike the warrior heroes of chivalric tales, who were denizens of a distant dream-time displaying forms of *virtù* that were often clearly fantasy, female leaders, intellectuals, and writers were increasing recognized in letters as living among the contemporary upper classes and displaying contemporary *virtù*. In fact, it became important in the fifteenth century to point out that contemporary women were capable of equaling not only the accomplishments of their modern male counterparts, but also those of ancient women and men, at least in the areas where women might compete with men. This meant, however, that making them heroic and exemplary helped to refashion them as special individuals worth considering more carefully. And, of course, as men pressed this status on a number of noteworthy women, it became increasingly important for every would-be major court or city to have its own women of note. In turn, at least at the level of the upper classes, there were a number of women who were already in fact playing roles of power or writing first-rate literature who were available to fill the role of heroic woman.

Many, both men and women, were not comfortable with this more public role for women as rulers, writers, and intellectuals. Certainly there was a strong tradition that required women to be passive, silent, obedient, and private. And women who acted otherwise could be, and were, attacked aggressively. Often they were portrayed as dangerously free and public, a portrayal that easily slid into typical misogynist claims of promiscuity and sexual license. Still, among aristocratic elites and especially at the princely courts, where high status served to a degree to protect women – a signifi-cant example of the way gender and status often intermixed – women rul-ers required respect, and women writers, if they chose their topics carefully, could be not only recognized but lionized. And in the process, proceeding with care, they too could contribute in a more instrumental way to con-structing their own heroic status as rulers, intellectuals, and writers, subtly transforming themselves from objects of art created by men to self-fashion-ing agents negotiating their own consensus realities as individuals.

Following Cox's lead, the career of Giovanni Sabadino degli Arienti (1445–1510) opens a masculine window on this world of power, patron-age, and celebration of women as individuals and works of art. Arienti is best known today for his *Novelle Porrettane*, a collection of sixty-one *novelle* in the tradition of the *Decameron* told by a group of gentlemen and ladies at the baths of Porretta, dedicated to Ercole d' Este (1431–1505), lord of Ferrara. Although for most of his life he served the Bentivoglio family of his native city, Bologna, in various roles, as a writer he carefully cultivated the Este family and their nearby court. It is even reported that in the mid-nineties, as his rapport with the Bentivoglio declined and his annual stipend was cancelled, he solidified his ties to the Este by secretly serving them as an informant about Bolognese affairs. Whether that is true or not, in later years his ties to the Este court became more open and direct. Before that open shift to the Este, however, he carefully cultivated the powerful women in the Bentivoglio family, especially the colorful (and, according to some contemporaries, often too colorful), Ginevra Sforza (1440–1507), illegitimate daughter of Alessandro Sforza and wife of the ruler of the city, Giovanni II Bentivoglio (1443–1508; ruled 1463–1506).

Ginerva's children were myriad, with thirteen living to adulthood. And, aside from a couple of daughters who became nuns, most played significant roles as *condottieri*, churchmen, and consorts of important figures. Giovanni contributed another seven illegitimate sons and at least four recognized ille-gitimate daughters. They were nothing if not fecund. Fecundity, however, was just a small part of Ginevra's fame in her day as she quickly gained notoriety as the real power behind Giovanni's rule. Her fame and power, in fact, were such that she was accused of associating with witches and practic-ing sorcery – accusations often aimed against powerful women. She was also widely criticized for her vanity and her penchant for sumptuous clothing and rich display, once again stereotypical attacks against powerful women. But perhaps most damning in the eyes of contemporaries was the cruel council she gave her husband in suppressing two of the conspiracies against his rule. The families of the accused conspirators, the Malvezzi and the Marescotti, in each case were aggressively punished with tortures, executions, and confiscations that seemed to many excessive, even at a time when excess was the rule. And once again the cruelty was attributed to the woman behind the man (in this case not all that behind). Beyond this virtually all-inclusive catalog of misogynist stereotypes against powerful women, it is difficult to know who Ginevra actually was, but it is clear that once again she had been constructed largely by males as a work of art – a cruel, evil, grasping work of art, but a work of art nonetheless.

Giovanni Sabadino degli Arienti, however, responded to her power in another way more typical of courtiers. In the 1490s he published a work he had written earlier titled *Gynevera de le clare donne* (*Ginevra, On Famous Women*). Dedicated to her, it celebrated the greatness of thirty-three famous modern women, who he claimed were as great in *virtù* as any women of the ancient world. In stark contrast to contemporary attacks, he proclaimed that the citizens of Bologna shouted Ginevra's name in the streets and lauded her *virtù* as surpassing that of the ancients; thus he had decided to write in praise of famous modern women like her who also surpassed the ancients. Summarizing her *virtù*, he gives space to the "fecundity of her womb" and the promise of her many children, but concludes by praising her "prudent councils," her manners, piety, charity, "and finally the discrete splendor of all her ornaments and regal presence," which made their city of Bologna "shine more [brilliantly] than gems or gold." Literally a woman constructed as a work of art, he insists that "for these reasons as a woman, you are in no way inferior to the immeasurable *virtù* of your family and your illustrious husband."

Once again there is room for considerable doubt about his imaginative account, but in presenting the opposite side of the coin to misogynist attacks, Arienti provides a clearer sense of the value of the coin itself. Ginevra makes or breaks her city. She is wife, mother, councilor, and literally the image of the magnificence of her Bologna and Bentivoglio rule. Perhaps no real woman could live up to either this praise or the opposing criticism, but there was no doubt that this woman was imagined as a powerful and important individual to be reckoned with. A contemporary painting in the family chapel in San Giacomo Maggiore in Bologna suggests this well, with Giovanni and Ginevra flanking the Madonna and Christ Child enthroned with their hands joined in prayer. She stands to the viewer's left, slightly below the Madonna, he to the right. Both are virtually on the same scale as the Madonna, and below them stand their children, seven girls on the left under their mother and four boys on the right under their father. Ginevra, richly dressed, is literally presented as the other half of the ruling couple, in no way inferior to her mate. If anything, with her dynastic fecundity on display, before the Virgin with her own fertile promise in the Christ Child on display, Ginevra almost seems to outshine her consort in *virtù* and certainly is presented as in "no way inferior" to him.

The thirty-three modern women whom Arienti presents as being similarly blessed with exceptional *virtù* include rulers, warriors, and writers. Among the literary lights he includes Battista da Montefeltro, Isotta Nogarola, Ginevra Nogarola, Angela Nogarola, Ippolita Sforza, Battista Sforza da Montefeltro, and Caterina Virgri. Isotta Nogarola (1418–1466), along with her sister Ginevra (1419–1465), followed in the tradition of their aunt Angela, a poet of some note, and while still young the sisters gained a reputation for learning. Their development suggests the way a few women of the upper classes were encouraged in their studies by their families and by supportive male intellectuals, all interested in gaining prestige by promoting their skills. While still young their father died. He came from a noble family of Verona that was no longer as important as it had once been before the fall of the city to the Venetians, but still notable. After his death their mother groomed her daughters for a future different from the norm for noble girls, sending them to private teachers to master Latin and the classics, evidently with an eye to cultivating their intellectual talents and apparently in the hope that scholarly success would single them and their family out.

Arienti depicts both young women as attracting attention early on for their exceptional abilities in Latin – literally youthful prodigies. Ginevra, however, abandoned Latin to marry a nobleman and move to Brescia, leaving Isotta to pursue her studies and fame on her own. Following in the footsteps of many of her male compatriots, she displayed her Latin learning via letters written to the more famous male scholars of her day and eventually produced a collection of twenty-six of her most important missives in Latin. Arienti reserved his greatest praise, however, for her dialogue composed in Latin as an epistolary exchange with the Venetian patrician Lodovico Foscarini, *Questio utrum Adam vel Eva magis peccavit* (*On the Question Whether Adam or Eve Was the Greater Sinner*), remarking: "[S]he was learned in theology and philosophy which she used to write a great dialogue on which was the more serious sin in eating the apple, Adam's or Eve's."

Lauding her familiarity with the Bible, which he claimed she knew almost "by heart," and the theology of Church Fathers, especially Saint Augustine, he proclaimed the work a treatise of profound significance. Isotta argues that Eve's was the lesser sin because she was a woman and more easily led astray – hardly a strong defense of female *virtù* or parity with males, but a clever argument in a dialogue that is rich with clever arguments on both side of the question. In fact, it has been suggested that Isotta may actually have composed both sides of the debate, merely giving the more traditional masculine argument to Foscarini, whom she had corresponded with and may have met while visiting Venice. Arienti summed up his compliments by claiming that "this Isotta was a religious and saintly woman … full of gravity and such great learning and eloquence that I believe that she surpassed every other most famous woman of antiquity." Claiming that the present surpassed the ancient world, and did so in the form of an unmarried female scholar living on her own – one could hardly imagine a higher compliment.

As usual, however, there were others who were not so complimentary. They portrayed Isotta's learning as implying her promiscuity and her dangerous freedom from the ties that normally bound society; for she had avoided the discipline of marriage and the family, required for women. In fact, Arienti's emphasis on her holiness and virginity almost certainly was meant to undercut such claims, which had circulated anonymously in the 1430s, when to most observers she had dangerously passed the age of marriage without marrying. Those attacks suggested that she was not only not a virgin, but actually living in an incestuous relationship with her brother. Cox pointed out cogently that class as well as gender played a role in such stereotypical attacks. Powerful women at court, and the daughters and wives of rulers, had a freer hand to take up intellectual endeavors, and often their successes were seen as triumphs for their families, their courts, and their cities. Lesser women, like Isotta, even if still aristocrats, had to tread more carefully. When their youthful status as prodigies passed, marriage seemed to be required; and if they failed to follow that virtually obligatory path, their chastity, religious commitment, and they themselves were doomed to be dogged by suspicion and censure.

Laura Cereta (1469–1499) and Cassandra Fedele (1465–1558) provide examples of similar difficulties faced by women below the very highest levels of society who attempted to carve a place for themselves as learned women. Once again, both were recognized as prodigies while still young and touted as great scholars by admirers eager to ride on their fame. But once they married, both were pressed to withdraw from public life. Cereta was born into an upper-class family in Brescia, an important Venetian provincial city, where her father was a lawyer. At seven she entered a convent school there, a venue that provided one of the primary opportunities for the education of girls whose families could not afford private tutors. Her serious training in the classics, however, began when she returned from the convent and expressed to her father an interest in continuing her education at a higher level. In her teens, like Isotta Nogarola she used her Latin letters as a vehicle to attempt to build her reputation as a scholar and eventually put together eighty-two of her most important as a collected work.

Unfortunately, those letters, written to the important scholars of her day, did not elicit much in the way of enthusiastic support, especially as she grew older and lost her youthful exceptionality. In fact, they did not circulate widely and were first published only in the mid-seventeenth century. Still, they blend an impressive range of classical knowledge, a practical insight into and understanding of the world around her, and a sensitivity to the problems that women faced that have led some to label her a proto-feminist. At the least she was a person, given her education and aggressive self-presentation, unusually insightful about the problems that women faced. In many areas, however, she upheld quite traditional values, even as she called upon women to support each other and pursue learning aggressively in order to play a more significant role in society. Briefly married in her teens to a merchant of Brescia who died in 1486, she spent the rest of her short life apparently lecturing in her hometown and striving, largely unsuccessfully, to gain entrance to the larger scholarly world of her day.

Among her correspondents was the slightly older and more successful Cassandra Fedele. From a family of Venetian *cittadini*, the legally recognized upper class, officially ranked just below the nobility, she was better placed for success. The special privileges the most powerful of that class enjoyed marked them out as a kind of elite beneath the nobility, and her family boasted doctors, lawyers, bankers, and at least one bishop. Once again she had gained note as a youthful prodigy. In her case studying with a private tutor, her mastery of Latin and Greek along with her training in rhetoric and natural sciences attracted attention. All made her quite exceptional, especially her interest in the natural sciences, and earned her a rare place as a woman in her twenties in the intellectual circles at the University of Padua, where such studies were being intensely cultivated. It appears that there was a moment when she was negotiating with rulers in the Iberian peninsula about taking up a university post there, but that fell through when the French King Charles VIII invaded Italy in 1494 and ushered in an age of warfare that disrupted Italy and Europe. It was even reported that the government of Venice attempted to block those negotiations, fearing to lose her youthful glory. Whatever was actually the case, she obviously had gained a major reputation for herself as a scholar and intellectual.

In 1499, at thirty-four – a surprisingly late age for a woman's first marriage – she suddenly married a prominent doctor. Apparently her acceptableness as a young woman prodigy had worn thin, and she bowed to the pressure to marry and take up a more traditional role for adult women. Supporting that supposition, after her marriage she cut off ties with Padua, largely shut down her scholarly career, and reportedly held that writing and the public life of a scholar conflicted with being a wife. If that was her reasoning, traveling with her husband to Crete also distanced her from Padua and the intellectual world where she had cut such an impressive figure. On the other hand, Crete was an important Venetian colony where, drawing on her husband's medical experience and her own interest in natural science, together they may have investigated local medical practices and cures at the behest of the Venetian government. That would certainly put her marriage and abandonment of Padua in a different light, although the archival evidence indicates that the governmental commission was his alone. Later, however, she was reported to have written a work on natural history and philosophy titled *Ordo Scientiarum* (*The Order of Knowledge*), now lost, which may have drawn upon those researches.

Their return to Venice in 1520 was disastrous. First they lost all their possessions in a shipwreck on the way back, and shortly thereafter her husband died (1521), reducing her to relative poverty at fifty-six. A woman on her own without much in the way of support, Cassandra found herself in a difficult position, one that she shared with many older women without children and limited family support. With her scholarly reputation, however, she attempted a solution not open to most, appealing to the Medici Pope Leo X, noted for his patronage of the arts, for aid – but as a mature woman, tellingly, without success. Finally, many years later in 1547, in her eighties, Pope Paul III responded to her plight, pressing the Venetian Senate to appoint her prioress of the Ospitale di San Domenico in Venice, which served primarily as an orphanage, a position that she held for the rest of her life until her death at ninety-three. But for most of her mature life, a period when a male scholar would have been at the peak of his productivity, Cassandra, a widow and no longer a child prodigy, suffered in obscurity.

Her collected letters were even more extensive than Cereta's, numbering 113; most were written before 1499, when she married. More formal and clearly aimed at making a higher mark, they were addressed to European rulers and the leading cultural figures of the day. And once again a male figure, the prominent Florentine scholar and poet Angelo Poliziano, recognized her learning while still young with a typical mix of stereotyping and enthusiasm for a woman's learning, addressing her, "You young girl are the only woman to emerge [as great], you work with the book instead of wool, the pen instead of rouge, writing instead of embroidery and you do not cover your skin with makeup, but instead paper with ink." But, after years of mature oblivion, shortly before her death her city remembered her youthful glory and asked her, at ninety-two, to deliver a Latin oration welcoming the queen of Poland to Venice. Perhaps merely as a form of modesty or perhaps – as one might wish was the case – with a deep irony, she pointed out that her Latin oration could hardly add to the queen's fame, but "I would hope that merely by honoring you, I also might be made immortal." From star to poverty, from fame to obscurity, from youthful darling of her city to forgotten old woman, Cassandra exemplified women writers and scholars who were not from the very highest ranks of society. Like most, she was a highly fragile work of art whose fame was contingent on a careful construction of self that teetered on a knife edge between the limited forms of fame that society was willing to recognize in women and the many evils that were associated with their renown, especially when they moved outside the traditional ideal placement of women in marriage or convent.

Isabella d'Este as a Work of Art

Although she was too young to be mentioned in Arienti's *Ginevera de le clare donne*, Isabella d'Este (1474–1539) was certainly one of the most visible women of the aristocratic Rinascimento. And, in fact, she was the one member of the Este family whom Arienti most assiduously cultivated. Not only an exceptional woman whose power and patronage made her worth his cultivation, she provides an excellent example of the way in which women at the very top of society were being reimagined as virtually works of art – in Isabella's case quite literally, as from time to time she quipped that her face must be the best known in all of Europe, as it was the most painted. Even Leonardo da Vinci sketched it for a painting that, as noted earlier, he never completed. But unlike Helen of Troy, whose beauty reportedly launched a thousand ships, Isabella's, along with her learning and patronage, launched at least that many compliments. One enthusiastic flatterer even labeled her the "first lady of the world," no small compliment for a woman who was officially merely the wife of the lord of Mantua, a small city in the center of the Lombard plain.

And while the parallel is not worth pursuing too far, like Helen, Isabella was born to rule. Her father was Ercole I d'Este, duke of Ferrara, her mother Leonora of Aragon, daughter of King Ferrante of Naples. Under their rule the court of Ferrara flowered into one of the most important in Italy. Among other things, they supported Battista Guarino, son of the noted teacher Guarino da Verona, and his school for the *studia humanitatis*; built a famed library; and patronized a series of important artists and writers. They were particularly supportive of vernacular writers such as Matteo Maria Boiardo (1441–1494), who wrote a chivalric romance in Italian, *Orlando innamorato* (*Orlando in Love*), which, although it remained unfinished at his death, traced the glorious Este family lineage back to the first times of Charlemagne and the love between a Saracen knight, Ruggiero, and the warrior maiden Bradamante. This highly popular work that celebrated the aristocratic and courtly world of the day would be finished in the sixteenth century by another recipient of Este patronage, Ludovico Ariosto (1474–1533), with his *Orlando furioso* (*Orlando Gone Mad*), a work that in many ways dominated the sixteenth-century literary imagination. Ercole and Leonora also supported the translation of Latin classics and were particularly supportive of a revival of the ancient Roman comedies of Plautus and Terence, which were performed with great success at their court and contributed to the rebirth of comedy as a popular literary genre in the sixteenth century.

Not only was their court a fertile place for its cultural leadership, their marriage was also fertile in more straightforward ways. For, although Isabella may have become the more important, her sister, Beatrice (1475–1497), one year younger, was perhaps better educated and more successful early on. As noted earlier, at fifteen she married Ludovico Sforza, known as Il Moro, the thirty-eight-year-old powerful leader of Milan, and quickly became an important political player and patron – promoting a lively court in that city – before her early death in childbirth at twenty-two. Isabella's first brother, Alfonso (1476–1534), was born a year after her sister and would succeed his father as duke of Ferrara, ruling the city and its increasingly brilliant court from 1505 until his death in 1534. Unwillingly, he took as his second wife yet another famous woman of the era, Lucretia Borgia (1480–1519), pressed upon him by her father, the Borgia Pope Alexander VI.

Ever fertile, Leonora gave birth next to Ferrante (1477–1540), who was considerably less successful. In his early career he served the French as a *condottiere*, apparently without great success, and eventually returned to serve the family by ruling some of their smaller territories. But his days ended unhappily after he and his illegitimate brother, Giulio (1478–1561), hatched a plot to assassinate their older brother Alfonso and take over Ferrara in 1506. When the plot failed, Ferrante, Giulio, and the other conspirators were condemned to die. Ferrante and Giulio were let off, however, and spent most of the rest of their lives in jail: Ferrante died there thirty-four years later; Giulio was "more fortunate," being released at eighty-one after having been imprisoned for fifty-three years. The next legitimate Este son, Ippolito (1479–1520), enjoyed an unusually meteoric ecclesiastical career, even for a scion of a notable family like the Este. An abbot at five years old, at seven he became the archbishop of Estergom in Hungary; at fourteen a cardinal; and at seventeen added to his increasing number of church offices the important position of archbishop of Milan. He also was a patron, who most notably supported Ariosto, although the latter complained about how modest that patronage was. In addition, he was noted for his interest in astronomy and mathematics and – perhaps less seemly, given his clerical status – women and violence. The last brother of Isabella was Sigismondo (1480–1524), who lived most of his life in Ferrara in the shadow of his older brothers and in their service.

Isabella, brought up at the brilliant court of her parents, apparently studied with Battista Guarino and as a child and a young woman made her mark as a person and personality of note. At six she was officially betrothed to sixteen-year-old Francesco Gonzaga (1466–1519; ruled 1484–1519), who would become duke of Mantua two years later, at eighteen, and was a noted *condottiere*. They married when she was fifteen, and their first children were girls who died young, but after ten years of marriage the sons she needed to consolidate her position as wife and mother of the future rulers of Mantua began to arrive: first Federigo (1500–1540; ruled 1519–1540), who would succeed his father as duke; then Ercole (1505–1563), who, thanks to the efforts of his mother, would become a cardinal in 1527, and Ferrante (1507–1557), who would serve the German emperor as a *condottiere*. Several other children died early on, and two daughters were placed in convents.

Virtually from the first, the lively Isabella dominated her husband's court and, with shrewd patronage of a number of leading intellectual figures, made it into one of the most famous in Italy. Certainly it did not hurt that she had grown up at the Este court of Ferrara, watching her mother and father enhance its European reputation with the splendor of their rule, something that Isabella carefully emulated in Mantua. Also, taking a page from her mother's book, and out of necessity, she quietly ruled for her husband when he was off earning his keep as a *condottiere*. Thus at an early age she gained a reputation as an effective ruler capable of handling both the internal problems of Mantua and the confused political world of her day, dancing diplomatically with the French, the emperor, and the various Italian states all jockeying for power and advantage at the expense of smaller cities like Mantua.

Isabella's eventual reputation as a virtually mythic figure makes it difficult to evaluate her actual life and the successes behind the legend. But as our interest focuses on her mythic figure as a work of art, it is Isabella as imagined by her contemporaries that really interests. Yet certainly reports of her as a child prodigy mastering Latin and Greek with Guarino appear to have been more imaginary than real, especially as in her letters later in life she referred from time to time to her ongoing study of Latin and her lack of success in mastering even that language at the level she wished. Evidently contemporary ideals required that she be a youthful prodigy, but, as a mere human being, she was actually more a lively young woman with wide-ranging interests and a position that she quickly learned to use to wield real power. Like her less politically powerful literary predecessors, however, her extensive correspondence played an important role in building her reputation, even if her letters were usually in Italian, not Latin.

And, significantly, those letters continued to amass across her life, running into thousands, not in the least curtailed by her marriage. Her pursuits and self-presentation there reveal her to have been a person whose interests spanned a wide range of subjects and levels that moved from the personal to the public. At one moment she could be writing to a public official to try to protect the poor or the humble women of her city, at the next to her agents to procure dwarfs for the mini-court of dwarfs that she kept in the ducal palace, or to obtain castrated boys to add their tenor voices to her choral group. Her letters also show her as an avid collector of Roman and Greek antiquities; thus (even without any exceptional ability in classical languages) helping to establish her reputation as an important collector and proponent of the cult of first times. And in the end they reveal both the positive and negative sides of the woman behind the myth that in many ways she helped to build with those very letters. She could invest considerable sums in her collecting efforts, paying agents across Italy and Europe to search out antiquities for her, but she was not above taking advantage of those in trouble when it came to securing what she wanted.

For example, when Mantegna, who had been a loyal protégée of her court, fell on hard times late in life and petitioned her for support in 1506, she was not above trading that support for an ancient Roman sculpture that was one of the artist's most prized possessions, one that he had previously refused to sell to her. Even more telling is the way she bought an antique fragment of a statue from Rhodes along with a Cupid reputedly carved by Michelangelo that had been in the possession of Guidobaldo of Montefeltro, *signore* of Urbino. It seems that in 1502, in the complex intrigues that Cesare Borgia was weaving to build himself a ministate in the heart of Italy, he had seized that city, driving out Guidobaldo and his wife, Elisabetta Gonzaga. Elisabetta was both a relative and a close friend of Isabella, and as a gesture of kindness she offered the deposed couple asylum in Mantua. In the meantime, however, aware that the pieces that she wanted for her collection had been carried off to Rome by Cesare, Isabella asked her brother Ippolito, then a cardinal in Rome, to secure the objects for her, noting in her letter that Cesare was not interested in such fine things. Apparently her evaluation of Cesare was correct; pressed by Ippolito he presented them to her as a gift. When Guidobaldo and Elisabetta asked for the return of their prized pieces, their good friend and protectress Isabella responded with silence.

She also could be rather ruthless in her dealings with those she patronized. Her letters often reveal her as less than generous and short of funds. Nonetheless, her wide-ranging patronage earned her increasing fame and the compliments of many who hoped to enjoy it. One of the most important was Baldassare Castiglione (1478–1529), whose famous *The Book of the Courtier* was set at the court of Urbino but included many figures who frequented Isabella's court. Although it will be discussed in more detail in Chapter 9, suffice it to say for now that this seminal work played an important role in elevating women who led courts, like Isabella, to an even higher level of visibility and magnificence. As a courtier himself in the service of Isabella and her family in Mantua, Castiglione was also active as a diplomat for the Gonzaga and even fought in the wars of Italy for them. Isabella's correspondence shows that she used him as well as her agent to purchase works of art and other objects that interested her as he traveled Italy and Europe. In addition, like her other agents, he was involved in commissioning works from the wide range of artists who were well enough known to have Isabella wish to add them to her collection.

In this she was one of the more visible to pursue a newer form of collecting that would eventually change the way art was produced; for she was willing to buy already completed paintings that interested her, thus making her in a way a collector of art and the works of specific artists rather than just a patron. In fact, she was more generally a collector. For while her collections were an expression of her fascination with a wide range of things – books, antiquities, gems, musical instruments, sculpture, paintings, and even humans (dwarfs, castrati, and courtiers) – they were central for the way she presented herself as a cultural leader. Carefully displayed to the correct viewers – aristocratic visitors of note and power – they also heightened her glory and fame. In this she was again fashioning a consensus reality of herself as a unique individual, a work of art in her own right; and in this she was following in the footsteps of, and would be emulated by, a number of other princely aristocrats who were becoming a new breed: the collector.

The writers, poets, and artists who frequented her court or cultivated her via their encomiums sought, in turn, to win glory and reputation of their own, basking in her reflected light and hoping for her ennobling praise. Her monetary support in the form of patronage was also appreciated when she was able to give it. Pietro Bembo corresponded with her and sent her poems; Aldus Manutius sent her a specially printed edition of his first printing of Petrarch's poems; Bernardo Dovizi – the future Cardinal Bibbiena – had his famous cross-dressing comedy, *La Calandra*, played for her in Rome; and both Boiardo and Ariosto shared their writings with her as they wrote them. The painters whose works she collected or attempted to collect were, if anything, more famous. Leonardo da Vinci visited her in Mantua in 1499, promising to paint her portrait, as noted earlier. Raphael eluded her grasp. Still, works by Bellini, Titian, Perugino, Mantegna, Bonsignori, Francia, Dossi, Costa, and a host of lesser figures graced her collection – some commissioned, some purchased after they were painted – as did musical instruments that were virtually works of art by the noted maker of same, Lorenzo da Pavia.

Once again, as was the case for aristocratic women of lesser fame, her extensive wardrobe and jewelry collection was especially important for demonstrating to contemporaries the glamour and significance of her court and herself. When in 1492 she was invited to Milan to visit her sister Beatrice and her new brother-in-law, Ludovico Il Moro, Isabella complained in a letter to her husband that she did not have a wardrobe sufficiently impressive to represent their city and court. Eventually she managed to put together clothing, jewels, and other adornments sufficient to the task, but she clearly understood that her self-presentation required careful investment – as she was quite simply a work of art in her own right who literally bought fame and wore glory. Her wardrobe and her jewelry also served from time to time in a more mundane way. When revenues fell short, jewels, expensive clothes, and even fine objects and antiquities could be pawned to secure loans to keep their rule afloat or, for example, to purchase a cardinal's hat for her son Ercole. That cost her 40,000 ducats in 1527 as Pope Clement VII was desperately trying to raise funds to defend Rome from what would be the famous Sack of Rome, money that she felt was well invested.

Actually, Isabella was in Rome at the time of the sack. And the story of how she managed to escape it is worth a short digression, as it provides a fine example of the complex and powerful role she played in the tumultuous political world of her day. Perhaps the best place to begin is with her tense relations with her son Federigo, which had reportedly led her to move to Rome in the mid-1520s. Following the death of her husband, apparently from the syphilis that had crippled him in his later years, Federigo became duke in 1519. A *condottiere* like his father, Isabella had politicked for years to have him named captain general of the papal armies, a position with rich potential and prestige. Her efforts were crowned with success in 1522, but with that feather in his cap, and securely in power in Mantua, the young Federigo got taken up with other youthful interests – especially a young and reportedly aggressive mistress, Isabella Boschetti.

The youthful couple enjoyed a more sensuous courtly style reflected in their patronage of Giulio Romano (1499–1546), a noted architect and artist who designed the pleasure palace they had built on an island near the city, the Palazzo del Te. The paintings that decorated the palace, especially the *Wedding Feast of Cupid and Psyche*, completed in the late 1520s, portrayed an imagined pagan court that featured free-flowing wine, sensuous nudity, and a sexuality that evoked a vision of the courtly ideal quite different from that depicted in two paintings Isabella had commissioned earlier, Mantegna's, *Pallas Expelling the Vices from the Garden of Eden* (c. 1499–1502) and Perugino's, *The Battle of Love and Chastity* (1503–1505), where chastity and virtue are definitely the order of the day. Federigo also hired Correggio (1489–1534), earlier patronized by his mother, to give the Palazzo Ducale a more erotic tone with a series of paintings of the loves of Jupiter, the most famous of which is probably *Jupiter and Io*, which depicts the god disguised as a cloud enfolding the beautiful young Io in a sexual embrace.

Adding spice to tales of the sensual style of the couple and their court were the rumors, apparently untrue, that the infamous paintings of Giulio Romano known as *I Modi*, published as engravings by Antonio Raimondi, were actually designed for the Palazzo del Te. The original paintings, which were destroyed, are known only through the Raimondi engravings, but if they are any indication of the originals, their explicit depiction of sixteen sexual positions in classical dress – or, to be more exact, classical undress – left little to the imagination; they were certainly far distant from Isabella's patronized ideals of courtly chastity and virtue. And although Romano seems not to have created *I Modi* for Federigo, it appears that, for all his classical training and cultural reputation, his interest in the erotic art he did commission was more than merely classical, as was the case with many patrons who displayed a definite predilection for erotic classical themes. Such a predilection suggests yet another, less-discussed reason for a fascination with the classical world, the fact that it was often frankly and openly erotic, making sensual pleasures safely ancient, sophisticated, and acceptable, at least for the aristocratic upper classes – and yet another *rinascimento*.

Isabella, in her late forties and no prude herself, nonetheless was much more conscious of her image as a chaste and pious widow, albeit still presenting herself as a beautiful and lively one. Perhaps, then, the tensions with her son turned on a conflict more of images than of values. But for whatever reason, seeing her influence on the wane in Mantua, she headed to Rome in 1525, where her second son, Ercole, was a rising power in the Church and concentrated on advancing his career. There she set herself up in a palace of her own, where she gathered a new court and deployed the courtly skills that had made her such a power in Mantua. She quickly gathered a group of courtiers whose prestige supported hers and reconfirmed her importance and influence in a Rome rich with important and influential figures. And the Sack of Rome in 1527 offered the opportunity she needed to turn her Roman glory into a cardinal's hat for her son with the help of some ready cash.

Her negotiations with the Medici Pope, Clement VII (1478–1534; pope 1523–1534) quickly ended in success as imperial armies intent on capturing the pope approached a weakly defended Rome. Badly in need of money to hire soldiers to defend the city and himself, Clement traded five cardinal's hats for the funds he needed, and Isabella simply bought one for her son. For Clement, as we shall see, the money was too little and too late as imperial troops, encountering little resistance, entered and sacked the city in 1527. The pope and much of his court holed up in the papal fortress on the bend of the Tiber, Castel San Angelo, and survived. But most Romans were less fortunate, as the sack was exceptional for its destruction, brutality, and terror. Isabella and her palace, however, were protected because another of her sons, Ferrante, happened to be serving the emperor and was a commander in the army that took the city. With his help and the soldiers she had hired to defend her palace, she not only held out, but reportedly gave refuge to many.

In sum, she emerged from the disaster not just successful in gaining the cardinal's hat for her twenty-two-year-old son, but as a still more glorious figure and leader of note. Her return to Mantua was punctuated by a series of triumphant entries along the way and by celebrations of her as a leader and a personality in Italy and Europe. At home again in Mantua, she crowned Ercole with his cardinal's hat with great pageantry and in that moment of triumph declared to all that she remained a major player even if her first son, Federigo, ruled. The lesson was underscored, if it needed underscoring, in 1529 when she traveled to Bologna for the visit of the Emperor Charles V (1500–1558; emperor 1519–1556), where many of the political and cultural leaders of the day congregated for his formal coronation as emperor in 1530. She participated in the visit and coronation as a widely recognized, powerful figure on a par with the male leaders of Europe and, as we shall see, a number of the leading women as well. Her glory was evident to all. She had fashioned it over the course of her life with her patronage and cultural leadership; with the power she had cultivated in the Church, via her cardinal son and her close relationships with many of its leaders; with her significant ties to the emperor; and with the ongoing brilliance of her family's court in Mantua. What role she actually played at the coronation in Bologna is unclear, but it is not without significance that the emperor visited Mantua shortly after his coronation and kept a promise he had made to her by officially investing Federigo with his title of duke on the steps of the cathedral. At fifty-six, the self-styled chaste and religious widow was still a power to be reckoned with and quite a work of art.

Consensus realities and the negotiation of self in terms of self-fashioning have allowed us to begin to rethink how glory and fame worked, not just among the great like Isabella d'Este, but more broadly in the more aristocratic and courtly world of the high Rinascimento. And while Burckhardt wanted to discover the origins of nineteenth-century individuals in the glorious figures of his vision of the Renaissance, he may not have been as far off base as some have claimed. For while the individual in one way or another is a regular part of human society and certainly was not discovered in the Rinascimento, a new emphasis was placed on the way the self was fashioned, negotiated, and constructed in the intimate urban world of the day. That complex process of forming, contesting, and maintaining consensus realities became yet more significant in the more courtly and aristocratic world that progressively dominated upper-class life in the fifteenth century and thereafter and was reflected in a myriad of ways associated with more traditional ways of seeing Renaissance art, literature, and life in general. Thus, rather than discovering the individual, we might claim that the period created the individual as a work of art, in aristocrats and their courtly ways and dress, in scholars and artists, in upper-class women, and in the end, in art itself. And perhaps not so strangely, the aristocratic glory that they sought to fashion *with themselves*, although different in crucial ways, was not so far from the aristocratic world that Burckhardt *imagined* as his own. Officially old, that Rinascimento self-fashioning was decidedly new in its emphasis on glory and the individual as a work of art. Other, more troubling novelties, however, were intruding on the aristocratic self-confidence and self-celebration so central to that fashioning – and with them came storm clouds for the very idea of a Rinascimento.

8

DISCOVERY: FINDING THE OLD IN
THE NEW (c. 1450–c. 1560)

Printing, New/Old Books, and Dangerous Ideas

The story goes that when Cosimo de' Medici decided to build a library of the basic books most necessary for being a learned individual, he turned to the noted book dealer Vespasiano da Bisticci (1421–1498) to produce it. Vespasiano was well known for his abilities in this area. He had also worked with Pope Nicolas V and the duke of Urbino, Federico da Montefeltro, a noted *condottiere*, patron, and scholar, to build their famous book collections. On his advice Cosimo commissioned two hundred books. To produce them in the minimum of time, Vespesiano hired forty-five professional scribes who took twenty-two months to complete the task. This works out to each scribe taking approximately five months to produce one book in manuscript form. Vespasiano prided himself on the high, virtually artistic quality of his books, and there were many shops that could have produced hand-copied books more cheaply and more rapidly, employing the assembly-line techniques used for textbooks or legal and medical reference works, where each scribe repeatedly copied a small group of pages rather than the whole book.

Shortly after midcentury, however, the printing press arrived in Italy from Germany, and relatively quickly printed books began to appear, produced more rapidly and cheaply. Vespasiano, outraged at this novelty, which he saw as undercutting the artistic and cultural aesthetics of hand-copied books, retired to his country estate to write a collection of lives of the most famous men of his day, his *Vite d'uomini illustri del secolo XV* (*The Lives of Famous Men of the Fifteenth Century*), which included a brief biography of Cosimo. Evidently he felt that printed books fell into that dangerous and to-be-avoided category, "the new" – a novelty that he despised, not a positive innovation.

He was not alone. The ancient world and its culture had not had printed books; the Bible made no mention of them; furthermore, there was no hint of them in sacred literature, no forewarning to be glimpsed in the past. Here was something definitely new and thus, from the perspective of the Rinascimento, self-evidently dangerous. Yet, as the time and expense involved in the production of Cosimo's two hundred volumes suggests, this novelty had its appeal to both the commercial spirit and the intellectual world of the day; for there was a growing market for books among the literate public. Moreover, the profits to be made producing them more quickly and at lower cost, and the promise of a larger supply of more affordable books, added to the attraction. The question remained, however, how to deny the new in all this and demonstrate that it was in fact safely old.

That unlikely program – denying the new in order to claim the old – played a major role in the early stages of printing in Italy. First, most of the pioneering printers did not attempt to print books as cheaply as possible. Markets were still perceived as captured by the highest-quality products rather than by the lowest-priced; thus small-quantity luxury production was seen as the most profitable mode of producing cloth, furniture, housewares, and other products. From this perspective, in the early stages of what we think of today as the printing revolution in Italy, print shops focused on producing high-quality books that mimicked handwritten ones as much as possible. Experiments with typefaces thus tended to focus on three quality issues; first, artistic merit; second, creating a typeface that reproduced as closely as possible ancient Roman script; and third, clarity. Especially preferred were typefaces that reproduced the form of the letters found in the most ancient manuscripts still in existence, which contemporary scholars had favored for handwritten books because it was assumed that they were closest to the original Roman letters – a literal rebirth of ancient Roman letters. As the oldest manuscripts still existent tended to come from the period of the Carolingian revival in the early Middle Ages, it was actually forms of that script, Carolingian Miniscule, that were favored – making the letters of printed books, at least, old rather than new.

Early printed books also tended to be printed in a way that required considerable hand work to finish them into elegant pieces of artisanal workmanship competitive with earlier and contemporary hand-produced volumes. Elaborate bindings costing more than the printed work itself were virtually required at first and remained fashionable, especially with more aristocratic buyers. Moreover, early printed books were often produced without capitals for opening paragraphs or new sections of the volume. Artisans would add the missing capitals by hand, once more creating a more expensive and upscale product that added to the impression that the aesthetic nature of the book had not really changed with printing. Finely made paper and hand-done illustrations also raised the cost of early books and added to their aesthetic nature. All this helped maintain the status of a luxury product for printed books produced for an aristocratic book-buying public. Finally, the book was a luxury product that had a crucial additional value: it was a luxury product that opened a door onto the elite culture of the day, and during the Rinascimento that culture was heavily reliant on classic first times. Thus that window provided vistas of the ancient world, once again looking back on what was perceived as an aristocratic past, even as it used new technology to do so. That reality was reified by the simple fact that the first books printed in fifteenth-century Italy focused heavily on works from first times, both secular and religious.

It appears that the first printers in Italy were German artisans, Conrad Sweynheym and Arnold Pannartz, who worked from a Benedictine monastery in Subiaco not far from Rome in the mid-1460s. No copy of their first book, *Donatus pro puerulis* (*Donatus for Boys*), a Latin grammar textbook printed in 300 copies, exists. It was soon followed by Cicero's *De oratione* (*On Speaking*), printed in a more modest 275 copies, one of the most popular works of that canonical ancient author. Their first dated publication was printed in 1465, an edition of three works by the early Christian author Lactantius (c. 240–c. 320). Finally, a printing of 275 copies of Saint Augustine's *City of God* added one of the most important foundational Christian texts to their list. Thus their first published works in many ways presaged the agenda of the early printing industry in Italy: two classical authors, one religious classic, and one classic textbook for learning Latin. Virtually nothing was new here if one focused on content and was willing to overlook how their books had been produced.

Soon after publishing these works Sweynheym and Pannartz moved to Rome, which offered a more likely market for their books with its lively classical revival, its university, and its rich clerical culture encouraged by the newly returned papacy. Nonetheless, by the early 1470s their press was failing, undoubtedly aided in this by small print runs that continued in the range of 250 to 300 volumes; by an inability to produce on demand, which meant tying up limited capital in books waiting to be sold; and, more immediately, by the expense of producing a five-volume edition of Nicolaus of Lyra's *Expositiones* (*Commentaries on the Bible*). When the secretary of the Vatican Library wrote to Pope Sixtus IV in 1472 requesting that he rescue the press, he spoke highly of its importance and listed twenty-eight works that had already been produced. Approximately two-thirds were ancient

Latin texts, with most of the rest being religious works. Once again virtually nothing of these early printers and their books was new under the sun. The pope did supply some funds to keep them afloat, but they soon went under anyway. Perhaps beyond all the other problems they faced, their failure was ultimately due to the fact that they were unable to fully appreciate the extent to which they were producing something new and thus could not imagine the need to develop new strategies, still thinking in terms of producing and selling high-quality volumes on demand.

The lure of a larger supply of books produced more quickly and potentially more cheaply, however, was quickly picked up by others. Venice, making use of its strong connections with Germany, and with the aid of artisans from north of the Alps, early on became a leader in using the new technology. In fact, there have been attempts to suggest that the Venetians actually "invented" printing. Usually these claim that reports of moveable type used in China brought back by Venetian merchants encouraged experimentation in the city. As unlikely as it might seem, even Marco Polo (1254–1324) has been suggested, and fanciful accounts have tried to connect his descendants to early printing in the city. Well after the introduction of printing, the Venetian scholar, librarian, and patriot Marcantonio Sabellico wrote in the 1580s, in his *History of Venice*, that during the first years of the dogeship of Pasquale Malipiero (1392–1462; doge 1457–1462), "Among the other happy events of his Dogeship, it should be noted that for the first time the method of printing books was discovered in Italy – the same invention which it is believed was made by the Germans." Venetian chauvinism aside, it appears that printing did not get started in Venice until 1469, when a German, John of Spires, printed Cicero's *Epistolae ad familiars* (*Familiar Letters*) there.

Although he died shortly thereafter, his press continued. But it faced rapidly increasing competition. It has been estimated that more than 150 presses opened in Venice in the 1470s alone. During the same period presses were set up in Florence, Milan, and at least seven other Italian towns. One of the early leaders in the industry in Venice was Nicholas Jenson, a Frenchmen who had served as metallurgist at the mint of the French King Charles VII before moving to Mainz, where he mastered the new technologies associated with printing. Jenson migrated to Venice in 1468 and was soon operating a press that produced a large number of Latin classics in the 1470s, using his own particularly impressive Roman script, often seen as the prototype of modern typefaces. The publishing boom moved so rapidly that by the mid-seventies one angry scribe complained that Venice was "stuffed with books," a claim supported by rough estimates that by the middle of the decade 176 editions had been published there and that by 1480 the figure had jumped to 593.

It has been plausibly argued that by the end of the century approximately 4,000 editions of books had been published in Venice.

Actually this explosion of publications created problems for the printing industry. A number of Venetian presses failed in the early seventies, victims again of overproduction and an inability to sell stocks quickly enough to recover the capital invested in their production. The failures of the early period did not prevent new competitors from joining the fray, however, probably because setting up a press was relatively easy. The technology was fairly straightforward, with the largest costs and skills being required for producing and maintaining the typefaces – both of which drew upon artisanal skills in metalworking already well developed in Venice and much of Europe. Early presses apparently involved less technical innovation and seem to have been adaptations of various forms of presses used in making wine, oil, or the more complex processes for making and finishing cloth. As a result, they required little in the way of skilled labor and minimal costs to maintain and operate. Also, restrictive guild legislation that often limited innovation in more traditional skilled crafts was less a factor in this new industry, allowing for considerable freedom to innovate, as well as to exploit cheap labor.

It is interesting to consider in this context that with the metalworking skills necessary for producing fine types and the gearing of clocks (developed in the fourteenth century), Italian artisans had created the basic mechanical techniques necessary for an industrial revolution, especially given the milling techniques, long available, that had harnessed the power of moving water and wind. Yet even with a society deeply committed to a wide range of entrepreneurial investments, skilled artisans, and an impressive number of artisan/writers and scholars, no such revolution occurred. Impressive astrological clocks were produced that recreated the supposed movements of the heavens, and fantastic automatons and toys were produced for princes and courts. On a more practical level, some forms of cloth processing made use of water-driven hammers and processing techniques. Why this did not turn into an industrial revolution is a question historians tend to avoid, as history rightly focuses on what happened rather than speculating about what did not. Still, such conjunctures, which seem like missed opportunities in the past, call for speculation.

And as – to a degree, at least – such speculation turns on the very nature of the Rinascimento, it warrants a moment's highly hypothetical reflection. First, it may simply have been that printing was one of the few proto-industrial forms that could be contemplated, because, for all its newness, it was so deeply connected to the old that its newness could be largely overlooked. The social organization of production also undoubtedly played a role. Guilds controlled production and had progressively limited the work of women and children – the heavy lifters of the later industrial revolution – placing the emphasis on craftsmen who produced high-quality luxury products. Skilled craftsmen were not ready or available to become the mere "hands" of industrial production in sufficient numbers to make such production imaginable. This in turn suggests an additional factor, the lack of a felt need or markets for cheaply made mass-produced products. Just as large numbers of inexpensive books at first created problems for distribution and marketing, other products that might be produced in large quantities could not be marketed widely enough without railroads, canal systems, or more efficient forms of sea transport to make mass production viable or at least perceived as viable. The cheaper products for everyday use that were produced by hand – either at home, by women and children, or by local artisans in more limited quantities – fit the scale and the way production was organized by the guild system. And significantly, in all this traditional production nothing else dangerously new had to be reimagined as old.

The introduction of printing in Italy is also interesting because it complicates traditional ways of understanding technological change. Some scholars celebrate the introduction of printing as a triumph of lower-class artisans, whose mastery of the technique of printing was based on artisanal skill and traditional modes of passing on technical knowledge. For these scholars, the real innovation in the printing revolution came from below and strikes a blow against any trickle-down vision of cultural and technological advances. And, of course, they are right. At the same time, those who favor the idea that elites set the cultural course of society tend to see printing as a triumph of high culture; for what was printed by the presses were the texts of a high and increasingly aristocratic culture, and thus printing slowly but surely allowed that culture to trickle down to a broader society. And, of course, they are right as well. Yet ultimately the innovation and successes associated with printing, like many major changes, were much more complex than such simple oppositions suggest.

Actually, before printing based upon moveable type could even be considered, a number of preparatory changes had to occur. Perhaps most notably, as long as books and documents were written by hand on parchment, a mechanical form of reproducing texts made little sense. Parchment, after all, was made from the hides of animals. As each folio or pair of folios was usually one hide, it was simply too expensive to meet the demand for an affordable printing surface that could sustain the higher levels of book production that printing offered. In sum, until there was a relatively inexpensive medium of high enough quality to print upon, printing multiple copies of anything made little sense. Paper, although it had long been known in the East, and was seen from time to time in the West, only began to be used more widely in the fourteenth century in Europe, although parchment was still preferred for hand-copied books. Toward the end of the century one begins to see more and more ephemeral documents done on paper, rough drafts of things such as wills and minor contracts. In fact, it was probably the increasing use of these kinds of documents and their penetration into the daily lives of more common people in the urban world of the day that created a demand for cheaper paper – paper that cost less but came as close as possible to parchment in terms of its ability to endure over time. Whether or not this was the case, it is clear that at the turn of the fifteenth century paper was slowly but surely moving up, from more humble documents and texts to more important ones, until eventually only the most important documents or texts would be written on parchment.

The growing availability of paper may have had a deeper impact on the intellectual life of the day, for writing, in a way not often considered in histories, is a significant way of thinking and analyzing ideas at a deeper level. One need only look at a scholastic text from the Middle Ages to see a way of thinking that to a great degree relied upon writing out ideas and then breaking them down via dialectic in written form. Without necessarily following a strict dialectical method, writing out ideas essentially allows one to break them down and to analyze them from an ever-finer perspective, taking things much deeper than most people are capable of doing when merely thinking abstractly. But thinking with writing is a strategy that is not particularly easy to follow or even to envision at a time when writing materials are precious and not widely available. Before paper, then, writing on parchment meant that very few had the opportunity to think with writing. Glosses on parchment texts were widely employed, of course, and they represent a good example of the ability to think more deeply with writing, but the number of parchment texts remained limited by the cost and time it took to produce them. It may be, then, that as paper became more readily available, this form of thinking became more widely practicable and that working with one's ideas on paper eventually became a powerful, if often unrecognized, tool in a new way of thinking more deeply and exploring ideas.

At a more straightforward level, paper was also very important in the Rinascimento for the development of record keeping and bureaucracies for both business and government. Well into the fourteenth century, most contracts, wills, and business documents were written in highly abbreviated Latin on parchment, adding significantly to their cost. As paper became more widely available and less expensive, less important documents quickly made the shift to paper, and that aspect of business record keeping became cheaper and more widely used. Moreover, the complex system of abbreviations originally developed to make it possible to write more words in less space on expensive parchment became less essential. Texts, as a result, became more fully and more accurately spelled out and required less training to read. A significant decrease in the use of abbreviations also made printing more feasible, as it cut down the number of different characters necessary to print a text.

But where one notices the change paper wrought even more dramatically is in the significant increase in the number of records kept by government and governmental bureaucracies. The most important documents continued to be written on parchment, a reflection of their perceived significance. But progressively more everyday government business was recorded and kept on paper, with the sheer volume of paper records creating a mini-revolution that seemed to significantly improve the ability of government to control and discipline society. It would be unwise to claim too much for this small, largely unnoticed revolution in the technology of government, however, because while more could be recorded, the increased quantity of records kept actually made them more difficult to use or keep track of. Still, paper changed the level at which governments and bureaucracies could attempt to function and in the process greatly increased the quantity of historical records after the last years of the fourteenth century.

As far as printing is concerned, however, as cheaper paper became widely available, the crucial missing ingredient was available to make it viable. Presses, already widely used for many purposes, along with the technical skills earlier developed in metalworking, made it possible for artisans to develop fairly rapidly a printing press and moveable type that could cover the many more pages of paper available with text. From this perspective the printed book might seem largely a change driven by the incremental knowledge of artisans coming together with the increased availability of paper. But, of course, without a market for books, there was little need for such innovation. Significantly, that market had more potential than is often assumed. First, of course, the long-standing demand for classical texts on the part of scholars and upper-class intellectuals, along with more aristocratic buyers anxious to demonstrate their elite status, played a crucial role, even as some were not eager to see books become too inexpensive or common. Less recognized, but important, was that large segment of the population that had a desire to read the early texts of Christianity, or at least have them read to them, motivated by the religious enthusiasms of the day. University students and those already practicing law and medicine also provided a growing demand. Moreover, in the urban centers of much of Italy, where, as discussed in Chapter 5, a large segment of the populace was able to read, there was also a large potential demand. In sum, the market was there.

A sense of this explosion of books in Venice is provided by Marcantonio Sabellico, who around 1490 wrote a work defending the purity of the Latin language in the form of a dialogue, *De latinae linguae reparatione* (*On the Renewal of the Latin Language*), that includes a description of a walk through what is still the main shopping district of Venice, the Merceria, which stretches almost a kilometer from the Rialto Bridge to Saint Mark's Square. One person in the dialogue, a Venetian named Sararisius, takes his scholarly friend Juliarius through the area to show him the city's riches. They find the Merceria lined with bookstalls, and Juliarius, overwhelmed by the selection, tarries to examine the books for sale. Sararisius leaves his visitor to his browsing, continuing on to the main square, Saint Mark's, to conduct his business. When Sararisius finally returns several hours later, he finds Juliarius loaded down with his purchases and still exploring the titles available. In fact, it takes some coaxing to get his friend to leave this paradise of books, which sets off a discussion about whether such easy access to learning is a good idea for the general populace – an issue that troubled many who felt that knowledge should be limited to those capable of mastering its complexities. Still, the very fact that the question could be raised – and Juliarius's armload of books – provides a sense of how decisively printing had changed the world of knowledge in barely a generation.

Given its emphasis on the classics, printing soon followed the developing trajectory of classical studies, expanding from Latin to Greek (and eventually to other ancient languages). Two problems had to be overcome in order to make this transition: first, a workable Greek type had to be developed; second, scholars with enough training in Greek to edit and correct texts had to be found. In Florence, an important student of ancient Greek, Janus Lascaris, designed a Greek type wholly in capitals. With the help of a Venetian printer there, he produced the first published edition of Homer's *Illiad* in 1496, and over the next two years brought out at least five more editions of classic Greek texts. At much the same time, in the early 1490s, Aldus Manutius (1449–1515) opened a press of his own in Venice dedicated to publishing the Greek classics, a press that would have a long and distinguished publication record, printing many of the first editions of ancient Greek works.

Although he made his reputation in Venice, Manutius was actually born near Rome, and his early studies there focused on ancient Latin authors. For a time, he served as a secretary in the papal curia and lectured at the University of Rome on Latin topics. During that period it seems that Manutius met and developed a working relationship with the noted Greek scholar and cardinal Bessarion, whom he reportedly accompanied on a mission to France. Whether he actually traveled to France or not, he later studied Greek intensively in Ferrara with Battista Guarino, toward the end of the 1470s. Guarino was the son of the noted educator Guarino da Verona, who had perfected his Greek in Constantinople and spent several years in the East searching for lost Greek manuscripts at the turn of the century. During these same years he also made friends with Giovanni Pico della Mirandola and the circle of intellectuals fascinated with Greek that Pico had gathered around him in his hometown of Mirandola. For a while Manutius even served as a tutor to Pico's nephews, one of whom, Alberto Pio, would eventually help finance his early printing ventures in Venice.

Many of the contacts made in those early years were essential to his success as a publisher in Venice and allowed Aldus, when he arrived in Venice around 1490, to be received as a recognized scholar of the classics, well schooled in Greek and with impressive connections. The timing of his arrival, much like his training and development as a classical scholar, was uniquely favorable for the success of his publishing endeavors. For in those same years the brilliant intellectual culture of Florence, with its emphasis on the classics and especially on Greek works, was already declining, along with the health of Lorenzo de' Medici and that of his bank as well. As we shall see, the fall of Lorenzo's son Piero in 1494 and the return of republican rule, which quickly fell under the sway of religious reform enthusiasm that called into question the pagan nature of classical scholarship, created an exodus of scholarly talent that Aldus drew upon to augment the local Venetian scholarly tradition of Greek studies. Particularly important for that tradition was the long, close trading and cultural relationship that Venice had had with Constantinople and the Greek-speaking East; the strong tradition of Aristotelian studies at Venice's university city of Padua; and, perhaps most immediately relevant for Manutius, the impressive collection of Greek manuscripts that Cardinal Bessarion had left to the city upon his death in 1472. Venice, with perfect timing, had become the ideal place to publish the most important ancient Greek texts, and Manutius was the ideal person for the job.

His home and print shop in Venice soon became a kind of rallying place for Greek scholars, with reports, perhaps overly optimistic, that even everyday conversations were carried on in Greek there. Still, under his direction a new Greek typeface was created, modeled on the hand of a Cretan scholar, Marcus Mursius. Aldus's printed Greek books were particularly impressive; his most important editions were virtually works of art, printed on expensive paper and handsomely bound. From 1494 to 1515 he printed first editions in Greek of Aristotle, Aristophanes, Thucydides, Sophocles, Herodotus, Euripides, Xenophon, Demosthenes, Pindar, Aeschylus, Athenaeus, and Plato, among others. And while these publications were perhaps his most famous, he also published an impressive range of books in Latin and Italian, many in less expensive formats, including works by Dante, Petrarch, Bembo, and even Erasmus, who visited his shop while touring Italy and penned a not entirely complimentary account of its bustling activity.

After a little more than a generation of printing, the industry was well established in Italy and well on its way to immortalizing in multiple print copies the learning of the ancient world as well as the Rinascimento. And, tellingly, it seems clear that these early printed books were yet again seen as a rebirth of the ancient world, old and safe, rather than new and dangerous. Of course, that did not make the danger of their newness disappear, and fairly quickly the world of written culture would be laid open to a much larger audience, with unexpected and quite revolutionary results. One only has to think of the reform movements that swept Italy and Europe a few decades later, based in part on the reading of the Bible and the early texts of Christianity, now printed for the first time. The larger audience reached, which included large numbers of everyday religious people not trained as theologians or intellectuals, seemed to many to play an important role in the violent conflicts that followed – leading many to fear the negative potential of the newly widespread print culture.

These fears were frequently expressed. In the first half of the 1470s Filippo di Strata, a Dominican friar and copyist, wrote a damning account in Latin of the dangers of printing addressed to the doge of Venice, Nicolò Marcello, full of warnings. Filippo played most of the chords of its menace, stressing its newness and the fact that it was an innovation brought by foreigners, and lamenting that those foreigners were boorish and drunken at that. Later in the 1490s Filippo rehearsed most of these same themes in a diatribe against printing written in Italian, adding fastidiously that one could not walk down the street without being harassed by book dealers selling cheap books – in a way, the obverse of Sabellico's proud depiction of the Merceria and its book-stalls. Moreover, he complained that these printed volumes were badly done, illegibly printed, and edited by "ignorant fools" who did not know what they were doing. Yet, because of their lower prices, they were driving off the market carefully done, handwritten manuscripts produced by skilled scribes (like himself, it should be noted). Filippo went on to argue that this read-ily available knowledge was dangerous, because it gave the ignorant access to ideas and learning that they were incapable of handling. Even if this was the claim of an irate scribe, it was one that struck deep chords for an elite intellectual tradition that saw knowledge as essentially esoteric, a privilege of the few and the best. But in the end he stressed the greatest negative of all – the dangerous newness of printing, pointing out that if the world had endured for six thousand years (the widely accepted age of the Earth at the time, based on biblical calculations), there was little need now to take up something new.

Filippo was not merely an irate conservative crying out against the new. There was considerable truth to his claim that unscrupulous publishers, rushing to print their badly edited editions of classical authors, often provided inaccurate and corrupt texts, distorting the classics, and that their cheap editions often made it harder for better ones to be produced or to survive. Like Filippo, a number of critics also worried about the impact of cheaper, more widely available editions of classical works that were seen as dangerously pagan or obscene. One of the favorite targets for such attacks, and one of the favorite and most profitable texts of early publishers, was Ovid's *Metamorphoses*, discussed earlier. With its short stories that were often quite provocative, and sexually suggestive, portraying ancient life and the often risqué relationships between gods and humans, it titillated as it conveyed a troublingly fascinating pagan world and its culture. Many scholars claimed that such works when read by those who had the intellectual background to "correctly" understand them were not really dangerous, but when read by the young or the ignorant were full of dangerous and seductive ideas and errors. Such dangers were made worse as printers began to print cheaper editions and to translate such literature into Italian, making it available to an ever larger market.

Beyond pagan and risqué material, however, printing the first texts of the Christian tradition was seen as particularly dangerous. Especially troubling from this perspective was the printing in the vernacular of the Bible and the popular classics of the Christian tradition, such as compilations of saint's lives and *florilegia* – collections of short texts by classical authors or the Church Fathers that were seen as particularly meaningful. These publications, it was feared, had the potential to convince even the most uneducated and gullible that they had the ability to read such texts and understand them on their own. This, in turn, meant that every person could consider himself (or, more dangerously in the eyes of authorities, herself) a theologian. It was not that many people did not already have their own understanding of Christianity, often quite distant from what the leaders of the Church and theologians held, but rather that they could now support their views with reference to the classic texts of Christianity. In essence, they too could return to first times, with texts in the language they used every day, to defend their own religious beliefs. This certainly gave added impetus to the religious ferment of the day; to various reform movements eventually labeled heretical; and ultimately to the Reformation and the Catholic Reformation as well. In sum, even as it disguised itself as old and offered to return to the beginnings of many beliefs and first times, this new beast of printing was disseminating the dangerous seeds of change and the new.

Invasions and New Political Realities

In contrast to printing, initially at least, the invasion of Italy in 1494 led by the young and inexperienced French King Charles VIII (1470–1498; ruled 1483–1498) to assert his dynastic claims to Naples seemed nothing new at all. European kings and emperors had regularly threatened to assert their dynastic claims to various parts of Italy and had even, every now and then, attempted to realize those threats, with little or no success. In fact, the results had frequently been disastrous for them, which, as discussed earlier, meant that the city-states of Italy had largely been left free to follow their own des-tinies in war and politics. If anything, trans-Alpine powers had been viewed for almost two centuries more as pawns of Italian city-states than as feared invaders. Charles also made the traditional and highly unlikely-sounding claim that taking Naples was just the first step in his crusading plans to free the Holy Land and Constantinople from the Turks. As such, it was easily dismissed as merely another sign of his youthful incompetence and the pro-jected failure of the whole unlikely venture. All this seemed to mark him out as an excellent pawn for more powerful and clever Italian leaders to use for their own immediate ends.

At the same time, the city-states of Italy seemed in many ways stronger than ever. Tuscany was dominated by an apparently powerful Florence, hav-ing executed a relatively smooth transition of power, following the death of Lorenzo de' Medici, to Lorenzo's yet more aristocratic and princely son Piero (1472–1503). Milan ruled with relative calm most of the western por-tion of the Lombard plain, under the increasingly powerful hand of Ludovico Il Moro Sforza (1452–1508), who governed in the name of the young heir Gian Galeazzo Sforza. Most of the eastern Lombard plain and much of the coast of the Adriatic, along with a maritime empire that cut deeply into the eastern Mediterranean, was controlled by the republic of Venice, reputed to be one of the richest and most powerful states in Europe. In Rome, the popes were back. And, although powerful families from the Iberian penin-sula had gained a foothold in the bureaucracy of the Church in order to compete with Italian and French prelates and had even managed to win the papacy itself, popes had been largely successful in their program of becoming Italian princes. Even the more contentious south of the peninsula seemed to have settled down, with the Aragonese in control of the kingdom of Naples and apparently quite capable of standing up to the young Charles's distant dynastic claims.

Appearances, however, were deceiving. Italian confidence that Charles would quickly fail was unwarranted. A closer look at the Italian situation in 1494 gives the lie to the rosy picture just sketched. Florence did control most of Tuscany. Pisa was under her direct rule, as was the port city of Leghorn (today Livorno), and although Siena and Lucca remained independent, they were essentially humbler companions of Florence. But economically, especially in the international arena, the power of the city had fallen off considerably. The Medici bank, following years of mismanagement and bad loans, was on the verge of collapse. Other banking families were in a stronger position, but the era of Florentine banking dominating the papacy and Europe was over. The once-powerful cloth industry of the city had also fallen into decline, with northern European producers undercutting Florentine markets with less expensive imitations of similar quality as well as with cheaper products. At the same time, more organized and aggressive northern European governments were taxing Italian cloth more heavily or actually restricting its entry into their lands, in order to encourage their own production. As part of this move to encourage local production, northern rulers were also making it more difficult to obtain the higher-quality raw wool so essential to the production of Florentine luxury cloth. Turning to trade, Florentine commerce was essentially a carrying trade, transporting goods to and from the city, and with the decline in cloth production and the international banking network that went with it, a good deal of this trade was drying up as well. Finally, Lorenzo's magnificent rule and his wars had been costly, and the government of the city was heavily in debt, which severely limited its ability to spend the money necessary to defend itself. In sum, although still rich in appearance, the city had feet of clay, and, in fact, many intellectuals were voting with their feet and deserting the city for richer climes and patrons.

In the end, however, Medici leadership may have been the biggest problem of all. The sixteenth-century statesmen, political theorist, and historian Francesco Guicciardini (1483–1540) certainly thought so, dismissing the young Piero de' Medici as "the eldest of Lorenzo's three sons, still very young and not qualified either by age or understanding to carry so heavy a burden, nor capable of governing with that moderation with which his father had ruled." In 1492, when he took up the officially invisible Medici rule of the city, he was barely twenty, still a callow youth by the standards of the day. Two years later, as Charles moved into Italy, Piero was already facing growing Florentine discontent caused by a number of unpopular and inept decisions. Perhaps most notably, early on he broke off Florence's alliance with Milan, which dated back to the time of Cosimo, in order to align with Naples.

Unpopular and perhaps as unwise as contemporaries claimed, that move had its logic when one realizes that Piero's mother was Clarice Orsini – from that old Roman noble family, long important power brokers in papal politics and allies of Naples. Moreover, his brother Giovanni de' Medici (1475–1521) was already a cardinal in Rome and, although only in his late teens, busily building a power base with Orsini support that would win him the papacy at the early age of thirty-eight, in 1513, as Pope Leo X. Still, the move was problematic. Significantly, it put him at loggerheads with the then Borgia Pope, Alexander VI (1431–1503; pope 1492–1503). The pope's election had been as strongly supported by Milan as it had been opposed by the Orsini; thus Piero, by following the Orsini lead and switching his alliance from Milan to Naples, angered both Milan and a dangerous Borgia pope.

But to appreciate fully the issues involved, a closer look at Milan in 1494 is necessary. Economically, its mini-empire in the western Lombard plain remained financially solid, with its balance of agriculture, local banking, local industry, and local trade. The main exceptions to this local economy were its highly-thought-of arms industry and its power over a number of the Alpine passes that to a degree controlled overland trade with northern Europe. Socially, it featured a well-established aristocratic society that at the highest levels had built significant ties with European aristocratic families outside of Italy. It was those aristocratic ties, however, that had placed the de facto ruler of Milan, Ludovico Sforza, known as Il Moro, in jeopardy and made him even more concerned about Piero's switching of alliances. Actually, before the aristocratic and courtly turn of the fifteenth century, *popolo grosso* elites had tended to intermarry locally, seeing non-Italian aristocratic families as largely irrelevant to their social and economic world and goals. Among the first to break this unwritten taboo were the families of *signori* who had risen to power in the fourteenth century, often seeing such foreign marriage ties as offering potential allies to help in local struggles, and as offering greater prestige and legitimacy for their rule. In fact, the Visconti lords of Milan were among the most aggressive in using what has been called bedroom diplomacy – marriage alliances to build dynastic strength that transcended the local.

From this perspective, Ludovico Il Moro's problems can be traced back at least to that famous enemy of Florence, Gian Galeazzo Visconti. Gian

Galeazzo, seeking allies against the anti-Viscontean league organized by the Florentines in the late 1380s, married his daughter Valentina to Louis of Orléans, brother of the French king, in 1386. The dynastic ramifications of that distant moment were haunting Ludovico il Moro more than a century later, which gives one some sense of the power and danger of such marriages. The problem was, of course, that the legitimate Visconti line of rulers had ended with the death of Filippo Maria Visconti in 1447. That succession crisis had been overcome with the marriage of Visconti's illegitimate daughter Bianca to Francesco Sforza, the founder of the Sforza line. But when Galeazzo Maria Sforza, son of Francesco, died in 1476, his heir was his son Gian Galeazzo Maria Sforza (1469–1494), who was too young to rule. Ludovico, the most aggressive of his father's brothers, quickly established himself as the tutor of his young nephew and slowly but surely pushed him aside, becoming the de facto ruler of the city.

To this point, although there may be more Galeazzos and Gian Galeazzos involved than might be desired for clarity, things were still relatively straightforward – Ludovico was doubly illegitimate. He was not the legitimate heir of the Sforza line, nor was the Sforza line all that legitimate in its own right, descending from a match between an illegitimate daughter of the Visconti and a *condottiere*, Francesco Sforza. Meanwhile, a legitimate branch of the Visconti line had moved to France with the marriage of Valentina to the duke of Orléans, and, to make matters more complex, that theoretically legitimate claim had passed down to the duke's grandson, Louis, Duke of Orléans, who, getting ahead of the story, would become king of France himself in 1498.

Unfortunately, things were not so simple. More immediately, Ludovico faced the claims of the family of Gian Galeazzo's wife, Isabella, for the young Sforza in 1494 was no longer a boy, but rather a young man in his early twenties who should have been ruling on his own. His wife, Isabella, was the granddaughter of Ferrante, King of Naples, and the daughter of his son Alfonso, Duke of Calabria. She, again in the style of aristocratic bedroom diplomacy, had been literally invested in marriage to the future duke of Milan. For her and her family, then, it was time for Ludovico to step aside so that they could reap the benefits of their investment. And here, finally, is where the deeper problem of Piero de' Medici's switching alliances comes in; for the Orsini family in Rome were not just tied to the Medici in Florence, they were also closely tied to Isabella and Ferrante of Naples. Thus, Piero's switching alliances clearly threatened Ludovico, proclaiming that he had lost an important ally to the very family that was contesting his hold on power in Milan. That meant in turn that Charles's planned invasion of Italy to make good his claims to Naples seemed to Ludovico a boon rather than a threat and was thus to be encouraged.

In turn, Ferrante (c. 1431–1494; ruled 1458–1494) in Naples had problems of his own, even before Charles VIII decided to assert his claims to rule his kingdom. Most notably, he ruled an unwieldy nobility made up of families that reflected the contested history of the region. Normans, Aragonese, Italians, and French had all tried their hand at dominating the area, with varying degrees of success; and Ferrante as king was merely the latest claimant, who had to work out his compromises with the various nobles who actually controlled the land. Many were of questionable loyalty, especially as Ferrante himself was noted for his aggressive attempts to strengthen his rule at their expense. In addition, his kingdom included a highly variegated mix of economies. Much of the land was held by his noble barons and farmed in a quasi-feudal fashion or used for pasturage. And although such areas produced significant amounts of food and raw materials for the rest of Italy, this was often accomplished using inefficient methods and a high level of exploitation that encouraged peasant unrest. Moreover, this agricultural economy did not produce the kind of tax base for Ferrante that the urban-based economies of the north enjoyed, forcing him to rely heavily on feudal levies along with a limited number of *condottieri* in his military operations. The city of Naples was, of course, a major urban center, and it was there that he centered his court. But it was mainly an administrative center and commercial hub, relying heavily on foreign bankers and foreign luxury products. As a result, it tended to be more a consumer than a producer of wealth, in contrast to the cities of the north.

The complex series of wars and marriages that had brought Ferrante's father, Alfonso, to power were recounted in Chapter 6. At his death, however, Ferrante, who was his illegitimate son, faced a number of opponents who were anxious to deny his claims to the throne, including the house of Anjou, led by Jean of Anjou, who had a strong hereditary claim, and much of the local nobility eager to escape what they saw as the heavy hand of the Aragonese. But Pope Pius II, seeking a crusading ally, eventually supported Ferrante's claim, both verbally and militarily. Thanks to Pius, with some of the most powerful papal *condottieri* at his side Ferrante eventually defeated Jean and put down his rebellious nobles; thus, six years after his father's death, he finally ruled. His reign followed much in the pattern of his father, with a mix of cruel repression, heavy taxation, and a brilliant court, although division and unrest plagued him at every level, from peasants and nobles in the countryside to plebs and nobles in Naples itself.

Turning to Rome, in 1492 a Spaniard, Rodrigo Lanzo e Borja, was elected Pope Alexander VI, reputedly helped by the votes of the Sforza family cardinal, Ascanio Sforza, in exchange for a promise of a large sum of money. Borgia, as his name was rendered in Italian, was perhaps both the most famous and most infamous pope of the Rinascimento. His nepotism was notorious, and not just for his son Cesare Borgia or his often-married daughter Lucrezia Borgia; for Rome and Italy were virtually overrun by Borgia family members seeking to make their fortune on the back of their pope. Recently scholars have attempted to rehabilitate Alexander, pointing out the brilliance of his court and his patronage, and his impressive building program. He was also a successful defender of papal power and the ideal of a princely pope, based upon a firm territorial base in the center of Italy. That he was ruthless in the pursuit of these goals, however, cannot be denied, and many who stood in the way of his plans for a strong papacy and a strong Borgia family in Italy found themselves pushed aside or simply dead.

The licentiousness of his court, his family, and his personal perversities may have been exaggerated by critics, and even by some of his supporters, but his numerous *nipoti* (a polite euphemism for illegitimate children) and acknowledged mistresses suggest that he enjoyed his sexual life and at times flaunted it. Yet in a way, an active and productive sexual life was just another aspect of the masculinity expected of a true Rinascimento prince. And Alexander played the role to the hilt. When he was made pope, he was so taken with his new mistress, the young and beautiful Giulia Farnese, wife of the Roman noble Orsino Orsini, that he made little attempt to keep the relationship secret, and it was the talk of the town. In fact, shortly after he became pope she gave birth to a daughter whom he recognized as his own and named Laura, perhaps after Petrarch's own love. Nonetheless, in his own way, he was also loyal to his earlier long-term mistress, Vannozza Cattanei, who had given birth to four of his children, including Lucrezia and Cesare, continuing to support her even as he found new companions.

In the tensions leading up to the French invasion, Alexander played a typically vacillating role aimed at gaining the maximum advantage for himself and his family. On the one hand, he continued a long-standing papal animosity to the Aragonese rule in Naples that stretched at least as far back as his uncle Pope Calixtus III (1378–1458; pope 1455–1458), who had turned against his former Aragonese allies in an attempt to reassert papal claims to the territory, apparently in order to reward his own rapacious branch of the family with lands there. Geography also played a role, as Neapolitan territory bordered the Papal States to the south and seemed to offer enticing opportunities for expansion that might benefit Borgia's voracious relatives.

Certainly Piero de' Medici's switching from Florence's traditional alliance with Milan to Naples, given the pope's obligations to the Sforza family, merely gave Borgia additional reasons to oppose the Aragonese in Naples. Thus in early 1493 the pope concluded an alliance with Milan and Venice as a means to counterbalance that between Piero's Florence and Ferrante's Naples. And to seal the deal, he married his daughter, Lucrezia Borgia, for the second time to Giovanni Sforza, lord of Pesaro, annulling her earlier marriage.

It appears that during this period he also encouraged Ludovico Il Moro, who needed little encouragement, to support the planned French invasion in order to put pressure on Ferrante to relinquish his daughter's claims to rule Milan with her husband, Gian Galeazzo. The pope, however, played both sides of the fence, as was his wont, by marrying his son Goffredo to Ferrante's granddaughter. This was followed in short order by an attempt to get all the Italian parties to agree to a pact to keep the French out of Italy, which failed as virtually everyone had already chosen sides. When Charles did invade in 1494, again Alexander played both sides of the fence, first aligning with Naples, but doing little to aid those attempting to block the invasion, then switching to the French side when Rome was faced by the French army at its gates and rebellion within, led by his old enemies the Orsini.

Venice might have remained neutral in this conflict, which was, at least officially, between distant France and relatively distant Naples, but Aragonese pretensions on the Adriatic coast of Italy and in the Mediterranean had created tensions between the two powers. Moreover, Charles's interest in a crusade to defeat the Turks and retake the Holy Land was attractive to Venice, even if there was a great deal about it that seemed unlikely. With the Aragonese as enemies of the French, if the crusading idea ever became a reality, Charles would need a naval power to aid him, and Venice stood to profit as a major naval power that he could rely upon. Once again, then, for the Venetians, using the French as a pawn in their political and economic strategies seemed attractive.

The young Charles VIII certainly seemed to most in Italy to be an ideal pawn. At twenty-four, he had just taken up rule, pushing aside his sister, who had served as regent since the death of his father in 1483. Guicciardini, with considerable exaggeration and more than a bit of wishful thinking, described the young man as physically weak and unhealthy, small in stature, ugly and ungainly, barely able to read or write, and totally dominated by his unworthy favorites. Although he wrote a generation after the invasion, his low opinion of the man was widely shared as Charles marched into Italy. This serious misjudgment reveals the weakness of judging a kingdom solely by its leader or his reputation. Great rulers, great generals – great men or women in general, for that matter – are all well and good, but often they are only as good as the resources they command. And there has been no shortage of mediocre figures who have triumphed over their personally superior adversaries because they commanded superior resources. In many ways, then, Charles's lack of acumen or good looks was irrelevant. The key to the success of his invasion was that it was not actually his invasion at all, but a French invasion with all that that implied, a reality that the Italians seriously underestimated.

For France was undergoing a transition from a semifeudal state, where the resources available in its vast territory were marshaled only with difficulty, to an early form of the nation-state, with considerably more effective revenue collection, bureaucracy, and ability to actually utilize its resources. Although it was still a long way from being one, it was becoming far more able to focus its extensive resources on prosecuting a war. In this context, scale had always been the heart of the matter and remained so. Previously the smaller scale of the Italian city-states and their more advanced bureaucracies, better suited to the more manageable size of their urban societies, had allowed them to mobilize their wealth for war more effectively, although wars, as we have seen, almost always pressed their economies to the limit. Larger-scale states like France and England, however, had lacked the economies, social structures, and bureaucracies to effectively mobilize the potentially much greater wealth available given their size; thus, although it may seem counterintuitive, in many ways the Italian city-states had been more competitive than their northern neighbors and Mediterranean powers across the fourteenth and fifteenth centuries precisely because of their smaller scale.

But that was changing. The northern European Hundred Years' War had ended in the early 1450s. The French King Louis XI (1423–1483; reigned 1461–1483) shortly thereafter aggressively began to limit the power of the French nobility and build an Italian-style royal bureaucracy, based less on court favorites and more on non-noble lawyers and notaries – innovations often pioneered in the Italian city-states of the thirteenth and fourteenth centuries and exported with Italian merchants, bureaucrats, and notaries in the years that followed. He also suppressed the Estates General, calling the body only once during his reign, and at that meeting he essentially took over the right to collect traditional taxes without the Estates' permission. Using these funds, he built up a standing army and, perhaps more importantly, paid the larger and more professional bureaucracy that he used to administer his realm more effectively and attempted to limit the power of the French nobility. Although Louis became less effective in his later years, the kingdom that Charles inherited was one in which the country's potentially great resources were much more available. And that meant that even if he lived down to Guicciardini's negative evaluation of him as a person and ruler, France was no longer a pawn.

Perhaps more immediately important was the fact that in the eyes of many contemporaries Charles had a better dynastic claim to rule Naples than did Ferrante. René of Anjou had been the adopted son and legal heir of Queen Joanna when she died in 1435. But he had not been strong enough to assert his claim against Alfonso of Aragon, as we have seen. Thus, after defeating René, Alfonso became king and passed his rule on to his illegitimate son Ferrante. Meanwhile, back in France, a sister of René married the French King Charles VII, who inherited the claim to Naples through his wife when René died. Thus Charles VIII found himself the legitimate heir to the Neapolitan throne as the legitimate son of Louis XI, who was in turn the legitimate son of Charles VII, faced off against an illegitimate son (Ferrante) of an illegitimate conqueror of that throne.

There is more that could be said about the messy dynastic complications of Charles's invasion, but suffice it to say Charles had a strong claim and, practically speaking, a surprisingly strong proto-nation-state to support it. In sum, the game had changed: the new was about to arrive, and it would be a new that would transform the Rinascimento across the board, finishing the political independence of most of the city-states of the penisula; beginning a long diaspora of its culture and political and social ideals throughout the West and the world; and setting off a gradual transformation of Italian society into what is often labeled the European Renaissance. As far as Charles was concerned, he had the power to succeed; he had the dynastic claims to succeed; and Italy offered him the riches to make his invasion possible and worthwhile. Unfortunately, for him and for Italy, he was not the only one in that situation. In these basic prerequisites, he was joined by Spain and the Holy Roman Empire. Together they would turn Italy into Europe's battleground for at least two generations, inaugurating what has been labeled the Age of the Italian Wars.

The French Invasion

Charles and his French army crossed the Alps in 1494. Almost immediately things did not conform to Italian expectations. Guicciardini noted in his account of the invasion that the advisors to the French king were "men of low condition" (*piccola condizione*) rather than "nobles." But that meant that it was an invasion that would be organized by advisors and a bureaucracy serving the crown and less subject to the intrigues and whims of aristocratic nobles and favorites. Guicciardini noted that the same was true of the army itself. It did have a significant number of traditional noblemen fighting on horseback and raised by feudal levy. But it also had a large, well-trained infantry capable of standing up to a cavalry charge, which brought the invading force up to about 20,000 men – a large but hardly overwhelming force. More importantly, however, it had small, light, mobile artillery that would play a crucial role in the French success.

The contrasts with the Italian armies that it would face, however, were significant and seemed to heavily favor the Italians. The famed Italian *condottieri*, still reputedly the best professional soldiers in Europe, fought mainly on horseback like the French nobility, but their superiority came from their better training and tactics, especially their ability to fight in tight formations, due in part to that training and in part to the crueler bit that was used to keep their horses under tighter control. Because of the expensive training and limited manpower available, these cavalry tactics tended to involve much smaller numbers or at least smaller corps of top-quality soldiers. The numbers of professional foot soldiers were swelled by local militias, poorly trained and lightly armed, that seldom were seen as crucial in gaining victories. The Italian powers were most sure of their superiority, however, in fortifications. Most cities and towns had strong walls that could withstand long sieges. In fact, often it was those who besieged Italian towns, whiling away long summer months in unsanitary conditions, who found their armies wasting away due to illness and lack of resources. Thus the Italian strategy was straightforward. As the French, in order to secure their lines of supply, would need to capture the major fortifications along the route from the north of Italy to Naples, they would simply allow the French to take on a series of sieges that would drag on for months, and sooner or later they would lose their enthusiasm or their lives.

Virtually everyone was confident that in the end a realignment in Italy that would reveal the true winners and losers would be worked out and that the French would slink home, once again used as pawns and discarded. As the invasion got under way Gian Galeazzo Sforza in Milan died of mysterious causes, some claiming that his death was caused by his insatiable sexual appetites, others concluding, more cynically, that he had been poisoned by his uncle and erstwhile protector, Ludovico Il Moro. Whatever the cause, this seemed to decisively change the political situation, as Ludovico gained control in Milan, and Naples, at least theoretically, was no longer a threat to his rule. It seemed to many that Ludovico had made good use of Charles to create a distraction that allowed him to eliminate his problems with his nephew and with Naples, and that Charles could now safely be abandoned to his fate, to lose and leave.

But that was not to be. Once again Guicciardini depicts the surprise and then the terror of the Italians when the first major fortified town that resisted the French army, instead of sustaining a long siege, quickly fell and was given over to a bloody sack. The French then moved on and rapidly took the next town, again putting it to the sword. With the advantage of hindsight Guicciardini attributed these rapid victories to the small, light artillery of the French, which he described as "lighter [than Italian canons] and all cast in bronze ... [which] shot at very short intervals ... and could be used as effectively in the field as in battering walls." Although Italian *condottieri* armies had used large cannons from the second half of the fourteenth century, they had never been particularly effective. Used more to create terror and confusion, *condottieri* tended to favor outsized cannon that, much like medieval *trebuchets*, fired large stones or iron balls. Unwieldy and slow, they were as likely to explode and destroy their crews as they were to actually damage the enemy.

The French light artillery, by contrast, fired a more standardized shot, fairly rapidly, and, wheeled and lighter, was quite mobile. Thus the French, faced with their first walled town, wheeled their artillery up to close range and, with rapid and repeated bombardment, quickly reduced the walls to rubble, entered with ease, and brutally destroyed the city and its populace. The lesson was clear. Things had changed. Once again the new had reared its ugly head, with disastrous results that were difficult to deny. Fortified towns could no longer count on their walls to protect them. And instead of the French army being mired in one siege after another as they moved south toward Naples, they found one town after another opening its gates and welcoming them before speeding them on their way south to Florence, Rome, and Naples.

The unexpectedly rapid advance threw all three cities into turmoil. As usual, Florence was unprepared to fight, and the weakness of Piero de' Medici only added to the problems. Most importantly, the city lacked the resources to field a major army, and there was little hope for much support from its allies. Meanwhile, the Borgia pope was switching sides with alacrity, attempting to find an alliance that would gain him some profit from the invasion while sparing Rome a sack. In Naples, Ferrante had picked the right time to die, early in 1494, before the invasion got under way, leaving his son Alfonso II in charge and the kingdom in turmoil.

In sum, with his opposition in disarray, Charles and his army moved south rather like a knife cutting through warm butter. As he approached Florentine territory Piero de Medici was faced with a dilemma: his alliance with Naples required that he oppose the French advance, but he lacked an army to do so. A defeat and a sack of Florence seemed imminent. Piero, like his father, Lorenzo, before him, tried what he hoped would be perceived as a courageous and heroic move. He left the city and went to meet the French army to negotiate a peace that would save the day. Unlike his father, however, he had little with which to negotiate. As a result, in the end he capitulated, promising to open the gates of the city to the French and ally with them against Naples in return for a promise that Florence would not be sacked. That essentially was the end of Piero and the first Medici rule, for after briefly returning to the city, he fled into exile. His opposition quickly reinstated a republican government to replace the theoretically republican sixty-year rule of the Medici (1434–1494).

The first problem the new government faced was Charles VIII and his army. For in early November 1494, when he marched into the city through the reluctantly opened gates with his army, he rode with his lance ostentatiously at rest, a traditional sign of a conquering general rather than a visiting ally. In a society acutely attuned to gestures, that gesture was not lost on the Florentines. Evidently Charles was claiming more than a mere alliance, perhaps even indicating that Florence was his by right of conquest. When the king's secretary confirmed Florentine fears by reading an ultimatum that claimed the city for the French, Piero Capponi, a leader of the new government, supposedly ripped the document from the secretary's hands, tore it to shreds, and threw it on the ground, proclaiming that Florence would never accept such terms. Almost certainly the French, better armed and better disciplined, would have won eventually had they decided to press their claims. But "eventually" was the key term that saved the day, for Charles was on the way to Naples, and he apparently did not want to be held up fighting a determined Florentine resistance, street by street and house by house, when he had already neutralized the city and was free to proceed to his real objective without any loss of troops or time.

In the end he negotiated a sizeable indemnity and the ceding of some important territory, and then moved south, leaving Florence to lick its wounds and try to work out the complicated process of reestablishing a republic. At the end of November the French army was already at the gates of Rome. Pope Alexander, like the Florentines, was unprepared. His last switch of alliances had been in favor of Alfonso II of Naples, and as the French army had advanced with one success after another, his opponents in Rome, seeing an opportunity to gain an advantage at the pope's expense, were in attack mode. The Colonna family had taken Rome's port city of Ostia. Within the city, the Orsini family had risen against him as well. As this left him in a difficult situation, he did what he perhaps did best: he changed sides once more and allied with the French, albeit very cautiously. He opened the gates of the city to Charles after securing a promise of their peaceful passage, but carefully locked himself in the papal fortress, Castel San'Angelo, just in case. Charles in turn negotiated a costly alliance with the pope and continued his inexorable march south.

If lack of preparation and internal dissension had bedeviled Florence and Rome, Alfonso's Naples made those cities seem models of organization and solidarity. Never popular with his barons or the city itself, the French army bearing down on Naples brought his family's popularity to an all-time low. Adding to the tension, upon entering Neapolitan territory Charles quickly took two fortified border towns and massacred the inhabitants. Alfonso sent his son Fernando II (1467–1496; officially king 1495–1496), called Ferrandino, along with his brother to face the French, but they were unable to stop Charles's advance and slowly retreated to Naples as the year ended. With things collapsing around him, Alfonso did the fatherly thing and abdicated in favor of his more popular son Ferrandino, withdrawing to a monastery where he soon died, perhaps even of natural causes. As the cities of Capua and Gaeta fell to the French, Naples rebelled and opened the gates of the city to the French army. Ferrandino fled to Sicily, which he would use as a base to regain his short-lived kingship.

But for the moment Charles and the French had traversed much of the Italian peninsula, easily overcoming some of the most important powers of the day, and taken Naples in less than a year. The lesson was not lost on other European powers. Rich and full of treasures, the cities of Italy seemed to be there for the taking. And, significantly, their riches would in the end more than pay for the cost of doing so. In the face of that new reality, the Italian city-states felt that they needed to make a show of their strength and drive the French from the peninsula immediately. Ludovico Il Moro, with Milan securely in hand, had been growing more worried as the French successes mounted; the Venetians shared his concern, especially as they saw their potential enemy Naples fall before the French; the pope was also anxious to see his new "allies," the French, driven out. North of the Alps, the Emperor Maximilian was worried that Charles might take more of Italy or even transform his new Italian "allies" into subjects, a concern shared by Spain as well. The result was a league comprised of much of Italy and Europe, known as the League of Venice or the Italian League, that forged an alliance against the French and began raising an army to drive Charles from Italy.

Recognizing the danger, Charles left the duke of Montpensier in Naples with a strong force to protect his conquest until he could return and headed north. As he passed through Florence, the city stayed loyal to its French alliance, but as the army moved north over the Apennines, the League raced to intercept and defeat Charles before he could escape from Italy. Their army, led by the noted Italian *condottiere* Francesco II Gonzaga, lord of Mantua and husband of Isabella d'Este, met the French at Fornovo di Taro on July 6, 1496. Had the French lost the battle, far from home and with little in the way of support in Italy, it might well have meant the demise of the young king and of French pretensions in Italy. In the end, however, both sides claimed victory, and in a way both lost. Gonzaga had the larger army and in many ways had the best of the fighting, with the French taking heavy losses and losing much of the spoils that they were carrying back to France. Yet the French managed to fight their way free and hurriedly carried their triumphant king back over the Alps. In the short run, notwithstanding French promises to return and support their troops left in Naples, Ferrandino, with the help of Aragon and Venice, drove the unpopular French garrison out of the city after only a year, in July of 1496.

For the moment it might have seemed as if the French invasion had been undone and that things had returned safely to the status quo. Ferrandino and the house of Aragon were back in Naples; Alexander and the Borgia clan were back in the saddle in central Italy; Florence was no longer in the hands of the Medici, but it was a republic again; Ludovico had Milan more strongly in hand than ever; and Venice remained strong, rich, and apparently invincible, at least in Italy. But almost no one was taken in by such appearances. The French clearly had every intention of returning and not only asserting their claims in Naples, but apparently also of taking advantage of dynastic claims to overthrow their enemies in Italy, especially Ludovico il Moro in Milan. The emperor was also deeply interested in reasserting his claims to Milan and making himself a power in the rest of the peninsula. And, of course, Aragon was anxious to defend its power in the south, and perhaps expand it northward, at the expense of the papacy. Moreover, the papacy remained rapacious with its own territorial goals. Clearly a return to the status quo was out of the question, and in the end the real question was how long Italy would remain a battleground before a new balance of power could be established. The most optimistic response to that question today would claim about two generations, until the peace of Cateau-Cambrésis (1559), signed by the major powers of Europe, carved up Italy into a limited number of city-states largely dominated by the Hapsburgs, with some under direct Spanish rule (Milan, Naples, and Sicily), some clients of Spain (Genoa), and almost all of the rest closely tied to the larger nation-states of Europe or the

Holy Roman Empire. The new had arrived, and Italy was no longer on its own, politically independent of the larger European powers.

Italy as a Battleground: The Unlikely War of the League of Cambrai (1509–1516)

The wars of those two generations are a quagmire of dynastic politics and incessant fighting that would require too much space to narrate here. But one of the more trying moments of those decades of war is worth a closer look, for it involved the fall and rise of Venice, the one Italian power that managed to survive independent across that period of travail and did so in a manner that confirmed its myth of republican longevity and stability – a myth that would have a significant impact on the political vision of the day and the Western republican tradition. On December 10, 1508, most of the leaders of Europe met at Cambrai, including Louis XII of France (1462–1515; ruled 1498–1515), who had succeeded Charles VIII; Maximilian I, the Holy Roman Emperor (1459–1519; emperor 1493–1519); Ferdinand, "the Catholic" King of Spain (1452–1516); and Pope Julius II (1443–1513; pope 1503–1513), former and future enemies all. Yet they formed a league to conquer and divide the one territorial state in Italy that seemed to remain a threat to their various plans for Italy. Their intended victim, Venice, appeared to be an unlikely mix of paradoxes: a republican city-state-empire in an age increasingly dominated by princely nation-states; a republic led by a nobility; a trading city with a substantial agricultural hinterland; a naval power able to field large and effective land armies; and an unusually open and free city that often was quite closed. It was also, more straightforwardly, rich and powerful – enticingly so.

Perhaps the most important immediate motivation for the formation of the League was Venetian expansion into territory in the center of Italy that had traditionally belonged to the papacy. At the end of the fifteenth century and in the first years of the sixteenth, Cesare Borgia (1475–1507) had taken advantage of the military and political confusion of the moment to ally with the French to carve out for himself a small state in the Romagna, with an unusual brutality and lack of regard for the traditional rules of war that made him hated, feared, and respected by many, including Machiavelli. When his father, Pope Alexander VI, suddenly died in 1503, Cesare, who was already making inroads into Tuscany, was caught unprepared. Ill himself, he was unable to influence the election of a new pope or to protect his conquests; thus he became the victim of those anxious to divide up his growing ministate. Venice was first in line. Uncomfortable with the power of the aggressive Borgia on their southern mainland borders, they gobbled up a group of cities in the area, including Faenza, Rimini, Ravenna, and Cervia. Many feared that this was part of a Venetian plan of expansion to gain control of the whole Adriatic coast east of the Apennines and become the dominant power in the peninsula, creating a territorial state that included the eastern half of Italy from the middle of the Lombard plain down the eastern coast of the peninsula, threatening not only the Papal States and the kingdom of Naples but all who hoped to rule in Italy.

Obviously this did not sit well with the new pope, Julius II, whose own goal was to reintegrate Borgia's mini-empire back into the Papal States. Julius was a different breed of pope and Renaissance prince. His lack of *virtù*, at least as Machiavelli envisioned it – especially careful planning and diplomatic maneuvering – deeply troubled the author of *The Prince*, who saw his impetuousness and penchant for direct, virtually unpremeditated action as totally wrong, but disconcertingly successful. In fact, Machiavelli's representation of the pope provides such a perfect foil for his own vision of the way a *virtù*-ous prince should behave that it must be taken with a grain of salt. Still, it seems clear that Julius was a warrior pope, who preferred action to careful preparations or negotiations. In 1505, feeling that negotiations with the French King Louis XII over dividing up the ex-Borgia lands in Italy were stalled, he reportedly put on his armor and headed north to personally take the territories he claimed as part of the Papal States.

Perugia was the first major city that he attempted to regain. Sitting atop an easily defended hill on the road north from Rome to the Apennine passes to the north, the city was well defended by its lord, Giampaolo Baglioni, who was noted for his violence, intrigues, and willingness to do whatever was necessary to maintain power – apparently a perfect foil for the impetuous Julius. Arriving before Perugia, the pope asked to meet with Baglioni; entered the city virtually without troops; and demanded that Giampaolo respect papal rights to the city or face the consequences. To Machiavelli's later amazement, rather than dispatching his enemy, as one might expect of a tough and unscrupulous tyrant, Baglioni, who had the undefended pope in his hands, capitulated. Later, in *The Prince*, Machiavelli pointed out that while Giampaolo had committed both incest and parricide in order to secure his rule, like many other princes famous for their lack of morality and cruelty he had lacked the courage or the understanding to use it wisely at crucial moments and simply eliminate Julius and his claims with one brutal deed.

Continuing north, the pope and his army attacked Bologna, which was held by another, more powerful *signore*, Giovanni Bentivoglio. Bologna was a crucial strategic stronghold and the largest city of the Papal States. Even Cesare Borgia, with all his military and diplomatic skill, had not been able to take it. But where Cesare's *virtù* had failed in Machiavelli's eyes, again much to his distress, the pope succeeded. Arriving with his army before the walls of the city and realizing that he had caught Bentivoglio unprepared, Julius attacked immediately. Machiavelli ruefully reports that the pope actually scaled the walls of the city in full battle armor and from their heights oversaw the attack. Although the sixty-four-year-old pope scaling the walls of Bologna in battle armor provides a striking and questionable image, it does say much about how Machiavelli and his contemporaries had come to see popes as warriors and princes, ready to defend their territorial claims. With the fall of Bologna, Venetian and papal territories had come face to face – and that meant, sooner or later, conflict. On the one hand, once north of the Apennines the pope was in a position to reclaim the cities that Venice had taken on the eastern side of the peninsula and block any further Venetian expansion to the south. On the other, as Bologna controlled the main passes to the south, the Venetians saw a threat not only to their expansion in the region, but also to their main north/south trade route.

As if this were not enough, the pope was unhappy with a well-established Venetian tradition of control of its local clergy and independence vis-à-vis the papacy. Like many Italian cities, it had taken advantage of the absence of the papacy in Avignon to assert a greater power over the local Church and to divert its resources to Venetian ends. Julius, however, was anxious to cut back such inroads on papal authority; thus, as an opening gambit, he attempted to deny the Venetians the right to appoint bishops in their territories. In theory, this had always been the right of the papacy, but Venice had long elected its own bishops, formally asking the papacy for approval only after the fact. As a result it had become a Venetian practice that local bishoprics were used to reward noble sons of powerful families, who had entered the Church to diversify family fortunes and as bishoprics usually included handsome incomes, such sinecures had become an important part of Venetian noble fortunes. But when the city attempted in 1507 to appoint the bishop of Vicenza, a major city in their mainland empire, Julius blocked the appointment, claiming the right to name his own bishop. The Venetians, in the end, won and successfully forced the pope to accept their appointee, but that was only the first battle in what would become a war.

As noted earlier, the pope had no lack of powerful potential allies who shared his displeasure with the Venetians. The other power with pretensions to world dominance, the Emperor Maximilian I, had his own immediate grievances with the city. It seems that Maximilian had become concerned that the French King Louis XII was growing too powerful in Italy and, along with his growing territorial claims, was planning to have himself made emperor, while at the same time making one of his French cardinals pope to replace Julius. To block any such plans, Maximilian aligned with the king of Aragon, with the aim of asserting his traditional claims to Milan and Genoa. This would have thwarted any greater plans Louis had in Italy and made the emperor a major power in the peninsula. But among other problems, his plan to make good his claims to Milan required that his army pass through Venetian territory. Obviously, Venice was not enthusiastic about the emperor becoming their neighbor ruling Milan and eastern Lombardy. Moreover, in their own mini-empire they held many cities that had traditionally been subject to imperial rule, to which the emperor could easily advance claims. Finally, he was a nearer potential enemy than the French, with lines of communication that required regular passage through Venetian territories, and this evidently increased the danger that he would decide to transform any alliance, even a short-term one, into dominance. Thus the Venetians drew a line in the sand and said, "No."

The emperor decided to pass through Venetian territory anyway, perhaps hoping that his boldness and the size of his army would force the Venetians to back down. But Venice was a rich city with an ability to quickly raise a significant *condottiere* army. And no sooner had Maximilian crossed the eastern border of their mainland territories in 1508 than he was soundly defeated by their army and forced to beat a hasty retreat. To make matters worse, the peace treaty imposed on the emperor was particularly humiliating and crippling for imperial pretensions in Italy, as he was forced to relinquish Trieste, his port city on the Adriatic, and other lesser cities in the area. Having come to Italy to establish himself as a major power there, he found not only that had his plans been thwarted, but that the Venetians had forced him to give up what foothold he had once had there. This humiliation led Maximilian to do the virtually unthinkable, to unite with his traditional enemy Louis XII to destroy Venice.

Louis had his own grievances with Venice. In the early stages of the wars following Charles VIII's invasion, France had expanded its territories in Italy, managing to take Milan and much of the western Lombard plain, asserting their dynastic claims there. As a result, his Milanese state was now bordered on the east by Venice's own mainland state, and the tensions along that uncertain border were palpable. Moreover, cities like Cremona, Brescia, and Bergamo, now held by Venice, had until fairly recently been under Milanese control, and Louis, never one loathe to demand territory that he believed belonged to him, was eager to assert his claims. Thus the

ambassadors of the emperor and the king came together at Cambrai, ostensibly to make peace between the two traditional enemies, but in reality to
draw up plans to carve up the Venetian mini-empire among themselves.
The result was the League of Cambrai, pitting the major powers of Europe
against Venice.

It was feeding time among the sharks. The League's plans envisioned that
the pope would get the Romagna; the emperor would get Friuli and the
eastern part of Venice's mainland empire; the king of Hungary would get
the territory Venice controlled along the eastern side of the Adriatic; the
duke of Savoy would get Cyprus; the king of France would get the rest of
Lombardy not taken by the emperor; the king of Aragon would get all the
Venetian territory on the eastern coast of southern Italy; and the smaller,
still independent cities of Mantua and Ferrara would get assorted tidbits in
their local spheres of influence. It seemed evident that Venice did not stand
a chance against this coalition. But there were chinks in the league's armor
right from the start. Neither the pope nor the king of Aragon had participated in the negotiations and thus might reject the agreement. In fact, Julius
did attempt to work out a separate deal with Venice, offering to withdraw
from the League if they would give him the territory and assurances he
wanted. But the Venetians refused, and the pope retaliated by officially joining the league and excommunicating the city for good measure.

Excommunicated and facing most of Europe, Venice mobilized its
resources for the impending war. They bought a *condottiere* army of about
20,000 professional soldiers, supplemented by light cavalry brought in from
Venice's territories in the east, primarily Greeks and Albanians. This army
was led by two *condottieri*: Bartolomeo d'Alviano, a young, aggressive rising
star; and the count of Pitigliano, older, more experienced, more careful, and
in command in the field. Final command, however, remained in the hands
of the Venetian Senate. Attempting to wage a war with an army led by a
large legislative body seems a dubious strategy. But the Senate's overall tactics made sense – avoid battle for as long as possible, confident that it was
only a matter of time before the unlikely group allied against them would
collapse. Those best-laid plans failed almost immediately, however, founder-
ing on the reported impetuousness of the young *condottiere* d'Alviano. Given
the Venetian preference for older, more experienced leaders and senatorial
control of the war, there may be some reason to doubt accounts that emphasized the Senate's wisdom and a young general's impetuous desire for glory.
Still, the story goes that d'Alviano, camped with his troops near the small
town of Agnadello and waiting impatiently for instructions from the Senate,
noted that the enemy forces gathering nearby were quite disorganized and

apparently vulnerable. Thus he decided to take matters into his own hands and strike before the League was ready.

As he attacked, the battle cry of the Venetian army, "*Italia e Libertà*," powerfully evoked the way Venice sought to present the war to contemporaries. "Italy and Liberty" made the city the defenders of Italian liberty in a way that emphasized their self-fashioned mythic role as an enduring and safely old republic in a new world of dangerous change. The cry of "Liberty" also evoked Venice's republican tradition, which had in an earlier day been the rallying cry of republics like Venice and Florence against Gian Galeazzo Visconti and other tyrants who had threatened Italian liberty and *civiltà*. Evocative battle cries do not by themselves win battles, however, and after some initial successes the League troops rallied and won the day. In this they were greatly aided by the fact that the other Venetian general, Pitigliano, did not bring up his troops to support d'Alviano. Unwilling to go against the Senate's orders not to engage the enemy, he held back his soldiers and eventually withdrew. The result was disastrous, especially as Pitigliano's retreating forces found themselves locked out of the cities of the Venetian mainland empire, apparently anxious to be liberated from Venetian rule. Thus the retreat turned into a rout, and the Battle of Agnadello (1509) became perhaps Venice's most ignominious defeat.

Venice, its mainland empire lost at virtually one blow and its army badly beaten, seemed to have lost the war with the first battle. The League's troops gathered victorious on the shore and gazed at their soon-to-be prize, the fabled entrepot of Venice lying virtually undefended on the open waters of the lagoon. But in this case nothing failed like success. With the city lying there for the taking, the leaders of the League hesitated, ostensibly to work out a strategy to cross the lagoons and take their prize, but in reality to maneuver among themselves to see who would gain the maximum advantage. As they jockeyed for position, the mainland cities of the ex-Venetian mainland empire began to get their first bitter taste of their liberation from Venice. The conquerors, having spent large sums raising their armies, were anxious to see immediate profits. Thus their new taxes and other excuses for raising revenues were unusually aggressive and made Venetian rule seem light-handed by comparison. Moreover, the local nobility, which had largely been kept in check by Venice, took advantage of the situation to try to reassert their old noble prerogatives, prerogatives that were often seen as the normal order of things by their new imperial and French overlords. Already by the midsummer of 1509 murmurings from the mainland were being heard in Venice, and on July 18 Venetian troops, suddenly appearing before the gates of Padua, were let into the city as the Paduans rallied the populace with the cry "Marco, Marco." The republic of San Marco was back.

This success not only threatened the League's lines of supply and communication, it also added to the climate of distrust among the unlikely allies in the League – a distrust that the Venetians were more than willing to exploit. The first to break ranks was Pope Julius II, who had never been entirely convinced by the idea of strengthening the French in Italy. He had designs on Ferrara, once at the northern edge of the Papal States. The city was particularly attractive because it controlled the main fords over the Po River and thus was in a position to block both the main east/west river artery that opened the Lombard plain as well as one of the main roads to the north where it crossed that river. The French in Milan would never have accepted Julius's gaining that city, but Venice was more than willing to encourage his hopes in order to break up the League. In short order the pope announced the formation of a new league, the Holy League, with the slogan "*Fuori i Barbari.*" The "*barbari*" or barbarians to be pushed out (*fuori*) were the French, even if the League in its enthusiasm apparently overlooked the fact that many of their number were themselves *barbari*. This new league included the pope and Venice, along with the king of Aragon and the Swiss (mercenaries who had previously been fighting for the French). Maximilian was content to sit on the fence and wait to see if the League would eliminate the French, saving him the necessity of doing so himself.

The Holy League eventually fought a major battle against the French at Ravenna in April of 1512. And although they lost, outmatched by the superiority of the French troops and their famous general, Gaston de Foix, fortunately for Julius and the Venetians, Gaston was killed in the battle, and the French troops withdrew without pressing their victory. In fact, without their best general, and also lacking the Swiss mercenaries who had played such an important role in their earlier successes, the French were slowly driven out of Italy. But for that to have ended the war would have been far too simple for the complexity of the European battleground that Italy had become. Venice took advantage of the Holy League and the retreat of the French to retake much of its mainland empire, but to finish the task they turned on their former allies and aligned with the French. After several more years of war and with the aid of a new French king, Francis I (1494–1547; ruled 1515–1547), they finally recovered virtually all of their mainland empire, which stretched once again from Brescia in the west to halfway down the eastern Adriatic coast in the east. Phoenix-like, the republic had risen from the ashes of defeat at the hands of virtually all of Europe and in less than a decade reestablished its former prominence in Italy and Europe.

The War of the League of Cambrai (1509–1516), however, was far from the end of the new European wars in Italy. As noted earlier, things settled down a bit only after midcentury with the Treaty of Cateau-Cambrésis (1559), when a new balance of power was established in Italy based on a series of dynastic alliances – bedroom diplomacy again – stabilized a new status quo in the peninsula. In the last years of his long reign, Francis I essentially gave up his Italian claims in return for Burgundy, nearer to home and one of the richest regions of Europe. Charles V (1500–1558; emperor 1519–1556), Maximilian's successor, was the ultimate winner, and through a fortunate and wise series of dynastic moves the Habsburg ruler and emperor gained Spain, most of the "New World" (new, of course, only from a European perspective), much of Germany, Austria, southern Italy and Sicily, Milan and the western Lombard plain, and exerted a strong influence over many cities in Italy, including Florence and Genoa. The papacy, weakened by the conflicts of the first half of the century associated with the Reformation, settled for as much of the traditional Papal States as they could hold against the interests of rapacious neighbors and powers from outside the peninsula.

But Venice remained a republic and the primary independent Italian city-state, a model of success and survival that to a greater or lesser extent would be copied by other states that saw themselves as republics, including England and much later the new United States of America. As an agricultural mini-empire in the north of Italy, Venice was unusually aggressive and entrepreneurial in its approach to farming, introducing new crops from the "New World" and the East and experimenting with new techniques to get the most profit from the land. Problems with the Turks would continue to plague the other major source of its wealth, the city's powerful international trade economy – problems that were compounded in the short run by the Portuguese circumnavigation of Africa, which created a direct trade connection with the Far East that allowed them to undercut Venetian prices for spices and silks, the staples of Venetian long-distance trade. Recent research, however, suggests that Venice continued to compete in both markets with some success. In the long run, however, it was the opening of the "New World" to European exploration and exploitation that would slowly but surely create an Atlantic economy and "civilization." That new future would literally change the geography of the world, leaving the Mediterranean basin no longer the sea at the heart of the West, but progressively a periphery of an Atlantic world – or, perhaps more accurately, a world of ocean empires – to which Venice's much more humble Mediterranean empire was no longer central. Once again the dangerously new struck at the heart of even the toughest of Rinascimento survivors like Venice.

"New Worlds" for "Old"

At first, given the Rinascimento view of the world, Europeans were reluctant to see the "New World" as new. The first explorers hoped and believed that the lands they had discovered were merely the outer reaches of the Far East, a territory long known. The people they encountered were seen as the lost tribes described in the Bible or other ancient texts or simply as "Indians" in the sense of distant tribes of the Indian subcontinent. But slowly, and unwillingly, the Rinascimento had to admit that the world that had been discovered was "new." Of course, it was actually old, but from the Eurocentric vision of the day, it was new, devastatingly so: it was not in the Bible; it was not in ancient Latin texts; it was not in the Greek classics; it was not in the supposed earlier texts that had impressed Ficino and many others (at least not without some extremely convoluted readings). This helps to explain why Europeans, even after they began to call it the "New World," and to marvel at the many new and wondrous things found there, continued with grim determination to attempt to force virtually every new thing encountered into a familiar ancient mold, almost as if it had to be old, had to be found in earlier first times until the contrary was absolutely undeniable.

In this ongoing quest to find the old in the new a great deal of intellectual effort was invested, now largely forgotten because, from a modern perspective, it seems so clearly a dead end. Yet, in a way, for our history of the Rinascimento, this was yet another and major sign of the beginning of the end – an unavoidable rent in a vision of the world that saw the return to the past glories of the ancient world or first Christian times as the correct answer to every question. Finally a "new" had arrived that could not easily be assimilated, and it came with teeth, an economic, social, and political bite that would change the order of Italian and European society irrevocably. The Rinascimento was being transformed from a powerful movement of return to a perfect first time into merely a chimera. Such a drastic rupture in the shared primary culture of the day, however, took time to sink in fully, and in the interim the challenges of the new – not just in the New World but across the board – helped to create an extremely fertile ferment of ideas and dreams in that shared primary culture, for, of course, endings can be as fertile as beginnings.

A closer look at this discovery of a "New World" is in order, then, even if the most important events apparently happened far from the confines of Italy and the Italian Rinascimento. For not only did those discoveries undermine the Rinascimento, they also helped open a broader world to it. The basic events are well known and require only a quick review. In 1469

Ferdinand of Aragon married Isabella of Castile, and the couple eventually inherited the two monarchies that had emerged from the conflicts of medieval Iberia, loosely uniting them. After many setbacks, the couple finished the physical reconquest (the famed *Reconquista*) of the last Muslim kingdom of Spain, conquering the kingdom of Granada in the first days of 1492, aided greatly in the last phases by divisions within the Muslim ruling family. But even before this success, they had been eyeing the northern coast of Africa as an area of potential expansion that would extend the powers that they already claimed in the central Mediterranean, most notably in Sicily and the south of Italy. This Mediterranean reach, as we have seen, had previously involved the new kingdom of Castile and Aragon in the Italian world, following in this a long Aragonese tradition.

Another important Mediterranean connection that was a significant factor in opening the Iberian peninsula to the Rinascimento was the role that the commercial and banking city of Genoa played in Spanish affairs. In fact, Genoese bankers and Genoese immigrants were deeply involved in the economic, political, and cultural life of the late fifteenth-century Iberian peninsula, a role that was to grow even more important across the sixteenth century as New World silver and gold flowed into Spain and Europe, radically changing the economic resources of European society. Although there is some debate on the matter, it appears that Christopher Columbus (Cristoforo Colombo) was one of these Genoese immigrants. For some time he had been trying to find support for his scheme to reach the spice-rich lands of the Far East by sailing to the west. Discounting the heroic myths of his trials in Spain seeking support, it appears that he actually found there a number of powerful patrons, including the queen's treasurer, several religious leaders, and members of the king's household, as well as the support of the powerful Genoese banker Francesco da Pinedo – all of whom were interested in his project.

With the support of these patrons, Ferdinand and Isabella were eventually convinced to sign an agreement with Columbus in April 1491 that divvied up the rights and responsibilities of both sides in the planned voyages and ordered the authorities at the port of Palos (Huelva) to provide the ships and supplies necessary. It appears, however, that the actual funding for his first voyage was largely provided by money raised in the Queen's name by her minister Luis de Santangel and funds provided by Columbus himself, with the support of the Genoese community and the seafaring owners of two of the vessels that made the voyage, the Pinta and the Niña. The third vessel, the Santa Maria, was provided by the seafarer Juan de la Cosa and, as the largest, served as Columbus's flagship. The ships sailed from Palos on

August 3, 1492, and, aided by the favoring South Atlantic trade winds that still carry hurricanes from Africa to the Caribbean in the late summer and early fall, they made first landfall on October 12 on an island that Columbus called San Salvador. It is generally agreed that this was one of the islands that today make up the Bahamas, but there remains debate about which one. He explored the area, never actually touching the mainland of North or South America but visiting several islands, including what would become Haiti and Cuba.

In a famed letter to Santangel that described the "great victory" he had won on that first voyage, Columbus wrote,

> As I know that you will be pleased at the great victory with which Our Lord has crowned my voyage, I write this to you, which will explain to you how ... I passed from the Canary Islands to the Indies.... And there I found many islands filled with innumerable people, and I have taken possession of them all for their highnesses, by proclamation and with the royal standard unfurled and no opposition was offered to me. To the first island which I found, I gave the name San Salvador, in remembrance of the Divine Majesty, Who has marvelously bestowed all this; the Indians call it 'Guanahani.' To the second, I gave the name Isla de Santa María de Concepción; to the third, Fernandina; to the fourth, Isabella ... and so to each one I gave a new name.

Perhaps unwittingly like Adam in Genesis, taking his power from his Spanish monarchs and God, he named the world he encountered and, tellingly, renamed it with names of the old world, making it safely old.

In his rich analysis of this letter and the first encounters between Columbus and the inhabitants of the new world, Steven Greenblatt points out the many levels of cultural miscommunication and misunderstanding involved and stresses the trope of the marvelous and wondrous nature of the things and people encountered. But the Italian's claims to ownership, also prominent in the letter, as Greenblatt suggests, were based on much more practical "realities." For the letter reports Columbus's "victory" (as if in battle) and how he took possession of the lands and peoples he encountered following regular juridical and ceremonial procedures: "by proclamation and with the royal standard unfurled, and no opposition was offered to me." While the subtleties of Greenblatt's argument cannot be reproduced here, it is worth pointing out that underlying Columbus's certainty that European legal forms applied and that his ceremonial deeds, along with God's support, actually allowed him to claim these lands, was his conviction that this was not a "new" and different world, but merely the uncivilized far edge of the old world that was already known, where traditional rules of that old world still applied. Of course, the real Indies did not subscribe to European legal and ceremonial forms either, but European contacts with the real Indies tended to reveal similar assumptions that European cultural norms were universal and God-given from the original first times of humanity.

This attempt to deny the new is suggestively underlined by formal instructions given to another explorer in the service of Spain two decades later, when it had become clearer that the "New World" was actually not the "old" Indies. These new, more aggressive, and carefully constructed legal requirements seem to suggest that part of the process of claiming new lands was to first make them old and European:

> The manner that you must have in the taking of new lands ... is to be that you shall make before a notary public and the greatest possible number of witnesses ... an act of possession in our name, cutting trees and boughs, and digging or making, if there be an opportunity, some small building, which should be in a part where there is some marked hill or a large tree ... and you shall make a gallows there, and somebody bring a complaint upon you, and as our captain and judge you shall pronounce upon and determine it, so that in all, you shall take the said possession.

To take the land literally involved transforming it from something new and unmarked by European ways into a space organized by traditional European culture – trees are trimmed; the land is dug; a building is built; and, most tellingly, a gallows is constructed and, if possible, justice is carried out. A dangerously "new" natural order required transformation into a civilized European space; thus in the process it was incorporated into the old world order, safely becoming no longer new and dangerous. In a way these instructions seem an eerie echo of the early fourteenth-century Sienese frescoes on good government by Ambrogio Lorenzetti in the Palazzo Pubblico – and not by chance, for the Spanish conquerors were using the forms of Roman law developed by that much earlier first Rinascimento in their attempt to reduce the new to an ordered old and secure.

Returning to Columbus's first voyage: after a little more than three month's sailing in the region, early in 1493, he caught the winter trade winds that carried him back to Spain in a voyage of just slightly less than two months. There he claimed "victory" and to have successfully reached the eastern edges of Asia. Columbus made three more voyages – the last in 1502 – to a world that from the very start resisted being what he and his supporters wanted it to be. With each voyage it became clearer that what they had found was not the far reaches of Asia, but a land previously unknown to Europeans, a "New World," at least from the perspective of the old. Columbus, however, died shortly after his fourth voyage, apparently still disappointed with his failure to find the riches of Asia. Some accounts report that in his last years he had become infatuated with his own central role in God's plan for human history, seeing himself in terms that seemed to echo the prophecies of Joachim of Fiore, claiming that he was the prophesized leader bringing humanity into a new last age. In a rather strange way there was some truth to his claim, for his "discoveries" and the impressive series of "news" that came with them eventually did usher in what might be called a new age, although perhaps not the last, and certainly far distant from the one Joachim envisioned.

In 1497 another Italian, born in Genoa but a Venetian citizen, Giovanni Caboto (more generally recognized in the English-speaking world as John Cabot [c. 1450–c. 1498]), sought to find a shorter route to the East, sailing for the English. Reportedly encountering Columbus after his return from his first voyage and reflecting on accounts of the lands that the latter had discovered, he doubted that the explorer had actually reached Asia. In turn, correctly surmising that a round Earth would be more quickly traversed by sailing as close to the poles as possible, because the distance would be reduced by the Earth's curvature, he offered the English king, Henry VII, a proposal to reach the East by sailing west via a shorter northern passage – something that presumably was attractive to the king because it would move England from the periphery of trade with the East to a central position. His proposal was supported by fishermen in the coastal city of Bristol, who had been sailing to the west in the North Atlantic for some time. Although they were secretive about the locations of the fishing areas discovered, it appears that they had been fishing off the coast of Iceland and perhaps Newfoundland, or even the coast of the future North America. Whether or not that was the case – and it has been used to suggest an earlier English discovery of the "New World" – it seems that they were ready to support Cabot. Thus, just five years after Columbus's more famous voyage, Caboto sailed from Bristol with one small ship, the Matthew, named after his Venetian wife, Mattea, and a crew of eighteen to discover a northern passage to Asia. What he found was the large island of Newfoundland, which he understood was not his goal, given its size and its small, non-Asian population.

The next year a larger expedition of five vessels was authorized to push on to the trading centers of the East. Tragically, only one ship returned, having left Caboto and his fleet as it pressed further west and disappeared from history. Following this failure there is some debate about whether this Italian/English quest for a northern passage was taken up by his son, Sebastian, in 1507. He claimed that a voyage he led in that year actually found a passage blocked by ice. Whether or not that voyage actually occurred, shortly thereafter, following the accession to the English throne of Henry VIII, who did not share his father's interest in exploration, Sebastian left England and managed to get himself appointed Spanish pilot major, thus continuing a Spanish/ Italian connection in exploration that remained important for much of the sixteenth century. With that title the junior Caboto was responsible for training and approving a generation of navigators in the fleets that Spain sent to the "New World." He also led an expedition to the Rio de la Plata region in what would become South America. Meanwhile, he maintained contact with his native city of Venice, reportedly attempting to sell the Venetians on the idea of financing further exploration for a northern passage. In addition, he corresponded with the Venetian writer Giovanni Battista Ramusio, who subsequently published one of the first collections of travelers' accounts of the new discoveries that were changing the very nature of the world. Its popularity gave those discoveries and the explorers who made them, like the Cabotos, an important Italian dimension.

Much the same was true of the Portuguese exploration of the western coast of Africa, begun early in the fifteenth century. Early on they too had made use of Italian sailors and sailing techniques. In the 1450s, for example, under the auspices of Henry the Navigator (1394–1460), the Italians Antoniotto Usodimare, Alvise da Cà da Mosto, and Antonio da Noli led voyages that reached and explored Senegal, Gambia, and the Cape Verde islands. Although exploration of the African coast is often cited as Henry's primary motivation for these expeditions, African slaves and gold made them profitable ventures. It has been estimated that in the second half of the century more than 17 metric tons of gold and some 150,000 African slaves were brought to Europe by the Portuguese, along with sugar, pepper, and ivory, with Genoese bankers serving as important middlemen in these transactions. Political and dynastic turmoil distracted Portuguese exploration for a time, but with the reign of John II (1455–1495; ruled 1477–1495; officially king 1481–1495) more aggressive exploration again became the order of the day. Even before John gained the throne, he had been put in charge of the exploitation of the African coastal territories that the Portuguese had opened with their voyages. Then, as king, he reinvigorated Portuguese exploration and pressed more aggressively to open a sea route to the Indies. Discoveries followed rapidly: 1482–83, the Congo and Cape Saint Mary; 1485, Cape Cross; and finally, in 1488, Bartholomew Diaz rounded what would later be called the Cape of Good Hope only to find another vast expanse of sea – almost 1,300 miles to be traversed before the East was actually reached. Once again political turmoil and the death of the king postponed what was becoming the inevitable, but finally, in 1498, Vasco di Gama succeeded where Columbus had failed, reaching the port of Calicut in India by sailing around Africa.

Even before this success, however, John had entered into negotiations with Spain over the division of the discoveries that Portugal and Spain were making. Spain, taking advantage of the fact that the pope at the time was a Borgia, Alexander VI, convinced him to issue a bull on May 4, 1493, that sidestepped the negotiations to Spain's advantage, officially dividing new discoveries between Spain and Portugal on a vertical line drawn from the North to the South Pole. Portugal, realizing that they had been had by the Borgia pope, threatened war. But in the end compromise won out, and with the Treaty of Todesillas (1494), the two powers agreed to a more equitable division that gave the Portuguese what would become the actual sea route to the East and much of what would become Brazil as well, while Spain gained what they hoped would be a shorter and more profitable route to the riches of the East. That hope turned out to be in vain. But, of course, what they actually gained would become the "New World," rich beyond belief with gold, silver, and a host of resources. In terms of gold and silver alone it has been estimated that these "new" lands supplied approximately 70 percent of the world supply of gold and 85 percent of its silver between the end of the fifteenth century and the beginning of the nineteenth. And within 60 years of Columbus's discoveries at least 100 tons of gold and some 16,000 tons of silver had been carried back to Europe, often extracted at a devastating cost to the native populations who did the mining and refining.

As Spanish and Portuguese adventurers explored the lands that the Borgia pope had given them, one of the most controversial and unlikely fellow travelers was the Florentine, and one-time follower of the Medici, Amerigo Vespucci (1454–1512). He found himself on a diplomatic mission in Spain when the Medici fell from power in 1494 and stayed on there, building a career as a navigator for the Spanish crown. But his fame was made by a number of richly detailed letters back to the Medici and friends in Italy, which were widely translated and circulated in Europe and expanded freely upon by others, often in his name. Scholars have debated how many of his claimed eyewitness accounts of what he labeled early on the "new world" (*mundus novus*) were actually witnessed by him and how many were imaginative elaborations of the accounts of others.

Vespucci's claims that he was the first person to actually set foot on the mainland of the Americas are merely the most highly contested. Still, in the letter titled *Mundus Novus*, supposedly written by him but existing only in a Latin copy from the first years of the sixteenth century, there is a clear statement that the world discovered was new and not old:

In the past I have written ... about my return from those *new* regions which we searched for and discovered ... and which can be called a *new world*, since our ancestors had no knowledge of them.... Indeed *it surpasses the knowledge of our ancient authorities* .... since *I have discovered* a continent in these southern regions that is inhabited by more numerous peoples and animals than in our Europe, Asia, or Africa. [italics mine]

Not one for modesty, Vespucci's claim that he discovered this new world, from a Rinascimento perspective, pales before his allegation that the "ancient authorities" had erred, with its implicit assertion that returning to the classics meant completely ignoring new lands and peoples more numerous than those found in Europe. This "new" contradicted at the most fundamental level the authority of the classics and the very ideal of a Rinascimento.

His much-copied letters, and the fame he gained through his writings, led the German cartographer Martin Waldseemüller to name the new territories America in his world map of 1507, after the Florentine. And the name eventually won out, as if Vespucci's claim that he had discovered a new world was actually true. Thus, ironically, the not-actually-new-worlds discovered by an Italian sailing for the Spanish, and an Italian sailing for the English, and an Italian self-promoter who claimed, probably falsely, to have beaten out his predecessors, was named by a German after the least likely of those Italians, from landlocked Florence, whose accounts may well have been largely imagined. Yet in a curious way this seeming chain of unlikely events with its unjust conclusion – naming continents that in the end were not really discovered at all for Amerigo Vespucci, who, even if he was not a fraud, was clearly not as important as he made himself out to be, suggests how even these events that occurred on the other side of a new, larger world were for many conceived in terms of Italy, Italians, and their leadership in the world. For even as the new was undermining it, the Rinascimento remained that world's ultimate point of reference, and thus it seems queerly just that the Americas were named after a Florentine member of the *popolo grosso* who was particularly apt at self-promotion and self-glorification – an individual who became once again a self-fashioned and complexly negotiated work of art, giving his name to a new/old world.

In a way, 1492 marked the start of another series of travels of discovery, less recognized as such. For in 1492 Ferdinand and Isabella, having driven out the last Muslim rulers of Granada, formally expelled the Jews from Spain. Actually, they required that all Jews convert to Christianity or leave; thus, in theory, Spain would become a society that was totally Catholic. Many officially converted to Christianity but continued to secretly follow their

Jewish beliefs, which quickly contributed to a society deeply suspicious of false Catholics, eventually labeled Marranos. The paranoia and persecutions associated with this attempt to purify Spanish society had profound negative effects on early modern Spain. But it also created a significant "new," especially for the Rinascimento in Italy, as many Jews from Spain migrated to Italy and literally discovered it – not surprisingly, as Italy, with its urban wealth and flourishing and apparently cosmopolitan culture, seemed a particularly attractive place. Moreover, most Italian cities already had a small but significant Jewish population, which eased the transition from Spanish intolerance to the discovery of what might be labeled an uneasy Italian coexistence with Italian Jews

Jews had long lived in the cities of Italy, providing services that Italians were unwilling or uncomfortable performing, and in many cases were fairly well integrated into their communities. In fact, some Jewish writers complained that they were much too well integrated. Perhaps the most important service they provided was making small-scale loans to the lower classes. In a society where many lived on the margins of subsistence, such loans were vital for getting through frequent moments of crisis, whether at the personal and family level or during more general times of economic dearth. The strategies discussed earlier for lending money at hidden rates of interest in order to avoid the sin of usury, such as letters of credit or exchange, really worked only for larger business ventures, not the small-scale needs of the poor. Without religious restrictions on lending money, Jews could and did provide small-scale loans to the lower classes.

And many urban governments had learned already in the thirteenth and fourteenth century how to take advantage of this situation. They allowed Jews to live in their cities and pay taxes on their economic activities, and periodically, when public unrest intensified over mounting debts and loan payments that burdened the lower classes, they garnered popular support by driving out the non-Christian moneylenders from their cities. Often these expulsions, encouraged by aggressive travelling preachers and tales of Jewish crimes and perverse religious rituals, were accompanied by violence. Here civic morality and the ideal of creating a Christian community became in a sense a civic immorality that made Jews the scapegoats for the endemic poverty that went hand in hand with an urban economy driven primarily with an eye to increasing the revenues of the rich and powerful. But, of course, the need for loans to the poor did not disappear with this scapegoating, and soon many were clamoring for the return of the Jews and their loans. Thus, usually after a short period of exile, Jews were invited back to perform once again the crucial services that they alone could provide.

In most cities the Jewish community made the best of a bad situation and adapted to this periodic repression. One result of this was that Jewish moneylenders calculated the periodic cancellation of the debts owed to them and the periodic disruptions and devastations of exile into the rates of interest they charged, once again making interest charges higher than they might have been in a society that did not make lending at interest so difficult and dangerous. Another result was that many Jews attempted to pass as Christians, creating a significant mixing of the Jewish and Christian communities that remained almost invisible from history, as people essentially attempting to go unnoticed rarely appear in the records of the day. But if one looks at cities like Venice, Florence, and Rome, while there were strict laws about intermarriage and social or sexual intermixing, the fact that such laws were passed repeatedly seems to indicate that they were frequently ignored. Occasionally, in fact, in criminal cases dealing with other matters a Jewish family or individual will emerge in passing living among Christian neighbors, practicing medicine or healing or a skill outside the normal guild structure of society, and virtually unremarked otherwise. How extensive such contacts were it is difficult to know.

But with the arrival of "new" Jews from the Iberian peninsula, this traditional coexistence was upset. On the positive side, Jews from Spain often brought a rich culture and wealth that had a significant impact on the Rinascimento. At times that Jewish wealth and culture were enhanced by contacts with other Jews who had fled Spain for the more welcoming and cosmopolitan Ottoman world in the eastern and southern Mediterranean, contacts that were of value to the Christian merchant community in Italy as well. On the negative side, Spanish Jews were seen as foreign and dangerous, not just by the Christian community, which was often not enthusiastic about Spanish influences anyway, but also by the established Jewish community in Italy, who often followed different religious traditions and who at times saw newcomers as upsetting the status quo in dangerous ways. Those fears were confirmed, for as more and more Spanish Jews immigrated to Italy, urban governments increased their surveillance and disciplining of all Jews. Eventually stricter restrictions resulted, and many cities set up special areas where Jews were required to live separately from the Christian community, often called ghettos, after the area in Venice first set apart for this purpose, as we shall see. Hand in hand with this went more aggressive programs to convert Jews to Christianity and to identify Jews passing as Christians. Essentially the impact of this was an attempt to create an increasingly "pure" Christian society even as the new in the form of new invaders, new religious confessions from the north of Europe, and greater contact with a broader world were making such purity less and less possible.

Syphilis a New Disease?

In 1494 the French troops invading Italy were struck by an extremely virulent disease that they associated with Italian camp followers and prostitutes
and hence labeled "the Italian disease." The Italians believed the disease had
been brought to Italy by the French and, returning the favor, called it the
French disease. Some in both camps decided to blame Spanish troops and
thus named it the Spanish disease. While debates would long continue about
who was responsible for the disease and deserved to have it named after
them, a more significant debate developed over whether it was new, old, or
suddenly reborn. Clearly conceptualizing the disease as an old one, reborn,
fit well with the Rinascimento view of things. Even disease was better conceived as originating in earlier times, especially as at the moment Europe
was working hard to incorporate a number of disconcertingly new things
into old paradigms. The disfiguring nature of the disease, similar to the disfiguring symptoms associated with leprosy, allowed many to see it at first as
a revival of that disease. Once the most dreaded disease of medieval Europe,
leprosy had declined and become less severe during the Rinascimento; thus,
its rebirth in a more virulent form seemed a likely explanation that made
the disease safely old. Doctors also scoured the classical medical literature to
find examples of earlier times when the disease had been more devastating,
with some success.

But the uncomfortable idea that the disease was a new one slowly gained
purchase. As early as 1497 the Italian medical writer Niccolò Leoniceno
wrote: "The fact that there was not only uncertainty regarding the name of
the disease, but also disagreement regarding its nature, led many to hypothe-
size that this illness was new ... and thus the Greek and Arabic doctors had
never spoken of it.... I absolutely cannot believe that this illness is born suddenly only now and has infected only our epoch." Guicciardini, however,
writing at the end of the 1530s in his *History of Italy*, accepted the idea that
the disease was new and came from the New World:

> It does not seem inappropriate to mention that [at that time 1494] ... an
> illness began that was called the Neapolitan Disease (*Male di Napoli*)....
> it was shown later that that illness had been transported from Spain to
> Naples. And it was not really from that nation, but brought there from
> those islands which ... began to be known in our hemisphere because of
> the voyages of the Genovese Christopher Columbus.

Perhaps the most definite early account of the New World origins of
the disease came from the Spanish physician Roderigo Diaz de Isla, in his

Treatise on the Serpentine Disease which in Spain Is Called Bubas, written in 1539. There he described an early outbreak of the disease that he had treated in Barcelona in 1493, which he claimed had originated among Columbus's sailors.

The debate still rages and in some suggestive ways has contours similar to the sixteenth-century debate. Medical historians examining skeletal remains from the ancient world seem to have discovered bone damage analogous to that caused by modern syphilis and evidence of a significant range of venereal diseases that might qualify as European precursors of the disease – bones in this case becoming the texts that modern science reads to support continuity and ancient origins. Equally telling, perhaps, is the fact that the disease appeared most devastatingly in Italy not in Spain and just a few months after Columbus's return from the New World – too quickly, many would claim, to fit a New World origin. Still, the concept of a "Columbian Exchange" involving disease as well as plants and animals that literally transformed the biospheres of both Europe and the Americas seems curiously incomplete without New World diseases having had a significant impact on sixteenth-century Europe. It is also suggestive that while European diseases like smallpox and later the more complex case of yellow fever (which apparently moved from Africa to the Americas and then back to Europe) were devastating to the native populations of the New World, the diseases of the New World seem not to have had a similar impact on Europe.

Estimates vary, and there is some question about whether population losses are entirely due to European diseases, but it appears that there were at least twenty million inhabitants in what would become Mexico at first contact and only one million left by the beginning of the seventeenth century. Similarly, the native population of Peru over the course of the sixteenth century seems to have fallen from about nine million to less than 700,000. Also troubling is the fact that although Old World diseases raced through native populations with devastating effect, syphilis apparently did not have much impact in the Americas. Yet it too should have been carried to that unprotected population by European explorers and conquerors with a similarly devastating impact. All of which suggests that syphilis was not another new European disease in the New World attacking a population that had not adapted to it, but rather a New World disease to which the indigenous population was already more resistant than Europeans. Returning to bones, recent comparative studies of skeletal remains in Europe and the Americas before first contact have discovered syphilis-like lesions in bones from the New World, but not in bones from Europe, again suggesting a New World origin.

The problem with this evidence, however, is that other diseases also produce syphilis-like bone lesions, so it remains more suggestive than conclusive. The continuity theory has recently gained a sociomilitary dimension, with scholars arguing that the nearly constant warfare of sixteenth-century Europe created a unique biological engine of disease transmission. Armies of professional soldiers, followed by camp followers and prostitutes, incubated and then carried with them and disseminated a much more virulent form of older European venereal diseases that became known as syphilis. This is a seductive idea, but it requires ignoring the fact that Europe had been devastated a century earlier by the Hundred Years' War between France and England and the Italian Hundred Years' War. One thing is clear, however: in the sixteenth century armies and prostitutes were certainly associated with the disease and undoubtedly played a significant role in its rapid dissemination.

Old or new, the devastating impact of the disease on those it infected was immediately perceived as new and terrifying. Reports of deformed genitals, great pustules and sores all over the body, or flesh and bones literally being eaten away by the disease convey a fear and loathing that went beyond a fear of the suffering caused by the disease itself – quickly evoking a deeper fear of a new order of punishment for the sins of the flesh and the immoral order of the Rinascimento world. Actually the disease fairly rapidly became less deadly and less virulent in Europe. And by midcentury, if not sooner, the greatest fear was passing, and treatment of syphilis was becoming a regular part of the shared primary culture of the day. Some even came to see infection as a sign of mature masculinity and virility.

Unfortunately, the most prevalent and apparently most effective treatments, based on mercury, did not cure the disease, merely ameliorating the symptoms. In turn, such mercury cures were devastating, causing bone damage and slow poisoning, often followed by mental disorders. One wonders what the impact of even the less virulent form of the disease and its treatment had on the mental world of the day, with a large portion of the population infected with it, especially the upper classes. It might even be tempting to attribute the violent tenor of the period and its troubling brutality and inhumanity in the name of faith, religion, and morality to a form of mass madness induced by this disease and its cures. Certainly it would be a comforting excuse for a period that, in both the New World and the Old, demonstrated a truly dark side of what has been optimistically labeled Western civilization. Unfortunately, however, it would be a difficult thesis to sustain in the face of a troublingly consistent record of inhumanity and brutality, both before the advent of the disease and after its slow demise, thanks to penicillin, in the twentieth century, the century of Europe's greatest wars and mass murder.

The Invention of the Courtesan

Perhaps one of the most important and most ignored (in traditional histories, at least) innovations of the late fifteenth and early sixteenth centuries was the courtesan: a new player who emerged and captured center stage in the aristocratic imagination of the day. There has been much speculation about how, why, and where these high-class prostitutes developed and quickly became famed for their beauty, wit, wealth, and courtly manners and graces, not just in Italy but across Europe. One hypothesis suggests that they developed in the second half of the fifteenth century in Rome along with the more vibrant court life of the city associated with the return of the papacy. It seems logical that a court dominated by males, most of whom were unmarried, and where women of court were in short supply would be a perfect place to establish a parallel social hierarchy in which courtlike women became available. That they also offered sexual services was, for many, merely a plus. The rapid rise of an impressive group of famous courtesans in Venice might also give that cosmopolitan and aristocratic city a claim of primacy. But wherever courtesans originated, they soon flourished in the larger cities of Italy because they filled a number of sexual and social needs for an increasingly aristocratic society. By the early sixteenth century, they were a major part not just of the illicit world, but also of the licit – an important new facet of the satyr in the Rinascimento garden.

Matteo Bandello (1485–1561), most noted as a prolific writer of *novelle*, across a long career in several Italian courts wrote a number of tales that lamented the evil ways of courtesans and their pernicious effects on society. But even in his negative accounts one sees his recognition of how important and brilliant they could be. In one novella he writes of the Roman courtesan Imperia, whom he portrays as virtually the embodiment of everything refined and aristocratic that sixteenth-century Italy had to offer. Her home in Rome, highlighting her name, was virtually imperial. "Her house was furnished," he wrote, "in a manner that was all carefully planned so that whichever foreigner entered seeing the furniture and the discipline of the servants would believe that here lived a princess." The perfect match in grace, wit, and courtly ways for the aristocratic men who visited her, Bandello also presented her as the ultimate judge of their status. In this she was much like the ideal court lady who not only selected the best men, but also confirmed their superiority for the rest of society.Yet significantly, while court ladies did this largely in theory, at least some courtesans did so in fact.

The black humor of the conclusion of Imperia's tale turns neatly on the power of this judging ability, as he portrays the discomfort of the Spanish ambassador to the pope in her imperial lodging and presence. Feeling the need to spit, this influential aristocrat could find no place to do so in the midst of so much finery and finally, saved by a suitably aristocratic inspiration, he turned and spit in the face of a servant. Then, once more with aristocratic manners and grace, he apologized to the youth: "I hope you don't mind [young man], but your face is the most base thing here." It was a perfect response and moment from the perspective of the patrician world of the day. Imperia measured men by judging their elegance, manners, grace, and *virtù*, and the Spanish ambassador lived up to her judging gaze. In a way, his spit and the servant's face measured the distance between those on the bottom of society and aristocrats, even aristocratic prostitutes. Imperia imperiously thanked the ambassador for his thoughtful and courteous gesture and informed him that if he felt the need again, he could instead spit on her elegant carpets, which were there for exactly that purpose. Whether this actually occurred as Bandello claimed, it aptly elicits the judging power courtesans had over the powerful in the imagination of the day as well as what is perhaps an often forgotten use for carpets.

Not everyone passed the courtesan's test of status. In another tale, Bandello relates the sad fate of a young Milanese aristocrat who travelled to Venice to enjoy the pleasures of one of that city's famous courtesans.Visiting her again impressive quarters, Bandello reports, "She ... seeing him richly dressed and looking like a man ready to spend, realized that he was a pigeon ready for plucking ... began to play him making eyes at him and giving him many sweet looks." Three months passed, three expensive months, as the youth courted her with presents and his best manners, with no reward beyond a kiss or two, as she reserved her favors for her more noble Venetian lovers. Finally, one day in desperation he threatened to kill himself by drinking poison if she did not yield to his pleas. She refused. He drank his poison. But he failed even in what should have been his dramatic moment, because the poison was slow-acting; thus the courtesan and her companions merely laughed at his futile gesture, and he fled back to his lodgings to die alone. For Bandello this was the ultimate tragedy, in a way more serious than the youth's death – for even his attempt at a last heroic gesture failed. Dying in private, the death went totally unnoted and thus virtually did not exist for the consensus realities of the day. For our purposes, however, the point is clear: a courtesan's judgment had its weight, and not every man, not even well-to-do aristocratic men, could count on one's approval. Courtesans were an attractive novelty with a decidedly dangerous edge – once again the dark side of the new.

A courtesan's power and success, like that of many scholars and intellectuals, however, usually hinged on the patronage and support of important men. They were necessary because they had the power to protect her when needed and to supply her with the regular income that allowed her to maintain the style and selectivity that being a courtesan required. With such protection the courtesan could escape the laws that hemmed in less elite prostitutes: circumvent sumptuary laws that limited the richness of their clothing and lodgings; avoid wearing the distinctive badges or articles of dress that were meant to identify prostitutes in most cities; move freely in areas normally forbidden to prostitutes; and, perhaps most importantly, bend the laws and courts to her advantage. In a way, this patronage was based on a symbiotic relationship: powerful patrons protected the courtesan, and a noted courtesan, by choosing to confer her favors on such men, confirmed their status and prestige.

The best courtesans provided even more. With their elegant lodgings and important patrons and clients, they provided a significant locus of male sociability, a minicourt or proto-salon where aristocratic males could meet and play in an illicit world that once again reinforced in many ways the licit. Gambling, sex, music, witty conversation, and even poetry were all ideally part of their aristocratic entertainments, each in its own way a form of elegant play that distinguished the mannered aristocratic world from the common. In fact, several of the most noted poets of the day were courtesans. Most famous, perhaps, were Veronica Franco (1546–1590) of Venice; Tullia d'Aragona (1510–1556), who worked in Florence; and Barbara Raffacani Salutati (b. c. 1500), a noted singer and composer of songs in Florence and a lover of Machiavelli in his later years.

Franco was, at least for a time, a star of the vibrant intellectual culture of Venice in the second half of the sixteenth century. She exchanged poems with some of the most important poets of the day, was lionized by a group of powerful Venetian nobles from the most important families in the city, and even had her portrait painted by Tintoretto. But perhaps her most famed moment was when the young future king of France, Henry III (1551–1589; ruled 1574–1589), on the way back to Paris to take up his crown in 1574, deserted the festivities the republic had organized for him to enjoy a few hours with her. Many of her poems were published in volumes of collected poetry with some of the other leading poets of the day. And in 1575 she published a collection of her own poetry, *Terze Rime*, which included verse that ranged widely, from love lyrics in the Petrarchan tradition to more personal and sensual poems that in many ways broke beyond the established canon, especially for women writers. In one of her better-known poems she wrote of her profession,

> And yet if you call me a prostitute
> Or might want to suggest that I am not
> Or again that among them [prostitutes] some are praiseworthy
> All that they have of the good
> All that they have of the graceful and mannerly
> The sound of your words describes in me.

Although she was ready to claim all the beauty and grace at the highest level of her trade as what set her apart, she was also acutely aware of the less glamorous reality of the profession, especially for those of lower status. In this context, as she grew older she worked to improve the condition of ex-prostitutes and also attacked the exploitation and inequities of a system that, as she pointed out, used up the bodies of women for the pleasures of men. For in reality few prostitutes joined the ranks of aristocratic courtesans, and even those few often ended up poor and broken when their beauty passed and they were forgotten by their former lovers, as Franco boldly reminded her aristocratic patrons.

New diseases, new aristocratic pleasures and victims, new books, new invaders and political realities, and ultimately new worlds that would render Italy peripheral and foundational at the same time – all these things undermined the very possibility of the Rinascimento. The new was breaking out all over, and in its growing undeniability the period was dissolving and morphing into something new and different in its own right, despite the valiant efforts of the best and brightest thinkers of the day. In fact, the clash between a new that could not be denied and an old whose certainty could not be given up, created an impressively creative period of cultural dissonance that in many ways was the fruitful conclusion of the Rinascimento in sixteenth-century Italy and the long-drawn-out dawning of a different society and age that has been labeled as the European Renaissance.

9

RE-DREAMS: *VIRTÙ*, SAVING THE RINASCIMENTO, AND THE SATYR IN THE GARDEN (c. 1500–c. 1560)

Re-Dreams of Virtù: *Machiavelli and Other Secular Prophets*

Niccolò Machiavelli (1469–1527) would become one of the most prominent secular prophets who presented a vision of social and cultural reform that might save the Rinascimento in its time of crisis, even as he was often portrayed as one of the most dangerous satyrs in its garden – if not the Serpent himself. But there was no lack of other prophets with competing visions for saving Italy. Along with Old Nick, three other important and controversial figures seem particularly significant in the rethinking of the *civiltà* of the day that was a much more general phenomenon in the early sixteenth century: Baldassare Castiglione (1478–1529), Ludovico Ariosto (1474–1533), and Pietro Aretino (1492–1556). Each in his own way wrestled with the underlying problem of the new that threatened Italy and its urban society and culture. Moreover, if at first sight their ideas seem profoundly different, at least for Machiavelli and Castiglione, their underlying answer to the problems of Italy was based upon a long established discourse that ran deeply in the shared primary culture of the Rinascimento.

Both called for a return to that *virtù* that had made Italy great, and both shared the vision that it was the lack of *virtù* that had opened the doors of Italy to conquerors from over the Alps: for it was a lack of *virtù* that had led to the corrupt and ineffective governments of the recent past, and it was a lack of *virtù* that had made the people of Italy "soft and effeminate." Thus in returning to *virtù*, and to the way Machiavelli and Castiglione used the term to think about the troubled nature of their day, rather than merely examining the vision of famous writers on *virtù*, we are once again tracing the parameters of a particularly significant discourse of the primary culture of the day – a shared discourse that drew much of its strength from its long tradition of defining moral and social superiority with a classical pedigree.

9.1. Veronese, *Mars and Venus United by Love*, 1570s, Metropolitan Museum of Art. ©The Metropolitan Museum of Art. Image source: Art Resource, New York.

In haunting lines of self-examination at the start of the second book of his *Discourses on the First Decade of Titus Livy*, Machiavelli worried about his conviction that the times in which he was living were the worst of times. At first, seeming to offer hope, he noted perceptively that old men – as he claimed to be, in his late forties – often saw the present as corrupt and degraded and tended to see the past as superior. This appeared to prepare the ground for an assertion that the present was not as bad as it might at first seem, especially to old men like himself. But ironically, that was exactly the point he rejected: "I do not know, therefore, if I deserve to be numbered among those who deceive themselves....Yet it is true that if the *virtù* which ruled in those times [the ancient Roman world] and the vices which rule today did not shine more clearly than the sun, I would not speak so strongly." Machiavelli, then, damned his day and presented a defense of his pessimistic position that drew on a central topos of the culture of the Rinascimento: Italians had lost the *virtù* of the ancient Romans that had made them great and had made the Rinascimento itself possible. Not surprisingly, then, he argued that a rebirth of that *virtù* would return Italy and its urban society to their previous glory.

Significantly, he argued this in his most famous (and infamous) work, *The Prince* (c. 1513), and in his less read but no less significant *Discourses* (written 1513–1517) – even if in the former he focused on a prince's need for *virtù* in order to rule and hold onto power, and in the latter on the need for the *popolo* to have *virtù* in order for a republic to resist a prince and survive. At first the *Discourses* may seem to concentrate primarily on the *virtù* of ancient Romans. Yet the *virtù* he presents as having made ancient Rome great, when looked at more closely, was less classical than contemporary. For, in fact, it was an evocative pastiche of the ancient read by Machiavelli through the lens of his primary shared culture, where *virtù* was, as we have seen, a measure of what made one man superior to another *in the Rinascimento*. As such, it was heavily reliant on contemporary civic values associated with the *popolo grosso* and civic morality. Indicative of this is the way Machiavelli felt comfortable using the term throughout the *Discourses*, to describe not only the positive ways ancient Romans behaved, but also the positive ways modern Italians behaved. And, in turn, the term, used in much the same way, and Machiavelli's contemporary examples of its success are central to his recipe for princely survival in *The Prince*.

In fact, *virtù*, and the success it brings, flourishes at the heart of much of his apparently less serious writing as well. In his famous comedy *La mandragola* (*The Mandrake Root*), for example, *virtù* cleverly deployed by a corrupt priest, Fra Timoteo, and a clever Machiavellian advisor, Ligurio, allows a young lover to succeed in bedding and winning the love of a young married woman, with the unwitting aid of her foolish old husband – *virtù* in the service of trickery and sin – hardly ancient Roman – or Christian, for that matter – but clearly Rinascimento. More subtly, perhaps, in his *Clizia* – a comedy that seems to poke fun at Machiavelli's own peccadilloes as an aged lover – an old husband, Nicomaco, blinded by his mad passion for a young woman, is saved from ruin by a clever plot that in its humorous humiliation of Nicomaco goes far beyond the ancient Roman comedy upon which it is loosely based. In the positive ending required of a comedy, he rejects the love that had rendered him a fool and regains *virtù* and the mature wisdom expected of the old men who rule families and society itself. Thus, he lives happily ever after as the *virtù*-ous patriarch of a reborn happy and well-ordered family. It might be suggested that just as *virtù* reborn in Nicomaco returned his family to its correct order, so *virtù* reborn in princes or the *popolo* offered the same possibility for the Rinascimento, in Machiavelli's eyes.

But to fully appreciate how deeply Machiavelli's vision of *virtù* was part of a historical moment and the shared primary culture of his day, a closer look at Machiavelli's life and career is in order. Both are fascinating, for when one begins to look more closely at the historical Machiavelli, he refuses to fit his modern Machiavellian stereotypes in ways that are revealing. First, of course, Machiavelli was a man of action, a man deeply caught up in his early sixteenth-century Florence. From this perspective it is much harder to think of him as an intellectual merely commenting on ancient political thought, or as a prescient proto-modern thinker able to see beyond his cultural context in ways that made him a precursor of modern political theory. Like most of his contemporaries, the former was what he claimed in his *Discourses*, presenting the work as merely a series of commentaries on the ancient historian Livy. The latter he could hardly claim, not being aware of the way his work would be singled out by later commentators, although he did claim to reject theory and the moral hypocrisy of earlier writers in order to speak directly to the future about the real issues involved in ruling. Yet such claims are usually just that, rhetorical claims, and Machiavelli, like most, had a series of agendas that drove his analysis that involved much more than a mere dispassionate description of the political reality of his day.

In 1498 a young Machiavelli (around twenty-nine) was appointed secretary of the chancellery responsible for foreign affairs and war. Historians have wondered how this young man from an old but no longer leading family was able to win such an important post. His father had been a moderately prosperous lawyer, and the young Niccolò apparently had already held some minor posts. But his jump to that prestigious post put him at one of the important centers of Florentine affairs at a critical moment. What seems clear is that Machiavelli made the most of his position and proved himself to the emerging leader of the republican government of the city, Piero Soderini, as an invaluable colleague and analyst of the political scene. A brief review of his more important diplomatic missions suggests just how important he had become. The year 1499 found him in Forlì meeting with

Caterina Sforza, an ally of Florence and the widow of Giovanni de' Medici, whose hold on that city was being threatened by Cesare Borgia. Cesare was busily trying to take advantage of the turmoil in Italy following the French invasion to carve out a state for himself in the region, and Forlì was one of his targets. It was in Florence's interest to see Borgia's plans thwarted, and their ally Caterina retain her power in the region. But notwithstanding his positive impression of Caterina's "manly *virtù*," Machiavelli reluctantly concluded that it would be trumped by Borgia's superior military power and his equal or superior *virtù*. And shortly after his mission, Forlì fell to Borgia, confirming his prognostication.

The next year (1500) he was sent to France, where he met with the new king, Louis XII (1462–1515; ruled 1498–1515) and was again impressed by his *virtù*, particularly in terms of military and political acumen. Louis, who had succeeded Charles VIII, during this period of early success had recently deposed Ludovico il Moro Sforza, claiming Milan by hereditary right, and would soon retake Naples (1501) only to lose it again (1503). Meanwhile, in 1502 and once more in 1503, Cesare Borgia and his expanding pretensions in central Italy would again claim Machiavelli's attention. In 1502 Cesare seemed about to succeed in establishing his ministate in the Romagna; thus Machiavelli was asked to evaluate how dangerous for Florence Borgia's success would be. In 1503, however, apparent success turned to failure with the unexpected death of Cesare's father, Pope Alexander VI. One last time Machiavelli was asked to evaluate Cesare's future, which he correctly judged as negative. Later, in *The Prince* he also used his observations on the rapid demise of Cesare that followed to analyze how it was that a leader who demonstrated such exceptional *virtù* could fall so quickly, obviously a problem for Machiavelli, who put so much emphasis on the power of *virtù*.

The year 1504 found him again travelling to France to evaluate the Florentine/French alliance, after the defeat of the French in Italy and their loss of Naples. In 1506 he journeyed with the new pope, Julius II (1443–1513; pope 1503–1513), on his successful military campaign to retake parts of the Papal States that had been lost under his predecessors. Once again in his political writings Machiavelli would return several times to the troubling figure of Julius, whose impetuousness and lack of reason and forethought seemed to doom him to failure – and, more importantly, appeared to make him the perfect figure of anti-*virtù*, winning out repeatedly where his impetuous lack of planning should have led to catastrophe. But in the end, with evident discomfort and some ingenious qualifications, Machiavelli managed to wrestle even this unlikely pope into a figure who grabbed the moment with *virtù* and won out over less courageous and hard-headed opponents.

Again in 1508 he was on the road, journeying to Bolzano in the context of the League of Cambrai's planned war on Venice, to meet with the Emperor Maximilian I (1459–1519; emperor 1493–1519); 1510 found him moving on to France as the League was breaking up and alliances were quickly being rearranged, requiring a careful analysis of where the French and Florence would fall in the new order of things. But these were only the most important missions of Machiavelli. He also travelled regularly to lesser hot spots and potential hot spots, sending back to his Florentine superiors important reports noted for their close and careful analysis of the leaders he met and the political and military situations he encountered. Many of his dispatches still exist and, supplemented by his letters, provide a fascinating picture of the political and diplomatic world in which he moved as a young man and upon which he based his later political writings.

During this same period Machiavelli was also intimately involved in Florence's military adventures. Foremost among them was its fifteen-year campaign to regain Pisa, lost after the fall of the Medici in 1494. Machiavelli took part in several ineffective sieges that apparently confirmed what would become his lifelong distrust and dislike of mercenaries. As he would later argue in his *Art of War* and more briefly in *The Prince* and *Discourses*, he was convinced that armies made up of professional soldiers were neither as loyal nor as committed as well-trained citizen militias. They were unwilling to spill sufficient blood or to fight to the end for employers, who were just that, employers, much preferring easy or at least secure victories or retreating to fight another day. Behind his apparently hard-headed analysis, however, there lay a deeper belief in the necessity of cultivating a citizenry imbued with *virtù*, along with a fairly traditional form of civic morality. Machiavelli believed that loyal citizens fighting for their *patria*, and for a cause in which they believed, with equal training and skill (military *virtù*) would always outperform mercenaries, because they had the more powerful *virtù* of good citizens defending their families and their homeland.

Like a true Rinascimento thinker, Machiavelli drew on the example of ancient Rome and its successful citizen armies to support his case, noting the special *virtù* they displayed in their many triumphs. But well before he wrote his famous tracts on the matter, he was busy trying to convince his superiors in government that Florence needed a civilian militia to fight its wars, rather than relying on the unreliable and costly *condottiere* armies that had produced so little for the city. Finally, in 1506, he convinced Soderini and was given the responsibility of organizing and training a citizen militia. Many were unimpressed with Machiavelli's plans, especially as they required the dangerous strategy of arming the lower classes. But it seems that his militia did play a role in the final taking of Pisa in 1509. And he, at least, claimed that victory as one of his greatest successes. With the fall of the Soderini government in 1512 and the return of the Medici, however, the militia was shelved, along with Machiavelli himself. Hard-headed economic and military realities won out over Machiavelli's idealistic beliefs – even if, ironically, the latter would live on in his writings, depicted as hard-headed and realistic.

With the return of the Medici, Machiavelli's active civic life was over. Too closely associated with the republican government of Soderini, and without strong defenders in the aristocratic faction that supported the returned Medici, he was fired. To make matters worse, shortly thereafter he was accused of having taken part in a plot to overthrow the new Medici regime. Arrested, he apparently successfully avoided confessing under torture; was eventually released; and went into a form of self-imposed exile at his family estate just south of Florence. At forty-three and, from his perspective, at the height of his political powers, Machiavelli found himself suddenly and unwillingly retired. His responses were several. And they virtually all turned around regaining the political place and prominence he had lost. Most notable, of course, were the famous works he wrote on government and politics, the *Prince* and the *Discourses* along with the *Art of War*, in an attempt to regain entrance to the political arena of his day. He also continued an important epistolary campaign to win friends, influence people, and maintain a circle of intimate friends who might support his return to power.

Although some of those letters have been lost, the significant body that remains provides a revealing record of the strategies of self-presentation of a man anxious to represent himself as a subtle analyst of the political situation of Florence, Italy, and the broader world that had so troublingly changed the political reality of Italy. At the same time, however, the letters represent Machiavelli not just as a man of *virtù* because of his political analysis and abilities, but also as a man of *virtù* because of his ability to cleverly laugh at himself and others. His illicit sexual exploits and fantasies, which are often quite explicitly detailed, provided a rich source of often self-mocking humor. In this way we might claim that he presented himself as the perfect satyr in the garden of his own attempted *rinascita* – half *virtù*-ous political mind, from the waist up, half *virtù*-ous licentious flesh, from the waist down. These same themes are central to his more literary works, the *Mandragola*, *Clizia*, and his egregiously misogynistic novella, *Belfagor*. Each presents its author as a man capable of laughing at the world around him and at himself, with a clever honesty that demonstrated to his contemporaries and their consensus reality judgments of him that he was literally one of the boys (albeit a bit old for the role) and full of *virtù*.

Yet the works that evoke *virtù* as the answer to the problems of an Italy overrun by foreign powers, *The Prince* and *The Discourses*, are Machiavelli's most famous. Both have been so carefully and diversely interpreted, often in ways that would have surprised Machiavelli, that it is difficult to say anything about them definitively. Actually, as argued more fully in my earlier book *Machiavelli in Love*, to a large extent the power of the term *virtù* for the Rinascimento and Machiavelli was to be found in the way it permitted multiple interpretations, its polysemous nature and flexibility. This gave it the ability to rhetorically evoke consensus, even as its meaning slid across a spectrum of meanings that included everything from the precepts of Christian morality to the ruthlessly rational calculation of self-interest. At first this might seem strange in a culture where social and moral values tended to be viewed as absolutes and where cultural relativity was not so much shunned as virtually unthinkable. But it is in just such cultures that a range of evaluative terms that are not closely defined, or that unwittingly allow for a broader range of meanings, become virtually necessary to deal with the complexity of life as lived. During the Rinascimento a number of especially significant terms fulfilled this need – for example, "old," "ancient," "honorable," "natural," "good," "beautiful," "customary," "mannerly," "courteous," and "honest." Each in its own way tended to be highly flexible and had a wide range of discursive uses that make precise definition impossible. Their very polyvalent nature, in fact, was one of their important strengths, as it allowed them to be adapted to the situation at hand with absolute certainty *and usually unnoted flexibility*.

Philosophers or theologians could perhaps deal in terms of absolutes and attempt tight definitions of such terms, but writers of the day concerned with practice, and with presenting a convincing argument, tended to use them with more flexibility – rhetorical tools to win support for often contending opinions. Thus a term like *virtù*, which at first glance might seem to have a straightforward meaning – the quality or skill that made one man superior to others – and which might seem to have endured unchanged from the ancient world up to and through the Rinascimento, as regularly claimed, was anything but unchanging and enduring, as we have seen. Significantly, the ability to sustain a complex discourse on what made one person better than another, rather than requiring a simple, straightforward definition, made the term one capable of changing dramatically – and not just over time, but also adapting to different cultural frames in terms of class, gender, moral values, ideology, and even pragmatic concerns.

In this respect, Machiavelli's use of the term provides a particularly good perspective on the equivocal nature of *virtù* in the Rinascimento. Like many a powerful rhetorician, he used the term to win acceptance for his arguments, even when they were troubling or questionable. Perhaps most regularly, however, he used the term in what might be deemed a rather traditional republican sense, drawing on the old *popolo grosso* values that had won out across much of northern Italy in the second half of the fourteenth and early years of the fifteenth century. As we have seen, that vision of *virtù* emphasized an ability/skill to successfully accomplish things via reasoned calculation, where calculation often slid over into cunning and tended to involve more problematic behavior in terms of honor or morality. Ghismonda's *virtù*-driven defense of her morally questionable affair to her father, the prince of Salerno, discussed in Chapter 5, which turned into a lecture on *virtù* in Boccaccio's fourteenth-century tale, seems to offer a foretaste of Machiavelli's own *virtù*-driven defense of the morally questionable deeds required to gain and hold power in *The Prince*. And neatly, both are presented in the form of lessons for a prince.

Perhaps the best example of this use of *virtù* in *The Prince* can be found in Machiavelli's depiction of the ruthless career of Cesare Borgia. Even Machiavelli was troubled by Borgia's cold-blooded brutality and lack of moral scruples. Yet Borgia, with his clever calculation, cunning, and success, also served as a perfect model of *virtù*, at least until evil fortune undermined even his *virtù* and led to his fall. That was a twist of fate at the expense of *virtù* that he was at pains to explain. For if *Fortuna* could sweep away the best laid plans of the *virtù*-ous prince, could *virtù* really be counted upon? His answer was a troubled yes. Comparing *Fortuna* to a flood that sweeps all before it, Machiavelli argued that with planning and forethought (*virtù*) even the damage of a flood can be contained by canals and dikes that would deflect its force – in the same way, the *virtù*-ous prince anticipated misfortune by preparing his political canals and dikes to deflect the force of evil fortune. Thus he noted that Borgia had planned ahead, only to be foiled by the one thing he did not anticipate, that he would be ill when his father, the pope, died and thus unable to put in motion his carefully prepared plans. Significantly, then, rather than drawing the conclusion that fortune had bested *virtù*, Machiavelli preferred to see Borgia's demise as merely a failure to foresee one particular eventuality and construct a plan to deal with it. *Virtù*, with a bit of tricky reasoning, then retained the power to overcome, or at least to limit, the damage of *Fortuna* and save the prince and Italy.

Still, Machiavelli had another recipe for dealing with *Fortuna* that has added to his reputation as a misogynist. Playing on the gendered nature of Italian nouns (*Fortuna* is a noun gendered feminine in Italian), he argued that *Fortuna* should be treated like a woman: grabbed and violently handled to keep her in line. Indicative of the slippery nature of the apparently clear language used, it should be noted, however, that *virtù* itself was also a feminine noun, and thus, to be consistent, Machiavelli might well have felt troubled in making it a crucial aspect of aggressive males. Of course, it did not hurt that the root of *virtù*, *vir*, meant "man," which may have made it easier to overlook its feminine gender as a word.

Fortuna, obviously, was not always negative. In fact, again thinking in terms of gender, Machiavelli envisioned fortune as a woman who tended to favor young men, especially young men in love. In *La Mandragola*, his best-known comedy, for example, the young would-be lover Callimaco – whose name in Greek suggests a once-upon-a-time youthful Machiavelli himself (*kalli* – young and handsome; *maco* – Machiavelli was referred to as "el Maco" by his friends) – appears at first glance to be a model of anti-*virtù* in action, with his wild and unlikely passion for a married woman whom he has barely seen and never actually met. He wanders the streets in a daze, mouthing lovesick lines that are clearly meant to elicit laughter. But in the end, with the aid of a clever plot designed with the best Machiavellian cunning by the sycophant Ligurio – who is, by contrast, a model of *virtù* – the young lover succeeds not only in bedding Lucrezia, the object of his desire, but in convincing her to overlook his trickery and accept him as her lover. In fact, he is so successful that she later describes her acceptance of his love as her own personal "*rinascita.*" That success in bed, however, undermines the easy reading of Callimaco as simply a young fool in love. Of course, he is presented as such, but once again, as was the case in much of the literature of the Rinascimento, love has the power to make even foolish young lovers capable of *virtù*-ous deeds and of winning the support of a smiling feminine *Fortuna*. Callimaco, in his ultimate success with Lucrezia, seems to fall into that lucky category.

In *The Prince*, *Fortuna* could also at times smile on would-be princes, catapulting them unexpectedly to power. But Machiavelli was not so enthusiastic about such unearned success; for what *Fortuna* gave, she could easily take away. Thus he was adamant that those who had gained power thanks merely to good fortune had to quickly develop the *virtù* necessary to maintain it. And the same was true for those who inherited rule. Clearly thinking of Florentines such as Piero de' Medici, along with other contemporary and ancient examples, he argued that the fatal flaw of those who inherited power was that they did so without having developed the *virtù* to rule effectively. By contrast, those who gained power without the aid of *Fortuna* had to develop *virtù* in order to act with the necessary forethought, skill, and cunning to succeed. Thus they were able to rule successfully using that *virtù*. The negative implications of this analysis, although rather quietly passed over in

The Prince, are carefully examined in *The Discourses* and are presented as a significant reason for the problems Italy faced in Machiavelli's day. In that work he sees governments dominated by princes or *signori* as having become progressively more corrupt and unstable, easy victims of more powerful and more *virtù*-ous foreigners.

This use of *virtù*, at least as presented in *The Prince*, seems to be, and is often interpreted as, quite amoral, although there are good reasons for questioning that too-easy conclusion. Even in the most apparently immoral moments of *The Prince*, Machiavelli is capable of a quick change of register that underlines the polyvalent nature of the term *virtù*. Undoubtedly the most notable example of this, and the most troubling for commentators, is his famous shifting judgment of the ancient Greek tyrant Agathocles. He introduces the tyrant with a description of his evil ways, stressing that Agathocles led an "infamous life" but nonetheless accompanied his infamy with such "*virtù*" of the "soul and body" that he won control of the rich city of Syracuse. He then briefly outlines the tyrant's strategy of rule, emphasizing his ruthless domination of the city and his willingness to use whatever means necessary to maintain power, which Machiavelli notes was based solely upon Agathocles' strong will and reasoned, amoral approach to rule – once again, his "*virtù*."

But without warning Machiavelli suddenly shifts registers and the meaning of *virtù* to claim: "Still one cannot call it *virtù* to kill one's subjects, betray one's friends, to be unfaithful, without pity, without religion. Such practices win rule, but not glory." When necessary, *virtù* could require the amoral rationality and cunning of a Cesare Borgia or even the ruthless cruelty of a tyrant like Agathocles, whose very soul demonstrated *virtù*, according to Machiavelli. Still, glory requires more, and Machiavelli's use of *virtù* shifts accordingly. In fact, in *The Discourses* the balance shifts decidedly toward a more moral use of the term, especially in the context of his deeper vision of civic morality. That work, which Machiavelli clearly saw as the summa of his ideal of how society and government should function based upon a life of service to the state, political action, and reflection on ancient and contemporary examples, was expressly aimed at recreating in his day a rebirth of the ancient Roman republic and its *virtù*.

Yet once again the actual *virtù* he described was less ancient than contemporary. To have an enduring republic, he argued, required a *popolo* imbued with *virtù*, a civic and moral *virtù* in the sense of the civic morality of the *civiltà* of the first Rinascimento. Citizens who lacked such *virtù* could not be counted upon to act *virtù*-ously, make wise decisions, live peacefully together, follow the law, or serve the republic honestly and faithfully. To encourage such *virtù* or actually require it, the republic needed *virtù*-ous laws that organized society in a rational and just manner, protecting the weak from the powerful and literally cutting off the offending members of society who did not follow the path of *virtù*. Such laws were necessary because Machiavelli unquestioningly accepted the Christian vision that people were inherently evil. He often referred to his contemporaries as *"triste"* – not so much "sad," as a literal translation might suggest, but inherently evil in the sense of having a stain on their souls that made them ultimately asocial. Not really antisocial, but rather constantly tending to pull apart and disaggregate society in order to gain their own personal desires or those of their family – something still seen by some as a deep problem in modern society. Overcoming that *triste* aspect of human nature was the essential problem of civil society and government for Machiavelli. And to succeed in that project, a republic required both *virtù*-ous citizen/leaders and *virtù*-ous laws to keep its populace *virtù*-ous.

In this vision of civic morality, in fact, there may lurk a potential single underlying definition of Machiavellian *virtù*. For, as Machiavelli notes often in *The Prince*, and from time to time in *The Discourses* as well, rulers when dealing with *triste* citizens cannot enjoy the luxury of a moral approach to rule. Agathocles or Cesare Borgia, dealing with subjects lacking *virtù* in a society without good laws or just government, in order to rule and survive had to make use of a sterner and more amoral *virtù*, one that was capable of overcoming the untrustworthy and ultimately evil populace they were attempting to control. Such stern *virtù* could secure their rule, and perhaps even provide the grounds for implementing better laws and eventually building a more *virtù*-ous citizenry, one of the goals of *The Prince*. But in *The Discourses*, discussing his ideal ancient Roman republic and his dream of its modern rebirth, he is clear that with truly *virtù*-ous citizens and rulers kept truly *virtù*-ous by laws, *virtù* could become finally moral. In such a republic violence and immoral actions would no longer be necessary, and the *virtù*-ous ruler could win glory and be virtuous in a truly moral sense. Whether or not that was Machiavelli's underlying vision, until that ideal state was reached, *virtù* remained polysemous and often amoral in Machiavelli's writings and in the shared culture of his day.

For Machiavelli, the question was obviously how to realize the rebirth of his dream of the ancient Roman republic and its *virtù* in the troubled days of early sixteenth-century Italy, where the new seemed to breaking out all over. One possible answer was *The Prince*. For behind the famous Machiavellian advice on how a prince might ruthlessly gain power and hold it, there may well have lain hidden a less recognized Machiavellian dream.

In *The Discourses*, which were written in the second decade of the century – before, after, and as he was writing *The Prince* – Machiavelli tackled the troubling question of how a corrupt state and citizenry where *virtù* no longer existed could be reformed and *virtù* reborn. After admitting the difficulty of the task, he argued that it could be done only by a truly exceptional prince. And he noted (sadly?) that such a ruler, in order to gain and hold power in a corrupt state where the people were *triste*, had to be ready to use the ruthless and amoral tactics that were necessary to subdue and control such a populace. But once in power, that same prince had to implement *virtù*-ous laws and slowly transform his *subjects* into *virtù*-ous *citizens* capable of sustaining a republic. With *virtù* restored and enforced, a true republic could be reborn. From this perspective the last section of *The Prince*, often dismissed as an afterthought or an attempt to soften the harsh message of the work, with its call for a strong leader to reform the states of Italy and lead them back to power, success, and *virtù*, seems less an afterthought and more an anticipation of the political dream of *The Discourses*.

That dream was based, in a way true to the Rinascimento, upon a suggestive mix of ancient history, philosophy, and contemporary ideals and observations that explained for Machiavelli the success and endurance of the ancient Roman republic. The issue was, in a world where everything seemed to decay and become corrupt, how had the Roman republic maintained and cultivated *virtù* for so long, and in turn how could an ideal state – or, ideally, the modern world – do the same? Reading Livy's account of the ancient republic and commenting on it in *The Discourses*, Machiavelli "discovered" that it was the mixed nature of that republic that had made it so successful. In essence, Roman republican government had been successful because it was based on a mixture of rule by the people as a whole, rule by the best people, and rule by a strong leader. In such a mixed rule the defects of each were overcome and held in check. For Machiavelli those defects were clear: rule by the people or democracy became mob rule; rule by the best people devolved into oligarchy; and rule by one man became tyranny. But when all three coexisted such degeneration was blocked by the interests of the other forms involved.

Whether or not the Roman republic ever actually functioned as a mixed government, this "discovery" of Machiavelli's was supported by the ancient Greek thinker Aristotle, whose well-known political vision of an ideal government was one that mixed democracy, aristocracy, and princely rule in order to avoid the same decay. One might be tempted to accuse Machiavelli of shamelessly stealing Aristotle's ideas and claiming them for his own. But that would be too easy, for the idea of mixed government had already been stolen (or reborn) to become a strong current in the political ideals and mythology of the Rinascimento. Venice had long touted its mixed government as one of the primary explanations for the city's success and peacefulness. Florentines had also tried from time to time to reimagine their government as somehow fulfilling similar ideas, with less success. In fact, when Machiavelli was a young man, the followers of Savonarola had toyed with similar ideas for their renewed republic. Even the Soderini government that he served experimented with adopting its own vision of mixed government based upon the Venetian model.

In sum, the shared primary culture of Machiavelli's day was awash with the ideal of mixed government, so the fact that he discovered it as the source of the longevity and success of the Roman republic and advocated it for his own ideal is hardly a surprise. More significantly, this demonstrates the complex way thinkers and writers of the Rinascimento actually interacted with the cultures to which they were exposed and how their supposedly original ideas were often overdetermined in ways that make claims of originality or of one ancient source difficult to sustain. Behind the complexity of that cultural interaction it is clear, however, that Machiavelli believed that *virtù* was the key to the success of ancient Rome and a necessity if the corruption and "effeminacy" of the Italians of his day were to be overcome. And although some may disagree, it seems that the prince of *The Prince*, or at least the prince of *The Discourses*, was to be the one to lead Italy back to *virtù*.

Castiglione: Re-Dreams of Love and Virtù

Baldassare Castiglione in his *Book of the Courtier*, written at much the same time as *The Prince* and *The Discourses*, once again offers *virtù* and a prince as the remedy for overcoming the crisis of an Italy overrun by invaders. Nine years Machiavelli's junior, Castiglione's political and diplomatic career in service to the lords of Urbino was also cut short by the Medici, in his case when the ruler of that city was ousted by the Medici pope, Leo X in 1516. Much like Machiavelli, before that date he had served as an administrator and diplomat, but for the lords of the cities and courts of Modena and Urbino rather than for a republic. He also shared with Machiavelli military interests and experience, but unlike him, he actually served as a military officer and fought in several major battles against both the Spanish and the French. Also unlike Machiavelli, his career as an administrator and diplomat was not cut short when he lost his post in Urbino. He merely transferred his services to new lords and actually ended up for a time serving the Medici pope, Clement VII.

Castiglione shared with Machiavelli and many of his Italian contemporaries a deep concern about the apparent fall from grace of Italy. Italy appeared unable to stem or even to respond to the ongoing invasions that seemed to be destroying not just its great cities and courts, but the very social and cultural fabric that had made it the leader and measure of Europe, at least from its own perspective. Thus, again like Machiavelli, in the second decade of the new century he took pen in hand to write *The Book of the Courtier*. On the surface the work was a handbook for life at court: a manual on how to be a successful gentleman or lady of court. As such, it might seem light years away from Machiavelli's princes, *virtù*-ous citizens, and republics. Yet, much as was the case with Machiavelli, the key to his vision of the successful courtier turned on *virtù*. And once again Castiglione's pivotal discussion of *virtù* opened the door for deeper reflections on how Italy might regain its lost glory, guided by the leadership of strong and *virtù*-ous princes, in this case advised by strong and *virtù*-ous courtiers.

Castiglione used the popular form of the dialogue to present an apparently wide range of views on how to form a perfect courtier and court lady. Set at the court of Urbino, the discussion was actually organized as a game, like many at court, to display the *virtù* and courtly graces of the participants. Speakers were chosen by a court lady, herself chosen by the duchess, who oversaw the conversation. They then displayed their rhetorical skills and brilliance and responded to the challenges and questions of other members of the court. The discussants, nineteen men and four largely silent women, were all well-known intellectual figures of the day, including the future cardinal Pietro Bembo (1470–1547, cardinal 1539–1547), at the time a famous love poet and lover; Giuliano de' Medici (1478–1516), the third son of Lorenzo the Magnificent, who lived for a time in exile at the court; Bernardo Accolti (1458–1534), known as L'Unico Aretino, noted for his extemporaneous poetry and courtly skills; Bernardo Dovizi (1470–1520; cardinal 1513–1520), called Il Bibbiena and best known today for his risqué comedy *La Calandra*; Ottavio Fregoso (1470–1524), briefly doge and then governor for the French of Genoa; and Gasparo Pallavicino (1486–1511), who had already died at the early age of twenty-five when the dialogue was written.

As a game showcasing rhetorical skill and the discussants' understanding of the culture of court, Castiglione's dialogue provides an interesting measure of the way *virtù* could be deployed to win arguments and elicit consent. In turn, the varied use of the term in those discussions provides a good measure of its flexibility and polysemous nature once again. The first three of the four books that make up the work focus on the *virtù* of the courtier (in books one and two) and the court lady (in book three). Although there was some difference in emphasis among speakers, the list of attributes that demonstrated the *virtù* of the courtier included noble birth, honor, masculine ways (in distinction to feminine, soft or effeminate ones), courtly manners, grace, *sprezzatura*, quick wit, playful spirit, military prowess, musical ability, artistic taste, ability as a lover, and, crucially, the ability to advise the prince. Clearly things have changed from the vision of *virtù* embraced by Boccaccio or the fourteenth-century merchant/banker elites and are far removed from ancient Roman ideals. Notably, noble birth, although questioned by some of the discussants, has here regained ground along with military prowess, while reason, calculation, and cunning, although underpinning many of the other attributes, are not nearly as visible as they were a century and a half earlier. Not surprisingly, the agenda of *virtù* at court emphasized more aristocratic values than those of an earlier day or those of Castiglione's contemporary Machiavelli. Thus, although they shared a faith in *virtù*, and both used the term as a measure of the behavioral changes that they felt would save their Italy, the different meanings they gave it suggests once again its polyvalent nature.

In the political world of Machiavelli, women figured only occasionally, although he does from time to time note particularly *virtù*-ous women, often with a "complimentary" and revealing nod to their virtually masculine *virtù*. Castiglione, by contrast, devotes the third book of his work to a discussion of the *virtù* of the court lady, suggesting a significant difference between the courtly and republican cultures of the day. At court, at least in theory, women played an important role as social arbiters, and especially in the courtly game of courtship, they exercised some real power over men, even if the extent of that power remains problematic. In fact, the problematic nature of such power is clearly on display in book three. The discussion heats up when a group of courtiers more sympathetic to women begin to argue that courtiers should not joke or gossip about a woman's behavior, pointing out that a double standard existed that allowed men the freedom to misbehave sexually while punishing women severely for any sign of promiscuity.

Gasparo Pallavicino, one of the most aggressive traditionalists and misogynists in the group (and safely dead), objected that if women were to be treated as equals, then they should be open to the same jokes and gossip as men. The future cardinal, Bernardo Dovizi, countered: "We men have ourselves made a law that a dissolute life is not considered a vice or a fault or infamous, but for women the same life is considered so shameful and worthy of great opprobrium that whether what is said about her is true or false ... [she] is forever disgraced." Castiglione then turns over the misogynist response to Ottavio Fregoso, who aggressively attacks Dovizi, "[It is] perhaps not as unreasonable as it seems to you. For given that *women are very imperfect animals* and of little or no dignity in comparison with men, by necessity they are not capable of any *virtù*-ous deeds." [italics mine] By arguing that women were incapable of *virtù*, and "imperfect animals" at that, he opened the way for a claim that they needed a different form of discipline than men, which in turn justified a double standard. Lacking *virtù*, they were not able to control their emotions or desires like men – even if men obviously did not always do so – and so, he concluded, they needed to be controlled by a sense of shame and fear. Shame and fear, in turn, worked to control those "imperfect animals" via the public evaluation of their behavior, and women who lacked chastity actually required gossip and negative comments from men – once again, here consensus realities structure the disciplining of behavior.

This essentially traditional sexual ideology, perhaps most definitively articulated in the ancient world by Aristotle and masquerading here as based on nature and natural, did not go unchallenged, however. In fact, most of the group advanced a decidedly different vision of the gender division between men and women, once again framed in terms of *virtù*. The defenders of women began a long series of descriptions of historical women who had displayed *virtù*, starting with classical times (much in the cultural context of the Rinascimento) and moving up to the present. But, of course, it was court ladies who were really the ultimate end of the discussion, and their *virtù* was crucial; a *virtù* that at first glance seemed quite similar to that of the courtier. Giuliano de' Medici argued, "I hold that many of the *virtù* of the soul that are necessary for a woman [at court] are much the same as for a man [at court]: the same nobility, the same avoidance of affectation, the same natural grace in all deeds, the same good manners, the same wit, the same prudence, avoiding pride, avoiding envy, avoiding insults, avoiding vanity, avoiding conflict, avoiding foolishness." Clearly Giuliano's list of *virtù*-ous qualities went well beyond the traditional vision of womanly virtue, with its emphasis on social attributes that were required of the courtier as well, such as courtly manners, grace, and, most notably, wit. Yet the inclusion on the list of behaviors that were more traditionally associated with unruly women and seldom attributed to men suggests how difficult it was to escape traditional gender ideology – court ladies, even their defenders admitted, must avoid vanity, envy, insults, conflict, and foolishness.

This lack of parity went deeper, for Giuliano continued, "It seems to me that it is more necessary that she [the court lady] be beautiful than is the case for the courtier, because to tell the truth a woman is most wanting who lacks beauty." In the face of that beauty, he warned, "She must also be very cautious and take special care not to do anything that would cause others to speak badly of her. She must act in such a way that she is not stained by misdeeds or even suspected of them, because a woman is not capable of defending herself against false accusations as is a man." Beauty and a lack of the ability to defend oneself against false accusations – apparently referring to a lack of physical ability to defend one's *virtù* via a duel or simple violence – allowed the double standard to reenter the discussion even from the perspective of the defenders of women. That return of the double standard and the emphasis on a woman's body as a "natural" limit on her freedom notwithstanding, Castiglione's supporters of women allowed them a much wider range of *virtù*. Giuliano concluded, aptly revealing this mix: "And although continence, magnanimity, temperance, strength of spirit, prudence and the other *virtù* may not seem important for social life [at court] I want [the court lady] to be adorned with all these not so much for social life as in order to be *virtù*-ous and so that these *virtù* make her a person worthy of honor."

All this was much too much for Gasparo. He returned to the attack with, "I am surprised that now that you have given to women literature, continence, magnanimity, and temperance that you do not want them to govern cities, make laws and lead armies" and continued with a famous diatribe against women that ended with his claiming on the authority of Aristotle that a woman was "a defect of nature." He conceded that for this they should not be despised but rather accepted for what they were, "a manifest error." Few of the discussants were willing to accept Gasparo's harsh judgment. But as far as ruling was concerned, even Giuliano, after noting that Plato had posited that women should rule along with men in his ideal republic, sidestepped the issue by insisting that he was talking about a court lady, not a queen. Yet Gasparo's challenge that the claims for the wide-ranging *virtù* of women implied that they were as capable as men of ruling was not addressed – perhaps because it was too dangerous an idea even for the supporters of women.

Significantly, however, that missed discussion of the relationship between *virtù* and the ability to rule presaged the crucial concluding discussion of book four. For much as in *The Prince*, the goal of Castiglione's ideal courtier was to encourage a prince to act with *virtù* and overcome the travails of Italy. Ottaviano Fregoso opened this theme by pointing out that he did not think that all the previous discussion was really worth much if the courtier sought only to make himself "noble, graceful, and pleasant" without offering "other fruits." In fact, such a courtier seemed merely "frivolous and vain." He thus suggested, in a manner that echoed both Aristotle and Machiavelli, that true *virtù* must be measured not simply by personal aggrandizement or accomplishments, but rather by "the ends" that it made possible. A pleasing personality, a winning lover, a noble disposition were not enough: "[O]ften these skills merely make the spirits of men effeminate (*effeminare la anima*), corrupt youth, and reduce [the courtier] to a most lascivious life" – once again the dangerous satyr in the garden. The courtier must instead use his *virtù* to pursue a more significant goal, or the game was not worth playing.

Fregoso's argument had called into question the whole project of Castiglione's ideal courtier as well as the significance of actual courtiers and courts. But, tellingly, Fregoso's critique opened the door to a vision of a critical goal that the *virtù* of the perfect courtier might serve, a goal that just might save the Rinascimento. "The end/goal of the perfect courtier," he argued, "I hold to be to win the grace and heart of the prince he serves." This, however, was not merely to dissimulate one's true nature, as is sometimes claimed, in order to win favor or power. For he explained,

> [I]n this way [the courtier] is able to tell him [the prince] and always say to him the truth of everything that he should know without fear or danger of displeasing him. And when [the courtier] sees that he [the prince] is inclined toward something that is unwise, he has the courage to contradict him thanks to the grace he has gained with those good qualities [of the ideal courtier]. Thus he leads [his prince] away from every evil intention and *onto the path of virtù*. [italics mine]

And he concluded leaving no doubt that the ultimate goal was *virtù* both for the courtier and the prince,

> [B]ecause the courtier has in himself the fullness [of *virtù*] … he will know in every situation how to smoothly make his prince see how much honor and utility he and his supporters can gain from justice, generosity, magnanimity, gentleness and the other *virtù* which are required of good princes and, in contrast, how much infamy and damage are the results of the vices which contradict them.

At virtually the same moment that Machiavelli was attempting to advise a prince on the way to succeed by following the path of *virtù*, Castiglione had given one of his central speakers an argument that required the ideal courtier to advise his prince and guide him on the path of *virtù*. And if one overlooks for a moment the flexible nature of the term, the projects seem exactly the same – a prince with the advice of Machiavelli, or Castiglione's perfect courtiers following the path of *virtù*, will overcome the "effeminacy" (both writers use the gendered term) and immorality of the day to return Italy to its lost greatness.

Machiavelli may have seen his prince as merely a transitional figure necessary to return to a republic of *virtù*, and at its most ruthless, his *virtù* was
probably much more amoral and aggressive than Castiglione's. But for both
men *virtù* was the key, and moreover, both saw it as creating a moral state
and society that might overcome the vices and "effeminacy" of the present.
Behind their shared hope for *virtù*, however, lay a deeper shared assumption,
for both agreed that the morality of true *virtù* was ultimately measured by
the state and its duty to create an ordered and disciplined society. Individuals,
both courtiers and princes, could act immorally at times in order to secure
the goal of a stable and moral state; in fact, Machiavelli saw clearly that that
was often necessary. Castiglione's courtiers were more circumspect, yet the
virtù that they saw as central required a careful tailoring of self to present a
personality that was pleasing to the prince, their peers, and their consensus
realities, in order to serve the purpose of guiding the prince in creating and
sustaining a just state. And while to a degree this tailoring may have required
a certain dissimulation and manipulation of appearances, for both men it
was driven at its heart by an honest deeper commitment to *virtù* in the
true prince or courtier. Thus in a deep way the civic morality of the shared
primary culture of the Rinascimento sustained by the state had become the
basis of morality for both.

Was this the discovery of the modern state? Or was it a step on a path to
a vision of the state as the ultimate arbiter of morality, a path that tends to
lead to modern totalitarian thinkers of both the left and the right? Or was it
merely a moment of perceived moral crisis, when thinkers who saw the state
as the only answer to that crisis reasserted its moral imperatives more aggressively? My guess is that the last option is the case and that as far as the future
of the ideal is concerned, periodically across the Western tradition the state
has had the potential to emerge as the ultimate arbiter of morality and occasionally has done so, if seldom with happy results. The irony in all this is that,
of course, for both thinkers the real arbiter of morality behind the state was
the social evaluation of *virtù* – a constant evaluation that ideally was carried
on in the daily life at court, in the halls of government, in the home, and in
the streets via consensus realities. A kind of regime of *virtù* – socially judged,
enforced, and reinforced by state, church, tradition, and the groups that surrounded one in daily life – actually ruled and created a relatively stable and
disciplined society, often much more powerful than the limited disciplining
powers of government. From that perspective it is hardly surprising that not
only Castiglione and Machiavelli, but a host of writers of the first half of the
sixteenth century turned to *virtù* as the unquestioned cure to overcome the
crisis of their society.

It is also worth considering that although the courtier's *virtù* is measured largely in terms of the court's perception of it, it seems that behind the self-fashioning and consensus realities involved, Castiglione's discussion implies that there was also an interior sense of self and inner *virtù* that had to be maintained. One played the courtier on the stage of court, but behind the poses of *virtù* there needed to exist a truly *virtù*-ous person. If this reading is correct, it would fit well with the views of scholars who see the court and its atmosphere of simulation and conscious self-fashioning as one of the sources of a stronger sense of self, an interior, self-evaluating self on the way to a modern, more inner sense of individuality. In an ironic way, the court as the quintessential place of appearances and judging action, in such interpretations, becomes the birthplace as well for a more careful evaluation of the inner "truths" of self; for as one carefully covered one's inner self with a courtly masquerade of mannered and refined behavior, one was forced in that external self-fashioning to face more squarely the internal self that was being restrained and masked. Discovering the origins of the modern inner self is a tricky business, but along with a more confessional emphasis – which, as we shall see, in the next chapter, was a major focus of the spiritual enthusiasms of the century and its reforms – the sixteenth century with its many crises seems to be one where a greater attention to a "true" inner self and self-evaluation was called for and made sense.

Returning to Castiglione and his courtiers, Gasparo, ever the contrarian, raised an objection to the courtier guiding the prince to the path of *virtù*. "Reviewing what has been said to this point," he observed, "one may draw one conclusion: that the courtier who leads the prince to *virtù* ... must almost certainly be old." Yet being a successful courtier turned on winning the love of the women of court; for all had earlier agreed that women were the judges of the perfect courtier and that winning their love was required. In turn, virtually all had agreed as well that young men were more attractive and successful lovers than old. To make his point Gasparo turned to a particularly popular ancient example, Aristotle, who had served as an advisor to Alexander the Great. At first glance Aristotle might have seemed from the perspective of the Rinascimento the perfect example of a courtier who had guided perhaps the most powerful prince of the ancient world on the path of *virtù*, with impressive success. Yet Gasparo mockingly noted, "If your old courtier Aristotle were in love and were to do the things that we see some young lovers do today, I doubt that he would find the correct harmony to teach his prince [*virtù*] and ... women would delight in making fun of him." Gasparo's irony threatened to return the court to an empty game and courtiers to young lovers, with wiser older men and their *virtù* condemned to the sidelines because they were not competitive as lovers.

Gasparo, however, had moved the discussion on to another crucial disciplining word of the day, *amore* (love), with his attack on older lovers. Rising to their defense was a champion Pietro Bembo, who took over the fourth book of *The Book of the Courtier* at this point with an impassioned monologue that not only defended old men as lovers, but also made them the perfect advisors to the prince. Bembo foiled Gasparo's irony, insisting that "the [older] courtier can love in a way that not only would not bring him any censure but rather much praise and the highest felicity ... something that the young seldom find; and as a result he would not have to give up on advising the prince." Following in the footsteps of a long tradition that included Ficino, Petrarch, Dante, and, of course, the ancient philosopher Plato and his followers, he exalted the love of truly *virtù*-ous old men that left behind the passions and sensual pleasures of the physical to seek the higher reality that stood behind those pleasures.

The beauty and love that young lovers found in the physical world, Bembo reasoned, were mere reflections of true beauty and love, which existed only in the real, unchanging world that stood eternally behind this world of change. The older courtier, with the true wisdom of that world, unclouded by youthful passions – once again ultimately *virtù* – understood that what he loved in his court lady was at its best merely a reflection of a true, unchanging beauty and goodness. Crucially, that love and that realization made him a lover of the enduring truth and beauty beyond this world and thus not only an ideal lover, but also a perfect advisor to the prince. He did not let his physical passions cloud his judgment, and his desires were all turned toward truth, *virtù*, and ultimately the author of that perfect spiritual world, God.

Bembo contrasted this lover with all the negatives of the young lover dominated by his emotions, detailing his unruly passions, dishonors, disgraces, and even violence, all of which he saw as stemming from the fact that his emotions and love were not yet disciplined by *virtù*. Young lovers were ensnared by a passion for "corrupt bodies," which were in the end merely "dreams and weak shadows of beauty," in contrast to true mature lovers and courtiers, who had discovered "the sweet flame," "the gracious fire," and "divine beauty" of the true spiritual world and ultimately of God. Although such a lover might enjoy a "spiritual kiss" or two with his beloved, his love and his finely tuned courtly graces merely served to elevate the courtier into a perfect lover of *virtù* whose ultimate goal was to lead his prince in a similar development. Thus court life and its games of love became, in Bembo's vision, a serious school of *virtù* for courtiers and ultimately for princes. Evidently this was a utopian vision and perhaps, with its addition of perfect spiritual love, an even more unlikely utopian vision than Machiavelli's ideal republic based on *virtù*-ous citizens and laws. Yet both thinkers, like many of their contemporaries, facing what they saw as a crisis that threatened their society and its cultural leadership in the world, turned to the promise and disciplining truism of *virtù* as the answer to regaining what had been lost.

Ariosto: Doubts about Re-Dreams of Virtù

Ludovico Ariosto might seem at first glance both the most noted literary figure of sixteenth-century Italy and the least interested in providing answers to the crisis of his day. His most famous work, then as now, was his long epic romance *Orlando furioso*. It returned to one of the favorite literary fantasies of the Rinascimento, the chivalric romances of Charlemagne and his knights, freely intermixed with the Breton heroes of twelfth-century French Arthurian cycles, to weave a rich tapestry of the adventures and loves of a number of already popular characters from that genre. Many at the time read it as escape literature, and among critics it long garnered a certain disregard because of its apparent irrelevance to the issues of the day and also because of its apparent indifference to the increasingly strict genre and language requirements of humanist critics. To those disciplinarians the work seemed to offer an escape to the wrong first time (a fantastic early Middle Ages) in the wrong language (Italian) and with the wrong heroes (chivalric knights) while breaking all the rules of genre as a narrative poem, a romance, or an epic, and moreover with what seemed like proscribed jumps in time, space, and action. To make matters worse, a certain irony shimmered barely beneath the poetry's soaring beauty to undermine its heroes, who often were seemingly being subtly mocked, undercutting even the pleasurable escape of the fantasy. Still, it was immensely popular, reprinted almost one hundred times in the sixteenth century alone.

Adding to its importance, its narrative served the needs of Ariosto's powerful courtly patrons, the Este family of Ferrara, because it traced their origins back to the heroic past of yet another first time, the first time of the Middle Ages. Bradamante, the impressive female warrior who spends most of the poem dressed in armor passing as a male paladin and who defeats in various battles most of the heroes of the genre, in the end appears to be tamed by the somewhat less impressive and heroic Ruggiero, descended, however, from the Trojan hero Hector. From their marriage Ariosto traces the foundation of the house of Este and his patrons, Alfonso d'Este and the Cardinal

Ippolito d'Este.Yet this impressive genealogy begins to suggest that the work and Ariosto's vision might not be quite so escapist and irrelevant to the big issues of his day as is sometimes claimed.

Certainly Ariosto was deeply involved in the political struggles and the courtly world of his day, even as he often lamented that fact and the way it interfered with his writing. Born in 1474 as the first of at least ten children (the number varies in different accounts), his father served the Este family, and he was raised in close association with their court in Ferrara. He studied law, unhappily, at the behest of his father, but early on moved on to the *studia humanitatis* with the noted scholar and Augustinian monk Gregorio da Spoleto. He also reportedly studied philosophy at the University of Ferrara, and one of his first letters in Latin that survives is written to Aldus Manutius in Venice in 1498 asking him to send him whatever he had by Ficino or the Greek Platonists translated into Latin. During this period it appears he also met the older Pietro Bembo at the Este court, whom he adopted as a mentor given their common interests in Plato, Ficino, and love poetry. Bembo would remain an important literary guide throughout his life, and his stout advocacy of the Tuscan of Dante, Petrarch, and Boccaccio as the foundational works of a literary Italian language would have a strong impact on Ariosto and his writing. In fact, in the 1520s we find him asking Bembo in his letters to help him correct the Italian for the final definitive version of *Orlando furioso* published in 1532 in order to bring it in line as much as possible with the former's vision of a literate Italian.

Ariosto's youthful studies were cut short in his mid-twenties when his father died in 1500, leaving him in charge of his large family. Although he had already received small subsidies from the Este family, he began almost immediately to work for them as a courtier and bureaucrat. In 1503 he joined the household of Cardinal Ippolito d'Este and served him – unhappily, according to his letters – for a number of years as the cardinal traveled around Italy. Ippolito was infamous for his violent, high-handed ways, a reputation that Ariosto confirmed in full. During this period Ariosto clearly experienced personally the many negatives of life as a courtier serving a difficult patron in the troubled times of the early sixteenth century – troubled days in which he was deeply involved at the side of a major player. And in those same years he began the *Orlando furioso*, probably in 1504. Shortly after he finished the first version of the poem, printed with the support of the cardinal in 1516 and dedicated to him, Ariosto finally abandoned him. In 1517, pleading illness and advancing old age at forty-three, he refused to accompany Ippolito when he moved to Hungary to take up a lucrative bishopric. His decision was probably influenced by an apparently unrelated event, the death in 1515 of the Florentine merchant Tito Strozzi. What made that so important to Ariosto was that Tito was the husband of his secret love, Alessandra Benucci. After her husband's death she moved to Ferrara, and the lovers took up a quiet life together (reportedly later formalized by a secret marriage), which Ariosto was apparently unwilling to abandon to follow his difficult patron.

Fortunately, Ariosto's growing literary fame, based on the first enthusiastic responses to the *Furioso* as well as a couple of popular comedies written for court and a large number of more ephemeral pieces, won him the patronage in 1518 of Alfonso I d'Este, Ippolito's brother and duke of Ferrara. Although Alfonso was less difficult than his brother, Ariosto soon found himself tasting once more the unhappy fruits of being dependent on a powerful patron. In 1522 he accepted the onerous task of serving as the governor of the Garfagnana for Alfonso. A mountainous territory on the disputed borders between Florentine territory and lands claimed by the papacy, it had long had a reputation for ferocious conflicts between local clans and a large population of criminals banned from neighboring states who added to the violent tenor of life in the region. Attempts at quelling that violence with reason and diplomacy brought few results, and Ariosto was soon reduced to adopting the expedients that Machiavelli had advocated in *The Prince* a few years earlier. For, as he lamented, the people he was dealing with were *triste*, in virtually the sense that Machiavelli had used the term – that is, lacking in civility and *virtù* and thus incapable of being ruled without recourse to deceit and violence. To make matters worse, it seems that his patron, Alfonso, and his agents were not entirely trustworthy or straightforward either. In sum, his experience was bitter and disillusioning in ways that seemed to call into question the unquestionable Rinascimento verities of *virtù*, reason, and even courtly aristocratic values.

Finally he stepped down, returned to the court at Ferrara, and lived out his last years working on revising his *Orlando furioso*, which in the meantime had made him famous. His third and last revision was published in 1532, the year before his death, and included a considerable amount of new material and a significant revision of the language to make it conform to the new ideal of Italian as a literary language. Not surprisingly, given Ariosto's difficult life and his disappointment with his Estense patrons, although the poem celebrates the distinguished founding of their family in a chivalric first time, lying just below the surface polish of the poetry and the swirling detail of its myriad adventures there runs a more disillusioned commentary on his contemporary world. Much as Albert Ascoli argued in his path-breaking work on the poem, *Ariosto's Bitter Harmony*, beneath the harmony of the work lies a bitter vision that was anything but escapist fantasy. At the most obvious level, rather than celebrating the beauty and excitement of warfare as was typical of the epic genre, he portrays it as brutal, bloody, and senseless. In fact, his descriptions of the violence and destruction of battles is at times so over the top, with shorn limbs and heads flying through the air and piling up in pools of blood, that it seems hard to escape the conclusion that he is mocking the chivalric tradition's celebration of martial violence and in the process making a strongly negative reflection on the Italian wars of his day.

But at a deeper level the tensions that lay at the heart of the Rinascimento vision of life, which both Machiavelli and Castiglione worked so hard to return to harmony, are presented in the *Furioso* as ultimately irreconcilable. Thus, although he shares both writers' vision that things have come apart and that Italy has lost its place as the leader and the measure of the world, over and over again in the *Furioso*, *virtù* fails to deliver. Reason is blown away by the whims of fortune, courtly grace and honor are cut short by the merely strong or the unjust, and love is portrayed as destructive and dangerous rather than as the tie that holds society together. Far from an escape into a realm of fantasy, the work, when looked at more closely, seems a denial of the Rinascimento, even as it dutifully provides Ariosto's patrons with a noble heritage in a glorious first time and in an artful way provides a series of fascinatingly intertwined tales and characters that grab and hold a reader's attention – bitter harmony indeed.

One thing that caught the attention of readers in the sixteenth century and that has recently reignited discussion of the work is the prominent role women play in the romance. Of course, this was part of a chivalric tradition in which women were required as the objects of desire and the prizes of noble paladins, where love drove much of the action. In fact, the Ferrarese author Matteo Maria Boiardo (c. 1440–1494), whose unfinished earlier chivalric romance *Orlando innamorato* Ariosto took up officially to complete, had already introduced the two dominating female figures of the *Furioso*, Angelica and Bradamante. Deanna Shemek has suggestively rethought the centrality of their characters in her important study, *Ladies Errant*, pointing out that the heroes and the action of the poem are largely driven by the two. Although she does not use the image, Angelica in her analysis appears rather like Helen of Troy – rather than the face that launched a thousand ships, she is the object of desire that launches a thousand adventures. The mere sight of her angelic visage evokes overwhelming love in the males who encounter her, and in the face of their serial mad passions Angelica flees through dark woods, deserted terrain, and many adventures attempting to escape their love. In turn, her would-be lovers desert their comrades in need, lose their way metaphorically in life and their lives literally in battles for her, while the supposed hero of the work, Orlando, even loses his mind (hence the *furioso* [mad] of the title) when she falls in love and marries another. Love of Angelica brings not harmony but disaster.

Bradamante, by contrast, was at once a more positive and more troubling character. Early in the story she has been informed that she will marry Ruggiero, founding the great Este family, a foreknowledge of that foundational match that awaits her at the end of the poem. But before that marriage she is one of the most impressive military figures of the poem, as perhaps befits the future mother of the Este line, which prided itself on its warrior virtues. Still, for a future maternal figure, she spends most of her time in armor, unhorsing one seemingly invincible warrior after another in a way that has troubled many in the sixteenth century and thereafter. In several episodes, in fact, she seems almost to deny that she is a woman, a decidedly uncomfortable claim for one destined to give birth to Ariosto's patron's noble family.

Recently, however, critics with a different vision of gender have come down hard on Bradamante, lamenting that after all her courageous breaking of gender codes and her adventures demonstrating her more-than-full equality with men, in the end she sheds her armor to become once more a loyal daughter and seems ready to bow down to her father's plans to marry her against her wishes to the son of the emperor of Constantinople. Yet it might be argued that her loyal daughter act reads more like just that, an act. She does shed her armor, and she does seem to give up her love for Ruggiero (and her promised destiny) in order to obey her father's wishes. But she does so only in the context of her clever strategy to thwart his plans, for she insists that she will marry only a man who can defeat her in battle. Thus she re-dons her armor and reenters the lists, only to be defeated apparently by the very man her father has chosen to marry her. But it turns out that that knight who bested her was actually Ruggiero in disguise, and thus she has her desire in the end, marrying exactly the person she loved with the approval of her father and Ariosto's patrons, who after all needed a mother for their line. They may have received a stronger and more martial one than they really appreciated, which may explain Ippolito's cool response to the first edition of the poem dedicated to him. In fact, if Bradamante has a weakness it may be the fact that she must give the poem a positive ending, and thus, for all the disillusionment and negative vision of Ariosto, the poem must end with a certain harmony given by her maternal promise, which partially obscures its deep pessimism.

The same cannot be said for Angelica. For, although she is a character who has fascinated not just the males of the poem, but males ever since in literature, art, and fantasy, with a minimum of reconsideration she seems considerably less attractive than her name and her famed beauty might suggest. Simply, Angelica is no Angel. Actually, for all her beauty, she is duplicitous and ever ready to con other characters into serving her in her never-ending times of need. Of course, as a character – and a plot-driving character at that – she can hardly be faulted. But the point is that with a name like Angelica a reader is set up to see her as Angelic, the epitome of beauty and all that goes with it. And therein lies the rub. In the vision of love and beauty that went back to Plato and more recently to Ariosto's own mentor, Bembo, the love of beauty in nature, in literature, or in a beautiful woman turned on the way in which that beauty reflected a deeper truth. Outer beauty was merely a reflection of inner beauty, and that, as we have seen, was merely a reflection of a deeper harmony and the highest truth. Angelica was the most beautiful woman any of the heroes had ever seen, immediately eliciting love; yet in her case, her beauty did not reflect a deeper truth. And love for her did not make men better. It made them worse and often destroyed them. Beauty, then, is not truth, Ariosto seems to be saying. And evoking that bitter realization, Angelica flees love through a series of dark woods that suggest that she and her beauty are constantly fleeing not just lovers but the light of knowledge. If this reading is correct, love did not make perfect courtiers, as Castiglione and Bembo opined, or offer a solution to the day's problems; in fact, it rendered heroes mad, as was the case with Orlando. Dante, lost in a dark wood, discovered Virgil, who brought him an ancient wisdom that helped him to find a modern paradise. Orlando discovered in a dark wood that his Angelica had deserted him for another once and for all and found only madness. In Ariosto's vision the certainties of the Rinascimento were dissolving in the dark woods of an Italy that seemed to have lost its glory and promise.

The Virtù of Exceptional Women and Recapturing Italy's Lost Glory

While for Castiglione the *virtù* that might save the Rinascimento was to be found in the aristocratic and courtly worlds that he imagined, for Ariosto, who had lost faith in that *virtù* and the life of a courtier, the only character whom he could imagine as consistently demonstrating its efficacy was a woman, Bradamante. And, in fact, the arbiters of *virtù* in the sixteenth century were over and over women. Not all women, of course, although from time to time a nod might be made in that direction, but rather those who were deemed the very best of women, the most aristocratic, and the most *virtù*-ous. Women like the imaginary Bradamante and the *apparently real* Isabella d'Este and the other women of aristocratic courts, who were seen as literally larger than life and works of art in their day. "Apparently real," for, as noted earlier, these outstanding individuals could hardly have existed as they were imagined and lionized. In a way, they were extraordinary Bradamante characters written on historical personages; thus, it is not surprising that historians and critics have easily picked holes in their heroic images. But in the way those images were deployed at the time and the way they played for contemporaries, we can begin to discover their importance for the hope of recapturing lost glory.

Significantly, the actual historical Pietro Bembo and Ludovico Ariosto agreed that a number of contemporary women demonstrated the *virtù* to help Italy regain its lost cultural and political leadership. Two that they singled out for leadership were Veronica Gambara (1485–1550) and Vittoria Colonna (c. 1490–1547). Ariosto, in his 1532 rewrite of *Orlando furioso*, named both as exceptional and styled Colonna as literally an archetype of female *virtù*, who in her person brought together the traditional ideals of chastity and love for her husband with learning and literary skill. In turn, not only was Bembo willing to exchange letters with both and include their poetry in his anthologies, he also selected what he saw as the most flattering of their letters to be published in his own collected letters. In addition, he actively encouraged the poetry of both, and Gambara even claimed him as a valued mentor. Finally, he also wrote a number of sonnets praising both women that portrayed them as heroic literary figures, as the titles dedicated to Colonna suggest: "Crown Her Temple with the Beloved Laurel," "Lofty Column (Colonna), Firm against the Storms," and perhaps most telling, "Beloved and Sovereign of the Honor of Our Age" – no small compliment.

Gambara and Colonna were from the very highest ranks of the aristocratic world of their day, which allowed them to move beyond the normal restraints that limited would-be women writers and intellectuals – although, as we shall see, even they never entirely escaped gender's disciplining power. Thus unlike many women writers of the fifteenth century, their literary careers and their fame did not end when their status as youthful prodigies passed after marriage. If anything, their fame grew, especially after they became widows (Gambara in 1518, Colonna in 1521). Both wrote love poetry early in their lives, for the most part safely dedicated to their husbands. Suggestively, their fame was even in a way confirmed together in Bologna in 1529–1530. There the two women, one literally (Gambara), one poetically (Colonna), were significant players in the political events that swirled around the Emperor Charles V, who, following the peace signed at Cambrai in 1529 that consolidated his power in Italy, came to Bologna to be crowned emperor by the pope.

Charles was greeted there by a host of Italian leaders, their representatives, petitioners, and the courtiers and supporters who swirled around
them. Even Isabella d'Este was on hand, playing politics; in return for her
support, it will be remembered, the emperor named her son while there
marquis of Mantua. When Charles arrived, Gambara was already on hand,
and not just as a well-known poet; for she was a major player as the countess
of Correggio, a title that she held officially from the emperor as a prized ally.
Making her position in Bologna even more significant was the fact that her
brother Umberto, who would eventually become a cardinal, had been made
papal governor of the city in 1528. Thus he was officially responsible for
hosting the emperor's visit. A second brother who had followed a military
career had also fought in Charles's armies. An indication of how close she
stood to the emperor is the fact that he visited her not once but twice at her
estates in Correggio during his time in Italy. Even her poetry proclaimed
their closeness, as she wrote at least four sonnets celebrating him and his
military successes.

While she was living in Bologna, then, where her brother ruled, she entertained a circle of noted intellectuals drawn from the diplomats and officials
gathered in the city to celebrate the emperor's coronation and work out the
realities of the new order of imperial dominance in Italy. Perhaps the most
famous was Pietro Bembo, who had been and was an active promoter of
Gambara's literary *virtù*. And while critics had long recognized that literary
virtù, it certainly did not hurt that Gambara was much more than an exceptional poet and intellect. She was a major political figure able to exert real
influence where it mattered. As such, she was cultivated and lionized and
returned the favor in ways that confirmed her significance.

Meanwhile, Bembo had been given copies of a number of Colonna's
love poems that celebrated her ongoing love and mourning for her dead
husband. Soon they were circulating among the intellectuals gathered in
Bologna, with Bembo's enthusiastic support. As Bembo was the recognized
master of the genre of love poetry, that support certainly attracted attention to her writing. But once again it did not hurt that her late husband,
Francesco Ferrante d'Avalos, Marquis of Pescara, had been one of Charles's
top generals, or that he had been from a prominent Spanish noble family
in Naples, or that her own family, the Colonna, had been one of the most
important families in Rome for centuries. Thus she was once again more
than a poet. Significantly, in her person and in her love poetry for her husband, she could be presented as representing a harmonious and loving union
between the old order of Italian aristocracy and the new order of imperial/
Spanish power in the peninsula, now in the hands of Charles V.

Virginia Cox points out in her study of Italian women writers of this period that Colonna's verse celebrating her husband was much more than the warm recollections of a loving wife; for it was rich with "political and ideological meanings" that literally married a leading Italian noble family of long standing with the new political realities of the peninsula. Cox goes on to point out another aspect of this complex celebration of her marital love, noting that her cousin via marriage, Alfonso d'Avalos, Marquis of Vasto, had been brought up by Colonna in her own household as virtually a "son." He too was a major figure, earning a reputation as a leader of imperial troops, and in 1535 would become Charles's governor of Milan and thus a prominent political figure in the new imperial order in Italy. Significantly, he was also another major promoter of Colonna. In this context it was he who in 1531 gave Ariosto a "generous pension," and thus it was probably not by chance that in the latter's 1532 revision of the *Furioso* the author added his fulsome praise of Colonna's *virtù* as a poet. Making things even more intertwined, we know that Alfonso had actually met Ariosto at, of all places, Gambara's estates in Correggio in 1531. Small world. It may have been from these contacts that a correspondence grew up between the two women in which they shared their poetry and which further increased their fame.

That exchange reveals, however, that their poetic interests were diverging. Gambara left her love poetry behind for what she saw as more serious themes for serious times. Colonna, by contrast, defended her continued emphasis on her love for her dead husband, progressively emphasizing the kind of Neo-Platonic vision of love as a path on the way to true knowledge that Bembo had long advocated. Later in life, however, Colonna turned her love poetry to more spiritual and reforming concerns. These later "*rime spirituali*," as they were known, melded Petrarchian and Bembian ideals of poetry with religious verse in a manner that became a model for many later poets. Her spiritual interests, however, led her to become a leading figure, along with Bembo, in the general currents of religious enthusiasm that were sweeping Italy in the forties and fifties of the century. In this she was treading on dangerous ground, and several of her friends at the time were actually questioned by the Inquisition about her beliefs on predestination and justification by faith alone.

Her spiritual poetry stressed the importance of Christ's passion and the central role his grace and faith played in salvation. This seemed dangerously close to what was being defined as heresy at the time, as we shall see, but it should be noted that an emphasis on love that had always been a strong theme in her poetic vision and the power of Christ's love for humanity could be used to defend her work as more traditional. Be that as it may, in her later years she was close to more radical reformers in the Church, especially the English Cardinal Pole and Bembo himself, and perhaps too close to reformers who eventually were declared heretics, such as Pietro Carnesecchi and Bernardino Ochino. But once again her status as one of the leading women in Italy, and also as one of the leading literary figures of her day, probably saved her from closer examination by ecclesiastical authorities. She, Gambara, and Bembo all died within a few years of each other in 1547, 1550, and 1547, respectively, and while neither their poetic or political *virtù* nor their various visions saved Italy, their lives and writings did highlight the new complex aristocratic order in Italy that was adapting to foreign rule and the spiritual enthusiasms of reform.

Re-Dreams or Nightmares? Aretino, the Satyr in the Garden, and Virtù

Even that order and the way it had been built upon the apparent verities of the Rinascimento did not go unquestioned in the crisis of the sixteenth century. For there had always been another side of that society, at times celebrated but more often uncomfortably ignored – a satyr in the Rinascimento garden that, like the satyrs of the ancient world, suggested that humans were divided between *virtù* and vice, reason and passion, half godlike and half animal. Perhaps the most famous critic of civic morality, the infamous satirist and irreverent wordsmith Pietro Aretino (1492–1556), might be seen as the defender and embodiment of that satyr. Almost a generation younger than Machiavelli and Castiglione, Aretino was literally a child of the crisis of the sixteenth century. And in his writing he touched critically on many of the day's largely unquestioned verities, attacking princes, courts, and *virtù* with a mocking and deeply prescient irony and laughter. Born into a lower-class family, he left home at an early age to seek his fortune as an artist. In the midteens, at about the same time that Castiglione and Machiavelli were writing their most important works, he returned to Rome (where earlier he had briefly served the rich Roman banker Agostino Chigi) after the election of the Medici pope Leo X (1475–1521; pope 1513–1521), who apparently enjoyed his irreverent wit and cutting tongue. And he soon gained the pope's favor, as a kind of racy court master of gossip and slander.

From that platform he launched his literary career with an impressive range of ephemeral writings that attracted attention because of its lively nature and its clever wordplay that often attacked contemporary events and personalities. Across his career his fame was reinforced by a series of works in praise of famous men and, perhaps more importantly, by others that offered cutting insults to the rich and famous who did not patronize him. These writings

were much feared for their clever, mocking, and often earthy humor, relying heavily on evocative wordplay that elevated the insulting sexual banter
of the streets into a complex pyrotechnics that captured the imagination of
contemporaries. In fact, they were so popular and feared that his older contemporary Ludovico Ariosto labeled him "the scourge of princes," perhaps
echoing a label Aretino had coined for himself in his quite successful attempt
to fashion himself as a decidedly dangerous piece of art – a satyr with both
a smile and teeth. It certainly did not hurt that his libels often had the ring
of truth, or at least probability. Evidently the rich and powerful had much to
fear, for many were willing to pay handsomely to avoid Aretino's clever cuts
or to win his praises.

It has been claimed that the young Aretino actually came to the attention
of the pope when he penned a send-up of the papal court in the form of a
last will left by the pope's elephant, Hanno. Whether or not that was the case,
the will's clever satire captures the rowdy and licentious tone of the papal
city in the early sixteenth century during the reign of Leo X and opens
another widely shared contemporary perspective on the Medici pope. For
while he was an aggressive promoter of his family and his native city, as well
as a major renovator of Rome and patron, he was also noted for encouraging a playful and licentious atmosphere at his court – once again the satyr
in the Rinascimento garden. That court included a number of buffoons of
note, a claque of mocking and laughing writers, and even Hanno, his pet
elephant, who was regularly celebrated up to and after his death. In his will,
then, Hanno left a series of bawdy bequests to notables at the papal court,
not sparing even the most important cardinals of the day. Starting off exactly
like a regular will, Hanno noted that he was of sound mind but near death,
perhaps because of the Roman climate or, more likely, because of "the avarice of Giovanni Battista Branconi," a papal favorite and courtier responsible
for his care.

Things quickly became more cutting. Hanno named as the witnesses to
his will "the most reverend, disgraced before God, Cardinal Adriano Gouffier
de Boissy, Bishop of Costanza, protector of the corrupt and all the hypocrisy
and stupidity of France; the most reverend Andrea Corner, Venetian, bastard, inadequate, presumptuous, and empty-headed Archbishop of Spoleto;
and the most reverend lord Jacopo di Nino di Amelia, Bishop of Potenza,
legal expert in matters of lies, calumny and insults." He then proceeded to
bequeath the various parts of his body to other victims of the will's humor.
To the cardinal of Auch (Francesco Guglielmo de Clermont) he bequeathed
his trunk "so that he could always carry it with him full of wine to water his
unending thirst" and to supply refreshment for his "continuous bacchanals."

He gave his jaw to Lorenzo Pucci, a cardinal noted for his expropriation of revenues, especially from the sale of offices and indulgences, "so that he can devour all the money of the whole republic of Christ and consume legally and illegally every convent and church by creating new offices [to sell]."

But perhaps most insulting and over the top were his bequests of his genitals to the cardinals Marco Vigneri and Achille Grasso. To Marco he left his testicles, "so that he will be more fertile in producing children and in generating the Antichrist ... with the reverend Giulia of the nuns at [the convent of] Santa Catarina di Senigalia." To Grasso he left his phallus, "so that he can be more able to incarnate bastards with the aid of Madonna Andriana of Bologna." What made these bequests even more cutting was the fact that Marco was widely reported to be carrying on a relationship with Giulia, even though she was a nun, and Grasso's relationship with Andriana de Scottis of Bologna was well known – so well known, in fact, that in the Roman census of 1527 she is listed as living near the cardinal and using the name Andriana di Grasis.

Whether or not Aretino wrote the will, he certainly referred to it approvingly in a number of other works, and it captures the tone and bite of his scathing letters, mocking poems, satirical texts, and pasquinades. In fact, Hanno's will has much the same tone and many of the same victims as a series of pasquinades usually attributed to Aretino. Pasquinades were lampoons, usually anonymous, that were posted on or near a badly mutilated ancient statue in the center of the city referred to by Romans of the day as Pasquino. These pasquinades became so popular in a city hungry for gossip and slander that eventually an annual festival was established, with the verses attributed to the statue published. Aretino became known in Rome as a master of the form and one of the most followed and feared posters. His reputation, in fact, became so great that it appears that he often was given credit for particularly clever and cutting pasquinades not written by him, as was perhaps the case with Hanno's will.

Nonetheless, in Aretino's case, the pen for once almost seemed mightier than the sword. Even the king of France, Francis I (1494–1547; ruled 1515–1547) was pleased to send Aretino a heavy gold chain in reward for his compliments, a chain that Aretino frequently referred to with pride in his writings. In his famous portrait painted by Titian, now in the Frick Collection in New York, Aretino prominently displays the chain. Apparently, however, by the early 1520s he had begun to overstep the invisible but very real boundary between being a successful cutting wit and being seen as a liability in Rome. During that period he was in and out of the city and involved in controversies with various powers there. When Giulio de' Medici was elected Pope Clement VII (1478–1534; pope 1523–1534) he returned, but soon found himself embroiled with Giovanni Matteo Giberti (1495–1543), a close advisor to the pope.

Giberti had arrested Marcantonio Raimondi (c. 1480–1543), a famous engraver, for engravings he had made of Giulio Romano's (c. 1499–1546) drawings of a series of sexual positions in a classical setting, known as *I Modi*. It seems that while such explicit images of sexual intercourse were not all that troubling for the classical tastes of the papal court, familiar with similar depictions on ancient coins (*spintria*) and in classical literature, disseminating them more widely via engravings that could reach a larger public was frowned upon. Apparently Aretino used his favor with the pope to have Raimondi freed, earning the enmity of Giberti. To make matters worse, he then published a series of sonnets to accompany the engravings, with his anything-but-classical language explicating their ins and outs. Aretino soon found himself briefly jailed in 1524; once freed, he left the city again. After a reconciliation with the pope, he returned, but this stay was literally cut short when he was stabbed, perhaps as part of a conflict over a love affair or at the instigation of Giberti, or both. When the pope did not come to his defense, Aretino read the writing on the wall and left Rome for good in 1525.

In those years he wrote one of his more famous comedies, *The Courtesan*, which was a typically Aretine cutting attack on contemporary Rome and the papal court. The plot involves a Sienese gentleman, Messer Maco, characterized as a "studier of books," suggesting once again a would-be humanist scholar who has been made more foolish than wise by his adherence to that discipline. He goes to Rome with the overly optimistic goal of being appointed a cardinal – a goal that Aretino's introduction promises will produce laughter on a par with the laughter inspired by Hanno's will or the best Roman pasquinades. In Rome, Messer Maco learns that he first must become a perfect courtier in order to succeed in winning the favor of the pope and a cardinal's hat. Thus his path turns leeringly into the world of the prostitutes and courtesans of the city, who he discovers are the true masters of the court and its arts. His adventures in that world in many ways provide a mocking *Anti-Book of the Courtier*, reading at times as if it were written by Aretino with Castiglione's book open before him. Needless to say, this attack on Rome and the papal court did not contribute to Aretino's popularity there.

Putting Rome behind him, he moved around northern Italy, eventually settling in Venice, where he wrote his most important works and enjoyed the reputed peace and freedom of the city along with close relations with a number of its leading intellectuals and artists. His attacks on the corruption of courtly society and culture remained an important theme of his work for the rest of his life, perhaps most notably in the comedy *The Marescalco*, set in Mantua but with many laudatory references to Venice. In that work he mocks the fawning self-effacement required to serve a prince and survive at court, laughingly rendered in the travails of the prince's Master of the Horse (the *Marescalco* of the title), who unhappily attempts to avoid the marriage imposed upon him by his lord, as discussed earlier. Adding to Aretino's perverse humor, the Master of the Horse is portrayed as a young man on the cusp of adulthood who is not in the least interested in marriage or women, being committed to the love of younger males. Thus, the comedy also involves an aggressive ongoing defense of sodomy and a telling misogynist attack on marriage, married life, and wives. Strikingly, then, Aretino manages to attack the court, the licit sexual order of the day, and the marital base of society, along with the civic morality that most saw as the underpinning of the Rinascimento itself, all in one darkly laughing comedy.

But his most virulent attack on marriage, civic morality, and the ideal of *virtù* that underlay the widely shared ideology of social order evoked by both Machiavelli and Castiglione, is found in his infamous *Ragionamenti* (*Dialogues*) or *Sei giornate* (*Six Days*, because its discussions occur over six days). On the first three days of the dialogue an ex-prostitute, Nanna, discusses with her friend Antonia the options for the best life that her daughter Pippa and women in general had in the Rinascimento, concluding that prostitution was the best and most honest profession. Over the next three days the conversation moves on to consider how to make Pippa the best prostitute possible. In this discussion, Antonia, after listening to Nanna's descriptions of her dishonest and dissolute life as a nun and a wife and her successes as a prostitute, concludes, "I believe that you should make your daughter Pippa a whore: for the nun is a traitor to her sacred vows, the wife an assassin of holy matrimony, but the whore attacks neither the convent nor the husband. In fact … her shop sells that which she has to sell.… So be openhanded with Pippa and make her a whore from the start."

It is easy to dismiss Antonia's words as the usual hyperbole of the irreverent Aretino. And certainly they qualify as such, but in many ways they actually sum up accurately a cleverly presented analysis of the inherent problems with love, marriage, and the very Rinascimento social order built on the ideal of civic morality and *virtù*. On the first day Nanna describes her experiences as a young nun. Entering the convent with some reluctance as a young girl, she discovered that the fervors of her sisters were anything but otherworldly. In one voyeuristic scene after another Nanna paints an erotic picture of the sexual life of the convent, eventually enjoying a wide range of encounters that might well be seen as a more imaginative and erotic prose replay of Raimondi's *I Modi*. Clearly Aretino could not have expected his readers to believe that all convents were as sexually active and perverse; but he and they were well aware that for many young women of the upper classes, life as a nun had been forced upon them by their families when a suitable dowry could not be raised to marry them. The problem was compounded by the fact that daughters had to be married fairly quickly once they reached puberty or the delay would put them beyond the acceptable marriage age and once again compromise family honor. In the face of such exigencies, daughters, especially second and third ones, often found themselves pressed to enter convents without a vocation. In fact, in many cities this reality was recognized, and there existed a range of convents that spanned the gamut from the spiritually committed, noted for their religiosity, to the more open, noted for their more mundane ways and often lively social life.

On the second day Nanna described her life as a wife. After fleeing the dishonesties of the convent, she decided to opt for the more honest life of a wife, the life generally held up as the ideal for women in the Rinascimento. She soon found that there was little honesty in matrimony either. Lacking a father to arrange her marriage, her mother took the matter in hand, spreading a series of lies that attempted to fashion a consensus reality of her as a pious young virgin ready to take up her role as wife and mother. Her lies soon bore unhappy fruit: "An old man, who only lived because he was still eating … decided to have me for his wife or die. And as he was well-to-do, my mother … concluded the marriage." This arranged marriage between the lively and independent Nanna and an old man "who only lived because he was still eating" was doomed from the start. Her old husband's sexual failings soon led her to learn from neighborhood women all the little tricks necessary to find sexual pleasure outside of marriage. And once again her adulteries, motivated by the unhappiness of her arranged marriage, underlined the dishonesty of marriage for many women who were married to much older men and the dishonesty of arranged marriages based on family goals and lies from the first.

Yet Aretino saved the best for last, for Nanna reported the end of her marriage with perfect symmetry. In the beginning her old husband had wanted "to have me for his wife or die." Discovered in bed with a lover and attacked by her husband, she coolly ended her marriage by burying "a little knife that I had in his chest and his pulse beat no longer." Once again Aretino pushed his satire over the top, but his critique of marriage had considerable weight and could be heard by many; in fact, Nanna's problems in her marriage were the moving force behind a great deal of literature, spanning the gamut from serious treatises on marriage, quasi-serious debates on the merits of matrimony, and more playful satires and comedies that focused on such themes. Quite literally, then, Aretino had turned the Rinascimento ideals of love, marriage, and family on their head, and, with clever irony, he had done so by attacking the very ideological base of society.

Did Aretino then reject *virtù*, as one might expect of one of the most caustic critics of the day? No. Actually, even he was too deeply inserted in the primary culture of his day to escape the explanatory power of *virtù*. As noted earlier, he had Antonia recommend the life of the prostitute for Nanna's daughter Pippa because, in contrast to the life of nuns and wives, that life was honest. Prostitutes "sold in their shops what they had to sell." Thus in the end Antonia, the friend who has listened to the discussion patiently, is given a concluding speech proclaiming the ultimate saving grace of the prostitute: "So [Nanna] your words force me to conclude that the vices of prostitutes are *virtù*." Indeed, even Aretino, the mocking critic – the ultimate defender of the satyr in the garden – defends his radical vision by returning to *virtù* and claiming that the sins of prostitutes, because they are open and honest, are actually more *virtù*-ous than the false virtues and dishonesties of marriage or the convent – almost certainly tongue-in-cheek, but *virtù* nonetheless remains the measure.

Aretino's critique was too outrageous and too well hidden behind a perverse and at times sexually explicit narrative to win many supporters, although it did have considerable impact on a group of writers often referred to as polymaths. These writers, like Aretino, attempted to use their critical vision, wit, and lively writing (usually in Italian) to actually make a living as writers. Often from quite humble backgrounds, they churned out a large volume of work whose impact has begun to be studied more closely following Paul Grendler's pioneering work, *Critics of the Italian World (1530–1560)*, which focused on the fascinating and controversial figures Anton Francesco Doni, Nicolò Franco, and Ortensio Landi. Actually, all three had troubled relations with Aretino, in part because of their similarity to him and their competition with him. Franco, who early on seemed to have been a kind of disciple, was reported to have been slashed and disfigured by his former friend after a highly public disagreement in Venice and to have fled the city, at least in part, to avoid the latter's ire. These polymaths, along with an increasingly vocal group of fellow travelers, critically and often mockingly broke free from the tightening ideals of humanist scholarship as a discipline and challenged the verities of the day, much in the mold of Aretino. In the process they helped to lay the groundwork for what was seen at the time as a new intellectual movement that consciously rejected the social values and traditions of their society. As the Rinascimento wound to its end, at least some of their number would be labeled Libertines and would become more important (and feared) in aristocratic and scholarly circles. Some of the thinkers in this group were taken by Aretino's claim that *virtù* was actually to be found in the illicit world of sex and pleasure and claimed that true *virtù* was limited to an elite who were capable of breaking all sexual and social taboos and traditions – not so much amoral as beyond morality and apparently well beyond the Rinascimento.

The Satyr in the Garden: The Pleasures and Dangers of the Rinascimento Illicit World

Yet Aretino claimed both less and more, for unlike many of the later Libertines, he ultimately argued that the illicit world of sex and pleasure was a central part of the Rinascimento. And from that perspective his open and celebratory relationship with that world warrants a closer examination of it. For across our period, in the larger cities of the peninsula, a complex counterculture of passion, pleasure, and what were often deemed the "natural sins of the flesh" had developed that had its own traditions, forms, and rules. In theory, of course, this culture was officially rejected by the primary culture's civic morality and Christian ideals; but in fact, it was deeply intertwined with both. In fact, with apparent paradox but actually a certain logic, the illicit world of the Rinascimento often adapted the forms of the primary culture to its own ends and, perhaps unwittingly, often reinforced the values of that culture even. In that world houses of prostitution could be organized like convents, with abbesses disciplining the life of the brothel; concubines could be treated as wives and actually live as them; wives could be prostitutes supporting their families; courtesans could function as true court ladies, judging the best men; prostitutes could substitute for Petrarch's Laura and Dante's Beatrice and become the object of love poetry as well as writers of it; and, virtually unnoticed or ignored by scholars, the world of illicit sex could provide one of the few "safe" environments for love in the Rinascimento.

And although there were plenty of negatives to be found in the illicit world, especially in the form of exploitation of woman and the young, along with violence and fraud, it must not be forgotten that the emphasis on them reflects the vision of the winners. Few were ready to point out the ways in which the two worlds worked together or the aspects of the illicit world that played a significant role in sustaining the Rinascimento – not even Aretino. For when he came to write about the strategies for making Nanna's daughter Pippa a truly *virtù*-ous prostitute in the last three days of his *Sei Giornate*, he mockingly stressed all the tricks and crimes of the trade and the world of illicit sex. But a closer look at that illicit world suggests that things were not so simple. Looking first at prostitution, in larger cities like Venice, Rome, Florence, Naples, and Milan, we find that there were multiple levels of the *arte* (craft), a virtual social hierarchy that paralleled that of the licit world. At the lowest levels, the alleys and back ways of cities were frequented by lower-class women who were forced by economic necessity to prostitute themselves from time to time. Given that in Rinascimento cities there was always a large underclass living on the margins of subsistence, this group was probably larger than generally assumed, especially in times of economic hardship. Some of these women were married and working to help support their families; others were young women pressed by hard times or seeking to raise a dowry in order to marry.

Already one can see how this type of formally illicit activity – by supporting families, raising dowries, or simply by helping the poor to survive – actually sustained the primary culture and its institutions. Archival documents occasionally refer to these women, often in terms of the crimes that victimized them, and it is suggestive that they were frequently described by their neighbors as "good women" and "good neighbors" – expressing a positive consensus reality about their status. Complaints against them tended to develop when they were too aggressive or too successful, especially with the husbands of their neighbors. But if their practice was quiet and largely unseen, it was largely ignored, and it appears that the personal sacrifice involved even engendered at times a certain respect, at least from other women. These "irregulars" were formally illegal because they were usually unregistered with the authorities, largely in order to avoid taxation and the "discipline" of the policing agencies that were responsible for controlling the trade in most cities.

Registered prostitutes who worked in brothels that were often publicly run, ideally as a sexual service for the young males of the city, were much more visible in the governmental records. In the fourteenth and fifteenth centuries they were usually located at the very center of the city and closely associated with the main markets and commercial areas, and at times they were even celebrated as one of the attractions of the urban scene. Across the sixteenth century, however, they tended to be moved to less conspicuous locations and even outside the city walls, at least in part in response to more aggressive calls for reform and civic morality. In a few cities this trend reached its logical conclusion with their closing. Actually, however, already at the beginning of the sixteenth century the larger brothels were in decline, replaced by a more diverse workforce that met the demand for a more socially and economically variegated trade and a less visible one as well.

Many registered prostitutes were managed or controlled by a *ruffiano* or *ruffiana* (a male or female pimp, respectively). In theory these relationships were supposed to be supportive, but it seems clear from the criminal records that many were not. Across the century legislation that tried to limit their exploitation proliferated, suggesting that the problem was noted and ongoing. Authorities were especially concerned about young girls, often just into their teens, recruited from the countryside by *ruffiani*, with a promise of marriage or a dowry, then held in a virtual slavery, unable to escape. Yet at the same time both criminal documents and literature also refer to married couples or enduring partnerships where a *ruffiano* and a prostitute both claimed to be in a loving relationship and to merely be, in Aretino's terms, "selling" the only wares that their shop had to sell.

Perhaps the most noted literary reflection of this was the popular sixteenth-century comedy by Ariosto, *La Lena*. In this play the character called only Lena (another term for a *ruffiana*), who has been prostituted by her husband with her consent in order to survive economically, is presented sympathetically as she contemplates becoming a *ruffiana*, a career choice necessitated by the fact that she is reaching the age when she feels she is no longer attractive enough to sell her favors. In the end she is saved from that fate and returns to her long-term paying "lover," with her husband's approval. But the fact that she is portrayed sympathetically by Ariosto and that one of the happy conclusions that makes the play a comedy is her continuing prostitution, suggests that things could be considerably more complex than mere exploitation in such relationships. Of course, one might suspect that Ariosto's positive portrayal of Lena and her sexual life is merely a male wish fulfillment, but, tellingly, he also gives Lena a number of bitter speeches in which she points out the negatives of her life as a prostitute with nary a nod to male fantasies. And, significantly, her life and her complaints are sympathetically presented, which make it harder to dismiss her, especially in light of the positive depiction of her happy return to her paying "lover." Lena in the end is a sympathetic character who by means of her formally illicit activities supports her husband who pimps her, sustains a paying relationship portrayed as loving, and in the main plot line brings together two young lovers in a happy marriage; thus in its own way the comedy ends with the happy marriage of the illicit and licit worlds at the heart of the Rinascimento.

Many prostitutes outside brothels frequented particular establishments or areas of the city. Baths, taverns, and inns were particularly important, as were the warrens of narrow streets and alleys of the old medieval centers, especially when they were near markets or commercial areas. In Venice, for example, the baths (*stue*) associated with prostitution were to be found in the narrow streets not far from the markets and commercial center of the Rialto Bridge, close to the old public brothel known as the Castelleto. In fact, if one wanders the back streets just off the main byway that links the Rialto with the large *campo*, San Polo, one can still see the buildings that housed the baths and the bridge known as the Ponte delle Tette (Bridge of the Breasts) where prostitutes were encouraged to display their breasts in order to encourage young men to select the "proper" sexual partners, women over boys. In Florence, again at the heart of the city, the small medieval streets just north of the Arno River, east of the Old Market (Mercato Vecchio) and southeast of the Duomo, featured a host of establishments that offered a wide range of sins, including gambling, drinking, and prostitution, along with violence and petty crime. In addition to the public brothel, baths, and inns, Florence also boasted a number of popular taverns, including the *Bertucci, Chiassolino, Fico, Malvagia, Panico,* and *Porco* – names that colorfully evoke the whole program of the illicit world.

It is easy to forget that prostitution in the larger cities was not limited to women. Although the phenomenon has been less studied, young males also offered their services, especially in cities such as Florence; there in that same area where female prostitution flourished one could also find young male prostitutes, although certain areas were apparently better known for them. For example, the Via dei Pellicciai, which went from the west side of the Old Market south past the Via Porta Rosa, was well known for the trade. There were also two taverns noted for offering male youths, the *Buco*, near the Ponte Vecchio on a small street that still bears this name, and the *Sant'Andrea* or *Del Lino*, which was located near the Church of Sant'Andrea, not far from the Old Market. Later in the sixteenth century the area around the Duomo gained such a reputation that young boys were legally forbidden to loiter there.

As noted in the last chapter, one of the most important innovations in prostitution was the invention of the courtesan at the end of the fifteenth century. Courtesans quickly became, at least in the imagination of the age, the glamorous apex of the profession, offering much more than sex and playing a significant role in the aristocratic life of the day. The relationship between Barbara Raffacani Salutati, a well-known singer, poet, and composer of songs in Florence, and her doting, aging lover, Machiavelli, offers a fine example of both their fascination and their unique role in both the licit and illicit worlds – once more the satyr that inhabited the Rinascimento garden. More noted as a singer than as a poet, Salutati was praised by Giorgio Vasari in the context of a brief discussion of a portrait of her painted in the 1520s by Domenico Puligo. Vasari reports, "[Puligo] painted a portrait of Barbara Fiorentina, famous at that time, a beautiful courtesan and much loved by many, not only for her beauty, but also for her fine manners, and particularly for being an excellent musician and a divine singer." Although some scholars today question Vasari's "courtesan" label, there is no doubt that Niccolò Machiavelli felt a deep passion for her that he labeled love. For although he was married, in his later years he moved on from earlier courtesan mistresses to have a highly visible affair with the much younger Barbara, a problematic relationship that, as suggested earlier, was perhaps humorously commemorated in his contemporary comedy *La Clizia*.

Barbara is often mentioned in Machiavelli's letters. And his passionate attachment shines through in his account of their working together writing new songs for his already famous comedy, *La mandragola*, and their plans to travel together to present them. Barbara, in turn, apparently felt a strong attachment to Machiavelli, defending him in his last years in Florence with powerful friends and seventeen years after his death still nostalgically recalling the pleasures of their love. There is much that might be discussed here, but it is easy to overlook a crucial term that comes up often in the Rinascimento in conjunction with courtesans and prostitutes. What was Machiavelli, long married to Marietta di Luigi Corsini, often portrayed tenderly in his letters, doing celebrating his *love* for Barbara?

The answer to that question requires a deeper exploration of the nature of prostitution in the Rinascimento from the perspective of love. For, unlikely as it might seem, prostitution was deeply intertwined with love. Once again this is not to deny the commercial or exploitative nature of the trade, but merely to suggest that sixteenth-century prostitution should not be too quickly identified with the modern. It existed, was conceptualized, and was understood from the perspective of the culture of illicit sex and the broader shared primary culture of the day. And *giovani* were in many ways the focus of that culture. The modern translation of *giovani* as "adolescent" is misleading because, as noted earlier, the age range denoted by the term was wider than it is today and also quite socially sensitive. Upper-class males entered this period as they began to mature sexually in their early teens, but continued to be *giovani* until they married in their late twenties or early thirties. Below the upper classes, as one moved down the social scale this period of male life became progressively shorter, with artisans often marrying in their early twenties when they had mastered their crafts and acquired the economic wherewithal to marry. Finally, at the bottom of society, marriage and independent status might never arrive, and many men remained "boys." Thus one could be a youth at the upper-class levels for fifteen to twenty years, and at lower-class levels for as little as eight to ten or permanently.

For all social levels, however, there was a definite perceived masculine development for *giovani*. In their early teens they were viewed as passive sexually and socially, feminine in appearance, and capable of displaying great beauty, as many works of art, such as Donatello's *David*, reveal. As a male moved into his later teens, however, and began to develop facial hair and the more muscular body associated with adulthood, it was assumed that he would also leave passivity behind and adopt a more dominating role socially and sexually. For the lower classes this transition ideally was quickly followed by marriage. For upper-class males, however, things were not so straight-forward. Unable to wield the wealth to be independent economically or socially, and unable to marry, they found that displaying their new, more aggressive social and sexual status was more difficult. One response was the violence associated with youth in most societies, frequently decried in the Rinascimento.

Two central aspects of the illicit world of the day were closely connected to this way of understanding the development of *giovani*. First, the percep-tion of young males as feminine and passive was a crucial component of the culture of sodomy. There, as we have seen, male/male sexual relationships were conceptualized as involving youths in their early teens in a passive fem-inine role, with older youths taking an active role. When these parameters were observed, especially in cities like Florence and Rome, the populace and authorities tended to look the other way, and more irreverent commenta-tors like Aretino could even celebrate such relationships in comedies like *Il Marescalco*. From this perspective the ideal of sodomy, although formally illicit, once again actually played a positive role in the dominant culture of marriage and family. For when young men were making the transition from passive to active roles, society frowned on any form of sex with respectable women that they might attempt outside of marriage – premarital sex, adul-tery, and rape were all crimes made more serious because they victimized the family, once again the building block of social discipline and society. Sexual relations with lower-class women and servants were less frowned upon for upper-class youths, but even they created a series of problems better avoided. Significantly, however, an older youth who expressed his new active sexual-ity with a younger male did not endanger either family or marriage. Such relationships produced no children or unwanted heirs and, because young partners grew up and became, in theory at least, active in turn, they would end naturally after a few years and not interfere with eventual marriage or family responsibilities. From the perspective of modern queer theory, there was virtually nothing queer about them, for although they were perceived as sinful, they were seen, much like premarital sex or adultery, as "natural" sins of the flesh and fit into a generally accepted vision of sexual and social development for males.

In this dynamic the prostitute offered a major alternative that many saw as preferable. Relatively inexpensive and widely available, prostitution offered the possibility for *giovani* to demonstrate an active sexuality – an opportunity to learn, practice, and demonstrate what the society saw as the ideal adult male sexuality. Thus males as they reached their late teens could take an active role in sex without endangering the virginity of daughters on the marriage market, the chastity of wives, the peace of widows, or the vows of nuns. And what made this even more positive, at least in theory, was that the prostitute as a master in the art or craft of sex could guide the young male and help with the difficult and dangerous transition from passive and feminine to active and masculine. As paradoxical as it might seem, from this perspective perhaps the most important transition in a Rinascimento male's life, from boy/youth to man/adult, was ideally in the hands of one of the most reviled, troubling, *and* celebrated figures of the day, the prostitute.

But there is more – for love also played a significant role in these relationships, both ideally and in fact. Machiavelli made no bones about loving Barbara Salutati; he actually celebrated that relationship in his correspondence and perhaps even in his literary works. In fact, the literature of the period is rife with references to the "lovers" of prostitutes at every level, from the bottom of the profession to the highest courtesan. And not just the literature – when the authorities of Venice asked the mother of the prostitute Andriana Savorgnan, who had recently married the noble Marco Dandolo, about her daughter's earlier noble customers, she labeled them "lovers," not clients, and pointed out that many were long-term lovers at that. Others, including those nobles, testified that their relationships with Andriana were much more than passing affairs and involved passionate love. A note of caution is warranted, however, as the accusation lodged against Andriana was that she had used love magic to win the hand of Marco, and thus the love of others helped to establish the claim that she was using love magic to win and hold her lover/clients. In fact, the case against her trotted out a wide range of love magic that many believed prostitutes used to win and hold their lover/clients – magic often referred to in other cases, in other cities, and in the literature of the day. Yet whether or not Andriana used love magic or was actually loved by Marco, the fact that such magic was believed to be widely used by prostitutes, even by the authorities, reveals that there was a widely shared vision that love played a significant role in their arts and relationships. The question remains, why? And the answer takes us back to Aretino and to Nanna's account of her marriage to an old man who was alive only because he was still eating – until Nanna terminated things with her little knife.

Without claiming, as Nanna's friend Antonia did, that "the wife was the assassin of matrimony," it is clear that the custom of arranged marriages made them hardly the ideal place for expressions of love. Virtually all forms of literature lament the lack of love in marriage as well as the great age differential that often found young women in their early teens married to much older men. Comedies laughed at the incongruities of such marriages and regularly offered their female characters other options for love. Adulterous love went hand in hand with the vigorous novella tradition of the day; poetry celebrated the love of other men's wives and almost never of one's own; epics celebrated the often epic search for love outside of marriage; and tragedy regularly suffered the negative ramifications of all of the above. Imaginative literature, in turn, was mirrored and confirmed in court cases involving marital disputes and adultery that regularly turned on the lack of love, although recent studies indicate that as the sixteenth century progressed there seems to have been a growing sense that love in marriage could at least be an ideal.

Marriage remained, however, an unlikely place to find the strong passions that the Rinascimento associated with love. In fact, in the eyes of most those passions were too strong, disorienting, and short-lived to make a solid base for such an important institution. In this context, prostitutes once again offered an ideal solution. One could fall in love with a prostitute at any social level, especially after the emergence of the courtesan, and thus that love could ideally be a passion as refined and aristocratic or as humble as desired. That the possibility of such relationships also turned on having the economic means to afford them merely strengthened their social measuring quality: at the upper levels of prostitution, only the wealthy could move in the rarefied circles of the courtesan; at more humble levels, the more humble could find more affordable passions. Moreover, because it was a paying relationship, in the context of a mercantile society it was in theory a free exchange for both parties – although clearly skewed toward men with the ability to pay. And when the strong passion passed, the buyer could stop paying and go his way, or his partner could theoretically – often very theoretically – refuse the relationship. Passion complicated this picture, however, as rejected male lovers were not always happy to keep their money and find another partner. And, obviously, for poor prostitutes refusal of a client was less of an option, although in criminal cases we encounter quite modest prostitutes rejecting potential client/lovers, often with violent results that caused their refusal to become part of the historical record.

This vision of prostitution and love once again fit particularly well with the long period of youth for males that typified the period. But as the sixteenth century progressed, even as courtesans were lionized and prostitution lauded as a positive necessity for society, there also grew apace a negative vision of the *arte*, in part in conjunction with a hardening of social boundaries and an attempt to define insiders and outsiders more narrowly. Added to traditional attacks on prostitution's exploitative nature for both women and men, its immorality, and increasing laments about the diseases it promulgated – most notably syphilis – were attacks on the way it undermined the family and in turn the very base of the civic morality of the Rinascimento. Youth and love were all very well, but when older married males fell in love with prostitutes, wasting their wealth and losing their honor and *virtù* in their pursuit of passions that served neither family nor society, many were not so willing to smile bemusedly at the passions of the illicit world. Even Machiavelli, the mature patriarch who enthused in his letters about his affairs with courtesans, could paint extramarital sexual relationships as a threat to *virtù* and social order in his comedy *Clizia*.

Many, like Machiavelli, were capable of arguing that sex for mature males outside of marriage was no longer acceptable and at the same time continue to frequent the illicit world of sex, even as mature married men. That notwithstanding, the stress on this ideal and its wider acceptance also accelerated the growing gap between the worlds of the licit and the illicit across the sixteenth century. And the gap was further expanded by the many religious reformers and a number of political and social commentators who were ready to see the defeats of the city-states of Italy at the hands of foreign invaders as a result, at least in part, of the negative effects of the illicit world – a world with dangerous passions that undermined the *virtù* of society and made men, and Italy itself, effeminate and easy victims of more martial and masculine foreigners.

Disease, morality, and reform went hand in hand in attempts to discipline prostitution more aggressively, both in its practice and in its impact on licit society, as the sixteenth century progressed. Particularly visible were a number of governmental initiatives to reclaim prostitutes and protect young women from being led astray and into the profession. Venice provides a good example of the broad initiatives that typified this reform movement, even if in many ways it was less an initiator and more an eclectic follower. Already early in the century the city opened a hospital to care for those suffering from syphilis, known as the *Incurabili*, where numerous prostitutes were interned. Although they were treated for the disease, the institution was mainly concerned with quarantining those infected and preventing the spread of the disease – in other words, separating the disease and the diseased from the rest of society. Soon it became more a place of internment for infected prostitutes, especially older ones, and satirical literature referred to it as the "courtesan's purgatory."

The *Convertite*, founded about 1530, as the name suggests offered the opportunity for prostitutes to rejoin licit society in return for repentance and personal reform. The original idea was that a prostitute who "voluntarily" entered the institution would be readied to reenter society as a wife or a nun. Living an austere, disciplined life, she would learn the skills required of a housewife or the discipline of a cottage industry (that helped to support the institution) along with the moral probity that came with a heavy dose of Christian training and, again, discipline. With time, however, the religious discipline of the institution came to dominate, and in 1551 the *Convertite* officially became a convent, where prostitutes were turned into nuns. One could hardly imagine a more impressive transformation from outsider to insider in Christian society. But perhaps it would not be wise to imagine too much, as at least in Venice the records suggest that the reality was less impressive than the ideal. In fact, after only a decade a major scandal broke out at the *Convertite* when it was discovered that several of the nuns were selling their favors from inside the walls of the convent, with their father confessor serving as their *ruffiano*. Even this was grist for the mill of reform morality as the priest, Pietro Leon da Valcamonica, made a public confession and preached a sermon against his sins and prostitution that impressed many. Nicely, the mother of Andriana Savorgnan, the courtesan discussed earlier, told her interrogators that one of her first memories when she moved to Venice was his powerful sermon, delivered before he was publicly executed.

In a more aggressive move to limit prostitution, a new home called the *Zitelle* (the House of Old Maids) was founded in Venice in 1560 with the goal of keeping poor young women from being lured into the *arte*. The Venetian government had long attempted to limit the recruitment of young women into the trade by law, but with little success; thus once again it moved to place them safely outside of society at the *Zitelle*. That goal was made clear by the requirements for entrance: candidates had to be at least nine years old, healthy and beautiful, and threatened with being forced into prostitution. The other side of the equation – unhappily married women who might enter the profession – was tackled by yet another institution, the *Casa del Soccorso* (the House of Support or Rescue), founded in the late 1570s. Its goal was to allow wives trapped in threatening family situations to escape without having to live on their own. To a great extent adult women living on their own were already outsiders in a society whose ideal was that every adult woman be placed in a family, and one of the major dangers of such a life was that a woman might be forced to support herself as a prostitute. Thus the *Soccorso* offered an opportunity for women with marital problems to escape the family and yet live a safely disciplined life within its walls. The potentially subversive nature of this institution, however, was recognized, and every effort was made to stress that it served not as a permanent escape but as a home that attempted to reconcile wives with their husbands and families or, failing that, prepared them to accept a new discipline as a nun.

This whole range of disciplines would have a long history and would be implemented with local variations across the cities of sixteenth-century Italy. In fact, it was copied widely beyond Italy and was reflected in institutions that interned women up through the last century. In some ways even the ideal of the modern penitentiary, with its theoretical emphasis on a mixture of penance and discipline, owes much to these sixteenth-century innovations in Italy. Be that as it may, however, it is important to recognize that these institutions were really unequipped to deal with the scale of the problems involved in eliminating or isolating prostitution and its impact on society. They were able to isolate and perhaps even to reform a few, at best dozens, while thousands plied the profession or moved in and out of its ranks, moved by poverty and their own marginality. More significantly, these institutions disciplined only one side of the problem, women. With a stubborn patriarchal myopia, they overlooked the fact that male clients created the demand and that the market would not disappear simply because a few women were locked up or even reformed.

But while scale limited the practical effects of these attempts to move prostitutes and dangerous women outside of society, each institution and its expressed rationale was a public reassertion of a heightened civic morality that ideally would save sixteenth-century Italy from the worst of the satyr in its garden. And prostitution and its diseases and irregularities as a source of the problem would progressively come to be portrayed in a more negative light. No longer was it just a minor and necessary evil. Rather, it was a trap for women that was difficult to escape, as institutions like the *Convertite* announced; it fed off the economic problems of the poor, the young, and the defenseless, as the *Zitelle* publicized; and, worst of all, it destroyed marriages and lured wives into a life of sin living on their own, as the *Soccorso* revealed. Moreover, it threatened to infect society with both a devastating physical disease and a (perhaps worse) moral one, as the *Incurabili* warned. In sum, these institutions broadcast in the cityscape the ideal that prostitution and its accompanying immorality should be excluded from society and the licit world once and for all.

In the end Machiavelli's re-dreaming of a return to Roman republican *virtù* and his perhaps less well recognized agenda of a return to the *virtù* of the early Rinascimento, both envisioned as a corrective to the effeminate ways of the early sixteenth century and as a means to recapture civic morality, were never realized. Returns, whether to the ancient past or to earlier, better times, make good ideology and better dreams, but they are rarely realized. And although many may cringe at the idea, Machiavelli's political vision was essentially a utopian one powered as much by a deep *faith* in *virtù* and government as by his practical experiences. Unfortunately for that faith, neither government nor the rebirth of *virtù* was capable of delivering the deep reforms he envisioned, and his utopia remained a dream. Castiglione's vision of the solution to the crisis of the early sixteenth century was, if anything, even more a dream, as it imagined returning to a courtly world of perfect courtiers and princes willing to be led to the path of *virtù*: an erotopolitical program set in an ideal courtly world that had never existed and was equally unlikely to exist in any future.

Aretino eschewed love in his often troubling dreams of the illicit world, with the result that they may seem more like nightmares. But that would be unfair to Aretino, because his vision was also a rueful, laughing critique powered by his linguistic fireworks. To gain and hold his reader, nothing could be or was sacred, and the more clever and irreverent his mockery, the more powerful his critique. Thus in the end he argued the hollowness of the vision that was the very foundation of his society, which saw civic life as based on civic morality and the familial organization of society. And from that point it was but a short step to claiming that true *virtù* was only to be found in the sins of a prostitute and the illicit world – the world of the satyr in the garden that had always been there, lurking behind the civic morality and discipline of the Rinascimento. If there was an implied utopia here, it was one based on egoistic passions and pleasures, perhaps on the order of that envisioned later by certain Libertines.

It seems more likely, however, that it was simply an irreverent replay of the inherent contradictions of the licit world and a mocking highlighting of the open secret that that world relied on and was deeply intertwined with its illicit world. In a strange way, however, it was Aretino's dream that at least had some future. As the sixteenth century progressed, Italy came to be noted in the European imagination as the place to find the illicit pleasures and excitements that were only dreamed of elsewhere – the satyr in the garden came to dominate the dream. Cities like Rome and Venice would become meccas of proto-tourism, with a thriving world of illicit sex and cultures perceived as wide open to free thought and free love (albeit, ironically, often quite costly in every sense). No matter that the reality was neither as lurid nor as free as perceived from abroad. But the other side of the coin was that these cities were also perceived as singularly corrupt and a threat to the moral order of the rest of Europe. Italy's Rinascimento garden with its flourishing culture came to be seen as coming at a dangerous cost – with a lurking satyr of illicit immorality personified by mythic figures of evil like the Machiavel and the Aretine.

But for the moment neither a return to earlier *virtù*, nor a rediscovery of true love, nor an escape to the many pleasures and dangers of the illicit world of the day would save Italy or disarm the new that was pressing on the Rinascimento from all quarters. Rebirth was still the dream, but it was a dream that was becoming ever less likely. Still, there was one more "re" word with a long history that seemed to many to offer promise for a future that would return the Rinascimento to its deserved preeminence – reform. And, nicely, it too evoked visions of love and *virtù*, but in a Christian and moral society reborn. Perhaps, as was the case with old Nicomaco, reform could save the Rinascimento and return it to the ways of civic morality and *virtù*.

REFORM: SPIRITUAL ENTHUSIASMS, DISCIPLINE, AND A CHURCH MILITANT (c. 1500–c. 1575)

Savonarola: Reform and Re-Dreams of Rebirth

One of the first reactions to the crisis of the new that inundated the Rinascimento at the turn of the sixteenth century was a traditional religious response – an appeal for reform. Once again a "re" word calling for a return, in this context to the Christianity of the early Church. As we have seen, this was a continuing refrain across the period, but it tended to grow in strength in times of crisis. Thus, although periodically across the Rinascimento fire-breathing preachers had elicited enthusiastic responses to calls for reform in the urban centers of Italy, one of the most famous, Girolamo Savonarola (1452–1498), emerged virtually in conjunction with the French invasion of Charles VIII. Called to Florence by Lorenzo de' Medici in 1490 and made prior of the Dominican monastery there that had been rebuilt and renewed by Lorenzo's grandfather Cosimo, Savonarola became progressively more popular and influential as a preacher as the decade progressed.

Actually, his success built on the French invasion, as he had preached well before Charles came on the scene that a "sword of God" from the north would be called to Italy to chastise the corrupt and immoral city of Florence. When Charles seemed to fulfill his prophecy, the already popular preacher, who had railed against the princely and ungodly ways of Lorenzo de' Medici and his circle, seemed to many to be confirmed as a prophet. And in the turmoil of the rebirth of the Florentine republic following Piero's fall, his sermons took on greater force yet, especially as they focused on traditional ways of calling for change: reform, renewal, and rebirth.

Clearly for a preacher like Savonarola it was not a Roman renewal that was the goal, but a moral rebirth, in which Florence guided by God and His prophet/preacher, would become not so much a new Jerusalem as a Jerusalem reborn or, better yet, a reborn Garden of Eden. The ungodly ways of the Medici and their followers – the satyr in Florence's garden – would be forcibly removed; and thus the first Godly Garden, where Adam and Eve lived in perfect harmony with God, would be reborn in Florence to serve as a model for Italy to reemerge as the spiritual leader of the world. In a way, his message provided a logical but significant twist to the traditional civic morality of the Rinascimento. Once again the government of a city would create a moral civic space in which a true Christian life could be led – but this time with the considerable advantage that that republican government would be guided on the path of *virtù*, true Christian *virtù*, by a preacher/prophet who could communicate to it God's plans for the city's rebirth as the leader of a re-formed Christian world. Disaster and defeat thus became merely the first steps on the way to triumph and a true *rinascita*.

But that return to the past required moral and spiritual reform, and that meant eliminating more than just Medici satyrs from the garden. Savonarola's famous bonfires of the vanities, where a wide range of art and literature, along with rich clothing and other things deemed immoral – such as cosmetics, wigs, carnival masks, and dice – were fed to the flames in public celebrations, were only the most famed aspects of a program that attempted to cleanse the city of vice in order to prepare it for its destiny as a reborn Garden of Eden, free of that old serpent, the Devil, and pagan satyrs. Under pressure from Savonarola and his supporters, who became progressively more powerful in the halls of government, laws were passed to reform and purify the city: expelling Jews and prostitutes and strengthening the punishments for sodomy, blasphemy, and superfluous luxuries. Moreover, the youth of the city, often seen as the instigators of the worst forms of immorality and vice, were recruited into youth brigades to monitor behavior and ensure that the city maintained its renewed moral fervor. This enthusiastic reform movement in the face of a crisis, in part real in terms of politics, economics, and military defeat, and in part imagined – but no less real for that – in terms of moral decay and corruption, won over many, creating a powerful group of supporters who spanned the social spectrum. The most active and visible were known as the *Piagnoni* (the weepers), apparently in response to their public tearful repentance for their sins and those of their fellow citizens.

Savonarola's reforming zeal and religious enthusiasm did not go uncontested, however, especially its political dimensions. By 1497 he was seen by a growing number of opponents as a dangerous political figure who was guiding Florentine government via his avid supporter Francesco Valori. Valori, serving as *Gonfaloniere* of Justice, visited him virtually daily at his monastery, San Marco, to get instructions on how to rule. Those opponents were divided into several factions: the *Arrabbiati* (The Outraged), an aristocratic group that looked to the pope for support and were committed to blocking any return of the Medici; the *Bigi* (The Grays), who called for a return of the Medici; and the *Compagnacci* (The Bad Boys), who as their name implies, were against Savonarola's strict moral reforms. Significantly, his fervent calls for more general Church reform – to literally burn the satyr of Rinascimento immorality out of the Church – also troubled many leaders in Italy and beyond, especially the pope, Alexander VI. The Borgia pope was not just concerned about Savonarola's calls for a radical reform of society and the Church, or even his Florentine-centric vision of a renewed Christianity that might call into question papal leadership. More troubling immediately was the fact that Savonarola's prophecies for the reformation of Florence required continuing the city's alliance with the French. With the pope staunchly opposing a return of the French and planning to help his rapacious relatives take over lands that the French claimed in Italy, Savonarola's support of a French alliance and calls for the king's return placed the prophet and his prophecies in direct conflict with the dangerous Borgia pope.

Not surprisingly, then, when Alexander summoned him to Rome in the summer of 1495 to discuss these matters, Savonarola wisely demurred. The pope then stepped up his attacks on Savonarola's prophecies, his diatribes against Rome, and his attachment to the French. He also took more direct action, attempting to stop his preaching and to force him to accept the discipline of the Church or, failing that, at the least the discipline of his Dominican order, with little success. Finally, in June of 1497, he excommunicated Savonarola, proclaiming that his claims and teachings were heretical and that he had been disobedient to his superiors. This immediately stopped his preaching, because allowing an excommunicated cleric to preach would have provided the pope with a rationale to place Florence under an interdict and would also have given him the excuse to adopt still stronger measures against the friar.

With Savonarola silenced, tensions escalated in Florence, with opponents of the friar pressing to break his hold on government and his supporters fighting to maintain his power and pressure the pope to back down. Things came to a head when a conspiracy was discovered to overthrow the friar's supporters and return the Medici to power. A number of prominent citizens were quickly arrested, tortured, proclaimed guilty of treason, and ordered executed. Although this was fairly standard operating procedure for conspiracies, one of the highly touted reforms enacted early on by Savonarola's supporters guaranteed the right to appeal convictions that carried the death penalty to the newly created Great Council, which theoretically included the most important families of Florence. Loud calls for an appeal, however, were quietly ignored. Executions, which many perceived as illegal, followed. And that, along with the friar's excommunication, seemed to suggest to a growing segment of the population that he and his followers were not quite as honest, moral, and holy as they claimed – politics as usual still seemed to rule, and the Garden of Eden remained distant.

With opposition growing in Florence, Savonarola and his closest followers decided that he needed to return to the pulpit to rally support; thus in early February of 1498 he preached a sermon in which he attacked his excommunication and the pope. Alexander VI, in the face of this open defiance, responded with firmness, asking that the friar either be silenced by Florentine authorities or be sent to Rome. It did not take much to realize that a trip to Rome would not be particularly favorable for his health; thus, after one last sermon attacking the pope, he once again stopped preaching. But behind the scenes he and his supporters, both in government and in the Church, intensified their attacks on the corruption of the Borgia pope and the Church, even suggesting that Alexander was not a true pope because he had bought his office.

As tensions escalated in Florence and factional fighting threatened to spill into the streets, an unlikely-sounding resolution was found. For some time Domenico da Pecia, a Dominican friar and one of Savonarola's most ardent supporters, had offered to walk through fire to demonstrate the power and truth of Savonarola's preaching and prophecies. The Franciscan order, traditional contenders with the Dominicans for spiritual leadership, unhappy about the preacher/prophet's popularity and questionable teachings, not to mention his troubles with the papacy, saw this as an opportunity to discredit Savonarola and his followers. Thus, toward the end of March, a Franciscan friar, Fra Rondinelli, challenged Domenico, offering to walk through the fire if Domenico did. Apparently Rondinelli did not claim that he would pass through unharmed, but he was willing to sacrifice himself in order to show that Domenico would not escape unharmed either and thus to give the lie to Savonarola and his supporter's claims.

Actually, both Savonarola and the pope opposed the idea. Both argued that the test demanded a miracle from God, and men, even very holy men, could not command God. Nonetheless, under popular pressure, and with the goal of easing the tensions that had built to an exploding point in the city, the confrontation was organized by the Florentine government. Thus on April 7, 1498, in the main square of Florence a large fire was lit and a path of burning coals cleared for the two champions to walk. Large crowds had gathered for the event, but almost immediately what seemed to offer a final clear trial of the prophet's message and power began to unravel, as supporters of both sides argued about the terms of the walk through the fire. The wrangling dragged on for hours, with the crowd growing more and more restive. Each side blamed the other for the delay. Finally, with what must have seemed like virtually divine irony or ire, a rainstorm intervened; the confrontation was called off, and the crowd dispersed.

Through the night more human ire seethed and plots thickened. The next day, Palm Sunday, found the people of Florence in the streets ready to settle Savonarola's fate once and for all with violence. Armed supporters and opponents fought pitched battles. Francesco Valori was killed; his followers were soundly defeated in the streets; and San Marco, Savonarola's monastery, was attacked. Finally, Savonarola and Fra Domenico were arrested, officially to save them from the mobs led by their opponents. The conclusion followed quickly. Although the pope requested that the friar be sent to Rome for trial, the Florentine government, now in the hands of his opponents, insisted on trying him themselves, apparently with an eye to showing that he was a false prophet and that he had used his preaching and prophecies to turn the government of the city to his own ends.

With a certain brutal irony, in the end the flames did decide the fate of the fiery preacher and his bonfires of vanities. For Fra Domenico and Savonarola were convicted and condemned to burn on May 23, 1498. Even as they were being "mercifully" first hanged and then burned, many present at the execution expected that a miracle would save the prophet. But there was no divine intervention. Florence was not to be a renewed Jerusalem or a reborn Garden of Eden; the new was not to be wiped out by a return to the origins of Christianity or a reformed Florentine church. And, tellingly, even the long tradition of Italian spiritual reform and religious leadership in Europe was soon to be challenged by a reforming wind from the north. Simply put, even religious reform and rebirth would not save the Rinascimento; the satyr would remain in the garden – perhaps because, when all is said and done, the Rinascimento garden as it had developed required the satyr and its illicit world of pleasures and passions as well as a Christian order, *pace* Savonarola. But where Florence's prophet had failed, many across Italy and Europe would not so much follow as attempt to lead with often similar disciplining visions and attacks on Rome and the papacy.

Roman Corruption and the Varieties of Reform

Once upon a time (before the papacy was carried off to Avignon) a "Jew ... rode off to the court of Rome ... [where] he began cautiously to observe the ways of the pope, the cardinals and the other prelates, along with the courtiers." What he found was troubling, for "from the most important to the least they were totally given to sexual sins and not only the natural kind but also sodomy, without any restraint, remorse or shame, thus the power of prostitutes and young boys to influence whatever grand affair was not to be underestimated." But that was not all. "[They were] all gluttonous, drunks, and primarily servants of their bellies like brute animals." Moreover, when he looked more closely he found "that they were all avaricious and lusted after money ignoring the divine and all that Christianity entailed." Thus he concluded that in Rome one could find "no holiness, no devotion, no good works or examples of the good life … and no cleric demonstrated anything but lasciviousness, avarice and gluttony, fraud, envy, pride and the like and worse."

This tale was told by Boccaccio in the *Decameron* as the second story of the first day. Like several others told by his young storytellers, behind its anticlerical and anti-Rome message it contained a crucial qualification that separated clerical corruption from the ultimate truth of Christianity. For the premise of the tale was that this Jew, Abraham, a rich Parisian merchant, had gone to Rome to observe the capital of Christendom after being impressed by the praises of Christianity of a friend and fellow merchant who hoped to convert him. When Abraham had suggested the visit, however, his friend had lost all hope of converting him, as he, like most, was well aware of the negative reputation of Rome and the papal court. Thus upon Abraham's return he was not surprised by his negative reports. He was very surprised, however, when Abraham confessed that his visit had convinced him that Christianity was actually the true religion. With a wry reasoning that does perfect justice to Boccaccio's sense of humor, Abraham had concluded that if Christianity had endured and prospered in the face of such corruption at its heart, it must truly be sustained by the Holy Spirit and be the one true religion. Otherwise it would have failed long ago. Thus Abraham requested to be baptized immediately and lived happily ever after "a good and valiant man of saintly life."

But Abraham's fictional faith notwithstanding, Rome remained corrupt in the eyes of contemporaries across the Rinascimento. And, if anything, with the return of the papacy to the city in the fifteenth century and the establishment of a more princely and courtly rule, the workings of the Holy Spirit behind the scene became increasingly hard for many to see, even if the city and the papacy grew apace, flourishing as the artistic and cultural capital of the Christian world. This perception of papal corruption was reinforced by the fact that the Church itself had become increasingly dominated by, and at the mercy of, Italian elites. Of the twenty-six popes who had ruled from 1417, when Martin V brought the papacy back to Italy, until 1600, twenty-three were Italian. A similar pattern, if slightly less extreme, can be seen among cardinals, where the proportion of Italians increased from approximately 50 percent at the election of Pius II in 1458 to thirty-four of thirty-nine in 1523, when Clement VII was elected pope. Much the same dominance was to be found among bishops appointed by the papacy and in the papal bureaucracy and burgeoning clerical office-purchasing class; thus, significantly, for many powerful Italian families the Church had become a lucrative investment. The response to this dominance and continued veniality and corruption was a virtually constant and increasingly demanding call for reform.

In Latin, Italian, and English we are faced with yet another "re" word that calls not for something new, but for a return or rebirth to a better, more perfect time – in this case, the correct first time. In the ancient and medieval Christian tradition that the Rinascimento inherited, reform tended to call for a return to one or both of two crucial beginnings for religion. The first, of course, was a personal return to the life of Christ. Saint Francis captured the essence of this vision of reform when he advocated that people should reform themselves and their lives on the model of Christ and his life in this world. As God had walked the streets of Jerusalem as a man, the question of the perfect Christian life was a simple one. One merely had to re-form one's life on his form and his life as revealed in the New Testament. Francis himself, after retiring to contemplate that life of the God/man, found that he himself had been blessed with the stigmata, the wounds that Christ had received during his crucifixion. One can hardly imagine a more impressive reform – his body had literally been re-formed and taken on the form of Christ's body.

Yet such personal reform, because it was individual, was not particularly radical in its implications for society, even if it required a radical personal change. Only if large masses of individuals independently reformed themselves on the model of Christ's life and, moreover, agreed on what that reform entailed would the shape of society change. Ultimately, if all were guided by the Holy Spirit in their individual reform, the outcome would be a collective reform that would change the world; but lacking that, reform could follow as many paths as there were self-reforming individuals. For most radical reformers, reforming the Church itself – an institutional reform – seemed a more promising goal. Perfecting a Church capable of organizing, disciplining, and defending a truly Christian society would return it to its original form as envisioned in the first days of the Church, the foundational days of Christ and his disciples. And those days were perfectly recorded in the New

Testament, the inspired writings of the Church Fathers, and the documents and institutions of the early Church; all that was necessary was to reform the institutions of the Church based on those texts.

Reform and Religious Enthusiasm in the Sixteenth Century

Both types of reform and *rinascita* of Christianity had their supporters in the sixteenth century. For the leaders of the Church, however, institutional reform seemed to offer the added possibility of reasserting their long-standing claims to a more dominant political role at the expense of rulers who had progressively limited their claims to discipline and guide Christendom. Significantly, however, reform itself was not a vision limited to theologians or ecclesiastical authorities. It was promulgated by popular Franciscan ideals, by the mendicant orders more generally and by fire-breathing preachers more particularly, as well as by confraternities and informal religious groups along with less-often-discussed spontaneous explosions of lower-class religious enthusiasm. Savonarola's ability to mobilize the religious enthusiasm of Florentines, from the humblest to the richest, from the uneducated to Pico della Mirandola and other jewels of the Medicean quasi-court, from the powerless and marginal to the most powerful families of the Florentine elite, is just one impressive example of the way spiritual reform was capable of powerfully touching deep chords throughout society.

In the fifteenth century mendicant orders, especially their Observant branches – committed to stricter discipline and observance of the orders' rules – had played a crucial role in reform, both institutional and personal. Thus, while they tended to advocate institutional reform for their orders and for the Church, in their personal lives, preaching, and ministry to the laity they stressed personal reform based on a life modeled on Christ. In Italy it has been calculated that the number of Observant communities among the various mendicant orders increased from about 30 in the 1420s to more than 1,200 by 1517. The Observant Franciscans provide a good example, with fiery preachers such as Bernardino of Siena (1380–1444) and Giovanni da Capistrano (1386–1456) crisscrossing the north of Italy denouncing corruption, sin, sodomites, and Jews. Still today one can see San Bernardino's famous symbol, the abbreviation in Latin for Jesus, yhs, surrounded by a sunburst, painted on the upper stories of buildings as a remembrance of his preaching in many Italian cities. Not all the religious enthusiasm that he or his fellows promoted, however, was positive, as demonstrated by the outbursts of repression and violence against Jews and those labeled sodomites that often followed his preaching. This was the darker side of the religious and reform enthusiasm of the day – an attempt to close out of the Rinascimento those perceived as unacceptable others. The isolation or elimination from the Christian community of those deemed "others" was a process that would progressively gain force across the sixteenth century, and it went hand in hand with calls for reform and the spiritual enthusiasms of the day.

Among the Observant Dominicans, a Spaniard, Vincent Ferrer (1350–1419), was a major reformer and influence on his order in Italy. Savonarola was only perhaps the most noted preacher in his order who followed in his footsteps. Egidio of Viterbo (1469–1523) pressed for similar reforms in the Augustinian Observants and had a major impact in Italy and beyond. In fact, the Augustinian Observants played an increasingly important role in the Holy Roman Empire, especially through the houses associated with a revival of Saint Augustine's teachings led by the Windesheim Chapter. One of their most important theologians was, of course, Martin Luther. Beyond the Observant mendicant orders, informal groups of people, both lay and clerical, came together locally to take vows that organized personal spiritual reform. Often drawing on traditional Italian confraternities and deeply influenced by northern European movements (such as the Brethren of the Common Life, the Devotio Moderno and, more troubling to authorities, the Hussites and the Lollards), these groups melded together clerics and a wide array of people from all classes, but with strong support among artisans and women, especially in the cities of northern Italy. Often building upon creative local traditions, some of which went back to the prophecies of Joachim of Fiore, these hotbeds of spiritual enthusiasm and popular Christianity flourished with an intensity that was worrisome, at least to those who feared their potential to transform reform into another "re" word, revolution.

Many leaders of the Church entertained similar fears about the religious enthusiasms and calls for reform led by women and devoted considerable time and attention to attempting to redirect that enthusiasm into channels deemed safe. Everywhere it seemed that holy women in religious orders and in the secular world were gaining visibility and not only calling for reform but serving as models for it. An indication of how successful they were is the fact that of the forty-four Italians made saints between 1494 and 1559, twenty-one – almost half – were women, a rare example of female equality during the period. The Franciscans and Dominicans actively publicized the numerous saintly women who populated their third orders, again with an eye to fomenting reform and claiming a leading role in it. The most noted model for such sanctity was Saint Catherine of Siena (1347–1380), associated with the Dominicans, whose active life, sanctity, and spiritual visions served as a model for a bevy of noted Dominican spiritual women, including most prominently Colomba of Rieti, Veronica of Binasco, Angela Merici, Caterina de' Ricci, and Lucia Broccadelli of Narni. Lucia Broccadelli of Narni (1476–1544), for example, had her personal reform confirmed by the appearance of her own stigmata, once again a telling sign of her self-reforming in Christ. She was widely famed as a living saint, and her prophesies were so impressive that the duke of Ferrara, Ercole I d'Este (1431–1505), brought her to Ferrara to serve as his court's quasi-saint and advisor.

Many women also gained notoriety for their sanctity outside formal religious orders. One example among many was Francesca Ponziani, daughter of an upper-class Roman family, who lived a saintly life as a wife and mother and progressively gathered around her a spiritual community of upper-class Roman women also committed to living a spiritual life without cloisterization or taking formal vows. But less famous women everywhere also played an important, if informal, role in the religious lives and spiritual enthusiasms of their communities. Little discussed but very important was the tradition of women healers, who used both herbs and traditional remedies along with an extensive repertory of spiritual cures that played a significant role in the everyday lives of virtually every city, town, and village. With their prayers and those spiritual cures, they often were seen as leading figures in the everyday religious life of their communities – and, significantly, it seemed to many that their spirituality delivered real benefits in the form of health, healing, and community harmony based upon Christian practices from the first days of the Church.

As the institutional reform supported by the established hierarchy of the Church gained momentum in the sixteenth century, however, these more humble and popular forms of religious enthusiasm, and especially female involvement with the spiritual, once largely ignored, became increasing suspect. In fact, one of themes of the religious reforms of the Catholic Church in the sixteenth century was an increasingly aggressive attempt to separate large segments of the spiritual world from the quotidian life of everyday people and to make the spiritual world accessible only through the mediation of clerics and the Church – potentially yet another great divide, separating in this case a religious elite from the Christian masses. A few women on the right side of the divide became saints, and many deemed to be on the wrong side became heretics or witches, while the great majority were pressed in the name of reform to express their spiritual enthusiasms within the stricter disciplinary confines of a male-led Church and to display a form of safely domestic piety deemed ideal for female spirituality. Not only did limiting the spirituality of women to the home return them to their "correct" place in society, to many Church leaders it also seemed to promise to eliminate the revolutionary potential of female spiritual enthusiasms, as they believed that few revolutions could be launched from domestic isolation, perhaps incorrectly.

The Florentine writer Francesco da Meleto (1449–c.1517) is an interesting if little-known masculine example of the religious enthusiasm and hopes that flourished at less humble but still nonclerical levels in early sixteenth century Italy. The illegitimate son of a Florentine merchant whose mother was apparently an ex-slave, he grew up and studied in Bologna. Returning to Florence at eighteen, he remained for a few years, but shortly after his father's death he decided to travel to the East to continue his studies. Perhaps influenced by the intellectual ferment of the Muslim, Jewish, and Christian communities he encountered there, he became convinced that great religious changes were in the offing that would unite those three great monotheistic traditions. Returning to Florence, his prophetic visions were reinforced by the Savonarolan prophecies that swept the city in the nineties along with the medieval Joachite tradition of the approaching last age of the Holy Spirit, which had enjoyed periodic revivals in Italy and Florence, especially in times of crisis.

It will be remembered that Joachim of Fiore had predicted that one of the signs that heralded the last age would be the conversion of the Jews and Muslims to the one true religion, exactly what Francesco believed was about to occur. Although Savonarola, with his own predictions of a new/last age, in the end died a fiery death in 1498, his religious prophecies and calls for reform certainly did not. Francesco, then, merely added his own personal vision to the broader reforming discourses of the day when he published in 1512 his dialogue, *Convivio de'secreti della Sacra Scrittura* (*Discussion on the Secrets of the Scriptures*). Much like his medieval predecessor Joachim, he predicted that a new leader would come forward to convert the Jews, reform Christianity, and open the way to a new age of peace and happiness for all and offered an exact date – 1517. Needless to say, with the advantage of hindsight, that date, the year in which Martin Luther supposedly posted his reform program on the church door in Wittenberg, makes our Florentine prophet's prophecy seem particularly prophetic.

But well before 1517 Francesco's prophecies attracted attention. In fact, in 1514 he was invited to Rome by Pope Leo X to "discuss" them. Although we know little of those discussions, clearly they were not a mere exchange of ideas. At the least he found his reform vision contested there by the Camaldolese hermit Vicenzo Querini (1478–1514), a Venetian noble and noted reformer himself. According to his fellow Venetian reformer and Camaldolese hermit Tommaso Giustiniani (1476–1528), Querini attacked Francesco's prophecies and visions as the product of the Devil. Apparently undaunted, Francesco returned to Florence and wrote a second work, which he dedicated to the pope, predicting more explicitly that the Muslims would be converted to Christianity in 1536. With Querini's death, Giustiniani took up the attack on Francesco, and, with a certain irony, finally in 1517 those attacks bore fruit with the condemnation of Francesco's prophecies as heretical. His books were ordered burned, and he was called upon to publicly abjure his calls for reform and his prophesies – something that he apparently never did as, perhaps conveniently, he disappeared from the historical record.

Francesco's attackers, Vicenzo Querini and Tommaso Giustiniani, were much better-known reformers, examples in their own right of the religious enthusiasms burning brightly even among the upper classes. Both were nobles from noted Venetian families who had been trained for public service in the Venetian tradition, studying at Padua and as young men holding important posts in government that seemed to mark them out as future leaders of the republic. But both at about the age of thirty – exactly the age at which a Venetian noble was expected to marry and take up the responsibilities of adult life – withdrew from public life to pursue their own personal religious reform. Although the details remain unclear, it appears that the two, moved by a shared religious enthusiasm, abandoned the political and civil world of Venice to experiment with withdrawing to Giustiniani's house on the island of Murano. There they lived a life of Christlike personal reform along with a group of like-minded young nobles that included yet another future figure of importance, Gasparo Contarini (1483–1542). What especially captured the imagination of their contemporaries was the group's rejection of the active life to take up a withdrawn life of contemplation and individual reform at precisely the moment when their city, Venice, was in the darkest days of the War of the League of Cambrai. Their withdrawal from civil life to follow the path of private reform seemed to reflect a total rejection of the civic morality and the ideal of active political life of an earlier day.

Finding that contemplative life unsatisfactory, however, Giustiniani eventually left his island retreat to journey to the Holy Land, once more searching for answers to the critical spiritual problems of his day in the past that mattered most to him, the first days of Christianity. Finally, in 1510, now back in Italy, he decided to join the order of Camaldolese hermits, a small reforming order, becoming a monk in their most important hermitage near Arezzo, just south of Florence. In 1511 he was joined by his old friend Querini, who apparently was less certain about becoming a hermit but was still committed to the older Giustiniani, who had been in many ways his spiritual mentor since their teens. As monks they took the suggestive names of Paolo and

Pietro (Paul and Peter), respectively, the two most important apostles of the early Church.

Their vision of reform, their views about the Church, and their own personal spiritual travails and concerns about salvation are richly documented in a triangular correspondence, recently rediscovered, between the two new monks and Gasparo Contarini, their old compatriot from Murano days who had decided to remain in the world and who would become a major figure in reform circles, both ecclesiastical and political. Contarini was the slightly younger contemporary of the two monks and a close friend of Querini, who often referred to their love for each other in their letters with an emotional tone not unusual between close male friends. These letters spanned the teens of the century, although after Querini's death in 1514 the correspondence between Giustiniani and Contarini became less frequent and more reserved. The early letters focused on the traditional Rinascimento debate on whether the active life of a Christian in the world or the withdrawn life of a monk was the best road to salvation, with Giustiniani aggressively pressing Contarini to join his two friends in their withdrawal. Contarini resisted, insisting that he was not capable of giving up his active life, even as he expressed concern about whether this put his soul and his salvation at risk. Perhaps what is most interesting in this often very intense correspondence is Contarini's vision that he would be saved by Christ's love and his own faith, not by his works in this world – salvation by faith alone, it appears, was in the very air breathed by many, a part of the larger shared religious culture of the day. And evidently this was much the same air that reformers like Luther, even in the distant north, were breathing in those same years.

One might well ask how Contarini, with his often-reiterated vision of salvation by faith and not works, eventually became a cardinal and an important reformer within the Church, while Luther and his followers were labeled heretics by that same Church. Therein, of course, lies a long, complex story far beyond the scope of this book. But from the perspective of Contarini and the Italian Church, one thing is evident: Contarini, like many other reformers, felt that reform would remain within the Church – a church that, after all, was theirs. For, as noted earlier, from the highest level of popes and cardinals down to the level of ecclesiastical bureaucrats and humble clerics, the Church that existed was largely Italian and thus essentially in their hands. In this context Italian elites both ecclesiastical and secular tended to share the view that their Church needed to be reformed, not overthrown; this meant that, especially at upper-class levels, similar reforming ideals produced very different results in Italy and beyond the Alps. Many northern rulers had much to gain and little to lose by aligning with reformers who were ready to break with the Roman Catholic Church. And, significantly, most of those who believed that they needed the Church, like the Emperor Charles V, remained loyal to it. In turn, when Italian reformers challenged that hierarchy or, worse, prophesized that its corruption promised change in the order of things, at least at first they were not seen as particularly dangerous. The Church responded hesitatingly, hoping such religious enthusiasms would fade or be incorporated into what they saw as their own mainstream reform visions. But with time that confidence waned, and Church leaders and the ruling elites in Italy came to fear that the religious enthusiasms that were breaking out everywhere were literally *breaking out*, with the real potential to leave them behind. And what reformers across Europe were labeling as a necessary return to the old, they began to fear was actually dangerously new.

The Sack of Rome: The Violence of the New

Certainly the relative novelty of foreign armies in Italy after 1494 helped to make these dangers crystal clear when on May 6, 1527, the unimaginable happened. Imperial troops led by the Constable of Bourbon, a renegade French noble in the service of the Emperor Charles V, swept into Rome virtually unopposed and sacked the city. It has been claimed with a certain justice that this was the real barbarian sack of the ancient city that truly finished its destruction. But at the time, it was perceived by many as the greatest calamity of the ongoing destruction of the wars that were devastating Italy and destroying the Rinascimento. Still, not all shared that opinion. Some in Italy and more in the north of Europe, where reforming sentiment was calling for a break with the Church of Rome, saw the sack of the city as its just reward for centuries of corruption and a sign of a deeper impending change – perhaps even a sign of the impending end of time and the return of Christ for the Last Judgment. Many of the German troops who pillaged the city, in fact, adhered to the new confessions of the north. And while it would be difficult to separate their typical mercenary lust for plunder and rapine from any religious enthusiasm that contributed to their violence, it seems that both were involved.

The sculptor, goldsmith, musician, and self-aggrandizing autobiographical author Benvenuto Cellini (1500–1571) was in the city at the time and has left a description of sack in his *Vita* (*Life* or *Autobiography*) that, typical of his writing, says more about his own heroic role in Rome's defense and the favorable impression he made on the Medici pope Clement VII than it does about the event itself. Still, he relates that along with three friends he went out to see what was happening as the imperial troops rapidly scaled the weakly defended walls and began pouring into Rome. It quickly became evident that the city was going to fall, and his friends were in a panic, ready to flee. But, ever the hero, Cellini called on them to show that they "were men," and, as they were armed with arquebuses, ordered them to shoot into the thickest group of enemy soldiers, where earlier he had noticed a leader standing. He reported that "we all fired twice in succession and … one of our shots killed the Constable of Bourbon … we learned later." Often dismissed as Cellini's typical braggadocio, his account is accurate at least to the degree that the Constable was shot and killed as his troops entered the city.

Cellini and his companions fled along with the crowds before the rampaging soldiers and barely made it into the Castel Sant'Angelo, the papal fortress lying on a bend of the Tiber that commands the center of the city. There the pope, many leading cardinals, and members of the papal court had holed up, hoping to resist the invaders. Always ready to boast of his military prowess and violent abilities, Cellini recounted his exploits in defense of the fortress, claiming modestly that on that first day, as most of the rest of the troops watched in terror while the city was being sacked, he fought on, harrying the enemy troops trying to break into the fortress so effectively that they were stopped and the pope saved. During the ongoing sack and the siege of Castel Sant'Angelo, he, however, gave few details of the disaster, preferring to recount his many adventures, including killing innumerable enemy troops; cutting in half an enemy officer at long distance with a shot that impressed even the pope with its impossibility; wounding another leader, the prince of Orange, with a masterful shot; and scaring (not quite the Devil out of) Cardinal Farnese (the future Pope Paul III [1534–1549]) with another clever shot that the cardinal thought was meant for him – something that Cellini believed contributed to the future pope's enmity toward him and his eventual jailing in 1538. But as Cellini pointed out, he was writing the story of his life and could not be distracted for too long by what were in the end mere historical events. Yet if the earlier French invasion of 1494 had signaled for many the beginning of a period of wars that would change forever the political order of Italy, the sack seemed to herald the end of Roman Catholic Europe as a religious entity and requires a closer look at those "mere events" and the players involved. We will return to Cellini and his more personal vision of the history that mattered later.

The relatively new pope at the time was Clement VII (1478–1534; pope 1523–1534). He was the illegitimate son of Giuliano de' Medici, assassinated in the Pazzi conspiracy of 1478, and had been raised by his famous uncle Lorenzo and educated by some of the most important scholars who surrounded Lorenzo in his later years. As was the case for his cousin, Pope Leo X (1475–1521; pope 1513–1521), the Medici family strategy of marrying into the Roman nobility and pursuing ecclesiastical office had once again paid off for Clement. He did not have quite the meteoric career of his cousin, who had rapidly scaled the heights of the Church hierarchy, being named a cardinal at fourteen and elected pope at thirty-eight. By contrast, Giulio, as he was called before he became pope, began his rise to power shortly after the fall of the Florentine republic in 1512; he was named archbishop of Florence in 1513 and later in the same year cardinal at the age of thirty-four. When Leo's hand-picked head of the government of Florence, Lorenzo II de' Medici, died in 1519, he asked Giulio to oversee the city. While a relative success in Florence, he was missed in Rome, where he had been an active participant in the lively court life of the city as well as an increasingly powerful figure behind the papal throne. Following the death of his cousin in 1521 and the brief interlude of the little-loved non-Italian pope, Adrian VI (1459–1523; pope 1522–1523), he was elected pope and took the name Clement VII at the still quite early age of forty-five.

His relationship with the Emperor Charles V (1500–1558; emperor 1519–1556), whose troops sacked the city and besieged him in Castel Sant'Angelo for almost eight months, was actually one of off-and-on alliance. Charles had supported his election as pope with the expectation that he would be an ally against Francis I (1494–1547; ruled 1515–1547), the French king who was the emperor's most powerful competitor for power in Italy and Europe. Clement, in turn, attempted to work with Charles to cut short the religious troubles in the emperor's Germanic territories and supported the Edict of Worms of 1521 that proscribed Martin Luther. Shortly after his election, Clement also demonstrated his support by aligning with the emperor as a new phase of open conflict broke out between the French and their supporters in Italy and Charles and his Italian allies. A famous victory for Charles at the Battle of Pavia in 1525 was crowned with the capture of the French king, who was carried off to Spain. But what looked like a definitive victory for the emperor was undone by an overoptimistic faith in the word of Francis. Signing the Peace of Madrid, which theoretically ended the wars between the two, Francis was released after pledging to give up all claims in Italy. Almost immediately, however, he repudiated his pledge, claiming that it had not been freely made – with some justice, obviously, as at the time he had been the emperor's prisoner.

This meant renewed hostilities. Clement, concerned about the growing power of Charles and seeing Francis as a necessary counterbalance, began secret negotiations with the French. And finally, on May 22, 1526, he formally dumped the emperor, joining the newly formed League of Cognac, led by Francis and including his own native city of Florence along with Venice and Milan. An imperial reaction was not long in coming. In September the Cardinal Pompeo Colonna, a member of that powerful Roman noble family and an ally of Charles, went into the streets of Rome with his followers, and with the cry of "Colonna and Liberty" plundered the Vatican while Clement fled to the safety of Castel Sant'Angelo. Charles, however, backed off from supporting this open confrontation with the pope and repudiated Colonna's attack. Having learned his lesson, the pope in turn repudiated his alliance with the French, and peace seemed to have broken out between the emperor and the pope.

But appearances were deceiving. Clement, overconfident about his rediscovered understanding with the emperor, unwisely sent home the troops supplied by his Florentine allies, leaving Rome dangerously undefended. Meanwhile, German and Spanish troops had entered Italy and were plundering their way through Lombardy, vaguely in the name of the emperor and his claims to Milan. But Rome beckoned, with its famed corruption and perhaps even more famous riches; thus, when the renegade Constable of Bourbon took command, those troops were ready to follow him south toward a richer prize. The pope was still not too concerned, because his Venetian allies had an army in the field, led by the duke of Urbino, that seemed more than capable of intercepting Bourbon's motley horde before they reached the holy city. Urbino monitored Bourbon's progress, apparently waiting for the right moment to intercept him or orders from Venice. But those orders never came; thus, although he followed the southward march at a safe distance, he never engaged the host. The result was that the impossible followed swiftly: virtually undefended, Rome fell and was brutally sacked.

As if the Sack of Rome were not enough, while Clement was besieged in Castel Sant'Angelo, Florentine republican leaders took advantage of the moment and threw out the Medici, reestablishing a short-lived republic in the pope's home city. Meanwhile, the emperor staked out the high ground, denouncing the sack, as disease struck the sacking army, carrying off many of the occupying troops along with many Romans. Finally, in June of 1529, peace between the pope and the emperor was formally reestablished. In the typical style of the dynastic diplomacy of the day, it was sealed by the marriage of Charles's illegitimate daughter, Margaret, to the illegitimate son of Lorenzo II de' Medici, Alessandro, along with a promise that the Medici would be returned to power in Florence aided by Charles. It also theoretically required the emperor to return Milan to the Sforza. Francesco II Sforza (1495–1535), son of Ludovico il Moro, who had been in and out of power in the city, found himself suddenly renamed duke. In reality, however, he was on a short leash, for the emperor married him to one of his nieces; thus when Francesco died (perhaps too conveniently) without heirs a few years later, the city became once again a part of Charles's empire.

Shortly thereafter Charles honored his commitment to Clement by besieging the recently reborn Florentine republic. It resisted heroically for almost a year, finally falling in August of 1530. Two years later the Medici were restored to power by the emperor, with Alessandro de' Medici named hereditary duke. His unpopular rule was cut short by assassination in 1537, and he was replaced by a young Cosimo I de' Medici (1519–1574; ruled 1537–1574). Over his long rule this new Cosimo ruthlessly solidified the Medici control of the city, once again creating an impressive court for Florence, drawing to it many of the artists and intellectuals of the day, even if he was not especially famed for his largess. Confirming his success, he was named grand duke of Tuscany by the emperor in 1570, a title which the Medici jealously defended down to 1737, when Gian Gastone de' Medici, the last Medici grand duke of Tuscany, died.

Clearly the major player in all of this was the Emperor Charles V, one of the most important political figures of the century. And he was also perhaps the best example of the power of bedroom diplomacy of his day, for his genealogy set him on the path to European domination. His father, Philip (1478–1506), was the duke of Burgundy when Charles was born and would become Philip I, king of Castile, through marriage. In turn, Philip was the son of the Emperor Maximilian I (1459–1519; emperor 1493–1519) and Mary of Burgundy. Charles's mother gave him an equally impressive pedigree, for she was the daughter of Ferdinand and Isabella, joint rulers of Spain. His younger brother, Ferdinand (1503–1564; emperor 1558–1564), ruled Austria and theoretically, through marriage, Hungary as well. Although this just begins to sketch Charles's genealogical power, things really began to come together for him with the death of his mother's father, Ferdinand, in 1516. At that point, already ruling Castile, he inherited Aragon and became king of Spain. This carried with it the Spanish territories in the New World and claims to Naples, Sicily, and Sardinia. Then, when his other grandfather, the Emperor Maximilian I, died, he inherited his Habsburg lands in the center of Europe and another series of claims in Italy.

The question that faced all of Europe with Maximilian's death was who would be elected emperor. Francis I, king of France, was not eager to see Charles's extensive powers and claims strengthened yet further, primarily because he was committed to pursuing his own claims to many of the same territories, especially in Italy. Thus he angled to obtain the title for himself, seeing it as both blocking Charles's ambitions and serving his own. Charles, however, won in the end, apparently aided by well-placed bribes to the electors, who selected him emperor. Crowned at Aachen in 1520, he rapidly found that he had little time to enjoy his title and claims to power. His territories in the north of Europe were embroiled in the confessional throes of the first days of what would become the Protestant Reformation. In Spain his heavy-handed program of establishing his own men in the most important offices of state, often German-speaking foreigners, quickly led to revolt in Castile (1520–1521). And in Italy open warfare with Francis began in 1521 over their conflicting claims to Milan and Naples, acerbated by disputes over Navarre and Burgundy.

Charles attempted to settle his religious problems via the Diet of Worms, which he called and presided over in 1521. Luther was summoned and appeared under a safe conduct, unsuccessfully defending his vision of reform. With the Edict of Worms, which Charles promulgated in May of that year, he proclaimed his support for the papacy and opposition to Luther, announcing, "[W]e forbid anyone from this time forward to dare either by words or deeds, to receive, defend, sustain or favor the said Martin Luther. On the contrary, we want him to be apprehended and punished as a notorious heretic." Clearly this was a victory for the papacy. But the emperor also attempted to stop Luther by taking up the cause of reform himself and pressed the Church for the reforms that he saw as necessary for healing the religious divisions in his territories. He pushed this agenda most directly by vigorously supporting the election of Pope Adrian VI (1459–1523; pope 1522–1523), who succeeded Leo X. This short-lived pope was Charles's own boyhood tutor, Adrian Dedel. Adrian's austere ways and reform agenda, strongly supported by the emperor, made him unpopular both in Rome and more widely – an unpopularity often couched in attacks on his non-Italian background and ways.

During Adrian's short reign, however, he did accomplish some significant reforms. Perhaps most importantly, he cut back aggressively on both the burgeoning bureaucracy of the Church and the extensive building programs of Leo. This saved the Church a great deal of money and had the potential to move it back toward a more spiritual institution, as reformers demanded. But it also sapped the lifeblood out of the rich and vibrant culture of the city. And, at a deeper level, it threatened to dry up the economic benefits garnered by many elite Italian families, who had literally invested their sons in ecclesiastical offices. Needless to say, this made him unpopular with both the leading families of Italy and the artists and intellectuals who had enjoyed Leo's largesse. Thus many were thankful that both Adrian and his reforms were short-lived. And with the election of the second Medici pope, Clement VII, Rome hoped to return to the glorious days of Leo. Many of those hopes, however, were not to be realized, for Clement was handicapped by financial problems, most notably his costly wars and the Sack of Rome itself.

Returning to Charles's own problems, although his attempt to reform the Church at its center with a pope of his own accomplished little, he was more successful in the political arena. He managed to put down the rebellion in Castile and gain effective control in Spain, which allowed him to concentrate on his claims in Italy and his most powerful enemy, Francis I. As noted earlier, it appeared that Charles had won out when Francis was defeated and captured at the Battle of Pavia in 1525. But his pledge to leave Italy to the emperor in return for his freedom was quickly broken, and in 1526 Charles found himself once again at war against the newly formed League of Cognac and his erstwhile ally, Pope Clement. The Sack of Rome followed. And things began to fall into place for him: the pope allied with him once again; Florence was retaken for the Medici; and Charles gained control of Milan, making him, in effect, the dominant power in Italy.

Yet even with all his successes, as he grew older it appears that he too was spiritually troubled by the religious and political turmoil of his day. Thus he startled Italy and Europe when in 1556, in his mid-fifties, he stepped down and renounced his imperial title as well as his several kingships in favor of his brother Ferdinand (1503–1564; emperor 1558–1564) and his son Philip II (1527–1598) and retired to a monastery. He died two years later, but over the course of his life he had dramatically changed the course of Italian affairs both through his wars and through his matrimonial alliances. While it may be true that the pen is not mightier than the sword, in his case it seems clear that the marital bed was, for a continuing adherence to bedroom diplomacy tied most of Italy and much of Europe and the world to his Habsburg family. In that context he married his relatives into the family lines of the Medici in Florence, the Gonzaga in Mantua, the Doria in Genoa, the Piccolomini in Siena, and the Farnese in Rome, not to mention the ruling families of Portugal, France, Denmark, Germany, Austria, and Hungary. In the larger world the conquests in the name of Spain of Cortes and Pizzaro in the Americas, which he also inherited, began the flow of tremendous treasure to Spain and Europe. And although its impact has been debated, that new wealth disrupted the economy of the Old World in the short run with its massive influx of gold and silver and began the process of creating both an Atlantic and a global economy that eventually shifted the center of the economic world from the Mediterranean and the North Sea to the Atlantic and beyond. Back in Italy, Charles had expanded Spanish power from the southern kingdom of Naples literally throughout Italy and accelerated the process of reintegrating the peninsula socially and culturally with the rest of Europe. The days of the Rinascimento and a unique Italian *civiltà* were numbered.

Reform and the Council of Trent

Whether or not the blame for the Sack of Rome can be laid at Charles's feet, that disaster, along with the Church's inability to contain the burgeoning religious enthusiasms of the north, which seemed to be raining radical new heresies in the name of reform almost daily, confirmed what had long been clear: the Catholic Church would have to seriously tackle the issue of institutional reform. Calls for such reform from leaders of the Church had continued to grow as it became clearer that gradual reform imposed from above would not deal with the deep structural problems it faced. Most lamented were: corruption, which might be more accurately read as clerical careerism, from the lowest priests and monks to the College of Cardinals and the papacy itself; nepotism, which turned on a loyalty and support of family over the Church's spiritual mission; a princely pope and higher clergy, much too eager to gain land and power; and what was widely thought to be the lack of a clear sense of the Church's spiritual mission.

As if that were not enough, many felt that the Church also suffered from a malaise that might best be described as being ultimately too catholic – catholic in the original sense of the world meaning all-inclusive. In the early Church this had been seen as positive, as it allowed the Church to include the many, often diverse strains of belief that memories of Christ and the teachings of his disciples had evoked. With time, however, that inclusiveness had begun to be seen as a problem, and to a degree the history of the medieval Church became one of defining what would be included and what would be defined as outside Christianity – catholic beliefs, in the original sense of the term, being progressively narrowed by eliminating those that were defined outside the pale, as being incorrect. By the middle years of the sixteenth century this process had come a long way. Protestant thinkers merely accelerated it, forcing the perhaps now misnamed Catholic Church to define yet more narrowly what was inside their once catholic boundaries, and labeling what they perceived to be outside as heresy.

Complicating things even before the challenge of the Reformation, a clergy with an uneven education (at times virtually none) meant that the official religion of the Church was frequently more honored in the breach than in practice, especially at the local level. This did not mean that everyday people did not consider themselves practicing Christians, but it did mean that the Christianity they practiced was often distant from the formal theology of Church leaders and theologians. From this perspective the beliefs and practices that made up the lived Christianity of many were much too broad and all-inclusive – too catholic again. And this was especially troubling in the face of Protestant beliefs and practices that had often grown out of and reflected similar everyday ways of understanding and living Christianity. Ultimately, as far as Church leaders were concerned, this was a problem of education and discipline. Most agreed that "true" Christianity had to reach the masses via a clergy capable of disseminating and disciplining a "correct" vision of the faith. The problem was that the clergy itself was largely unprepared to carry out this task, and at the local level they were often the problem, encouraging exactly the practices that leaders saw as dangerously outside of acceptable Christianity. Institutional reform from the top down, with an emphasis on education and discipline, was thus necessary to gather the flock back within the fold of the one true Church, at least from the perspective of the hierarchy of that Church, making it, ironically, safely less all-inclusive and catholic.

Finally, in 1545, Pope Paul III (1468–1549; pope 1534–1549) called a reforming General Council of the Church that would become known as the Council of Trent. In many ways, then as now, he seemed an unlikely reformer. Born Alessandro Farnese to a rich Roman noble family noted for their *condottieri* and patronage of the city's lively cultural life, both licit and less so, he was educated by the best scholars of the day and originally aimed at a political career. In Florence, as a young man at the quasi-court of Lorenzo the Magnificent he was close to Giovanni de' Medici, the future Pope Leo X. Following in the latter's footsteps, he entered the Church and advanced rapidly, apparently thanks to the more illicit side of papal Rome. For at twenty-five he was made a cardinal, reportedly at the insistence of his sister Giulia, who was Pope Alexander VI's mistress. Thereafter he played significant roles in the rule of the popes who preceded him, even sitting out the Sack of Rome in Castel Sant'Angelo with Clement VII and Cellini. As pope, however, Paul was noted for his nepotism, love of pomp and ceremony, patronage of artists and intellectuals such as Michelangelo, and his building program for Rome, which included the construction of the famous Farnese Palace and important restructuring of Saint Peter's. This was exactly the expensive and glorious Rome that reformers objected to and that continued in the costly tradition of his Medici predecessors. It also demonstrated that the Rinascimento, although pressed on all sides, was far from over, at least in Rome.

But Paul also had reforming credentials. He was reputed to be a good administrator, and he had apparently taken his responsibilities quite seriously when he was bishop of Parma as a young man. As pope he also advanced and supported a number of important reforming leaders from the ranks, making them cardinals, most notably Gasparo Contarini, Pietro Bembo, Jacopo Sadoleto, Giovanni Morone, Reginald Pole, John Fisher, and Giovanni Pietro Carafa, the future Paul IV (1476–1559; pope 1555–1559). He also tried to reform the functioning of the papal curia by limiting the sale of offices and dispensations, meeting stiff resistance from entrenched interests in both cases. He even endeavored in the early 1540s to order absentee bishops living in Rome to return to their dioceses, without much success. Perhaps his most notable attempt at reform before convening the council was his appointment in 1536 of a committee of leading clerics presided over by his new cardinal, the Venetian reformer Gasparo Contarini, to look into the problems of the Church and propose reforms. The resulting *Consilium de emendanda Ecclesia* (*Recommendation for Correction of the Church*) of 1537 minced no words, listing an impressive number of abuses and problems and pointing the finger directly at Rome and a tradition of papal leadership that emphasized the political and material over the spiritual. In essence it called into question the whole development of a princely papacy based on a territorial base in Italy and the powerful taxation system that supported the Church's large bureaucracy. After a pirated copy was leaked in 1538, which caused Protestants to gloat over the listed abuses, it was shelved, although not forgotten.

In 1542 reform in the form of stricter discipline gained center stage when, pressed by Cardinal Carafa and a number of other leaders of the Church, the pope renewed and strengthened the Roman Inquisition. Actually a medieval ecclesiastical tribunal, it had been established in 1229 to deal with a series of heresies that then threatened the Church. In the late thirteenth and fourteenth centuries in Italy it had moved on to deal with conflicts over radical Franciscan teachings on spirituality, clerical poverty, and Joachite prophesies of the impending destruction of the Church and the arrival of a last age of the Holy Spirit. In the fifteenth century it had continued, but was less active. Toward the end of that century, in 1478, Pope Sixtus IV, however, allowed Ferdinand and Isabella to set up their own special branch of the Inquisition in Spain, a local Iberian Inquisition. It rapidly became very important in that realm, focusing its attention on Jews, Muslims, and the deep fears of false converts from those religions. Theoretically under the control of the pope, it became a powerful and feared institution in its own right in Spain, working closely with political authorities there to discipline society much more broadly.

After 1542 the reformed Roman Inquisition (as distinct from the Spanish) remained more directly under the control of the pope. That tighter control by the papacy also meant that the Roman Inquisition was more carefully monitored and more legally limited than most other tribunals of the day. This is not to argue that it did not operate with a heavy hand at times, or that it was not ruthless and often short-sighted and repressive. In fact, it rapidly spread a climate of fear and intimidation in Italy. And with its reformed institutional base and more effective procedures, within a generation it was reaching out even into the rural areas of Italy to discipline the faith of peasants and humble women and discovering that the religious enthusiasms that underlay many popular cries for reform were far from the official beliefs of the Church.

Closely related to this disciplining drive to stamp out religious error, often labeled heresy, by the renewed Inquisition was an attempt to shut down what we might label the wider world of literature, which had gained a much broader purchase in society as printing was producing cheaper books for a broader reading public. Religious enthusiasm created a profitable market for books that dealt with an eclectic range of religious topics, from the most traditional and orthodox to the most adventuresome and heretical. Clearly the latter were perceived as a danger, and the renewed Inquisition moved to eliminate them. But books that seemed immoral or that seemed to question the proper order of society were also seen as threatening; thus, for example, Boccaccio's *Decameron* was censored and bowdlerized, most aggressively for its anticlerical sentiments, but also for its perceived immorality and sexual permissiveness. In this context the sometime Inquisitor and Papal Nuncio, Giovanni della Casa, in 1549 drew up for the pope a list of books to be prohibited in the name of reforming Christian society, which was followed in 1559 by the first official list of prohibited books, the *Index librorum prohibitorum* (*List of Prohibited Books*).

While widespread censorship followed quickly, eliminating many books and making it difficult for others to be published or circulated, for upper-class readers and the powerful much of the literature officially banned by the *Index* remained available and was read, perhaps with even greater interest given its now formally illicit nature. Publishers also developed clever schemes to avoid this censorship. Nonetheless, it became more difficult and costly to print or read a wide range of material that spanned the spectrum from the erotic and pagan classics of the ancient world to heretical or even merely reform-oriented works on religion. From this perspective Paul III's reform platform was coming to envision the Church as a fortress to be defended against the dangers of the new – new heresies, new books, new ideas – a vision that, given the Rinascimento's negative vision of the new, was widely accepted at the same time that it was closing off much of the excitement and creativity of the period. Rather than the Rinascimento being an opening to the past, it was becoming a disciplined closing limited to one officially correct past – ultimately quite a different project.

Returning to the council called by the pope, the city of Trent was finally selected as a compromise site for tackling a serious reform of the Church. A small city on the road that led from Italy over the Brenner Pass to northern Europe, it was seen as a promising neutral location – not quite in Italy, yet not quite over the Alps. Even in a neutral place, however, as much as reform was seen as needed, it was also feared. Thus from the start the council was called together with some difficulty and eventually devolved into three separate sittings: 1545–1547, 1551–1552, and 1561–1563. The first attempted to deal with both doctrine and discipline within the Church and ended without great success. Perhaps the most important accomplishment was a decree on the key theological issue of salvation. Against Luther's claim that salvation was a gift from God requiring faith alone, the council returned to a traditional claim that free will was crucial to being saved. Salvation was not simply a matter of God's grace, conferred without reference to a person's deeds, or foreordained given God's infinite power and foreknowledge of all that would happen in His creation. Humans had to will to accept God and to demonstrate through good works that they deserved to be saved. Thus the council argued that they were upholding a long-standing doctrine of human free will against those who in essence denied it. The council, however, avoided the deeper theological complexity of their position, largely because the ecclesiastics who gathered there held such a wide range of views on the relationship between grace and free will that consensus was hard to find. Nonetheless, free will, accepting God's grace, and earning it were to become the key elements of what distinguished the Roman Catholic vision of salvation from the Protestant. On other issues the first session of the council was less successful, and few meaningful decisions were made on institutional reform or in discussions of the nature of the sacraments. After moving for a short time to Bologna in 1547, the first session closed in 1549 at the death of Pope Paul III.

In 1551 the second sitting was called, again at Trent, by the new Pope Julius III (1487–1555; pope 1550–1555). Although a small group of German Protestants was invited with an eye toward promoting a reunion of the Church, the division between Protestants and Catholics was too deep; thus it was short-lived and largely ineffective. Contributing to its lack of accomplishments were the strong political divisions between the religious leaders who supported the French king and those who supported the emperor. When warfare again broke out between the two, the council shut down in early 1552. Hopes were raised, however, with the death of Julius, as it seemed that a strong non-Italian pope might be elected, the noted English advocate of reform, Cardinal Pole. But he lost out, reportedly by one vote, to an Italian cardinal who took the name of Marcellus II and lived only three weeks. His successor, Paul IV (1476–1559; pope 1555–1559), was more interested in papal-driven discipline and reform; thus, although he took Paul III's name, he did not recall his council.

Instead, as noted earlier, he strengthened the Roman Inquisition and instituted the *Index*. He even took the disciplinary move of formally forbidding the reading of the Bible in the vernacular, widely seen by conservatives as a perilous source of independent lay thinking about Christianity and of many dangerously new ideas that were fueling popular religious enthusiasms and heresies. Restricting the reading of the Bible to those who could read it in Latin essentially limited its reading to the educated upper classes, who were believed to be more capable of dealing with its subtleties and, realistically, often had more to lose if religious reform became too radical. Paul's repressive approach to reform and, more generally, to Church governance, however, was seriously weakened by his political failures, most notably his ill-advised alliance with the French in 1556 in their war against Philip II of Spain (1527–1598; ruled 1556–1598). The allies were soundly defeated by Philip, and with the Treaty of Cateau-Cambrésis (1559) his claims in Italy were recognized to the detriment of the pope and the French. All in all, Paul's papacy seemed to confirm to many that reform needed to rely less on popes; and with his death, once again the idea of a general Church council gained wide support.

His successor, Pope Pius IV (1499–1565; pope 1559–1565), apparently accepted this logic and reconvened the council in 1562. This third session, lasting from 1562 to 1563, was by far the most important, in terms of both doctrinal matters and the reorganization of the Church. As far as doctrine was concerned, the central meaning of the mass, as a celebration of Christ's sacrifice that turned on the real transubstantiation of bread and wine into the flesh and blood of Christ in the eucharistic ceremony was confirmed. This was a crucial distinction. Protestants almost universally had come to believe that the ceremony involved merely a symbolic remembrance, not a real transubstantiation – that is, that the bread and wine were not actually transformed into the substance (trans-substantiation) of the flesh and blood of Christ. The council also confirmed the priest's role in this, thus emphasizing the distinction between the priesthood and believers. Only a priest could carry out this central re-creation of Christ's body and blood – a concept that was most significant for the future of the institutional Church, where with increasing insistence direct access to the spiritual would be restricted to, or at the least closely monitored by, the priesthood. The existence of Purgatory was also confirmed, again an important rejection of the position of most Protestants, who held that Purgatory was a medieval invention, unmentioned in the Bible or by Church Fathers. Finally, the sacraments of holy orders and marriage were officially added to baptism and communion, establishing four sacraments (of an eventual seven) that the institutional Church offered its followers, organizing Christian life virtually from birth to death.

Although central to the way the Church would define itself and crucial for confirming the deep divide with the Protestant movement, none of these decisions were in themselves particularly reform-oriented; rather, they tended to confirm medieval traditions and practices. In this, then, they harkened back to an earlier time and thus qualified as reform, but largely insisted on what was already current practice. The decisions of the council on institutional reforms, however, were another matter. There was intense debate about whether bishops should be required to reside in their dioceses, argued in terms of whether this was a matter of divine law or divine precept. Those who favored a strong pope held that this was merely a divine precept, which meant that the pope could decide on an individual basis who had to remain in his diocese and who would be free to live elsewhere – for instance, at the papal court. By contrast, many bishops, especially those from Spain and France, along with the more radical reforming Italians supported a hard-line position claiming that this was a divine law, which meant that the pope did not have the power to overrule it. In the end Cardinal Morone, who was papal legate at the council, won the day with the council agreeing that this was merely a divine precept, not a law, leaving the door open for the pope to decide when bishops might leave their sees.

While the more radical proponents of institutional reform failed to win on this issue, the debate revealed a more general consensus that bishops were destined to be key players in the institutional reform envisioned by the council. This was especially important in the area of education, where local priests were often not well enough educated to lead their flocks or at times even to perform the most basic rituals of the Church. Thus the council ruled that bishops were responsible for setting up and overseeing seminaries to train priests. They were also required to perform regular visitations and hold annual synods to make sure that local clergy were performing as they should. The goal of these reforms was to create an institutional structure in which bishops disciplined their flocks, making sure that the Church actually functioned in a hierarchical and regular manner. Ideally, at every level discipline would flow from above through a spiritual organization staffed by clergy capable of actually serving the ultimate goal of Christianity – making it literally the perfect vehicle for the unfolding of the Holy Spirit in this world and the dissemination of a modern social discipline from the center to the periphery.

As a result, not just any reform-minded individual could redirect the religious enthusiasm of believers, for even the Holy Spirit would now work through a hierarchical bureaucracy that informed the Christian community through the medium of the Church, its institutional hierarchy, and its local bishops. With a tighter organization and a more disciplined and educated clergy from top to bottom, the council's reforms prepared the ground for a church militant that could combat what was perceived as the Protestant menace, a church militant that would ultimately take control of the religious enthusiasms of Christians and direct them on the "correct" path, making the clergy the final masters of the spiritual in this world. Significantly, behind this project of reform lurked a virtually modern division of the world between the spiritual, controlled by the clergy, and the material, open to all. This division would ultimately result in a slowly developing de-spiritualization of everyday life and a demystification of secular life in the world – never entirely complete, but crucial nonetheless for what we see as modern science and, more subtly, for the modern search for a material-based, yet moral, social order in forms such as capitalism, socialism, and anarchism.

Books also played an important part in this program of education, with handbooks for clerics at all levels and catechisms and instructional religious tracts for the more humble being encouraged. Art, often seen as the teacher of the illiterate, was a target of the council's disciplining drive as well. It considered carefully the role of art in Christian society, insisting that it be straightforward and emotionally powerful for its viewers, so that "through the saints [depicted] the miracles of God and salutary examples are set before the eyes of the faithful, so that they may give God thanks for those things, may fashion their own life and conduct in imitation of the saints, and be moved to adore and love God and cultivate piety." The emphasis on the saints, with the clarification that they were merely exemplary, leading to the worship of God and His miracles (and thus His power, not theirs), not only insisted on the didactic power of painting, but also reiterated the Church's stance on the importance of saints. Many Protestants had aggressively contested the Catholic cult of saints and the images associated with it, claiming that those images encouraged a form of idolatry, with believers worshipping saints and their images rather than God – saints had become essentially a new pantheon of pagan gods. Thus the council made it clear that images of saints merely led to and evoked the true power of God as expressed through His saints and had no power in their own right.

It appears that such disciplinary rulings, reinforced by polemical writers like the powerful cardinal and bishop Carlo Borromeo, actually had an impact on religious art, for the second half of the century saw some decline in the influence of the often-convoluted style in religious art labeled Mannerism in favor of a more simple and emotive representation of the saints and the Virgin. Even representations of the human body appear to have been affected. The glorious nudes of Michelangelo and a host of others lost ground to more chastely dressed saints or at least artfully displayed figures that managed not to suggest, even in their nudity, anything that might offend prudish observers, although there were some significant and contested exceptions. Perhaps the best-known example of this trend was the dressing of the nude figures in Michelangelo's *Last Judgment* in the Sistine Chapel, originally represented as God had made them, without clothing. Shortly after Michelangelo's death one of his pupils, Daniele da Volterra, was hired to paint "*braghette*" or pants on those nudes, earning him and his coworkers the contemptuous nickname of "*Braghettoni.*" In fact, the pants were actually more like loin cloths, as can still be seen in the Sistine Chapel today, for even after the recent cleaning the *braghette* have been retained, apparently protecting modern viewers from the ongoing danger of seeing humans as God made them.

Even the Inquisition got involved in the disciplining of art. One of the best-known cases involved the Venetian painter Veronese's famous painting, which started out as a *Last Supper* but ended up as merely a *Feast in the House of Levi* (Illustration 10.1). Although commissioned as a *Last Supper* for the Dominican Monastery of Saints Giovanni e Paolo in Venice, the Venetian branch of the Inquisition, known as the Holy Office, apparently received complaints about the painting. Rather than nudity, the issue raised was that instead of a simple and direct representation of the theme that made clear to the viewer the meaning of this crucial event that presaged the mass and the sacrament of the eucharist, Veronese had painted a lively dinner party replete with modern characters, including jesters, German soldiers, drunks, and even a pet dog. Not only did all that unlikely detail seem to create confusion about the meaning of the Last Supper, some worried that it might even be seen as a mockery of claims for transubstantiation of the bread and wine in the eucharistic ceremony as promised at the Last Supper. But while the Holy Office did ask about potentially deeper theological issues in a rather vague manner when they called in the painter in 1573, in the end they focused on the way the painting unfaithfully represented the scene and confused

10.1. Veronese, *Feast in the House of Levi*, 1573, Galleria dell'Accademia, Venice. Photo: Cameraphoto Arte, Venice/Art Resource, New York.

its meaning for viewers with all its unseemly details and ordered Veronese to change it. That he did. Perhaps not quite as the Holy Office envisioned, however; for rather than painting out the offending details, he simply and elegantly eliminated the whole issue by renaming his painting *Feast in the House of Levi*, removing once and for all questions about unnecessary details or religious messages.

As far as the institutional Church was concerned, in the long run the Council of Trent's reforms dramatically transformed the Catholic Church. But "in the long run" is a necessary qualifier; for even if the leaders of the council understood that top-down reforms and discipline were only as effective as the bureaucracy and church leaders that implemented them, their ability to implement them was curbed by the simple limits of the technology of governing a large, unwieldy organization and the resistance of those most affected by such changes, within both the clergy and the broader Christian community. As a result, while it is true that "in the long run" the Council of Trent was a crucial turning point in the history of the Catholic Church, its actual impact in the short run may be overrated. In theory it was impressive and perhaps even modern in its disciplinary drives, even as officially it looked back and claimed to be traditional. Yet as actually implemented, it might well be argued that the idea that it was the key turning point for religion in the sixteenth century may be stealing the thunder from the most immediately important driving forces of the century, reform and its closely related spiritual enthusiasms. Together they were breaking out all over and at all social levels and deeply transforming Christian society and Italy, while the Council of Trent and the Church tried with limited success to ride their tsunami.

Yet for some modern theoretical thinkers those spiritual enthusiasms and reforming drives that began well before Trent and continued to be a force long after the council were, if anything, more than a tsunami; for they have been hypothesized as major factors in what was perhaps the greatest transition associated with the development of the modern psyche and modernity itself – the development of a modern inner sense of self. Certainly the confessional debates and the violent furor and repression that accompanied them forced many at all levels of society to deeply evaluate what their personal beliefs actually were. In that inner self-evaluation the question became not just how do I seem to those who judge my consensus realities, but rather, more intensely, what do I believe, what is my faith, and how does it relate to God? In fact, in the older tradition of consensus realities that would obviously continue to coexist with a deeper sense of an inner self, some in Italy adopted what was known as Nicomedism. Named after the biblical figure Nicodemus and coined by the Genevan reformer John Calvin, those who followed this strategy, like the biblical character, disguised their true faith and followed the outward forms of religion that their society required of them – protecting their consensus realities – while secretly adhering to what they really believed. This dissimulation of true belief seems to be the essence of the inner/outer conflicts that characterize the modern psyche. And when the many others who carefully considered their true inner convictions and how to act on them in a society increasing committed to policing confessional faith are added to those who dissimulated, it seems to imply a much deeper awareness of one's inner life and its significance.

The Church's move to emphasize more regular confession is often seen as further enhancing this emphasis on interiority. When confession and the examination of one's conscience that was theoretically at its heart was irregularly practiced and poorly understood by many, often uninstructed in its deeper meaning, it may have been seen as more of an outer duty than a deep reflection on one's inner self and faith. But as faith became more contested and confession became more aggressively pushed as a repeating crucial time in life when true penance and confession garnered forgiveness and personal renewal, a careful examination of the inner self became at the least an ideal. Some have argued, in fact, that in the context of such regular self-evaluation there developed an inner-directed culture of guilt that largely replaced community judgments as the primary guide for behavior. That may well overstate the case for the sixteenth century, but the idea that in a time of crisis individuals were developing a more inner and self-evaluative sense that extended well beyond the religious seems a likely hypothesis. In the face of such monumental changes or, more simply, in the face of the powerful spiritual enthusiasms and reform sentiments of the day, the modest ability of the Church to apply the discipline and reforms of Trent to Italian society appears to be merely an episode in a much broader sea change.

Discipline and Attempts to Control Religious Enthusiasms

In the short run, however, after the council closed in 1563 its educational and disciplinary goals were only as effective as the human and material resources available to carry out the reforms envisioned. As already noted, bishops were theoretically to be the key in implementing many of Trent's reforms, and a number in Italy took up the challenge with considerable success, perhaps most notably the cardinal and bishop of Milan, Carlo Borromeo (1538– 1584). Born into an important Milanese family, Borromeo's early career was helped by the very nepotism that deeply troubled reformers. Shortly after his uncle became Pope Pius IV in 1559, Carlo was called to Rome and given a number of important posts. A year later, at the age of twenty-two, he was appointed archbishop of Milan and became a cardinal, thus following in the pattern of youthful cardinals, multiple office holding, and absentee bishops. But for all that, he quickly gained visibility in Rome as an able administrator and reformer and played a significant role in the reopening of the Council of Trent for its last and most productive session in 1562. Some claim that the death of his brother in that same year led him to radically reform his personal life, adopting an asceticism that emphasized poverty and spirituality. Whether or not that was the case, with the death of his uncle Pius IV at the end of 1565, he left Rome and took up residence in Milan with an eye to administering his diocese in the spirit of Trent.

Perhaps it would be more accurate to say that he administered his diocese as his own reforming spirit interpreted the goals of the council. An important qualification, for more often than not Trent's reforms were implemented as local clerical authorities interpreted them in the context of their own vision and at times their own personal interests, significantly deforming the top-down vision of the council. Borromeo provided discipline with regular visits of inspection, as well as with a series of local councils and synods that he called, designed both to investigate and to discipline local practices.

Convents and monasteries were also aggressively reformed with an eye to improving their spiritual quality and enforcing a strict cloisterization of nuns. The lack of both had been seen by many at Trent as one of the blackest marks on the moral reputation of the Church. In turn, he started a number of schools and academies, reportedly often using his family wealth to help finance them, and stressed the importance for the laity of catechism overseen by an educated clergy. He also founded hospitals, orphanages, and shelters for the poor and abandoned, especially women.

In his zeal, however, he also revealed a number of the more negative aspects of the reforms that divided and disciplined society by creating stricter boundaries between those defined as inside the Christian community and those seen as outside; thus he used the renewed Inquisition to hunt out those who entertained religious views that seemed to question the ideas of a new, more militant Church; to strictly limit the freedom of Jews; and to repress those whom he and his inquisitors saw as misusing or misappropriating the spiritual powers of the Church. These aggressive disciplining reforms, which often seemed more like repression, earned him many enemies and at least two assassination attempts. But his approach to reform also appeared to many to be the correct way to implement the top-down discipline imagined by the council, an approach that he laid out in print in his *Acta Ecclesiae Mediolanenesis* (*The Works of the Church of Milan*) published in 1582, frequently cited as a model for reform. In the end, what was considered his saintly life and his evident successes made him a prototype for the ideal reforming bishop, a fact confirmed by his rapid canonization as a saint in 1610.

The flourishing growth of new religious orders also played a significant role in reform following Trent, even if many were more a product of the general reforming enthusiasm of the day and were founded during or even slightly before the council. The Theatines, for example, were founded by a small group in Rome in 1524 who took vows of poverty, chastity, and obedience, with an eye to reforming the Church and serving its needs in the world. This new order was led in its early years by the Venetian Gaetano Thiene (1480–1547), who eventually became a saint (Saint Cajetan), and Pietro Carafa (1476–1559), who became Pope Paul IV (1555–1559). Beyond a commitment to establishing confraternities and hospitals (especially concerned with the new disease of syphilis) and stressing frequent confession and communion, they wanted their community of reformed priests to inspire piety and promote spiritual enthusiasm among the laity. The Capuchians, formally recognized by Pope Clement VII in 1527, were actually just another reforming order that had broken from the Observant wing of the Franciscans.

They grew rapidly in Italy and focused on living an exemplary life of poverty, working with the poor, and advocating frequent communion; they were also noted for their selfless care for the ill during outbreaks of the plague. But they were less concerned with teaching or leading the Church and thus were less involved in the institutional reforms that followed Trent. Other orders, such as the Barnabites, founded in Milan in the 1520s, and the Somaschi, founded in Venice in 1534, flourished in a limited way after Trent and were joined by small orders founded in the second half of the century, such as The Clerks Regular of the Mother of God (the Matritani), founded in 1574, The Clerks Regular Minor (the Caracciolini), founded in 1588, and the Poor Clerks Regular of the Mother of God of the Pious Schools (the Scolopi), founded in 1597.

It was the Jesuits, however, who were most closely associated with the work of disseminating the reforms of Trent and prompting reform more generally. Formally recognized by Pope Paul III with a papal bull of September 27, 1540, the movement had actually begun at the University of Paris, where a group of young students led by the Basque ex-soldier Ignatius Loyola (1491–1556) had taken a vow to go to the Holy Land to convert Muslims. From early on they professed strong support for the papacy, which won them important backing from a number of popes. They also stressed institutional reform and an active ministry in the world. But, perhaps most importantly, from their first days they followed a strict discipline, much more clearly spelled out in their rule than in those of other orders. At times, in fact, their discipline and organization appeared to border on the military, with a highly centralized administration under a Superior General who lived in Rome in close contact with the central powers of the Church. The rapid growth of the order, along with its exceptional discipline and unusual power and success, however, alarmed some. This included not only the better-established monastic orders like the Dominicans and Franciscans, who frequently saw them as dangerous competitors, but also several popes, including Paul IV (1555–1559), Pius V (1566–1572), and Sixtus V (1581–1590), as well as secular authorities in a number of Italian cities.

Still, the widely felt need for a better-educated lay public that could lead society with the Christian values of the reformed Church helped to make the order a major player in the second half of the sixteenth century. In many ways their educational ideal advocated what might be seen as a Jesuit form of civic morality, updated for an Italy in crisis and a militant Church. The colleges that they founded throughout Italy and beyond were officially open to all, but, as the teaching was in Latin, in reality most of their students came from families rich enough to have trained their sons in Latin. The education provided was based on the classics, both of the ancient world and of Christianity, fitting well the Rinascimento ideals of education, but with the crucial addition of a strong grounding in Catholic discipline and an evolving sense of fraternal solidarity among those who studied with them. A few of these colleges developed into full-fledged universities of great import, but most remained local schools with an emphasis on what might be labeled secondary education. They were so successful that they virtually exploded in number, with 144 colleges established by 1579 and 372 by 1615; in fact, the Jesuits claimed that they lacked the numbers to staff all the schools that were requested – the Superior General at the turn of the seventeenth century lamenting that he had had to turn down at least 150 petitions to found new colleges because of such a lack. A Jesuit education quickly became an important part of the educational experience of many of the leaders of Italy and the Catholic world – a common training and discipline whose import would be difficult to gauge, but should not be underestimated.

The Jesuits were also noted for their missionary work in the rural areas of Italy and in the broader world. The latter work has been more often studied, but the former was also important in its attempts to bring the spirituality and religious enthusiasms of the rural laity under the discipline of the Church. In the order's early days, however, its reputation was enhanced by missionary successes in Asia such as those of the Portuguese Francis Xavier (1506–1552), who would eventually be sainted for his proselytizing in India, Malaysia, Indonesia, and Japan. One of the original Paris founding group who, along with Loyola, had pledged to go on a mission to Palestine, his actual career in Asia setting up networks of Jesuits who worked to win over the rulers and upper classes there seemed to offer great promise. Matteo Ricci (1552–1610), noted for his accounts of his life in China, is perhaps the best known of the many who followed in Loyola's footsteps. Meanwhile, in the Americas, Jesuits often took over the pioneering work of other orders, using their tighter discipline to considerable advantage. Especially in Brazil and Paraguay they created their own minisocieties, where the native population was theoretically protected from enslavement while being Christianized, with results, however, that frequently did not live up to the high ideals expressed in their founding. At the same time, they founded colleges in the major cities of South America with the mission of Christianizing and transporting their own vision of the Rinascimento to the new elites of a now much larger world. In many ways a Jesuit form of the Rinascimento quietly conquered the elites of much of the world and set the stage for a diaspora of its culture and values that would underlie a developing ideal of "Western civilization," for better *and* worse.

The order's worldwide experience as missionaries and teachers was also reflected in their important publishing endeavors. Not only did they print key spiritual and educational works, they also published widely read accounts of the new worlds and the new ways of life they encountered – new, of course, only from the perspective of Europe. These accounts added to the increasing realization that the world was larger than the ancients or Church Fathers had realized and that much of it was, in fact, new and troubling to the apparent certainties of both traditions. With time, this again helped to make the dream of a Rinascimento just that, a dream. In the face of a world full of new things and new peoples, lands, and cultures, it was becoming a dream that simply did not apply, even for those who were officially committed to it and attempting somehow to fit the world within its much too narrow confines. Ironically, then, the new was breaking out all over even in the very heart of the religious order committed to reform and the Rinascimento. And even its militant view of reform and its many successes in the wider world would not bring the return of the Rinascimento or the first times of a no longer unquestioned superior past.

The Quasi-Saint Benvenuto Cellini: Religious Enthusiasm and the Great Social Divide

In many ways the spiritual life of the often violent sinner Benvenuto Cellini (1500–1571), whom we encountered defending Pope Clement VII during the Sack of Rome, suggestively evokes this and the religious enthusiasm of the last years of the Rinascimento. And at the same time, it rather strangely evokes how deeply such spiritual reform could connect with the tensions created by disciplining drives across society that were often unwittingly contributing to reestablishing a Great Social Divide that separated the "best" from the rest. For while many were grappling with the new religious and social realities of a Rinascimento in crisis, Cellini made their struggles surprisingly, if strangely, explicit in his *Vita* (*Autobiography*). In a work that seems to fit particularly well the modern label of an ego document, along with his self-described murders, brawls, beatings of women and servants, highhanded ways, and illicit sexual preferences, the self-promoting Cellini also presents a rich description of his own ennobling spiritual reform that suggests at one level the wide reach of the spiritual enthusiasms that often fueled reforming thought in the shared culture of midcentury, and at another his virtually saintly, if not Christlike, experiences.

From the start of his autobiography, in true Rinascimento fashion, Cellini made a point of noting his family's ancient aristocratic origins, which he traced back to the very first times of Florence. He also related the numerous miraculous signs that foretold his own ennobling accomplishments and future. Moreover, having inherited his father's skill as a horn player, which had provided the latter a solid career supported by Medici patronage, Cellini rejected pleas to pursue that profession because he felt it did not offer the glory and status that he believed was warranted by his greater *virtù*. Instead, he opted to take up what he saw as his destiny, creating great works of art and winning fame and elite status as an artist. If the road to that fame, as he described it in his autobiography, was hard and cluttered with misadventures and setbacks at the hand of *Fortuna* – often in the figure of powerful women who did not appreciate his aggressive masculine ways – it was still the heroic and ultimately ennobling road. Fame, heroism, and great works of art, along with high-handed masculine manners, however, all demonstrated for Cellini one thing, his *virtù* – that which made him an artist rather than a mere artisan.

Describing that path of *virtù* in his autobiography, Cellini demonstrated, at least to his own satisfaction, that he had literally lived up to his own model of the elite artist, Michelangelo. Like Michelangelo, Cellini's skills (*virtù*) were so exceptional, as he insisted regularly, that he deserved to regain his family's aristocratic heritage. Unfortunately, as his autobiography inadvertently shows, few real aristocrats were willing to grant him that status, even as they reportedly praised his skills. In fact, it is not hard to read between the lines of his account that the high-handed masculine ways that he believed were necessary to demonstrate his aristocratic manners rubbed many of his patrons the wrong way. For while they may have been forced by codes of honor and aristocratic ideals to treat such behavior by those they considered their peers carefully or risk the violence of duels or more complex confrontations, with Cellini, the great gap between their status and his allowed them to respond more negatively. In essence they could do without his art, finding other more humble and respectful artisans, and thus they could and did replace him in his correct social place regularly when he overreached.

Obviously, Cellini did not present his clashes with his patrons in that light. His emotionally violent confrontations with popes, princes, and kings, not to mention the merely rich and powerful of Florence, Rome, and even France, produced a series of setbacks – including loss of commissions, loss of favor, and even banishments – as well as almost two years in papal prisons. That time in prison, however, reveals how even this would-be aristocrat and often unrepentant sinner could also present himself in the guise of one committed to a level of individual spiritual reform that suggested a yet higher status, a virtually saintly one. The tale as Cellini relates it actually takes us back to

his account of the Sack of Rome, when he mentioned in passing that during his defense of the city, one of his clever shots came so close to Cardinal
Alessandro Farnese that the cardinal harbored the suspicion that it was actually meant for him. Cellini insisted, with typical braggadocio, that those who
knew his abilities (*virtù*) would never have thought such a thing, given his
excellent marksmanship; but nonetheless he warned his readers that that shot
would come back to haunt him.

Eleven years later, in 1538, when Farnese had become Pope Paul III,
Cellini was accused of having taken advantage of the turmoil during the
sack to steal a large fortune in papal jewels. Paul, hoping to regain that fortune, ordered Cellini arrested and pressured to return what he had stolen.
According to his own account, Cellini brilliantly defended himself and his
innocence against the charges. The pope, however, thanks to a lethal combination of his ongoing grudge, his evil advisors, his greed, and his inability
to admit his error in accusing Cellini, rather than freeing him, had him jailed
in the papal fortress and prison, Castel Sant'Angelo. Ironically, it was the very
fortress that he had earlier defended during the Sack of Rome.

At first his imprisonment was rather loose, and Cellini continued with
his work on commissions while in jail. But time passed, and rather than the
pope relenting, his confinement became stricter, until finally Cellini decided
to take advantage of his metalworking skills to escape. Thus he dismantled
the door to his cell and, using strips of sheets, climbed down the walls of
the castle to almost carry off a brilliant escape that once more demonstrated
his manliness and *virtù*. Almost. For although he reported proudly that his
escape was the talk of Rome and that everyone was impressed by his *virtù*,
even the pope, he admitted that due to the strain on his arms and bleeding
hands he lost his grip during his descent and fell the last part of the way
to the street, breaking his leg. Found there, he was carried to the house of
Margarita of Austria, the illegitimate daughter of Charles V, who, although
she was married to a relative of the pope, had been married previously
to Alessandro de' Medici and in theory was a friend of Cellini's through
their shared Florentine connections. Through a complicated series of noble
intrigues, however, he found himself quickly reconsigned to the pope and
prison, with the promise that a papal pardon would soon follow.

That promise was not kept. Rather, Cellini found himself in much stricter
confinement "in the prison of those condemned to death," with a dangerously broken leg and a guard who sympathized, "Oh my, poor Benvenuto
what have you done to *them* [the great] to warrant this." [italics mine] In
the face of what looked like impending death, Cellini found religion in his
own spiritual reform and – typically, given his enormous self-esteem – in

his special relationship with God, which ultimately made him superior even to the guard's "them" – those of unquestioned power and authority on the other side of the Great Social Divide. In the vein of a spiritual hero, he replied to his guard with Christian resignation, "The sooner I escape the jail of this world, the happier I will be, especially as I am sure that my soul is saved and that my death is unjust. Christ in his divinity and glory will gather me to his disciples and friends, who like Him, and they, were unjustly executed as I will be." Suggestively, even when anticipating his martyrdom Cellini sees it in terms of his finally joining the most elite of the elites, the circle of Christ and his disciples. If his craft and art no longer seemed able to confirm his superior status as he lay dying in the papal prison, his special relationship to God and martyrdom would win him a place in the ultimate elite – at the side of God in Paradise.

Clearly, a placement in one of the lower circles of Dante's Paradise, contemplating the Divinity from afar, was much too humble a spiritual placement for Cellini. But he put off – momentarily, at least – sitting at the side of God in Heaven thanks to the pleas of his important noble supporters who pressed his case with the pope. Taken from his death cell, he was given a slightly better one that contained only "quite a bit of water and many tarantulas and poisonous worms." But it also came with a book or two, including, interestingly, given the Church's suspicion of vernacular Bibles, a copy of the Bible in Italian, which provided the inspiration for Cellini's final Calvary. Reading it, as he contemplated suicide, he was visited by an angel as he dozed off, who admonished him not to damage God's great work done in creating him and not to lose faith in Him or in his own *virtù*. In response, he began to write religious poetry on the blank pages in the Bible, overcome by just the kind of religious enthusiasm that the Church feared Bible reading tended to awaken in the uneducated.

In his growing spirituality he prayed and sang hymns to pass the time as his body steadily deteriorated, with his nails growing so long that he could not touch himself and his teeth rotting and falling out. Nonetheless, his broken leg healed "miraculously" after four months, a foretaste of the greater miracles to follow. His spiritual fervor continued to grow, with dreams and visions taking up more and more of his prison life. One of his most powerful occurred after he prayed to God and begged the same angel who had saved him from suicide to be allowed to see the sun just once after months in his dark cell. One night his angel came to him to answer those prayers. But even Cellini's description of "his" angel is revealing, given his own self-depiction as a "noble" lover of youths; "my Invisible [angel] there revealed himself in human form as a youth [*giovane*] with just the first signs of a beard, with a most beautiful and splendid face, but austere, not lascivious." His angel had the beauty of the youths who had attracted him in the everyday world, but he was careful to note that it transcended that world, for the experience that was to follow turned on the spiritual and transcendent, not on the sensual pleasures of the material world.

After guiding him through a space that contained the "infinite thousands" of people who had lived up to that time, his angel led him outside to where ladders leaned against a wall, allowing Cellini to climb up out of the shade and view the sun directly. When he first saw it, he closed his eyes, for like normal mortals, he feared that its direct light would blind him. But then he opened his eyes, willing to risk blindness in order to take full advantage of the miracle granted him. And as he looked directly at the sun, its blinding rays separated to reveal the disk of the sun itself looking like molten gold, described very much in the terms of the goldsmith that he was. But the true miracle in all its material spirituality had just begun for this more and more transcendent artisan and artist, because as he watched the sun, it began to bulge, and from its surface emerged a magnificent golden Christ on the Cross. Cellini could not help crying, "Miracles, miracles! Oh God, your forgiveness, your infinite *virtù*, what a great thing you have made me worthy of." The grace of God was literally shining upon him.

Then Christ moved off to the side, and there appeared from the disk of the sun the Madonna with a playful Christ Child in her arms, accompanied by two beautiful angels and worshipped by Saint Peter, the first pope. Cellini watched for a time, and then the vision disappeared and he was back in his dark cell. Still overwhelmed by his vision, he began to cry loudly, "The *virtù* of God has made me worthy of His showing me all His glory, which perhaps has never been seen by any other mortal eye; from this I know that I am free and happy with the grace of God." Once again, even in this moment of extreme spiritual ecstasy, Cellini presented himself as having virtually unique status in the eyes of God. And he made this clearer yet by noting that a vision of the first pope, Peter, praying to the Virgin and Christ Child revealed him praying to them to intercede for none other than Cellini himself. He even claimed that his vision had allowed him to learn the exact date when their prayers would be answered and he would be liberated from jail. The strangeness of Cellini's spiritual election masks an important point that requires emphasis in the context of our earlier discussion of a sense of interiority and an inner self. For while Cellini's account of his life and suffering as a would-be artist and quasi-saint seem to be the quintessential self-presentation for constructing a consensus reality about himself – often a highly unlikely one – all the events of this truly miraculous moment, his spiritual apotheosis, are told in terms of his inner feelings and inner self. A consummate man of action and self-fashioning, he fashions even his inner self for posterity at the heart of his autobiography – ego document indeed.

Before his prophecy came true, however, as it must in such miraculous accounts, he described one last spiritual experience:

> Still I do not want to leave out one thing, *the greatest that ever happened to any person* – [a thing] which attests to the divinity of God and his ineffable ways, which he deemed me deserving of being made worthy. Ever after that vision [perhaps the dream just described] there remained a glow [or a halo (*uno isplendore*)] over my head, a thing marvelous to behold. This is visible to every person to whom I wish to show it, even if they are few in number. [italics mine]

Evidently Cellini's halo was the crowning glory of the deep religious enthusiasm that his suffering in jail brought out in him, and suggested that he had leaped the greatest gap of all in Christian society, becoming a spiritual being, with his halo modestly visible only to a chosen few. Before that saintly halo the distinctions between orthodox and heterodox, artisans and artists, commoners and aristocrats, inner and outer self, and the Great Social Divide itself simply paled, and he was ultimately beyond the discipline of this world.

Once freed from the papal prison, however, his elite pretensions returned to more mundane dimensions; he again focused on his great art, his superiority to his artistic competitors, and his largely unrecognized but nevertheless true equality with the most important men of his day. In a way, however, Cellini's successes and failures serve as an evocative metaphor for the coming successes and failures of the second half of the sixteenth century in Italy and the slow dissolving of the Rinascimento in the larger and newer world that denied its uniqueness and dreams of a return to the past. His personal reform and religious enthusiasms, like those of his day, while impressive, were not enough to bring back the past or overcome the more powerful forces arraigned against him and the *civiltà* of the Rinascimento. For all his striving and posturing he, like most of his contemporaries, could not jump a Great Social Divide that was making Italy socially and politically much more like the rest of Europe. Yet he anticipated, with his often asocial ways and demands for a special status as an artist and intellectual, a future vision of intellectual elites and genius that would soften that divide for those recognized as exceptionally talented – although, as his many failures reveal, that status would require the recognition and approval of those actually on top of society. At the same time, his dreams of a return to his

family's ancient noble origins that would bring him greatness in the future
eerily echo the very dreams of the Rinascimento itself and their failure.
Cellini would not return to those origins, and even his momentary deep
spiritual reform would deliver no more than a halo that only a chosen few
could see. And the same was true of the Rinascimento; its halo was seen by
fewer and fewer, and the deep empowering return to a series of first times
was becoming more and more a dream. Admittedly it would be re-dreamed
regularly, but the times were doing the one thing that they can be counted
upon to do, changing. And the new, in the form of new disciplines, new and
stronger social and religious divides, and new powers in Italy, was undermining dreams of return and reform whether spiritual, social, political, or
Cellini's reveries of saintliness.

II

RETREAT: THE GREAT SOCIAL DIVIDE
AND THE END OF THE
RINASCIMENTO (c. 1525–c. 1575)

From Spiritual to Political Reform: Prophets of
Reestablished Italian Glory

Reformers and reform sentiment were abroad in the sixteenth century and pressing for change well beyond the religious arena. In fact, many of the same people who were concerned with the spiritual reform of the Church were also profoundly concerned with reforming the political world of the Italian city-states in order to revitalize the traditional political order of the peninsula in the face of invasions and a deplored loss of political autonomy. As we have seen, these were crucial issues for the important political thinkers and social critics of the first decades of the century, like Machiavelli and Castiglione, and were deeply embedded in the apparently less political writings of writers like Ariosto, Aretino, Bembo, Gambara, and Colonna. They remained crucial even in the years of the Council of Trent and after, in fact, for the rest of the premodern period.

Gasparo Contarini (1483–1542), whom we have already met as a religious reformer, provides a good example of the way in which church reforming ideology and state reform often intermixed in fertile ways. Although he rejected for himself the spiritual withdrawal from the world of his fellow Venetians Vicenzo Querini and Tommaso Giustiniani, he remained committed to religious reform even as he became a major figure in the crucial political events of the day. Thus he played an important role in Venetian politics, serving as a diplomat representing Venice in the negotiations forming the League of Cognac, and after the Sack of Rome helping to reestablish peace between the emperor and Clement VII. At the same time, however, he gained a reputation for his Christian reforming ideals and was appointed a cardinal in 1535 at the age of fifty-two.

In that capacity he became a leader of a more moderate group of reformers and was widely recognized as one of the few Church leaders still hopeful that a reconciliation with Luther and his followers might be worked out. Given his views on salvation as expressed in his correspondence with Querini and Giustiniani, discussed earlier, where he had leaned toward a form of justification by faith rather than works, he certainly had a position on that vexed issue that might have made reconciliation possible. Pope Paul III, Cellini's nemesis, may have hoped to take advantage of Contarini's noted diplomatic skills and reputation as a moderate to divide the followers of Luther at the Diet of Regensburg in 1541, called in an attempt to reunite Christianity, where he sent him as papal legate. But Contarini's desire for compromise was severely limited by the pope's instructions, which restricted what he could propose; thus his more moderate stance went largely unexpressed and the council failed, as had earlier attempts at compromise and reunification.

In the political realm, however, Contarini's vision of reform had a more lasting impact. As a political figure, not only did he serve on numerous important diplomatic missions before he became a cardinal, he also held some of the most important offices in Venetian government, serving as senator and even head of the famed Council of Ten, often seen as the small committee that dominated the government of the city in the sixteenth century. He also wrote a famous political treatise, *De magistratibus et republica Venetorum* (*On the Commonwealth and Republic of Venice*), that presented Venice and its government as the ideal mixed republic that implicitly might serve as a model for the reform of Italian city-state governments in the face of the political crisis of the day. In the spirit of the Rinascimento, Contarini claimed to look to the first times of Venice to discover what had enabled the republic to endure so long and so successfully. What he found expressed repeatedly in the chronicles of the city were the basic components of the myth of Venice – a myth that stressed the unusual *virtù* of the city's merchant elite, who wisely had been willing to sacrifice their own self-interest for the broader welfare and well-being of the republic.

In turn, building on a vision of the ideal republic based on medieval and ultimately Aristotelian ideals of mixed government, he argued that the Venetian republic had long been a virtually perfect expression of that ideal. Essentially, in Venice a self-effacing closed nobility ruled in the general interest of the commonwealth with a mix of princely power (in the form of the doge, the city's chief executive and ritual figurehead), aristocratic power (in the form of the Senate, the elite council representing the best men of the city), and democratic power (in the form of the Great Council, representing the *popolo* of the city). All this was maintained by a well-established tradition of law that kept Venetians virtuous and moral, and those laws were in turn followed by virtuous Venetians – guaranteeing Venice's own superior civic morality. These ideas were hardly new. Not only were they sprinkled generously through the Venetian chronicle tradition of the early Rinascimento and the city's self-representation and civic rituals, they were much more widely accepted – even grudgingly countenanced by political thinkers such as Machiavelli, as we have seen. But, of course, the fact that they were not new, that they were already a part of the shared primary culture of the day, only made them more attractive for the Rinascimento.

Unfortunately, however, they were not particularly accurate, as Contarini must have been aware, having actually served in the government and experienced on a daily basis the much more complex reality of the messy business and corruption of Venetian politics. In fact, the Venetians of his day even had a technical term in the local dialect for the corruption that they felt actually made their government function, *broglio* – a term that, although seldom used today, actually made it into English as a name for political corruption. Yet here once again reality was in many ways less important than appearances, as Machiavelli would have argued. For to contemporaries it was clear that Venice was, in fact, unusual in its longevity, peacefulness, prosperity, and well-ordered success, and Contarini's treatise simply explained why, without novel claims or dangerous innovations. In fact, his recipe for successful governing was point by point satisfyingly old and traditional, based on claims (also untrue) that the city had endured as a virtually unchanging republic for a thousand years. From the perspective of this imagined reality, others who sought success and stability could argue that reform and rebirth on the Venetian model offered the answer.

Significantly, Contarini's work was so convincing that it was quickly translated from Latin into Italian, French, and English and thus had a much wider impact. Most notably, perhaps, it had a profound influence on English and American political thinkers, as the masterful studies of J. G. A. Pocock and William Bouswma have shown from slightly different perspectives. In fact, the subsequent history of Venice only heightened the attractiveness of Contarini's presentation of the Venetian myth. That story does not belong here, but events like the Venetian surprise victory over the Turks at the Battle of Lepanto in 1571 and the writings of later Venetian political thinkers like Paolo Paruta, at the end of the century, and Paolo Sarpi, early in the seventeenth century – thinkers who tied the myth of mixed politics and civic morality into a richly suggestive package that also advocated resistance to the claims of power by religious institutions – made the Venetian model particularly attractive. That potent mix, promising stable government, peace, and civic morality, prepared the ground for political ideologies that could argue for the separation of church and state without being open to charges of supporting an immoral secular order or dangerously new ideas. And it had a profound impact on political thinkers like Thomas Jefferson, who had clearly read his Contarini and Sarpi along with Machiavelli and who, at times, could see the new country he was involved in founding as not so new after all, but rather a reassuring rebirth modeled on the successes of the Rinascimento.

Returning to Italy, however, and looking back at 1494 from the mid-1520s, Machiavelli's younger friend and correspondent Francesco Guicciardini (1483–1540) described in his *Dialogo del Reggimento di Firenze* (*Dialogue on the Government of Florence*) another, more pragmatic vision of potential political reform. The work, set in 1494 just after the fall of the Medici, presented a supposed discussion between a group advocating reestablishing the old Florentine republic and a wise old supporter of the Medici, Bernardo del Nero, who agreed reluctantly with their proposal and suggested reforming the city's old institutions in order to create a more ideal republic. The republicans, represented by actual historical figures who had played major roles in the renewed republic (1494–1512), were won over by del Nero's logic, which cleverly displayed Guicciardini's own famed "realism" and "anti-theoretical" approach to politics. Del Nero argued that while republican forms of government had more problems and defects than one-man rule, given the particular circumstances of the moment, a return to such rule under the Medici was not possible. Thus particular circumstances, not historical rules or ideals of returning to first times, forced del Nero to opt for a new republic, and, not surprisingly, it was very similar to the mixed republican government advocated by Machiavelli in the *Discourses* and later by Contarini. This neatly allowed Guicciardini to defend what he saw as a better form of republican government that might have been established in an imaginary past without stepping on the toes of the current Medici rulers of his city.

Giucciardini, unlike Machiavelli, was born into one of the major old aristocratic families in Florence with deep and illustrious roots in the city's history. After studying law and the classics both in Florence and at the University of Padua, he married Maria Salviati in his mid-twenties, apparently without the consent of his family. Their lack of enthusiasm for the match seems to have been due to the fact that even if her family was old and prominent, it was temporarily out of power during the revived republic (1494–1512), given its Medicean sympathies. His marriage and political career became considerably happier and more prosperous, however, with the return of the Medici in

1512. After working briefly in their restored government, he entered the service of the papacy and spent most of the papacies of Leo X and Clement VII working for them. In that capacity he played a significant role in the ill-fated League of Cognac and as papal governor in various cities of the Papal States. With the death of Clement in 1534 and the papacy of Paul III, however, Guicciardini found his favor waning in Rome. Unfortunately for him, the same was true in Florence, where the new Medici duke, Cosimo I, found the ex-papal official with his anti-imperial reputation a problem for his rule, which was heavily reliant on the emperor, Charles V.

Given the political climate, Guicciardini opted, much like Machiavelli, to retire to his Tuscan villa near Arcetri in 1537, devoting his last years to his historical writings and his practical reflections on life in a work known as *Ricordi* (*Records* or *Memories*). *Ricordi* had long been popular among Florentines: beginning as annotated account books, they slowly developed into diarylike works with the addition of progressively more personal detail. It appears that Guicciardini's *Ricordi* were written early in his career in this typical chronological form, but late in life he reorganized them so that they appeared more like short aphorisms on his vision on life. Although not published until much later, they provide a revealing critique and rejection of the Rinascimento. The idea of a return or rebirth of first times, he argued, was an empty dream; moreover, there were no models, ancient or modern, for living a good life. Instead, one needed to use "*discrezione*": the ability to distinguish the nature of each situation and decide what needed to be done case by case. Not surprisingly, then, he was also unenthusiastic about the Church and its reforms, arguing that religion made the world "effeminate" – once again that gendered value judgment – and was best kept separate from politics and the pragmatic decisions that mattered.

Much the same vision can be found in his major history, still unfinished at his death, the *Storia d'Italia* (*History of Italy*). A multivolume work that carefully detailed the history of the peninsula from 1492 to 1534, it focused on the events and individuals that Guicciardini saw as critical for the crisis that Italy faced. And in many ways it can still be read as a political history of that period from the perspective of the ruling elites of Italy. In fact, with its reliance on documents and a close, often personal knowledge of events and diplomatic maneuvers, it is frequently referred to as one of the first truly modern histories in the Western tradition. Firsts, of course, are notoriously temporary, enduring only until someone finds a newer first; and first "moderns," if anything, tend to be very short-lived. Yet there is much in his history that makes it read differently than most other histories of his day, even if it wrestles with the same big question that troubled everyone, the apparent

demise of the Rinascimento. He too related the events and the context of
what were seen at the time as the disasters that had ruined Italy, from the
invasion of the French King Charles VIII in 1494 through the Sack of Rome
in 1527, along with the wars that had wracked the peninsula between the
French kings and the Habsburg emperors, and on to the eventual dominance
of Charles V.

But, significantly, he relates these events without an evident overall theoretical frame or classical model. Rather, he provides a close individual analysis on a case-by-case basis without offering lessons or a general overview of
history itself; thus Guicciardini's tale tends to turn on the deeds of individual
actors motivated by human emotions and historically particular factors. In
sharp contrast with Machiavelli's historical reflections in his histories and in
his *Discourses* and *The Prince*, Guicciardini's past offers no rules, aside from
the very significant rule that history offers no rules. In this, then, Guicciardini
rejects one of the basic underpinnings of the Rinascimento, for one cannot
return to the past to find lessons, rules, or models for living in the present in
an historical past where none exists. In the end, history is too complex, and
historical events involve too many individual conjunctures, meaning that the
past is absolutely unrepeatable. Reform and rebirth in the deep sense of the
Rinascimento were ultimately chimeras.

Guicciardini had developed similar ideas in his *Considerazioni intorno ai
Discorsi di Machiavelli sulla prima Deca di Tito Livio* (*Considerations on the
Discourses of Machiavelli*), written earlier in 1529, shortly after the death of his
friend Machiavelli. In that work, echoing the letters the two had exchanged,
Guicciardini argued that Machiavelli's analysis was actually driven by a
deeper theoretical vision, rejecting his claims that he was merely analyzing
things as they were and as they worked. Most notably, he pointed out that
Machiavelli believed that the Roman past actually provided ongoing rules
that could be discovered for the way events and histories developed rules
that could be applied in the present. Once again Guicciardini argued that
such rules simply did not exist. Machiavelli, because he did not realize this,
missed the real trees for an imagined theoretical forest, even as he denied
that he was doing so.

Perhaps most indicative of Guicciardini's distance from Machiavelli, however, was his discussion of the relationship between *Fortuna* and *virtù*, developed most fully in the *Ricordi*. Given the impressive power most thinkers
attributed to *virtù* in human affairs and in the very organization of society,
fortune's widely recognized ability to overturn *virtù* was a perennial subject
of reflection. Machiavelli's worries about *Fortuna* are merely among the best
known, but Guicciardini's reflections on the subject may be read as a rejection

of what he saw as his friend's overly optimistic conclusions on the subject. For although Machiavelli gave fortune great power, in the end he claimed that the truly *virtù*-ous could control it. As we have seen, he argued that while fortune was like a flood that swept all before it, the *virtù*-ous person could be wise enough to carefully plan ahead and build the necessary dikes and canals to control the force of that flood, thus avoiding the worst of its destructive power. Guicciardini countered that the best-laid plans were often simply overwhelmed by fortune, and given that the past never repeated itself, *virtù* was incapable of using the past to foretell where fortune would strike. In this pessimistic vision, another lynchpin of the Rinascimento primary culture, *virtù*, was once again undermined. In the end one had to judge each situation on its own and accept that even this approach would not always be enough to overcome fortune. In all this Guicciardini might be seen as anticipating the modern world and is often presented in that light. But perhaps it would be better to see him in the terms of his time, for in many ways he was more a disillusioned aristocrat, who, like many of his peers, had lost faith in some of the most important givens of the Rinascimento, without, however, actually being able to leave that world and culture behind.

As an aristocrat and conservative, Guicciardini's vision of the ideal society was strongly conditioned by a measured rationality intermingled with nostalgia for a past that he ruefully realized could not return or be recreated. Yet for all its unrepeatability, it was at the heart of the future he hoped for, even as he doubted it would arrive. Telling in this regard is his often-cited hope for the future of Italy: "I wish to see three things before I die, but I doubt that ... I will see any of them: a well ordered republican life in our city, Italy liberated from all the barbarians, and the world freed from the tyranny of those priests." His first two wishes actually seem to imply a return to the glories of the Rinascimento, even if he had argued cogently that they could not return. His last fit well with his suspicion of religion and its negative impact on society. And to a degree it seemed to echo the more radical reformers of his day, who called for divesting the Church of its material wealth and political power, even if he would probably have been uncomfortable in their company.

In contrast to Machiavelli's call for a strong leader with the *virtù* to unite Italy and drive the barbarians from the peninsula, Guicciardini seemed to desire merely a continuation of the city-states of Italy. Each, led by aristocratic elites made up of men like himself, would follow its own local political and cultural path, a diversity that promised continued greatness and leadership, culturally and politically. To overcome the barbarians, the only hope was for city-states to band together to drive them out of Italy and at the same time to divest the papacy of its temporal powers, thus eliminating once and for all its continuing destabilizing maneuvering with powers from outside the peninsula. Guicciardini presented what was ultimately a fairly traditional vision as merely the result of a careful analysis of things as they were, even if paradoxically, in its own way it was a call for a return to an imagined past that had been lost with the invasions. In all of this Guicciardini seems symptomatic of a period of transition. He rejected many of the key concepts of the shared primary culture of the Rinascimento: *virtù*, optimism, reform, return, and ultimately the very possibility of a rebirth of the ancient world or even of the immediate past, while ultimately hoping to return to an imagined better past. And at the very heart of his way of seeing the world, there lurked that most scary of all the fears of the period – the new, which in his pessimistic vision seemed to be destroying the world in which he lived.

The Great Social Divide: Aristocrats and Academies

In his firm belief that the Italian aristocracy as it had developed across the Rinascimento offered the ideal leaders to overcome the crisis Italy faced, Guicciardini may not have been entirely correct, but he was on target about who the major players would be. For in many ways the middle years of the century in Italy were ones that formalized what we have labeled the Great Social Divide. Of course, from the first days of the Rinascimento – and well before, for that matter – there had been a strong sense of social hierarchy in the cities of Italy. But, as we have seen, in that urban world of relatively rapid social change there had been considerable uncertainty and competition about who the most important people actually should be. Eventually the question was settled in favor of a mixed group of merchants, bankers, and owners of larger artisanal enterprises such as the great cloth producers of Florence, along with a liberal dash of the old nobility who joined their ranks – the *popolo grosso*. This new elite, with its claim to be re-founding the glories of ancient Rome, along with the way of life of the ancient world based on their own *virtù* and ideals as rediscovered in ancient texts, both classical and Christian, asserted that they were definitely not new. In fact, they presented themselves as safely and successfully the best of the old, leading a rebirth of ancient society and *virtù* – a Rinascimento.

Across the fifteenth century we have seen how this elite became progressively more aristocratic. In turn, the series of crises of the sixteenth century accentuated this process. With a greater emphasis on bloodline and family tradition; with increasing competition from the rest of Europe in banking, trade, and neoindustrial production; with a New World and a developing

world economy that threatened to transform the Mediterranean from center to periphery; with a renewed emphasis on the Church, warfare, and the
land as the most secure economic motors for the upper classes; and with
tighter and tighter marriage strategies within class, the gateway to elite status was becoming narrower and narrower. Moreover, at the highest level
of the aristocracy, the best families of the most important cities and courts
were increasingly breaking away from the custom of marrying locally, or at
least with other Italian aristocrats, and rediscovering the prestige and power
that came with marrying into powerful European noble families, a tendency
encouraged by the new political realities of the peninsula, where foreign
families like the Habsburgs and countries like Spain dominated. Those few
below this more narrow and powerful aristocracy who managed to gain the
wealth or the power and visibility to join their ranks faced a long and often
fruitless struggle to actually be allowed in – in essence, a divide that had long
existed was becoming a yawning chasm in Italy. To a great extent that Great
Social Divide was the last piece of the puzzle that aligned Italy once more
with the dynamic of the rest of Europe and prepared it to follow on the
path to a new European order, becoming a part of a more general European
Renaissance already under way and eventually developing into what would
be labeled the *ancien régime*.

One area where this growing divide seemed to be eased somewhat was
in the rapid growth of academies dedicated to learning and intellectual play
in the sixteenth century. Informal groupings of intellectuals drawn from the
upper classes, scholars, and even an occasional artisan/artist noted for his
virtù had long been a part of the cultural life of Italy. One thinks of the circle
of scholar/bureaucrats and upper-class intellectuals that Coluccio Salutati
and his protégé Leonardo Bruni gathered around themselves at the turn of
the fifteenth century; the group that gathered around Marsilio Ficino; or
the so-called Roman Academy led by Pomponio Leto that incurred the
suspicious displeasure of Pope Paul II, which he broke up in 1468. Even
Machiavelli was associated with an informal group that met in the Rucellai
Gardens to discuss ideas and politics, where he read to his fellows parts of
the *Discourses* as they were being written. His *Art of War* was actually set
as a dialogue that took place in those same gardens. Examples could easily
be multiplied in virtually every cultural center of Italy. What changed as
the sixteenth century progressed, however, was that an increasing number
of these groups transformed themselves from informal gatherings that met
outside universities or courts, into formal academies that elected members,
met regularly, and had officers and rules – in essence attempting to create
their own urban pseudo-courts without a prince for what was increasingly

a self-styled intellectual elite. The aristocratic, elitist nature of most academies was clearly one reason for their rapid proliferation across the sixteenth century. It has been estimated that in 1530 there were probably about a dozen or so formal academies in Italy. By 1600 the number had ballooned to almost 400, and it continued to grow to at least 1,000 by 1700, with virtually every major population center having at least one academy and larger cities usually having several.

Status, both social and intellectual, was clearly an important aspect of the academies, yet it is unclear just where they actually fit in the social hierarchy of the day. Although their pretensions often aimed at elite status, many did not match up with the unquestioned social superiority of the high aristocracy who frequented the important courts of the day or often even of the most powerful aristocrats of formally noncourtly cities like Venice and Genoa. And clearly there were numerous academies, especially in smaller cities or at a second-tier level in larger ones, where most of the members were on the wrong side of the growing Great Social Divide. It may well be, however, that this rather unclear social placement fit well with the increasingly strict social divisions that typified the second half of the sixteenth century. In their way, the academies, perhaps in a largely unrecognized manner, provided an apparent softening of that divide, offering a type of elite status to those who socially and in terms of power no longer would find a real place among what was now a new, much more aristocratic elite with a growing European reach and visibility.

In essence the academies created a slightly less elite social environment that ran parallel to the courts of the day, rewarding, at least in theory, the more traditional *virtù* associated with accomplishment, usually intellectual. There was some crossover, of course, with some more intellectually accomplished notables joining or patronizing academies and a few of the most impressive members of academies adding their luster to the most important courts. Significantly, although real power and status seemed to go first to the courts and their increasingly notable notables, in ways perhaps unrecognized at the time, this gave a different, less visible power to the academies. Without the necessity of serving a prince or competing for his favor or moving in international circles, the gaming and play of academies could focus more easily on scholarship and the intellectual play that would provide the basis for intellectual innovation, especially in areas like the natural and mechanical sciences.

With time, a hierarchy of academies developed, with the greatest offering their members a badge of high status and lesser ones at the least marking a person out as an aristocrat locally. In a few, notable local artists, and even an occasional artisan respected for his skills, mixed with intellectuals and aristocrats, sharing interests in natural philosophy or more practical learning to create a rich blending of ideas across social distinctions. But more often these academies reflected the virtually unquestioned assumption that both gender (masculine) and class (aristocratic) determined who the truly *virtù*-ous were. This aristocratic tone was reflected in the playful titles and names given to these groups – the Ardenti (Impassioned Ones) in Naples; the Addormentati (Sleeping Ones) in Genoa; the Gelati (Frozen, Frigid Ones) in Bologna; the Confusi (Confused Ones) in Viterbo; the Infiammati (Burning Ones) in Padua; the Innominati (Unnamed Ones) in Parma; and the Intronati (Dazed Ones) in Siena – for even the exchange of ideas and intellectual pursuits were seen by the upper classes as aristocratic play or games, not work. Work was for the lower classes, and thus, in order to be truly aristocratic, intellectual activities virtually by definition had to be at least playful. In fact, the association of play, games, and what would become scientific investigation made what is often labeled early science a very different project than the modern, both socially and intellectually.

With time, however, the most successful academies became more serious, and as they did, they tended to reinforce the Great Social Divide with a series of significant intellectual divides. The Accademia della Crusca (The Academy of the Chaff) in Florence, founded officially in 1583, provides a telling example. It grew out of an informal group that referred to itself as the Brigata dei Crusconi (The Bad Chaff Chums), from the term *cruscate*, which referred both to a playful form of lecture that seemed to wander around a topic without openly coming to a conclusion and to the chaff left over when grain was milled, *crusca*. This Brigata had begun to meet as a more playful alternative to the Florentine Academy patronized by the grand duke of Tuscany, Cosimo I, which they saw as too serious and pedantic. Thus, they sought to wear their learning lightly, something indicated by the names the group took for themselves, most of which played upon references to food and, more specifically, flour and grain.

The most famous founding member, Anton Francesco Grazzini (1503–1584), noted for his racy and humorous poems, his comedies, and his collection of *novelle*, Le cene (*The Dinners*), which followed in the tradition of Boccaccio, took the name Il Lasca, a small freshwater fish noted for being difficult to eat because of its many spiny bones, probably to suggest his notoriously difficult character. This name might seem to go against the grain of naming members after foods with a grain dimension, but as Lasca himself pointed out, in order to be eaten this fish had to be dusted in flour and fried. In fact, Lasca had a reputation for being hard to swallow on his own, as in

1540 he had been one of the founders of an earlier academy in Florence, the Umidi (the Damp or Sweaty). But he was expelled in 1547 as his irreverent and more popular style of humor, especially with its mocking of the Latin and Greek classics, made him unpopular with the increasingly disciplinary approach of the humanists who progressively dominated that academy. The first days of the Accademia della Crusca were more amenable to his playful erudition and his preference for writing in a rich and inventive Tuscan rather than in Latin.

But it was Leonardo Salviati, known as the Infarinato (Coated with Flour), who led the academy in a commitment to promulgate Tuscan as a full-fledged literary language, Italian, on a par with Latin – in the process making it less common and more aristocratic. Early on it republished the great writers of that dialect, such as Dante and Boccaccio, and focused discussions on their use of the language and its rich potential for creating a high literature. Before long their discussions became less humorous and more disciplinary in nature, a process that was accelerated early in the seventeenth century with the publication of the first edition of their *Vocabulario della Lingua Italiana* (*Dictionary of the Italian Language*, 1612). In the title lay a program, for the work claimed to be not a dictionary of one dialect of Italian, Tuscan, but the dictionary of the language of all of Italy. Although that clearly was not the case, the claim involved the academy in what might be termed a linguistic crusade to make Tuscan the formal, learned language of Italy – the modern equivalent of ancient Latin. For that it needed a formal dictionary to discipline usage and spelling, along with recognized models of fine writing and a literary tradition, all of which the academy aggressively promoted, following in this the lead of earlier defenders of Tuscan like Pietro Bembo.

This was also reflected in a rethinking of what the name of the academy itself meant. No longer were they self-effacing chaff; rather, they began to claim that they were the academy that winnowed the chaff from the grain, separating out the pure flour of a great language; thus they adopted a motto freely adapted from Petrarch, "*il più bel fior ne coglie*" ("the most beautiful flower is chosen"). The most beautiful flowers of the Italian language were chosen by the academy to make the fine flour of a pure language, and the chaff was left behind. And the flowers chosen, crucially, were also social, as lower-class would-be intellectuals were winnowed out as well, while the academy, like most others, accepted only the flower of the intellectual elite – yet another reflection of the hardening Great Social Divide. One imagines the irreverent Lasca turning over in his grave at the new linguistic discipline that he had helped to create and the increasingly pedantic academy that he had helped to found. In this program, however, the academy itself flourished, maintaining itself as the self-appointed arbiter of the Italian language down to the twentieth century, reprinting and updating their dictionary many times and serving as a model for similar language-disciplining efforts such as the *Dictionnaire de l'Académie française*.

The disciplining of language was not without a social agenda as well. Printing had created a dangerous blurring of the lines of social division, making the book, its learning, and its access to culture available to a much wider public. From the first printing had its critics, who focused on just this socially promiscuous nature of the printed book. Scholars with aristocratic pretensions lamented this sharing of knowledge with a wider public, complaining that even artisans could play at being learned with the aid of printed books. The religious enthusiasms that disrupted Italy and Europe in the sixteenth century, encouraged in part by printed religious works in the vernacular, merely confirmed the danger in the minds of many. "Vernacular," however, is the key word here, for one significant factor that limited the spread of ideas, even after printing, was that the most important intellectual works were printed in classical languages. Without a university training – largely limited to the upper classes – most were unable to read works printed in those languages even if they could buy them. Moreover, humanists and their new lingual discipline, with its emphasis not just on any form of Latin, but on the elegant Latin of Cicero and a few other chosen classical authors, made the writing of those who copied those styles once again less available to a wider public, even those who were able to read the everyday Latin of business. In this way humanists and their disciplining of Latin contributed, along with the academies, to strengthening the Great Social Divide in the cultural realm.

But it might well be argued that the creation of a formal disciplined vernacular based on the Tuscan dialect had a similar impact and that the rules and canonical texts of the academies played a notable role as well. Significantly, from this perspective, as authors felt more and more compelled to write in "correct" Tuscan Italian, abandoning their local dialects, writing and reading in that "high" vernacular became more difficult. In fact, even writers like Ariosto and Castiglione felt the need to apologize for their non-Tuscan usage and hired editors to correct their attempts at Tuscan Italian. For a time in the sixteenth and seventeenth centuries that version of Italian became the learned language par excellence among elites at court and the sophisticated across Europe. At the same time, writings in other local dialects tended to assume a lower, often more bawdy, register and intellectual tone – suitable only for "popular" literature, in the value-laden sense of that term, from the perspective of the aristocratic sixteenth century. In this way one strain of the vernacular, Tuscan, became a learned language, and printed texts in the refined forms encouraged by academies became less available to a general public, thus reinforcing social divisions even as printed texts became more and more widely available.

The Intronati (Dazed) of Siena was one of the earliest academies to formally organize (between 1525 and 1527) as well as one of the most visible and successful to recognize the complex importance of the vernacular. Their name referred to their claim that dazed by the confusion of the rapidly changing world around them; they had decided to withdraw to a life of literary pursuits and wooing the women of their city. The registers of the academy claim that the original founders were six of the leading literary figures in Siena: the Archbishop Francesco Bandini Piccolomini, Marcantonio Piccolomini, Antonio Vignali, Francesco Sozzi, Giovan Francesco Franceschi, and Alessandro Marsi. The two Piccolomini stressed the aristocratic nature of the group, as they were scions of one of the oldest and most important families in the city, who could trace their literary fame back at least as far as the fifteenth-century scholar and pope, Pius II, Aneas Silvius Piccolomini. Vignali was undoubtedly the most controversial, and soon was forced to flee the city because of his outrageous satire, *La Cazzaria* (*The Book of the Prick*), published in Italian by the academy shortly after it was formed. The work had something to upset virtually everyone as it defended sodomy, both philosophically and in immediate graphic detail, and at the same time managed to use those graphic details as metaphors for the political conflicts of Siena, which were critiqued bitterly. Recently translated and published with an important introduction by Ian Moulton, with this work we are definitely back in the playful world of the satyr in the garden of the late Rinascimento, where the play had a serious bite on several levels.

The Intronati minus Vignali, however, won fame for their production of literature in Italian; their salonlike gatherings (called in local dialect *veglie*); and their proclaimed interest in supporting the intellectual endeavors of women. They were perhaps most famous, however, for the comedies they wrote and produced. In fact, the comedy that they officially wrote as a group shortly after Vignali fled the city and performed in 1532, *Gl'ingannati* (*The Deceived*), became one of the most successful and influential comedies of the sixteenth century. The intriguing plot stars a cross-dressed young woman, Lelia, serving the man she loves, Flamminio, as his male page. She roams the streets passing as a young man, and even successfully courting another woman and in the process performs as a more-than-passable male lover. All this questionable behavior notwithstanding, she eventually wins Flamminio's love, in no small part due to her *virtù*-ous lack of traditional feminine virtue.

In the end Lelia marries, and everything may seem to reconfirm with that happy ending that a quite wayward young woman has been safely returned to her correct place, securely under the yoke of matrimony. But, as Laura Giannetti points out in her study, *Lelia's Kiss*, that may be just the last and biggest deception of the *The Deceived*, for throughout the comedy a young woman breaks most of the rules that kept women subservient to men and in their secondary roles in society, and in the end her plotting, along with a bit of luck, brings her, against the wishes and plans of her father, her desire – marriage to the man she loves.

And, crucially, the women of the audience have seen in the play of the play her successes and tasted her dangerously delicious freedom – imaginatively, at least. At the same time, the comedy barely hides behind its fast-paced action and humor a critique of a number of things that restricted upper-class women at the time, most notably arranged marriages in pursuit of family goals, restrictions on their movements outside the home, and a lack of concern for their feelings and desires. That people enjoyed the comedy, and enjoyed imagining its more challenging moments, is indicated by the fact that it was widely performed and imitated, spawning a slew of Italian comedies that borrowed large portions of its plot. It was also quickly taken up in other countries, especially Spain, where it served as a model for a number of successful comedies and ultimately became, either directly or indirectly, the basis for Shakespeare's *Twelfth Night*. All this seems to suggest a deep, uncomfortable awareness that the traditional restrictions on women were not without their problems, not just for women but also for men and for society as a whole.

Such successes helped to focus the Intronati's activities on the literary, and across the sixteenth century they continued to write and produce a number of popular comedies. They also continued with their theme of supporting women and their intellectual interests. Right from the start, one of their focuses had been on providing literature written in Italian, claiming that such literature was more available to women than literature written in Latin, as few women had been exposed to that classical language at a level that allowed them to appreciate its literature. One response was translating the Latin classics into Italian, but equally important was creating a literature in Italian that was great in its own right and worthy of upper-class aristocratic women. Some modern scholars have expressed doubts about just how serious these claims were, and certainly works like Vignali's *La Cazzaria*, which in many ways demeaned women, add to that doubt. Still, behind the misogynist topoi of some members, and the more playful sexual courting and wordplay of others, there was a definite strain of writing produced by male members of the academy that supported a more significant role for aristocratic women, at least, in the intellectual life of the day and the academies themselves. But it should be remembered that this support of learning for women was strictly intended for an elite of aristocratic women at the top of society. Thus it reflected in its own way the hardening social divisions of the day and their crucial gendered dimension; nonelite women were on the wrong side of the divide and therefore too insignificant to really matter.

At another level the Intronati, like other academies, also had a less apparent political agenda, for as the real power of government fell more and more into the hands of tighter oligarchies, absolutist local princes, and foreign powers, especially Spain and the Habsburgs, the old ideal of an active life in service to the state became an increasingly empty dream. In the case of Siena and the Intronati, the city fell in 1555 to its perennial enemy Florence, which in turn was a client state of the Habsburg emperors; thus, although local government continued under the watchful eyes of Florence and its more distant Habsburg supporters, it was clearly no longer the feisty preserve of local aristocrats exercising their power over their community. In that context, academies in many no-longer-independent cities, with their meetings, rules, and debates, offered a form of civil institution parallel to government where one could not only engage in civil conversation and make decisions in a pseudo-republican setting, but even do so in the name of influencing the life of one's city. In fact, the organization of academies is sometimes compared to that of guild organization, although it might be more accurate to claim merely that virtually all cooperate bodies that restricted membership to a select group – whether that was masters of a craft, the citizens that mattered in a city-state, or a select group of intellectuals and scholars – followed much the same organizational model. Thus an academy could seem to mirror guild structures for a select upper-class membership at the same time that it functioned like a republic of letters or ideas in world where republics were largely a thing of the past.

Actually, the way academies seemed to parallel courts and offer to some degree the civil life that was less available in the more closed government and society of the day provides a necessary qualification against overestimating the increasing strictness of the Great Social Divide. It was becoming more real and more definitive, certainly. But while true aristocratic status on a European level was becoming increasingly difficult to gain unless one was from an established major family, there was still a lively economic life that allowed a few to gain riches and a certain status. This was especially true in the second half of the sixteenth century, when Spanish rule over much of the peninsula during a relatively peaceful period allowed the economy of many cities to flourish. Moreover, in many rural areas a more capital-intensive agriculture apparently provided a more secure balance to the wealth of the upper classes in general, allowing a significant number of the newer rich to adopt a more rural lifestyle consonant with the more aristocratic ideals that were shared across Europe. But few with new wealth were capable of jumping to true aristocratic status or true political power, and in that situation academies offered a significant opportunity to claim status and exercise power.

Divide and Discipline

At more humble levels, the hardening social divisions and an increasing concern with social discipline in a more strictly divided society were also stimulating an increasing concern with problems that had long troubled the cities of the Rinascimento, and often the rest of Europe as well. One of the most important was the question of poverty and the poor. There was a time when scholars argued that the Protestant Reformation created a new attitude toward poverty. To simplify greatly, the argument ran that in Catholic lands where good works were required for salvation, charity for the poor was one of the primary good works that guaranteed salvation. Thus, before the Reformation and in Catholic lands after it, the poor were an accepted part of society who, as members of the community, offered the necessary opportunity to those who were better-off to win salvation through charitable works. By contrast, in Protestant lands, where new confessions held that salvation was through faith and the grace of God alone, the poor lost this positive dimension and, rather than being seen as necessary members of society, were increasingly seen as people who did not belong, requiring discipline or even expulsion.

In Protestant lands, as a result, government took over from private charity the newly perceived problem of dealing with the poor, setting up programs of poor relief – especially in urban areas, where they were increasingly seen as a major problem. While these programs tended to be styled "relief," they attacked the problem primarily by dividing those labeled "the deserving poor" from those who were not, aiding the former and disciplining the latter. The deserving poor were those viewed as regular, hard-working members of the community who had merely fallen on hard times and required temporary assistance until they could get back on their feet and return to being productive members of society. The rest of the poor comprised a more diverse group who shared the unfortunate characteristic of being perceived as unwilling to work and largely outsiders, either because they lacked a true work ethic or because they were from somewhere else and had joined the community in the hope of taking advantage of its poor relief. Needless to say, those poor people came to be considered outsiders who did not deserve the community's charity, and numerous disciplinary schemes were developed to force them to work or drive them away.

While this dichotomy between Catholic lands and Protestant lands has a certain logic, actual historical developments in neither area fit it well. And, in fact, the last generation of research on the subject has demonstrated that much of the governmental poor relief in northern Europe was actually based upon programs developed in the cities of Catholic Italy. Natalie Davis, for example, in a classic study on poor relief in Lyon, was actually able to show how an influential Italian immigrant working in Lyon played a crucial role in setting up poor relief there on Italian models. And, in a magisterial work based on massive archival research, *Rich and Poor in Renaissance Venice*, Brian Pullan demonstrated in detail how that Catholic city developed a complex system of poor relief, if not in anticipation of Protestant lands, at least in much the same time frame. In reality, given the turbulent life of Rinascimento cities and the long-term desire to create a more peaceful and secure urban environment, it is not surprising that the poor were an issue that concerned governments in Italy early on.

As we have seen, in the fourteenth century, if not earlier, most cities created grain offices that attempted to provide grain for the poor during periods of dearth in order to avoid the disorders associated with hard times and famine. In the fifteenth century, many also created dowry funds to aid poor young girls whose families did not have the wealth to supply them with dowries and thus allow them to get married. Ideally, this was to help them set up families and live a more secure life that would save them from destitution or prostitution. Such governmental initiatives, however, were supplemented by nongovernmental practices that better fit the charity model of helping the poor, with confraternities playing an important role in distributing charity in times of need; guilds setting up funds to support poor people working in their crafts and professions; and many wills, especially those of richer women, bequeathing money to allow poor young girls and orphans to marry. Hospitals, usually funded by individual donors, confraternities, or even occasionally guilds, also provided poor relief, sometimes directly in the form of handouts to the poor or taking in the destitute until they could productively return to society. In the vision of the day the "*male*" (meaning both illness and evil) of illness was seen as in many ways sliding easily into the "*male*" of poverty, making hospitals much more all-purpose institutions that dealt both with the sick and the indigent.

These initiatives were supplemented by others that mixed governmental and nongovernmental projects, such as foundling homes, often supported by government, as well as by donors, which grew in importance from the fifteenth century on, providing a form of poor relief not always recognized as such; for one of the primary purposes of such homes was to raise the offspring of the poor, who were not able to feed their children because of their poverty. In a similar vein, the numerous sixteenth-century institutions discussed earlier to protect poor women and keep them from being forced into prostitution, supported by both donors and by government, also aimed at ameliorating the problems of poor women. And finally, the Church provided charity to the poor as well. This mixing makes more sense when one remembers that we are dealing not so much with a distinction between private charity and governmental charity, but rather, as argued earlier, with a situation where government was still regularly seen as one corporate fictive individual competing for power and control with a series of other corporate fictive individuals, such as guilds, confraternities, the Church, and individual donors.

To a degree, then, well before the sixteenth century most urban governments in Italy were beginning to rethink the nature of poverty and their role in dealing with it. And in the process they began to take into account the growing perception of a distinction between those poor people who were seen as members of the community who had fallen on hard times and those who were seen as merely unwilling to work and living off the charity of others. But in the sixteenth century this distinction became more widely accepted and prompted more aggressive action and disciplining of the poor by government. Obviously, the crisis of the early decades of the century and the dislocation and disruption that accompanied it helped to make the problem increasingly visible and a matter of concern. But clearly more was involved. A larger and more complex government with a stronger sense of its mandate to discipline society and control social disorder certainly played a part as well. The desire for a more decorous society better suited to a more aristocratic urban life may also have contributed to increasing pressure to remove beggars and the unsightly poor from the streets and squares of cities. And more traditional values such as civic morality, accentuated by the spiritual enthusiasms and reform sentiments that were the order of the day, also encouraged such governmental action in the name of reform. Finally, most difficult to gauge was a growing sense among the upper classes that the lower classes were meant to work and that those who escaped that imperative endangered the proper order of society and its underlying social hierarchy, literally as a disease and disease-carrying group (a *male*), that threatened to infect society, both morally and physically.

In fact, such reforming zeal, combined with an increasingly strong sense of who belonged in the moral community and who did not, contributed to an ongoing series of attempts by government to weed out, or at least to divide out from their urban world, all those deemed to be unworthy or outsiders. Thus, for example, going hand in hand with an increasing emphasis on the negative stereotypes associated with those considered foreigners, most particularly Spaniards and Germans, governments made every effort to isolate, where possible, at least the nonaristocratic members of such groups. Obviously that was not entirely possible in cities that were governed by or closely aligned with Spanish or Germans rulers, but in such cities, what government could not do the populace attempted to enforce with insults and violence. Isolation was perhaps more effectively deployed for those groups who were not Catholic, such as Protestant or Muslim merchants in trading cities like Venice, who were more strictly confined to special enclaves. The same was true for the Jewish populations of the peninsula, which had noticeably increased after the 1490s following their expulsion from Spain and Portugal.

Once again Venice took the lead in this movement to divide and discipline, creating what would become known as the ghetto, where Jews were forced to live in isolation from the larger community on a series of islands that had once served as an isolated area for iron foundries and their dangerous forges. The entrances to the group of islands that made up the area were fortified, and Jews were required to retire within the locked gates and walls that isolated their lodgings and their family life from those of the Christian community. The insistence on such division and isolation suggests the way in which the opposite was becoming increasingly true: Italian society was becoming more European, with more and more "outsiders" – merchants, refugees, conquerors, and even tourists – changing the nature of its cities and its once distinctive *civiltà*. For, of course, the technology of governance was not up to the task of enforcing such isolation, and prejudice and slurs were not entirely up to the task either; thus it appears that such isolation and division was never entirely successful. As a result, some Jews, Protestants, and even Muslims managed to live outside their enclaves and interact more regularly with local communities that, for all the resistance, were becoming theirs as well. And, of course, for all the slurs and insults, foreigners governed much of Italy and along with their foreign bureaucrats and courtiers they were gradually setting a different tone for upper-class society. For, in a way, the Rinascimento as an Italian phenomenon was coming to an end, to be replaced by a Renaissance that would be European and eventually worldwide.

In a similar attempt at division, although usually with even less success, communities attempted to limit prostitution by means of stricter laws and once again to divide it from licit society, both by legally restricting the areas where prostitutes could practice and often by moving the munici-pal house of prostitution outside the walls of the city or closing it down entirely. Moreover, most governments, as part of theoretically charitable initiatives to deal with poor prostitutes and women forced into prostitution by poverty, created a series of institutions meant to protect such women. But, significantly, these institutions also isolated them from the community until they had mastered the discipline that was deemed necessary to be recovered as moral members of society. For many, that meant becoming virtual prisoners of those institutions until they had reformed, or at least until they had convinced their "benefactors" that they had done so. And in the process, such institutions became an often-overlooked precursor of the modern idea of penal institutions that are *supposed* to discipline and reform criminals, changing them from dangerous outsiders into productive mem-bers of the community.

More generally, sexuality was also more strictly monitored and disciplined. In most cities penalties for sodomy were made stricter – even in Florence, famed for its more relaxed attitude toward the range of practices associ-ated with the "sin." At the same time, however, it appears that for the upper classes the ancient pedigree of male love gave it a classical and aristocratic veneer that allowed some at the top of society to claim superiority to such laws. In fact, aristocrats were often protected by their status from the sterner strictures on sexual behavior more generally. Of course, different treatment before the law had a long tradition for the upper classes, but the upper-class rake and sexual predator victimizing lower-class women seemed to be gain-ing ground even as such activities were being more severely condemned more generally, not just by harsher laws, but also by a growing ideal that adult male patriarchs should confine their sexuality to marriage. As we have seen, even Machiavelli ruefully defended this ideal in his comedy *Clizia*, perhaps at his own expense. Suggestively, in much literature and especially in comedies and *novelle*, male sexuality outside of marriage was increasingly associated with low or base characters who were either laughable or sorry, more ruined by their passions than rewarded, or with virtually heroic aristo-cratic characters, masters of upper-class perversions beyond the ken of those who lacked their status. When aristocrats and lower-class characters mixed in literature, it was usually with the lower serving as the obvious victims of their betters. Once again the illicit world mirrored licit society and in this case its increasingly strict social divisions, at least imaginatively.

Even language followed this disciplining and dividing drive with an eye
to creating a truly moral society and civic world. Attempts to transform the
Tuscan dialect of Dante, Petrarch, and Boccaccio into a literary language
following the dictates of Bembo and other sixteenth century lingual disciplinarians, as noted earlier, both uplifted it into a superior language capable of
competing with Latin and made its use the mark of a true intellectual elite.
In the realm of poetry we see how this could take on a sexual dimension,
with those writing in the Petrarchian tradition, often in the refined Tuscan
Italian, squaring off against those who wrote ostentatiously in a lower register in their local dialects, extolling the more sensual and physical pleasures
increasingly associated with the baser instincts of the lower classes. Often
depicted as exaggeratedly gross and bawdy, such poetry, however, did not
always demean the lower classes and their passions. In fact, in an increasingly mannered and disciplined aristocratic society, it and a sizeable portion
of vernacular literature in a similar "low" register enjoyed a popularity even
in the face of censorship that attempted to curtail its reach – perhaps as an
escape, perhaps simply as a celebration of the more earthy pleasures required
to give the satyr – still lurking in what was left of the ever more disciplined
Rinascimento garden – his due.

Be that as it may, even at the level of everyday speech, restrictions and discipline also increased in the sixteenth century. The dangerous violent power
of words had long been respected in the urban world of the Rinascimento,
and most cities had laws not only against seditious speech, but also against the
kind of violent speech that seemed to encourage vendetta or require private
retribution. Governments, by stepping in to formally restrict such speech,
apparently hoped to limit the escalation of insults into violence and vendetta
by punishing insults in court rather than leaving matters in the hands of the
individuals and families insulted. In the sixteenth century, however, these
laws were reinforced with the creation of magistracies specifically concerned
with punishing blasphemy and words that were deemed to threaten the civic
morality and moral order of the city. Those who would swear or insult were
no longer fit to be members of the community, and that was especially true
of those who swore at or insulted their social betters, once again hardening
the social divisions lurking behind such moral imperatives. The formaliza-
tion of the *Index of Prohibited Books* by the Church in 1559, when added to
local efforts at the disciplining of words, was merely the frosting on a much
more substantial cake – a range of disciplinary drives that officially sought to
create a moral society that divided the local community into the pure and
deserving and eliminated those deemed to threaten that unity and purity.

Not to be ignored, an increased emphasis on what might be called the rituals of polite speech and politeness itself also played a significant role in disciplining society and reinforcing stricter social divisions. Anyone who has read letters or other documents from the sixteenth century will have been impressed by the proliferation of titles and the honorific superlatives of polite address. Long past were the days when a simple *"messer"* was enough of a title to express respect and status. The important had become *"Onorato,"* *"Egregio,"* *"Illustre,"* *"Spectabile,"* and often what we might label *"issimo-ized"* (most-ified), as in *"Onoratissimo, Egregissimo, Illustrissimo,* and *Spectabilissimo"* often elaborately combined to reach the airy heights of verbal display to fit the occasion or convey the social respect deemed necessary. Politeness at upper-class levels also required a greater attention to social rituals of personal interaction. Perhaps to a degree growing out of and reinforcing the rituals of court, all levels of social interaction increasingly developed rituals that coded and disciplined conduct.

This increasingly important aspect of life, however, was a much broader and deeper phenomenon that has too easily been dismissed as merely strange or a curious obsession of the age. The studies of Norbert Elias and many historians of court have begun to seriously challenge such dismissals, but it seems clear that this development of what seems an extreme attention to etiquette and the rituals of life, requires more study that moves beyond the court and the aristocracy of sixteenth-century Italy. And it should not be forgotten that in transforming the practices of everyday life into rituals governed by an increasingly demanding etiquette, we are encountering another form of discipline that attempted to organize and control life. Virtually every form of social interaction, from eating to playing, developed its etiquette and its disciplining rituals, and a plethora of manuals followed in the footsteps of these developments – manuals for courtly behavior, polite conversation, table manners, playing games correctly, and even for being violent, with manuals for dueling. In fact, in all these areas and in the manuals that codified such behavior, Italians and their manuals, although challenged by the Spanish and French, long remained the gold standard.

Obviously, not all subscribed to these programs, and resistance, often enlivened by mockery, was widespread and frequently rich in its creative inventiveness, both in the realm of literature and in everyday life. But, suggestively, even this aided in reifying the Great Social Divide, for at the level of the aristocratic upper classes, increasingly beyond the reach of the law and beyond the "common herd," resistance or simple flouting was relatively easy. For a few, in fact, it was virtually the order of the day, at least when compliance was not enforced by peers, as in the case of etiquette and the rituals of polite language. Lower-class denizens of the city and the increasingly controlled countryside were less able to ignore these disciplining drives, although even at that level attempts at discipline were limited by the inability of institutions like government and Church to actually implement the controls that they saw as necessary.

Still, as the ideal of a moral and disciplined society gained purchase and support among a wide swath of the community, these same values, even eventually a more humble form of politeness, were also policed by society itself in a process largely invisible to history because it produced few records. At the edge of criminal and inquisitional cases from the second half of the sixteenth century, however, one does see an increasing attention to these matters on the part of the everyday people who appear as witnesses – a tendency to measure others with comments about their goodness or neighborliness that reveal who were insiders and belonged in the community and who were not. Obviously, such anecdotal information does not prove the case; yet in the face of the numerous disciplining drives of the century in Italy and the stricter divides the separated the best from the rest, both socially and morally, it seems that rethinking the sixteenth century as one of discipline and division has merit.

Beyond the Great Social Divide: Michelangelo

A few intellectuals and artisans/artists from more humble backgrounds did create challenges for the stricter social divides of sixteenth-century society and the patronage system that still controlled their lives and, to a degree, their accomplishments. But even for outstanding individuals who claimed to be artists or exceptional intellects and thus warranted a higher status, real status became harder and harder to achieve. More and more they found themselves placed in a sort of limbo outside the regular social hierarchy that would eventually be reserved for that rarest of breeds, the genius. Superior, but not truly to be numbered among the aristocratic elite of society, they were in fact often portrayed as notably different from the rest of society, and especially from the true elite, in their behavior and manners. Eccentric, disorderly, and lacking the required bloodline and politeness of true aristocrats, they were well on the way to becoming the stereotypic undisciplined and disorderly creative personality allowed to live beyond the social order of the day – the genius. In fact, again much like works of art, they were carefully negotiated and constructed in the imagination of their society as special, but safely unequal. And although we could consider numerous examples of artisan/artists who were marked out as special and increasingly beyond the normal social order – such as Leonardo da Vinci, Raphael, Giulio Romano, Pontormo, Bronzino, Giorgione, Tintoretto, Veronese, and Titian – the first half of the sixteenth century saw one figure who represents the apogee of this phenomenon: Michelangelo Buonarroti (1475–1564).

Michelangelo made his reputation as an artisan and at the same time as a difficult and troubled character on his thorny path to being recognized as an exceptional artist. Sculptor, painter, architect, and more, he was first known primarily as a sculptor, a profession that in many ways was harder to liberate from the label of artisanal labor, as it required heavy physical work that made it seem more like manual toil than art. William Wallace, whose studies of Michelangelo and his workshop have transformed how we look at the man and the artist, pointed out how the critic Giorgio Vasari (1511–1574), who in many ways established the first canon of Rinascimento "artists," tried to represent his physical labor as something sublime and ennobling when he described the sculptor "liberating" a figure from a block of marble or "peeling away" stone to discover the form within. Yet, as Wallace pointed out, carving a large statue was hard work requiring "tens of thousands" of blows, precisely directed, with one mistake capable of destroying in a moment weeks of work and a valuable piece of marble. Whether or not Michelangelo was actually Vasari's ethereal intellectual contemplating the inner forms lurking in a block of marble, he was a workman whose trade required heavy manual labor, which made it a difficult task to convince aristocratic elites that he might share their status. They definitely did not work with their hands and carefully avoided heavy labor. From their special superior social position they knew that artisans were at best skilled hands at work, while they themselves were ideally graceful minds at play.

Key in Michelangelo's transformation into something more was the young craftsman's being taken up by Lorenzo de' Medici and joining the circle of intellectuals and artists that made up his unofficial court. It is not clear how Michelangelo came to Lorenzo's attention, but after a period of apprenticeship with the workshop of the noted Florentine painter Domenico Ghirlandaio, at fifteen he left to join Lorenzo's household for the last two years of the latter's life. Much has been made of his association there with intellectuals like Ficino and Poliziano, the painters Botticelli and Luca Signorelli, the architect Giuliano da Sangallo, and the sculptor Bertoldo di Giovanni. But equally important may have been his relationship with future patrons: Lorenzo's son Giovanni, who would become Pope Leo X, and his nephew Giulio, the future Pope Clement VII. After the fall of the Medici in 1494, he went to Bologna for a short time, further honing his skills as a sculptor. When he returned to Florence, the city had fallen under the sway of the prophet Savonarola, and it appears that his fiery preaching deeply influenced and troubled the young man.

During this period Michelangelo reportedly became skilled enough to pass off as an ancient statue a *Sleeping Cupid* that he had carved. Its adventures evoke the world that the sculptor, just turning twenty, was about to serve and impress in his rise to fame. Sold to Cardinal Riario in Rome as a Roman original, it then passed to the noted *condottiere* and collector of antiquities Guidobaldo, duke of Urbino, from whom it was stolen as part of the loot taken when Cesare Borgia sacked that city. In turn, as we have seen, when Isabella d'Este realized that Cesare had taken it, she instructed her contacts in Rome to ask him for it, noting that Cesare was not interested in such fine things anyway. Cesare, apparently confirming her opinion, gave her the statue. In sum, cardinals, *condottieri*, a pope's son, and finally one of the cultural icons of the day all appreciated the young craftsman's artistry. He was well on the way to becoming an artist for those whose opinions mattered and literally made artists out of artisans.

Riario invited Michelangelo to join him in Rome, reportedly curious to meet such a talented young man and become his patron. Rome, as it would do repeatedly over the course of his long career, confirmed both his promise and his artistry. There, amid the ruins of the ancient world, a wider public came to see him as truly extraordinary as he carved some of his greatest masterpieces. The most famous was his *Pietà*, which depicts a full-grown Christ taken down from the Cross and lying in the Virgin Mary's lap (Illustration 11.1). In the contract for the work Michelangelo promised to produce the most beautiful statue in Rome, and many would argue that he delivered. The potentially ungainly composition of a grown man lying in a woman's lap is portrayed with a grace that captures the grief of the moment with a technical virtuosity that seemed to take sculpture to a new level. Or, to be more accurate, it seemed to take it to a new/old level, rivaling the greatest sculptures of the ancients and the remains of their work found in Rome. The erotically charged body of the dead Christ makes it fully clear – with its lifelike flesh, veins, and muscles showing through, along with its highly polished surfaces – that Christ was fully God and fully man – a powerful Christian message that Michelangelo's sculpture conveyed not so much in spite of, but rather because of, its erotic charge.

Returning to Florence in 1499 after the fall of Savonarola, he was given in 1501 the commission to do a large statue of David by the wool guild, as part of a major program of reappropriating for the new republic civic iconography that had been co-opted by the Medici (Illustration 11.2). David

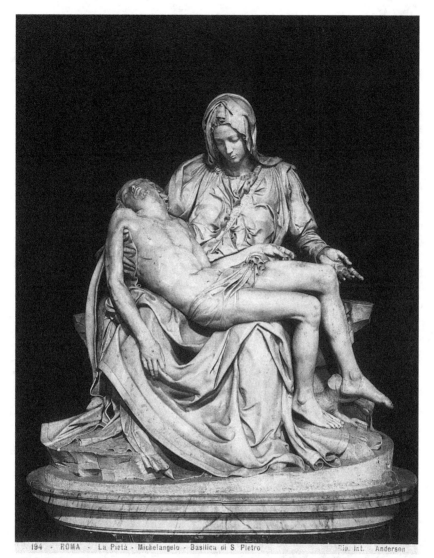

11.1. Michelangelo, *Pietà*, 1498–99, St. Peter's, Rome. Photo: Alinari/Art Resource, New York.

had long been a popular theme of Florentine painting and sculpture, as it evoked a powerful vision of the *virtù*-ous youthful David defeating the evil giant Goliath and, in turn, the *virtù*-ous republican Florence defeating the evil tyrants who had so often threatened the city. Reportedly his task was made more difficult by the fact that the massive block of marble he was

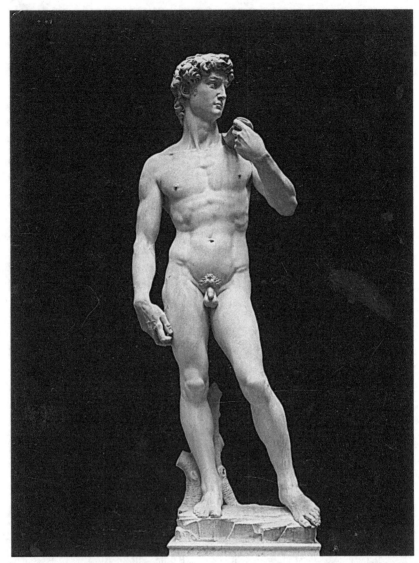

11.2. Michelangelo, *David*, 1501–1504, Accademia, Florence. Photo: Alinari/Art Resource, New York.

given had been partially worked already and had internal flaws limiting what he could do with it. Once again the finished carving was such a success that it has become virtually iconic, so much so that it is very difficult to see its originality or even to appreciate it today. It is also difficult to see today because its surface polish, which was once much like that of the *Pietà*, has been lost due to years of weathering standing before the Palazzo della Signoria, a problem compounded by unfortunate nineteenth-century restoration attempts.

At three times life size and with a powerful masculine body that gives little suggestion of being boyish, time, weather, and familiarity have not undercut the fact that Michelangelo created a dominating male figure that seems quite unlike the biblical David. Some critics have actually suggested that it was supposed to be a classical Hercules, which Michelangelo refigured at the last minute as David. Also curious is the way the hands and the head of the figure seem out of proportion, too large for the rest of the body. Both apparent anomalies have given rise to debate about what Michelangelo was actually trying to do with the sculpture. At least we know that although the statue was originally commissioned to be placed on the cathedral along with a number of other statues by great Florentines sculptors, it was so impressive that it was moved to guard the entrance of the Palazzo della Signoria, reminding all who entered of the masculine power of the city. And once again in that public setting it confirmed for a discerning Florentine public, not just the male-gendered power and stature of the republic, but the stature and power of the sculptor. Not only was Michelangelo, who worked with his hands in a dusty and dirty craft becoming an artist, he was becoming a great Florentine artist.

It was during this period of growing recognition that we also have his first attempts at poetry, both profane and religious, which would occupy more and more of his creative energies as he grew older and once again demonstrate to his aristocratic contemporaries that he could play with words as well as work with stone. But soon it was Rome that commanded Michelangelo's attention and the new Pope Julius II, with an aggressive program for aggrandizing his capital and himself. Given Julius's high sense of self-esteem, as a powerful patron he challenged the young man to create an exceptional monumental tomb for himself. Michelangelo, as an artist with a strong sense of his own value, accepted, countering with a challenge of his own − offering an extraordinary plan for a massive project that would include over forty major pieces of sculpture and require years of work. Less a case of patron commanding client, the moment seemed more like one of great individuals squaring off to see who would dominate in the production of a monument that was originally conceptualized as glorifying its patron but was in danger of becoming a monument to the artist who created it. Nonetheless, the pope accepted the project, and Michelangelo, as was his wont, headed off to the marble quarries at Carrara to oversee the quarrying of the marble that he would use. On his return to Rome, the pope's visits to his workshop, which had originally been frequent, slowly decreased. Michelangelo interpreted this as a sign that enemies in Rome had turned the pope against him and his ambitious project. He feared what he saw as the machinations of the architect Donato Bramante, who was working on the new Church of Saint Peter's for the pope, as well as the young painter Raphael (1483–1520), also a papal favorite. Unlike Michelangelo, however, Raphael's presumed machinations and competition for artistic glory were short-lived, at least as a living artist, for he died at thirty-seven, leaving Michelangelo to live on in increasing fame to almost ninety.

At the time, however, apparently suspecting the worse, in a huff Michelangelo closed his shop, deserted his patron, and returned to Florence in 1506. While Julius may have lost some enthusiasm for the willful sculptor who clearly lacked the humility of an artisan, he still wanted his tomb and wanted to keep Michelangelo in his stable of courtiers. Thus, shortly thereafter, when he retook Bologna with his usual impetuosity (much to Machiavelli's distress), he pressed the government of Florence to make Michelangelo return to his service. A reconciliation was worked out, but not without a certain humbling of the artist, perhaps required from the perspective of traditional elites, and almost certainly from that of the strong-willed pope. Thus Julius ordered *his* artisan Michelangelo to cast a bronze statue of him, celebrating his conquest of Bologna – in one blow apparently reestablishing the correct order of things. Michelangelo was to be the obedient hand and the pope the celebrated leader and patron. But Michelangelo found artistic glory even in this papal humbling, for many doubted that the statue that he planned could actually be successfully cast in bronze, especially by someone who was inexperienced working with that tricky medium. In the end, however, Michelangelo triumphed, producing an impressive work that was placed over the door of the Basilica of San Petronio in Bologna as a memorial of the pope's conquest of the city. Neither the pope nor Michelangelo enjoyed their respective triumphs for long, however, for in 1511 the papal occupying forces were thrown out of the city, and the bronze figure was removed to be melted down and recast as a cannon, which reportedly was mockingly named Giulia after the pope.

Meanwhile, the pope and the sculptor had moved on to new tests of will. In 1508 the pope ordered Michelangelo to put aside his work on his tomb in order to paint the ceiling of the Sistine Chapel. Michelangelo objected that he was a sculptor, not a painter, and apparently feared once again that the task had been suggested to the pope by his enemies, Raphael and Bramante, in an attempt to ruin his reputation. The pope insisted, and the artist demurred, but once more in a way that marked his own independence and glory in

11.3. Michelangelo, Sistine Chapel ceiling, 1508–12, Sistine Chapel, Rome. Photo: Erich Lessing/Art Resource, New York.

the face of his patron's demands. Essentially he rejected the original plan for the ceiling and substituted his own, much more complex and ambitious one, promising to depict the history of humanity's relationship with God from the creation to the moment when Moses received the Ten Commandments. In this way his ceiling completed the program of the side wall paintings done in the 1480s that portrayed Moses receiving the commandments and the life of Christ. And, neatly, it literally and figuratively overarched them (Illustration 11.3).

The central panels of the ceiling begin with God the Father checking the darkness with His light at the beginning of creation, followed by Him imperiously creating the planets, and then separating land from water. There follows the famous and often reproduced image of God creating and empowering Adam with knowledge as he reaches out from Heaven to touch the beautiful figure of man – in a scene that seems to hauntingly echo the vision of creation that Ficino found in the pagan Egyptian Genesis of Hermes Trismegistus (Illustration 11.4). Next, the creation of Eve rising from Adam's side leads inexorably to original sin and the expulsion from Eden. After the Fall human history begins with sin and suffering, which means that the last three central panels represent that tragic reality with the sacrifice of Abel, the Flood, and the drunkenness of Noah. But that is just the start of his design, for the central panels are bordered by lunettes and inserts between the lunettes that portray the pagan and Jewish prophets, who, inspired by the

11.4. Michelangelo, *Creation of Adam*, 1508–12, Sistine Chapel, Rome. Photo: Erich Lessing/Art Resource, New York.

Holy Spirit, had played a crucial role in preparing the world for the coming of Christ.

When at the end of October 1512 the work was revealed to the public, it was immediately hailed as a masterpiece, even as many worried about the nudity of the figures portrayed, especially the male bodies. Those nudes notwithstanding, if Michelangelo's enemies had pressed the pope to give him the project in order to damage his reputation, he had turned the tables on them; for he had created an impressive masterpiece that trumpeted his reputation as an exceptional painter as well as sculptor. Yet despite the extraordinary success of his painting, Michelangelo became increasingly worried about those in the papal court who he feared were jealous of his success and trying to undercut him with his powerful patron. Whether that jealousy and the plots against him were real or paranoia, his desire to proceed with the tomb project for Julius was blocked once more, this time by the death of Julius in 1513. His new patron became Leo X, the first Medici pope, whom Michelangelo had known briefly when both were youths in the household of Lorenzo the Magnificent. And Leo had new plans for him, Medici plans.

Even before he had become pope, Leo had been instrumental in the overthrow of the republican government in Florence and saw Michelangelo as being more useful to his family there, recreating the visual ideology of Medici rule. There followed almost two decades of on-again-off-again work in Florence, much of it concerned with glorifying the main church associated with the Medici, San Lorenzo. The first project Leo ordered was a glorious marble façade for it, but for reasons that are unclear the pope lost interest in the project in 1520 and cancelled it. In fact, a marble façade was never added, and the church still lacks one today. Whether it was his slow pace, his always feared enemies, or his own grandiose and costly vision of the project, Michelangelo lost years working on it and in the end Leo's patronage as well. Cardinal Giulio de'Medici, the pope's cousin and the future Pope Clement VII, however, soon hired him and asked him to design a new sacristy for that same church with a series of Medici tombs to memorialize the family's glory. Michelangelo's impressive plans again were never completed, perhaps because they were once more too costly and time-consuming to finish. Nonetheless, shortly after Clement became pope he commissioned Michelangelo to design a library next to San Lorenzo that was actually completed. The Laurentian Library, as it was called, added to his creative reputation, in this case as an architect.

With the Sack of Rome in 1527, Florence threw out the Medici one more time and momentarily instituted a renewed republic, disrupting Michelangelo's not always happy relationship with his Medici patrons. He sided with the republic against his Medici patrons, even helping to design the fortifications to defend the city against the imperial troops who, supporting the Medici, lay siege to the city in 1530. But Florence soon fell to the besieging armies of the Emperor Charles V, who shortly thereafter returned it to the Medici. They in turn forgave Michelangelo and encouraged him to continue his work on the sacristy of San Lorenzo, but when Clement died in 1434 he left Florence, never to return. Soon back in Rome, Michelangelo hoped that the new pope, Paul III (1468–1549; pope 1534–1549) – the same pope who had imprisoned Cellini – would support his resumption of work on the tomb of Julius II. But a new pope meant a new patron and new plans for the artist yet again. Thus in 1435 he gave Michelangelo the title of official sculptor, painter, and architect of the Vatican, with a substantial salary of 1,200 *scudi* a year and set him to painting on the altar wall of the Sistine Chapel his *Last Judgment* (Illustration 11.5).

Unlike the masterpiece that Michelangelo had earlier painted on the ceiling, this vast panorama of Christ separating the saved from the damned – the ultimate division and discipline, one might point out – lacks an architectural frame, seeming to open the altar wall of the chapel to an infinite space and the end of time. Moreover, the twisted and tormented nudes seem to reflect

11.5. Michelangelo, *Last Judgment*, 1534–41, Sistine Chapel, Rome. Photo: The Art Archive at Art Resource, New York.

a spiritual unease, rather distant from his earlier, apparently more confident ceiling depicting humanity's special relationship with God. Instead, his *Last Judgment* seems to roil with the terror and fear about salvation and damnation that typified the debates about Christianity and reform at the time and Michelangelo's concerns about both. In fact, these were issues that he returned to insistently in his deeply spiritual and troubled poetry written during the same period. Interestingly, although the formal structure of the work is perhaps one of the most traditional that Michelangelo ever adopted, with figures arranged hierarchically in a vertical space and identified both by size and by a generally familiar iconography, the painting is so powerful that once again it was immediately recognized as a masterpiece and the artist as extraordinary.

Once again many were troubled, however, by the artist's depiction of nudity and by the whirling bodies, some of whose positions seemed questionable. Saint Catherine of Siena, for example, below and to the right of Christ, now safely sporting a green dress, was originally painted nude, with a Saint Blaise hovering behind her and looking down at her in a way and in a position that could easily be misread. A student of Michelangelo a few years later repainted this scene, turning Saint Blaise's gaze away from the crouching, naked Catherine, safely upward toward Christ, and clothing her. Various genitals were also covered with loin cloths and remain so today, even after recent restorations. Some were also scandalized by two men kissing on the lips, placed safely among the saved. This was not "corrected," perhaps because it could be viewed as a kiss of peace or celebration at being saved.

That kiss and Michelangelo's fascination with male nudes, along with his quite well-known passions for a series of young men, have led critics to speculate about his "homosexuality" and have served to make him in some circles today, if anything, even more of a hero than he was in his time. While most scholars now are convinced that Michelangelo's letters, poems, and paintings confirm his fascination with the male body and attraction to and desire for a series of young men, debate rages about whether or not he acted on those desires or expressed them in his art. There seems little room for doubt, however, that he saw the male body with great clarity and was able to represent it with impressive intensity and feeling. Critics have frequently pointed out that even his female figures seem to have male bodies, vaguely feminized with breasts and feminine hair styles, but much too muscular and thick to create a comfortable recognition of them as women (at least for those critics). Yet recent scholarship has raised some interesting questions about a too-easy association of his fascination with nude male bodies in his art and his sexual interests. Most notably, as we have seen, male/male sexual desire and practice were culturally constructed during the period in ways that are different from what is generally seen as homosexuality in the modern world; thus, finding modern sexual desires in his work is potentially more anachronistic than accurate.

Most people at the time saw same-sex desire and sexual activities as belonging to adolescence or youth, a period that stretched from the early teens to about thirty for the courtly upper classes in which Michelangelo tried to move. And the objects of those adolescent desires were youths in their early to midteens, idealized as slim, feminine, and passive, as discussed earlier. What creates the greatest problem for those who would see Michelangelo's sexual interests driving his depiction of male bodies, then, is the fact that the male form to which he returned over and over in his art was not the teenage body of the ideal sexual partner for an older male or, for that matter, the body type of the younger men with whom he corresponded and for whom he expressed desire in his poetry and letters. There is nary a Donatello-style youthful, feminine David, or Ganymede, in any of his works. His males are adult, well-muscled, and very masculine – just the kind of men he apparently was not attracted to in his personal life. Have scholars, then, been wrong in identifying his interest in the male nude body in his art with his sexual interests? Or was he perhaps so anxious not to reveal what to contemporaries would have been his questionable continuing sexual interest in young men that he carefully avoided depicting them in his art? Or might it be suggested that he was fascinated by his vision of his own mature body, imagining it as an ideal, which he hoped would be attractive to young men? Such speculation makes for fascinating conjectures. But what remains are the impressive and deeply troubled bodies of his *Last Judgment*.

His letters to the young men who attracted his desire and his poetry do seem to indicate that, while Michelangelo was willing, and even eager, to express his desire in writing, he was also concerned to place it on a less sexual and physical plane – attempting, it seems, to ennoble it by associating it with the platonic ideals of Ficino, Bembo, and others. Such writers, following in the footsteps of Petrarch and Dante, had used an ennobling ideal of love to detach it from dangerous associations with adultery and sodomy, transforming it into a desire for beauty, truth, and ultimately God. This was an association that, while it had strong classical precedents, was also attractive to an aristocratic elite interested in male/male love and anxious to separate it from the increasingly strictly punished common crime of sodomy, as we have seen. Still, his spiritual turmoil and deep concerns about salvation, which swirl through his later poetry and his *Last Judgment* like an open wound, seem to suggest that his worries about his own personal fate after death were driven by a concern with salvation akin to some of the most troubled meditations of contemporary religious thinkers. Perhaps adding to his concerns was the fact that sodomy, beyond the disciplining drive of government, was coming to be considered one of the most damning sins of the day, and whether Michelangelo was a sodomite in deed or merely in thought, he seems to have worried that his desires placed his salvation in serious jeopardy.

The troubling story of one of his last works may suggest the tragic depth of his anxiety. In his seventies he began work on a statue that for once did not involve a demanding patron, as it was to adorn his own tomb. It depicted Christ as he was being taken down from the Cross, *The Deposition* (Illustration 11.6). In traditional representations of this crucial moment in Christian iconography, the Virgin is usually in the center of the scene, but Michelangelo moved her to the right side of the collapsing body of Christ. Behind the body and supporting Christ is the hooded figure of Nicodemus, who, according to the Bible, helped with his burial and, perhaps more importantly, also supported him secretly during his life, hiding his own belief in order to live safely in a society that denied his teachings. Nicodemus's face looks down sadly on Christ. And, hauntingly, it is Michelangelo's own.

Christ in Christian theology, of course, died to save all of sinning mankind, and one wonders if Michelangelo saw himself in the guise of Nicodemus as the ultimate sinner, who hid his true beliefs and desires, hoping he would be saved by Christ's sacrifice. Beyond his sexual beliefs and desires it has been suggested that the use of Nicodemus also signals the artist's secret acceptance of the Protestant doctrine of salvation by faith alone, something that he kept secret, not unlike the biblical figure, in order to live successfully in his more strictly disciplined Catholic society that held such beliefs to be heretical. There certainly are indications in his poetry that his deeper spiritual anxieties often turned to the question of the role of grace and works in salvation. Whether those concerns are at the heart of the work or not, his relationship with the sculpture was a troubled one, for in 1555, before it was finished, he took a hammer to it and smashed it.

Was the work too evident an admission of his personal beliefs or doubts? Was it too troubling to countenance for a worried old man? Was it too audacious a self-representation, even for an extremely famous sculptor, celebrated by all and immortalized as the greatest artist of his day? Or was it simply that the marble was too flawed, and he was not satisfied with it? Once again we do not know. In the end, however, one of Michelangelo's pupils pieced the statue together from the fragments and finished the carving, although the face of Mary and a number of details remain unfinished. In a way, that makes it a perfect metaphor for Michelangelo's fame, life, and his salvation, at least in an historical sense. For although his spiritual uncertainties in many ways paralleled the spiritual enthusiasms and turmoil of the day and perhaps its more disciplined moral climate, as a creative artist, even in

40369 · FIRENZE · La Pietà di Michelangelo in S. Maria del Fiore - (Stab. D. Anderson)

11.6. Michelangelo, *Deposition*, c. 1546–55, Museo dell'Opera del Duomo, Florence. Photo: Alinari/Art Resource, New York.

the face of ongoing conflicts with demanding aristocratic patrons, he was so successful and so widely recognized for such a wide range of work that generations of scholars and enthusiasts have repeatedly rebuilt his reputation and guaranteed his salvation, at least as a great artist and genius. Yet, for all that, the real Michelangelo will probably always remain a mystery, wrapped in his myths and the evocative nature of his accomplishments, much like the Rinascimento itself.

In his sixteenth-century myth, Michelangelo was portrayed by Vasari as realizing the rebirth (*rinascita* is the term he uses) of ancient art and at the same time surpassing it. In his enthusiasm, it may well be that Vasari did not fully realize that with that compliment he was denying the very *rinascita* that he celebrated, for his claim implied that in surpassing the ancients Michelangelo had created works of art that were both *new and better.* Exceptional artists like Michelangelo, then, were new and ultimately made returning to earlier first times no longer the measure of true artistry; new artists and their superiority implied ultimately that the new and novel could be better, as they were in Michelangelo's case. And they were a novelty with a future, as the eccentric, creative artistic genius who created a special status for himself outside traditional social categories – even the Great Social Divide – would come to be celebrated and cultivated by the most elite circles of society without really having to conform to or accept their values. Certainly many were not happy with this novelty, as it seemed to overthrow the proper relationship between patron and client, gentleman/noble and artisan, refined/courtly and manual/ unmannerly, as even Michelangelo learned in his relationships with Julius II and the Medici. But Italy and its social and cultural worlds were changing. And although mythic artists like Michelangelo rode those changes with a mix of angst and success, the Rinascimento as a period and a movement was coming to an end, to be replaced by a more disciplined and aristocratic Italy whose trajectory of development fit more and more easily into the general trajectory of a European Renaissance.

An Ending and a Beginning: Carnival and Lent

But in history every ending is a beginning. And while the ending of our Rinascimento was in many ways a beginning in terms of the macro changes discussed, it was also, of course, significant in the virtually infinite number of small micro events of everyday life, each rich with implications of change and continuity.

The evening was just beginning on one of the last days of carnival, *Giovedì Grasso* (Fat Thursday) in Venice in 1571. The weather was good, and it was the season of license still dedicated to celebrating the satyr in the garden of the Rinasimento and the pleasures of the senses, especially their illicit variety; for carnival was the period when passions and the flesh ruled, before Lent arrived with its traditional period of fasting and penance that led up to

Easter and the yearly celebration of the Christ's self-sacrifice for humanity and the yearly renewal of Christian society. In theory carnival was a time when everything could be laughed at and the licit world was turned on its head.

Much in that vein, two young men dressed as priests were enjoying themselves, lustily singing their way through the streets near Saint Mark's Square, the ceremonial center of the city where during carnival large crowds gathered to frolic in costume. Masked, they accosted passersby making obscene gestures with a broom and parodying the mass. One outraged priest reported that he heard the youths chanting what sounded at first like a priest's words at mass, but actually went, "Who will be that devoted soul who will give herself to me to be screwed one time? Who will be that soul of God who will give herself to me to be screwed for the love of God?" This was certainly a refrain that evoked the irreverence and illicit erotic atmosphere that carnival traditionally unleashed. In fact, continuing the theme, one of the pair actually admitted that his friend in the priest costume went through the streets with "a broom in his hands and when we encountered other people dressed in masks he said making [an obscene gesture] with the broom, 'Lord sprinkle me' [*Asperges me Domini*]." Clearly these youths were displaying some of the most irreverent themes of carnival.

But worse was yet to come. For as they wound their way through the crowds of other maskers crowding the streets, the youths apparently had a new idea for increasing their evening's pleasures. One of the revelers, Giacomo Zorzi, scion of a powerful noble Venetian family, suggested to his friend Zaccaria Lombardini, a young lawyer and minor official, that they seek out the wife of a certain Antonio Banchini, Letitia, who had recently been his mistress. Both men were in their early twenties, and although Zaccaria was recently married, he came from a non-noble family with little in the way of aristocratic pretensions; and when powerful young nobles of high status suggested a plan, young men with a desire to advance in life listened. Thus the two stopped their playful wandering through the streets and moved with a purpose to the nearby house of Letitia, in campo San Luca barely a five-minute walk away.

Before the house where she lived they continued in their singing ways, serenading her beneath her window. When she heard their voices she came out onto her balcony and greeted Zorzi as the old "friend" that he was, asking "Zorzi, do you want to come to the festivities with me?" Evidently ex-mistresses, even if they had been left by their upper-class aristocratic lovers, saw a certain value in continuing to cultivate them. Zorzi answered with a simple "sure," and Letitia went inside, apparently to prepare for the evening.

It looked like the evening of the young men was about to take off, as it should during the last days of carnival. And from obscene priests they were about to become the partners of a young woman of free morals who might well change their obscene songs into deeds.

But events, as Guicciardini noted, seldom follow rules, and the rules of both aristocratic power and carnival were about to be momentarily over-turned by a young woman of the lower classes. For after a few minutes inside, Letitia reappeared on her balcony to say rather lamely that she had decided to go to bed rather than join the youthful revelers. Apparently Zorzi considered that excuse as unlikely then as it seems today, more than four and a half centuries later. Thus they moved off to a nearby square to join the festivities there, but also to keep an eye on her house to see what might happen next. Their suspicions were rewarded when shortly thereafter Letitia emerged from her front door with four masked youths and headed out to enjoy carnival. Zorzi and Zaccaria followed, at first discreetly, but eventually their anger won out and they began to display their aristocratic aggression outside a mask shop where Letitia had stopped with her friends to allow them to buy her a mask. Her jilted ex-lover and his friend outside loudly sang obscene songs and insulted passersby with lewd remarks and gestures in a manner that suggested worse was to follow.

Letitia and her friends fled the shop and headed for Saint Mark's Square where presumably the large crowds that gathered there on *Giovedì Grasso* might have offered them some protection or perhaps even the opportunity to escape the unwanted and increasingly unpleasant attentions of Zorzi and Zaccaria. If that was their plan, it did not work, for in the square they noted that their two followers had picked up four armed ruffians. At that point it appears that Letitia decided that home and bed were as attractive as she had originally claimed, and she and her friends hurriedly left the square to head back to San Luca and her home. Things quickly unraveled. For as soon as they left behind the crowds of the square, they were set upon by their fol-lowers with arms drawn, crying, not too promisingly, "Kill! Kill!"

Her masked companions did the politic if not the gentlemanly thing by fleeing as Letitia was bustled into an alley with a knife at her throat. After considering acting on their threats and dispatching their despairing prey, calmer heads prevailed, and Zorzi and Zaccharia eventually opted to return a badly shaken Letitia home. That was probably a sound decision, for while the aristocratic upper classes were increasingly free to act beyond the laws in the sixteenth century, murder committed in the public streets was not so easily ignored, even during carnival. Thus Letitia perhaps lived to reconsider her unwise decision to cross a powerful noble ex-lover like Zorzi and to show more respect for the social divide that set such men on top of society, and definitely on top of young women of limited status and power. Her *Giovedì Grasso* was over, and she was probably happy to snuggle in her bed and anticipate the last days of carnival and the coming of Lent.

What Zorzi and Zaccharia did with the rest of their carnival is not recorded, but their Lent almost certainly brought at least some repentance for their violent acts of prepotency. For within a few days, as Lent began, they were called in by the disciplining powers of Venetian government to answer for their deeds. It is unlikely that Letitia or her husband would have complained to the authorities; they were probably happy to have escaped the ire of Zorzi so easily. But one of her masked friends turned out to be the son of a minor official in government and he decided, perhaps unwisely, to file a complaint against the pair for their assault. Thus the two were called in to explain their actions, but it appears that Zorzi's noble status and powerful family did the trick – a minor carnival assault without blood drawn was not serious enough to warrant prosecution of such powerful men, and the matter was quietly dropped. One wonders if Zorzi and his family treated the minor official who had accused him of assault with the same moderation.

But perhaps they were distracted from seeking retribution by larger problems that soon raised their dangerous heads. For a few days later Zorzi and his friend found themselves before the Holy Office of Venice – a special branch of the renewed Inquisition that Pope Paul III had reformed in 1542. Venice, concerned about allowing a non-Venetian disciplining body like the Inquisition to operate in its territory, had worked out a compromise with the papacy that created a special local court, the Holy Office, to act in the name of the Inquisition in its territories. Thus in 1547 the doge and the Collegio (the top executive committee of Venice) appointed three nobles called the Savii sopra l'Eresia (the Wise Men Overseeing Heresy) to work with the papal nuncio to the city, the patriarch of Venice, and an inquisitor appointed by the Church to act as the Inquisition in Venetian territories. Known as the Holy Office, it was a unique institution, Venice's own Inquisition. By 1571 this institution, like the regular Inquisition, had largely reined in the threat of Protestant "heresy" in Italy and gone on to become an important arm of a more militant and disciplining Church, aggressively investigating a wide range of activities and spiritual enthusiasms that church leaders perceived as dangerous or merely incorrect.

In that context even the rowdy conduct of a powerful noble during carnival, with its admittedly blasphemous implications, was seen as warranting the attention of the Holy Office. As a result, Zorzi and Zaccharia found themselves explaining their hijinks before a decidedly less sympathetic disciplining body. The Holy Office framed their case with a troubling accusation that the two had dishonored the Church, God, and religion – honor once again raising its disciplining head – by "putting behind them the fear of the Divine Lord and the justice of the world, dressed with the surplices of priests, they went about screaming the litany with most evil and dishonest words dishonoring the saints of heaven and doing other things against the honor of God and religion." Their carnival was definitely over, then, when at the beginning of March 1571 they responded nervously to their accusers. In fact, Zaccharia quickly attempted to dissociate himself from his powerful friend, testifying that the really blasphemous and obscene acts were carried out by Zorzi. He participated by merely following in the footsteps of his powerful friend – an excuse for his deeds that almost certainly made sense to the powerful men who heard his testimony.

It has been suggested that, in the sterner disciplining climate of the last years of the sixteenth century in Italy, carnival was coming to an end and Lent beginning for the Rinascimento with the closing down of its lively and creative society. And certainly there is much to support this position, as we have seen, but history refuses to be neat, and while carnival was more and more limited – both in the literal sense, to one period of the year, and in the more general sense that there were many and wide-ranging attempts to discipline and close down those areas of life that were seen as illicit, immoral, socially incorrect, or merely new and dangerous – even discipline and newer, more powerful institutions to enforce it reached only so far. To put it simply, carnival, both literally and metaphorically, continued even as discipline seemed to dominate the day. And the case of Zorzi and Zaccharia not quite neatly, but actually rather messily, symbolizes that well.

For while the first people called in to testify about the sacrilegious carnival pranks spoke with outrage and an evident desire to see such practices eliminated even from carnival's special season, as time passed their disciplining passions cooled. Witnesses, who had proclaimed that they would tell the whole truth without fear about the horrible blasphemies that they had seen, slowly remembered less and less and were pressed by their interrogators less and less aggressively to remember. With the passage of time, the Holy Office found few who were willing to stick to their guns and support their earlier claims against the two. Perhaps even the feared inquisitional discipline of the Holy Office lost some of its enthusiasm for defending the honor of "God and Religion," at least when a powerful noble was involved, and blasphemy morphed gradually into harmless carnival pranks.

Finally, as Lent dissolved into spring as it regularly does still today, the case against the two was quietly dropped. It appears that the power of the nobility and the Great Social Divide won out in the end, along with the more ubiquitous business-as-usual and avoiding unnecessary conflict. In a much larger historical frame, carnival survived as well, never truly replaced by Lent. It did so, however, in a more disciplined society politically, socially, and internally that increasingly looked more and more like the rest of Europe. And in the process the Rinascimento dissolved into a more general European Renaissance and what would eventually be labeled, rather misleadingly, the Ancient Regime. Thus in the end the Rinascimento really did not end – rather, it seeded a series of new beginnings and new histories, perhaps the final irony for an age that feared and rejected the new. And we today are still harvesting its fruits, both sweet and bitter.

EPILOGUE: THE DIASPORA OF
THE RINASCIMENTO

In August of 1572, as the infamous slaughter known as the Saint Bartholomew's Day Massacre raged in France, in Lyon an Italian printer working in the city, Alessandro Marsigli, apparently took advantage of the uproar to murder an Italian merchant, Paolo Minutolo. Although the religiously driven massacres probably killed between ten and twenty thousand people, Paolo's murder was not motivated by confessional differences. Rather, it seems that Alessandro hoped to use the murder of Minutolo, banned from Lucca, to win a pardon for his own crimes and to be allowed to return to Italy from exile. Alessandro's hopes were apparently based on the fact that Italian governments regularly offered pardons to those who dispatched criminals who had fled and been placed under a ban. If that was Alessandro's motivation, it was thwarted by the fact that the authorities in Lyon were not particularly enthusiastic about supporting Italian justice by overlooking murder in their city; for we know of his crime only because the authorities there prosecuted him, creating a trial record that Natalie Z. Davis cited in a footnote to her path-breaking book, *Society and Culture in Early Modern France.*

Suggestively, in her many studies of Lyon in the sixteenth century Davis often referred to the Italians who were living in the city: silk workers, who had played an important role in founding the industry there and sustaining it; printers, who were significant in establishing the city as an important center of printing; bankers, who had helped make the city a major financial center; along with merchants of all types, lawyers, bureaucrats, and ecclesiastics. Not surprisingly, she noted that these Italians brought with them their Rinascimento values, intellectual fascinations, and ways of living. Even in the first half of the century, she notes, one of the major figures in the attempts at reforming poor relief in the city was the Dominican Santo Paganini, also from Lucca. As a young man this Santo had been a protégé of the Medici in Florence, then briefly a follower of Savonarola, and later had taught Greek and Hebrew in Rome under Pope Leo X. With the death of Leo he joined an increasing tide of Italians seeking to escape the uncertainties of war-torn Italy and its shaky patronage for greener pastures. In his case, finding them in Lyon, he became a leading cultural figure and reformer there. Throughout Europe figures like Santo were transporting the values and culture of the Rinascimento to a broader world just as, on a more material level, Italian bankers, lawyers, bureaucrats, artisans, artists, and architects were doing much the same.

But this brief nod to Davis's treatment of Italians in Lyon and a more general suggestion that Italians at all social levels were spreading the Rinascimento throughout Europe might leave an impression that Davis would certainly reject. For the Italians just described as bearers of what we might label a Rinascimento diaspora seem to be primarily males, and that misses the crucial role that women played in this dissemination of the Rinascimento. As Italy became more aristocratic and more dominated by powers from beyond the peninsula, local *popolo grosso* traditions of marrying within local elites were progressively dropped in favor of marrying daughters into the powerful aristocratic families of the invading powers. Often these wives, pawns in the bedroom diplomacy of the day, moved to their new families throughout Europe carrying with them Rinascimento ways of living, values, and expectations. Their arrival in their new homes and families was not always a happy one, but it was ubiquitous, and when it took place at an aristocratic level their manners and styles were often seen as enhancing elite status and frequently became the mode.

Returning to the Saint Bartholomew's Day Massacre murder leads back to one of the most powerful and important Italian women of the sixteenth century, Catherine de' Medici (1519–1589), at the time widow of Henry II, king of France (1519–1559; ruled 1547–1559) and mother of the reigning ruler of France, Charles IX (1550–1574; ruled 1560–1574). She is often accused of having encouraged or even organized that massacre from behind the scenes in a Machiavellian fashion – an accusation that once again turned on the perception that Italians, and in this case an Italian wife, were exporting their political ways to a broader world – dangerous Machiavellian ways at that. Serious doubts have been raised about such accusations, but it is clear that her life and international career literally spanned, and at times dominated, much of the sixteenth century in France and were often seen, then as now, as playing a significant role in Italianizing upper-class French society and culture.

Once more her origins take us back to Florence and her famous family, the Medici. Her great grandfather was Lorenzo the Magnificent; the Medici pope, Clement VII, was an uncle; and even Pope Leo X was a distant relative, an uncle of her father, Lorenzo II de' Medici. Both he and her mother, Madeline de la Tour d'Auvergne, died young in 1519 shortly after Catherine was born, victims of the plague, although some claim that Lorenzo died from a particularly virulent form of syphilis, then spreading devastatingly through the Italian upper classes. Be that as it may, as a child she was raised by her Medici relatives, primarily in Rome. And crucially, although her father had not lived long enough to have an impact on her upbringing, he left her, as his only heir, a large portion of the Medici family fortune, making her an extremely attractive object of marital desire and decidedly influencing the course of her life.

With her large inheritance and the support of her uncle, Pope Clement VII, she had considerably more to offer a young prince than that orphan of the seventeenth-century Italian fable, Cinderella; and her sixteenth-century prince – perhaps not all that charming – soon arrived. The royal family of France, strapped for cash to cover its burgeoning debts and anxious for a papal alliance in order to continue pursuing its claims in Italy, proposed a prince indeed: Henry, the son of Francis I, king of France, who became her husband in 1533, when both had reached the marriageable age of fourteen. He became Henry II, king of France, in 1547, and she became queen at twenty-eight. The couple's teenage marriage may have created problems for Catherine, as her primary purpose from the perspective of her royal family, after providing a rich infusion of money into the royal coffers with her inheritance, was to produce royal heirs, and early on none was forthcoming. Nonetheless, over the course of those first years in France she developed from being a well-educated Italian novelty at court who attracted attention because of her overly refined manners – reportedly even using a fork to eat – and her stylish Italian retinue, who reputedly outshone the French nobility, into a savvy political player and cultural leader.

Her position improved significantly when, after more than ten years of childless marriage, Catherine finally produced a son, Francis (1544–1560), heir to the throne as Francis II (ruled 1559–1560). Although controversy swirled around her, enhanced by Henry's interest in other favorites who competed with her for power at court and behind the scenes, especially Diane of Portier, once she began to produce heirs she continued at an impressive rate, guaranteeing herself an increasingly important role in the political world of the second half of the sixteenth century. Two other sons would rule France after Francis's death, Charles IX and Henry III (1551–1589; ruled 1574–89), and it seemed to many that with each son Catherine's power behind the throne became greater and more insidiously Italian. Elisabeth

(1545–1568), her second-born, although she died young at twenty-three, lived long enough to be married at fifteen to Philip II (1527–1598), who not only ruled Spain (1556–1598) but was effectively ruler of much of Italy along with a major portion of the New World. The marriage was actually part of the negotiated settlement of the Treaty of Chateau-Cambrésis in 1559 and ended the on-again-off-again marital negotiations that Philip had pursued with Queen Elizabeth of England. Given the relatively short duration of the marriage, perhaps its most immediately significant ramification was the fact that it further confirmed what Philip had gained militarily, his status as the leading foreign power in Italy.

But it was through her daughter Margaret (1553–1615) and her complex and conflicted life that Medici and Italian influence continued in France at the highest levels of society, albeit in a rather convoluted way. For in 1572 Margaret reluctantly married a French Huguenot, Henry of Bourbon, who became in that same year king of Navarre. When the French royal line of the Valois died out in 1589, rule fell to the Bourbon family; Henry of Bourbon became king of France as Henry IV (1553–1610; ruled 1589–1610), and Margaret, the daughter of a Medici, became queen – albeit a strange one. Her marriage had started out badly as reportedly she was unenthusiastic about marrying the leader of the Huguenot opposition and apparently found Henry unattractive as well. For many years it continued unhappily, with both partners rather openly enjoying a series of lovers. Margaret was actually imprisoned for a time by her brother Henry III, accused of a series of misdeeds – political, religious, and sexual. Moreover, the couple was frequently divided physically and emotionally by the Wars of Religion (1562–1598). Their marriage's turbulent course was cut short when in 1599 Henry repudiated his childless wife and queen. With a certain irony, he then married another Medici, Marie de' Medici (1573–1642), daughter of the grand duke of Tuscany, Francesco I, in 1600. She produced six children and started the Bourbon family French royal line, becoming in the process the next Italian leading woman in France in the seventeenth century.

This quick summary of Catherine de'Medici's children overlooks her complex machinations in the power struggles of the political world that swirled around her, her husband, and her three sons who became kings of France. And, in fact, her role behind the scenes from her own day up to the present has been the stuff of scholarly battles, with some arguing that for most of her life she was virtually the evil Italian Machiavellian manipulator working behind the throne, initiating complex plots that were central to much of the turmoil, religious and political, of her day, and even from time to time poisoning a relative or enemy to secure her goals – again, behavior widely associated with Italian women of the evil and wily type. Others have seen her as negotiating a complex path in order to survive as both a wife and a significant player over a long period of highly conflicted French history. But those debates about her actual role need not detain us here, as for the purposes of this discussion Catherine provides a particularly suggestive example of the way Italian women, especially aristocratic women, intermarried Rinascimento culture and social ways into the broader aristocratic world of Europe. To bedroom diplomacy we might well add the trope "bedroom culture" in order to highlight the way marriages between Italian aristocratic women and the scions of European aristocratic families created cultural alliances that spread the Rinascimento not just to France, but throughout Europe.

If anything, this "bedroom culture" was an even more central aspect of the Rinascimento's close relationship with Spain, which in many ways was much more important for the diaspora than the Italian-French connection. As discussed in Chapter 6, although the first Aragonese king of the kingdom of Naples, Alfonso I, conquered the kingdom by defeating his French opponents, his claims to rule were family-based and dynastic – relying upon Aragonese family ties to the Hohenstaufen emperors of the thirteenth century and more immediate and questionable family ties to the queen of Naples, Joanna II, who had temporarily adopted him in order to protect her rule. From the kingdom of Naples there developed a long and increasingly close association between the Iberian peninsula and the Italian, which accelerated with the increasing domination of the north by Habsburg emperors in the sixteenth century, also predicated in many ways on Charles V's marital alliances and dynastic power. This close relationship deeply influenced Spain, and through it, the broader world that Spain dominated. But, of course, the contact went both ways, with some even arguing that the sixteenth century was really the Spanish century in Italy. The relationship used to be characterized too neatly with the claim that while Spain dominated most of Italy in the sixteenth and seventeenth centuries, Italy dominated Spain culturally. Although in a general sense there is some truth to this, the reality is that there was a cross-fertilization, with both positive and negative results for both societies. In fact, to a degree the influence of Spanish styles and values played a significant role in the sixteenth century in dissolving the distinctive urban values of the Rinascimento into a broader European culture, along with the more visible and decried political and military triumphs that so disrupted Italy. But in many ways Italy and the Rinascimento became at the same time the measure of early modern Spain.

Many Spaniards were deeply influenced by the Rinascimento when they studied law at the major Italian universities or served as bureaucrats or diplomats in Italy. They returned to Spain with a strong bureaucratic and legal vision that was incorporated into Spanish legal reform and the country's burgeoning bureaucracies, along with cultural experiences that contributed to Spain's own Renaissance. Also crucial were the close ties with Genoese banks, which became stronger yet in the sixteenth century as that republic fell increasingly under the influence of Habsburg emperors. Those contacts brought the sophisticated culture of money developed in Italy to Spain, and it was that culture that handled much of the banking for the Spanish crown and the exploitation of "New World" resources. Money and the Rinascimento definitely went hand and hand in Spain. But more visible was the high cultural influence of the Rinascimento. Titian, who never actually traveled to Spain, as perhaps the favorite artist of Charles V literally dominated his collection of art, and an impressive list of Italian artists journeyed to the peninsula drawn by the rich patronage to be gained there, including Sofonisba Anguissola, Luca Cambiaso, Federico Zuccaro, Pellegrino Tibaldi, Bartolomé and Vicente Carducho, Giovan Battista Crescenzi, Francesco Rizi, and Luca Giordano; sculptors such as Pompeo Leoni; and architects and engineers ranging from Juanelo Turiano to Francesco Paciotti. Italian literature and theater were also quickly copied and extremely popular in Spain, although occasionally censored when deemed too threatening to the sterner Christian morality typical of the peninsula.

Once again marriage and wives played a crucial role in this diaspora of the Rinascimento in Spain. In fact, Spain even had its Medici connection, although at first it went in the opposite direction, with Eleonora of Toledo (1522–1562) marrying Cosimo I in 1539. She was the daughter of Pedro of Toledo, who ruled Naples as the viceroy and who, in an attempt to consolidate his power there, married his family into the most important noble houses of Italy. In turn, Cosimo needed the marriage to Eleonora to secure his alliance with the emperor, Charles V, whose support was crucial for his power in Florence. But perhaps more important were the dynastic policies favored by Charles himself, which over time helped to form family networks in Italy that definitively ended the tradition of city-state isolation from the dynastic politics of the rest of Europe. Aristocratic families from Florence, Parma, Ferrara, Mantua, Urbino, Turin, and even the republics of Genoa and Venice, along with those of the papal court and cardinals, all intermarried with the nobility of Spain, the Low Countries, and other Habsburg lands, often with Charles's active support, and the Rinascimento went forth with the wives who left Italy to build these aristocratic networks.

Of course, not all Italian wives outside of Italy were queens or even aristo-crats. As Davis noted for early modern Lyon, Italian artisans were ubiquitous there, especially printers and workers in the cloth industry, the latter aggres-sively recruited from Tuscany and other cloth-producing regions. Moreover, in the latter Italian women figured not just as wives, but also as skilled arti-sans in their own right, especially in the silk-producing industry. In fact, artisans of all types, both women and men, escaped the turmoil of sixteenth-century Italy or moved to what appeared to be more lucrative or promis-ing locations throughout Europe, often riding on the reputation that Italian artisans enjoyed at least in part as a reflection of the glory and fame of the Rinascimento. More visible in this human diaspora were the famed artisans/artists like Leonardo da Vinci and Benvenuto Cellini who were invited to the courts of Europe to glorify them with their artistry. But even they brought more than artistry. Cellini, perhaps in an attempt to belittle Leonardo or per-haps just honestly, noted, for example, that Leonardo actually accomplished little in the French king's service, but spent a great deal of time with him discussing ideas. Cellini may not have seen this as very impressive, but it sug-gests the broader way in which artisans from another land with a reputation for being culturally superior disseminated that culture.

But artisans and artists also ventured beyond Europe. The Ottoman court was particularly interested in Western artisans and artists during periods when ongoing tensions abated enough to make contact easier. Already toward the end of the fifteenth century, as part of a temporary peace between Venice and the Turks, Gentile Bellini, of the famed Venetian family of artists, was sent at the request of Sultan Mehmed II – who had conquered Constantinople at midcentury – to paint his portrait and serve as a Venetian cultural ambassa-dor to his court. Although there is some debate about whether he actually painted it, a painting of the sultan dated about 1480 and attributed to Bellini now hangs in the National Gallery in London. During his visit Bellini reportedly demonstrated his artistry for the sultan with numerous pictures and was in turn influenced by the Turkish world and artists.

Legends about the visit quickly grew up, especially as the Turks long con-tinued to be the primary perceived threat to Italy and Europe. In fact, Bellini and his visit figured in one of the more negative legends that stressed the inhuman cruelty of the conqueror and of Turks in general. As reported by Carlo Ridolfi in *Le maraviglie dell'arte*, a mid-seventeenth-century series of biographies celebrating Venetian painters, Bellini had impressed the sultan with his lifelike paintings that virtually seemed to make the figures painted come alive. But ever ready to show his superior knowledge, the sultan pointed out that in a painting of the beheading of John the Baptist, the artist had incorrectly rendered the severed head. And to prove his point, he ordered one of his servants beheaded then and there to demonstrate what a beheading actually looked like, to the horror of the more "civilized" Westerner. Clearly apocryphal, the story illustrates well that contact could be used not just to disseminate culture but also, at times, to make further contact seem dangerous or impossible.

Be that as it may, between regular periods of open warfare, economic and cultural contacts continued. In fact, many of the soldiers and bureaucrats who served the sultan were actually Westerners captured as youths and pressed into his service, often as eunuchs. Many became important figures in the Turkish world, and although it is difficult to speculate about what they brought from Italy and Europe to the East, in some cases it may have been meaningful. Literary contacts, although often downplayed, were also clearly important. Walter Andrews and Mehmet Kalpakli in their recent book, *The Age of the Beloveds: Love and the Beloved in Early-Modern Ottoman and European Culture and Society*, have presented a series of translations of Ottoman love poetry in a suggestive attempt to show that, in fact, in the early modern period there was a general circulation between the West and the East of ideas about love that created a common vision of ideal love throughout the region. It seems clear that for all the warfare and fear that separated the two worlds, there were significant cultural contacts between the Rinascimento and the East to go along with ongoing economic relations.

Actually, from the Eastern perspective, the Rinascimento could well seem merely a sidelight on a golden age of Ottoman power solidified during the long and impressive reign of Suleiman the Magnificent (1494–1566; ruled 1520–1566). Suggestively, Suleiman's remarkable rule and many successes, both culturally and militarily, overlapped almost perfectly with the last days of the Rinascimento, and much like the earlier and the considerably less magnificent Lorenzo the Magnificent, Suleiman was famed as a love poet, patron of the arts, and builder. Moreover, in the best style of the Rinascimento, he based his rule on one of the favorite tools of the *popolo grosso*, a revival of law; in his case his famed reordering and revising of the law code of his empire. Yet what is perhaps most striking, if one is seeking parallels, is Suleiman's cultivation of glory for himself and his court, much in the tradition of the courts of Italy. He was not content with his conquests, which far outshone those of potential rivals like Charles V – conquests that won him much of eastern Europe and brought him to the gates of Europe at Vienna (in 1529) and gave him control of much of North Africa and the Mediterranean as well as the Persian Gulf and the Red Sea, thus creating an empire that rivaled that of Alexander the Great. To confirm his glory he attempted to attract to his court the greatest artists and writers of his day from throughout the world and to make Ottoman society and culture world leaders. Whether or not he accomplished those heady goals, in the process the culture of the Rinascimento seeped into the East.

Less visible to history, but perhaps even more important, were the highly permeable borders between the East and the West in the Balkans, where Ottoman lands and ways rubbed shoulders with lands that had been ruled by Venice or were at least deeply influenced by the Rinascimento. There and in Venice itself many moved quietly between societies and cultures. Over his long rule Suleiman also increasingly encouraged the Jewish populations who had been pushed out of Spain and Portugal to settle in his empire. Many had for a time lived in Italy, but as restrictions multiplied there and harassment from secular and ecclesiastical leaders worsened with reform initiatives, many moved on to live under Suleiman's more protective and cosmopolitan rule, in the process also bringing with them the Rinascimento values, culture, and learning that they had picked up on their way, albeit often deeply colored by a rich Jewish heritage. Historians are just beginning to look more closely at these exchanges, but it is becoming increasingly clear that the Rinascimento travelled east in many ways, just as the East infiltrated the West, adding another set of new challenges. As Carlo Ginzburg noted with surprise more than a generation ago, even the humble Italian miller Menocchio, of *The Cheese and the Worms*, seemed to have garnered some of his most challenging ideas from a copy of the Koran that he had some-how read in rural Friuli. Perhaps, then, it is not so surprising that Suleiman the Magnificent in many of his glorious accomplishments seemed to echo Rinascimento values in an Ottoman context.

Italian theater troupes that traversed Europe in the sixteenth and sev-enteenth centuries were also visible sources of the Rinascimento diaspora. Early on they brought vernacular translations of ancient Roman comedies along with the first Italian comedies, known rather misleadingly as "eru-dite comedies." Rather than erudite, they presented the urban world of the Rinascimento in a playful, rule-breaking way that intrigued Italian specta-tors and similarly caught the imagination of European ones, and of a broader European readership as well, for many were soon translated and rapidly revi-talized the theater in Europe. One of the most successful was *Gl'Ingannati* (*The Deceived*), written collectively, it was claimed, by the Sienese academy known as the Intronati (Dazed), discussed earlier. Featuring a young girl in her teens cross-dressed as a male and courageously braving the streets of Modena to pursue her love and thwart her father's plans to marry her to a much older man, the play presented a delicious and clever fantasy of overturning the power of patriarchs and arranged marriages in the name of love and pleasure. In the process it broke most of the taboos of the day with a smile and a wink, and as a result it was one of the most popular comedies of the day, spawning dozens of imitations in Italian and most European languages. Even Shakespeare, who was not averse to borrowing his plots from Italian sources, took the plot (probably from a translation) as the basis for his very popular *Twelfth Night*. Although the Rinascimento world depicted for the rest of Europe (and more broadly) in such comedies was to a degree a wish-fulfilling fantasy version of the Italian urban world, it nonetheless added to the attractiveness of Italian culture and things Italian, aiding in their diffusion throughout Europe and the world.

Perhaps the most famous travelling theater group in the second half of the sixteenth century was the Comici Gelosi (Jealous Comic/Players), led by the poet and actor Francesco Andreini (1548–1624) and his probably more famous wife, Isabella Andreini (1562–1604). Isabella was noted for her beauty, her poetry, and as one of the first great actresses; until midcentury most plays (in Italy and elsewhere) were performed with male actors playing female roles. The Comici Gelosi were also important pioneers in a newer form of comedy known as the commedia dell'arte. Although a literal translation appears to be "artistic comedy," that is misleading as the name actually refers to stage improvisation by master players in the sense of guild (*arte*) masters rather than to artistry in the modern sense. In these comedies stock characters, working with just a plot line, developed the dialogue and action on stage, improvising as they went along. The stock characters – Arlecchino (Harlequin: a poor, witty counterculture survivor), Pantaleone (a rich, greedy merchant), Scaramouch (a clever, cowardly soldier/lover), Pucinella (a philosophical dreamer, sliding through life somehow), Zanni (Giovanni: a poor, ignorant everyman who was often clever in his own foolish way) and Il Dottore (The Doctor, a learned fool closely related to the earlier pedant/humanist character) – were so popular throughout Europe that they were regularly portrayed in art and served as stereotypical labels, in both literature and daily life, for the character traits with which they were associated. Significantly, these comedies once again were deeply imbued with the urban life of the late Rinascimento and its cultural world, often featuring its playful and racy illicit underside – the satyr in the garden once more. As such, they were particularly attractive to those who wished to imagine a more open and pleasure-oriented society than usually existed.

Of course, not all who left Italy brought with them artistry or play. Italian masters of the craft of war, *condottieri*, and more humble soldiers also travelled widely to ply their trade and often settled down, once again with Italian values and ways of life, in a larger world, not just in Europe but also in the "New World." The latter offered many opportunities for the adventurous to move ahead rapidly by using their military skills and their *virtù*, in the more traditional sense of the term favored by Machiavelli. As noted earlier, many of the earlier explorers were Italians, and the "New World" was even named for the rather questionable Florentine adventurer Amerigo Vespucci. But there were other militants, fighters for the Catholic Church, who were at least equally important, especially the Jesuits. Although founded by a non-Italian group of students in Paris led by the Basque ex-soldier Ignatius Loyola (1491–1556), the Jesuits were quickly recognized by the pope as a new order, in no small part because they pledged themselves to supporting the papacy and Roman leadership of the Church. They also made a name for themselves for their virtually military discipline and their strong support of the papacy's vision of institutional reform. Their Italian credentials and close relationship to the papacy were also strengthened by the fact that their Superior General and administration were centered in Rome. After Trent, as we have seen, they were especially important for their educational reforms and missionary activity in Europe and around the world. Both were high priorities of the final reform agenda of Trent, and in both areas they virtually served as the front-line troops of a church militant that exported the Roman Catholic Church and its often Rinascimento values to the larger world.

Jesuit colleges were an immediate success. Shortly after Loyola's death in 1556, close to 150 had opened their doors in Europe, Asia, and the Americas. By 1615 their number had more than doubled. In Europe and South America their colleges were especially important in educating the upper-class leaders of society, providing them with a curriculum that emphasized Latin, Greek, ancient literature, poetry, philosophy/theology, and natural sciences – virtually the educational ideal of the Rinascimento placed at the service of the Catholic Church and its goal of creating a Roman Catholic World. To a great degree, then, they helped to seed the Rinascimento in Europe and the New World. And "seeding" is a particularly apt term, for they planted the seeds of that culture in a foreign soil where, to continue the metaphor, the plants that grew were also deeply influenced by that local soil and climate, producing a cultural harvest that was never purely European or Rinascimento, but rather a hybrid, at times rich with creative potential, at times disturbingly deformed. For it is easy to overlook the fact that diasporas bring with them and often emphasize the deep problems of their culture along with more celebrated positive features. Moreover, diasporas are virtually never a one-way street. And, in fact, Jesuits and other travelers to foreign lands who returned to Italy and the Rinascimento often returned with new values and new visions that both enriched and changed, slowly but irrevocably, its complex cultural mix. In a very real way, in the process of its own diaspora the Rinascimento was dissolving into a larger series of new worlds.

The Jesuits and a few other competing mendicant orders in more isolated areas of Brazil and Paraguay went well beyond education and conversion, actually attempting to create ideal theocratic societies, known as *Reducciones*, on the local level. These attempts at Christian utopias, distant from European control, often developed in strange ways that troubled authorities both ecclesiastical and civil, although some of their reported excesses must be treated with a grain of salt, as both civil and ecclesiastical authorities were often ready to depict them in the worst possible light, seeing them as dangerous competitors for power. Sometimes Jesuits and other missionary orders were also seen as problematic because of their defense of native populations against the exploitation that often victimized them, including the virtually genocidal slavery associated with mining and certain types of agriculture. At the same time, however, almost everywhere they were active in forming a new Europeanized society in South America, even playing a leading role in founding cities such as Sao Paolo and Rio de Janeiro.

In Asia the Jesuits attempted to convert the upper classes with some initial success. Francis Xavier (1506–1552), one of the founders of the order, arrived in Portuguese-controlled Goa in what is today India in 1541 to convert and teach. By 1545 he was petitioning the pope to establish a branch of the Inquisition there. In Japan, after some initial success – actually being granted for a short time their own feudal state – the Jesuits were driven out as a dangerous outside influence. In China they had greater success, even establishing a Western-style university in the Portuguese-controlled territory of Macau; in fact, in the seventeenth century they eventually became powerful enough to be banned by Portuguese authorities from the territories they controlled in the East as a dangerous competitor for power. Although dreams of Christianizing the East remained illusory, they did strengthen a cultural contact with much of Asia that had never really disappeared across the Middle Ages. From the second half of the sixteenth century, however, slowly and with many reverses, that contact along with ongoing economic relations established a deeper awareness of yet another "new" world.

If the Jesuits and to a lesser degree the other mendicant orders of the Church that took up missionary and educational activities throughout the world were the warriors of Catholicism, the regular clergy who went out to serve as church leaders were the bureaucrats who followed those troops in an attempt to convert their "victories" into more stable control and discipline.

And as the Church was still largely led from Rome, and Italian, many of those leaders had grown up, studied, and begun their careers in Italy and were deeply imbued with the ideals of the Rinascimento that they brought with them. They too, in turn, often returned to Italy with new ideas and new ways that contributed to dissolving the Rinascimento. It should be noted, however, that some, threatened by what they discovered abroad, returned more committed than ever to defend their traditional culture and values. But in the long run that culture was dissolving into the new and the broader worlds they encountered.

One of the most dangerous "news" encountered, however, was the one that had so troubled Vespasiano da Bisticci back in the mid-fifteenth century, the printed book. Little did he realize just how dangerous it would be for his Rinascimento world. Of course, as we have seen, in the early years of printing many were worried about the effect of making the knowledge contained in books more widely available. Knowledge was power, often dangerous power, and making it available to the masses threatened the aristocratic control of society and perhaps foreshadowed mob rule. For many, this had been confirmed in the radical religious reform movements that were often seen as having been spread by the printed word and by reading the Bible in the vernacular. The response was censorship and discipline, by both government and the Church. But the printed word was loose in the late Rinascimento, the genie was out of the bottle, and the results were dramatic and at times revolutionary.

Yet it might be argued that in the complex societies that had evolved across Europe since the end of the Middle Ages many controls had developed that made revolution or radical change difficult. Thus the profound changes that did occur were often the result of not seeing the broader implications of choices that seemed innocuous or of limited import. The shorter route to the East that Columbus promised had serious economic import, certainly, but it led to the totally unexpected "discovery" of "new" worlds, a revolutionary shift in the focus of the West, and a deep restructuring of the world as a whole. Those dangers were simply unimaginable at the time when his proposal was accepted and funded. By contrast, Copernicus's placing of the sun at the center of the solar system and Galileo's proofs that the heavens were not unchanging and not made up of a fifth perfect essence that made them eternal were rapidly seen for what they were, potentially revolutionary proposals that threatened the whole edifice of ancient knowledge, Church dogma, and the Rinascimento. Thus, although much more was involved, both were aggressively and harshly rejected and continued to be so until long after those theories had been well established and confirmed. The difference is clear. In one case the confrontation was unmistakable; in the other it was virtually unrecognized until its revolutionary potential could no longer be avoided.

In many ways the printed book represented an intermediate ground. Some realized that it presented a danger, but on the whole they were unaware of how wide-ranging that danger could be. Eventually, with the establishment of the *Index of Printed Books* and local censorship offices, that deeper danger was at least partially recognized, but once again it was too little and too late to block its radical potential. From the perspective of the diaspora of the Rinascimento, much of that radical potential might seem positive, although in the receiving cultures at the time many saw the dissemination of Rinascimento values through the printed book as decidedly negative. The well-known diatribes against the political works of Machiavelli and Machiavellianism and against the erotically charged works of Aretino in England, France, and Spain are only the best examples. The amoral Machiavel and the pornographic Aretine in the late sixteenth and seventeenth centuries came to represent all that was evil in the Italian version of a broader European Renaissance, while Castiglione's manual for the ideal courtly aristocrat became an attractive ideal of upper-class sophistication. Italian comedies and *novelle* offered fantasies of an urban world of adventure and intrigue that was at once attractive, illicit, and fascinatingly dangerous. The list could easily be augmented. But the point is simply that the Rinascimento was disseminated throughout Europe and the world by that powerful new cultural force, the printed book, as well as by Italians. In fact, the literature of the Rinascimento in all its forms was quickly translated and circulated, reflecting at least to a degree the attractiveness of things Italian and Italy's ongoing cultural leadership.

In turn, in the seventeenth and eighteenth centuries the cities of Italy became the featured venue of the European Grand Tour, where aristocrats from around the continent and a few from the New World as well journeyed to that promised land of culture (and the illicit) that they and their peers had read about in order to gain the sophistication associated with that culture and society. In that Grand Tour the Rinascimento itself enjoyed a rebirth among the ruling classes of Europe in a ritual that is to a degree distantly reflected today at a more humble level, in the mass tourism that overruns Italy in the summer months and cities like Rome, Florence, and Venice year round.

Significantly, as the rest of Europe also sought precedents for their rapidly evolving nation-state governments and royal pretensions of absolute rule, much as the earlier Italian city-states had done, they turned to their own claims of ancient origins and classical political theory. But they also had, closer to hand and closer in time, another highly regarded model, the political order and political theories of the city-states of Italy. Their riches and evident success, becoming yet more apparent as European powers were busily despoiling them in the sixteenth and seventeenth centuries, made them models that demanded and received respect. Venice, with its mythic claims of longevity and stability, won pride of place for its supposed perfect mixed government. But political theorists throughout Italy who described the success of their city-states by citing similar Aristotelian theories of an ideal mixed government were particularly attractive to political leaders and thinkers beyond Italy, especially those who dreamt of creating lasting republics. In the 1960s and early 1970s a series of exceptional historians – led by Felix Gilbert with his 1965 study, *Machiavelli and Guicciardini: Politics and History in Sixteenth-Century Florence*; William Bouswma in his massive 1968 work, *Venice and the Defense of Republican Liberty: Renaissance Values in the Age of the Counter Reformation;* and, perhaps most significantly, John Pocock in his seminal 1975 volume *The Machiavellian Moment: Florentine Political Thought and the Atlantic Republican Tradition* – showed the deep ways in which European political thought and practice were rethought and remodeled on a Rinascimento vision deeply influenced by Italian thinkers such as Machiavelli, Guicciardini, Contarini, and their compatriots, based on the ideal and to a degree the reality of Italian city-states. One need only look at the Palladian architecture of Washington or the ideal mixed vision of government in the United States – with its president, representing one-man rule; its Senate, representing rule by the best; and its House of Representatives, representing rule by the *popolo* – to see Rinascimento echoes at the heart of modern government. And these examples could easily be multiplied.

Practice, of course, was another matter, but once again Rinascimento political writing was rich with practical advice, and historical works described, often in detail, the intricacies of effective governance. In turn, in areas where the Catholic Church remained dominant – perhaps the most powerful and tightly organized bureaucratic organization of the day – that Church provided a Roman/Italian model of bureaucratic control and discipline easily copied by governments who interacted with it daily and often relied on its leaders to serve as their own officials. In sum, across the board, from government to the humble folk on the grounds of a Shakespearean theater, from famous artists and artisans to silk workers in Lyon, from wives of kings to camp followers of the armies that traversed Europe, from slaves of the Ottoman sultan to Jesuits ruling theocratic utopias in Paraguay, from Spanish bureaucrats in Italy to Genoese bankers in Spain, the Rinascimento reached out to a broader world in a largely unrecognized and unquestioned diaspora. In turn, across the sixteenth century at home the great themes of the Rinascimento were changed irreversibly by a rapidly increasing deluge of the undeniably new and of a broader, richly diverse world. It might seem legitimate to claim, then, that the Rinascimento ended slowly, dissolving into a wider world that would find new ideals first in French, Spanish, and Habsburg aristocratic "civilizations" in a Spanish and Portuguese colonial world, then in English "bourgeois" "imperial rule," and eventually in U.S. "democratic" "hegemony" over an Atlantic and world economy and a far more material culture. But this is not the place to make such claims.

And in the end, periods do not end. Obviously, it would be difficult to argue that a thing that does not exist has ceased to exist. For periods are merely useful heuristic devices for gathering together central aspects of the society and culture of particular times, and when those central aspects change, or at least when their importance wanes (or increases) and new factors enter and skew the mix, eventually the balance and weight of those things that were once central, change as well. Thus, slowly but surely, a period label no longer serves as a heuristic tool. In this case the major factors that made the Rinascimento such a significant and rich period did not disappear; rather, they dissolved into a broader European and developing Atlantic culture and society (for better and worse) which may at present be dissolving into a broader worldwide culture, sometimes quietly, sometimes painfully, with strife and bloody discord.

Once upon a time and not so long ago, in a more self-satisfied and decidedly less culturally aware European world, the great cultural successes and accomplishments of the Italian Renaissance were seen as foundational for Western civilization. Today a more measured claim might be that well beyond the notable cultural accomplishments of the day, the Rinascimento incorporated new ways of imagining and living with social hierarchy and conflict, political power, religious discipline, urban life, spiritual enthusiasms, and creativity across the social spectrum, which over and over again were legitimated by returning to the past and privileged first times with a success that has had a lasting impact on the West and the world. That impact has not always been positive, but rethinking the Rinascimento in such terms makes it a period whose successes and problems speak to us in ways that are suggestive for critically rethinking the past and the present, hopefully more subtly, usefully, and creatively.

BIBLIOGRAPHY: A SHORT LIST OF WORKS USED

Abulafia, David. *The French Descent into Renaissance Italy, 1494–95: Antecedents and Effects*. Brookfield, VT: Ashgate, 1995.

Abulafia, David, ed. *The French Descent into Italy, 1494–1495*. Burlington, VT: Ashgate, 1995.

Amelang, James S. *The Flight of Icarus: Artisan Autobiography in Early Modern Europe*. Stanford: Stanford University Press, 1998.

Andrews, Walter G., and Mehmet Kalpakli. *The Age of the Beloveds: Love and the Beloved in Early-Modern Ottoman and European Culture and Society*. Durham: Duke University Press, 2005.

Arrizabalaga, Jon, Jon Henderson, and Roger French. *The Great Pox: The French Disease in Renaissance Europe*. New Haven: Yale University Press, 1997.

Ascoli, Albert Russell. *Ariosto's Bitter Harmony: Crisis and Evasion in the Italian Renaissance*. Princeton: Princeton University Press, 1987.

Dante and the Making of a Modern Author. Cambridge: Cambridge University Press, 2008.

Astarita, Tommaso. *Village Justice: The Community, Family and Popular Culture in Early Modern Italy*. Baltimore: Johns Hopkins University Press, 1999.

Baron, Hans. *The Crisis of the Early Italian Renaissance: Civic Humanism and Republican Liberty in the Age of Classicism and Tyranny*. Princeton: Princeton University Press, 1966.

Barzman, Karen-edis. *The Florentine Academy and the Early Modern State: Discipline of Disegno*. Cambridge: Cambridge University Press, 2000.

Baxandall, Michael. *Painting and Experience in Renaissance Italy*. Oxford: Clarendon Press, 1972.

Black, Robert. *Humanism and Education in Medieval and Renaissance Italy: Tradition and Innovation in Latin Schools from the Twelfth to the Fifteenth Century*. Cambridge: Cambridge University Press, 2007.

Boer, Wietse de. *The Conquest of the Soul: Confession, Discipline and Public Order in Counter-Reformation Milan*. Leiden: Brill, 2000.

Bossy, John. *Christianity and the West 1400–1700*. Oxford: Oxford University Press, 1985.

Boswell, John. *Christianity, Social Tolerance, and Homosexuality*. Chicago: University of Chicago Press, 1981.

The Kindness of Strangers: Child Abandonment in Western Europe from Late Antiquity to the Renaissance. New York: Pantheon, 1988.

Bourne, Molly. *Francesco II Gonzaga: The Soldier Prince as Patron*. Rome: Bulzoni, 2008.

"Renaissance Husbands and Wives as Patrons of Art: The *Camerini* of Isabella d'Este and Francesco II Gonzaga," in *Beyond Isabella: Secular Women Patrons of Art in Renaissance Italy*, ed. Sheryl Reiss and David Wilkins. Kirksville, MO: Truman State University Press, 2001: 93–123.

Bouwsma, William J. *Venice and the Defense of Republican Liberty*. Berkeley: University of California Press, 1968.

The Waning of the Renaissance, 1550–1640. New Haven: Yale University Press, 2000.

Bowsky, William J. *A Medieval Commune: Siena under the Nine, 1287–1355*. Berkeley: University of California Press, 1981.

Braudel, Ferdinand. *Out of Italy, 1450–1650*, trans. Sian Reynolds. Paris: Flammarion, 1991.

Brotton, Jerry, and Lisa Jardine. *Global Interests: Renaissance Art between East and West*. Ithaca: Cornell University Press, 2000.

Brucker, Gene. *The Civic World of Early Renaissance Florence*. Princeton: Princeton University Press, 1977.

Florentine Politics and Society 1343–1378. Princeton: Princeton University Press, 1962.

Bullard, Melissa. *Lorenzo il Magnifico: Image and Anxiety, Politics and Finance*. Florence: Olschki, 1994.

Burckhardt, Jacob. *The Civilization of the Renaissance in Italy*, trans. S. G. C. Middlemore. New York: Penguin, 1990.

Burke, Peter. *The Historical Anthropology of Early Modern Italy*. Cambridge: Cambridge University Press, 1987; especially "The Presentation of Self in the Renaissance Portrait," pp. 150–167.

The Italian Renaissance: Culture and Society in Italy. Princeton: Princeton University Press, 1986.

Caferro, William. *Contesting the Renaissance*. Oxford: Wiley-Blackwell, 2011.

"Warfare and the Economy of Renaissance Italy, 1350–1450." *Journal of Interdisciplinary History* 39 (2008): 167–209.

Campbell, Lorne. *Renaissance Portraits: European Portrait-Painting in the Fourteenth, Fifteenth and Sixteenth Centuries*. New Haven: Yale University Press, 1990.

Cantimori, Delio. *Eretici italiani del Cinquecento e Prospettive di storia ereticale italiana del Cinquecento*, ed. Adriano Prosperi. Turin: Einaudi, 2009.

Carmichael, Ann. *Plague and the Poor in Renaissance Florence*. Cambridge: Cambridge University Press, 1986.

Carroll, Linda. "Who's on Top? Gender as Societal Power Configuration in Italian Renaissance Painting and Drama." *The Sixteenth Century Journal* 20 (1989): 531–58.

Castelnuovo, Enrico. "Il significato del ritratto pittorico nella società," in *Storia d'Italia 5*. Turin: Einaudi, 1973: 1035–94.

Celenza, Christopher. *The Lost Italian Renaissance: Humanism, Historians, and Latin's Legacy*. Baltimore: Johns Hopkins University Press, 2004.

Chastel, Andre. *The Sack of Rome*. Princeton: Princeton University Press, 1983.

Chojnacki, Stanley. *Women and Men in Renaissance Venice: Twelve Essays on Patrician Society*. Baltimore: Johns Hopkins University Press, 2000.

Clark, Paula. *The Soderini and the Medici: Power and Patronage in Fifteenth-Century Florence.* New York: Oxford University Press, 1991.

Cohen, Elizabeth S., and Thomas V. Cohen. *Daily Life in Renaissance Italy.* Westport, CT: Greenwood Press, 2001.

Words and Deeds in Renaissance Rome: Trials before the Papal Magistrates. Toronto: University of Toronto Press, 1993.

Cohen, Sherril. *The Evolution of Women's Asylums since 1500: From Refuges for Ex-Prostitutes to Shelters for Battered Wives.* New York: Oxford University Press, 1992.

Cohen, Thomas V. *Love and Death in Renaissance Italy.* Chicago: University of Chicago Press, 2004.

Cohn, Samuel. *The Black Death Transformed: Disease and Culture in Early Renaissance Florence.* London: Arnold, 2003.

Creating the Florentine State: Peasants and Rebellion, 1343–1434. Cambridge: Cambridge University Press, 2000.

Cox, Virginia. *Women's Writing in Italy 1400–1650.* Baltimore: Johns Hopkins University Press, 2008.

Crum, Roger J., and John T. Paoletti, eds. *Renaissance Florence: A Social History.* Cambridge: Cambridge University Press, 2006.

D'Amico, John. *Renaissance Humanism in Papal Rome: Humanists and Churchmen on the Eve of the Reformation.* Baltimore: Johns Hopkins University Press, 1983.

Darling, Linda. "The Renaissance and the Middle East," in *A Companion to the Worlds of the Renaissance,* ed. Guido Ruggiero. Oxford: Blackwell, 2002: 55–69.

Davidson, Nicolaus S. *The Counter-Reformation.* Oxford: Blackwell, 1987.

Davis, Natalie Zemon. *Society and Culture in Early Modern France.* Stanford: Stanford University Press, 1965.

De Roover, Raymond. *The Rise and Decline of the Medici Bank, 1397–1494.* New York: W.W. Norton, 1966.

Eamon, William. *Science and the Secrets of Nature: Books and Secrets in Medieval and Early Modern Culture.* Princeton: Princeton University Press, 1994.

Edgerton, Samuel Y. *The Renaissance Rediscovery of Linear Perspective.* New York: Harper & Row, 1975.

Eisenbichler, Konrad. *The Boys of the Archangel Raphael: A Youth Confraternity in Florence, 1411–1785.* Toronto: University of Toronto Press, 1998.

Eisenbichler, Konrad, and Olga Zorzi, eds. *Ficino and Renaissance Neoplatonism.* Ottawa: Dovehouse Editions, 1986.

Eisenstein, Elizabeth L. *The Printing Revolution in Early Modern Europe.* Cambridge: Cambridge University Press, 1983.

Epstein, Stephen. *Economic and Social History of Later Medieval Europe, 1000–1500.* Cambridge: Cambridge University Press, 2009.

Wage Labor and Guilds in Medieval Europe. Chapel Hill: University of North Carolina Press, 1991.

Fenlon, Dermont. *Heresy and Obedience in Tridentine Italy: Cardinal Pole and the Counter-Reformation.* Cambridge: Cambridge University Press, 2008.

Ferguson, Wallace K. *The Renaissance in Historical Thought: Five Centuries of Interpretation.* Cambridge, MA: Riverside Press, 1948.

Ferraro, Joanne. *Marriage Wars in Late Renaissance Venice.* New York: Oxford University Press, 2001.

Venice: History of the Floating City. Cambridge: Cambridge University Press, 2012.

Findlen, Paula. *Possessing Nature: Museums, Collecting and Scientific Culture in Early Modern Italy.* Berkeley: University of California Press, 1994.

Finucci, Valeria. *The Lady Vanishes: Subjectivity and Representation in Castiglione and Ariosto.* Stanford: Stanford University Press, 1992.

The Manly Masquerade: Masculinity, Paternity, and Castration in the Italian Renaissance. Durham: Duke University Press, 2006.

Foucault, Michel. *Discipline and Punish: The Birth of the Prison,* trans. Alan Sheridan. New York: Vintage, 1995.

Fragnito, Gigliola. *La Bibbia al rogo. La censura ecclesiastica e i volgarizzamenti della Scrittura, 1471–1605.* Bologna: Il Mulino, 1997.

Fubini, Riccardo. "Renaissance Historian: The Career of Hans Baron." *Journal of Modern History* 64 (1992): 541–74.

Garin, Eugenio. *Italian Humanism: Philosophy and Civic Life in the Renaissance,* trans. Peter Munz. Oxford: Basil Blackwell, 1965.

Gavitt, Philip R. *Charity and Children in Renaissance Florence: The Ospedale degli Innocenti, 1410–1536.* Ann Arbor: University of Michigan Press, 1990.

Geary, Patrick J. *Furta Sacra: Thefts of Relics in the Central Middle Ages.* Princeton: Princeton University Press, 1978.

Gentilcore, David. *Healers and Healing in Early Modern Italy.* Manchester: Manchester University Press, 1998.

Giannetti, Laura. *Lelia's Kiss: Imagining Gender, Sex, and Marriage in Italian Renaissance Comedy.* Toronto: University of Toronto Press, 2009.

Giannetti, Laura, and Guido Ruggiero. "Introduction," in *Five Comedies from the Italian Renaissance,* ed. and trans. Laura Giannetti and Guido Ruggiero. Baltimore: Johns Hopkins University Press, 2003: xi–xlii.

Gilbert, Felix. *Machiavelli and Guicciardini: Politics and History in Sixteenth-Century Florence.* Princeton: Princeton University Press, 1965.

Ginzburg, Carlo. *The Cheese and the Worms: The Cosmos of a Sixteenth-Century Miller,* trans. John and Ann Tedeschi. Baltimore: Johns Hopkins University Press, 1980.

The Night Battles: Witchcraft and Agrarian Cults in the Sixteenth and Seventeenth Centuries, trans. John and Ann Tedeschi. Baltimore: Johns Hopkins University Press, 1983.

Goldthwaite, Richard A. *The Economy of Renaissance Florence.* Baltimore: Johns Hopkins University Press, 2009.

Wealth and the Demand for Art in Italy, 1300–1600. Baltimore: Johns Hopkins University Press, 1993.

Gombrich, Ernest H. *Art and Illusion.* Princeton: Princeton University Press, 1960.

Gouwins, Kenneth. "Perceiving the Past: Renaissance Humanism after the 'Cognitive Turn.'" *American Historical Review* 103 (1998): 55–82.

Grafton, Anthony. *Leon Battista Alberti: Master Builder of the Italian Renaissance.* Cambridge, MA: Harvard University Press, 2002.

Grafton, Anthony. *New Worlds, Ancient Texts: The Power of Tradition and the Shock of the New.* Cambridge, MA: Harvard University Press, 1992.

Grafton, Anthony, and Lisa Gardine. *From Humanism to Humanities: Education and the Liberal Arts in Fifteenth- and Sixteenth-Century Europe.* Cambridge, MA: Harvard University Press, 1986.

Greenblatt, Steven. *Marvelous Possessions: The Wonder of the New World*. Chicago: University of Chicago Press, 1992.

Renaissance Self-Fashioning from More to Shakespeare. Chicago: University of Chicago Press, 1980.

The Swerve: How the World Became Modern. New York: W.W. Norton, 2011.

Grendler, Paul. *Critics of the Italian World 1530–1560: Anton Doni, Nicolò Franco and Ortensio Lando*. Madison: University of Wisconsin Press, 1969.

The Roman Inquisition and the Venetian Press 1540–1605. Princeton: Princeton University Press, 1977.

Schooling in Renaissance Italy: Literacy and Learning, 1300–1600. Baltimore: Johns Hopkins University Press, 1989.

Grubb, James. *Provincial Families of the Renaissance: Public and Private Life in the Veneto*. Baltimore: Johns Hopkins University Press, 1996.

Gundersheimer, Werner L. *Ferrara: The Style of a Renaissance Despotism*. Princeton: Princeton University Press, 1973.

Gundersheimer, Werner L., Craig Kallendorf, John M. Najemy, and Ronald Witt. "AHA Forum: Hans Baron's Renaissance Humanism." *American Historical Review* 101 (1996): 107–44.

Hale, John. *War and Society in Renaissance Europe, 1450–1620*. Baltimore: Johns Hopkins University Press, 1985.

Hale, John, and Michael Mallet. *The Military Organization of a Renaissance State: Venice c. 1400 to 1617*. Cambridge: Cambridge University Press, 1984.

Hall, Bert. *Weapons and Warfare in Renaissance Europe: Gunpowder, Technology, and Tactics*. Baltimore: Johns Hopkins University Press, 1997.

Hankins, James. *Humanism and Platonism in the Italian Renaissance*, 2 vols. Rome: Edizione di Storia e Letteratura, 2003–2004.

Hankins, James, ed. *Renaissance Civic Humanism: Reappraisals and Reflections*. Cambridge: Cambridge University Press, 2000.

Hay, Denys, and John Law. *Italy in the Age of the Renaissance 1380–1530*. London: Longman, 1989.

Henderson, John. *Piety and Charity in Late Medieval Florence*. Oxford: Oxford University Press, 1994.

The Renaissance Hospital: Healing the Body and Healing the Soul. New Haven: Yale University Press, 2006.

Hennessy, J. Pope. *The Portrait in the Renaissance*. Princeton: Princeton University Press, 1966.

Herlihy, David. *Medieval and Renaissance Pistoia: The Social History of an Italian Town 1200–1430*. New Haven: Yale University Press, 1967.

Herlihy, David, and Christiane Klapish Zuber. *Les Toscans et leurs familles*. Paris: Foundation Nationale des Sciences Politiques, 1978; abridged English version, *Tuscans and Their Families: A Study of the Florentine Catasto of 1427*. New Haven: Yale University Press, 1985.

Hughes, Diane Owen. "Sumptuary Law and Social Relations in Renaissance Italy," in *Disputes and Settlements: Law and Human Relations in the West*, ed. John Bossy. Cambridge: Cambridge University Press, 1983: 69–99.

Huizinga, Johan. *The Autumn of the Middle Ages*, trans. Rodney J. Payton and Ulrich Mammitzsch. Chicago: University of Chicago Press, 1996.

Imber, Colin. *The Ottoman Empire 1300–1650: The Structure of Power*. New York: Macmillan, 2002.

Jedin, Hurbert. *Crisis and Closure of the Council of Trent*. London: Sheed and Ward, 1967.

Johnson, Geraldine, and Sara Matthew Grieco, eds. *Picturing Women in Renaissance and Baroque Italy*. Cambridge: Cambridge University Press, 1997.

Jones, Philip. *The Italian City State: From Commune to Signoria*. Oxford: Clarendon Press, 1997.

Jurdjevic, Mark. "Hedgehogs and Foxes: The Present and Future of Italian Renaissance Intellectual History." *Past and Present* 195 (2007): 241–68.

Kelly, Joan. *Women, History and Theory: The Essays*. Chicago: University of Chicago Press, 1984.

Kelly, Samantha. *The New Solomon: Robert of Naples (1309–1343) and Fourteenth-Century Kingship*. Leiden: Brill, 2003.

Kent, Dale V. *Cosimo de'Medici and the Florentine Renaissance: The Patron's Oeuvre*. New Haven: Yale University Press, 2000.

Kessler, Herbert L., and Joanna Zacharias. *Rome 1300: On the Path of the Pilgrim*. New Haven: Yale University Press, 2000.

King, Margaret. *Venetian Humanism in an Age of Patrician Dominance*. Princeton: Princeton University Press, 1986.

Kirshner, Julius, ed. *The Origins of the State in Italy, 1300–1600*. Chicago: University of Chicago Press, 1995.

Klapish Zuber, Christiane. *Women, Family and Ritual in Renaissance Italy*, trans. Lydia Cochrane. Chicago: University of Chicago Press, 1985.

Kovesi, Catherine. *Sumptuary Law in Italy, 1200–1500*. Oxford: Oxford University Press, 2002.

Kraye, Jill, ed. *The Cambridge Companion to Renaissance Humanism*. Cambridge: Cambridge University Press, 1996.

Kristeller, Paul Oscar. *Renaissance Thought and Its Sources*. New York: Columbia University Press, 1979.

Kuehn, Thomas. *Law, Family and Women: Towards a Legal Anthropology of Renaissance Italy*. Chicago: University of Chicago Press, 1991.

Lane, Frederic C. *Venice a Maritime Republic*. Baltimore: Johns Hopkins University Press, 1973.

Lane, Frederic C. *Venice and History: The Collected Papers of Frederic C. Lane*. Baltimore: Johns Hopkins University Press, 1966.

Lane, Frederic C., and Reinhold Mueller. *Money and Banking in Medieval and Renaissance Venice: Coins and Moneys of Account*. Baltimore: Johns Hopkins University Press, 1985.

Lansing, Carol. *The Florentine Magnates: Lineage and Faction in a Medieval Commune*. Princeton: Princeton University Press, 1991.

Larner, John. *Italy in the Age of Dante and Petrarch, 1216–1380*. London: Longman, 1980.

Lopez, Robert. *The Commercial Revolution of the Middle Ages, 950–1350*. Cambridge: Cambridge University Press, 1976.

Lowry, Martin. *The World of Aldus Manutius: Business and Scholarship in Renaissance Venice*. Oxford: Basil Blackwell, 1979.

Mackenney, Richard. *Tradesmen and Traders: The World of the Guilds in Venice and Europe, c. 1250–c. 1650*. London: Croom Helm, 1987.

Maclean, Ian. *The Renaissance Notion of Women: A Study in the Fortunes of Scholasticism and Medical Science in European Intellectual Life.* Cambridge: Cambridge University Press, 1980.

McClure, George W. *The Culture of the Professions in Late Renaissance Italy.* Toronto: University of Toronto Press, 2004.

Mallet, Michael. *Mercenaries and Their Masters: Warfare in Renaissance Italy.* Totowa, NJ: Rowan and Littlefield, 1974.

Martin, John Jeffries. *Venice's Hidden Enemies: Italian Heretics in a Renaissance City.* Berkeley: University of California Press, 1993.

Martin, John. *Myths of Renaissance Individualism.* New York: Palgrave: Macmillan 2004.

Martines, Lauro. *Fire in the City: Savonarola and the Struggle for the Soul of Renaissance Florence.* New York: Oxford University Press, 2006.

Lawyers and Statecraft in Renaissance Florence. Princeton: Princeton University Press, 1968.

Power and Imagination: City States in Renaissance Italy. New York: Knopf, 1979.

Martines, Lauro. *Strong Words: Writing and Social Strain in the Italian Renaissance.* Baltimore: Johns Hopkins University Press, 2001.

Martines, Lauro, ed. *Violence and Civil Disorder in Italian Cities, 1200–1500.* Berkeley: University of California Press, 1972.

Mesquita, Daniel Bueno de. *Gian Galeazzo Visconti, Duke of Milan, 1351–1402: A Study in the Political Career of an Italian Despot.* Cambridge: Cambridge University Press, 1941.

Mignolo, Walter D. *The Darker Side of the Renaissance: Literacy, Territoriality, and Colonization.* Ann Arbor: University of Michigan Press, 2003.

Miskimin, Harry A. *The Economy of Early Renaissance Europe, 1300–1460.* Cambridge: Cambridge University Press, 1975.

Mormando, Franco. *The Preacher's Demons: Bernardino of Siena and the Social Underworld of Early Renaissance Italy.* Chicago: University of Chicago Press, 1999.

Moulton, Ian Frederick. *Before Pornography: Erotic Writing in Early Modern England.* New York: Oxford University Press, 2000.

Muir, Edward. *Civic Ritual in Renaissance Venice.* Princeton: Princeton University Press, 1981.

Mad Blood Stirring: Vendetta and Factions in Friuli during the Renaissance. Baltimore: Johns Hopkins University Press, 1993.

"The Virgin on the Street Corner: The Place of the Sacred in Italian Cities," in *Religion and Culture in the Renaissance and Reformation,* ed. Steven Ozment. Kirksville, MO: Sixteenth-Century Journal Publications, 1989: 25–40

Muir, Edward, and Guido Ruggiero, eds. *History from Crime: Selections from Quaderni Storici,* Baltimore: Johns Hopkins University Press, 1994.

eds. *Microhistory and the Lost Peoples of Europe: Selections from Quaderni Storici.* Baltimore: Johns Hopkins University Press, 1991.

eds. *Sex and Gender in Historical Perspective: Selections from Quaderni Storici.* Baltimore: Johns Hopkins University Press, 1990.

Najemy, John M. *Corporatism and Consensus in Florentine Electoral Politics, 1280–1400.* Chapel Hill: University of North Carolina Press, 1982.

"Guild Republicanism in Trecento Florence: The Success and Ultimate Failure of Corporate Politics." *American Historical Review* 84 (1979): 53–71.

A History of Florence 1200–1575. Oxford: Blackwell, 2006.

Nelson, Jonathan Katz, and Richard Zeckhauser, eds. *The Patron's Payoff: Conspicuous Commissions in Italian Renaissance Art*. Princeton: Princeton University Press, 2008.

Niccoli, Ottavia. *Prophecy and the People in Renaissance Italy*, trans. Lydia Cochrane. Princeton: Princeton University Press, 1990.

O'Neil, Mary. "Ecclesiastical and Superstitious Remedies in Sixteenth Century Italy," in *Understanding Popular Culture: Europe from the Middle Ages to the Present*, ed. Stephen Kaplan. Berlin: Mouton, 1984: 53–83.

Ottokar, Nicolai. *Il comune di Firenze alla fine del Dugento*. Florence: Vallecchi, 1926.

Paoletti, John T., and Gary M. Radke. *Art in Renaissance Italy*. London: Lawrence King, 2011.

Partner, Peter. *The Pope's Men: The Papal Civil Service in the Renaissance*. Oxford: Clarendon Press, 1990.

Peterson, David S. "Out of the Margins: Religion and the Church in Renaissance Italy." *Renaissance Quarterly* 53 (2000): 835–79.

Pocock, John G. A. *The Machiavellian Moment: Florentine Political Thought and the Atlantic Republican Tradition*. Princeton: Princeton University Press, 1975.

Po-Hsia, Ronnie. *The World of Catholic Renewal*. Cambridge: Cambridge University Press, 1998.

Pomeranz, Kenneth. *The Great Divergence: China, Europe, and the Making of the Modern World Economy*. Princeton: Princeton University Press, 2001.

Prodi, Paolo. *La crisi religiosa del XVI secolo: Riforma cattolica e Controriforma*. Bologna: Riccardo Pàtron, 1964.

Prodi, Paolo, ed. *Disciplina dell'anima, disciplina del corpo e disciplina della società tra medioevo ed età moderna*. Bologna: Il Mulino, 1994.

Prosperi, Adriano. *Tribunali della coscienza. Inquisitori, confessore, missionari*. Turin: Einaudi, 1996.

Pullan, Brian. *A History of Early Renaissance Italy*. London: Allen Lane, 1973.

Rich and Poor in Renaissance Venice: The Social Institutions of a Catholic State. Oxford: Basil Blackwell, 1971.

Rabb, Theodore K. *The Last Days of the Renaissance and the March to Modernity*. New York: Basic Books, 2006.

Rabil, Albert, ed. *Renaissance Humanism: Foundations, Forms, and Legacy*. 3 vols, Philadelphia: University of Pennsylvania Press, 1988.

Restall, Matthew. "The Renaissance World from the West: Spanish America and the 'Real' Renaissance," in *A Companion to the Worlds of the Renaissance*, ed. Guido Ruggiero. New York: Oxford University Press, 2002: 70–87.

Richardson, Brian. *Print Culture in Renaissance Italy: The Editor and the Vernacular Text, 1470–1600*. Cambridge: Cambridge University Press, 2004.

Printing, Writers and Readers in Renaissance Italy. Cambridge: Cambridge University Press, 1999.

Rocke, Michael. *Forbidden Friendships: Homosexuality and Male Culture in Renaissance Florence*. New York: Oxford University Press, 1966.

Rosenberg, Charles M., ed. *The Court Cities of Northern Italy: Milan, Parma, Piacenza, Mantua, Ferrara, Bologna, Urbino, Pesaro and Rimini*. Cambridge: Cambridge University Press, 2010.

Rosenthal, Margaret F. *The Honest Courtesan: Veronica Franco, Citizen and Writer in Sixteenth-Century Venice.* Chicago: University of Chicago Press, 1992.

Rotondò, Antonio. "La censura ecclesiastica e la cultura," in *Storia d'Italia.* Turin: Einaudi, 1973.

Rubin, Patricia Lee. *Images and Identity in Fifteenth-Century Florence.* New Haven: Yale University Press, 2007.

Ruggiero, Guido. *Binding Passions: Tales of Magic, Marriage and Power at the End of the Renaissance.* New York: Oxford University Press, 1993.

The Boundaries of Eros: Sex Crime and Sexuality in Renaissance Venice. New York: Oxford University Press, 1985.

Machiavelli in Love: Sex, Self and Society in the Italian Renaissance. Baltimore: Johns Hopkins University Press, 2007.

"Mean Streets, Familiar Streets, or The Fat Woodcarver and the Masculine Spaces of Renaissance Florence," in *Renaissance Florence, A Social History,* Roger J. Crum and John T. Paoletti, eds. Cambridge: Cambridge University Press, 2006: 295–310.

Violence in Early Renaissance Venice. New Brunswick, NJ: Rutgers University Press, 1980.

ed. *A Companion to the Worlds of the Renaissance.* Oxford: Blackwell, 2002.

Salvemini, Gaetano. *Magnati e popolani in Firenze dal 1280 al 1295.* Florence: G. Carnesecchi, 1899.

Shaw, Christine. *Popular Government and Oligarchy in Renaissance Italy.* Leiden: Brill, 2006.

Shemek, Deanna. *Ladies Errant: Wayward Women and Social Order in Early Modern Italy.* Durham: Duke University Press, 1998.

Simons, Patricia. "Alert and Erect: Masculinity in Some Italian Renaissance Portraits of Fathers and Sons," in *Gender Rhetorics: Postures of Dominance and Submission in History,* ed. Richard C. Trexler. Binghampton, NY: Medieval and Renaissance Texts and Studies, 1994.

Simplicio, Oscar di. *Peccato Penitenza Perdono Siena 1575–1800.* Milan: Franco Angeli Storia, 1994.

Skinner, Quentin. *The Foundations of Modern Political Thought,* 2 vols. Cambridge: Cambridge University Press, 1978.

Starn, Randolph, "A Postmodern Renaissance?" *Renaissance Quarterly* 60 (2007): 1–24.

Starn, Randolph, and Loren Partridge. *Arts of Power: Three Halls of State in Italy, 1300–1600.* Berkeley: University of California Press, 1992.

Steinberg, Leo. *The Sexuality of Christ in Renaissance Art and Modern Oblivion.* Chicago: University of Chicago Press, 1996.

Syson, Luke, and Dora Thornton. *Objects of Virtue: Art in Renaissance Italy.* London, British Museum Press, 2001.

Talvacchia, Bette. *Taking Positions: On the Erotic in Renaissance Culture.* Princeton: Princeton University Press, 1999.

Terpstra, Nicholas. *Abandoned Children of the Italian Renaissance: Orphan Care in Florence and Bologna.* Baltimore: Johns Hopkins University Press, 2005.

Lay Confraternities and Civic Religion in Renaissance Bologna. Cambridge: Cambridge University Press, 1995.

Trexler, Richard. *Public Life in Renaissance Florence.* New York: Academic Press, 1980.

Trinkhaus, Charles. *In Our Image and Likeness: Humanity and Divinity in Italian Renaissance Thought,* 2 vols. Chicago: University of Chicago Press, 1970.

Von Martin, Alfred. *Sociology of the Italian Renaissance.* New York: Harper and Row, 1963.

Weaver, Elissa B. *Convent Theater in Early Modern Italy: Spiritual Fun and Learning for Women.* Cambridge: Cambridge University Press, 2002.

Weinstein, Donald. *Savonarola and Florence: Prophecy and Patriotism in the Renaissance.* Princeton: Princeton University Press, 1970.

Welch, Evelyn. *Shopping in the Renaissance.* New Haven: Yale University Press, 2009.

Witt, Ronald. *In the Footsteps of the Ancients: The Origins of Humanism from Lovato to Bruni.* Leiden: Brill, 2003.

Woods-Marsten, Joanna. *Renaissance Self-Portraiture: The Visual Construction of Identity and the Social Status of the Artist.* New Haven: Yale University Press, 1998.

Yates, Frances A. *Giordano Bruno and the Hermetic Tradition.* Chicago: University of Chicago Press, 1964.

Zardin, Danilo. *Riforma Cattolica e resistenza nobilare nella diocesi di Carlo Borromeo.* Milan: Jaca Book, 1983.

INDEX

CPSIA information can be obtained
at www.ICGtesting.com
Printed in the USA
LVHW082004251121
704214LV00015B/440